The Man
Who Listens
to Horses

The Man Who Listens to Horses

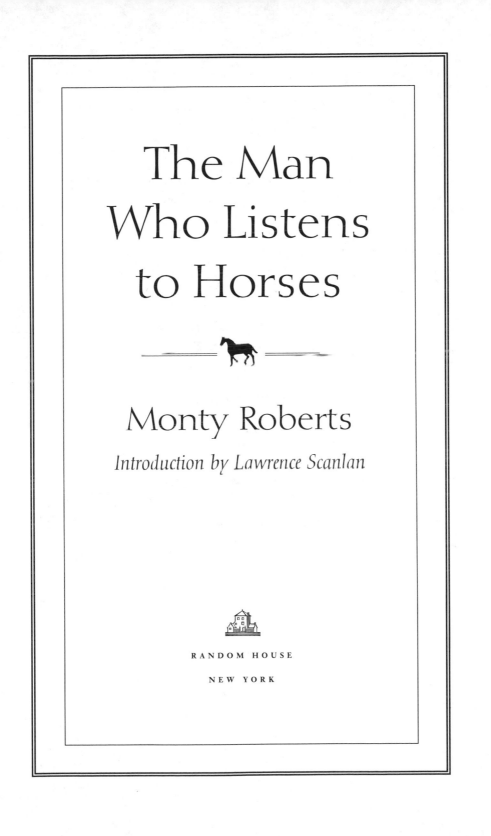

Monty Roberts

Introduction by Lawrence Scanlan

RANDOM HOUSE

NEW YORK

Library of Congress Cataloging-in-Publication Data
Roberts, Monty
The man who listens to horses/Monty Roberts; introduction by
Larry Scanlan.—1st ed.
p.   cm.
ISBN 0-679-45658-9
1. Roberts, Monty.   2. Horses—Behavior.   3. Horses—
Training.   4. Human-animal communication.   5. Horse trainers—
California—Biography.   I. Title.
SF284.52.R635A3   1997
636.1'0835'092—dc21
[B]   97-17318

Random House website address: www.randomhouse.com
Printed in the United States of America on acid-free paper
Book design by J. K. Lambert
8 C 9 7

DEDICATION

I could think of no other choice than to dedicate this book to *Equus: The Flight Animal.* It is my opinion that we owe this species an apology for causing it to endure our lack of understanding for thousands of years. Equus has been my teacher, my friend, and my provider.

WITH WARM AND LOVING APPRECIATION

It must be said with utter sincerity that the partnership with my wife, Pat, has been the strongest contributor in the advancement of my career. Her hard work in the management of our operation allowed me travel time and the time to study my art. Her sacrifices have been monumental.

Pat, along with our children—Deborah, Laurel, and Marty—deserve my deepest thanks for their love, patience, tolerance, and incredible work load.

THANK YOU TO MY TEACHERS

While Equus has been my greatest teacher, Marguerite Parsons, Sister Agnes Patricia, Bill Dorrance, Don Dodge, and Dr. Bob Miller must take a lot of credit for creating an environment in which I could learn.

AND A WORD TO MY READERS

While horses are friendly animals, mistreatment and fear can render them hostile, and caution should be used if you are unsure of a horse's temperament.

Acknowledgments

I owe a debt of gratitude to those who gave great effort to create this book: Deb Futter and Louise Dennys, my editors, who courageously and solidly supported me throughout this project; Larry Scanlan, who traveled from Canada to spend time with us and worked brilliantly to edit copious pages and still have them read in my vernacular, as well as to share with us and describe our "mustang adventure"; and last of all but not the least, Jane Turnbull, my enthusiastic and totally supportive literary agent, who believed in me from the start.

A special thanks must go to Her Majesty, Queen Elizabeth II, who brought light to my work and who shows continuing interest; to Sir John Miller, who was instrumental in making the Royal connection; and to Terry Pendry, my friend and ardent supporter, and his lovely family.

My nine students who have risen to the level of Advanced Professional must be acknowledged: Crawford Hall, Sean McCarthy, Kelly Marks, Richard Maxwell, Terry Pendry, Tim Piper, Satish Seemar, Simon Stokes, and Hector Valadez.

Contents

Introduction

There is nothing new under the sun, the saying goes. And then along comes a man or a woman to remind us that while there is some truth in those words, they also deny the human imagination and capacity for change. The relationship between humans and horses, for example, has been much the same for more than 6,000 years, but in that particular world there *is* something new under the sun, and it comes to us from an extraordinary man named Monty Roberts.

Dr. William O. Reed, the dean of North American track veterinarians, may also have thought he had seen it all—until he and several thousand others watched Monty Roberts work with an unbroken horse. The demonstration took place in December 1995 at the annual meeting of the American Association of Equine Practitioners, or horse veterinarians, in Lexington, Kentucky, the virtual hub of the world's Thoroughbred horse industry. A New York–based veterinary surgeon with a Kentucky horse farm of his own, Dr. Reed has worked during his illustrious career on many of the finest Thoroughbreds in the world. Ruffian. Northern Dancer. Secretariat.

He vividly remembers that December day. "I thought it was the greatest communication between man and animal I had ever seen," he told me. "Monty Roberts is definitely a pioneer. In the past, horse breaking has been man against horse, checking his will, dominating him. Monty does something quite different."

Beating a horse into submission is less fashionable now than it was even a few decades ago, but there have always been infinitely more men and women inclined to the whip than to the kind word. "Horse breakers" and "broncobusters" are friendly, even romantic terms to describe methodical savagery. Breaking horses sometimes meant breaking bones—the buster's, the bronco's. This was a cruel and dangerous event in the life of the horse and of the first human he ever felt on his back.

To the art of gentling a horse, Monty Roberts brings wisdom and a lifetime of observation, along with a new and quite exhilarating sense of discovery. Since the beginning of recorded history, one of humankind's great challenges has been the gulf that divides humans and animals. How do you communicate with animals—especially ones that play a part in our daily lives—when we share no common language? Clearly, it is still a challenge; it still matters. The longing for kinship with a horse, for example, is ancient (and, in this highly technical age, perhaps more powerful than ever).

As this book attests, Monty Roberts has not just set out to change the way we communicate with animals, but—as a result—how we communicate with each other. Recently, thousands of corporate officers—from Disney, Xerox, General Motors, A.T.&T., for example—have gone to hear this horseman speak at his farm in California. It's a tantalizing notion: the horse as teacher. The lessons Monty Roberts learned from horses may one day influence the way that managers and workers, parents and children, relate to each other. What works with horses, he says, also works with humans. The name of the game is communication, and at that Monty Roberts is an old pro.

He was only seven years old when he made a remarkable discovery: that you can communicate with a horse by reading his body language and sending similar signals back. He would eventually call this silent tongue "the language of Equus"; he would codify it, break down its grammar. I count it his greatest achievement: to show the world that when a horse does *this* with his body, it means something quite specific; and that when a human does *that* with his body in response, that action also conveys a particular message to the horse. Now sixty-two, Monty wonders if another boy in another era ever chanced upon similar knowledge.

"Horses are such good teachers," he says. "There *had* to be people before me." Was this other boy rebuffed, as Monty was most of his life, for trying to learn the language of horses? Or was he just ignored? You can put a message in a bottle at sea, but the odds of someone reading it are remote.

To know even a little of traditional horsemanship is to appreciate the nature and extent of Monty Roberts's achievement. History has had its gentlers, too, but they have been few and far between. Three hundred years before the birth of Christ there lived a Greek cavalry officer called Xenophon (meaning "a person who speaks strangely"). He wrote a tiny classic called *The Art of Horsemanship*; educators with the British Horse Society call Xenophon's observations as relevant today as when written. Be firm but not harsh, Xenophon urged, and *never* lose your temper while dealing with a horse. He wrote,

> A fit of passion is a thing that has no foresight in it, and so we often have to rue the day when we gave way to it. Consequently, when your horse shies at an object and is unwilling to go up to it, he should be shown that there is nothing fearful in it, least of all to a courageous horse like him; but if this fails, touch the object yourself that seems so dreadful to him, and lead him up to it with gentleness.

Here was a man training horses for war, warning riders that aggression (with horses, anyway) does not pay. Close to Monty Roberts in his thinking but more than two thousand years his predecessor, Xenophon seems attuned to horse psychology: "...reward him with kindness when he has done what you wish and admonish him when he disobeys." On the other hand, "riders who force their horses by the use of the whip only increase their fear, for they then associate the pain with the thing that frightens them."

Such considerate advice would seem only to make sense, but sense is far from common. Our long association with the horse is like a road that here moves cleanly forward and there twists inanely back on itself. The history of horsemanship is less about sugar than pepper, less about light than dark, less about mindful kindness than thoughtless cruelty. Horse trainers of the Roman empire seem not to have read Xenophon. They would force the horse to the ground, sit on his head, and tie his legs together. The idea was to demoralize the horse, to break his spirit and will (and more if necessary). Icelandic sagas from the tenth century describe how stallions were pitted against each other, much like cocks and pit bulls are in more recent times. Stallions need little prodding to spar; it is in their nature. And if it is human nature to devise sport and entertainment, then what animal offers more drama and wagering opportunities than the very symbol of grace, beauty, and power—the horse.

By the sixteenth century, the business of schooling horses had taken a decidedly harsh turn. England's Thomas Blundeville, for example, advised that for recalcitrant horses one should take an iron bar set with prickles and suspended from the horse's tail. Pass it, he instructed, between the horse's legs and link it to a cord, so the rider may draw it up and mete out punishment as required. If this fails, "let a footman stand behind you with a shrewd cat tied at one end of a long pole with her belly upwards, so as she may have mouth and claws at liberty. And when your horse may stay or go backwards, let him thrust the cat between his legs so as she may scratch and bite him, sometimes by the thighs, sometimes by the rump and often times by the stones."

The Renaissance, meanwhile, had elevated riding into an art form, alongside the visual arts, music, and literature. Tactics used to create *haute école* horsemanship may well have been dubious, but riding became part of every noble person's education. And by the eighteenth century some equestrians at least appear more enlightened, more Xenophonic. The Duke of Newcastle, builder of riding academies in Paris and Brussels wrote:

A boy is a long time before he knows his alphabet, longer before he has learned to spell, and perhaps several years before he can read distinctly; and yet there are some people who, as soon as they get on a young horse, entirely undressed and untaught, fancy that by beating and spurring they will make him a dressed horse in one morning only. I would fain ask such stupid people whether by beating a boy they would teach him to read without first showing him the alphabet? Sure, they would beat him to death, before they would make him read.

Nevertheless, the fate of the horse rested then, as now, with his owner. Where proper food and lodgings were traded for equine services rendered, the life of the horse may well have been decent and long. But the horse in abject servitude, the horse beaten because his owner knew no alternative or starved because his master lacked the means: this was the fate of many.

And when not pulling carts or hauling his master over mountains, the horse was often a fierce instrument of war. The warhorse's lot can barely be imagined, but best not be misled by those triumphant equestrian statues or the great paintings of sleek horses under captains of war, and emperors with field glasses monitoring distant battlefields on the plains below. The numbers of horses in battle alone give pause. In 1286 B.C., a battle between the Hittites and the Egyptians involved 7,000 horses pulling half that many chariots. At the Battle of Waterloo in 1815, the French and English cavalry numbered 30,000. Napoleon had twenty horses killed under him in battle, another arresting number.

In the First World War, the horses used as cavalry and to move supplies and guns numbered 1.5 million; one-third died. Heavy guns blasted battlefields into gruel. With grooming forsaken, mange and parasites spread like a contagion. Against mange, the army scrubbed and clipped horses, who then shivered in the cold and rain and snow. Water troughs froze; food supplies dwindled. Desperate horses choked trying to eat the blankets of their stablemates; horses chewed ropes, others' manes and tails, even the epaulets on men's shoulders.

I remember seeing a photograph taken before that war of Canadian officers buying horses from a farmer. It was a sunny warm day for horse trading. Those horses went overseas and did not return; save for a minuscule number of officers' favored charges, any horses not killed in battle were sent to European slaughterhouses for human consumption when peace was restored.

Even in peacetime, the commerce in horses was often cruel. In the nineteenth century it was common practice, and still is today in some areas, to "fire," or soundly whip, a horse to make him frisky before a sale. One observer remembers seeing "a poor brute stone blind, exquisitely shaped, and showing all the marks of high blood, whom I saw unmercifully cut with a whip a quarter of an hour before the sale, to bring her to the use of her stiffened limbs, *while the tears were trickling down her cheeks.*" The italics were in the original text and clearly constitute hyperbole: a horse may shed tears from dirt in the eye but does not weep in the human sense. Countless horses, though, have had cause to cry.

Horsewhipped. Horse knacker. Horseflesh.

The words conjure a triptych: horse as slave, horse at slaughter-house, horse as dinner. Look into a horse's eyes and you will some-times see there resignation. I find it sobering to ponder an individual horse's life, the spirit he was surely born with, and who or what might have stolen it away.

The most traumatic event in the life of many horses remains that first ride. A two-legged creature with bad manners enters the paddock with a long list of commands and the spurs, whip, and cruel bit to en-force them.

But the gentling philosophy had its practitioners here and there, now and then. The Indians of the North American plains in the eigh-teenth and nineteenth centuries tended to be firm as horse breakers but slow and easy. Like many modern gentlers, they used touch and voice to reassure the horse. Some tribes rode mustangs into a lake or river; the water helped tire the thrashing horses and offered a softer landing for tossed riders. What a clever notion: marry water, horse, and rider. Such insights about horses are a little like prehistoric in-sects locked in amber; if only someone would chance along and turn a certain rock over, the secrets would be passed on. And it seems that some were.

During the First World War, a "reclamation camp" was established in England to deal with "untamable" army horses. Otherwise slated to be destroyed, the horses were entrusted to horse-wise young women, the daughters of wealthy country gentlemen, who had lived around horses from childhood. The ladies did as Sioux boys had done: they rode into deep water where the horses soon became docile. It never failed.

Why, I once asked Monty Roberts, do horse trainers cling to the old way of the whip and the spur? Why did schooling a horse gently become fashionable at various points in history, only to be replaced by the iron fist for centuries at a time?

We were in the weight room of his farm in California with its commanding view of the Santa Ynez Valley, me writing at a rough-hewn antique table, he lying four feet away on a white-leather beanbag—the most forgiving chair in the house for his woeful back. You have to understand, he said, that most trainers are burdened with the great weight of the male ego.

"You walkin' on the fightin' side of me," he began in a fine west-Texas accent put on for the occasion, "when you say my daddy didn't know what he was doin'. I got horses—you couldn't get close to 'em. You admit to me now, that there's a time when a horse needs a good whippin'."

Imagine that bruised ego when along comes someone who can enter a fifty-foot round pen with a wild or unbroken horse and by communicating with the animal win his trust to such an extent that the horse accepts saddle, bridle, and rider—all within thirty minutes, with no hand raised or harsh word spoken. Dr. William O. Reed clearly learned a great deal when he watched Monty Roberts that day in Lexington. "Let me put it like this," he told me. "If I had twenty-five yearlings, I wouldn't school them any other way. This method is innovative and, from the point of view of potential injury to the animal, foolproof."

So-called crazy horses are brought to Monty Roberts to be made sane again, and owners of prize racehorses fly him all over the world to work with their seemingly irretrievably "damaged" animals. Monty hates this work with what he calls "remedial horses," but he loves it, too. When he can, he is happy to save such horses' lives; but he is frustrated by the persistent human folly that churns out all these terrified animals. He once described himself as a marathon runner dealing with weekend joggers who *think* they are marathon runners. There exist parents who freely admit they should never have had children; there exist horse owners who have no business owning horses. Monty will often "fix" the horse, address and overcome the horse's fear—whether of starting gates or of being tied to a rope—but the owner-trainer, lacking Monty's patience, will let the horse slide back into old terrors, then privately slam Monty for a job badly done and eventually have to kill the animal.

In other instances, trainer and owner may be different people. The trainer may have failed utterly with the horse and it is the flustered owner who calls Monty Roberts. The trainer, then, has a vested interest in seeing the horse fail: "Must be a crazy horse 'cause *I* sure couldn't work him." Monty explained this sad and chronic process to Nicholas Evans while that author researched his novel *The Horse Whisperer,* and Monty rather liked the way Evans put it in the book.

Often seen as witches, Evans wrote, horse whisperers/healers, those with the touch,

> could see into the creature's soul and soothe the wounds they found there.... And those who truly had the gift were wont to guard it wisely, for it was said that he who drove the devil out might also drive him in. The owner of a horse you calmed might shake your hand then dance around the flames while they burned you in the village square.

There are no superstitious bones in Monty's body, only sentimental ones. He is very clear that he has no magic touch, no physical genius by virtue of the Cherokee blood that flows in his veins, that he is simply a man who has spent a watchful life with horses. Were you or I to spend a year with him he could teach us everything he knows about horses; with similar patience and skill we too could then solve the dilemma of horses who dread ropes or gates.

"What I can do with horses," says Monty, "is the result of long hours observing them in the wild. It's essentially a simple thing based on common sense. There *is* something magical about it, but it's the magic of an undiscovered tongue—primitive, precise, and easy to read. The silent language uses movements of the body—"signs" that can be read. I've called it Equus but I believe this is a universal tongue understood not just by all wild and domestic horses, ponies, mules, and even donkeys but also by other "flight" animals such as deer. Once learned, the language allows a new understanding between human and horse. But it doesn't need to be, nor is it, exclusive to me." Monty bristles when people assign him mystical qualities, call him horse healer and horse whisperer. Diligence taught him all he knows about the horses he loves.

Monty has "started" (never "broken"—he loathes the word) some 10,000 horses at his farm in California and all over the world. These horses are green, absolutely raw—they have never previously been ridden. Monty calls the process "join-up," and it's a vivid word to describe what happens. He enters into a communication with the horse that will result in the horse *voluntarily* (a critical distinction from the past) deciding to work with this human in this new endeavor. Join-up has the feel of ritual, or a one-act play. The exhilaration Monty displays at the end is genuine and heartfelt, though the ending is ever the same.

I have observed this process, and it is both astonishing and moving to watch. Monty is alone in the round pen (about the size of a small pond) with the unbroken horse—a powerful, potentially dangerous animal. When the horse enters the pen, clearly nervous, Monty flicks a light cotton line at him—but never actually *touches* him with it—to send him round and round the perimeter. "Don't go away a little," he invariably tells the horse, "go away a lot." The horse soon learns to respect, but not fear, the tossed line, which he had at first instinctively perceived as a threat.

The alternative to being "pushed away," the horse will come to realize, is first a conversation—then a contract—with this man. The key "signs" then come, one after the other: the horse, still trotting in a circle, eventually locks one ear on Monty, later sticks out his tongue and makes chewing motions, and, finally, lowers his head until it is inches from the ground. "I want to talk," says the horse, a herd animal now in solitary and therefore fearful, for to be alone is to be exposed to predators. His powerful instinct, the herd instinct, is to join another herd. Maybe Monty's herd. When to face the horse and make eye contact, when not to, where to touch the horse first, whether to move slowly or quickly: all this Monty knows, for he has learned his equine manners and grammar.

The communication has never failed Monty, though doubters are forever testing him and his methods with cantankerous horses. His equine language—which he now teaches around the world and explains in depth in his book—is coupled with an uncommon sensibility and a richly inventive mind.

When I was at Monty's farm, he was working with a Thoroughbred called Gospel Hill, owned by a friend of Monty's—actor John Forsythe (he starred in the television series *Dynasty*). Unable to break the apparently incorrigible stallion, another trainer had hoped to calm him by gelding him, but the horse was still nervous, still impossible.

Call Monty.

After a normal join-up with Monty, he and his students, working slowly and always by degrees over the course of several months, had Gospel Hill agreeably entering the gate, then exploding out of it. I (never mind Forsythe) took great joy in witnessing that event. I have seen many races, but never stood twenty feet from a starting gate. When the gates clanged open, it was like watching a great arrow released from a bow. The earth at my feet shivered, the air divided to let the streaking horse and rider through.

Ever the student, Monty a year ago got the idea of positioning his portable starting gate in the far corner of his track and *facing* the barn, not away from it as is the custom. He was close to giving up on one horse phobic about gates when it hit him: why make the horse run *away* from the barn, his comfort? Why not let him run for home? As he told me the story, Monty smacked his forehead with the heel of his hand as if to say, How could I have been so thick? He is an old dog still teaching himself new tricks about horses.

Curious about the intransigence of horse trainers, I spoke with John Franks of Shreveport, Louisiana, the only four-time winner of the Eclipse Award—granted annually to America's premier Thoroughbred horse owner. ("How many horses do you own?" I asked him. "Unfortunately," he drawled, then paused. "I have six hundred.")

"Monty's method is outstanding," said Franks, who cottoned on to it a decade ago. "I don't know why his method isn't *the* method for breaking horses." But he does know: "I'm a geologist and when something new comes along in geology, about drilling for oil, say, we all jump on it. But the horse world is so splintered. Everyone goes his own way, and it's *hard* to change a trainer who has done it his way all his life. It's like trying to change the tide."

And yet the tide is turning. To understand how revolutionary Monty Roberts's way is, only consider the advice that Monty's own father was offering in *his* book—a little blue hardcover called *Horse and Horsemen Training,* self-published in 1957 under the name Marvin E. Roberts. The copy in Monty's possession smells musty, its contents unnervingly casual. One page displays a black-and-white photograph of the necessary bits and halters and ropes, the latter, though new, clearly stained with blood.

For the bucking horse, urged Roberts Sr., fill a burlap sack with tin cans and attach it to his saddle: a little terror so the bronc knows who's boss. For the horse ill-inclined to leave the herd or enter the barn ("herd-bound" or "barn-sour"), "put your left hand on the saddle horn and hit him on the top of the neck right up between the ears as hard as you can." Where to hit, what to use, and when ("some colts have to be hit more than others"): it's all there.

Monty's father—as you will see in the pages that follow—must also have felt that some sons have to be hit more savagely than others. But it is important to understand that his thoughts on curbing the horse were very much in line with most of his contemporaries. He was not *seen* as a horse basher; on the contrary, for the gift of his horsemanship to children, the grateful citizens of Monterey County, California, named a rodeo arena after him.

In global terms, little has apparently changed in the way that horses are taught and disciplined. Some three-quarters are likely schooled the Marvin E. Roberts way. But in North America, there has been a dramatic change. A headline in *The New York Times* in October 1993 caught the mood: "Broncobusters Try New Tack: Tenderness." The notable lions in these kinder, gentler dens are sometimes long in the tooth, suggesting that tenderness is not necessarily new practice on some ranges. Tom Dorrance, sometimes dubbed "the horse's lawyer," is eighty-six. Ray Hunt, his protégé, is seventy-something. Both have written books that stress cooperation and harmony between horse and rider, and the number of their followers is legion.

It is almost certain that these modern-day gentlers read, as children, the novel *My Friend Flicka*, written by Mary O'Hara and published in 1941, in which a boy longs for a young mustang filly he spots on the range. A Swedish ranch hand calls her Flicka—"little girl" in Swedish. What struck me as I reread it recently was how progressive it now seems. The boy's father, Rob, is a hard-nosed rancher who harbors no sentiments about mustangs, but he abhors the traditional way of breaking horses. "It ruins a horse!" he says. "He loses something and never gets it back. Something goes out of him. He's not a whole horse any more. I hate the method, waiting until a horse is full grown, all his habits formed, and then a battle to the death, and the horse marked with fear and distrust, his disposition damaged—he'll never have confidence in a man again."

The horse breaker Rob admires most is a woman—his wife, Nell. She is patient, lets the horse smell her, and then, significantly, it seems to me now, turns her back to the horse, just as Monty will do in the round pen. The message to the horse? I trust you enough to turn my back on you. Trust me, too. Follow me.

"Under the eye of a human being," Mary O'Hara writes, "an unbroken horse is in terror." When Nell feels the horse nuzzling her back, she slowly turns and begins talking to her, stroking her, leans on the saddle and places her knee under the mare's belly as if to mount, and only when the horse shows no signs of fear, only then does she rise into the saddle.

Women more than men, Monty told me, are generally receptive to his thoughts on the nonviolent schooling of horses. He believes that that is because women and horses share something—a feeling of vulnerability. "The horse," he says, "is a flight animal who feels vulnerability twenty-four hours a day. It's the same vulnerability that a woman may feel when she's alone in an elevator and a burly man gets on."

My Friend Flicka offers just one more reminder that some people have, in their own way and for a long time, been "listening" to horses. Monty Roberts would read this novel now and want to correct a few notions: he would remind the reader, for example, that the language of the wild horse is a silent language. But he admires the spirit of the book and how open it is to the possibilities for horse/human communication. Here is the rancher teaching his son about the ways of horses, and how trust will conquer fear:

> "Remember, a horse can tell you a lot of things, if you watch, and expect it to be sensible and intelligent. Pay attention to all the little signs—the way it moves its body, the ears, the eyes, the little whinnies—that's its way of talking. There is the neigh of terror, the scream of rage, the whinny of nervous impatience (that's a very funny sound), the nicker of longing or hunger or friendliness or delight or recognition. She'll talk to you, and it's for you to understand her. You'll learn her language, and she'll learn yours—never forget that *they can understand everything you say to them.*"
>
> "*Everything* Dad?" This was really exciting.
>
> "Everything. And when you once realize that, friendship with an animal begins to be quite a different thing. Communication, see?"

— —

It can be somewhat unnerving driving in a car with Monty Roberts. He wears a national championship rodeo buckle on his belt and for much of his life competed in the showring. When you ask him (as I did) to relive some of those moments, competitive juices bubble in him and then his wife, Pat, will diplomatically remind him that he is over the speed limit. More disconcerting, though, is the urgency in her voice when she says on approach to an intersection. "Monty, the light's red!"

Monty is not just color-blind—born with a confused sense of color as many men and some women are. He is what an ophthalmologist would call achromatopic: he sees no color at all, but a rich array of blacks, whites, and tonal grays. And Monty wonders now if he ever could have learned the pure, silent language of horses had he not been born with this so-called "deficit." The neurologist Oliver Sacks writes, with awe and wonder, about people with such deficits—deafness, blindness, autism, bizarre disorders of the brain. He is forever musing on the silver linings in the dark clouds of pathology.

(A very small percentage of people—one in thirty or forty thousand—are achromatopic. In his book, *The Island of the Colorblind*—Dr.

Sacks describes an expedition to the remote and tiny Pacific atoll of Pingelap where, by some extraordinary coincidence of history and geography, virtually the entire population is achromatopic, and has learned to inhabit their world with particular delicacy and subtlety.)

A deaf person who uses sign language—a visual grammar—sees in a remarkable and unique way: introduce her into a room and ask her seconds later to recall the objects and their arrangement and she will typically remember far more than a hearing person will. It's a kind of spatial genius. What's more, the owners of deficits feel a terrific allegiance to their deficit-defined culture. Deaf individuals granted hearing are sometimes appalled at the cacophony and if possible return to their familiar silent world.

Monty was once provided with contact lenses that allowed him to see the world in what we call living color. He, too, was appalled. The colors screamed at him, distracted and disoriented him. He parked the lenses in a drawer at home. "Military camouflage," he told me, "is a confusion of color. It stirs the eye up so you don't see the shape. The color blind just see the shape, but it also means we see so much more than the normally sighted."

When he was a child, Monty's father used him as a scout on hunting trips: the boy could spot deer moving on a distant hillside long before the rifleman, who boasted of his son's eyesight. The American military heard about Monty's unusual skill and wanted him to fly as a passenger in a spy plane over enemy territory during the Korean war: with his eyes he would not be duped by camouflage. Monty declined.

His color blindness (which he hid, by the way, most of his life) meant that as a boy of twelve observing wild mustang herds for weeks at a time in the Nevada desert, he saw patterns of movement that you or I might have missed. In *The Man Who Listens to Horses,* Monty watches spellbound as a mustang mare excommunicates an unruly colt from the herd: it is a compelling story in a book that teems with stories.

But perhaps we would have neither that story, nor this book, had Monty seen color as most of us do.

When I consider Monty's accomplishments in the world of horses (the depth and breadth of his personal experience—in rodeo competition, Thoroughbred racing, showjumping, polo, eventing—may have no equal in the world), I find myself asking, What if?

What if he had not been born color-blind?

What if his Cherokee grandmother had spoken English? "I understood her body language more than anything," Monty told me. "She used words, not sentences, with lots of gestures and sounds." Perhaps that training proved useful when he sought to understand what horses intended. Only a careful eye could have deciphered their signals when no one else noticed them, never mind knew what they meant.

What if Monty had not had the chance to study *wild* horses? The first thing I noticed about a wild horse is how wary and watchful and silent he is. Though a domestic horse is far more inclined to communicate by nickering, he is also far less inclined to communicate at all. In a given period of time, says Monty, a mustang may deliver fifty signals with his body to every two by his stabled counterpart. (I find it intriguing that a wild horse domesticated will soon start to nicker like his stallmates, while a domestic horse gone feral will soon learn about predators and the wisdom of quiet.) In the deserts of Nevada, then, Monty was seeing extremely "talkative" horses: the desert as language lab.

(In March 1997, Monty returned to the high desert terrain to attempt what many said was impossible: to gentle a mustang in the wild. It was a high stakes gamble, for a documentary film crew from BBC television was on-site to record his success, or failure. The afterword to *The Man Who Listens to Horses* presents my eyewitness account of that bold and memorable undertaking.)

What if his father had not been the kind of person he was? A man of the old school, Marvin sought to make a true horseman of Monty—a chip off the old block. But when the son, at seven years of age, showed no faith in that philosophy and already looked to be going his own way with horses, the father turned on him. Talk to Monty for a time, get a little close to him, and he will often twist conversations back to his father. The wound is still raw. His father did not beat traditional horsemanship into him; he beat it *out* of him. Where Monty was walking, in any case, his father caused him to run.

Monty Roberts has many stories, and often they made me laugh.

Stories about elaborate pranks at the farm, about cowboy characters named Wendell and Doc, Slim and Slick, about calamitous cattle roundups that pretty near killed him, but since he survived, became amusing anecdotes—fodder for a book. He has deep pockets full of stories about horses, like the well-named Prince of Darkness who literally ran over Monty several times while Monty puzzled through the stallion's starting-gate phobia. About his days as a child prodigy in the showring and on Hollywood film sets. He draws his life and times with a fine and detailed pen; his memory for racehorse pedigrees, and for the character and personality of horses he has known, is staggering. But many of the stories about his father were gut-wrenching to bear witness to. The telling sapped him, left him wet-eyed and trembling. A bear, I thought, in need of a hug.

When I first shook Monty's hand at the airport in Santa Barbara, mine disappeared in his and I was secretly glad to get it back. Later that day, I watched as he worked on stretching a rope, tying one end to an elm tree on his lawn and the other to his truck, and for all his thick, strong hands, the fingers nimbly worked the ropes. Monty is squarely built, and, at 240 pounds on a five-foot-ten-inch frame, much heavier than he looks. He favors checked shirts, blue jeans, and that belt buckle the diameter of a grapefruit, a brown-and-black oilskin jacket, maybe a ball cap or straw cowboy hat, cowboy boots. There's a line across his nose—white above, brown below—that says he always wears a hat in the sun. When he bends down to pluck something off the ground, he genuflects like an altar boy. After all the beatings he took as a child, after all his rodeo days riding bulls and wrestling steers, his back will have it no other way.

In 1981, he endured lower back surgery so radical that walking again was offered only as a possibility; his riding days were over. The surgeons reckoned wrongly. I have not encountered a tougher specimen of a man (mentally or physically). I wondered if his bones might be made of mesquite, that notoriously heavy wood of the Southwest. He is tireless, always relentlessly focused on the task at hand, and possessed by a deep work ethic. "*He* was a worker," Monty once said of a writer friend who had earned the ultimate compliment.

He is not without a sense of fun, or showmanship for that matter.

On a long train ride, he is someone I would want for company: smart, thoughtful, passionate and mettlesome, full of opinions, full, as I say, of stories. But he does seem ruled overall by a high seriousness and missionary zeal: his calling has always been to make the world a better place for the horse. His son, Marty (who once signed a birthday card to his father, "Your son, Marty R. Roberts"), called his father on the car phone one day and I heard Monty ask him, "Why are you so somber?" "I'm *always* somber," came the reply, and Monty—who loves his son dearly—laughed as heartily as I ever saw him laugh in all the time we were together. Sometimes a father sees his son in a certain light and chuckles at the resemblance.

Key to his health are the fourteen natural supplements he takes daily to compensate for a lifetime of pain that elevated his adrenaline levels and damaged his pancreas, spleen, liver, and kidneys. He takes a natural enzyme to carry oxygen to the tissues, vitamins C and E, ginseng, magnesium, zinc, and melatonin, along with a coated aspirin to thin the blood. All contained in a little black suitcase.

Call it a modern diet. And yet, like many horse people, he loves tradition and fine old things. Hates plastic and modern gadgets built to break. Loves wood, admires craft, and surrounds himself with it. Those six-hundred-year old church doors in the stone wall by the house, he says, will still be glorious when his Lincoln Continental is rust.

"The ladder-back chairs in the living room," he tells me, "were made by craftsmen who studied their art for years before ever making a chair. The drawers I keep my clothes in are four hundred years old, with dovetail corners and hand-sawn boards. There's beauty in that and you can't find it in modern things." The patience, love, and care that he admires in the work of craftsmen are the same values that he brings to his work with horses.

Monty is a proud cook who often uses his great-grandfather's black cast-iron skillets that hang on one wall of the ample, sky-lit kitchen. And in the saloon he built by the garage is a black-and-chrome cookstove from Elmira, Ontario, an old gray spool-to-spool Royal typewriter that once belonged to John Steinbeck, and a framed photograph of Geronimo over the chief's rifle. (Notched into the stock in an in-

verted Braille-like code is the Apache chief's name, along with dozens
of other dots to spell the word MEN—each dot a recorded kill.)

When I first saw Monty Roberts, he looked vaguely familiar. During
the 1970s he had been in dozens of commercials—drinking Coke, driving a Chevy, about to sip a Miller Light. But when you read his book,
it is not his perhaps familiar face you should have in your head, but the
sound of his voice. I have noticed that people who work around horses
and cattle often speak slowly, as if the pace of a walking steer or quarter horse had come to guide their speech. And he always speaks distinctly, with more drawl than I imagined a Californian would ever
possess. He is an educated, articulate man: his schooling is grounded
in the practical world—agribusiness, biology, psychology. When he
speaks, he speaks with great purpose; seldom does he falter in his
phrasing, restart a sentence or story. He will take deep breaths or pause
as necessary, and for comic effect dip into a repertoire of accents.

I have the sense that Monty Roberts is a reasonably happy and con-
tented man. His is the joy of someone who knew to follow his passion
when he was seven years old, come hell, come high water. "Horses,"
he says, "are my blood, my lifeline." But he does talk about "a lifetime
of rejection." People only began to heed in recent years what he had
been saying for so many: that you can communicate with horses, win
their trust, school them without whips and spurs.

You would not be holding in your hand *The Man Who Listens to
Horses* had Elizabeth II, Queen of England, not read an article in a
horse magazine about Monty Roberts. He might still be a minor draw
at horse shows, a literal voice in the wilderness, had Elizabeth II not
heard about him and invited him to demonstrate his horsemanship at
Windsor Castle in 1989. The royal stamp of approval—warm endorsement would be more accurate, because the Queen's horses are
now all trained Monty's way—bestowed immediate and international
legitimacy. And by the way, said Her Majesty, you should write a book
about your discovery.

Since then, Monty has met with the Queen on twenty other occasions. He seems as protective of her privacy as he is plainly delighted
by her company. They often converse alone in the palace garden,
sometimes for hours—about horses, people, the philosophy of educa-

tion. More than that he will not say; this was the *only* time he was ever guarded when I asked him a question. "It is an amazing relationship," says Monty, who also calls the Queen Mother "one of the most humane beings ever to walk the face of the earth."

But Monty Roberts was not the first American horseman to be summoned to the palace; more than a century ago another gentler, John Solomon Rarey, took the European horse world by storm just as Monty did, and he, too, had turned his back on conventional horse breaking. He also wrote a little book (the copy I read in the rare books section of the Toronto reference library was four inches by seven inches): *The Farmer's Friend, Containing Rarey's Horse Secret, With Other Valuable Receipts and Information.*

Rarey's secret? One breathtakingly simple governing principle: you need not abuse a horse to earn his cooperation. Rarey, I think, would be astonished at what Monty Roberts and the new tribe of gentlers can accomplish, but for me the striking thing about Rarey was how his ideas mirror those of Monty and the moderns and Xenophon and the ancients.

Rarey had farmed in Ohio and there wisely sought the advice of old cowpunchers, circus trainers, Indian riders, and any horseman with answers to his questions. Eventually he devised a system of training horses that relied on gentleness, fearlessness, and simple devices (such as soft-leather hobbles) that worked even on hostile horses. He made a name for himself. In time, despite several tests put to him by disbelieving trainers and horsemen, he arrived in England. There he faced a stallion called Cruiser, a steeplechaser not ridden in three years and who wore an eight-pound iron muzzle; his groom always carried a bludgeon. Cruiser's owner, Lord Dorchester, conceded that it was "as much as a man's life was worth to attend to him." But attend to him Rarey did, showing infinite patience, perseverance, and savvy. He gentled the horse, forced him to lie down, talked softly to him, and touched him all over. He "set to work ...," as one observer put it, "to tame him limb by limb, and inch by inch." Any show of hostility would prompt Rarey to lift the horse's head and shake it, as a father would scold a daughter by lightly grabbing her chin. Cruiser the crazy horse would be calmed.

Word spread. Rarey taught cavalry officers and riding masters; he lectured London cabmen on treating horses humanely. Queen Victoria had Rarey tame one of her more fiery horses, and the prime minister, Lord Palmerston, sought a word. A contributor to the *Illustrated London News* in 1858 predicted (wrongly) of Rarey that "his name will rank among the great social reformers of the nineteenth century." Instead, his little book, *The Farmer's Friend . . .*, was forgotten. But clearly he had sketched there a kind of gentler's guide to the equine galaxy. Appeal to the horse's intelligence, he urged, let the laws of his nature rule your thinking. Use a system, haste makes waste, leave fear and anger behind.

———

There is about the Roberts farm an air of quiet solidity. Fear and anger have no place here. You must ascend a winding road to achieve the low-slung board-and-batten and adobe house. A rough-looking mesquite-wood wagon, called a "stone boat" and once pulled by oxen to haul rocks, is the first thing you see as you approach the house. Set on an elevated island of lawn surrounded by a low stone wall, the great wagon—a clear centerpiece—at night is bathed in floodlight. Ceilings on the house's south side are all high, and windows there equally high: the honeyed light from California skies pours in, day after day. From up here one has a commanding view of many horses in their paddocks below.

If it sounds restful, it is. By day, the light warmed my northern soul. My first night there, the frogs commenced their chorus and I admired the fireflies down in the valley. Then Pat Roberts kindly set me straight. The "fireflies" were the headlights of cars on the road, their beams broken by the trunks of thirty-foot cedars that line the edges of Flag Is Up Farms.

The blinking lights are like a pulse. "We don't run the farm," Monty and Pat's daughter Laurel once told me on the fly. "The farm runs us." When the farm office shuts down after business hours, calls are routed to the house and start every morning at six-thirty.

The patio and terraced lawns overlooking the valley are protected by an Alamo-like wall on the west, with inset doors that open to let in sea breezes and a view of the sun as it drops below the mountains. In that wall, in its own grotto, is a statue of St. Francis of Assisi, the patron saint of animals.

Monty smiled when I asked him about the statue. A good choice, he conceded, but not one picked with any solemnity. A stone Dr. Doolittle might also have done the trick. Perhaps Monty's greatest gift to us will be his heartfelt plea that we all *can* and *should* "talk" to the animals. On that lawn where St. Francis, bird in hand, casts his gaze, Monty learned—using precisely the methods he used to communicate with horses—to "talk" to wild deer. Even does and newborn fawns, once he has made his introduction, abide his close proximity.

Monty's work with deer began in 1977 when he was riding in the hills overlooking the farm and chanced upon an old wounded doe being attacked by coyotes. That rescue of the deer he would call Grandma paid handsome dividends. Monty devotes an entire chapter to his experience with deer: in part, because deer use the same body language as horses, and they taught him many surprising subtleties. You may finish that fascinating section in the book, as I did, with a new respect and appreciation for Grandma and her kin.

When I was at the farm a young antlered male called Cyrus came up the hill every morning to have his neck rubbed. Doors must be closed when he is about, for he will now wander inside the house as if it were his. Simply put, Monty communicates with deer by deploying an advance-and-retreat, hello-and-good-bye system that draws on most animals' conflicting tendencies—first to flee an apparent threat, then, out of curiosity, to investigate it. A horse, for example, feels security in numbers. Isolate him and he will want to "join up" with another creature, even a human (any port in a storm), if the trust is there. While fly-fishing (his favorite pastime is to go fly-fishing in northern British Columbia, always catch-and-release), Monty noticed that fish, like deer and horses, initially fled him and then circled back in the stream. You *can* talk to the animals. And we do. A recent study at the University of Pennsylvania found that ninety-eight percent of pet owners talk to their animals, as if to a sympathetic friend. Convinced there is more there than meets the eye, those of us who own dogs or cats or horses have grown increasingly fascinated with the inner lives of these and other animals.

How else to explain the extraordinary success of *When Elephants*

Weep: The Emotional Lives of Animals by Jeffrey Moussaieff Masson and Susan McCarthy, or *The Hidden Life of Dogs* by Elizabeth Marshall Thomas, or *The Intelligence of Dogs* by Stanley Coren? Nicholas Evans's novel, *The Horse Whisperer,* was one of the memorable publishing successes in the mid-1990s. The story in a nutshell: a magazine editor from New York embarks on a quest to Montana where she desperately hopes a "horse whisperer" can heal her teenage daughter's horse, crazed and badly scarred after a highway accident. Somehow, the mother intuits, healing the horse is the key to healing her distraught and now partially disabled daughter, even to healing herself.

The whisperer is a character inspired by Evans's long conversations with Monty Roberts, Tom Dorrance, Ray Hunt, Buck Brannaman, and others. *The Horse Whisperer* is a novel about hope, but mostly it's a novel about horses, and connecting with horses. "I don't do it for the people," the whisperer explains. "I do it for the horse." Sift through the words of actual gentlers and you hear echoes: gentlers talk, not about people with horse problems, but about horses with people problems. About the horse as teacher, about the slow way with horses as the quickest way. This is a horse-centered worldview that gentlers say offers a nice spinoff: It makes humans more humane. Horses, creatures of flight, are *so* sensitive and aware; humans, more inclined to fight, have lost that acuity. The horse has much to teach humans about listening.

In the span of human/animal interaction, our position—until quite recently—has been either utilitarian (How can I exploit this animal?) or egomaniacal (Don't I look handsome/tall/successful on this fine gray horse?). Up until ten or twenty years ago, most doctors believed that newborn infants neither felt nor remembered pain; no need, then, to use analgesics for painful, invasive procedures. And if we dismissed babies as sentient beings, then doubly did we dismiss animals.

In the 1950s, when Monty Roberts went to California Polytechnic State University, San Luis Obispo, and wanted to study animal behavior, no such course existed. The countless books written about horses throughout history make repeated references to "our dumb companions" and "the noble brutes." And while some writers of the Old West took an interest in mustangs, no one until fairly recently observed the herds as a biologist would in a field study. We already knew about the horse, didn't we? Barely a ripple was raised earlier this century when some two million wild horses on the American plains were wiped out—mostly for pet food.

For most of human history, a strict hierarchy put God at the top and humankind below, with animals near the bottom. Man, says the Book of Genesis, would have "dominion over...every creeping creature that moveth upon the earth." Most cultures gave little thought to whether the animals they were busy hunting and bossing also remembered, felt, feared, or sorrowed.

Many of us no longer think that way. The rising tide of vegetarianism, especially among young people, suggests a startling new awareness of animal consciousness. In academic circles, many thinkers—among them Elizabeth Atwood Lawrence, a former veterinarian and now cultural anthropologist who has written widely on the connection between horses and humans, and Edmund O. Wilson, a world-renowned ant specialist and the only two-time winner of the Pulitzer Prize—are among those advancing a philosophy they call *biophilia*.

Biophilia contends that as we come to understand other organisms—how a herd of horses interacts in a pasture, the various social tasks of insects in the jungle, the mood of your dog walking ahead of you during your evening constitutional—we value them, and ourselves, more. The reward is in *observing* nature, not in *controlling* it.

Monty Roberts, in *The Man Who Listens to Horses*, describes a fellow and highly successful horse trainer named Greg Ward. What should amaze trainers of the old school is how he eases young horses into work: for the first twenty days that a rider is on their backs, the horses call *all* the shots. If the horse wants to graze, trot, roll—the wish is granted. There is no chance for resentments or neuroses to form.

"A new beginning in the relationship between man and horse," Monty calls it. Generous praise. But if anyone has ushered in a new relationship, it is Monty Roberts himself—the man who heeds and understands horses like no one else before him.

One of the patriarchs of Thoroughbred racing in North America is Joe Taylor, seventy-three years old when I talked to him early in 1997.

At his Taylor Made Farms in Lexington, Kentucky, are stabled 550 horses. Fifteen years ago he had gone to a round pen in an open field near his farm where a man was going to demonstrate breaking a horse in a new and different way. A great many farm managers had been invited, but none came. Only Joe Taylor.

"I couldn't believe it," said Taylor of what he saw Monty Roberts do that day. "I've been around horses all my life, but I had no concept that horses had their own language. I would love to have known about this when I was a kid. The old way—putting a horse in a corral, lassoing him, tying him to a post and then getting on him with a pair of spurs—unbelievable. Now we use round pens, we teach the horse that we're not going to hurt him, that we're his friend."

"Twenty years from now," Taylor predicts, "everybody will be using Monty Roberts's methods. We've got to. It's the right thing."

My sense is that the name Monty Roberts will have an enduring currency. He will be remembered as the horseman who learned the language of horses; as the author of a sophisticated yet simple system of bringing the horse amiably to that first rider; and as an animal psychologist who bade us ground the schooling of the horse in the very nature of the horse. He is a wise teacher, a man of unyielding principles and uncommon courage, and one of the best friends the equine species ever had. My hope is that he is the one to lead us, for good this time, into a gentler and deeper connection with horses.

—Lawrence Scanlan
April 1997

The Man
Who Listens
to Horses

CHAPTER 1

The Call of the Wild Horses

It all dates from those summers alone in the high desert, me lying on my belly and watching wild horses with my binoculars for hours at a time. Straining to see in the moonlight, striving to fathom mustang ways, I knew instinctively I had chanced upon something important but could not know that it would shape my life. In 1948 I was a boy of thirteen learning the language of horses.

In the wilderness of Nevada, the soil is silky and cool to the touch at dawn, and at midday will burn your skin. My summer vigils were marked off by the heat of the day and the cold of the night and a profound sense of solitude. It felt right to be there under those vast skies on that dove-gray moonscape in the company of wild and wary horses. I remember, especially, a dun mare with a dark stripe along her back and zebra stripes above her knees. Clearly the matriarch of the herd, she was disciplining an unruly young colt who had been roughing up foals and mares. I vividly recall how she squared up to him, her eyes on his eyes, her spine rigid, her head pointed arrowlike at the adolescent. No longer full of himself, he knew exactly what she meant. Three hundred yards from the herd, the outcast would know by her body position when he could return to the fold.

If she faced him, he could not. If she showed him part of her body's long axis, he could begin to consider it. Before her act of forgiveness had to come signs of his penitence. The signals he gave back to her— the seeking of forgiveness—would later be fundamental to a technique I would develop to introduce young horses gently to saddle and rider. It was the mustangs who taught me their silent body grammar, and the dun mare was my first teacher.

I grew up in Salinas, California, where wild horses were annually put to other uses. In 1948, the Wild Horse Race was a featured part of the Salinas Rodeo. And because I lived in a house on the rodeo grounds (or "competition grounds," as I called it) where my parents ran a riding school, rodeo was part of our lives. Normally, wild horses were cheap and plentiful. Doc Leach, a short, bespectacled man who was our dentist and also president of the association that governed the competition grounds, would have called the usual people and said, in effect, "Come on, folks, I need a hundred and fifty mustangs to be delivered to Salinas by July the first"—and it would happen. But with horsemeat used so extensively during the war, mustang numbers had dwindled significantly, and by 1947 the herds in northern California, Nevada, and southern Oregon had diminished by as much as two-thirds, with the horses now located almost exclusively in Nevada. That year Doc Leach's calls had fallen on deaf ears. "What mustangs?" the Nevada ranchers had countered. "You come up here and see if you can get them yourself." The wild horse race was usually no race at all but a kind of maniacal musical chairs played with mustangs, but that year the Salinas Rodeo Association had to scrape together what they could find, and so it was a fairly tame wild horse race, with too few horses and too many old ones to put on the show required.

The following year I saw an opportunity to provide Doc Leach with a service that would both salvage the reputation of the wild horse race and save the lives of a hundred or more horses. I was only thirteen; he might not listen. But I was driven by both a fierce young entrepreneurial spirit and my love of the horses. In previous years, after the rodeo, the mustangs were sent to Crow's Landing to be slaughtered for dog food. If I could somehow make them worth more than that...

"What if," I proposed to Doc Leach, "I go to Nevada and get the mustangs?"

Doc Leach's eyebrows popped up above his glasses. "How you going to do that, walk?"

"No, I've made a lot of friends from trips to horse shows there. I know I can ask for help from the Campbell Ranch." Bill Dorrance, a remarkable horseman in his mid-fifties who would become my mentor, had contacts at the ranch and would make the arrangements. Ralph and Vivian Carter, good horse people and friends of the family, had business to conduct near there and had agreed to help. Finally, I had a truck driver lined up.

"Good for you," Doc Leach came back, a hint of mockery in his voice. I was, after all, little more than a boy.

"I'd ride up to the ranges with some of the day hands from the Campbell Ranch, and I bet I could secure one hundred and fifty head."

"Head of what? Chickens or horses?" He had a sophisticated sense of humour.

"Strong and healthy mustangs, Dr. Leach." I explained to him that my younger brother, Larry, and I could care for them at the competition grounds until the rodeo was held. "They'll be ready on the spot, with the pair of us on hand to see they're all right." Doc Leach shifted his pipe from one corner of his mouth to the other and blinked a couple of times. That meant he was cogitating.

Finally he asked, "What's in it for you?"

"I was thinking, sir, that after the rodeo Larry and I could break in the mustangs and maybe have an auction sale, so they'd be worth more than Crow's bait." That was the euphemism for animals taken to Crow's Landing for slaughter.

This year, I told him, he would not have to send any animals to the abattoir. "There'd definitely be more than a few that would go through the sale ring ridden by my brother or myself and maybe provide someone with a useful mount, sir."

He was still cogitating, so I went on.

"And perhaps the rodeo association could show a profit at the end of the day, more than the slaughter value anyway." Doc Leach weighed the arrangement, turning it over in his mind. He was like the buyer of a used car, kicking the tires and looking for the hidden defect. When he could find none, he agreed.

He offered to call up Irvin Bray and contract him to provide me with transport for the return journey. Finally, we agreed that the net proceeds of any sales were to be divided equally between the rodeo association and the Roberts brothers.

I was on my way to Nevada to gather 150 head of mustangs. It would prove to be the most important opportunity of my life: to study horses in their natural groups, in the wild. For the next three years I would be crossing the Sierra Nevada to the high desert beyond, to live alongside wild herds for several weeks at a time. From that experience I would begin to learn a language, a silent language which I have subsequently termed "Equus." With that as a springboard, I would assemble a framework of ideas and principles that would guide my life's work with horses. I would have none of this were it not for my time as a teenager spent in the company of mustangs.

In June 1948, Ralph and Vivian Carter and I put our horses and our equipment in the van and headed off. The Carters were an odd couple. Older than Ralph by fifteen years, short, stocky and strong, Vivian had been an exceptional rider as a teenager and very successful in the showring, but in her late twenties a horse bucked her into the trunk of a tree. She would still ride well, but walk with a decided limp for the rest of her life. Nevertheless, the smile on her face was constant and spoke of her inner beauty. She was far and away a better horse person than Ralph was, and I learned to listen more to her than to him. Ralph had the appearance of an all-American/Scandinavian cross: blond hair and eyebrows, blue eyes, tall and handsome, broad at the shoulders, narrow at the hips.

The van carrying us weaved back and forth around the foothills before climbing the Sierra Nevada, following roads cut by our forefathers into the stern, harsh landscape 400 miles north and west of Salinas. North beyond Battle Mountain lay the high desert and the Campbell Ranch, and the vast, empty tract of federal land owned by the Bureau of Land Management.

What I noticed first as the door of the truck swung open was the air, how thin it was. Climbing down from the cab, I knew already that this landscape would be like nothing I had ever encountered. The horizons, the sky, stretched endlessly. I had the sense of being on a different planet. The lunar landscape was covered in sage and rough grasses and cut by deep barrancas (ravines) overgrown with stunted trees. Somewhere in this vast natural wilderness were wild horses.

Indian day hands at the Campbell Ranch were detailed to help us. I was half expecting them to recommend the same trick my Cherokee ancestors had apparently used—before driving the mustangs toward the trap, push them in the opposite direction for a day or so. The horses' tendency is to press back against the control inflicted on them. The day hands, though, had another plan.

Some fifty miles from the homestead, they had built a corral about a quarter of a mile long. They had searched for a heavily traveled canyon and set the corral at the bottom end. From the air it bore the shape of a keyhole, with two sides angled into a narrow gap and a circular area beyond. The posts and fencing were camouflaged with sage and brushwood.

It was a two-day ride to reach this makeshift structure, and when we got there the day hands walked us around and explained how the mustangs should be driven into the wedge at the bottom and funneled through the narrowest part into the circular area, where they would slow up and be forced to turn. Riders, meanwhile, would come down the wings and close the gate across the narrowest part of the keyhole. Familiar with this canyon, the horses would not have seen a vehicle, a building, or even a fence post to scare them off.

But where were the horses?

They were not to be seen by any casual scanning of the earth's surface, a large part of which seemed to lie spread in front of us, a fissured plateau baking in the sun. The Indians pointed here and there. The whereabouts of the wild-horse herds could not be guessed accurately, and the ranch hands were happy to allow the Carters and me to head off and start bringing them back ourselves. They had work to do, but they would help us complete the job.

For this undertaking I had two saddle horses and two packhorses.

The latter were piled high with blankets and utensils. Brownie was my number-one saddle horse, but in addition I had Sergeant and Burgundy as well as a second packhorse, Oriel. The going was stoney and rough; the barrancas, in particular, made for precarious riding, so I would be leading Brownie on foot much of the time. He was precious to me, and I wanted to save him from too much wear and tear if I could.

I was anticipating the adventure of a lifetime, and Brownie caught my excitement and shared it, or perhaps it came from deep inside him. When he took his first steps into this cracked and thirsty land, this son of a mustang was heading home.

Brownie was always a steady and well-mannered horse, but the conviction with which he carried me into his home territory hinted that he knew something I did not.

Ralph, Vivian, and I broke camp at dawn and hurried to stamp out the remains of the fire and bury it, kicking at the loose earth, enjoying the burst of activity if only to warm ourselves in the chill air. We wore yesterday's clothes, and as we mounted our horses and started to peel the oranges that my mother insisted I eat every day, the sun rose like a golden disk, watery at first but then burning with increasing strength as the morning wore on.

Things began to go wrong, or so I thought, as soon as we saw the first herd of fifty or so wild horses.

Brownie caught their scent as we traversed a barranca. Large stones littered its slopes where stunted trees struggled to suck enough water and take advantage of the shelter. Though it was dangerous, you could ride the bottoms of these canyons, along natural paths formed by the scouring action of flash floods. As we descended, Brownie's heels dragged behind him when he tried to load more weight onto his hocks to take the strain.

At one point he stopped dead, concentrating on something I could not see or hear. I knew from his lack of agitation—and the fact that he was keen to move on in the same direction as his ears were pointing— that he had scented this herd of his brothers and sisters, the mustangs of northern Nevada.

But when we caught up with them—and they were already moving away, fully aware of our presence—Ralph and I had different ideas on how to proceed. The Carters, not unreasonably, wanted to press on and simply drive the horses back toward the ranch. Because we had to cover fifty or sixty miles of ground on the return journey, we would have to go relatively fast to stick to our schedule.

I, on the other hand, wanted to stop and simply observe the horses. There was something compelling about seeing them as a family, the alpha male or breeding stallion circling and lifting his tail, stepping out with a high, proud action, and acknowledging our presence. It made me want to melt into the background and see what could be seen, without subjecting them to our interference. It was almost as if I wanted to be a horse myself, so thoroughly had I taken their side. These horses were not only Brownie's brothers and sisters, they were mine, too. I wanted to understand them, and I was more than ever certain that I knew less than I thought I did.

This unspoken conflict of interest between the Carters and me generated an unspoken compromise. They hurried me along, and I slowed them down. We none of us got what we wanted.

As we pressed the mustangs ahead of us, we saw the signals that would be obvious to anyone with experience of horses. A pair of forward ears shows interest in something anterior or in front. Forward ears with head high denotes interest in something in front but far off. Forward ears with the head held low indicates interest in something up close, near the ground.

The mustangs we pursued held their heads in normal position but with a "split ear," one forward and one back, signifying interest in something in front, but also concern for anything to the rear—us. The ears were like beacons that told us the direction of their focus. If their ears were hanging relaxed and the horses stood with one hind leg bent and resting, we could assume we were unobserved. At that moment, the signals said, these horses had no concern for their safety.

If a horse pins his ears back on his neck, he is angry. We watched one mustang, ears pinned, maneuvering to position his rear legs and take action against another animal. He was angry, aggressive, and dangerous.

Once or twice we saw the stallion pin his ears back and stick his nose straight out as far as he could reach; he had his head lowered to just below wither height, so that from the shoulder forward the neck and head looked like an arrow; his eyes were steely, and he was moving forward in a stalking mode. He must have possessed very active testicles, for this stance is exclusive to the full-grown adult male. Only as the male reaches potential for supremacy within the family group are you likely to see this particular display.

As Ralph and Vivian and I circled this first group, turning them this way and that to point them back toward the trap set for them, I learned that a horse's field of vision is nearly 360 degrees, with only a slim cut of land right behind him, which he cannot see, and an even slimmer cut directly in front.

Watching the stallion badger the mares in his defensive role, we could confirm that when he switched his tail—other than when clearing insects off his body—he was not content. This we knew already. A trainer who puts too much pressure on a horse with spurs or whip will create what is called "a switch-tail horse," and in Western competition significant points are lost if a horse switches his tail while performing.

Perhaps the most important piece of knowledge that my first foray into the high desert of Nevada indelibly engraved on my mind was this tenet: there are two types of animal, the *fight* animal and the *flight* animal. It bears repeating that the horse is a flight animal. If I knew it before, I understand it now in a more profound way.

It sounds obvious, but it is critical to remember that given the slightest excuse a horse will say, "I don't want to be near you. I feel there is danger if I stay!" The flight animal wants only to reproduce and survive; fear is the tool that allows him to survive. This has to be respected in any dealings with a horse, or he will be misunderstood.

Humankind, however, is a fight animal. Our preoccupation is with the chase, and having dominion over other creatures in order to eat them or use them for our own ends. The horse, then, sits at the far end of the flight animal spectrum, while humankind, the supreme fight animal, is his clear opposite.

In order to gain a horse's trust and willing cooperation, both parties must meet in the middle. However, it is totally the responsibility of the human to achieve this. The only way is to earn the trust of the horse and never abuse his status as a flight animal.

If I learned anything on that first trip, it was that I needed a much longer time if I was to get what I was looking for: a true understanding of how horses behave in the wild.

My frustration was that it could not happen under these conditions. When we got back to the trap in the barranca, we merely jammed a bunch of horses into the circular pen, brought up the hired transport, and carted them off. We did not select suitable animals, grade them by age or sex. Along with the more suitable, younger adolescent colts came older animals and even lactating mares—meaning that somewhere behind was a foal facing certain death.

In short, we were distressingly insensitive. At least I knew what I wanted to do next time.

———

With our convoy of trucks hauling 150 mustangs—all of them banging and kicking in the trailers—we arrived back at the competition gounds in Salinas. When we dropped down the trailer ramps, the horses scooted into their new home, a huge stock corral near the track. The horses were seeing, for the first time, barns and other buildings, and the arena where they would be racing in just a month's time before thousands of people. The mustangs snorted and blew and ran round the perimeter of the corral, astonished at their new circumstances.

I rushed into the house, proud to tell my parents what we had done. "And," I said, "I'm going to take more time next year, and then I can see what those horses are all about. They're barely going to know I'm there."

My mother was receptive and listened intently. "What do you think you'll find out?"

"I don't know, but something. The way they communicate as a family. That's what I hope."

My father was not pleased at all. "About all you'll find out is it's cold at night and hot in the day. You'll find out those mustangs don't want to have much to do with you or your fancy notions." Horses understood one thing only, my father barked, and that was fear. If you did not hurt them first, they would hurt you.

As for the 150 mustangs, we—that is to say, humankind—were going to hurt them quite badly in the wild horse race. But it was not until later that I realized how responsible I was for that. For all my entrepreneurial spirit, I was, in the end, a child, with much to learn.

Some 20,000 spectators came to watch this popular part of the rodeo each of the four days. Larry and I were in among a crush of people pressed against the fence. Waiting on the track were a number of teams of three men each, all of them dressed in full cowboy regalia. They were as likely to get hurt as the horses were, and you could tell they were nervous by the way they fidgeted. The teams milled about some distance apart from one another, waiting to have their wild horse delivered to them, each team with a Western saddle parked ready on the ground nearby.

Riders would come onto the track on their saddle horses, each one literally dragging a wild mustang on the end of a fifteen-foot lead rope connected to the horn of his saddle. At the sight of this, the crowd started to holler and cheer and stamp their feet. Behind the mustangs and pushing them forward were more riders.

Wild with terror, the mustangs were bucking and running, diving and pulling on the ends of their ropes. I imagine the Roman circus generated something like the same hysteria; convinced they were coming to a savage end, the horses raged as they were dragged in. The crowd was whooping.

The riders then handed the lead rope of each mustang to the first member of each team, called "the anchor"—the biggest and heaviest of the three men. The anchors dug in their heels and set about trying to keep these 900-pound wild animals as much as possible in one place.

The second man is called "the mugger," and his is probably the most dangerous job. The mugger travels down the lead rope, hand over hand, turning this way and that to follow the line as the mustang fights and plunges like the wild animal he is. As fast as he can, the mugger has to grasp the horse around his neck, try to put him into a headlock, and pinch his top lips. The idea is to hold him still long enough for another man to put a saddle on him.

My heart was in my mouth as the battle began. Some of the men were thrown off the ropes before they reached the horses; others had better luck and were already hanging in there, wrestling with these animals like they were in a barroom brawl. The third member of the teams, "the rider," began to dart in, carrying a saddle on his arm, trying to throw it on and cinch it down.

Imagine the noise and the confusion. My nerves were screwed to the highest pitch, just watching. Several men limped off, too injured to continue, while others ran forward to take their places. One man was dragged out unconscious from under the feet of a horse and carried off.

By now, some riders had managed to tighten the cinch and were jumping up and aiming to stay on long enough to be handed the lead rope, which is their only method of guidance. It was a scene of utter chaos, with horses bolting in all directions, some with riders on board, some without. Riders who had managed to get mounted were attempting to race each other once around a half-mile track, and were using whatever methods of hazing they could. They were shouting and spurring their horses and pulling at the rope to try to turn them the right way.

I lived the excitement as would any thirteen-year-old raised in the culture of rodeo, but at the same time I recoiled against the mad cruelty. There were some crashing falls, and I felt the impact of each and every one of them as though it was happening to me. One horse, I learned later, had broken his jaw. An excited voice exclaimed behind me each time there was a horse writhing on the ground—"Crow's bait, Crow's bait!"

By the time some riders were up in the saddle and racing around the track, the roar of the crowd doubled in volume and the horses were running for their lives, their heads held low and ears pinned back to their necks. They raced once around the half-mile track and the winner threw one hand in the air and continued sailing around until his horse had slowed enough for him to leap down and take his applause. He would stand to face the audience, his expression one of utmost excitement and triumph.

The wild horse race causes several deaths among horses every year in Salinas, and it is the same at forty or so other rodeos around the country. I believe it should be abolished.

———

The task now was to make the mustangs worth more alive than dead. Larry and I had just sixty days, August and September, to break as many of them as possible. A schooled mustang might fetch a buyer at the October auction; an unbroken one was destined for Crow's Landing. Their lives, and our hopes for a profitable arrangement with Doc Leach, were in our own hands.

Owing to injuries and deaths in the race, only 130 of the mustangs were left to us. We turned them out in the corrals, where they were no doubt glad to relax after the trauma. Their rest would be brief. My brother and I agreed that I would take roughly two-thirds of them, to his third.

My first concern, though, was to hide my new ways of thinking from my father, who broke horses the traditional, violent way. Happily, a pair of barns ran down either side of the pen where I would school the mustangs, so I was sequestered from his view. Despite the impending deadline, I wanted to continue experimenting with the communication skills that so intrigued me. My aim was to refine a technique that used the horse's respect and cooperation, not the one that forced its servitude.

I believed it was important to concentrate on this, in part *because* of the deadline; I was sure my way would be quicker. But I also felt in my bones that I had chanced upon something new that would change the way human beings relate to horses. Although my technique would improve dramatically after the following year's expedition to Nevada, even at this stage I had come to think of my process as entirely different from that of "breaking" horses. That word has connotations of violence and domination.

I changed the nomenclature. From that day on, I called my method "starting" horses. If traditional breaking was designed to generate fear in the horse, I wanted to create trust. If the old way involved ropes and tying horses' heads and legs, I wanted no part of that either. A significant moment came when I realized I could cause trust in a horse without pain or restraint.

In short, instead of telling young horses "You must," I wanted to ask them "Will you?"

I knew from the very beginning that engaging the horse's trust would work. My technique was still haphazard and unrefined, but I got there. After the starting process, I recruited from our riding school four or five of my top students and so brought on to a good standard about eighty of my one hundred mustangs. The students were willing volunteers, and together we learned a great deal from every horse.

On the day of the sale, my eighty horses were ridden through the ring and my brother's were ridden as well. Altogether, the sale took in just under $6,000.

Doc Leach was happy with the results. He got back his $5,000 investment in the herd and made a small profit. This was unprecedented; acquiring mustangs for the wild horse race traditionally meant a substantial loss.

My brother and I were less happy, at least financially speaking. For two months' work, our share of the profit amounted to $250 each. Even in those days, this was not a wage to brag about. It was more like a nod and a thank-you. But given what I had started to learn about wild horses in those first few months, I had an even better feeling of time well spent. This was just the beginning.

———

The following summer was perhaps the finest of my life. I would spend much of it alone in the high desert, in what I came to see as an outdoor university. I was a freshman at Mustang U. But first I had to make some new arrangements with Doc Leach.

"What can I do for you, son?"

"I have an idea how to improve the wild horse race this year."

"You didn't do so badly for us last time."

"How about we reduce the number of mustangs we haul back here?"

"And that's to improve the race, is it?"

"Well," I explained, "I noticed that you didn't use all hundred-and-fifty head. You picked out the best two-thirds of them."

"That's right, we did."

"What if we choose the best two-thirds of them up there in Nevada instead of down here in Salinas? Then we'd only be transporting a hundred head instead of one-fifty, and we could lower the overhead."

Even at fourteen, I had a pretty firm grasp of cost.

Doc Leach looked down at me. "Who's going to judge the best one hundred head—you?"

"That's right, sir. Then we can avoid bringing the lactating mares and the older animals in the first place."

Doc Leach smiled. "You've got a point, I have to admit."

I recommended that we gather 500 head and select the best 100 adolescent colts and fillies. ("Adolescent" in mustang terms means an animal three to five years old, since the limited nutrition and harsh desert environment delay their maturity. Mustangs cover vast territories to feed, and the saying is that they can graze—at twenty miles an hour.)

I paid a trucker to transport myself, Brownie, Sergeant, and Oriel up to the Campbell Ranch. Ralph and Vivian Carter agreed to join me later on this adventure; the helpers and truck convoy would come up with them. But for three weeks I would be alone in the Nevada desert with the mustangs. I would have the time to move slowly and observe them without interfering in any way. The Campbell Ranch had prior information on the location of family groups, which were sometimes ten miles apart. I intended to bring each family group toward the trap in the barranca one by one, very slowly, observing them as I went.

Once again, I was glad to have Brownie as one of my saddle horses for this all-important experience. I patted his neck as we rode out over the high desert ground. Oriel and Sergeant walked along behind, and in addition I had our black-and-white stock dog, called Bobby, three pairs of binoculars (two spares, for I would have been lost without them), a handgun and a rifle.

When we reached the first horizon I twisted around in my saddle and watched the outbuildings of the Campbell Ranch disappear from sight as we moved down the opposite side of the slope. We were on our own.

It felt good to be riding across this open ground again, with its rocky barrancas where the cottonwood and aspen trees grew. I would have to be extra vigilant for rattlesnakes. Worse were the invisible crevices: you might be galloping across what looked like a flat, unbroken expanse of desert in pursuit of a herd when, suddenly, a six-foot crevice yawned at your horse's feet. The mustangs, who usually spotted you before you spotted them, used these depressions cleverly. They would travel in them at the slightest suspicion of danger, and from my vantage a mile away it seemed that the horses in my sights had suddenly vanished.

My father was right, at least, about the weather: the days were hot, the nights cold. Occasionally, rainstorms would lash me and the horses for an hour. Big, billowy, high-desert clouds would give rise to electrical storms. I was living on a diet mostly of jerky—a cured meat—plus pancake mix and salami, as well as oranges.

To find the first family group of horses, I had to consider their food source. The mustangs would eat the sage and the chamise if they were desperate, but they preferred the gramma, brome, and rye grasses.

When I caught up with my first group, my aim was to integrate with the herd as closely as I could. Either they would accept me as no threat, which meant staying more than a mile distant, or I could try to get closer without their knowing I was there. The latter option quickly evaporated. The horses caught my scent from a mile away and began to move off. They were little more than dots on the plateau, and already they were going away.

I left Oriel, my bay packhorse, behind because he was proving rather clumsy and often stumbled over stones, the noise of which carried over vast distances—not that he cared. I was beginning to wonder about this Oriel character. His ears were always at half-mast, neither forward nor backward. He was either a deep thinker or a little dumb, maybe both.

After lightly hobbling him and leaving Sergeant to keep him company, I continued on foot, leading Brownie. We used the barrancas as cover and stayed downwind, moving quietly. Given the time to move slowly and think about what was happening, I was surprised by how hypersensitive the herd was to our presence. If Brownie just scuffed a rock, I could see their ears flick in our direction.

I could get within a quarter mile of the herd, but no closer. I was running out of cover and even though I was downwind of them, they would cede us no more ground. Brownie and I settled down by a cottonwood tree and I counted the horses, trying to log their markings so I could distinguish one from another.

My binoculars were key. When I see young people today strapping on virtual reality helmets, entranced by the world they enter, I am reminded of how I felt when I looked through binoculars at that herd of wild horses. They seemed close enough to touch. I could see subtle shifts of the eyes, ears, tongue. These were pure movements, untainted by human intervention. That day I would watch for eight continuous hours.

I noticed, in particular, the dun mare. Older than most of the others, with a heavier belly that hinted at many pregnancies, she seemed to issue a lot of commands. She ordered her group to move off. She started, the others followed. She stopped, they did likewise. It seemed she was the wisest, and they knew it.

What I was observing, in fact, was the dominant mare. Many people likely still think that the stallion runs the show. The breeding or dominant stallion, sometimes called the alpha male or lead male, will skirt the herd and defend it from marauders. His motivation is to prevent anyone or anything from stealing his harem. But it was the dun mare who was in charge of the day-to-day running of this group. There was no mistaking it.

And then I saw an extraordinary sequence of events. A light bay colt was behaving badly. He was about twenty months old, I guessed, with a vast amount of feathering around his fetlocks and down the backs of his legs, and a mane running down well below his neckline. He took a run at a filly and gave her a kick. The filly cowered and hobbled off, and the colt looked pleased with himself. He was only about 550 pounds in weight, but very aware of the fact that he owned a pair of testicles.

Then he committed another crime. A little foal approached him, moving his mouth in a suckling action to indicate he was no threat but subservient. Just a foal. That cut no ice with this colt; he launched himself at his younger cousin and took a bite out of the foal's backside. The bay colt was a terrorist. Immediately after the attack, he pretended nothing had happened; he went neutral, as though trying to avoid blame.

Each time he behaved badly, the dun mare—the matriarch—weaved a little closer to him. I became certain that she was watching for any more of this behavior. She showed no apparent sign of interest, but she had left her station and was edging closer to him all the time.

The mare witnessed about four such episodes before she finally made her move. Now she stood within twenty yards. Still, the cream-colored colt could not help himself: he launched at a grown mare, grabbed the nape of her neck, and bit down hard.

The dun mare did not hesitate. In an instant she went from neutral to full-blown anger; she pinned her ears back and ran at him, knocking him down. As he struggled to his feet, she whirled and knocked him down again. While this chastisement unfolded, the other members apparently took no notice.

The dun mare ended by driving the colt 300 yards from the herd and left him there, alone. Amazed, I tried to fathom what I was seeing. The mare took up a position on the edge of the herd to keep him in exile. She kept her eyes on his and faced up to him. She was freezing him out.

It terrified the colt to be left alone. For a flight animal, this was tantamount to a death sentence; the predators will get any horse long separated from the group. He walked back and forth, his head close to the ground, several times executing this strange, uncomfortable gait. It looked like a sign of obedience, similar to a human's bow.

Then the colt made his way around to the other side of the herd and attempted to sneak back in that way, but the dun mare had followed his circle. Again she drove him out, running at him until he had fled another 300 yards. Returning to her post on the edge of the herd, she kept her body square on his, and never once took her eye off him.

He stood there, and I noticed a lot of licking and chewing going on, although with all this drama he had eaten nothing. I remembered the foal and how he had snapped his mouth in an obvious signal of humility, as though he were saying, "I'm not a threat to you." Was this colt now saying the same thing to his matriarch?

By this time, it was getting dark, and I would have to get back to the other horses. I wanted the moon bright that night; I wanted desperately to see how the tale would end. I scooped up Brownie's reins and rode back to where Sergeant and Oriel were waiting. My intention was to camp there and continue observing the dialogue between mare and colt.

When I got back, Oriel was standing with his nose in a bush. Then he lifted his head sharply, his whole body tense with surprise. A cloud of bees surrounded his head. This was an emergency, for the horse was clearly being stung. Oriel took a few paces backward and then tried a couple more sideways. He tried it with his head held low and then jerked it up again.

No luck.

Then he shook himself like a dog emerging from water. The bees still hovered, a cloud hooked on a mountaintop. This was a puzzle, and Oriel had nearly run out of tricks. There was only one left: he tossed his head up and down, evidently figuring that if he did this long enough the bees would get bored and leave, which is what they did.

Oriel did not seem unduly perturbed by the experience. It was one of life's many mysteries: the one and only time I ever saw a bee swarm take such a shine to a horse's head.

Oriel was an accident-prone, affable character who always got into trouble but somehow made it seem funny. Once he spiked himself by walking into a shard of wood. I am unsure how he did it—and only he could have done it—but a two-foot-long splinter was driven through his nose and the roof of his mouth. It was a painful sight: not at all amusing, but this was Oriel we were dealing with. He was most apologetic and sorry for himself and allowed me to perform the grisly task of pulling out the splinter. He was then left with a hole in his nose the size of my thumb, blood pouring from the wound.

I took off the bright red bandanna I customarily wore around my neck and used it to plug the hole and stem the bleeding. There stood Oriel with a red flag flying in the middle of his face, and every time he took a drink the cloth would soak up the water. Then it would drip, like tears. It was a sorry sight, but I had to laugh.

The sun now sank surprisingly fast down the western slope of the sky, as though itself desiring rest from a hard day's work. I made camp and hurried to settle Brownie, Sergeant, and Oriel with their feed.

From its place in that vast sky, the moon cast the landscape in a new and surprisingly generous light. I picked up my binoculars and found I could see clearly for quite a distance. I did not realize it then, but my night vision was likely helped by the fact that I am totally color-blind. I know that the color of the high desert is dove-gray only because others have told me. Mine is a rare condition, quite separate from the more common one in which an individual cannot properly distinguish colors.

When I was young, no one believed that I could see only in black and white, but I have subsequently learned that I see in a way very different from normally sighted people.

Oliver Sacks, in his study of "The Case of the Colorblind Painter," describes how his subject had a car accident that caused him to lose all perception of color. But along with that terrible loss came an unexpected gift: "People's figures might be visible and recognizable half a mile off...his vision had become much sharper, 'that of an eagle.'" Distressed by his condition, the artist became nocturnal and at night his extraordinary vision allowed him to identify a license plate four blocks away.

Using the binoculars, I caught sight of my herd. To my astonishment, the dun mare was now grooming the troublesome colt. She was giving him little scrapes on his neck and hindquarters with her teeth, and generally fussing over him. She had let him back in; now she was keeping him close by and giving him a lot of attention. She worked away at the root of his tail, hips, and withers.

Purgatory was behind him. This was heaven.

As it turned out, night was a better time to watch the wild herds. Mustangs fear attacks from predators mostly at dawn and dusk; at night they relax and their social interaction is more marked. It became a habit to watch them by the light of the moon, and I would usually sleep from about one-thirty A.M. until five-thirty A.M.

For the next two summers, I would round up mustangs for the Salinas rodeo, and nothing I saw ever matched the exchange between the dun mare and that light bay colt. It was educational to watch the matriarch disciplining young, adolescent horses because so much happened. The youthful energy and inexperience of the gang of adolescents drove them to make mistakes, much like the young of any species.

Often, like a child, the colt would reoffend immediately after being let back in, to test the disciplinary system and to gain back lost ground. He might fight another colt or bother the fillies. The dun mare came right back and disciplined him again. Each time he sinned she drove him out and kept him out before letting him back in and welcoming him into the group with extensive grooming. The third time he sinned, he practically owned up and exited by himself, grumbling about it but accepting his fate.

Then, finally, his teenage rebellion ceased. Now cloyingly sweet, he had become a positive nuisance, wandering about and asking every horse, "Do you need any grooming?" when all they wanted was to be left alone to eat. For four days the dun mare had made the education of this awful brat her number-one priority, and it had paid off.

As I watched the mare's training procedures with this adolescent and others, I began to understand the language she used, and it was exciting to recognize the exact sequence of signals that would pass between her and the younger horses. It really was a language—predictable, discernible, and effective.

The silent aspect of her commands is worth dwelling on because we often underrate a language that uses a different medium from our own. As I was to learn much later, the most common form of communication on this planet takes place silently—in the dark of the deep sea, where animals use intricate lighting systems called bioluminescence to attract mates, ward off predators, attract prey, and otherwise convey all the signals necessary for their existence.

Body language is not confined to humans or horses; it constitutes the most common form of communication between all animate objects.

In the desert, the dun mare constantly schooled the foals and yearlings, and they responded to her, without a sound. The stallion's security system required near absolute silence, and his investigations of mating potential were also conducted soundlessly. The mustangs were happy with one another, upset with one another, guided and advised one another—all in silence.

I learned that in the equine universe, every degree of a horse's movement has a reason. Nothing is trivial, nothing is to be dismissed. A horse raised alone, I now know, will still speak Equus: genetics imparts much of the language. But the lone horse's communication is dull, less defined. A mustang raised in the wild in a herd, on the other hand, displays as pure a form of the equine tongue as I could have hoped to find anywhere.

I would learn, much later, while starting horses in a round pen, a rich code of signs and subsigns. Keeping my mouth closed invited the horse's discomfort, opening it slightly was fine. Opening a fist on the side of my body away from the horse drew him in, while opening a fist close to him sent him away. Fingers open stirred one response, fingers closed another. Hands above my head with fingers splayed provoked true panic (perhaps it triggers primordial memories of cat claws). Whether I am moving, standing still, facing the horse, or away: all this matters as the horse reads my body language and I read his. I can now enumerate about one hundred or more signs the horse will respond to, and the vocabulary is still growing.

The key ingredient in the equine language is the positioning of the body and its direction of travel. The attitude of the body relative to the long axis of the spine and the short axis: this is critical to their vocabulary. It *is* their vocabulary.

When the dun mare squared up and faced the colt, she was holding up a Keep Out sign. If she showed him part of her long axis, he could begin to consider returning to the herd. But before she would say, "I forgive you," he had to say, "I'm sorry." If the colt paced with his nose close to the ground, then he was asking for a chance to end his isolation and to renegotiate his position with her. He was saying, "I am obedient, and I'm willing to listen." If he showed her the long axis of his body, then he was offering vulnerable areas to her and asking to be forgiven.

Their eye contact also spoke volumes. When she was holding him out there, she always kept one eye directly on his, sometimes for uncomfortably long periods of time. When her eye slid a short distance off his, he knew he might be allowed back in. I came to realize how subtle was this reading of eye contact. Even when I was unfamiliar to this herd, I could cause a horse to alter his direction and pace of movement by changing which part of his body I looked at—even from a distance.

When the colt trotted out to suffer his exile, he would throw his nose out in a circular motion. Translation: "I didn't intend to do that. I'm sorry. It wasn't my idea. It just happened. It was the other guy's fault." The dun mare had to judge whether or not to believe him. I could see her thinking about it. Sometimes she bought it, sometimes not. The licking and chewing action of the colt's mouth was a signal of penitence. He was saying to her, "Look, I'm a herbivore. I'm no threat to you. I'm eating over here."

Observing all this, I could make sense of the "yo-yo effect" once described by my Uncle Ray. Cherokee hunters had for centuries exploited the tendency of prey animals, once chased, to circle back and "hunt" the hunter. Press the young horse away, and his instinct is to return. The dun mare advanced on him, then retreated. When I made this connection between the mare's discipline and Uncle Ray's story, it was as if synapses in my brain all fired simultaneously. A term sprang to my mind—"Advance and Retreat."

In time, I would grasp just how exact a language it was. There were precise messages, whole phrases and sentences that always meant the same thing, always had the same effect.

Perhaps, it occurred to me, I could use the same silent system of communication myself. If I understood how to do it, I could effectively cross over the boundary between human (the ultimate fight animal) and horse (the flight animal). Using their language, their system of communication, I could create a strong bond of trust. I would achieve cross-species communication.

"Advance and Retreat" also offered a psychological explanation for why horses are "into pressure" animals. In my twenties, during a short career riding bucking horses, I once waited in the chute on a horse who was leaning hard on one side, pinching my leg against the boards. Six cowboys were pushing against the horse's body trying to move him over, but the harder they pushed, the more the horse leaned.

Finally, one wise old horseman chanced by and put one finger against the horse's *other* side, as if pushing against it. Instantly, the horse moved into that little bit of pressure and my pinched leg was just as instantly grateful.

Horses, as a natural response, do not move away from pressure, they move into it—particularly if the pressure is applied to their flanks. The wild dogs that prey on horses on every continent attack the horse's belly, aiming to tear a hole in the stomach wall so the intestines will drop out. The dogs can then fall back and track the horse, confident that a meal is imminent.

Once flight is no longer a clear option, the horse's best defense is not to run but to turn into the onslaught and kick: if they run from a bite, their skin will more likely tear. I am convinced that this explains a phenomenon recognized by all good trainers: poke a forefinger into a horse's side and he will move against the pressure rather than away from it. It is perhaps the single most important thing to remember in training horses. *Horses are into pressure animals.*

Go into pain, nature told the horse. And the horse heeded the message. Over the years I would expand my Equus vocabulary, but even the more refined signs would exist within this all-important umbrella concept of Advance and Retreat that I learned at the age of thirteen.

———

Later that same summer I witnessed a fight between two stallions.

Water was in short supply that year, and I watched, fascinated, as the matriarchs made frantic efforts to get their families watered and fed. The different family groups were lining up at a water hole like airliners in a holding pattern. The groups had to keep their distance because the stallions would not tolerate it otherwise. Their territorial instincts were in conflict with those of the matriarchs, and this made all the horses edgy.

Among them was a bachelor group—young males who had left their family groups and were now scrimmaging among themselves, honing their fighting skills for the day when they would make a challenge for a herd of their own. Then the inevitable happened. A bachelor clashed with the alpha male of a family group waiting in line for water. A stallion fight is one of the few times you will hear sounds from a mustang.

I found the noise of battle chilling, but the mares took no notice of the terrible squealing and screaming at the perimeter of their group. This was a contest that one horse would win; a draw was not in the cards. The two males reared and pawed each other with their hooves, plunged and kicked and bit. It continued for five or six hours, well into the night, and though my eyelids were drooping, I had to watch.

Just when it seemed the stallion had won and the bachelor was about to hobble off, the latter redoubled his attack, though his leg was torn and bleeding from the teeth raking his hide. Limping toward the stallion, practically carrying his hind leg, the bachelor waded in again.

When the younger stallion finally left, he did not return. Before long the predators would gather round him and he would be their meal for the next day or two. The bachelor knew it, too. A vanquished male will often commit a kind of suicide, deliberately seeking the areas where the cats are, almost offering himself.

Even the victor, on this occasion, was a sorry sight. He was left battered and limping, and he walked as if he was a century old for the next day or two. Another challenger would have finished him, but none came and he nursed himself back to strength.

———

It took Brownie and me about three weeks to gather the different family groups. When we were five miles from the trap in the barranca with one group, a team of six day hands from the Campbell Ranch would ride out, circle the mustangs, and help drive them into the enclosures where a feed of alfalfa awaited them. They would then tell me where the second group had been last sighted, and take Brownie, Oriel, and me in the van as close as dirt roads would allow, maybe fifteen to twenty miles. When they left us and were driving back, they would drop a trail of alfalfa every mile or two back to the trap, as bait for the horses.

At the end of the three-week period, we had about 500 mustangs corralled. We culled lactating mares, obviously pregnant fillies, breeding stallions, and older animals, then loaded about one hundred young colts and fillies into the trucks and drove them back to Salinas as before.

That year, they had a much better wild horse race. The horses were suitable for the task at hand, and fewer were injured. Once again I watched from the grandstand, but took no pleasure in it. I vowed to train myself as quickly as possible to communicate with horses; I was beginning to realize that there was a lot of apologizing to be done to the equine species.

Euphoric from my time in the desert and bursting with what I thought were critical insights about horses, I looked forward to telling my mother and brother about my discoveries. My mother was a quiet, competent rider who genuinely liked her horses, and she was naturally intrigued by my tales. But the one person who understood better than anyone my sense of excitement, if not precisely what I was saying, was Bill Dorrance, who had helped me connect with the Campbell Ranch.

Bill was born in 1903. He was a slim six-footer, and always wore round glasses. Were you to see him in a three-piece suit and hear him talk, you might take the straight, stiff man for a banker or an accountant, certainly an educated man. In fact, like his brother, Tom, he had little formal schooling, but there was a remarkable brightness about them both.

Now in his mid-nineties, Bill is still a fine rider and roper but as a young man he was nervous when he competed under pressure in the showring. Bill Dorrance was all about careful calculation. In terms of the psychology of a horse, the study of the horse's mind, he was light-years ahead of his time. He was the only one who believed in me, and when I was seventeen my father finally forbade me to see him. "Bill Dorrance will destroy you," he predicted one memorable day in Salinas. Bill was a progressive man with new ideas, ideas I shared and understood. When I got back from the desert, I went right to him. He was like a grandfather to me, an armchair philosopher of horsemanship. He was ridiculed for some of the things he said, but I now see how far ahead of his time he really was.

"You have to cause your horse to be mellow," he once told me, "to be in unison with you, not against you." It was a breathtaking notion for someone of his generation. I owe Bill a great deal. What we shared was a keen awareness of the possibilities between horses and humans, a sense that we had barely scratched the surface of that ancient connection. "I'm discovering things about horses," he once told me, "and I don't want to die before I pass them on. You're young and talented, and I want to pass them on to you."

I felt I did possess a special affinity with horses. Now that I was beginning to understand their silent language, I could turn a great corner. My ambition was immense: change the way humans relate to horses.

The one hundred mustangs at the competition grounds would be the ideal test of my theory: how to form a natural bond with a wild horse; how to convince the horse you are an ally, not a predator; how to cast myself as the dominant matriarch and speak her language.

I would have to work fast, and with one eye on the whereabouts of my father, because I did not want him to interfere—although, underneath it all, I still sought his acceptance and approval.

As it happened, in the course of starting the mustangs, I discovered something so exciting that I began to believe I could persuade even my tradition-bound father to see things my way. I had identified a phenomenon that I called "join-up." As I lay in bed at night I could hardly sleep, so convinced was I that I had stumbled on something that truly would change the way we operate with horses.

Surely, I reasoned, my father would see it. He was too experienced a horseman not to. But I knew better than to go to him and show him directly. Instead, I settled on showing Ray Hackworth, hoping that he could prevail upon my father because he had my father's respect.

Ray Hackworth leased facilities at the competition grounds where we lived. Soft-spoken but also a disciplinarian, he was a noted trainer and a gentleman: I asked him to come and watch what I could do. I told him I had discovered a phenomenon that I could explain only in terms of the horse's own language. I promised him that I could dissolve the natural barrier between horse and man, flight animal and fight animal.

He reminded me that my father had often warned me over the years that my ideas could be dangerous and I should stick to the conventional ways of doing things. But I continued to implore that he come and see for himself what I could do. If I could please Ray, I could surely please my father....

Eventually he agreed.

When we arrived at the round pen, Ray strolled up the ramp on to the viewing deck and leaned against the fence. "OK," he said, tipping his hat to the back of his head. "Let's see it."

I stood in the middle of the pen, together with a three-year-old colt not long past the trauma of the wild horse race. The colt wore no halter, rope, or restraint of any type. The door to the round pen was closed; it was he and I.

From practicing this a hundred times over, I knew what to do. I confidently waited a moment or two to let this unnamed mustang get accustomed to the round pen. He was too nervous to take a single step toward me, although his attention was on me as the main threat currently confronting him. "What I'm going to do," I said, "is use the same language as the dominant mare in his family group." The silence from the viewing deck told me Ray was not going to ask questions, so I continued. "That language is a silent language, a body language, and the first thing I'm going to ask him is to go away from me, to flee. I'm only doing this because then I will ask him to come back and join up with me."

I moved, quite abruptly, toward the colt. I squared my shoulders and fixed my eye on his eye. Straight away, he went into flight, taking off in a canter around the perimeter, staying as close to the wall as he could—and as far from me as possible.

I continued to press him into flight, in the same way that I had observed the matriarch driving away the adolescents in the wild. I remained square on to him, I maintained direct eye contact. For Ray's benefit, I continued to explain what I was doing. "In his own language I'm saying to him, 'Go ahead and flee, but I don't want you to go away a little. I want you to go away a lot. For now, I'll call the shots, until we can form a partnership. You see, I speak your language.' "

I had a light sash line, and I pitched it at the colt—not to hit him, but to encourage him to flee. Which he did. As he cantered around the pen I used the line and my body posture to keep him in flight; my shoulders were parallel to his long axis. I was facing directly toward his head and, with my body, pressing him away. My eyes were locked on his.

This continued for several minutes. I was watching for the signals—the same signals I had observed in the wild, when the adolescents would ask the dominant mare to be released from their enforced exile. Meanwhile, as a test, I allowed my eyes to drop back to his neck. When I did, he slowed.

I let my eyes drop back farther, to his shoulder...and he slowed a bit more; his head started to come off the rail a bit to look over at me. When I let my eyes drop back to his hip, I saw a further reduction in speed, and he began to angle off the wall even more.

Then I took my eyes back to his eyes, and his speed increased immediately; he moved back toward the wall and was in full flight again. He was reading me. He knew we were dealing with each other in *his* language.

I called to Ray, "I'm waiting for his ear to open onto me, for him to start licking and chewing, and then for him to duck his head and run along holding it a few inches off the ground." It was important that Ray realize I could *predict* what would happen.

"Here's the first one, now!" I called. "See?"

The colt's inside ear had opened toward me and stayed fixed in that position. The outside ear was tuned to the surrounding areas, flicking forward and back. The colt was saying, "I don't really know what this is all about, but I'll pay attention to you and we'll see where it goes from here."

The colt had made approximately eight revolutions of the round pen before the ear closest to me was adequately locked on. At this point, I pitched the line in front of the colt and stepped a bit to the front of his action, keeping my eyes locked on his to prevent his coming off the wall toward me. Quickly, he reversed field and fled in the opposite direction. In a moment or two, the ear closest to me was locked onto me as before. It was going according to pattern.

Since Ray could not know what to look for down in that pen between the kid and the colt, it was important that I explain my actions and expectations, but I suddenly sensed this might all be a mistake. A fourteen-year-old explaining things to an older man? It might be seen as arrogant. Still, I hoped, the value of what I was doing would counteract that.

I began to take the pressure off the colt. First, I reduced the number of times I cast the line at him. Then I coiled the line and held it in my hand, slapping my leg with it to encourage him to continue. The colt came back to a trot. By this time he had made twelve revolutions of the round pen.

The next signal came right on time. He started to lick and chew. His tongue actually came through his teeth and outside his mouth, then he pulled his tongue back and chewed with his teeth. There was a ripple effect across the large mandibles.

"There!" I called to Ray. "You see that chewing action with his mouth? That's exactly what I saw them doing out on the range. It means he's ready to discuss this situation. He's gone away and I've pressed him away farther. He's recognized my desire to communicate with him, and now he'd like the chance to renegotiate. This licking and chewing action of the colt is a message to me, it's saying something like, 'I am a herbivore; I am a grazer, and I'm making this eating action with my mouth now because I'm considering whether or not to trust you. Help me out with that decision, can you, please?' "

Then came the final signal I was looking for. As the colt trotted around, he dropped his head so his nose was traveling only an inch or so above ground level.

"And there you go!" I called to Ray. "His head's dropped. I can't tell you the times I've seen this out there in the desert, and it always means the same thing—it means 'Let me back in, I don't want to flee any more.' "

It was time for me—like the dun mare—to turn passive, to let this colt come and join up with me. I allowed my eyes to travel to a point maybe fifteen to twenty feet in front of him. I moved my shoulders around to follow my eyes until they were on a forty-five-degree angle to his long body axis. I was avoiding eye contact and showing him my flanks, as it were.

Immediately, he stopped. He came off the wall and faced me. I maintained my position, my body and my eyeline at forty-five degrees to his. He took a step or two toward me. I waited.

Then he walked right up to me, not stopping until his nose was inches from my shoulder. I could not speak. I wanted to shout to Ray, "Look, this is what I mean. How *about* this? Isn't it fantastic?" But I could not afford to break the spell. It was indeed magic: this colt trusted me. No longer a predator, I was his safety zone. The moment of acceptance, or join-up, is what I had discovered, and I felt a shudder of heartfelt emotion. I have felt the same thrill with every one of the 10,000 or more horses I have started this way. I fervently hoped that Ray felt the same way.

To test the strength of the join-up, I took a slow right turn. The colt followed me into the circle, his nose to my shoulder. Then I took a left turn. He hesitated, and looked to be going the other way.

Immediately I knew to return to a dominant stance, and I began to drive him away. He did not like that, and before he had completed one circuit of the round pen he was flicking his nose out and apologizing, asking to be let back in.

I allowed him back, soothed him and talked to him, and gave him a good stroke between the eyes. It is not essential to use the area between the eyes as the stroking point, but it seems to be more effective to touch the horse here than any other part of the body. There is general consensus that for a horse to let you into a part of his anatomy that he cannot see is the ultimate expression of trust.

Now I had the colt walking comfortably behind me and I knew Ray would be amazed. I imagined him saying to my father, "I tell you, Marvin, that boy of yours had a wild horse walking along behind him like it was his best friend after only twenty-five minutes. He's on to something. Come down and see for yourself."

I called out to Ray, as quietly as possible now that the colt was standing next to me, "Ray, you know, now that he's joined up with me and we're on the same side, it's pretty much of a formality." When I was confident the colt fully trusted me, I brought in another long-line, a saddle, bridle, and a saddle pad, as well as a long stirrup leather—all of which I put on the ground in the middle of the pen. With the click of the gate, the colt's stance changed. He saw something different—a pile of equipment—and became frightened. He had justification for being skeptical, so I waited. I allowed him to choose between me and the equipment. He chose me and calmed down. He stood still while I carefully lifted the saddle pad and the saddle onto his back. He let me fix the girth—slowly, smoothly. After taking a step or two away, he steadied and let me continue.

Before any rope or lead had been attached to his head, let alone a bridle, he was wearing his first saddle. He was asking me lots of questions, his ears flicking back and forth and his nostrils blowing, but he trusted me.

At this point I stepped away from him and squared up to him, driving him away, not aggressively, but with the confidence I had developed over the last 200 or so horses. He went into flight and began to canter around the perimeter of the round pen. I wanted to familiarize him with the saddle before a rider was on. He bucked hard for several minutes, which I was glad to see because I did not want Ray Hackworth to think this was a fluke. Within a few minutes the colt was cantering steadily around, the bucking over. I saw the same signals—the licking and chewing, the inside ear settling on me, his coming off the wall to get closer to me. For a minute or two I worked him around the outer limits of the pen, and let him find comfort in carrying the saddle, first one way, then the other. After three or four revolutions in each direction, the colt was telling me he was ready to come back in. I let him join up with me, adjusted his girth, and generally soothed him with my voice. He was doing fine. There was nothing to be frightened about, if he stuck with me. I would look after him and have fun with him, love him like I loved all his brothers and sisters. I took the bridle and lifted it over his ears. The colt accepted the snaffle with no more than a brief lift of his head. I secured the reins under the rear portion of the saddle and took the stirrups down to prepare for long-lining. Then I sent the colt back to work, cantering him around the perimeter, first one way, then the other. He was fully tacked-up, wearing a saddle and a bridle and the long-lines.

I called out, "I want to gain his confidence and make him happy to follow the bit and bridle—as he'll be doing just that for the rest of his working life. I want to make it a happy experience for him."

I turned the colt six or seven times before stopping him and reining back one step. I again adjusted his girth; I brushed the saddle with my hands, rubbed his neck and belly. Then I put my left toe in the stirrup and prepared to lift myself on to his back. I felt the strain in my thigh muscle as I asked the colt if I could put my full weight into the stirrup, testing for his reaction. He took a sideways step to help redistribute the extra weight, but he held firm.

I lifted myself up. Instead of swinging a leg over, I lay across his back for a while, waiting to see if he was comfortable with this. I hoped I was answering any questions he had with the things I was saying to him. I would find him a good name. We would find him a good home. Perhaps he would enjoy being a ranch horse, or maybe he would go into a Western show, in the pleasure-horse category. He might end up with a kid like me, learning to ride. I let the colt catch sight of me out of both eyes before calmly swinging a leg over and sitting up. I was riding him after only forty minutes.

I sat there jubilant on the back of that horse. An idealistic youth, I was convinced that it was only a matter of weeks before I would enjoy the respect and admiration of my elders and betters all over the county. And especially, my father.

"That was a fluke!" Ray barked out.

He was staring at me, a concerned look on his face. The sound of his voice coincided with the colt's first steps, and I did not try to stop him. As the colt and I walked around together, I heard Ray say, "You're wrong to go against your father. He's worried about you getting hurt—and you could be hurt. These horses are dangerous. I suggest you stop it now."

He walked from the viewing deck and disappeared from sight. I rode the colt, feeling crushed at the very moment I should have felt triumphant. The people whose respect and guidance I needed were refusing to give it. I vowed never to mention my ideas to anyone again.

CHAPTER 2

Growing Up
with Horses

My first and most vivid childhood memory has me on the back of a horse. The ears of a horse flicking back and forth, the neck bobbing in front of me, the mane bouncing as the horse's rhythmic stride carried us along—well before I could walk, horse geography was as familiar to me as the human kind.

I was not like other toddlers, lifted onto a saddle as a diversion or so that a photograph might be snapped. I sat on a horse in the crook of my mother's arm for many hours at a time, while she gave riding lessons at the horse facility where she and my father lived. The feel of leather reins and horsehair, the sound of a horse blowing, the smell of fresh hay and horse lather: my senses first stirred in the world of horses.

I was born in the midst of the Great Depression, on May 14, 1935, in the little town of Salinas, one hundred miles south of San Francisco. John Steinbeck grew up in Salinas and set many of his classic novels—*The Grapes of Wrath, East of Eden, The Red Pony*—in this region. Perhaps he drew inspiration for his characters from my ancestors, among the immigrants and natives who came to settle in edenic California.

The first thing I would have seen when I was carried outside our little gray house would have been 2,300 acres of prime land situated in the so-called Salad Bowl of America. I remember the smells of the valley: the awful sweet, fermenting smells from Spreckels, the big sugar plant; the pungent hothouse smells of broccoli, onion, garlic, and the other cash crops growing in the alluvial topsoil that was twenty feet deep in places.

In *East of Eden,* Steinbeck talks about the Salinas River valley, how the river raged in spring, then went underground in summer—"a part-time river" he called it. The novel describes how a man bored a well in that lush valley and up came white sand full of shells and pieces of whalebone, along with bits of redwood—proof that the valley had once been a forest, and later an inland sea. Steinbeck sketches the flowers that grow there, the California poppies the color of gold—"if pure gold were liquid and could raise a cream," the blue lupines, the buttercups, the stands of Indian paintbrush, the yellow violets with black centers. He describes the valley's yellow mustard, once so tall that, if a man were to ride a horse in a field of it, only his head would be visible.

The valley is prone to extremes: occasionally too much water in winter, too little in summer. Topsoil thick in the valley bottom, scant on the mountainsides. Spring grasses were luxurious, but in summer the hot wind—"a rasping nervous wind," Steinbeck called it—forced men working in the fields to wear goggles over their eyes and kerchiefs over their noses to keep out the dust.

And Steinbeck refers to the place names, like Wild Horse Canyon and Mustang Grade, a reminder for me of how horses figure prominently in the valley. And in my life.

We did not live in a rural setting. Our place was set on the edge of town in a built-up area, but every one of our buildings was horse-inspired—from box stalls to a showring with bleachers to enclosures and breeding barns.

By the time I was two, I spent most of the day on a horse, having graduated to a mount of my own. My childhood was unique: few people can say they were born and raised on a rodeo competition grounds. The grounds came to exist when Eugene Sherwood died and willed to the city of Salinas 2,300 acres to be used solely for horse-related activities.

When the estate and the city called on my father to manage the land, he agreed, and shortly thereafter construction began on more than 800 box stalls and a competition arena with a 20,000-seat grandstand. At the time, it was the largest equestrian facility in North America. It still exists but was recently rebuilt: I plucked as a souvenir a slab of concrete from the old grandstand.

In addition to managing the facility, my father, Marvin, also operated his own riding school on the grounds. Physical education classes in Salinas grammar and high schools offered horseback riding. And so every day my mother, Marguerite, would make her rounds in our big station wagon, picking up students and bringing them to the grounds for their lessons, then returning them to class. Marvin Earl Roberts also trained and boarded horses for private clients, and leased the facilities to various horse trainers, as stipulated by Eugene Sherwood in his will.

My first horse was called Ginger. No one asked about his breeding: he was that kind of horse. Ginger was a red roan, with a bit of Thoroughbred in him, some Spanish pony blood, and maybe some Belgian four generations back, judging by the bit of feather on his legs.

He was thirteen years old when I first met him, a reined cow horse from the Uhl Ranch who in his time had been a fair entry in Western competition. Now, in his retirement, he was required to be both my baby-sitter and my teacher. Ginger had the perfect temperament: well-disciplined and steady, and marvelously calm, collected, and amiable. "Bomb-proof," as horse people say.

He had done all the cowboy stuff for years, and he knew it intimately. Even with a three-year-old kid bouncing on his withers and flapping his arms and legs in every direction, Ginger was patient. He knew me and nickered for me. His was not a noble or a peaceful retirement, but I think he too had fun. In my eyes he could do no wrong.

I can remember people saying, "That boy's just three years old"—but I could walk, trot, and canter a horse, do flying lead changes, and perform figure-of-eight maneuvers without a great deal of trouble.

My father soon noticed my riding abilities and made plans to exploit them. Before I had even started kindergarten, my father told me I had to practice harder and spend more time riding than I already did. He seized on me rather than on my brother because Larry was younger and born with a condition that, during his early years, made him somewhat frail. Larry was a gifted rider, more gifted than I was. But where he needed looking after, I could be pushed to the limit. I entered horse shows regularly and competed almost every weekend. I still have some shaky old footage of Larry and me entering the junior stock-horse class when I was four years old. The grainy, flickering film shows us running our horses around, spinning and stopping them, and racing them back and forth like miniature versions of the cowboys who had taught us—all in eerie silence.

When I see how I hauled Ginger around by his mouth and mistreated him, it makes me sad. I hope he understood that I was only a small child who knew no better.

In the Salinas junior stock-horse competition most of the children were older, but I had Ginger on my side and he knew how to score high marks in these events; he had been doing it for years against stiffer competition than this. The publicity that accrued from this unlikely win on Ginger had an intoxicating effect on my parents. Their business suddenly expanded—Mr. and Mrs. Roberts were plainly the best teachers because they had a boy of only four who won a trophy. It confirmed my father's belief: I was the child who would make the Roberts name famous in the world of show horses.

My father was an important figure, both in my personal life and in my working life with horses. Everything I achieved came to me because of the early and concentrated exposure to horses that he gave me. But if my professional life can be described as having a direction, it is one that runs absolutely counter to my father and his thinking.

Eventually my stance against him and his methods amounted to outright rebellion, for which I paid dearly. My father died in 1986, but calling him up even now, all these years later, is a bitterly hard thing to do. To understand *who* I am and *how* I am with horses, you must understand who my father was and how he was with horses.

My father was a tall man of a slim, muscular build, with chiseled features and light brown hair. He was as neat and orderly as circumstances allowed. If he met a friend in Salinas, he could be friendly, even inviting. Later in life he showed great tenderness to members of my family, but I never saw that side of him. I never shook hands with him, never got hugged by him. He would pass me on the street and not say hello. From the outset, he turned a cold and critical eye on me. Generous with others, he demanded perfection of me. He was unforgiving and scrutinized everything I did, more often than not holding it up to ridicule. As a boy I was serious and polite, and when I look back on those times I see that I never was a child. Child prodigy, perhaps. My father's protégé, yes, for a time. But a child? Never.

My father's methods of dealing with horses were what I would describe as conventional—but that is to say, cruel.

The standard way of breaking horses in those days remains popular even today. A television program from 1989 celebrated twenty years of space travel and made the point that while outer space is the great frontier of our era, the "Wild West" was its previous counterpart. As the program noted, some things have not changed since those times. Among their featured examples was how we break horses.

My father had a special corral built, with six solid posts fixed at equal distances around its perimeter. This way he could break half a dozen horses simultaneously. First he put halters on them. This might involve running horses through a squeeze chute to gain close enough access. Next, he attached strong ropes to their halters and tied each horse to a post, wrapping the rope around the post about six feet off the ground and tying off the end on the rails. Imagine, then, six animals tied thirty feet apart around the edge of the corral. The horses were already terrified and the process had only just begun.

Next, my father stood in the middle of the corral with a heavy tarpaulin or weighted sack attached to the end of a rope. He threw the sack over the horses' backs and around their legs, moving from one horse to the next. When the sack dropped on their hips and around their rear legs, the horses panicked. They rolled their eyes and kicked, reared, and pulled back against the ropes as though their lives depended on it.

Who could tell them that this was not some awful precursor to death? What primordial fears of attacks by predators were provoked?

Fear is in the horse's nature, and they were driven wild with it. They plunged back and forth and sideways on the ends of the ropes. Their necks and heads swelled up and frequently they injured themselves. It was, and remains, a desperately cruel sight.

This process is called "sacking out." It continued for perhaps four days, its purpose to break the horses' willpower and thwart their capacity for resistance. In the next stage, a leg—usually the near hind—was tied up. (Originally to accommodate swords, riders mount and dismount on the horse's left; so the "near" side of a horse is the left side, the "off" side is the horse's right.) A rope would be caught under their rear pastern and pulled tight to a collar placed around their necks. With the horses now disabled, a second period of sacking out further reduced their ability to resist. They struggled valiantly, heaving their weight pitifully on three legs and groaning in pain at the pressure on their halters. Each leg in turn was tied up; sacking out now took less and less time to sap their spirit. Then, with the hind leg again tied off, a saddle was fixed on. The horses renewed their resistance, fighting the girth. More sacking out wore them down. Some fought for many hours; others gave up more quickly and descended into confusion, waiting for more pain.

By now, eight to ten days had passed. The horses had blood tracks on their pasterns where the ropes had worn through the skin; in places, friction burned off the hair. Bruising and more serious leg injuries were common. The horses' relationship with their human masters was now defined: they would work out of fear, not willingness.

To destroy the willingness in a horse is a crazy, unforgivable act. Inherent generosity is among the dominant characteristics of the horse, and if nurtured can grow into the most rewarding aspect of their working lives. Of the horses I have been close to in my life, I have marveled most at their willingness to try for me, over and over again.

At this stage in the sacking out process, the six horses were untied one by one and fitted with a hackamore—a rawhide noseband without a bit. For a further week, the horses were long-lined. Essentially, lines are attached through the stirrups to the horse to get him used to the bit. The aim is to introduce the horse to the notion of brakes and gas pedal, ideas that do not come naturally to him. The rider to come will need the horse to know about stop and go.

I have a dramatic black-and-white photograph of my father long-lining a horse in the corral. He is bent low, hinged forward at the waist, his whole body tensed and focused on the poor horse at the end of the two lines. One might think a charge of electricity runs along the lines between man and horse. The horse kicks up great clouds of dust and reels off the corral fence. The whites in his eyes showing, the horse desperately tries to escape my father, and one eye looks back at him in fear and dread.

When my father came to ride these horses for the first time, their rear legs would be tied up again to prevent bucking. He mounted and dismounted, kicked them in the belly, tried any way he could to provoke some fight in them. If they moved, they were whipped.

If convinced they were "broken," he would untie them and ride them in the round pen. Those not yet ready to ride spent part of the day with their legs tied up, groaning in pain and despair. The whole process took a minimum of three weeks.

Given those same six horses today, I would have them ready to ride without tethering and whips, and without inflicting a moment's discomfort. I would communicate almost entirely with my body language, using my voice in only a minor way, and the result would be a willing partner that would try hard throughout his working life. All this and all six horses in just three hours, not three weeks.

— —

My father was standing next to a stranger, beckoning me over to him. "Monty, this is Mr. Don Page."

The man loomed above me, holding out his hand for me to shake. It was 1939, and I was four years old; I was in competition at the Pickwick Riding Stables in Burbank, California. This area was also home to many Hollywood movie studios such as MGM, Paramount, and Warner Brothers. My father continued, "Mr. Page works at Warner Brothers, Monty."

They were both looking at me expectantly, and I waited to hear what was coming. Mr. Page dropped to his haunches to bring his face level with mine. "You know, horse stories are real popular at the moment. You seen any? Everyone's hungry for stories with kids and horses and nice things like that, so they can forget all the trouble we're in, what with the Depression, and the war in Europe. And we haven't got enough kids who can ride for us."

I squinted across at him and began to think I knew what he was after. "Your dad tells me you can ride pretty well. How do you feel about coming along to show us what you can do?"

Mr. Page suggested we stay over for a day and visit a nearby location where the studio's stunt team kept their horses and perfected their routines. At the appointed time for my audition, we turned up at this studio facility and were greeted by a line of people—likely stunt directors and casting directors. They had a steady, predictable horse ready for me, one presumably accustomed to the peculiar demands of Hollywood film directors. He was a bay gelding and led the low life of a studio mount in those days when the film industry was not so concerned about the safety of animals.

Someone called out, "OK, Monty, just canter past from left to right." I did. "And now back the other way, if possible." I successfully completed this difficult maneuver; difficult, that is, for most four-year-olds. "Now, can you pull up to a dead stop, and jump off?" This time he sounded more questioning; he was no longer issuing instructions. But I had been jumping off horses for some time now.

There was some whispering between my father and the line of studio observers. The man issuing all the orders came over to where I was standing by my horse. He looked at me and asked in a serious tone, "You see the sandpit over there?" I looked to where he was pointing.

"If you're comfortable about it, could you just ride over the sandpit and sort of...fall off? While the horse is moving?" I cantered the gelding over the sandpit and took a dive off the right-hand side. The sporadic outbreak of applause was no doubt led by my father. I stood up and brushed the sand off my clothes; someone had caught the gelding and was bringing him back. Next they had me doing all sorts of tricks. "Can you fall off the rear end?" "Could you just canter him past us and be invisible, hanging off the other side?"

Like most kids, my brother and I watched motion pictures on Saturday mornings. We would then go home and try to copy the stunts using a trick riding saddle our father had found for us. I left that studio facility pretty sore, but I had literally tumbled into the movie business, and over subsequent years I would appear in a hundred or so films.

I doubled for Roddy McDowall many times. On one occasion the crew was setting up the massive film camera they used in those days, pointing the wide-angle lens into the corral. We all gathered round. "OK, Monty," said the director, "you rope the horse here in the paddock. The pretty little girl is watching you from over there, sitting on the fence. Got that?"

"OK."

"The horse yanks you off your feet, but you cling to the end of the rope as though your life depends on it." He frowned. "Now don't forget to let the horse drag you around the paddock for quite a while, because we have to get coverage of that."

"No, I'll hang on to the rope until you tell me to stop."

This cheered him. "Great! And we'll cut the sequence back-to-back with Roddy bringing the girl here and then taking off with her afterwards. Go along to wardrobe now, and they'll fit you out in the same clothes as Roddy's wearing."

It was a simple requirement, although my father was shaking his head and telling the producers how dangerous this was going to be for his son and suggesting that the fee should reflect the level of risk. I roped the horse and dug my heels in to make it seem like I was being pulled over by the horse. I bit the dust, literally, and was dragged along the ground as planned. Then came a shredding sound; the pants given me by the costume department were of a thin, crepelike material. With this rough treatment they had bottomed out, and my bottom was equally out for all to see.

I got to my feet mortified. No one could help me out of that predicament quickly enough.

There was some consternation among the crew and much running about. They needed more shots of me being dragged, so I was to carry on, but wearing my own jeans instead. No new clothes to match

Roddy's could be found—they would worry about the continuity problem later.

But it seems they did not worry much. In the finished movie, Roddy McDowall wears off-white pants one moment, and in the next a pair of jeans while he ropes a fairly wild-looking horse, and afterward he is back in his off-white pants again.

I doubled for many child artists. I was Elizabeth Taylor in *National Velvet*—though I never actually met her until much later in life; they simply gave me a wig and a horse, and I followed instructions. I was Mickey Rooney, Charlton Heston, and Tab Hunter, and you can spot me, if you look carefully, in *Thunderhead* and *My Friend Flicka* and scores of other films. It was a good career for a boy just starting grade school, although my father made all the decisions in dealing with the studios. He negotiated and signed the contracts. He was not legally obliged to consult me or to inform me how much I had earned, nor were there laws governing the use of minors in film production. Provision for schooling, minimum wage, and safety rules did not exist then. And today, the parents of such a child actor would have to follow certain ethical standards.

As my filming schedule increased, my father often congratulated me on how well I was doing financially. He told me he was investing the money on my behalf, that it would be waiting for me when I was old enough to use it wisely. If I asked for some of it to buy a new saddle, for example, he would shake his head. "Monty, I'm telling you, I'll keep the money for you."

He stuck to his word; I never saw a penny.

———

For a seven-year-old child, a horse auction is a heady atmosphere. The crush threatened to carry me away, and I had to keep my father in sight or lose him. There was much squealing and calling, the auctioneer hammering away in his high-octane sales patter, and horses of every description were hurried into the ring to be put through their paces.

We squeezed into a spot near ringside and watched the first few horses, my father impassive. Then a skittish chestnut filly listed in the auctioneer's program as eight years old entered the ring. She was playing up and pushing her nose in the air, bothered by the halter rope and walking into the back of the man leading her as though she were only a two-year-old. She was undoubtedly a horse with problems, and no one was interested. My father was. He raised his hand and bought her for peanuts.

He signed the bill of sale and then took hold of my shoulder. "Monty, time to go to work. Follow me," he said. I thought, Here we go again. I ran along behind as he scooted around to the stalls to find the chestnut filly he had just bought. Filly in hand, we hurried to a spot out of sight of the sales ring.

On the way, my father had picked up lunge ropes, a saddle, bridle, and whip. He put on the saddle and bridle and attached the lunge ropes, then ran the filly around in a circle, turning her in both directions for about ten minutes before reining her in and removing the lunge ropes.

"Overfed and underused," he said, making a snap diagnosis of the animal's unsociable behavior. "Ride her hard for about an hour, then bring her down to a walk and cool her off. Have her take backward steps every quarter of an hour. Clean her up, and we'll put her back in the ring in three hours' time. We'll do the usual show."

For the next three hours, it was just me and the chestnut filly. My affinity with problem horses—or, as I call them, remedial horses—dates from these early, rather dubious experiences with my father at the sales ring. Horses whose difficulties he thought stemmed from maltreatment by youthful riders—"child-spoiled horses," he called them—came my way. He felt that I was the best person to ease the horse's transition to a regular rider.

I took the chestnut filly and did as instructed. But every time I worked with such a horse, I also felt compelled to figure out for myself what was causing the behavioral problem.

When my father returned, he watched as I rode the chestnut filly steadily in circles at walk, trot, and canter. Then I slipped off, ducked my head, and walked repeatedly underneath her belly. "OK," said my father. "Let's go."

Back in the sales ring, buyers looked on as I rode what appeared to be a well-broken, gentle animal and put her through some impressive maneuvers. I dismounted and walked back and forth underneath the horse's belly. Buyers pressed closer; they were impressed.

The voice of the auctioneer quickened and rose a notch as the figure rose to twice, then three times what my father had paid earlier in the day. The auctioneer must have been aware of what my father was doing. There was nothing illegal about it, of course, but clearly the horse's problems had not been solved, only quickly masked over. However, the sheer range of horses I rode made it an experience hard to equal. In time I developed the ability to read and understand problem horses quickly and accurately.

By observing the horse's actions and reactions, I developed an inner ear. I believed the horses were telling me something and, most important, I learned, with rare exceptions, never to believe the people connected with the horse. The rider was not lying, simply not listening.

Over the years this came to be the cornerstone of my thinking, so much so that it became like a mantra, and one proven by experience to be true: *A good trainer can hear a horse speak to him. A great trainer can hear him whisper.*

———

Early in 1942 the California sun was baking the dry earth as my father and I moved across the corral where he broke horses. He leaned against one of the six upright posts used to tether young horses. The posts were even taller and thinner than he was.

He was coiling a rope neatly on the post, ready for the next poor animal who would dance on the end of it like a fish on a line.

"Maybe it's time," he said, "you learned how to break a horse." I offered no reply, for I wanted no part of sacking out. The posts in the corral were like grim sentries guarding the reputation of this terrible procedure.

"There's nothin' much you can't manage," my father told me, "despite you being only a kid." We walked over to a nearby corral where my father pointed at two young horses. "There. Those two."

They seemed of a gentle enough disposition. Then we climbed the rail and got closer. The two young horses stirred and moved away quietly, but they were receptive to our voices. They had been handled before.

"We'll have you do the pair of them together, OK?"

No, I wanted to reply, I was not ready to sack out and tie up a horse; I wanted to avoid it completely if I could. My father continued, "I'll let you know when I've got the time to take you through it and instruct you."

I asked, "Can I have a few days?"

He did not sense my reluctance. To him, it would have been incomprehensible to want to "break" a horse in any other way. "A few days for what?"

"You know, maybe get to know them a bit first."

"To get to *know* them?" he asked, mystified.

"Maybe."

"Well, OK, but don't go messing it up. And don't go trying any fancy business. A horse is a dangerous machine, and you'd be wise to remember that. You hurt them first—or they'll hurt you."

I took the horses to a distant round pen and simply familiarized myself with them. I was in no danger; adults were working on their horses nearby and keeping an eye on me. I merely walked around the pen following the horses and trying to cajole them into letting me closer. It was all trial and error, but on the third day I was surprised to find that one of the horses was following me around. Where I went, so did this gelding. To my astonishment, I could stand on my tiptoes and push a saddle on his back. There seemed to be no rhyme or reason to it, but it happened.

Wildly excited by what I had accomplished, I ran immediately to the house to tell my father. I asked him to come and watch. He reminded me what he had said about not messing around as he followed me to the pen. I could not judge his mood. Maybe he was reluctant to waste his time walking 200 yards for nothing. Perhaps he had sensed my disobedience already, and was angry about it.

When we arrived, he said nothing. He simply took up position on the viewing stand just above the fence and waited. I was confident as I brought the gelding into the round pen. The horse and I wandered

here and there together. It was an odd sort of dance, with neither partner knowing what the moves were, but eventually I was standing next
to him.

Then, moving quietly and calmly, I reached up as high as I could
and slid a saddle on his back. It was, for me, a magical experience. At
this point, I looked up at my father, who was staring at me with his
mouth open. I was uncertain how to read that look, but I was hoping
it was astonishment and maybe pride at my accomplishing this after
only three days.

Slowly, he stood up, still fixing me with this look that could have
meant any number of things. "What the hell am I raising?" were the
first words he uttered. As he jumped off the viewing platform, I saw
that he had in hand a four-foot stall chain; such chains were often
slung over the fences, and he may have gathered one up as he was
watching me. He burst into the pen and grabbed me by one arm.

"What am I raising?" he said again, as if I had done something evil.
Perhaps he expected me to cleanse myself, to apologize for veering
from his methods. Instead, I said, "You saw it work. I was right."

Then he raised the stall chain and brought it down hard, again and
again, on my thighs and buttocks. I reeled with the shock of it and
the blood drained from my skull until I felt faint. I can still remember the iron grip of his left hand on my upper arm as he used his
right hand to wield the chain. The beating seemed to continue for
several minutes while I writhed in his grasp, my eyes closed, my spirit
shattered.

I was left in a pitiful, grieving state. He whipped horses into submission and now he was giving me the same treatment, and I felt the
same anger and sense of failure that the horse must have felt. A
lesson in how *not* to win respect and allegiance, it only enforced a reluctant obedience, instilled fear, and left me with a lifelong sense of
resentment.

I was put in the hospital so my parents could call my injuries horse-
related and to keep me from the glare of friends and relatives. The
term "child abuse," and the will to deal with it in society, were still
many decades away. Large areas of my body were swollen, and I
could neither walk nor stand. The beatings continued weekly for

three more years before finally starting to taper off when I was ten. Only when I was fifteen did they cease altogether. On three other occasions, injuries from beatings required medical attention. I am sure the doctor knew, but nothing was said. Amid this blur of pain and disappointment, I learned a second lesson. I promised myself I would never again show my father any part of my work in starting and developing young horses.

Forty-four years would pass before I once more took him into my confidence. In 1986, just before he died at the age of seventy-eight, I would invite him to take up a position on the viewing deck of a round pen. But by then, everything had changed. Even him.

Later that year, in September of 1942, a stranger appeared at the gates of the Salinas rodeo and competition grounds. A man in a jacket and tie and carrying a briefcase was not a usual sight in Salinas. My father and mother greeted him, and they stood in a knot, talking.

From a discreet distance, my brother and I watched as my father raised his hand and pointed in different directions. When they started to move off, we followed, poking our noses around the corners of barns to see where they were going next. We soon realized that this stocky stranger was visiting areas of the competition grounds not normally used. From time to time he would stride up and down the lengths of the barns, measuring off distances. He examined the perimeter fencing. More pointing, more note taking.

A month later a letter arrived. My father read it aloud as we all listened: "It has been confirmed that the competition grounds owned by the city of Salinas are to be requisitioned and used by the U.S. Government as a Japanese-American internment camp."

What was an internment camp? Pearl Harbor had brought America wholeheartedly into the war the previous year, but I had no idea what this meant. My father and mother explained it to us by turns. We were at war with Japan, so Japanese immigrants and their families were considered enemies of the state and were to be interned for the duration of the war.

But these people were our friends and neighbors; some had been living around here for as long as we could remember. We were confused and stunned. Uncomprehending, we asked, "Where will they all live?"

"The government plans to house them in the box stalls."

"In the box stalls? What about the horses?"

My father was silent, looking again at the letter. Then he read out, "Other buildings will be constructed to provide communal facilities." My father folded the letter and explained that we were being asked to choose the lesser of two evils. We could reduce our riding school and horse-training activities almost to zero if we wanted to stay living at the grounds. Or, we could leave.

This was a traumatic experience for us all. If we chose to stay in our house, we would be living under cramped conditions behind barbed-wire fences, as though we, too, were prisoners, and whether we stayed or left, we would have to sell most of our horses. I remember the arguments going back and forth; the atmosphere in the house blackened. There was no option: we would leave.

My life had come to an end. I could not sleep, and cried through most nights. Many of my concerns were selfish, as those of a small child tend to be. I already believed I was to be a champion rider, with a future in showing horses. Now, all our horses and equipment were to be sold. Larry and I watched resentfully as an endless line of vehicles came and went. Some brought materials to convert box stalls into the most basic of living quarters and to erect makeshift communal facilities. Other trucks carted off our equipment and our horses.

Many of the horses were sent to be slaughtered at the notorious Crow's Landing. I would later go there myself dozens of times, and I remember once seeing men with their lunch boxes open on the carcasses of horses. All my life I have believed that the time of a horse's death is a sacred one. You tip your hat, you think about it. Crow's Landing was a horrible place, but that was the final destination of these truckloads of horses as they rolled out of the competition grounds in clouds of dust.

Larry and I were beset with anguish. To help assuage our grief, our parents told us that horsemeat was required for the war effort. All over the world, American soldiers not much older than ourselves were living in desperate conditions. The outcome of the fight against tyranny depended on keeping these young soldiers fit and well fed. Horse-meat would go toward saving their lives and winning the war.

In truth, there was nowhere else for the horses to go. No one could afford to buy them or, with gas rationed, even transport them. On one of those trucks bound for Crow's Landing was my faithful red roan, Ginger.

———

We moved to a small house in the center of Salinas. It had concrete curbs out front, and was the only house I would ever live in with a number on the door: 347 Church Street. Dating from the 1920s, the clapboard house had three bedrooms and an elevated floor; you navigated a lot of porch before you finally arrived inside. In the backyard grew a large magnolia tree; its blooms, though exquisite, made me sneeze.

Living here, on this city lot, with neighbors in every direction, was unlike anything I had ever known. My mother tried to console me and always lavished affection on me. In one photograph, taken early in her marriage, she wears a suit with fur epaulets, and the ringlets in her hair spill in a coy sort of way from her elegant hat. She was the oldest of eight children, born of the union of a Portuguese farmer and an English/Irish schoolteacher. Her family called her "Flick," because of the way she darted about. My mother was also a subservient soul who walked in my father's shadow, but later on she stood up to him many times and literally threw herself around me to protect me.

We had not been in that clapboard house long when she picked up our large globe of the world, brought it to my room, and asked me to find Japan. I eventually did. Then she asked me to find America.

"Now, Monty, look at those two places. Japan is a collection of tiny islands. The United States is a massive country, isn't it? So you can understand why, in just a few months, the war will be over and we can return to the competition grounds." It helped, but there was plenty of evidence to the contrary, and I began to doubt my mother. If the war was winding down, why were people putting stickers in their car windows asking, "Is this trip really necessary?"

Meanwhile, my father was thirty-four years old and therefore not

eligible for service in the armed forces. But when he was younger he
had policed the mountains on horseback for the forest service, riding
a horse and carrying a badge and a gun. The shortage of young men
and the fact that he had once been a forest ranger made him an ideal
recruit for the Salinas police department.

———

When the news came of his appointment, it seemed to me that we
would never get back to the competition grounds. But one thing prevented my life from straying too far from the course that I had so
firmly fixed for it: my father managed to rent a small holding on the
edge of town. It was only a barn surrounded by a few acres, and nothing like what we were used to, but it would allow us to keep ten to fifteen horses in training.

We cleaned it out thoroughly with a hose. We hammered up partitions, mended gates, and scrubbed concrete floors until they glis-
tened. We walked over the ground inch by inch to clear any nails and
the remnants of fencing wire that might damage the horses' feet. We
connected the water supply, set gates back on their hinges, contrived
a bin for the feed. The smell of horses was in my nostrils again, and
that meant happiness.

Although my father was a frightening man, he had given me back
what I wanted most in the world: a future with horses. More specifically, my future lay with the brown gelding called Brownie, who was
one of the first arrivals at the Villa Street facility.

Brownie was 15 hands, his mother a mustang mare and his sire a
Thoroughbred—one of the government remount stallions. This was a
project whereby the U.S. Cavalry took Thoroughbred stallions and set
them loose to run with the mustangs on the open range. The ranchers
got a payment if they shot a mustang stallion: the Thoroughbred
stallions could thus take over the females and breed a class of horse
suitable for the military. The cavalry had first call to come back and
capture the young males for themselves, while the ranchers could
keep the fillies as further payment for their cooperation.

As his name implied, Brownie was medium brown all over, except
for about eight inches of a softer, doeskin color on his muzzle and a

small white dot between his eyes, which gave him a concentrated, pointed look. He had well-shaped feet with flint-hard hooves—a legacy of his mustang heritage. Domestic horses raised on soft ground need regular visits from the farrier to keep their feet healthy. But owing to the minerals mustangs eat and the constant teasing of the feet from running over rocks, mustang hooves are so strong a nail could hardly penetrate them.

The minute Brownie arrived and I knew he was to be mine, I wanted to bond with him closely.

"OK," said my father, "let's break him."

My heart sank. How could I be this animal's best friend when his tentative trust in human beings was about to be abused? But I was too frightened of my father to stop it. As Brownie waited in his stall, my father rooted among some old slatted boxes used for the commercial transport of vegetables. He found what he was looking for   a cut of heavy, crepelike paper used to line the crate. He twisted one end and tied it to the end of a rope.

Brownie was tied to a single post that had been driven deep into the ground. He stood patiently while my father walked around behind him, coiling the rope with the paper tied to the end of it. My father lobbed the paper and Brownie jumped sideways as if his life depended on it, which to his way of thinking it did. His head snapped around, brought up short by the rope. This was just the beginning.

As I watched Brownie's eyes widen and roll in fear, I felt dread and sympathy in equal doses. I cursed inwardly and wanted more than anything to untie the rope. I tried in vain to think how I might make it up to him.

Years later, while Brownie and I were trekking over the high desert for days at a time, I felt compelled to offer him an apology for the vicious sacking out and the paper terror he would feel until the day he died. I talked to him, tried to put things right and hoped he understood.

Brownie never forgot the sacking out: all his life he was phobic about paper. Anything that sounded remotely like paper would send him into a panic, and he would be dangerous to himself and to others. He would bolt, and no one could tell him that it was only paper, nothing to fear. Never angry with Brownie for this blind spot in his nature, I accepted it as our fault, our crime against him.

———

When my father became a policeman, our car became a police car. The war had made vehicles of any description difficult to come by. When he joined up, my father was told he would earn a higher salary if he offered to equip his family car for police work.

Consequently, many policemen's private cars were fitted with red emergency lights, sirens, and radios. Special spotlights and lighting systems were installed to adapt the car for driving in blackout conditions. The West Coast was vulnerable to enemy attack and blackouts were common.

I recall my father coming home one day—we were then still living at the competition grounds—and saying we needed a larger vehicle to pick up riding students. The Mullers, who owned a mortuary in Salinas, had just the car for us: the limousine used by the immediate family in the funeral procession.

The huge 1932 Cadillac sedan, with enormous running boards, was like a car from a gangster movie. Fitted with every option under the sun, it had acres of space inside and would accommodate many more riding students than any new car we might have bought for the same price. As with many automobiles of its day, the trunk consisted of a large metal box, like a footlocker, which bolted onto the back of the car. Now the black Cadillac was a patrol car for my father.

I sometimes accompanied him to his training sessions. My father could handle every man there, and most instructors, with a smile on his face. He was fearless. There was never a cell of fear in that man. I can remember riding with my father when he got calls over the radio, or when he saw someone violating the traffic code. The red light would come on, the siren would sound, and we would race off to "apprehend the suspect." He carried his badge with him always, and kept a citation pad and handcuffs in the glove compartment. There was also usually a handgun.

Late in the evening of one spring day in 1943, we were driving home from caring for some pasture horses. It had been a long day of riding and attending to their keep. Now it was getting dark. Near the city limits, a call came over the radio concerning an armed robbery in progress at the Golden Dragon saloon on Soledad Street in Chinatown. My father picked up the hand microphone and responded, "I'm just a block and a half from the Golden Dragon and I'll answer that call." The radio dispatcher asked, "Are you armed?" My father replied, "Yes."

A bolt of fear ran through me. In all the times I had been with him when he answered police calls, he had never had to defend himself with a gun. He flipped the switches for the siren and the flashing light. The car veered wildly from side to side as it covered the distance. The headlights picked up people leaping out of our way.

He barked at me, "Get down on the floor!"

The tone of his voice conveyed the seriousness of the situation. I quickly slid from the seat and into the foot well underneath the dash, and waited. My heart was beating loud and fast, and I could almost smell my own fear.

What happened next changed me forever. I would push the incident I am about to describe into a dark corner of my mind, until one day, returning from a horse sale on a mostly empty airplane, I took out a tape recorder and the truth poured out of me. Fresh blood from an old wound. There are days when I regret disinterring these memories. The whole picture remains crystal-clear, as if it had happened yesterday.

Some members of my family advised me that this incident should have no place in the book, and I weighed their counsel carefully before making the decision to reveal it—probably the single most important influence in my life. But what I saw on that day had a profound impact on the way I deal with horses, though not a single horse featured in the events of that night.

Before then I was a different person. In a way, I was born that evening, at the age of eight.

My father, you should know, had been brought up in the tough, sometimes cruel, world of the American pioneer. So much changed during those early decades of the twentieth century that the single generation between my father and me felt like a great chasm. During his childhood, he would have faced almost daily the natural law of "kill or be killed." In later years he mellowed. When my wife, Pat, came to know him, he was no longer the cold, rigid man I had known as a child; the fight had drained from him. My children remember him as a fine grandfather.

I am also at pains to point out the difficulty my father had with the issue of race. Half Cherokee, he had suffered racial abuse in his youth, and he felt a deep shame about his Cherokee mother. (Ironically, a little Cherokee blood ran in his own wife's veins.) Yet he was angry that the Second World War had brought black people to our otherwise white community. Fort Ord was a twenty-minute drive away, and many black servicemen were stationed there. Given the chance, victims of racial prejudice are sometimes the first to inflict it on others.

This is not to excuse what happened, and neither am I trying to vilify my father. But for as long as I live I will go on trying to understand what he did that night and how it shaped me.

As the car sped toward the crime scene, my father issued a second order: "Get me the gun and the handcuffs."

I flipped the latch on the glove compartment and quickly removed the handcuffs, but I could not feel the gun. Frantically, my fingers swept through the maps, pens, and other detritus, but in vain. He was cursing at me to hurry. "Damn," he said, "I was sure I brought it with me." He had already grabbed the handcuffs and shoved them into his pocket.

The Cadillac slid to a halt a few doors down from the Golden Dragon. He leapt from the car almost before it stopped moving, shouting to me just before he slammed the door, "Stay in the car, *on the floor!*"

I lay there, curled under the dash, as the flashing neon lights of the saloon's facade filled the car with an eerie pulsating glow. It was cramped where I lay, with its smell of barn dirt, sweat, and damp wool from the carpet. I wrestled with the urge to sit up, partly to escape the smell but mainly to see what was happening. As I crept up to the seat, my eyes were now level with the bottom of the driver's window. I had a direct view of the bar entrance some twenty yards away. The street was lined with people, some talking to my father and pointing to the saloon. They were agitated, whispering among themselves as my father went inside. Though stiff with panic, I reached over to the door handle and eased it open. Everyone was focused on what was going on just inside the saloon doorway, so no one saw me crawling along. I crabbed sideways to gain a spot near the door. It seemed like everything had gone silent, because all I could hear was the thumping of my heart as I peered into the bar.

Inside, no more than five feet away, I saw my father with his back to me. The bar's patrons were scattered to the farthest corners of the room. A tall, heavy-set black man in army fatigues was the only person moving. I seldom encountered blacks in Salinas; he was not a man to me, but a *black* man. He swerved to point a knife that looked the size of a sword—maybe it was a bayonet—in the direction of the bartender and shouted, "Put the money on the bar!" The frightened bartender pulled bills from the register, scattering coins to the floor in his haste.

The robber, who may have been twenty years old, had spread his coat on the bar and collected a small heap of watches, rings, bracelets, and wallets. Evidently he had been cleaning out the patrons. The plan was to use the coat as a sack and then make his escape.

At this point my father lifted his badge high in the air so everyone could see his authority, and he shouted, "Police! Stand where you are. Put down the knife and place your hands on the bar." All time stopped now.

The black man turned to face my father, his knife pointing directly in front of him. My father was a big man, but the man at the bar was huge. I silently begged my father to give way. He did not. He stepped forward, walking toward the knife. Serious injury or even death awaited him. It was a brave act. Terror overtook me; in those few seconds I saw myself fatherless.

"Don't do this to yourself," my father said as he kept walking forward. "Put the knife on the bar, turn around and put your hands in the air, give it up."

When they were inches from each other, and just when I thought the man would give way after all, he struck. He made a quick thrust with his knife hand, aiming for my father's ribs. My father's hand snaked out and grabbed the man's fist exactly where it closed on the knife handle.

With a quick folding action he locked the robber's elbow backward and sent the knife spinning to the floor. The pressure on his twisted arm caused the man to fall back, and his head cracked on the edge of the bar. He continued his free fall to the floor and hit his head again, this time on the brass foot rail. He lay motionless, in a heap. It was over.

I experienced a rush of emotion. My father was alive and, though unarmed, had brought down a knife-wielding thief. He was a hero.

But it was not over. At this point, my father—a powerfully built man who weighed about 220 pounds—put the cuffs on the man and stood over him. He raised one foot and locked his heel behind his thigh, elevated his body, and then dropped, driving his knee into the chest of the unconscious black man. I was shocked, but my father's next move was even more appalling. He lifted one foot, took aim and, with all the force he could muster, slammed the heel of his cowboy boot into the mouth of the fallen man. He then picked up the knife and handed it to the bartender, asking him to carry it for him. Turning to his prisoner, he grabbed the chain connecting the handcuffs and hauled on it, dragging the black man who was limp as a sack of feed, his hands high over his head.

As my father turned toward the doorway, it struck me, almost too late, that I was not where I was supposed to be. I turned and ran. As I slid into the driver's seat and closed the door behind me, I saw my father emerge from the bar, surrounded by onlookers. He gave the torso an extra lift and then released the chain, dropping the back of the man's head onto the sidewalk.

When my father arrived at the car, dragging his prisoner behind him, he went round and opened the passenger side of the car, taking the knife from the barman and placing it carefully on the seat beside me.

Then he went to the rear of the Cadillac and opened that big, trunklike box. He took empty grain sacks and laid them over the rear floor space so the black man's blood would not stain the interior.

He opened the doors wide, heaved the man inside, then got in the car himself. The knife was an object of fear for me. But I was torn between sitting close to the knife or sitting close to my father. My father instructed me to pick it up by the blade and place it in the glove compartment. A measure of the size of a 1932 Cadillac's glove compartment is that this long knife fit inside.

As we drove off, I could hear sounds coming from the man's throat. But my father said he was faking his injuries: "He'll be just fine." By now, other patrol cars had joined us on our way to the police station. Their sirens joined ours in a wailing that precisely caught my own inner mood of anguish and despair.

My father used the car radio to tell his colleagues how the thief had attempted to cut him with the knife. The tale was told with bravado. Turning around, I looked down to see if the man was still breathing. I could only see bubbles of blood around his mouth. I pleaded with my father to take him to the hospital, not the police station. He simply repeated that the man was faking his injuries.

On arrival at the station my father opened the car door and dragged the man onto the sidewalk. For good measure, as if testing for resistance, he again drew the black man's shoulders up a few feet and dropped him with a crack onto the cement. Other officers, emerging from the station or their patrol cars, laughed and hooted at this display.

My father picked up the chain again and hauled, so the unconscious prisoner's hands were once more over his head, as if in surrender. Lifting the man's head and torso off the sidewalk, he used the handcuff chain to drag the man backward up the concrete steps fronting the police station. "Get the knife out of the glove box," he barked to one of the officers. "Don't touch the handle." He would take a few steps, hoist his prisoner, take a few more steps, and repeat the process. The man was being conveyed into jail like an awkward piece of furniture.

No one made any attempt to find a stretcher, or to help my father. This was his trophy. He had bagged it, and now he was bringing it home to display before his brother officers. They hollered and laughed behind him, sidestepping the trail of blood.

Inside the station, at the top of the stairs, was the sergeant's desk. Dragging the black man the last few feet to a point opposite the desk, my father dropped him on the concrete floor. "I've pulled an I.D. from his pocket," he said. "Here's his name; book him, and send someone to get his prints." By this time in his police career, my father was a sergeant talking to a fellow sergeant. His imperious manner was that of a hunter after a kill.

The sergeant fed a sheet of paper into the typewriter and the keys began their staccato beat. Officers lit cigarettes and gathered to hear my father's tale. There was a second telling, this time with more violence and drama.

The man lay unconscious on the floor and I feared he was dying. I pulled at my father's coat to beg him to do something. My father looked down and shouted, "You get back in the car and shut up. The man is just faking it! There's nothing at all wrong with him." At this point the man seemed to regain consciousness and struggled to stand. Still handcuffed, he staggered forward toward the shaft of light coming through the door. No one made a move to stop him.

"Get in the car, Monty," said my father, who almost casually turned to follow his prisoner. The man did not go very far; he stumbled at the top of the steps and dove headlong, striking his head against a tree. Again he lay motionless. By now I was crying uncontrollably. My father again yelled, "Get in the car!" as he approached the prisoner. Through the window I saw my father kick him repeatedly in the ribs with the toe of his cowboy boot. This last display seemed for the benefit of four or five officers standing at the entrance. Finally, he dragged the prisoner up the steps and deposited him through the door.

Back in the Cadillac I buried my face in the upholstery, sobbing. Soon I heard the sound of the car door opening and slamming shut, then the scrape of the key in the ignition. We were going home.

Four days later I summoned enough courage to ask my father what had happened to the man he had arrested in the saloon. He replied, "Oh, he died." He must have felt my shock, because he quickly said, "He didn't die of his injuries. He died of pneumonia. That boy refused to pull the blankets over him at night, and he caught pneumonia and died."

I believed the story and I believed him. From then on, throughout my boyhood, I was careful at night to pull the covers up to my chin. Years later, I was told that the black man had lain for two days with his ribs broken, his lungs pierced and his skull cracked. He died without ever seeing a doctor.

Later, in psychology courses, I would learn how kidnappers and child molesters kill small animals in front of their victims to instill in them such fear that they are unable to fight back. My father's brutalizing of the young soldier was not aimed at me at all; he tried, in fact, to hide it from me. But the effect on me was the same as if he had forced me to watch.

I understand now that I became a victim of my father's aggression—then I only knew how much I feared him. But from that point forward, I knew I had to direct my life away from him.

There is a postscript to this incident.

Two months later, my father asked me to come with him one evening. "We're going to the fights," he said, "and you're going to meet a very special man there." We drove to the National Guard Armory, passing crowds of people as we pulled up outside. We entered a room at the back of the exhibition hall where a large black man was seated on a table.

My pulse shot up. He was the first of his race I had seen since the robbery. My father drew me closer and said, "Come on, Monty. Meet Joe Louis, he's the heavyweight champion of the world."

Joe Louis greeted my father by name. My father had been hired as one of the bodyguards to protect the champion.

"Hi," said my father. "Meet my son, Monty."

I refused to go closer. "Come on," said the boxer. "I won't hurt you."

I shook the hand of Joe Louis, but I could not look him in the eye. Hoping to get past my shyness, he pointed at his shoulder and said, "Hey, little man, hit me, I dare you."

It was a game I could not play. In the end he took my hand, folded it into a fist and tapped it against his shoulder, feigning injury. "Now," he said, "you can say you knocked out the world champ."

A photographer setting up nearby signaled his readiness. My father lined up beside Joe Louis and the flash popped. I still have the photo of Louis—an imposing man—flanked by four uniformed, hatted men at least his size or bigger. It is hard to read Louis's look, but the others, all white, seem more pleased to be in his company than he is in theirs.

On the way home, my father was remembering how Joe Louis, a celebrity bystander that night, had signed autographs while sitting in one corner of the ring. He would sign hurriedly, then drop the paper onto the floor of the ring so the autograph seekers had to pick them up. "The nigger in him had to come out, didn't it?" railed my father.

A woman named Nola Hightower worked for us in our house, and though my father treated her well, behind her back she, too, was a "nigger." Later, when I played high school football, his advice to me was to hit the black players hard early in the game and they would not bother me again, because "niggers lack courage." My father was a racist, and the black-and-white photograph of him smiling, with his arm around Joe Louis is, for me, a powerful memento.

———

When I was eight, I started riding quarter horses in sprint races, and my education in horsemanship moved up another notch.

Quarter horses were, and are, stout, easy keepers with well-developed feet and calm dispositions. Typically small, the quarter horse possessed a conformation one might call the muscular "bull-dog" type, with exceptionally well-rounded hindquarters and a deep chest. "A deep heart," as horsemen say.

The breed was originally known in the 1930s as Copper Bottom and, later, as Steel Dust—after the two principal sires who launched this specialist breed. Easily trained, they were bred for ranch work because their terrific acceleration made them ideal for roping cattle and cutting a cow out of a herd. During the week they would work on the ranch, and during weekend rodeos they would be entered in the roping events and steer wrestling competition. After a few minutes' rest, the quarter horses would swap their heavy Western rigs for the jockey's "postage stamp" saddle, and they would be raced on the bush tracks that surrounded the rodeo arenas. In shorter races, no horse could beat them: they were the equine equivalent of drag racers. In fact, many of these horses never drew a breath until after they crossed the finish line; only as they slowed did they realize the need for a change of air in their lungs.

Because of the distance involved, a quarter of a mile, the breed became known as the quarter horse. This new type of competitive event was called sprint-horse racing. I loved the excitement of it. To minimize weight on the back of the animal, the smallest boys were picked as riders. My fee, which the owner paid, was five dollars to ride and ten dollars to win. Little towns up and down California—Salinas, King City, Fresno, Victorville, Stockton—held these "short horse" or "quarter horse" meets. The gambling was unregulated and unsanctioned. Like any backroom gambling, it made for a charged atmosphere. Riders were also unlicensed, nor was much concern shown for their safety. I had no serious accidents, despite riding in some 200 sprint races, mostly quarter horse races, until I was thirteen years old, although I did fall off a time or two, and I often rode in races without a protective helmet.

In 1949, no longer able to keep my weight down below the 130-pound mark, I rode my last race in King City. It was just a ranching town, but for quarter horse racing two owners there had become important: Gyle Norris and the McKensie brothers. The latter owned a top-class mare named Lady Lee, whom I was lucky enough to ride a few times. They also owned Dee Dee, who was 1946 champion older male of the quarter horse breed.

One of my fellow racers in those days was the aptly named Tucker Slender, a tall, thin fellow three or four years my senior and a much better jockey than me. He went on to become the head starter at many of the major tracks in southern California, and at Santa Anita and Del Mar he is still the head starter. Slender knew, and I would learn, that horses and starting gates do not always mix.

One day, I was at Frank Vessels's track—then still quite rustic—as his trainer, a man named Farrell Jones, coped with a young quarter horse. The horse wheeled about behind the starting gate, eyeing its doors as he might the jaws of a crocodile. The track spooked him, the blocks of hay where we sat spooked him, the sky itself rattled him.

Accompanying this young horse was an older stablemate who knew the ropes.

"Right, then," said Farrell calmly, "let's load him into the gates." Farrell was a ruddy fireplug who lost his hair early.

In training quarter horses to bolt from the starting gate, it was then common practice to shut the novice horse inside and put the whip on him. The thinking was to drive the horse into a frenzy so he would be anxious to escape once the gate flipped open. And, every subsequent time in a starting gate, he would remember the fear, and the instinct to run would guarantee a better performance. Occasionally, electric shocks were applied to achieve the same effect.

I watched as Farrell Jones now took the nervous horse and walked him *through* the starting gate. Then he went around again. And again. This continued until the few of us watching began to get dizzy; the horse himself must have been on the edge of being bored with these endless circles. Finally he led him in and shut the front gate, offering a mouthful of feed in a bucket to make him feel at home. His stable-mate was nearby, easily visible through the slatted sides. And there they stood.

I was confused. Was the training session designed to make the novice horse learn effective starts in a race? Or was this, in fact, his new stable?

However, once the horse had grown comfortable behind closed gates, they were opened. But he was not led out. No, he was allowed to take his time and to decide for himself whether he wanted to leave, if ever. When he did so, it seemed to me like an exciting moment.

Farrell Jones was eliminating every ounce of pressure from the training procedure. I also began to see another reason for having the stablemate on hand. With the gates closed and the novice horse in-side, the stablemate was walked down the track a ways. The gate was opened and, without any encouragement, the novice stepped daintily out of the stall and strolled up the track to join his friend. A while later, the older pace horse was set going at a faster walk and allowed to get farther down the track. Now the novice had to shrug into a gen-tle trot to catch up with her.

Not many hours later, Farrell Jones had his novice horse entering the stalls without the slightest fuss, waiting with his nose pressed against the front gate in a state of great anticipation. The horse's only thought was to go forward, to fly out the gate of his own free will, and to canter down to the pace horse—who was always held back a touch to allow the novice to overtake him and "win" the race.

The once nervous horse was having fun. I was deeply impressed by what I had witnessed, and I wanted to know all about it.

"You know," said Farrell as he sucked on the wad of tobacco parked down the side of his back teeth, "I've watched a whole lot of these races, and I've watched them pretty carefully—as you do when there's maybe a sum of money riding into your pocket if you make the right choices. And I saw an interesting thing. It ain't the horses who're all jazzed up who're starting the quickest. Those ones are so busy banging about from side to side and running on the spot and thinking about what evil-doer is behind them, that they have less time to notice whether the gate's flying open. No, it's the animals who are the most relaxed—they're the ones making the flying starts."

Farrell proved to me that the cruelty of whipping horses in the stall to make them afraid and want to escape was not only unnecessary, it was counterproductive. It made the horses *slower* off the mark.

I learned a great deal that day. My way of thinking about horses was enriched by this critical idea: a rider or trainer should never say to a horse, "You *must*." Instead, the horse should be invited to perform because, "I would like you to." Taking that a step further—to ask a horse to perform is not as clever as causing him to *want* to perform.

Horses naturally want to run, and if they are trained correctly we can harness their willingness to do just that, to race to their potential. As it turned out, I would work for most of my life in the Thoroughbred racing industry, and to this day I am fervent in my belief that whips should be banned; there is no need for them if training procedures take advantage of a well-bred horse's overpowering desire to run.

At Flag Is Up Farms, exercise riders sometimes carry a crop: we are, after all, training horses for the track, and a horse that has *never* seen a whip may throw the first jockey to use one. A rider at our farm, then, may tap a horse; but if that rider raises a welt, that rider is gone.

Trevor Denman, the track announcer at the Santa Anita and Del Mar racetracks in California, has actually timed horses under the whip; he has determined that most horses slow down when they are whipped. The whip is simply a bad tool. We have no need for it.

Farrell Jones would become the leading Thoroughbred trainer in the United States several times over; his son, Gary, one of the top trainers in North America. Farrell's methods and original thinking have stood me in good stead since I learned that first lesson from him.

Frank Vessels, one of the major quarter horse owners in the United States, would launch the Quarter Racing Association in 1945—and soon he would elevate sprint racing into the same class of event as Thoroughbred racing. By 1946, the American Quarter Horse Association had formed, with a team of inspectors touring the United States adding to their register those horses with the right conformation.

From hanging on to the neck of a quarter horse as it blasted down those rough tracks, we all started the quarter horse racing industry. And I learned something about horses and starting gates.

———

When I was nine years old, my uncle Ray told me a story from our Cherokee ancestry—an old way that would have a place in my new way of thinking about horses.

My grandfather, Earl Roberts, was born in Wales in 1870. My love of horses may have come from him, because he farmed with them and also used them for foxhunting and pleasure riding. But at seventeen he was lured to the West by the promise of steady work, building roads over the Sierra Nevadas. In Spanish, Sierra Nevada means "snow-covered mountains," an unassuming phrase for the massive natural barrier that forms the border between California and Nevada. In North America only the Rocky Mountains are bigger.

In the Sierras, crews could work only six months of the year. Passes were otherwise closed. In 1846, the ill-fated Donner Party wagon train tried to cross the Sierras in the fall and were swallowed by one of its fierce, early winters. I can barely imagine the work involved in cutting through those mountains using only man and beast. Young Earl was hired to supply the horses that pulled the equipment on these road projects, as well as to provide saddle horses for the foremen directing the crews. The laborers were typically immigrants like my grandfather, but also among them were Indians of the Cherokee nation, who were brought to Nevada from their reservations in the Midwest by the federal government.

In that number was the woman who would become my grandmother, a young Cherokee girl in her late teens. I wish I knew her Indian name; they called her Sweeney, after the agent who had transported her family to Nevada. Among her few possessions were papers qualifying her as a full-blooded Cherokee entitled to specific native-born rights. Earl petitioned her family for her hand in marriage and in quick succession she bore him nine children—five of whom survived, including my father and my uncle Ray.

When Ray, her youngest child, was eleven years old, Sweeney decided that her marriage contract with Earl had been fulfilled. One day when the family got up in the morning, they found her gone.

Months passed while they searched for her. In the end, they discovered that she had walked from Tulare back to the Cherokee Indian Reservation, a distance of 600 miles. When I knew her, she had gone salt-and-pepper gray. She was about five feet six inches tall—fairly tall for a Cherokee woman of the late 1800s.

My father told disparaging stories about her and was not pleased that I sought her company. She was forbidden fruit. My grandmother spoke little English, words, not sentences, and she never said anything in front of my mother, but she seemed to come alive when we were alone together and she would rattle on in Cherokee, holding me close.

But in her life she was not content.

Shortly after she walked away, Ray developed pneumonia. Earl decided to take the boy back to Sweeney on the reservation, where Ray was adopted into the Cherokee tribe and raised to adulthood. He thus had the benefit of learning the Indian way as well as the white man's way.

Uncle Ray told me that when the Cherokee wanted to capture wild horses on the great plains, their problem was how to get close enough to rope them. They overcame this obstacle in remarkable fashion. Instead of driving them into the neck of a valley or building other traps of that sort, difficult given the landscape, they used a much quicker method. First of all, they followed the herd of horses. They did not drive them hard, but simply walked after them, pressing them away. This would continue for a day or two. Then, when the time was right, the Cherokee would turn and walk in the opposite direction. Invariably, in a kind of yo-yo effect, the horses would turn around and follow them. The Cherokee would then simply lead the wild herd into corrals between two and five acres in size.

Apparently the Cherokee used similar tactics to get close to the beasts they hunted—deer, antelope, and buffalo. To be effective with the bow and arrow, the hunter needed to be within forty or fifty feet of his target. He would press the animals away from him for a while, then turn around and head back the other way. The animals would turn and follow. After this pattern between hunter and prey had been repeated several times, the hunters found themselves near enough to make an easy kill.

When my uncle Ray told me the story of hunted animals circling back to check out the hunter, it was a mystery to me. Later on, when I had the opportunity to observe horses in the wild for myself, I would come to understand the reasons for their curious tendency to turn back and seek intimacy with their pursuers. I would give the phenomenon a name, "Advance and Retreat," and it would form the basis of my technique in working with horses.

———

The years of the Second World War had been filled with death. In one way or another, whether actual or metaphorical, war brings darkness. I was ten when the war finally ended in 1945, and in my small world the death of my dreams seemed as certain as it had when we first moved away from the competition grounds. I had seen my Japanese-American classmates rounded up and interned at a prison camp located at my former home. I had witnessed the death of the black man at the hands of my father, which caused me to lose respect for him and to seek my own path in life. Ironically, while I was trying hard to dissociate my life from his, he was giving me what I wanted more than anything else—a life with horses.

With the war over, it was a mad scramble to return to normalcy. For my father, this meant gearing up to return to our business at the competition grounds and entering me in as many equestrian competitions as he could find around the country—which was exactly what I wanted to do. But it was frantic. The grounds were in a horrible state. We dragged magnets around for weeks because the workmen who had dismantled the living quarters had left nails and roofing tacks on the ground, where they posed a threat to the horses' feet. We put the stables back in order, restored the feed stalls, repaired floors, and mended roofs. My mother's entire family turned up to volunteer their help. We sawed the back off the Cadillac to turn it into a pickup, and it went back and forth to the dump, carting away rubbish.

I recall the day when the new saddles arrived—twenty or thirty of them, all dumped in the yard at the same time. I tore at the packages to get them out and ready for the start of lessons the following day. We were back in our old house, back in business. But with the cost of all this equipment, not to mention the horses themselves, came heavy overhead. We held grave family conferences around the kitchen table. It was decided that my father would remain in the police force because he had risen to the rank of lieutenant and his salary could help to fund our debts. If we were to succeed, my father told us, we would have to do it on our own and without much hired help. We could afford only one man, the same Wendell Gillott who had worked for us beforehand.

Wendell was jockey-sized and claimed a jockey past, but no one could find a trace of it. He was full of stories whose details shifted with his moods. Wendell also claimed he had boxed, and he certainly had the face of someone who had been on the receiving end of many punches. His ears were elephantine and cauliflower, his nose flat and pushed off to one side. People said he had the look of a monkey: he would use his knuckles to rise up from a table.

His were the hands of a worker, and few worked as hard and fast as he did. Wendell was not vulgar, did not drink like so many ranch hands. He was a good man, not the brightest, but always with a joke or a laugh, and we could not have gotten along without him.

To fit in the necessary work of helping Wendell, schooling for Larry and me was cut back to bare bones. Wendell would arrive at the stables at four-thirty A.M. and immediately start feeding the sixty horses we were now stabling. I rolled out of bed some time before five o'clock and struggled into the same working clothes that had lain in a heap on the floor where I had dropped them the night before. I scooted, for I had twenty-two stalls to muck out before breakfast. Because he was younger and not as strong, Larry had ten stalls to clean.

I barely paused to call out a greeting to Wendell before cleaning and raking each stall, rolling back the bedding, adding straw—and on to the next one. As I went, I counted the seconds: the aim was to take no more than three and a half minutes, or 210 seconds, for each stall; ideally, all twenty-two stalls were done in just under an hour and a half. It was like a race; when I finally threw the pitchfork back against the wall I would raise both hands in the air like rodeo calf ropers do to stop the clock.

Breakfast was at six-thirty. As Larry and I ate, our father issued instructions on which horses to ride and what exercises each required. After breakfast, Wendell cleaned out the remaining thirty-odd stalls while Larry and I were out riding. From seven to nine, I rode perhaps six horses with a variety of training programs and tasks to be accomplished. After that, we trotted back to the house and showered and changed, ready for the start of school at nine-thirty.

At one-thirty we returned to the competition grounds and were straight back in the saddle training five to six horses apiece, so by mid-afternoon I had four hours of riding behind me. Then all of us—my father, mother, my brother, and I—gave riding lessons to classes ranging from six to twelve people. Some were scared stiff of horses, others were above it all, some were attentive. We pressed on, doing the best we could. At five-thirty P.M. my mother took the Cadillac and delivered the children back home.

Larry, Wendell, and I would finish up by stabling and feeding the horses, and cleaning the tack. By six-thirty my mother was preparing dinner and I was her helper, which got me interested in cooking. Then, after dinner, there was schoolwork. Even though I was only in school for between ten and forty percent of the normal time, my father insisted I keep up the best possible grades. By anyone's standards, he was a hard taskmaster.

A child's capabilities are elastic at that age, and he stretched mine to the limit, but perhaps as much credit should go to the tutor hired for me—a Miss Marguerite Parsons. That I wanted to take the school tests at all is a credit to her kindness and understanding. Despite my prolonged absences from the classroom, I would achieve near straight-A grades at school.

Like a cartoon character, I had the carrot in front of me, the whip behind.

———

The end of the war created a surplus of cheap military hardware, and among local ranchers it became fashionable to zip around in nearly new military jeeps or armored cars. My father joined in this craze, but in his own remarkable way: he leased a railroad car once used by the U.S. Cavalry. Framed in metal, its wood painted dark green, the car bore military numbers on the outside and, barely discernible beneath the paint, the American eagle.

A minimal payment secured it for several years. Designed to take officers' horses around the country on the rail network, it came equipped with shipping stalls for fifteen horses. My father reasoned that though competitions were few and far between, and even less publicized, the railroad car would get us there. He was also confident that the competitions would inevitably increase in number when normal life returned and he wanted to be prepared to take full advantage.

Builders removed six stalls in the car and constructed in their place a bunk room and a feed room with a bin for the grain and a large container for water. A minimal kitchen area offered a hot plate and a spot for making coffee. For the next few years, this railroad car would crisscross the United States. It was my home away from home during long spells in summer.

My father and I would consult the advertised schedules for horse shows, select the best ones, and then take our itinerary to Southern Pacific. Railroad officials would give us a series of pickup times and siding numbers; we might be car twenty-one in siding number fifty-six, for example, and at the appointed time—the railway did run on time in those days—a switch engine would pull us from the siding onto the main track. The train would back up to us, our car would be hitched up, and off we would go.

My father stayed behind to attend to his duties as a policeman, and as a trainer/manager of the horses. Traveling in the car with me were my favorite horse, Brownie; anywhere up to eight other horses; a groom (sometimes Wendell); and Miss Marguerite Parsons.

She was a central figure in my life. I still own a striking portrait photograph of her: she has her hair up in the 1940s style—we called it the "Rosie the Riveter look" after a cartoon character of the day—and what a luxuriant mane of hair it is. The chin is slightly pointed, the nose prominent. She has deep brown eyes, kindly eyes. You would look at that photograph and say, Here is a woman of character.

In the bunk room of the railroad car, the tiny-waisted Miss Parsons slept on the other side of a curtain strung along a pole. When we had all retired for the night, I would hear a strange whispering sound from her side of the curtain. It was not a human sound, and no horse ever made one like it. It had to be emanating from Miss Parsons. I did not know what it was, and I never asked. It was only some years later that the whispering was made plain to me: it was the pleasing sound of a woman's underclothing, silk on silk or the rustle of nylons. But in my bunk I could make no sense of the whispers, which only added to the quality of mystery that enveloped Miss Marguerite Parsons.

She had been our baby-sitter since I was two or three years old, and now she became my teacher as well. Neat, clean, and steady as a rock, she read me stories and made learning fun. Always in long skirts and dresses, she was strict and serious, but very caring and warm. Above all, she was instructive. If Miss Parsons had a fault she kept it hidden from me, and I loved her as pupils always love their favorite teacher.

She was only in her mid-twenties, but mature beyond her years, even wise. It seemed to me that she was always right in what she said and did. She would not leave us until 1949 when I was fourteen years old. She understood me better than my parents did and sympathized with my problems. She gave me lessons I value now: she taught me how to communicate with people; she encouraged me to relax; and she made me understand that if I was to pursue a career as a horseman with such single-minded dedication and from such a young age, I would have to pace myself—or burn out.

I remember heading for a show in Pomona, in southern California; it was one of the first times we used the railroad car, and simply preparing for it put me in a state of high excitement. We cleaned and sorted the saddles and bridles and arranged them in boxes fitted to one wall of the railroad car. In this way, we could simply lift out the boxes and stack them in the van so the equipment would not be damaged or soiled en route to the show ground.

"Ramp up, ramp up!" exclaimed Miss Parsons as soon as the horses and equipment were loaded and we were all inside. There was some urgency in her voice; a ramp was a welcome mat for mice. She worried obsessively about rodents, which were plentiful at all the railway sidings. Grain spilled during transport offered them a healthy food supply. Miss Parsons maintained a keen mouse vigil as well as a comprehensive extermination program inside the railroad car. And when not chasing mice she continued a brave but futile crusade against dust as we rolled from one siding to another.

A perfectionist, she posted lists of rules and regulations around the car, which we were asked to read every day. Many signs had mice in mind:

- Keep Doors Closed.
- Spill Grain, Clean Up Every Kernel.
- Horse Droppings Are to Be Cleaned Immediately.
- Keep Lids Tightly in Place on Manure Cans.

Before heading off, Miss Parsons would sort out the homework she would take with us to let me keep pace with my schooling.

She prepared my homework and wrote out tests for me at the little desk she set up in the car. She performed her task and I mine during long stopovers, and at night when the train was stopped, lest both of us become too ill with motion sickness from trying to read and write while underway.

The switch engine would pull us onto the main track, and a gentle bump and the clink of the hitch told us we were now one of many wagons hitched to the engine that we could hear steaming away at the head of the train. Southern Pacific took us down through San Luis Obispo, Santa Barbara, Ventura, and on toward the Los Angeles basin. Peering out through the heavy wire mesh guarding the windows, we could look ahead as the train snaked around a mountain or into the dozen or so tunnels that went right through the mountains. Rolling along the then pristine, unpopulated coast, we could look out to the tranquil beauty of the ocean. This was train travel, but wind-in-your-hair train travel, which most people never experience. The slow rhythm of the wheels rolling over the tracks settled all of us—horses, Wendell, Miss Parsons and me—into a routine as we made our way south.

After the tunnels and the slow route beside the sea, Los Angeles was an eye-opener: so many cars and buildings and people squeezed together constituted an alien land. But finally, we arrived at Pomona. This was an upscale, fiercely competitive show, and I faced it with trepidation. I could be reasonably confident of winning in some of the shows I went to, but Pomona was different, and, in one way, unique.

The owner of the facility—Dr. John Harvey Kellogg of Kellogg's cereals—had built a spur line connecting his grounds to the main Southern Pacific network. No need to park in a siding and transport horses and equipment to the show ground. We simply chugged down the spur line, dropped the ramp, and the main arena lay right before us. The other contestants, who had to stable their horses a mile away, looked on in amazement at this kid who just parked next to the arena in his own train. It was a good psychological tactic. I had already won pole position.

But I would need any advantage. This was a serious event, with a 2,000-seat stadium and a parade of superbly equipped competitors mounted on expensive horses. I would have to give Brownie all the help I could muster to cut a path anywhere near the top. A current of excitement coursed through Brownie, too; he was as charged up as I was. Because of his breeding—part aristocrat, part mustang—his nerves were always highly tuned, and he knew this was something special.

As I led him out and then returned to help Wendell with the other horses, a line of children began to form a small audience. They continued to observe impassively as I—only eleven myself—warmed up Brownie, putting him through his paces as any athlete would—to warm up the ligaments and tendons and to push his blood around his body a bit faster after the long journey with inadequate exercise.

As the children watched, I had the sense that Brownie and I were the "other team," tagged as the opposition. During the warm-up, something caught my eye in a ring some distance away—a horse coming to a dead stop from a gallop, a cloud of dust under his belly, the hind feet tucked neatly underneath and taking the strain of the sliding halt. I was impressed, even elated at the sight, but depressed, too. Surely, I thought to myself, there is the winner of my junior class.

As I rode over I saw, with no small measure of relief, that the rider was an adult; he would compete in a different division. Drawing closer, I recognized Clyde Kennedy riding Rango, the southern California champion reined cow horse. I had been impressed, even from afar, with good reason.

Still somewhat daunted by the professional atmosphere, I felt uncertain and unsure of our prospects. When it was time for my class, Wendell brought Brownie across to me. Watching my horse stride over, the single white dot like a third eye as he carried himself along in his usual, steady fashion, I suddenly knew I had the best horse. In the saddle with my hand on his neck, I sensed his low pulse rate and his capable attitude and adopted it myself to calm my nerves. I had doubted him, but no longer. We felt like professionals.

Figure eights were Brownie's Achilles' heel, but he hit the flying changes on this occasion unusually well. I knew Clyde Kennedy was watching me. I had found a new hero, and I wanted to impress him. When it came to do the stops, Brownie accomplished the first two reasonably quickly, but without any reaction from the crowd. The third stop I can remember to this day because I asked Brownie 'Whoa!' when we were galloping in the center of the ring, and he slid to a quivering, perfect halt in thirty feet. We stood in that cloud of dust while the crowd roared; it was the kind of applause that goes up at a football game after a touchdown, and I knew then, before the backing up and the offsets, that we had done fine.

At the out gate, Clyde Kennedy was there to congratulate Brownie on his performance and to ask me if I had a trainer. I told him no, but that I had seen him on Rango earlier and I would take any lessons I could from him. Clyde came over to the railroad car and looked around inside, intrigued by the arrangement. That night, he joined Miss Parsons and me in the railroad workers' cafeteria a short way up the track. As we sat down to our meal, I learned about the rivalry between Clyde and Jimmy Williams, the local favorite in Pomona.

Clyde continued to ask questions about the railroad car. Miss Parsons was proud to tell him how we were strictly tied to a low budget. There was no candy or soft drinks for young Monty Roberts; if he was lucky, he might get to open the box of scrap leather and mend some of his equipment—if he ever had a spare moment after collecting used Coca-Cola bottles so he could get the deposits back. Clyde shook his head in amusement.

That night as I lay in the railroad car I could hear children whispering and running around outside; they were looking for Brownie, who had become something of a hero. On the outside of the railroad car was pinned a line of rosettes, as well as spurs and belt buckles and other prizes. Brownie took this celebrity in stride, as though he thought it was his due. He was not an arrogant horse, simply one unfazed by almost any experience that did not involve paper.

On the last day of the show, the rivalry between Jimmy Williams and Clyde Kennedy was played out in the open division. Jimmy's horse Red Hawk could spin like a top. His sliding stops could be seen for miles around, the dust like Cherokee smoke signals. The crowd was rooting for him.

Clyde Kennedy, though, was superb on Rango. With only Miss Parsons, Wendell, and me to cheer him on, Rango executed the figure eights with style, effortlessly flying from one lead to the other as if he were ambidextrous. His pirouettes were a blur—all the while holding his head and neck straight, and never allowing his front feet to tangle while spinning in both directions. I had already seen his marvelous stops, and was not surprised when he won, but it was thrilling to witness nonetheless.

Wendell, Miss Parsons, and I loaded ourselves and our horses back into the railroad car, ready to be hauled back to the main line. Next stop: Tucson, Arizona, more than eight hours away. My whole life, invariably a life with horses, seemed to stretch out before me, as straight and as uncomplicated as the railway track itself.

Recently, I had occasion to revisit Pomona to give a lecture at a breeders' symposium. As I drove the car past a wild grassy area and a broken-down fence line, I had a flashback. I said to Pat, "Hang on, I've been here before. Follow me and I'll show you." I cut a path through the tall grass and we went about one hundred yards up the valley.

"I bet you," I said, "there's a disused single-track railway line up here." Pat followed me but gave me a doubting look. A little way off, I found the old length of iron and some wasted railway ties. We walked down the track to the spot where the show ground had been. The spectators' grandstand had been dismantled but the main ring itself was still discernible as an oval shape, the railings grassed over and choked with weeds. Suddenly, that day half a century ago, its clear sense of triumph and excitement, came back to me. The reality of the place, the show ground itself, was eroding; the event lived on only in the minds of those who had taken part. In a few years all trace of it would be gone.

It was a powerfully nostalgic feeling to stand where I had stood as a boy. It stirred my soul and took me totally by surprise.

I had once thought that life would be a straight progression, like an iron line through the wilderness. I knew better now, but looking out to that faded oval, with my arms around Pat, I felt a certain joy in our maturity. After forty years of marriage and raising a family, we had made it. To stand in Pomona, amid the ruins, was to make a neat and tidy circle.

———

Small wonder that entrepreneurial instincts were strong in me even as a boy: I had been riding for prize money at horse shows and working as a stunt rider in movies since the age of four, and even school was shaped around work in the stables. By the time I was twelve, money-making schemes—some quite epic—began to hatch in my brain. One involved Coca-Cola bottles.

My brother and I had been picking up bottles at horse competitions and bringing them home in the railroad car to earn the two-cent deposits. In 1947, it was announced that the first big postwar rodeo was to be held at the competition grounds in Salinas, and visions of all those empty Coke bottles were too tempting to pass up.

The outdoor grandstand was five stories high with a concrete wall behind and bench seating from top to bottom. The 20,000 spectators each day would stuff wrappers and spent bottles into the cavity below their seats—and down into the off-limits area below.

I went to Doc Leach in the competition grounds office with a proposal. Larry and I would clean up under the seats when the rodeo ended—"just for the coins and stuff we might find." Doc Leach wondered vaguely why we might volunteer to do so much work just for the odd coin, but he agreed. He would not have known about either the deposit system or Coke itself: inventions too new for old Doc Leach.

After the rodeo, however, our profits appeared to be in jeopardy. Before taking the measure of our haul, I had asked my father to call a representative of the Coca-Cola Bottling Company. I had in mind a very busy scene: wooden crates stacked by the doors, a line of trucks to take them away, with Larry and me in charge. But a Mr. Carlson of Coca-Cola warned us that people were catching on to the deposit idea and taking bottles home. We might do a great deal of work for almost nothing.

When, after the rodeo, my brother and I first entered that cavernous space below the seats, we were greeted by an amazing spectacle. Sunlight filtered through the slatted seats, like light through a Venetian blind, throwing wide stripes across ground that was ankle-deep in rubbish.

Anxious to find that first bottle, we held it up to a shaft of light. It was not broken, and few were. We were safe. We were also knee-deep in work: it took us two and a half months, working mostly at night, to complete the task! But at the end was a glass bonanza—80,000 bottles, one for every ticket sold over the four days. A convoy of trucks did indeed cart the bottles away. Larry and I earned $800 each, then a small fortune.

A tribute to the glass then used, only a thousand bottles had broken: some, remember, were dropped from a great height.

In the local newspaper, Doc Leach cheerfully conceded: the rodeo association had missed out on quite a profit and two young entrepreneurs had taken an old guy for a ride. He would not make the same mistake again.

The next year, when I went up to the high deserts of Nevada to bring back wild mustangs for Doc Leach and the rodeo, our partnership would be more equitable. But the heady Coca-Cola success certainly led to my life-changing encounters with the wild horses through the summer that followed.

CHAPTER 3

East of Eden

By 1949, when I was fourteen years old, I had essentially been a professional rider for a decade. I never really had a childhood; my youth had been an apprenticeship dedicated almost exclusively to horses, and my amateur competitors in the showring could not have known that the fuzzy-cheeked kid opposing them—on Ginger or Brownie— was a pro in every sense. Small wonder the trophies often went my way.

I had grown up on rodeo grounds, and it was inevitable that one day rodeo competition would beckon and that one day I would heed the call. My father's credo was simple: if there was prize money, I was to try for it. And so I entered skeet-shooting contests, chuck-wagon races, I rode bulls and even bucking horses—though I loathed riding broncs and had no talent for it. At fourteen, I began to practice the rodeo event called "bulldogging," which would prove to be the one at which I was most capable. Bulldogging started on ranches in Texas. Cowboys would have to hold herds of cattle together for hours at a time while various animals were singled out and roped—for veterinary treatment, perhaps, or for branding. Occasionally, a grown animal would run out of the herd, and the cowboys would chase after him and turn him back. For their own amusement during the long hours on the range, they started to compete among themselves in this chase-and-turn work. Some tried jumping from their horses onto the animal's neck, turning him back using their bare hands.

One day a black cowboy named Bill Pickett rode after a steer, jumped on its head, leaned over and grabbed its upper lip in his mouth, and bit down hard. The animal was so surprised by the pain that it fell. This was the very method that the English bulldog used to drop deer. Pickett would then turn the animal around and drive it back into the herd. The ranch put him on a tour to demonstrate his remarkable methods, which evolved into the event that we know today as bulldogging.

In the modern version, two men on horseback dart after an adult horned steer. One stays on the right and hazes the animal to keep it going in a straight line. The other runs alongside it on the left-hand side and leaps off his horse. The aim is to land on the steer's neck. His goal is to "throw" the steer. The bulldogger will want to stick to the animal like glue to prevent falling underneath his hooves. He wraps an arm around the animal's horns and takes its nose in the crook of his elbow, then gives an almighty twist to the steer's neck. The forward impetus of the animal causes it to flip on its side. It's like performing a judo throw with a 700-pound steer at breakneck speed. When the steer's flanks hit the dust, the clock stops. Injuries to the animals are virtually nil; the cowboys are often not as lucky.

I won the National Intercollegiate Rodeo Association (NIRA) bull-dogging championship in 1957, and I did well to win it—generally, rodeo championships go to cowboys from inland states such as Texas, Idaho, and Montana. My first steer was a bad draw. He was a big, slow-handling animal, and by the time I had thrown him I was placed seventh in the event, with a time of 6.2 seconds. But I could still win the championship if I placed well in the second round (the two rounds are averaged to produce a final score). I drew for my second steer, and got myself perhaps the best on offer. However, I drew in the "slack," which meant my second round would fall late at night, long after the public had left the arena.

Worse, by ten P.M. a sleet storm blew up. Particles of ice dripped off our hats. There was no cover, and I piled whatever clothing I could find on my horse and myself. Every now and again, I would run around in circles for ten minutes to keep my muscles warm. I would trot my horse, called Miss Twist, in circles for the same reason. Just past midnight, with only two more bulldoggers to go, I got the call for my second round. My college crew (my teammates) were all drinking hot coffee, and they swore it was the best thing for me in these crazy conditions, so I took half a cup and drained it, though coffee and I did not agree.

The bulldogger before me was in the chutes and ready to go. With the steer set on its way, the hazer's horse slipped on the muddy ground and failed to keep up. The young bulldogger found himself galloping alongside the steer with no one on the other side to keep it in a straight line. The steer peeled off to the right and the boy got his horse over and alongside the steer as best he could. But by now the steer was running alongside the fence and just as the boy leaned out to pitch from his horse, the steer carved a line to the left, toward the horse, and the rider was upended, bounced over the top of the steer, and into the metal pipe-and-rail fencing. He hit his head on an upright post and lay still where he fell.

The ambulance was called, and there was a sorrowful delay. The realization sank in that the boy had died instantly; the sound of his head hitting the upright had been ominously final.

The weather further blackened our spirits. And to add to these increasingly desperate circumstances, I began to feel nauseous; the coffee was working away in my gut and producing the allergic reaction that I subsequently learned to avoid at all costs. While my stomach churned, I backed Miss Twist into the box and threw off the sheets keeping her more or less out of the sleet and rain. I signaled to my hazer, Jack Roddy, that I was ready.

The steer was let out and I blew after him as fast as I could, Jack Roddy's horse maintaining his grip in the mud and keeping the steer in a straight line for me. I leapt from my saddle onto the steer's neck and with a giant twist of his head I brought him down in 4.3 seconds. I knew as soon as I felt him hit the turf that this great score meant I had earned myself a national championship in bulldogging.

When my college crew ran over to applaud me they found me staring at the ground, almost embracing it. The allergy had taken effect
and I was more sick than I believed possible. I threw up everything,
even my heels. The crew put it down to overexcitement, and I could
not draw a breath to tell them otherwise and to plead: could they
please stop pounding on the back of such a sick and sorry man.

———

Of all the events performed in the rodeo, perhaps the most dangerous
is bull riding. In bull riding, your life depends on the draw. After your
ride, the bull receives a score between one and fifty for his efforts, and
the rider receives a score in that same range for his. You might even
call it a team event. Each contestant has eight seconds to stay right
side up on a professional rodeo bull. Bulls are more ferocious in their
tactics than bucking horses. Horses arch their backs, curl their heads
between their front legs and jump, stiff-legged, in a pogo-stick type
of action, all of which is difficult enough. Bulls, on the other hand,
have extraordinary strength and traction in their cloven feet that
allows them to dive, then twist up to the left, come down again, crack
into a right spin, and so on. A bull is like a hairy, snorting roller
coaster. You hold on to the braided rope around his middle, and eight
seconds on a bull's back can seem like a lifetime.

Of course, once you jump off or are thrown the bull straightaway
turns and heads for you. His intentions are clear; he wants to see
you as dust under his feet. So-called clowns run into the ring and
distract his attention, which they do with any number of humorous
antics. The clowns are amazing athletes and bullfighters who risk
everything to entertain the crowd and save cowboys from injury.

When I got married, Pat asked me to give up bull riding since competitors are particularly prone to serious injury. She argued that
my other rodeo events would improve without the stress and strain of
bull riding. I agreed, and it took no more than one rodeo event to
prove her right. Still, long afterward I would have strange flashes
about bull riding. At a rodeo I would find myself worrying about
which bull I had drawn, then remember. Without knowing it, I had
been suffering from enormous tension, and I was glad of Pat's advice.

———

Most rodeo events evolved from common working practices on the ranch. In team roping, a pair of day hands would rope the steer's head and hind feet and stretch him out on the ground. Using a medicinal kit carried in their saddlebags, the two might have to deal with a hunk of barbed wire around his leg or a foxtail in his eye. Ranch horses were trained to maintain the tension on the rope until the job was done. Rodeo took that task and turned it into a competition—team roping. I was to win the NIRA national championship in team roping in 1956. To win that title requires a year of preparation.

Once, in Scottsdale, Arizona, Jack Roddy and I had drawn a perfect steer; he was steady and moved in a straight line. In my mind, this steer was important if we were going to get things going for the year. The steer was in the chute; Jack, the header, was behind the barrier to the left; I, the heeler, was in position on the right.

A piece of string is attached to the steer. When he takes off, he goes a prescribed distance before the string trips the latch holding a cord across the front of the header's horse. A ten-second fine is imposed if the header breaks through the cord. The trick (an art, really) is to have the horse moving forward just as the cord is released.

On this occasion, Jack Roddy timed it perfectly. In the arena he threw a great loop: a time below ten seconds and the championship trophy appeared before me like a vision. I was on a horse called Berney, and we shot off after the steer that Jack was drawing across our path. I leaned out, my loop built and whirling above my head, well within range and, suddenly, I had no horse. Berney took a dive and somersaulted, throwing me onto my chin.

In my hands was a rope, one end of it tied to the steer's hind feet. With a neat bucking action, the steer pulled it through, and the palms of my hands were like hamburger, practically smoking. Logically, I should have let the rope go but my subconscious had taken over. I had to apologize to Jack Roddy. No trophy.

Albuquerque, New Mexico, was a different story. We drew a steer that rodeo competitors call "a blue screamer." He was more like a racehorse than a bovine. "Don't worry," said Jack, "we'll beat these pot lickers." *Pot licker* was a derogatory term for the competition; when everyone else had finished lunch, a pot licker got to lick the pot.

The steer was in his chute wringing his tail, anxious to run, and Jack and I were lined up. Jack had his horse, Chongo, backed all the way up in the chute, aiming to time it so he pushed through the cord at a full gallop.

The steer lit out of the chute like it was on fire, and Jack rolled Chongo forward just as the string was tightening. He had Chongo flat out after only a few strides, and he roped the steer's head with a superb long throw. However, the long rope meant it was more difficult for me because the steer was swinging back and forth in a long arc. I had Berney on his tail and I could see his hind feet going quicker than I thought possible. I faced a twelve- to fourteen-foot throw instead of the usual four or five. Berney was practically scratching his inside ear on the ground, leaning that hard into the corner to get me close enough to rope the critter's heels. But this was the only chance I would get, and I had no time to widen my loop. I made the throw of a lifetime, and the steer's hind legs ran into the coil. We had him laid out flat on the ground and the field judge dropped the flag in less than eight seconds. The world championship was mine.

As a young man in the rodeo arena, I did more calf roping than I care to admit. In the calf-roping event, a small, 200-pound bovine scatters from the gate, moving more nimbly than the bigger animals. Dexterity is the name of the game. A cowboy races after him. As he builds his loop and closes in, the calf knows he is there. He ducks his head and flattens his ears, expecting his pursuer—as a predator—to catch him on the back of the neck. The cowboy throws the loop around the calf's head, keeping the other end of the rope tied around the horn of his saddle. All in one motion, the horse stops hard, the roper dismounts, and the calf is jerked off its feet and lands with a thud on its side.

The cowboy runs at him with a small length of rope in his teeth, waiting for the calf to rise to his feet. The roper's task is to throw the calf to the ground again and then wind the rope around any three of his legs—usually one front leg and both rear legs. The instant the cowboy completes the tie and throws his hands in the air, the field judge drops the flag and the clock stops.

Calf roping is not a pleasant event, and bears no comparison with what actually happens on a ranch. Roping calves is a necessary practice—for branding, castration, and medical purposes—but the calf is allowed to run with the rope and is brought to a halt slowly. Usually calves are roped by a team, to minimize stress on the calf.

I recently did a day's roping on a neighboring ranch and my horse, Dually, a champion reined and cutting horse, never broke out of a walk during the whole day's work. Ranchers prefer it this way: these babies, after all, are their livelihood. Protests against calf roping on the rodeo circuit have increased to such an extent that now the event is seldom seen by the paying public. It still takes place, but in the slack when the seats are empty.

As for bronc riding, another competition that has stirred an outcry, the distress that some people feel for broncs is misplaced. The bronc is not just any wild animal; he is a highly prized specialist. Not many horses are suited for the work. Far from being a cruel sport, this is a competition event in which the horse truly enjoys himself.

The champion bronc is a valuable animal who gets the best care and nutrition. He is not bored by repetitive exercises, like many horses working in other rodeo events or in the Western show-horse categories. He is respected as a bronc. He is a wild thing, and nobody spends hours trying to bend his will. He quickly learns that he has nothing to fear.

He is taken into the chute, a man gets on him, and the gate opens. The bronc then does as he pleases, and what pleases him is to put that rider on the ground. It's a good life.

———

In 1949, a group of American amateur equestrian associations banded together and established rules for a new amateur contest called "horsemastership," open to anyone under the age of eighteen. They laid a grid on the map, and each state was divided into districts. The winner would climb a ladder, from district to state to regional competition. At the end of this long trail of hard work, the reward was to be invited to the international final of the horsemastership contest, held in New York.

Parents across the country entered their children in this enormous and comprehensive competition. Surely the nation's gross national product dropped during the few years the all-consuming contest was held. My brother and I entered the first year. It was a hot day in Santa Rosa, California, and we were roasted in more ways than one. We were unprepared and came home losers.

Within days, we began to prepare for the 1950 horsemastership title. Next time I did better. Victorious in the district, I went to the state competition at Palm Springs. Judges had numbered different bits and bridles and ancillary equipment, and we were asked to name them. For every buckle and strip of leather, I gave a crisp answer. The judges might have taken my confidence as patronizing, but they liked the philosophy behind the phrase I repeated over and over, and they gave me full marks. "The most important part of any bit or horse headgear," I told them, "are the hands that hold it."

I won, but it was no surprise—I had been training horses for this event obsessively for two years in the manner of an adult professional yet I was pitched against young people who undertook their horsemanship more as a hobby. When I traveled to New York to win the final event with points to spare, I was still only fifteen. Nearly all the other twenty finalists were at the maximum age of eighteen. Fifteen of them came from various states in the United States; the rest were from Canada, Mexico, Panama, Puerto Rico, South Africa, and Argentina.

Between the rodeos and the show grounds and the horsemastership contests, and all the traveling on the railroad car, I did manage to fit in a little time at school, but my attendance record was slim. It consisted mostly of turning up on examination days to prove that I was up to standard. I was, though, registered with the local Catholic school administered by Notre Dame nuns. One nun, Sister Agnes Patricia, was the most influential teacher I ever knew. What I will always remember about her is her statement that there is no such thing as teaching—only learning. She believed that no teacher could ever teach anyone anything. Her task as a teacher was to create an environment in which the student can learn.

Knowledge, she told us, standing very straight in her long black habit, her face framed by her white wimple, pointed at the top like the spire of a cathedral, needs to be pulled into the brain by the student, not pushed into it by the teacher. Knowledge is not to be forced on anyone. The brain has to be receptive, malleable, and most important, hungry for that knowledge.

I apply the same philosophy to training horses. To use the word "teach" implies an injection of knowledge. Like Sister Agnes Patricia, I came to agree that there is no such thing as teaching, only learning.

———

When I was sixteen, Larry and I were part of a mad enterprise: a roundup of wild steers that had the look and feel of a wild goose chase—in the dark.

A woman named Dorothy Tavernetti owned the Laguna Seca Ranch, fifteen miles south of Salinas and some 6,000 acres in size. In 1950 she became the financial backer of an enthusiastic rodeo cowboy, Trevor Haggeman, who specialized in team roping, and they may have been connected romantically as well. She bought batches of young "Mexican Corianti" steers with long horns on which Trevor could practice his roping. My brother and I would go over three times a week to practice as well.

Within three or four months the steers got too heavy and stopped running; they grew weary of being roped all the time. Instead of selling them, Trevor would turn them out on the range and Dorothy would buy another batch of steers for him. The cattle lived on the range and grew bigger and bigger. When, a year later, Dorothy grew disenchanted with Trevor and asked him to leave, she decided to sell all the steers that had been put out on her ranch. The first group of 400 steers were easy to round up, and were shipped off to market. But the remaining one hundred head were now quite wild. You were lucky to glimpse them in the daylight hours and only rarely at night. Dorothy's hired hands concluded it was impossible to catch them.

She did not accept this defeatist attitude, however, and contracted Ralph Carter to catch her renegade cattle. Ralph and Vivian had been our partners in the mustang roundups, and since roping was a part of our lives, Ralph asked Larry and me, then fifteen and sixteen, to help. We felt like rustlers, for the roundup would take place under cover of darkness. The first few nights we were able to gather about forty head without too much difficulty. The remaining sixty head, however, were elusive. Ralph devised a plan: he would drive out with a load of hay in the pickup and feed them on open, flat areas five miles from the ranch house.

It was high summer, and food was in short supply. The cattle quickly found the new hay and would listen for the pickup as it came at nine or ten at night. They grew to like the sound of the truck's engine. Once this routine was established, Ralph hid Larry and me, on horseback, in the trees nearby. While the steers were eating the dropped hay, we were to break from the trees and gallop through the darkness, heading them off before they could reach the safety of the brush. The task was to rope a steer in near darkness.

It was hair-raising to be riding hellishly fast over broken ground, trying to see enough by the scant moonlight to rope some of the wildest steers known to humankind. You only knew you had caught one when you felt the sudden yank on the line. It was like fishing in the dark.

We would hold the captured steer with a dally—the rope wrapped around the horn of the saddle—until Ralph arrived with the truck and trailer. We then passed the ropes through the front of the trailer, so that by pulling from in front and pushing from behind, the steers were drawn up and into the trailer. Over six nights, we captured twelve steers in this fashion. The remaining forty-eight grew wise and would not be tempted from the brush. Ralph had to devise another plan. This time, Larry and I left headquarters on horseback, heading north of the cattle. We then pressed south, driving any cattle ahead of us through the brush into the open areas where we ran the horses flat out to catch the steers before they thought to circle back to cover.

I was chasing a steer I could barely see when it ran into a small clump of oak trees. I was concentrating hard on not riding into a low-hanging limb. The steer obviously knew that in the center of this clump of trees lay a deep pit. He also knew (though Brownie and I did not) about a trail that skirted round the edge of the pit. When the steer suddenly veered off, we continued on—airborne—down into the pit.

I was thrown over Brownie's head and, as I passed over his ears, accidentally caught my hand on the crown of the bridle. I found myself at the bottom of a sixteen-foot pit, standing in sand up to my knees. In my left hand was the whole bridle and part of a rope; in my right hand was my loop, still built. Brownie stood beside me in sand up to his knees and hocks.

Outwitted by a steer! I felt sore about this, but I was less pleased to discover that this fifty-foot-wide pit was truly a sand trap. I would scramble up the side, hang on by the tips of my fingers, then slide back down again. Once or twice I reached the top, but could not persuade Brownie to join me. I was spitting dust, and my boots were full of stones. It took me half an hour to fight my way out of there, horse included. Back at the pickup, they were wondering what had happened to me.

Larry and I began to make inquiries about our salaries, and whether danger pay ought to be included. Our fee was a meager ten dollars per steer. But we carried on anyway because we were having fun. Finally, there remained about twenty steers to capture, and Ralph had yet another new plan.

We had learned that the steers were frightened only of the horses, whom they could smell from afar. Horses were their nemeses. But they still liked the sound of the pickup and the hay that came with it. We would use subterfuge.

Ralph stowed me in the back of the pickup, well hidden but with a loop already built. The other end of the rope was attached to the trailer hitch. Ralph drove slowly through the herd, while I tossed flakes of hay over the side from my position lying supine in the bed of the pickup. Ralph was muttering out the side window in a low voice, "Three coming up now on the left side..." At an opportune moment, I leapt from my hiding place and roped a steer. Ralph gunned the accelerator and jerked the steer to the ground. Larry and I jumped on the steer and held him down while Ralph got a rope around his horns. We then tied him to a tree, to be picked up later in the trailer. We were doing very well with this method until the accident.

I reckoned the steers were going to be on the right side of the truck, but they turned and approached us from the left. As usual, I jumped up, but then had to face in the other direction to throw the loop. I did not stop to think about where the rest of the rope was lying. As Ralph accelerated, the rope—caught around me—whipped up, crossed over my left cheekbone, and slammed my head into the tailgate.

He dragged the steer for thirty yards, while the rope massaged my head. I was unconscious for several hours; I awoke in the hospital with bandages covering my head and wondering what had happened. We eventually caught all the steers and made a fair amount of money for those nights' work. We were lucky to live through it, but it was fun and taught us to see in the dark.

———

During my trips to Nevada, I had become acutely aware that Brownie was due an apology from us. In the high desert, I had seen how he must have been brought up. Predators aside, it had looked to me to be idyllically happy. Brownie would have been been raised in a close family group, with affection tempered by discipline, and with all the security of a large extended family communicating effectively with one another.

He had then been wrenched into an alien environment, and right away beaten and frightened into submission. I had taken it upon myself to try to make up for the sacking-out procedure. I talked to him all the time, listened to him, gave him the best possible care; I wanted to do everything right for him. His health was always good; I thought carefully about his diet, I read his every mood. And he had responded. He had become as close as a brother to me. Save for his paper phobia, he was a steady and well-adjusted horse. He had recovered, I think, as well as could be expected.

However, not long after our steer-roping adventure together, when he was fourteen and I was seventeen, I began to notice a sorrowful air come over him in the stable, a certain reluctance when I swung into the saddle. He was not crisp and ready for the day as he usually was. Concerned, I began to experiment with his diet and exercise.

One of Brownie's favorite exercises was one I had devised to practice for the heeling event in rodeo competition. I did not always have a header to work with me, so I trained one steer to cooperate with us in these training sessions. The steer's job was to hold in one corner of a large rectangular pen; we would gallop toward him, and the steer would run toward the center. Brownie's task—and he excelled at it—was to execute a U-turn placing his right shoulder near the left hip of the steer, giving me a perfect opportunity to rope the hind legs. Both Brownie and the steer seemed to enjoy the game.

But when I included a touch more of this favorite activity in Brownie's training schedule, his apathy seemed worse rather than better. Suddenly, it hit me. He was bored with me; he needed a holiday. A young person as driven as I was will almost always overwork his horse, and despite all the attention I gave Brownie, it had proven too much. I had crowded his life with my own.

I realized this only weeks before the biggest horse show of the year in Salinas. Were we to duck out of it, and give up all we had worked for? More than ever, I wished that we shared the same language.

One day I leaned into Brownie's stall and had a conversation with him. I put an arrangement to him: "Brownie, I will love you from Monday to Friday, feed and exercise you from Monday to Friday, but I won't badger you or bother you. You can do what you want during the week. In return, can you give me everything you've got on Saturday and Sunday?"

Knowing he could not understand, but fresh with the knowledge I had gained in Nevada, I made a promise to him that I would dedicate my life to understanding his language. This was a vow made to a horse, but solemn nonetheless. I meant to keep it. On that day, which was a focal point in my life, I set out my goal. My ambitions became focused from that point.

Brownie won everything at the Salinas show. It was as though he did understand.

———

These were the last summers spent on the railroad car traveling to horse shows.

The shows themselves were a flurry of activity and hard work. My father employed an advance man to sort out transportation from rail yard to show ground, to identify where we could restock with provisions and, more important, to sell as many tickets as possible to a "clinic" I would put on after the weekend shows, often on a Monday evening. Miss Parsons took the gate money and banked our share; she kept accounts in a steel box that would then be pored over by her and by my father, though I was not privy to that. The advance man also secured the venue for the clinic. Often the tickets were sold to clubs and schools. The advertised appeal was: "Monty can show you how to win." My father no doubt hit on this initiative to help cover the considerable costs involved in hauling the railroad car around the country with all those horses and two full-time employees. He must have needed more than my prize money to keep that show on the road.

At the shows, I generally won everything. And why not? I had Brownie, plus up to eight highly trained horses to mop up any prizes left over. I was a professional with years of experience behind me. The American Horse Shows Association recognized me as a professional but did not exclude me from entering amateur competitions as long as I was within the qualifying age. I competed against boys and girls who might enter two or three horse shows a summer and only ride on weekends. Horsemanship was their fun, not their life's work. In a way, I was a freak occurrence on the show circuit in those years. At the clinics I was supposed to reveal the secret of my success before what we hoped was an enthusiastic audience. Brownie was on hand so young riders could see the famous champion horse. I listened hard to every question and gave as much advice as I could.

I spoke about equipment, work ethic, training. I watched my pupils' horses and counseled what should be done with them next. I learned to project my voice and speak clearly. I felt a great weight of responsibility, because all these riders had paid and deserved the best attention. But, for all that, the clinics could never deliver what they promised. The "secret" of my success was a life obsession with horses. I would look at the eager young faces lined up before me: no youngsters were going to dedicate six to seven hours a day to riding, and no parents would let them. Sometimes I felt sorry for those kids, but just as often I felt sorry for myself. My life during those summers was like that of young evangelists who travel the country preaching; in many ways, it was a trying existence.

Not having had the opportunity to behave as a child, I was separate, isolated, with a different set of values from most young people. I had never visited a toy shop, for instance, never possessed a toy as a child; only much later did that fact strike me as odd. I would see a child go into a shop, point at a train set or a doll, and say, "Can I have that one, please?" It struck me that I had never done that, and I felt an overwhelming sense of regret. On the other hand, because my world was focused so tightly on horses, I was prone to think I was better than anyone else and that I possessed unique qualities. After all, I was *the* high-profile junior horseman on the North American showring circuit. Behind my father's back I had started to investigate the silent language of Equus. I could not wait to be free of him and to start using my own methods.

Luckily, Miss Parsons kept my feet on the ground, reminding me that the whole circus of our operation offered tremendous opportunities for both adventure and education. She kept me humble, pointing out that my success owed a great deal to the many hours of work I put in, which my competitors could not. There were no magic wands in my possession, no mystical qualities unique to Monty Roberts.

But I was already more man than boy. In terms of my life experience, my travel, and my education, I was a man in his twenties. Even my body carried the message that I was older than my years. I had turned to weight lifting, and my 190 pounds was spread over a powerful frame with a forty-eight-inch chest. Silently, I was conveying a message to my father: "I will be bigger than you." When I won the "Mr. Salinas Junior" bodybuilding contest, my father ridiculed me. We were like two bulls, and though the younger one still feared the older, time, as it always is, was on the side of the young.

The already strained relationship between us grew increasingly difficult. As a boy reaching manhood, I had good reason to believe I should be testing my wings. We had many aborted conversations about starting to train horses using my own methods. What was wrong with his methods? he would ask. He had done pretty well with them—what was there to change? He wanted his ways to be my ways; he could not conceive that I might do anything other than what he had taught me. The mere thought of it stirred anger in him.

At fifteen, I had wanted to play football and try out for the wrestling team, but he would have none of it. I might as well have asked his permission to fly to the moon. Anything that took me away from the life he had made for me was beyond contemplation. He had given me first breath, and he owned the ones that came after.

I would try again. "Maybe you could release some of the income I earned from the motion pictures I did, so I could buy some equipment?"

"What money? You used that up long ago."

"OK, what about the clinics we just held?"

He would counter with a question of his own. "Who paid for your education, who paid for your room and board, who paid for your upbringing?"

Then he made the point crystal clear. "I, as your father, am responsible for everything you've done, and you owe me, not vice versa."

Sometime later, I was in the house talking with my mother, explaining to her how working with the mustangs over the last few years had taught me a great deal.

"Like what?" she asked.

"Something very important. For instance, I just know that no one needs to sack out a young horse anymore. I'm doing it a different way. I don't even hit a horse once, not ever —not the way I do it. I don't even tie a rope to their heads before I ride them."

"Well," she said, "that sounds like a lot happier way of doing things." Just then, a movement caught my eye and I turned and saw my father. He was staring at me from the doorway, and I knew he had caught the drift of my conversation. He stepped forward wearing a hard, unforgiving look. I knew what that meant. He stepped in front of us, his color heightened by his terrible fury. The veins stood out in his neck as he shouted, "I don't want to hear any more of this sort of talk."

"Dad—"

He shouted louder, one of his hands curling into a fist, the other jabbing at my chest. "You are ungrateful to me."

"I'm not."

"You are too stupid to do anything without my help." I swallowed hard, knowing what was coming, as my mother pleaded, "Marvin, please…"

"You owe everything to me!" With that, he raised his fist to his opposite ear and brought it back across my face, knocking my jaw hard. On this day, finally, I was not going to take it. I advanced on him, my hands on his arms, and backed him against a wall. I looked him in the eye, and he seemed to grow a little smaller. I had anger now to match his, and I came within a hair of unleashing it.

I felt then what I have occasionally felt since but always resisted: an urge to strike. But at that moment the chain of violence was broken. I would not be like him—either with other humans, or with animals.

I registered that my mother had screamed, briefly. I heard my mother say to him, "Marvin, stop at once." She had his arm and was staring at him hard, like she wanted to turn him to stone.

"Listen to him for once," she said. "Let's just see what he has to say. He's not a child."

We moved slightly apart, and he dropped his shoulders. He was not afraid of me, but he wore a look of shock and resignation. "Listen, uh?" he said, as though anything I said would not be worth much. Nevertheless, he went quiet. We moved to the living room and he sat on a couch by himself while my mother stood close by me.

Something clicked; I recognized my opportunity. This was no conversation now. I was telling him what was going to happen. "I want to start up on my own. I figure there are people who will give me work training their horses, and I want to be left to do as I think fit. I want a chance to prove I can do it. It's not much to ask, it's only what anyone in Salinas could do—lease some facilities from you so they can work with horses here at the grounds. Same as Ray Hackworth or anybody else."

There was a moment's pause while my father digested what he had just heard. A look of disbelief stole over his face, then he said, "Good! You can do just that! I'll rent you barn number eight, course I will. And we'll see how you get on." Then he stood up and pointed a finger at me. "And while you're about it, since you're so damned grown-up all of a sudden, you can pay us money for your board, you can buy your own vehicle and your own clothes." His parting shot was: "The rent for your room here is thirty-five dollars a month!"

The rent for the entire house on Church Street had been thirty-five dollars a month. He wanted to show me the kind of payments he faced, and by setting such a high rent he thought he was sowing the seeds of my failure. Nevertheless, I eagerly accepted the arrangement. He named my mother as administrator for all the various charges, and the days she was to expect them.

I took him at his word and opened for business as a trainer of show horses and cutting horses.

In other ways too I made it clear that I was now in charge of my own destiny. Rodeos would no longer dominate my time: I joined the football and wrestling teams at school. As far as making a living, I was a world champion horseman, was I not? Surely there would be more than enough work training other people's horses.

Reality struck home quickly: had it not been for my mother helping me out surreptitiously most of the time, forgetting a month's rent here and there and slipping me some cash when she saw I needed it, I certainly would have crashed quickly and would have had to find myself a job digging ditches. But my mother cheated on my behalf in ingenious ways. She bought pants, supposedly for my father but in my size, so she could give them to me instead. Without her adjusting the accounts in this way, my father would have been right and I would not have survived.

Thanks to her, I was out from under him for the first time in my life. It was a start.

———

I was mounted on Brownie, standing in one corner of the corral. In the other corner stood one steer. While Brownie jigged on the spot, wanting to be set loose and run at the steer, I counted the seconds and judged when to give the command. I gave a cluck and he jumped forward in the usual gleeful way. Brownie ran in, rolling the steer out of the corner and bouncing it out from along the rails—his particular skill.

Suddenly, he felt all wrong beneath me. As if his nervous system was plugged into mine, I felt the sharp, fearful breakdown within him just as he did. When he stumbled and made a crashing fall, this was no horse tripping over a piece of rough ground; this was the rug pulled out from under his feet.

By the time I stood up, I knew he was dead. He was lying on the ground, not moving a muscle. A terrible grief overtook me. I could not imagine life without this horse as my friend and companion. I suffered true bereavement, as bad as any I have known. I stood there for a long while in dumb silence, not doing a thing.

As I stood there, I remembered. I remembered first seeing that single white dot between his eyes, remembered hearing his name. Brownie. Standing nose to tail with Oriel in the pale moonlight up on the high desert in Nevada. Rocking back and forth in the railroad car, keeping his balance. Walking forward to collect many, many championship trophies as a working horse. Spinning calves out of the corner of the corral...

I set about to bury him where he died, at the south end of the competition grounds. The ground was rock hard, and I went at it with a pick and shovel. To my surprise, my father understood my sorrow. He rented an air chisel for me so I could break through; it was the kindest thing he ever did for me.

The old grounds at Salinas were recently rebuilt and one of the mementos I plucked from it was a board from Brownie's stall. Not that I needed anything to remember him by.

It is a bitter pill to watch a horse die, but to lose one you love is to lose a part of yourself. The tears do not stop coming for a long time.

"Rest in peace," I said to Brownie as I laid him in his grave. I meant it.

———

Mr. Fowler paced back and forth at the head of the class, while we waited with our pencils sharpened and our paper at the ready. A tall man with an erect bearing and an olive complexion, he always dressed immaculately.

"I want you all to think about this very carefully," the teacher said, waving his long, elegant hands. "It should be like painting a picture of your lives in the future, as if all your ambitions had been realized."

A voice piped up. "How much detail do you want, sir?"

"As much as possible. It should be a complete portrayal of what you envision for yourself in the future." He turned to gaze at us calmly.

"And my last instruction to you is perhaps the most important: This vision should be realistic. I don't want to hear about some crazy, off-the-wall plan. I don't want to know about any Hollywood dreams, either."

There was a smattering of laughter at this. We were in California, after all. Mr. Fowler ended, "It should be a fair and accurate assessment of where I might expect to find you if I were to visit you in your mid-thirties. It's to be called "My Goals in Life" and should be returned within three weeks."

In my last year of high school, I knew precisely what I wanted to do in life; from the time I was nine I had been sketching plans for stables and training facilities. Mine was no Hollywood dream. I turned in what I thought was a good paper that captured my life's ambition: a ground plan and associated paperwork for the operation of a Thoroughbred racehorse facility. Five days later, the paper was returned to me with a big red F printed across the top of the page, along with the traditional words: "See me."

This was a shock, because I normally got good grades. Essay in hand, I went immediately to see Mr. Fowler after class and asked him what I had done wrong. He leafed through the pages. "You know that my last instruction to you was to be realistic in this projection of your future?"

"Yes, I did realize that."

"Do you realize that the average annual income of a person in the United States is sixty-three hundred dollars?" I had a clear idea of what was coming. "So how many years would you have to work and save up to earn the amount of money you'd need for your plan?" he asked me.

"I don't know."

He snapped his finger against the red F and advised me, "It's a wild, unattainable dream. I gave it a failing grade based on the instructions I issued at the outset." He handed me back the paper. "I know your family and background; it would just not be possible. Take it home, think about it, change your vision to an appropriate level, and hand it in again. The last thing I want is to fail you based on a misunderstanding."

It felt like he had driven a knife into me, so unexpected was his re-action. I was suddenly awakened to the reality of finance, and I faced the prospect that my dream was of the impossible kind. The next few days were depressing. I agonized over what to do. My mother saw I was troubled and inquired, so I confided in her.

She read my paper and suggested, "Well, if that's truly your life's dream, then in my opinion you can achieve it. I think you ought to consider turning the paper back in just the way it is, without any changes." She added, "If you think it's unattainable, then you can change it yourself. But I don't think it's for a high school instructor to set a level on your hopes and dreams."

My mother was a meek woman, but this is one of the few times I saw her angry. I felt renewed. I returned to school and handed the paper back, this time with a note attached to Mr. Fowler. I told him that while he had every right as my instructor to call my life plan un-attainable, I did not see it that way. I further suggested that he did not have the right to put a cap on my aspirations, but that he should grade the paper as he saw fit.

When the grades were mailed to us at the end of the year, I got an A for that particular course. I never did find out to what extent my teacher changed the mark, but clearly an F on the project would have scuttled any chance for a top grade. I would encounter Lyman Fowler much later in my life: he would have more to say on the subject of hopes and dreams.

———

One night in the summer of 1953, I was in the railroad car, winding through the Imperial Valley in California. It was still strange not hav-ing Brownie with me—we had spent so long together in this rattling wooden structure as it rolled around the vast countryside. His was a ghostly presence, especially at night.

I had gone back over the roof of the train to the caboose where the railroad crew rode. Nothing much was happening. The cards were put away and no one was drinking or eating. I was looking out the window into the moonlit desert of southern California. Quite sud-denly the image of a young lady named Patricia Burden came into my mind as clearly as if I had invited her to sit by me. It struck me that she was going to be a major factor in my life. Pat Burden had been one year behind me through primary and secondary school. Her father owned a major company that drilled and installed water wells, but she had relatives who were involved in the horse business and in rodeo as well.

What to do next preyed on me. This was not a decision I had made; it was as if someone else were pulling the strings. Once home, I went up to her in the corridor of Salinas Union High School and simply informed her that she was my "chosen woman," or words to that effect. She had a different reading and shooed me away.

Pat was then involved with someone in an on-again, off-again relationship. Curiously, I discovered later that in grade school she *did* have a crush on me and even named her black cocker spaniel Monty Blue. But that was then; Monty Blue the dog had since been run over. This was now.

Soon after my announcement in the corridor, Pat was with friends, Sally and Jim Martins, who happened to be related to my family and she told them I was pestering her every day for a meeting of some sort, suggesting no end of things we might do together. They dared Pat to go out with me just once. Not being the type to turn down a dare, she said she would. The next day, I made my usual overture. This time she said yes to a date—dinner and a movie. Since then we have been together for more than forty years.

———

A major Hollywood picture was scheduled to be shot in and around Salinas in the summer of 1954. It was to be called *East of Eden,* from the book by John Steinbeck, who had been a Salinas resident in the early years of the century. I had gone to school with members of his family.

The director was to be the noted filmmaker Elia Kazan. He had cast a kid from a New York stage school in the main role, and naturally the producers were worried about asking a city boy to play the part of a small-town Californian. Our old friend Don Page was the first assistant director on the film, and he suggested that I take this young, unknown actor under my wing and show him around, let him live with me for a while, to help him soak up the local atmosphere. I thought it was a terrible idea, imagining some drama school graduate slowing me down. But when Don pointed out that there was a $2,500 payment for the three months, plus food allowances, I saw what a sensible plan it was after all. "What's the actor's name?"

"James Dean."

He turned up at the competition grounds with a little suitcase, wearing jeans, a T-shirt, and a leather jacket. He was disheveled and careless, goofy and irreverent, unstructured and confident. He was twenty-three years to my twenty, but it seemed the other way around; he was young for his age. I took his bag and showed him to my room, where I gave him the top bunk. Then I noticed his boots. They were a city-slicker's idea of cowboy boots, with the jeans an inch too short to show more of the leather. I said nothing at first, but then could bear it no longer. We had a clothing allowance for him, and I suggested we go to the Garcia saddlery store to buy him some real boots.

Jimmy was stoic about it, though he wanted to hang on to his original pair. "If you don't burn them by the time we're through," I told him, "I won't have done my job properly." A little later, when he was comfortable with his new footwear, he gave the original boots away. The boots episode tipped us into a firm friendship. He would sit on the fence and watch Pat and me riding, either at shows or in the practice corrals. We went to Mac's Cafe and had dinner; we introduced him to everyone we could. He would melt into corners and sit balled up, running his fingers through his hair. I advised him to straighten up, to come out of his shell, not to slink back all the time if he wanted to appear like a Salinas-born Steinbeck character. "Yeah, yeah. I'll do that," he replied, unconcerned. Then with genuine interest he would ask, "Can you show me how to spin that rope?"

We sat up till three in the morning teaching him to do the "butterfly." Jimmy thought that mastering that spin would be his ticket to local social acceptance. He was right. He did it everywhere, showing off his new trick while the assembled company nodded their heads in approval. He also wanted a pair of chaps. He would borrow mine and wear them to horse shows, but for a spectator to wear the uniform of a competitor was considered poor form, and he soon stopped. He was pleased when I gave him an old pair of my father's chaps.

Jimmy fell in love with Pat and followed her around like a puppy. He was never a threat because he never advanced his case—he simply looked at her all the time, and wherever she went he would go too. After the three months were up, Don Page and Elia Kazan called me in for a meeting. They were close to shooting now, and they wanted to know how their young prospect had fared.

I told them I really liked him, that he was like a brother to me, and that I was impressed with his character, with everything about him. I had to add one caveat, though. I knew plenty of actors from my film work, and James Dean was not like John Wayne or Roddy McDowall. He was not gregarious, did not engage people in conversation, did not evoke enthusiasm. He just did not seem to me like an actor.

The two men thanked me for my report, and I went away to begin my various tasks on the shoot. I was the wrangler looking after the horses my father had provided for the movie, as well as a stuntman and an extra. Soon the film crews turned up. Jimmy moved out of my bedroom and into the hotel with them, although we still formed a threesome, still went out every night.

Filming started and after two days Elia Kazan and Don Page asked me if I would attend what are called the "dailies"—a session to view footage shot the day before. They wanted me to comment on the authenticity of all aspects of the film. I felt a certain dread because I was sure that Jimmy's acting ability, or lack of it, was about to be cruelly exposed. I pictured the scene: when they asked, "What are we going to do to save this movie?" I would have to stop myself from saying, "I told you so."

I could not have been more wrong. I went back to being an environmental consultant and never breathed a word about his acting again. It was immediately obvious that James Dean brought a new and magical presence to the screen. He was absolutely electric.

When we were out together at night, Jimmy would act out scenarios for our amusement. First he would pretend to be on the telephone to someone, describing his spectacular success. He was the Hollywood star who did not know what to do with all his money—there were girls beating down the door to see him; he was going to buy a huge ranch in the area; Pat and I were going to manage it for him; he would fly in from whichever part of the world he was shooting in. Then he would act out a darker scenario. *East of Eden* was a terrible failure. No one watched it; the studios wanted their $150,000 fee back; they wanted the clothing allowance back; they came and took the boots off his feet.

None of us knew then which it was going to be.

History recorded the answer. Over the next year I was with James Dean when he shot *Rebel Without a Cause*, as well as *Giant* with Elizabeth Taylor and Rock Hudson. As it turned out, Jimmy's Hollywood star scenario was the right one, and he gained the fortune to go with it. And he really did want to buy a ranch that Pat and I would manage for him. There was a property for sale near Salinas, and we had even driven out together to look at it.

Late one summer, Jimmy called to say he was due to take part in a road race in Salinas. He would drive up from Hollywood with his mechanic in his Porsche Spyder, and stay with us at Pat's parents' place. We would begin looking at property in earnest. Pat and I felt our future was decided—through our friendship, we were following a promising new track in our lives.

On September 30, 1955, we were waiting for his telephone call. We had told him to call us when he was near to let us know his estimated time of arrival. His mechanic, Wolf Weutherich, had our names and telephone numbers in the pocket of his overalls and was getting ready to stop when the Porsche collided with another car. The other driver walked away with a bruised nose. Weutherich broke his leg and jaw. James Dean died of a broken neck.

In the aftermath, Wolf was so dazed and traumatized that the first call he made was to us. Through his fractured jaw, he mumbled that James Dean was dead.

It was a numbing experience. What made it even harder was that Pat and I were alone with our grief. We had known him for only a year. We knew none of his family, and they were unaware that we existed. His body was taken back to the Midwest and we never attended the funeral. The life that we had been expecting to lead with our friend closed down in front of us. We simply went back to school.

In 1955 I won a football scholarship to the California Polytechnic State University, San Luis Obispo (better known as Cal Poly), where I would major in three areas: biological sciences (specializing in psychology), animal science, and agri-economics. The "full-ride" scholarship meant that both tuition and living expenses were paid for. However, because of a football injury, I declined the scholarship and joined the rodeo team instead. They welcomed me, a four-event man, with open arms.

I had registered for the military draft but had not yet been called up. Their medical examination confirmed that I was completely color-blind. I was glad to have it proven that I saw in a way that most others did not—that I perceived movement more clearly and from a far greater distance, and that I could see better at night.

Many years later, when I was sixty-one, I went to a specialist in Britain who gave me contact lenses that offered a taste of what it is like to see color. The vibration of energy that resulted caused me enormous agitation. If this is what normally sighted people have to put up with, I thought to myself, small wonder they are so distracted and nervous. It was a revelation that left me certain: I could not have done what I have in my life had I seen color. (And when I describe colors in this book, say the coppery color of a horse I may be using what others have told me. But the most delicate shadings and depths of shadows and light I do see. I see density of pigment, which allows me to see the sheen and sparkle of a healthy horse's coat.)

Woody Proud, who owned the Proud Ranch near the university, allowed me to live there while I was a student. Convinced my reputation would bring him significant business, he let me occupy a house rent-free if I agreed to share it with two other rent-paying students. It was not so much a house as a hut—Woody had bought several old motel cabins and parked them on his land.

Nevertheless, this arrangement let me keep my three horses—Miss Twist, Finito, and Poco Hyena—and still afford to go to college. From the outset, I practiced hard with the college rodeo team. As we drove to competitions far afield, I became interested in how horses transported in trailers countered the stress and strain of road travel. A year or two later, I would team up with Sheila Varian and conduct an in-depth study of horse transportation, hauling horses over twisting roads for long periods of time. We used an open truck with no partitions, reasoning that loose horses would be free to find the most comfortable position. Almost all the time they chose to arrange themselves at forty-five degrees to the roadway, with about half facing forward and half facing backward. The common element, though, was the clear preference for forty-five degrees. At that angle, they were better able to brace themselves against the stopping and starting and against the pull of the corners.

Subsequently, in 1960, I took my old trailer to a welding shop and had them change the partitions so all were hinged to one wall and would swing open. I could then haul my horses at forty-five degrees. To my knowledge, mine was the first trailer adapted in this way. I made inquiries about taking out a patent on the design, but never pressed the matter. Years later, forty-five-degree-angle trailers were being factory-built, and now half of all horse trailers built in the United States follow that design.

——

On June 16, 1956, Pat and I got married and together moved into something on the Proud Ranch that was a little closer to a real house. Our first child, Deborah, arrived less than a year later. That day was the greatest in our lives, to be matched only by the births of our other two children, Laurel and Marty.

Suddenly, money disappeared more quickly. The dollars left my pocket and I waved good-bye to them, then wondered where the next ones would come from. I simply could not win enough at competitions to pay for our own needs and the upkeep of the horses. I was a twenty-two-year-old rodeo competitor who brought back prize money maybe four days a month during summer, but only one day a month in winter.

While Pat was pursuing a diploma in business, we opened a shop to which we were able to give the famous "Garcia" name; the arrangement amounted to an early franchise operation. Garcia made the best Western equipment in North America, and our store was conveniently located between Cal Poly and the Proud Ranch.

Toward the end of our college years, the economic climate for us appeared to brighten with the arrival of one Homer Mitchell. He had put a horse or two my way for training and had been impressed. Now he wanted to find a property near the ocean and San Luis Obispo. The plan was that I help him build a training facility there, which I would then manage for him. When he was older, he would retire there.

I found him an eighty-acre property near Edna, California, five miles inland from Pismo Beach. In those days the whole area was as beautiful and unspoiled as any along that coastline. Homer agreed that the property, called Laurellinda, was perfect.

Pat and I watched Homer as he reached into his coat pocket and took out a checkbook and pen. It was a simple thing to write a check for $160,000, but to us he was walking on water; we did not think that kind of money existed, even in a bank. We agreed in writing to lease the property. Homer would put three horses into training for a fixed amount per month, meaning that we started out already halfway to covering our costs. We counted ourselves lucky. By now our second daughter, Laurel, had been born. We were about to leave college and make a living doing what we loved. We were young and rightly optimistic. All was well.

———

The 1960s marked a period of great upheaval: men burned their draft cards, women burned their bras, and students—especially in California—started leaning far to the left on the political spectrum. We seemed not to be touched by any of this. Our concerns were elsewhere, and we had too much else on our plates. We had two infant daughters, Debbie and Laurel, with our son, Marty, on the way. We had to finish constructing a 2,000-square-foot ranch house and the outbuildings. And we had our horses. What we did not have was money.

Laurellinda was just eighty beautiful acres with a couple of broken-down shacks on it. Homer pointed at one shack and said, "A nickel box of matches will do the job here." It was his way of instructing us to torch the buildings.

"Where will we live?" we asked him.

"You'll have to rent a place in town and drive out here to work. Money dictates that we build the horse facility before we build the house." Pat and I had no money for rent, and running back and forth was out of the question. Horses are not nine-to-five; horses are all hours.

Since the pair of little shacks stood where the training barn was to be built, we moved them away a short distance. One was a very old, very small railway car, and the other was a garage-shaped box. We nudged them together and plastered over the holes. I saw this as a temporary arrangement—surely, with my reputation, horses in need of expert training would arrive any minute. We could then rent a big house trailer until a proper house could be built. But the horses did not arrive. And we had given up our saddle-shop franchise now that our third baby was on the way. I had a few mares to breed and I gave a few lessons, but with only four paid horses in training I was desperate. I was trying hard for prize money in rodeos, but the figures just did not add up. I had to find more work.

It was then that someone said to me: "Go live with Don Dodge for a while." Don Dodge was possibly the most successful trainer of Western horses in the United States, and he did have a line of vans waiting to turn into his place. "Study hard with Don," the advice went. "Give him one hundred percent. If he believes in you, you'll have it made. He'll recommend people to you." Then came the warning: "He's impossible to impress!"

With nothing to lose, I called him up and asked to work for him for a while.

"Yup. Come up if you want. Prepare to go to work, though. You can bring a couple of your own horses, and when it's time for you to leave I'll figure out what you owe me. 'Cause I'm going to teach you something. God knows you need it. Oh, and Monty, you have to promise to do exactly as I tell you. OK?"

"I promise."

I took two of my horses in training, Selah Reed and Finito, and drove north to 3400 North Del Paso Boulevard, North Sacramento, California, an address forever engraved in my memory.

Don Dodge was about forty-four, a six-footer with dark hair. He had a slim build, a beaky nose, and close-set eyes that gave him an intense look that women seemed to adore. He cut a good figure on a horse, and he had about forty horses in training for some of the best owners in the world. Bad owners do not pay their bills; they dictate to the trainer and make sore losers. Good owners, on the other hand, pay bills on time, get involved enough to take good or bad news in stride, and they let the trainer train. Don Dodge was blessed with a fleet of such owners.

I had no sooner pulled up in his yard than he had me working. "Glad you're here. Billy Patrick here could use some help." He waved at a red-haired kid scurrying back and forth with water buckets. I backed out my two horses, and they were allocated open booths of distinctly inferior quality to the box stalls occupied by Don's horses.

I helped Billy feed all forty horses and topped off their stalls (removed the top layer of manure). More bucket carrying ensued because Don did not believe in automatic watering systems. After that, we had to clean all the tack used that day.

At about seven P.M. Billy and I were through, and I went indoors. I was looking forward to a wash and brushup, changing into some clean clothes, then maybe having dinner with Don. I imagined we would share a drink and a chat, and during the meal I could begin to cultivate his friendship.

"Where you going to stay?" Don asked me.

My jaw dropped. "I thought you might have a bunk room for me somewhere."

"Nope. You can go down the road a way, and there's a sort of rooming house. Old Mother Harris." Don telephoned to tell her I was coming. He added, "She'll fix your meals for you." Cursing in disbelief, I drove to Mother Harris's place. A room with board included would be . . . a figure I could not dream of paying. A room without board was two dollars a night; I had no other option.

I telephoned Pat. The children were crying in the background; the shack was falling down around her ears; and there was, she assured me, no more money. The only thing I could afford to eat was a product called MetreCal, a liquid meal designed for people trying to lose weight. It cost ninety cents a can, and I lived off it for ten weeks.

On the bright side, there were different flavors. I had a choice of chocolate MetreCal, vanilla MetreCal or strawberry MetreCal. I would make my decision, punch holes in the top, and suck out the contents.

I had to be at Don Dodge's at four-thirty in the morning to feed the horses and attend to their stalls. Don would appear at seven-thirty and start barking orders. I would ride a minimum of ten horses for him during the morning, then crack another can of MetreCal and keep going. At some point in the afternoon, he would always spend time with me as I worked on my two horses. A hard taskmaster, Don Dodge would shout at the top of his lungs. I did what I was told. I learned a lot.

During these afternoon sessions, he would pepper me with questions about the other two horses left at home. Surrounded by his sleek horses, it sounded pitiful to talk about the four I had in training. I told him about one of them, a stallion owned by Lawson Williams called Panama Buck, who tried to mate with his reflection if he caught sight of himself in glass. I told him many other details, including who their owners were and how much I was charging for their keep and training. I could not fathom his interest. Did he like hearing how badly I was doing?

For the rest of the afternoon, Billy and I would finish the chores and top off the stalls and clean the tack. Work ended at nine P.M. I would swallow some more MetreCal and head back to Mother Harris's place. Occasionally, Don asked me in for a meal and I fell on the food like the starving person I was. Once or twice we went to a rodeo and I won enough for a few meals, but basically I was on a MetreCal diet. I turned into a skeleton; my ribs popped out and I had a deathly pallor. My hands were calloused from carrying water buckets, and I was worn down by Don's constant shouting.

As the time for my departure drew near, Don invited me into his office for a formal meeting to settle up—and he warned me that he would tell me how much I owed him. After his stern treatment of me and my unflagging slave labor for him, I looked forward to the payoff—he would say he was going to recommend me to everyone he knew and my labor would all have been well spent.

He sat down on the opposite side of the desk, stared at me, and said, "Well, Monty, I have you figured. You have a little talent, which maybe you could build on. But it's a lot different now. No college bullshit rodeo team."

"No, I realize that, but I hope I'm ready to do it on my own."

"You're going to have to work a lot harder than I've put you through if you want to make any progress at all."

I could not believe what he had just said. Suddenly I was so tired and dispirited I could have chewed nails.

"Now then," he went on, "there is this matter of your promise to do exactly what I instructed."

I nodded in agreement. "Sure." A promise was a promise.

He leaned forward and spoke slowly and precisely. "Go home, call Lawson Williams, and tell him his horse is no good and you're wasting his money. Tell him he's to come and pick him up immediately. Then do the same with that other horse you got back there."

I went into a tailspin. "How can I do that? I've only got four horses, and you're asking me to cut my income in half? Why? Why on earth should I do such a thing?"

"I don't owe you an explanation, but seeing as you ask—you're going to do it for a very good reason. You're going to do it because he'll be impressed with you. That horse of his isn't going anywhere. You know it; I know it. You'll tell him the truth, and he'll respect you for it and send you five horses right back again."

I let this sink in. I could see his psychology, but it seemed too risky for someone with only four paid horses-in-training to send two of them away.

"Now," he added, "the reckoning."

I waited for him to congratulate me on my hard work. He might even weigh the poor straits I was in and press a few dollars into my hand. Instead he said, "You owe me fifty dollars per day; that's a total of thirty-two hundred dollars." And he wrote out a bill. "Pay me just as soon as you can. You'll realize some day it's the best bargain you ever had."

Driving home with my tail between my legs I was devastated, but not totally surprised. When I showed the bill to Pat she was *absolutely* devastated. But perhaps because I had paid so dearly for Don's advice, it began to sound good. I started to like the feel of it. I delayed for a while, trying to work out the best way of saying it, but there was no other way but head on. I rang Lawson Williams.

"Mr. Williams, I don't want to waste your money, and it's my judgment that Panama Buck isn't worth spending any more on. I'd like you to come up and collect—"

Lawson Williams cut in. "You useless son of a gun, you wouldn't know a good horse if it leapt up between your legs. That's the last horse you'll ever get from me!" He slammed down his receiver, and the next day a man arrived to take away Panama Buck. I had a vision of all of us—Pat, the children, and me—on MetreCal.

Shortly afterward, Selah Reed, the one paid horse-in-training I had with any promise, fractured her hind leg and had to be taken out of training. I was now running on empty. I walked about the place thinking about suicide the whole time. Life was all wrong, and I was letting my family down. Then I got a telephone call.

"Hello. Joe Gray here. I'm a pipeline contractor."

"Hello, Mr. Gray." Who *was* this?

"I was having lunch with Lawson Williams yesterday. He was complaining about you, but from what I understand you must be about the only honest horse trainer I ever heard of."

A wave of emotion overtook me. I remembered Don Dodge's intense stare, and his advice. It had seemed harsh at the time.

"What can I do for you, Mr. Gray?"

"Well, I know that Panama Buck wasn't any good, and I just want to take a flyer on you. I have this horse I want to send you; she's called My Blue Heaven."

In my heart I felt I could glimpse daylight.

"I'm a little worried for the safety of my daughters," he said. "My Blue Heaven is a six-year-old quarter horse mare. I thought she would be a good show horse for them, and she has been trained extensively. But she went wrong, and no one can stop her now."

"Is she dangerous?"

"Extremely. They can't pull her up."

At shows with one of his daughters in the saddle, she would apparently take the bit between her teeth, run away, and crash into fences or try to avoid fences by turning sharply and falling down at high speed.

Joe Gray sent the little gray mare to me with the instruction that she be sold. The family was going on a three-week vacation, and no matter how low the sum offered, I was to find a buyer before they returned.

When she came out of the van I saw she was a pretty mare with a good action and a lively eye—highly sensitive to the bit and bridle. Joe had used increasingly fierce bits to try and get her to stop. I put on a hackamore, a bitless bridle, and rode her into the arena.

To my surprise, My Blue Heaven was a well-trained mare. When she was frightened, she would indeed run out of control—I discovered that soon enough—but she also performed better than any horse I had ridden in the showring up to that time. I removed the hackamore and saddle and turned her loose in the round pen. I wanted to earn her trust, then perhaps I could encourage her to enjoy stopping and thus end the vicious circle of crime and punishment.

I squared up to her and sent her away, cast the light sash line in her direction and pressed her away harder, until she was traveling at a smart canter. I fixed my eye on hers; she began to drop the odd signal that she was prepared to talk—I saw her tongue briefly, and her large mandibles rippled, showing the chewing action. She was keeping one ear fixed on my position, then she dropped her head. After one more turn of the round pen, I turned my shoulders through forty-five degrees to the front of her action. She stopped immediately, and my eyes left hers. Although I was not looking at her, I could sense her waiting. I could hear nothing but my own heartbeat.

She was wondering whether to trust me or not. She was asking herself, Where would this lead? Moments later, she took her first step toward me. Then another. She was tentative, and all I could do was wait. Eventually she was there, standing by me. I soothed her and told her I would not abuse her trust. Together we would work it out; we were going to help each other. She would help me make a reputation as a trainer; I would help her avoid harsh bits in her mouth.

Her early training for stopping had been conventional: if enough pressure is put on a horse's mouth, the horse can be forced to stop. As her riders had become increasingly frightened of her, increasingly severe bits were deployed. It was an unhappy progression. The worse the bit, the worse she got.

My aim was to get her to like stopping, schooling her with signals from my body and voice that would cause her to ease into stops. I tried to put as little pressure on her mouth as I could. I created a situation whereby she herself wanted to stop, by pushing her on until it seemed like stopping was her idea. My Blue Heaven began to welcome the stop signal—the word "Whoa" and my weight pressing down into the back of the saddle—once she learned that she could avoid the pressure if she made the stop comfortably and without resistance. Though her problem was deep-seated and fairly long-standing, she was smart enough to sort it out, and she became extremely effective at stopping.

About two weeks after the Grays left for their vacation, I decided to enter My Blue Heaven in a popular, high-quality show at the Alisal Guest Ranch in the Santa Ynez Valley. If I put in a good performance there, the mare would bring a better price for Mr. Gray and his family. Unable to reach the Grays, I made the entry myself and continued to school her.

The winner of the event would get a fair bit of money, and, more important, a Jedlicka saddle, a Western saddle made of hand-tooled leather. Letters depicting the trophy embellished the fenders—the part of the saddle above the stirrup and below the seat. Today the saddle would be worth $5,000.

There were close to twenty good horses in the competition. My Blue Heaven performed like a professional and won. Don Dodge's advice was working well. I was getting what I wanted, so was My Blue Heaven, and the Gray daughters might get what they wanted, too: a top-flight show horse. I called friends of the Gray family and was able to get into their house. I put the saddle in their dining room, with a note on it to the effect that I needed to discuss My Blue Heaven with the family before selling her.

When they returned, Joe and his family were elated with My Blue Heaven's win. The daughters particularly were excited, and the family agreed that she should stay in training. The following year, she ranked second in the world for the reined cow horse division. Twice she finished second in the world, and only because she happened to come up against Mona Lisa, one of the greatest reined cow horses of all time. Mona Lisa was owned and shown by none other than Don Dodge.

My Blue Heaven was the first horse I campaigned in open professional competition, and she was a significant part of my learning process. After I showed her for two seasons, she went on to compete under the two daughters successfully throughout the western United States.

I did eventually pay Don Dodge's bill—and I wrote and thanked him for the best advice I ever had. Within six months I had fifteen horses in training.

———

In 1961 we moved out of the shack and into the now finished ranch house at Laurellinda. On February 1, our son Marty was born, and it seemed a good time for my mother and father to drive the 125 miles south from Salinas to visit us and their three grandchildren.

I took my father to view the horses I had in training, but as we walked around the property he sang the same old song: "You wait, I'm telling you, that bastard horse is going to go the other way with you. He's going to come loose and get you. You've got to keep them tuned up."

I looked at the lines now carved more deeply into his face. I was twenty-six; he was nearly fifty-four. He could not hurt me anymore. I had escaped him, and his opinions were almost irrelevant. Even so, I felt anger as new as the day he created it. I never wanted any horse of mine to suffer that same anger, fear, and resentment.

During the visit, he played with his grandchildren—Debbie was then four, Laurel two, and Marty a newborn. The two older children had their little responsibilities around the house, such as keeping their rooms tidy. Each had a horse whose stalls they helped muck out daily. At one point, my father said, "You know, Monty, you're too tough on these kids."

Incredulous, my mother left the room. The world briefly stopped turning.

"Me, tough?" I replied. "Do you by any chance remember how tough you were on me?"

"I know, but these are good kids."

I was startled. "And I wasn't?"

He added, "And they're little girls."

What deflated my father more than anything was the undeniable fact that my method of training horses worked. It was especially effective in dealing with remedial horses.

Hey Sam was a Thoroughbred who came to me that same year. He was raised on the Parker Ranch in Hawaii and purchased by Robert Anderson. I started him and gave him his pretrack training before he went to Hollywood Park for racing. Hey Sam started well and went to the track in exceptional form, but he was then sent to a trainer who was not Anderson's first choice.

Something was going wrong. I was called to come and see the horse at Hollywood Park about three months after his arrival, and I quickly identified the root of the problem: The rider had been pulling up Hey Sam on the racetrack at exactly the same place—the half-mile pole—every day, so the horse had begun to anticipate this. Insisting on going back to the barn, Hey Sam would pull off the track in dramatic fashion, whether his rider wanted him to or not. He would run up against the outside part of the track and almost bury himself in the hedge, a quivering wreck. The rider thought to correct this habit by severely whipping Hey Sam before he got to the half-mile pole so as to beat him past the troublesome area. Then, when the horse started veering to the outside of the track to pull himself up, the exercise rider would whip him on the right side to drive him back to the inside rail.

These methods appeared to work for a while, but by the time I arrived to see him all that had been accomplished was that Hey Sam would quicken his pace when approaching the half-mile pole. When he saw his chance he would veer violently outside and stop at the hedge, bracing for the whip but refusing to go anywhere. It was a dramatic display, and the stewards ruled him off the track.

This was distressing for me since I had sent him from my establishment in good order and ready to begin his training for his racing career. My reputation as well as the trainer's was at stake. I had no choice but to take him home and reestablish communication.

Once again I harked back to the lessons I had learned from other horses, like Brownie. Horses do not move away from pressure, they move into it—particularly if the pressure is applied to their flanks. *Horses are into pressure animals.* I knew that the whip inflicted by Hey Sam's riders on his outside flanks was causing him to go the opposite way to the one that might be expected, and we had to change that. I worked for about six months, taking all pressure off the outside. Instead, I started to use my leg well back on the inside, schooling him to bring his head more toward the rail and to be happy doing it.

He was not a bad horse and had no evil in him. He learned, and he changed significantly. When he went back to the track, I sent him to Farrell Jones. I had known Farrell for so many years and we communicated well with each other. It was the best thing that could have happened to the horse. Farrell watched me ride Hey Sam on the racecourse at Golden Gate Fields in northern California, and then he put a rider on him who employed the same techniques. Soon enough he was entered in his first race, and he won at odds of fifty to one. My heart lifted; he was on his way. I also felt a personal triumph. Hey Sam went on to win twelve races, and earned his owner more than $100,000.

It was a success story, and the start of my love affair with the American Thoroughbred racing industry.

———

The horse I loved perhaps more than any other had the all-boy name of Johnny Tivio. He was a registered quarter horse stallion, fourteen hands, three inches high, and weighing 1,200 pounds. He was a light bay, but his coat had a brilliant coppery sheen that made it almost glitter.

I had seen him at the show grounds and had been eyeing him for a long time. Though he was not kept in top condition, his coat seemed to outshine any other horse's, as though the polish came through from the very heart and soul of him rather than from constant grooming.

His trainer, Harry Rose, had enjoyed a lot of success with Johnny Tivio. Harry was a rough, tough kind of man who lived hard and played hard. One day Pat and I were on the horse-show circuit, driving to a competition in Watsonville, California, when we saw a horse trailer parked outside a scuzzy, honky-tonk bar. Inside the trailer I could see Johnny Tivio and another horse.

I said to Pat, "There's Harry, drinking the town dry again."

We were in Watsonville to compete in a show for working horses. We unloaded Fiddle D'Or and My Blue Heaven and put them away for the night at the grounds, then drove back the same way. Harry Rose's trailer was still parked outside the bar, the horses still inside.

The next morning we turned up early to prepare our two horses for the competition that day. Two blocks from the bar, the trailer was now parked outside a house, with Johnny Tivio and the other horse still inside. They had been standing there all night.

After the usual preparation with our horses, which included an exercise or two to warm them up, we were ready for the eight A.M. start. Minutes before the hour, Harry Rose came tearing down the hill, his trailer swerving behind. He jerked to a halt, dragged out a girlfriend, then backed out the two horses.

He threw a saddle on Johnny Tivio and sprang onto his back; then he hauled the girl up behind him and the pair of them started prancing around.

Johnny Tivio won everything that day. Locked up in a trailer all night and without a moment's preparation, he beat my horse for fun. He walked into the arena as if he owned the place and we were lucky just to rub up alongside him. I was amazed and angry that Harry Rose would treat such a wonderful horse so badly.

"That horse is solid gold," I said to Pat. "Some day he'll be mine."

Only months later the local humane society got a telephone call about a horse left in a trailer outside a house for two days. Horse and trailer were impounded and the registration number led the police to the home of the owner, Carl Williams. They attempted to arrest Carl for cruelty to a horse called Johnny Tivio but he put them right and set them on the trail of his trainer, Harry Rose. Then he rang me because he knew I had been angling to buy his horse. He asked me for

$6,000. I leapt at the chance, though I had to call George Smith, a customer and an old friend, to put up half the money.

Johnny Tivio had foundered, his feet were sore and inflamed, and his shoes were grown in, but he was mine. We looked after him and cared for his feet. He was always a willing animal, but he grew stronger and better with every kind word and every kind deed.

But from the minute he joined us at Laurellinda, he was in charge: we were working for him and not vice versa. He had several complaints about his stall, and we had to shift the bedding around so he could drop his manure in one particular corner. With his fastidious stable manners and superior attitude, he was quite the best horse he himself had ever seen. Other horses were allowed to exist but only with his approval. Palominos were out of the question: early in life he had had a palomino stablemate, and now he could barely tolerate the sight of one.

Johnny Tivio became a monumental success; year after year I could enter him in any category of the Western division, and he would win. He was one of the few horses on the show circuit who everyone would agree was the best on the face of the earth.

——

Sometimes a horse comes along who is too troubled, too mean, to engage in conversation. Barlet was a horse made mean by humans.

A movie studio had hired an actor, Slim Pickens, to feature in a film for Disney called *The Horse with the Flying Tail*, about a palomino jumping horse. They would use a foal, called Barlet, to depict the early years of the equine star. I was on the set as a stunt rider at a ranch in the Salinas valley where much of the footage was shot. I had known Slim since I was a child; he was like an uncle to me.

"Hey, Monty, look at this!" Slim called to me. "Isn't this the cutest foal you've ever seen?" Slim was toying with a stick, and the little palomino foal was trying to nibble at it.

"Watch this," he said. He tossed the stick and the foal turned and ambled over to where it lay, picked it up in his teeth and brought it back like a retriever. Then the foal wandered back to where Slim was standing.

"Incredible," I agreed.

"He's like a little puppy," said Slim. "Watch this as well." He turned to the foal and slapped his own chest, calling, "Hup! Hup!" The foal jumped up and put his front legs on Slim's shoulders. "See?" said Slim. "Ain't this going to be the brightest Walt Disney horse?" While it did seem fetching at the time, Barlet also thought it was fun to perform the same tricks as a two-year-old, whether he was asked to or not.

By then his owner, Marten Clark, had been showing Barlet throughout the western United States, and he was virtually undefeated as a halter horse, an in-hand competition judged only on the horse's conformation. He was in line to be the national champion that year; it was almost a certainty. But when I next saw Barlet at the championship show in 1962 at the Cow Palace in San Francisco, I found that Marten Clark had him in a box stall with an electrical circuit. Two wires had been set up: one all around the stall and halfway up the wall, and a second wire around the top. Astonishingly, if the electric current were switched off, Barlet would climb right over the wall.

The palomino was smart. When he heard a pulsating sound, a signal that the charger was on, he posed no problem at all. When Marten wanted to take him out of the stall, however, he had to turn off the charger to open the door. Once the switch was thrown, Barlet became more like a tiger than a horse, and he literally attacked Marten.

During the days before the competition, Marten could not get Barlet out of the stall; handling the horse was impossible. Marten made me an offer: "If you can catch Barlet in the stall and get him through the show ring and win with him, I'll give you a half interest in him; then you can take him back to San Luis Obispo and put him in training." Since Barlet's value stood in the $35,000 range, this was no mean offer. I was excited by the challenge and convinced there was no horse I could not handle. Still, I was disconcerted when I arrived at the stall and saw the security arrangements. After shutting off the power, I opened the door and Barlet bolted toward me from the rear of the stall with his ears back and his teeth bared. He wanted to hurt me.

I jumped back and closed the door before he got hold of me. Unable even to look him over, I had to reassess the situation. This horse was too far gone to even ask for his trust. From a very young age he had been spoiled, not through cruelty in his case, but through unintended psychological abuse. He had been trained as a lapdog, and something had gone terribly wrong.

Using a lariat rope, I was able to swing the rope around in such a fashion that it kept Barlet at sufficient distance. I got him roped in the stall and was able to put on his head a piece of equipment Don Dodge had taught me to use; we call it the "come-along." The come-along is a cute phrase to describe a useful but dangerous tool. The rope is put over the horse's head and arranged in halterlike fashion: the rope applies pressure to nerves above the horse's cheekbones and behind the ears. Too much pressure at the wrong time can be exceedingly dangerous for horse and person. But with some remedial horses, the come-along is the only option if they are to be introduced to a better life, or any life at all.

I led Barlet out of his stall and started schooling him, using the join-up method. I was trying to restore his trust. It took a good deal longer than it did with My Blue Heaven, and the results were not as consistent, but he did eventually come to trust me a little. I was then able to show him in hand at that show and when he was named national champion, I became half owner. I took him home, and he went on to win a great deal. But he was never a mentally balanced horse after being spoiled as a foal. As is so often the case with horses made mean, even by well-intentioned people like Slim Pickens, they can seldom be trusted. This type of chronically distrustful horse should be handled only by professional horse trainers fully aware of what they are dealing with. The consequences can be too grave otherwise.

Barlet was a truly mean and severely troubled horse who attacked me on several occasions. One can only guess at what had triggered his disappointment with human beings. He and I had an understanding built around a well-developed discipline-and-reward system, so I was able to control his neurosis for three or four years. Unhappily, his problems eventually got the better of him, and he died in a fight with a gelding on my farm at Laurellinda. He smashed a fence to get to the other horse and broke his front leg during the ensuing skirmish.

CHAPTER 4

The Sand-Castle Syndrome

Imagine a beach on a blistering day in August. Down at the water's edge is a child with shovel and pail building an elaborate sand castle. The child has taken great delight in this creation, fussed all day over its turrets, fashioned moats and stairs and dwelt on every intricate detail. But at the end of the day, when the tide comes in, the greater joy is in watching as the waves level it all.

Now imagine an adult who acts like that child on the beach, an adult with the power and the wealth to construct on an epic scale— and a dark urge to crush the very thing he has so lovingly created. Such people bear no distinguishing marks, no telltale warning signs. No one told the crewmen of *The Bounty* before they set sail that her captain was a madman; no one told me that the bold dreamer I cast my lot with would be so keen years later to destroy.

In 1964, when I was thirty-one years old, I fell in with just such a man. He would take my family and me to dizzying heights and bring us lower than I ever imagined possible. I would find my fiber tested as never before; I would find what friends are made of; and I would find the courage to continue.

That year, at a quarter horse sale in the Santa Ynez Valley near

Solvang, I watched one man buy several horses. His name was Hastings Harcourt, son of the founder of a giant textbook publisher, Harcourt Brace & World. Married, with a grown son, Hastings Harcourt was in his sixties and had gained a reputation as an eccentric and difficult millionaire. He owned property at Juniper Farms in the Santa Ynez Valley, and in Montecito—among the most exclusive residential areas in all of California.

A few days later, after hearing about me through a veterinarian, Mr. Harcourt called and asked if I would be interested in training his recent acquisitions. Within a day I was transporting three young quarter horses the sixty miles from Santa Ynez north to my place at Laurellinda.

After a week, I reported back to him that one three-year-old gelding, in particular, a horse called Travel's Echo, possessed talent. Mr. Harcourt seemed pleased and invited me to meet him at Juniper Farms.

Juniper Farms stood at the end of a long, treed driveway. The place was a tangle of architectural styles tacked onto a 1920s early-California house, but the property was immaculately maintained. On first impression, Hastings Harcourt struck me as an unfortunate-looking man. A skin condition had marked and pitted his face. He wore thick, black-rimmed glasses; he carried too much weight on his six-foot-two-inch frame; and I was acutely aware that his smile touched only his mouth, it never reached his eyes.

If he seemed possessed by a boyish enthusiasm, bouncing up from his lawn chair to greet Pat and me like old friends, his wife, Fran, was impassive. Uninterested in our arrival and disinclined even to get up from her chair, she bore the look of someone who had seen many like us come and go.

Hastings Harcourt admitted that he knew nothing about horses, but his desire to learn seemed genuine, even refreshing. He struck me as a nice man enjoying the first flush of excitement at becoming involved in the horse business. I mentioned that I would show Johnny Tivio at a show in Santa Barbara three months away. Why not, he pleaded, show Travel's Echo, too? Putting a green horse in a high-caliber show with little time for training was not my style, and I warned him to keep his expectations low. But I was also grateful for the work, and it seemed there was the promise of more.

Both Pat and I had some solid horses to show in that event, so at the very least the Harcourts could see his trainers competing on three world-class horses. I had Johnny Tivio, who would no doubt organize all the major trophies for himself, and Night Mist, who could be almost as good. Pat had Julia's Doll, a well-established mare competing in the pleasure-horse division. Travel's Echo was progressing so rapidly that I thought maybe there was a chance that I could show him, and I covered my bets by entering him just in case.

On the appointed day, the Harcourts had rented an exclusive box seats at the center of the ring. They brought along a party of eight to ten friends, all prominent in the Montecito society circuit. The entourage was as much on display as the horses.

Johnny Tivio performed as expected; Night Mist was her sterling self, winning both her events; and Julia's Doll was in top form, winning with Pat in the saddle. I was due to show Travel's Echo in the Western pleasure-horse division, open to horses four and under. Entering the arena, I was stunned when I saw that we were up against more than fifty competitors. But Travel's Echo surprised everyone, including me and those of Harcourts' guests who were savvy about horses and who could appreciate the achievement. Travel's Echo made the ten-horse finals. In the runoff, he finished third to two of the nation's top competitors, defeating other horses who had already won many championships. As I rode forward to collect the trophy and the rosette for third place, I was looking straight at the Harcourts. They were beaming, their friends all standing and applauding.

Afterward, they all came to the out gate to stand with Travel's Echo and pat him. It was embarrassing because this was the exit for competitors in the arena, and the Harcourt party seemed oblivious to the traffic jam they were creating. Because of his standing in the community and his reputation as a philanthropist, photographers and journalists crowded around to chronicle both his enthusiasm and the spectacular success of his young horse.

Sparks were flying now. Three days later the Harcourts flew in their private plane to San Luis Obispo to see our modest operation and discuss a greater involvement.

"Have you got any experience with the Thoroughbred racing industry?" he asked me. He owned a few Thoroughbreds, but he had the feeling they were not of the highest quality. I told him that we always had a few Thoroughbreds in training, but never the class of horse needed to win top races in California. Two days later he had me flown in his plane to three different locations to see his Thoroughbred stable: some brood mares, three foals, two yearlings, and two horses-in-training. He was right to doubt their quality. Now Harcourt upped the ante yet again. He proposed sending me to the Del Mar Thoroughbred yearling sale with a budget of $20,000 to buy two horses of my choosing.

Harcourt was offering me a chance of a lifetime. I had bought Thoroughbred yearlings for other clients who imposed limits of $2,000 per horse—low-class, fair-track horses, but they had done fairly well considering their breeding, and it seemed I had the ability to choose horses who could run and stay sound. Harcourt's offer meant a chance to leap into top-flight racing on California tracks: it was like a professional baseball player moving overnight from single "A" ball to the big leagues.

At Del Mar, where the restaurant menus included champagne, I decided that my cowboy hat should stay at home, and I wore instead a soft tweed cap. During the auction I saw a chestnut colt walk by at a distance of fifty yards. I will never forget that moment. He caught my eye as no young Thoroughbred had. Stock still, he had perfect symmetry and balance, but the extraordinary thing was how those qualities did not diminish when he moved. I went immediately to the stable where the chestnut was kept. On closer inspection, he proved even more impressive. No one else much fancied him. The nameless horse was brought into the auction ring and I won the bidding at just $5,000. When the hammer came down, Sharivari—as we later called him—was mine. I was now in business with Hastings Harcourt.

Sharivari would later be ranked the best three-year-old in California prior to the Kentucky Derby where he was the early book favorite. He would later become a champion sire many times over. At Del Mar,

I also purchased a bay colt, whom we called Bahroona. As it turned out, the bay was the more precocious of the two horses and was ready to run by June of the following year. Gifted with blinding speed, he won his first start at Hollywood Park by ten open lengths. Harcourt was euphoric about Bahroona's success and insisted that I come in his plane to Montecito: he was holding a victory party at his home.

The pilot and I took off, settling into the journey. Flying over the gleaming black waters of Lake Cachuma in the Santa Ynez Valley, the engine died and we immediately started plummeting toward the water. I was certain we would die. The pilot switched over to the second fuel tank and started the engine again, and we pulled out of the dive. This incident did nothing for my nerves, but later it struck me as a symbolic moment in the roller-coaster ride I was now embarked on.

A driver took me from the Santa Barbara airport to their house where a party was in full swing. Over the noise and laughter, Mr. Harcourt shouted out to me, "We must have a major operation!" With those words, the noise of the party seemed to recede as I latched on to what he was saying so loudly. "I have property in the Santa Ynez Valley. What do you think of that area for creating a full-scale Thoroughbred facility?"

It had been my life's dream to be a part of a horse operation in that valley. While the party continued on its high-spirited course, I offered my opinion that the climate and the soil there were superior to any in the United States, and that it would be a wonderful choice of location for a Thoroughbred breeding and training farm.

Harcourt was bursting with plans. "Start studying the area," he advised, "and I will purchase enough property to encompass a world-class facility."

My education had prepared me well for my scouting mission. I knew about soils, forage grasses, fertilization, facility design, conformation, pedigrees, and most of all, training techniques. None of the various properties that Harcourt already owned in the Santa Ynez Valley was right. One was too heavily treed, another too stony, a third lacked water. We needed land along the river; just outside the town of Solvang I pinpointed a microvalley three miles long by one and a quarter miles wide. The valley bottom was almost level, and the top-

Wedding photo
of Monty's parents.

On Ginger in 1939, age four,
winning the junior stock horse
competition for age sixteen
and under.

Monty in football uniform.

Monty's father with Joe Louis.

Monty's father long-lining a young horse.

Pat and Monty in costume
on the set of *East of Eden*.

James Dean with a pair
of Monty's chaps.

Monty and James Dean on the *East of Eden* set.

Future wife, Pat, presenting Monty with hackamore champion trophy in 1955.

Monty and Pat on their wedding day, June 16, 1956.

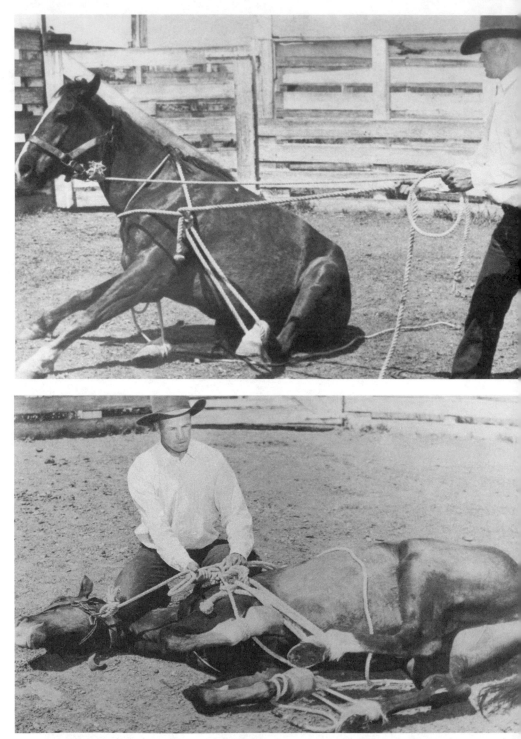

Monty's father's methods of breaking a horse: tying a horse to gain supremacy.

Monty achieving join-up.

Monty and Pat on Flag Is Up Farms, October 1966.

Johnny Tivio at home on
Flag Is Up Farms, 1967.

Monty cutting cattle on Johnny Tivio in Monterey, California.

Pat with a quarter horse
mare, 1996.

Flag Is Up Farms, late 1980s.

Monty and Pat releasing the first horses on the new pastures at Flag Is Up Farms, October 1966

Alleged winning the Prix de l'Arc de Triomphe with Lester Piggott. As a team, they won in 1977 and 1978.

Lomitas refusing to enter the starting gate the day he was banned from racing at the end of May 1991.

Lomitas, with Monty leading him to the starting gate June 23, 1991, ten days after Monty met him. He went in like a lamb, got the best start, won the race, and was reinstated.

Lomitas in winning form in the following months.

Her Majesty Queen Elizabeth II with Monty and Pat as they presented her with a copy of the British edition of *The Man Who Listens to Horses.*

Monty with one of Her Majesty the Queen's horses at Windsor Castle.

Grandma, early 1990s.

Monty joining up with
deer on Flag Is Up Farms,
January 1995.

Monty and Dually in competition, January 1996.

Monty on Dually with the mustang Shy Boy at side.

soil averaged seventeen feet in depth. Even better, below the topsoil lay a generous layer of diatomaceous material—microscopic sea-shells or crustaceans compressed into a chalky, calcium-rich earth, the legacy of a prehistoric ocean. In addition, ample underground aquifers near the surface meant wells with extraordinary flows, up to 600 gallons a minute. The climate was ideal: the influence of the nearby ocean kept the valley cool in summer and relatively warm in winter.

Harcourt began buying in one-hundred- and fifty-acre parcels, making offers no property owner could refuse. Within ninety days we sat down to discuss design concepts. As keen as I, he marshaled his considerable resources into a frenzy of activity. The train was rolling fast; then came a derailment, the first of many.

The day before a scheduled meeting in Santa Barbara, I got a call from his private secretary. In a roundabout way, she indicated that Mr. Harcourt had had second thoughts about building his sizable horse farm, and she advised me to consider him out of the picture.

Once it had sunk in, I was both devastated and dumbfounded. Only hours before, he had been plunging ahead as if his life depended on it. I spent that night pondering my next move. So much was at stake. It occurred to me that the secretary had implied, but not specified, that my meeting with Harcourt was canceled. I decided to go to his home at the designated time, as if the secretary had never called. At least I would hear him explain his decision to withdraw. Next day I drove the one hundred miles to Montecito, unsure of what to anticipate at the journey's end.

When I stopped at the gates and spoke into the security intercom, I half expected to be refused entry, but a voice buzzed me through. I drove down the driveway, the gravel crunching under my tires as I followed the circular drive around an imposing fountain. I parked by the guest house and walked to the front door of the main house where I rang the bell and waited. Clearly someone was in—I had been let through the gate. I reminded myself that it took a while to get from one end of such a large house to the other, so I waited longer than usual before ringing the bell a second time. No one came. It was deathly quiet. After some minutes, I gave up hope. I had one hand on my car door handle when a sudden movement caught my eye. I turned and saw Mr. Harcourt scuttle across an open area of ground on the far side of the fountain. He disappeared through a side door.

I was alarmed because he looked to be deliberately trying to avoid being seen. But perhaps he was hurrying into the house to be punctual for our meeting? I rang the bell again, but the house remained silent and uninviting. Clearly, I was persona non grata: it was all over. I tried calling him that evening, but the maid, not unkindly, said he was unavailable.

Pat took the philosophical attitude that we should get on with our lives as if Hastings and Fran Harcourt had never existed. Even if he did call to apologize, he was evidently unstable and we should ignore him. Four days later, while I was working horses at home, Harcourt called. I dismounted and went to the telephone, my stomach in knots.

Offering a cordial greeting and an apology, he said he had endured a psychological downturn and something untoward had befallen his family's publishing business. However, he had sought professional counseling and was once more ready to proceed with the farm. Full throttle.

Our whole family plunged into the effort to create the classiest Thoroughbred facility anywhere. The sudden emotional shift was enormous. Proof of his new seriousness was that he now had a name for the farm he envisioned. "I have always been intrigued," he said, "by that moment at the races when the announcer says, 'The flag is up.'" At one time, tracks employed someone literally to hold up a red flag—a signal that all the horses were in the starting gate. At that moment, no more bets were possible, and everyone paused to focus on the gate. "That's the moment," said Mr. Harcourt, "that this whole farm enterprise—the breeding, the selection, the training—is preparing for. At that moment, what will be will be."

But in his grand plan, I was no mere overseer. "I want you to be more than a manager, more than a horseman," he told me. "I want you to become the managing partner of Flag Is Up Farms, and for your input you should be entitled to five percent of the operation going in and have the right to buy deeper into it as we progress. I will create a contract with you, and I will pay for the legal work. You should go to the offices of my lawyer and outline for him all that you want in the contract. I will read it, but you can create it."

I did as instructed and outlined a contract that I believed to be fair and equitable to both sides.

Then he asked me if I would fly to Europe to tour the best horse operations there, and with that knowledge press ahead quickly with planning the facility. I had never been outside North America before and eagerly boarded a plane to England, where I hooked up with Tim Vigors. He was a bloodstock agent, a gentleman farmer, and a former fighter pilot in the Second World War. With Vigors at the controls, we flew to stud farms all around Britain and landed on most of the major racecourses. I made notes and took photographs. In France we toured more facilities, including the Guy de Rothschild breeding farm. The trip was better than a university course in the design and management of racehorse facilities. Then we flew to Germany and on to Ireland.

While I had been away, Harcourt had been reading about operations in other parts of the world, so I was not long back before I was sent off to Argentina, Australia, and New Zealand on the same mission. When I returned, I made a final report and recommendations to him. Both Pat and I prepared ourselves and our family for a twelve- to eighteen-month cyclone of activity to plan, construct, and open the operation of Flag Is Up Farms, Incorporated, Solvang, California.

The 1,250-acre property, then far and away the classiest Thoroughbred facility in California, had four main areas. First, there was a breeding and foaling operation with a stallion barn, breeding pens, laboratory, round pen, office complex, eight-stall foaling barn, and residential quarters for up to eight employees. The second area—a training and starting facility for adolescent horses—incorporated a covered riding arena, two covered round pens, box stalls for eighty horses, a five-eighth-mile training track, a two-and-a-half-mile cross-country gallop, three large hay- and straw-storage barns, a feed mill to make our own feed, a main office, and residential quarters for up to fifty employees. Third, a hospital and rehabilitation area included space for forty horses, a swimming pool for water therapy, an X-ray therapy facility, an office complex, turn-out paddocks, plus residential quarters for six employees.

Last, there was the main house. It sat on top of the "mesa" or 150-foot rise on the north end of the property. Designed in the early Californian tradition, though with much more glass than usual, the house looked south out over the valley.

We moved the first horses on to the farm in July 1966. Johnny Tivio strolled in and booked the best room in the place. In October of that year our family moved into our beautiful new home. We were all working hard, but we felt like we had stepped into paradise.

Not long afterward, my father and mother came to inspect our new digs. I gave them a guided tour.

My father criticized the fencing ("Should have got oak from Kentucky and made plank fencing.") and the many thousands of cedars and other trees I had planted ("Get in the way if you want to move anything around. You wait. They'll just knock your hat off every time you ride underneath."). The racetrack was too small. The training-barn loft badly built. The aisle floors ill-conceived. The round pens too costly. "Keep a foot in the show-horse business," he advised me before leaving. "This racehorse thing will eat you up."

Meanwhile, our horses were performing well and we won our share of good races, mostly from horses I had selected as yearlings: Cathy Honey, champion three-year-old filly of the United States; Gladwin, a beautiful First Landing colt purchased at Saratoga, was a Group I winner (that is, he won at the highest level in Thoroughbred racing); Aladancer, another Group I winner, was among the first crop of Northern Dancer foals; *Petrone, purchased as a three-year-old in France for $150,000, later won more than $400,000; Sharivari, eventual Champion Sprinter and Horse of the Year in New Zealand; and Bahroona, a major stakes winner, along with many other winners, were among the early residents of Flag Is Up Farms. The years 1967 to 1970 were successful ones for the farm.

One day early in 1971, Mr. Harcourt came to the house. He had had a drink and asked for another as we retired to the patio overlooking the farm. He took off his spectacles and I could see his eyes, now watering from all the emotion welling up. "It's no way for anyone to live, having this disease," he confided, striking his own chest. Then he described the effects of what he termed "bi-polar disease." From a very early age, he had suffered from manic depression.

It had driven him out of the family business and broken up countless business partnerships. People were not willing to cope with him. I felt sympathy for his plight but had no idea how to help. I sensed, however, that he was asking me to look after him and understand his every whim, however illogical.

"Do you know," he said, "I've had thirty years of therapy? How does that sound?"

"Expensive," I suggested, trying for a little levity.

"Fran knows how to handle me. When I swing on the moon, she knows to draw me back down. When I'm stumbling through the cellar in the dark, she knows to bring me back up. Do you know, Monty," he said suddenly, "my relationship with your family and what we're doing at Flag Is Up Farms is the most important thing in my life, and I don't want to encounter these problems with you."

"I agree," I said, and meant it. We had already had a hint of it, and it had been devastating.

"I want you to know how to handle me. If we can do this, I see our relationship lasting all my days. I'll make an appointment for you to visit my psychiatrist. You can learn from him how to track me. I'm confident your intelligence will allow you to do that. You'll be just like Fran."

While I felt relieved that the situation was out in the open and that some kind of a plan to cope was taking shape, I also felt a great weight of responsibility for this sorry man.

His psychiatrist in Santa Barbara did not seem pleased to see me. A tall, lean man in his late forties with a sophisticated and soft-spoken manner, he queried me carefully—no doubt concerned about breaching patient confidentiality, even with Harcourt's consent. But on my second visit to the clinic, it became clear that he now knew everything about me and was more inclined to be candid. He described Harcourt's condition as "sand-castle syndrome": he used the curious metaphor of the child on the beach taking as much joy in destruction as in creation.

Standing on the terrace later that evening, I looked down on the barns caught in the last rays of the sun slipping below the mountains, and I remembered Harcourt's wild enthusiasm as we planned and built. And I knew then we had built a sand castle for Hastings Harcourt.

In September 1971, I was at the racecourse in Del Mar, 250 miles from Flag Is Up Farms, when I received a call saying that the private plane would pick me up and fly me back to the farm. Mr. Harcourt wanted to see me that afternoon. He and another man were already waiting for me in a car outside the house. Pat was out with the children, so I was to face them alone on the back patio overlooking the farm.

They appeared to choose the seating arrangements carefully. I sat on one side of the table; they sat together on the opposite side. Harcourt was in a stern, somber mood. He introduced his companion as a business associate who was working with him on some new projects.

Harcourt produced from his jacket pocket a silver pillbox that he ceremoniously placed on the table between us. He opened it to reveal about twenty tablets of varying colors, shapes, and sizes. When he looked at me, the hairs stood up on the back of my neck. It was a cold, ominous look. What we had been dreading was about to unfold.

"I just want you to realize," said Harcourt, "that it takes me this many pills to get through a day. You know my doctor, and you know my problems. I won't bore you with a lot of the details, but I am sure that you realize I am in a grave condition."

He paused, then continued, "I must sell the farm and all the horses as soon as possible. It is devastating to me, but it must be done. I am saddened to give up my farm and my horses, but it is particularly painful to give up my relationship with you, Pat, and your family. You have been an important part of our lives for almost six years now, but where my health is concerned I can let no one get in the way."

I knew the signs. Hastings Harcourt was heading into free fall.

"My associate here will coordinate with you over the disposition of the assets. If you can find someone to buy the farm, obviously you could remain here under similar circumstances. And possibly that same person would be interested in buying some or all of the horses. Whatever I can do to assist in your quest to keep the farm together, I will do, so long as I can get out of everything very soon. I will leave you now and wait in the car for my associate, who will explain to you some of my ideas for disposition."

His speech over, he walked round the table toward me with his arms outstretched. I stood and waited while he threw his arms around me and squeezed. "I'm sorry," he said. "I have failed you and your family, but this must be done."

He turned and disappeared through the house. I felt sorry for this poor old man. I also felt an inexplicable wonder—awe, even—that such a destructive psychology could exist and continue to take such ruinous effect, even in a man who knew himself and who could afford the best possible treatment.

Harcourt's man ordered me to sit down. I felt like a student in the principal's office. He announced, "Mr. Harcourt is getting out of this thing in short order, so don't get in his way. We can work together on this, and I can help you make the transition."

"Mr. Harcourt," he went on, "feels the people in this industry would be more responsive to buying the property and horses if you remain involved in the sale. Your reputation and approval will bring significant value to the deal and increase the speed with which we can push it through."

"Fair enough."

"He would like you to explain to any potential purchaser that you have a five percent interest in the property, money they wouldn't have to come up with. You should also say that you will buy in on the horses to at least ten percent, which Mr. Harcourt would not require you to pay. So you would end up with ten percent in the horses as a commission. He might even consider fifteen or twenty percent, depending on price and conditions."

"That's fine, thank you." I prayed it was going to be as easy as this. It appeared we had our escape route and that Harcourt was acting sensibly. Harcourt's business associate wanted a list of horses I would not buy in to, since they would be consigned to the earliest sale possible. I said I would do that right away.

Then he dropped the first bombshell. "In addition to this, Mr. Harcourt has instructed me to tell you that he wants his riding horse, called Travel's Echo, shot dead . . . and disposed of."

His words stopped me cold.

"Why on earth—"

He cut in. "Mr. Harcourt doesn't want anyone else to have Travel's Echo. He wishes you personally to shoot him, rather than have him go to another home."

I said nothing. Wanting Travel's Echo not to go to anyone else was a sentimental notion—but to place such a cruel sting in the tail of it? I could not bear it. The image came to me of Travel's Echo doing so well for the Harcourts at that first show almost five years ago...and their smiles as they accepted the applause of friends.

"He also wants you personally to shoot Mrs. Harcourt's driving ponies. She, also, doesn't wish them to go to anyone else." Fran had bought a pair of driving ponies, thinking she might like to come out from time to time and use them; she never did, though the ponies were kept in good condition by farm staff.

He paused and consulted some papers in front of him. "Mr. Harcourt has also been extremely disappointed with the performance of two horses, Veiled Wonder and Cherokee Arrow. He wants you to shoot them, preferably today. He does not want you to try to sell them to someone else; he feels they have disgraced him because he had high hopes for their performance and they let him down."

Gone was amazement, sorrow, or incomprehension. Now I felt anger and determination. No horse in my care was going to be sacrificed on the whim of an unstable man. Harcourt's henchman prepared to go. "I will be in touch with you on a daily basis to facilitate the disposal."

I heard the door shut with a click. I sat there, hollow with shock. I knew this much: There was no time to feel sorry for myself, because if I failed to move quickly, things would be taken out of my hands. Since I was empowered to sign papers, certain options were open to save the lives of these animals. The man's words squirreled around in my head: "...disappointed with their performance...a disgrace..." Cherokee Arrow and Veiled Wonder were young colts—well-bred stakes winners—who had only "disappointed" us because we had set our hopes extremely high for them. I went down to their stalls and looked them over. I stroked their muzzles and tried to think.

Just a month before, Veiled Wonder and Cherokee Arrow had been appraised along with all the other Harcourt horses. I double-checked at the farm office: Veiled Wonder was valued at $3,500 and Cherokee Arrow at $3,000. I had one option: sell them this instant and ensure that the money was logged as usual in the Flag Is Up Farms accounts. I could not leave myself open to any accusation of theft.

I called a friend and asked him to send me a check for $6,500, naming the two horses. I promised him I would get the money back to him. He agreed, and I quickly arranged to ship both horses to England for quarantine, then on to Alton Lodge in New Zealand, where Sharivari and Bahroona were standing at stud. As the trucks pulled out with the horses, I wondered how Harcourt would react when he found out I had refused to destroy them. No wrong was done to Harcourt since the farm received their full appraised value. I told myself that he was a sick man making irrational decisions, and I could not allow the animals to be the victims of this malady.

Next, the driving ponies. I telephoned a friend who would give them a good home, and she was at the farm within the hour to take them. Then I called a neighbor who lived close by.

"Can I park a horse with you, in secret?"

"What's going on?"

"I can't tell you, but if you can trust me that this horse's life is in danger, will you take him and not tell a soul?"

"Send him over, then. What's his name?"

"It's best if I don't tell you."

I led Travel's Echo out of his stall and loaded him into one of our vans. He would stay hidden until some sense could be made of these events.

This frenzy of activity occupied me through the afternoon and well into the night. I finished by visiting Johnny Tivio in his stall, just to check he was still there, alive and well. As usual, his stall was in immaculate condition, the dung piled neatly in one corner. He rarely urinated in his stall. I said to him, "You're almost house-trained, aren't you, boy? You want to come and live with us in the house, a room of your own, huh?" It felt good to break the tension a little. Johnny Tivio regarded me silently, impassively.

Early next morning, I got a call.

"Mr. Roberts?" It was a woman's voice, distant and cool. By her tone, she might have been calling about a malfunctioning dishwasher, not to cross horses off a death list. "I'm calling on behalf of Hastings Harcourt."

"Yes."

"Can you confirm for me that the horse named Travel's Echo has been destroyed?" I needed to lie but the nuns had taught me well. I hated lies, yet now it was imperative that I deceive, or at least stretch the truth.

"He's gone."

"And the two colts, Veiled Wonder and Cherokee Arrow, have they also been destroyed?"

"I can confirm they've gone, too."

"And can you confirm that Mrs. Harcourt's driving ponies have also been destroyed?"

"They're no longer here."

"And lastly, I need to confirm that you personally undertook the disposal of these animals."

"Yes."

"Thank you, Mr. Roberts." The phone clicked and the disembodied voice was gone. The next few months were chaos for us as we prepared brood mares, yearlings, foals, and racehorses for sales conducted over a radius of 3,000 miles. The children were now ten, twelve, and fourteen years old, and they had a difficult time making sense of events. They were not alone.

I desperately contacted potential buyers for Flag Is Up Farms. If one was not found quickly, the farm would be broken up and sold in lots. Although the family was tense and worried much of the time, I was reasonably confident that things would go well. I had avoided having to shoot the animals, Harcourt had obviously believed my story, and a Mr. Rudolf Greenbaum, from Los Angeles, had surfaced as a possible buyer for the farm.

Two months later, in the first week of December 1971, Rudolf Greenbaum finally agreed to buy Flag Is Up Farms, most of the horses, the rolling stock, and the equipment—in other words, the ongoing business. The price was negotiated, and by the third week in December, Greenbaum had deposited $200,000 in an escrow account

opened at a title insurance company in Santa Barbara. The deal was
done. We were safe, and on a better footing than before. We took comfort, knowing that the sand-castle man was behind us.

Then he came roaring back, and I learned that hell hath no fury
like a Harcourt scorned. On January 3, 1972, his emissary called to say
that everything was on hold and he needed to meet with me in my office at the farm. He arrived with a large briefcase and delivered what
sounded like a well-rehearsed speech.

"Mr. Harcourt is very upset. He has discovered that you didn't
shoot Veiled Wonder and Cherokee Arrow, and that you had a friend
buy them only to transfer them to your name. It looks as though you
stole them."

"I paid their fair market value," I said, "and since he wanted to
shoot them, he got $6,500 more than he should have."

Harcourt's man paused and then said quietly, "By the time he gets
through with it...he'll make you look like Jesse James. If that's the
route you want to go."

The Greenbaum deal was crushed, like a match underfoot. Moving
with speed and power, as his wealth allowed him to, he used his web
of contacts to "disappear" the records of the escrow account, and to
send the $200,000 back into Rudolf Greenbaum's account as if it had
never been sent. If Rudolf Greenbaum sued, as surely he would, I was
the only third party who could testify in court that the deal had ever
been struck.

"Mr. Harcourt," said his colleague, "has been very nice to you and
to your family, and he can make it very easy on you or he can make it
tough on you for the rest of your life. Mr. Harcourt needs you to
come to court and testify that there was never an agreement to sell the
farm."

I saw what was happening. The sale of the farm had gone too
smoothly. Harcourt had not yet made enough waves. His castle still
stood by the seashore. When I told this pacing hireling that I would
not lie in court, and that I wanted nothing more to do with Hastings
Harcourt, he sighed and bade me polite farewell.

There followed three weeks of calm before the inevitable storm.
Whenever I saw Harcourt at the farm, he was saccharine, pleading for

my cooperation. He even asked me to speak with Rudolf Greenbaum and tell him I had changed my mind. I told Harcourt that during the transition period I would cooperate in every way I could, but that my days of doing business with him were over.

A few days later, on January 24, his secretary called. Sharivari and Bahroona were to be sold in New Zealand and I was to go there immediately to consummate the deal. Pat would join me on the trip: during these turbulent days we needed each other close. We were to meet Harcourt at a certain barbershop in Santa Barbara, as a send-off. It was indeed that.

While Pat went down the street to buy me a hamburger, for I was famished, I entered the barbershop. Two hulking men who announced they were from the district attorney's office put me in handcuffs. "You're under arrest," said one. "We're acting on a complaint that you've stolen two million dollars and that you're about to flee the country." As we left I spotted Harcourt's black Lincoln across the street; he was behind the wheel in almost comically oversized dark sunglasses.

Pat, meanwhile, burger in hand, got the alarming news of my arrest from the equally bewildered barber. She drove frantically to the sheriff's office in Santa Barbara where she would take up an agonizing vigil from mid-afternoon to ten P.M.

That night, she and the children watched in horror and disbelief as the charges led off the eleven o'clock news. So many friends called Pat that finally she let the answering service take over while she tried to calm the children. They had so many questions and their mother had so few answers. They held each other like a family huddled in a tent while a windstorm rages outside. What happened that day belongs in film or fiction. But it did happen, and it happened to me.

The two hulking men took me into an all-white booking room with marble-top counters, first pulling rank on the attendants and shooing them away like flies. The two had clearly never booked anyone before, but the comic air soon evaporated. They wanted a guilty plea from me, and quickly. I said I would never plead guilty when I was not. One squeezed my bicep to the bone. "I must tell you," he said, "that we have a murderer waiting in a cell for your company, and he is there to convince you to plead guilty."

They took me down a long hallway, past cells full of men, some lying down, some pacing or playing cards, many shouting profanities. The noise was insane: the iron doors, the metal cups being banged on the bars, the screaming, the shouting—something you must experience to know. Bank robbers, town drunks, and druggies were all thrown together like sticks in a tornado. My jailers would stop along the way, ask me to reconsider. They seemed oddly sincere when they said they did not want me to go through with what lay in store.

I was taken to a solitary confinement cell, eight-foot-square, with a solid concrete front and a black iron door. The only light source was a bulb recessed into the ceiling and covered with a cage. Inside was an enormous chained man who looked like a cross between a grizzly and Bigfoot. I was introduced to Buffalo Babcock.

He was about six feet, four inches tall, and weighed at least 300 pounds. He stank in his jeans and undershirt. Red hair grew in tufts out of his neck; his arms were as big as my thighs and busy with dark tattoos. On the right arm was a snake's head, its body extending over to the man's pectorals. On the left arm was a woman, long and waistless in shorts and high heels. I was shackled to him, face-to-face through a floating ring, with heavy metal collars at our wrists and ankles. An X formed between us. The men showed Babcock a button near the door, which he was to press when I was ready to plead guilty. The noise of the door closing was deafening. My pulse was racing out of control, but I knew I had to think if I was to survive this. I wanted this man to talk.

"Why are you in here?" I asked him. Smiling at first, he said he "blew a jukebox," then explained what that meant: You enter a bar with a double-barreled shotgun and shoot out the jukebox, then announce that the next blast is for the first guy who moves—in this case, an unfortunate bartender who went for a hidden gun.

Babcock turned his attention to me. "I know you, Monty Roberts. I know all about you. You're my passport. I don't really want to hurt you, but my life is on the line and I couldn't give a damn about yours." The deal was this: He would convince me, nicely or not, to plead guilty and thus win for himself a dismissal of charges.

My mind turned somersaults. I had to get him talking again. As he spoke in rapid-fire fashion about his abusive father, drunken mother, his stint in Korea, this giant would stand up, then sit down on the iron bunk. Ranching and rodeo work had taught me to stay clear of ropes that might entangle you and kill you when a steer or mustang was on the other end.

Buffalo was too immersed in his tale to notice the chain sliding around his right knee, and as he bent to sit down again, I moved. I had been bulldogging in the arena, and I was quick and strong. With a power reserved for fathers lifting cars off children, I hoisted the chain around his ankles and he came crashing down, banging his head on the corner of the iron bunk. While he lay there, motionless, I went for the buzzer.

Help came in the form of a sheriff's uniform. "This has gone far enough," he yelled. They unchained me, took Babcock to the infirmary and me to a jail cell. Along the way, the several hundred prisoners were yelling and applauding, banging their metal cups against the bars in celebration. "Good man, you survived," praised one. It seemed I was a hero for vanquishing Babcock, whom they knew as a bully.

I mentioned to a cell mate that I was hungry—my last meal had been breakfast. All fifteen prisoners in my cell once more created pandemonium with their cups. A guard came, and soon after, a sympathetic young man who, oddly enough, had once worked for me in the broodmare barn at the farm. He brought me the most delicious roast-beef sandwiches I had ever tasted, along with a toothbrush, toothpaste, a washcloth, a bar of soap, and a towel. After the brutality of the day, this simple and humane act touched me deeply.

I paced the cell all night and had no appetite for breakfast in the morning. By then my hero's halo was fading: some of my cell mates, now deciding I was a millionaire, were showing signs of aggression. At nine o'clock came further evidence that even in dark times like this, my guardian angel—the one the nuns had told me about as a boy—was looking after me. I was taken to a small room with a telephone on the wall, the receiver off the hook.

On the other end was Glen Cornelius, a cattleman I had done business with. Harcourt's office had tried to sell him cattle that Glen knew belonged to me. Glen was on his way to a meeting at my home of concerned friends. But first, he had to know something.

"Did you take anything from this man?"

"I took nothing from him," I said. "It has to do with him wanting me to lie for him in court." He asked me again, and I made the same answer. "I knew you were honest," Glen would say later, "and I knew you worked for a man who wasn't." After Glen met with Pat and the others that morning, he came with a paper bag and $50,000 in bail money.

Within days, after hearings to plead for a reduced bail, and huddles with lawyers, I was out. When I finally got back to the farm, it was lit up with floodlights everywhere, and armed guards were patrolling the property.

Late that night, there was a knock at the front door; when I stepped outside a guard put a shotgun to the back of my head. He instructed me to lie on my stomach; his foot against my neck was meant to ensure I stay there. This fellow, too, wanted my guilty plea and perhaps a bonus for procuring it. But once again, my angel was on duty. At that moment, the guard's boss showed up and called off the uniformed thug.

In the days that followed, the friends who rallied around us saved our lives in every way. The help was emotional, logistical, financial, and if I name names here it is by way of thanks: to John and JoAnn Jones, Marge and Vince Evans, George and Kathy Smith, John and Glory Bacon, Dr. Jack and Cae Algeo, Peggy and Slick Gardner, Raymond and Rosalie Cornelius, as well as Glen and Ora Cornelius.

One loaned us a car, for we had none; the farm owned everything. Another took in our children for several months while the legal firestorm raged. Another housed Pat and me when our lawyers advised us to leave the property.

On that day, I ran down to the stables and immediately saddled Johnny Tivio, Jess, and Cadillac—the three horses I knew we had to get away from Flag Is Up Farms. While I was saddling Johnny Tivio, one of my office staff came to say that the horses should remain until everyone knew who they really belonged to. I smiled at her and continued tacking up. She knew who these three horses belonged to, and that an army could not separate me from Johnny Tivio, short of burying me a distance from him.

I put as much of my tack and equipment as I could on my horses. Then I mounted Johnny Tivio and led the other two down the long straight drive, past the buildings I had so carefully planned and the paddocks I had cultivated over the past six years. I wondered if I would ever return. It looked peaceful and orderly, and its beauty had the usual effect on me. I was proud of it.

In the paddocks grazed some of the horses I had trained or started. Horses know nothing of our troubles and we know too little of theirs. But I wanted to know more, and I felt renewed resolve to focus on my work with remedial animals and in starting young horses. The acres that spread out on either side of me would exist long after Harcourt was dead and gone, and long after I was too.

Johnny Tivio walked on, toward the safe haven of the Gardner Ranch, in charge as always, his ears flicking back and forth. At that moment, Johnny Tivio's belief in himself and his natural superiority to everyone around him seemed to me like gold dust—magical and priceless. I loved that horse.

During the following year, the case against me unraveled; the charge of theft languished in court. Harcourt panicked and started selling off pieces of Flag Is Up Farms for much less than their actual value. There followed a protracted legal battle: Rudolf Greenbaum sued Harcourt for $10 million; I filed a wrongful prosecution suit against Harcourt for $30 million.

A judge was hauled out of retirement to sort it all out. C. Douglas Smith was a slight, gray-haired, distinguished-looking man with a deliberate manner and a cool gaze. In his chambers, the judge said that he had read all the documents and he did not see a felony here—at least, not on the part of the accused. Pointing at me, he said, "I want to see that man smile." I liked this judge.

In the end, my attorneys came to me with a deal. They were not sure it was good enough, but the alternative was years more of legal wrangling and a full trial. I was to plead a *nolo contendere* to a misdemeanor for signing the two horses' ownership papers over to myself. Both horses would be given to me by Harcourt as final proof that I had committed no intrinsic wrong. And the California Horse Racing Board agreed that my licence—suspended early in these proceedings—would immediately be restored and a letter of apology sent to me.

Last, but not least, Flag Is Up Farms would be ours. The compensation paid to us by Harcourt allowed us to buy the farm. It was over.

A year later, Hastings Harcourt contacted me to say that he was terminally ill and wanted to meet. We sat in the den overlooking the farm. The first thing he did was congratulate me on being such a formidable opponent. He asked forgiveness for the injustice he had tried to perpetrate, and I said I appreciated the gesture, adding that two of my children, Deborah and Marty, had decided to take up law, hoping to bring some integrity to a legal system that sometimes seems to have none. Harcourt died not long afterward.

What a study in the variables of human psychology that tortured tale was. It drew me closer still to horses—the most wonderful and the most predictable creatures on earth.

CHAPTER 5

Flag Is Up Farms Regained

For Johnny Tivio, Jess, and Cadillac, the barn at the Gardner Ranch had been home for a year. Now I loaded them in the van and drove them back the short distance to Flag Is Up Farms. Johnny Tivio was pleased to see his real home again, with its gracious stabling and spacious paddocks laid out side by side in this stunning valley.

When Pat and I, with Debbie, Laurel, and Marty, walked back into our house, it looked to have lain empty for one hundred years, not twelve months. Our footsteps echoed as we walked over the wooden floors. Cobwebs hung from the rafters, and everywhere we felt the ghostly residue of all that had transpired before our hurried departure.

We switched on the electricity and the plumbing, opened the windows, and blew some life back into the place. We liberated our furniture from the storage company. A gifted artist, Pat started painting pictures and hung them all over the house. She wanted to bring light and color back into our lives. Later, she took up sculpture too, studied human and equine anatomy, and began to work in bronze.

We walked the farm, reintroducing ourselves to each paddock and building. Much of the original land and the site of the breeding barn had been sold off, but the core remained. We still had 154 acres. In time, it sunk in that Flag Is Up Farms was ours and we began to mend as a family. I was keen to get back to what I was good at: horses. Perhaps this renewed sense of energy led to overzealousness, and a critical error of judgment with a horse called Fancy Heels.

I had been talking to our friends Dave and Sue Abel of Elko, Nevada, about my coming to the Elko horse show to look over the large contingent of reined cow horses who compete there every year. These ranch horses work long hours each day, honing their skills without suffering the drudgery of exercises specifically geared for the showring, which tends to make horses resent their jobs. The Elko competition often showcases wonderful equine athletes, with sound work ethics and good attitudes.

I soon spotted a horse that impressed me. Tall, copper-red in color, with an unattractive head, Fancy Heels looked like a classic mustang/Thoroughbred cross, with a fair bit of feathering on his legs. He showed an enormous amount of cow sense and good athletic ability, with a light, responsive mouth. A little work, I thought, could turn him from a good working horse to a top show horse.

Fancy Heels won his class on the Saturday, which earned him a place in the championship on the Sunday. I was anxious to buy him before he started winning any championships outright, so that afternoon Dave Abel and I sought out the horse's owner, Randy Bunch.

"Well, he's for sale all right," said Randy. "That's why I brought him to town in the first place."

"How much do you want for him?"

Randy paused before saying $3,500. I was surprised at this low figure and agreed immediately. We shook hands and I wrote him a check.

"You looking forward to the championship tomorrow, just the same?" I queried.

"Uh-uh. Hang on. You own the horse; you show him tomorrow."

Startled, I said, "Now wait a minute, I've never even sat on him yet, and I don't even have any clothes or equipment." Randy crooked a finger at me and said, "I want to show you something." Fancy Heels shifted to one side as we walked to the back of his stall.

Randy raked back the bedding from one corner to reveal a half-empty bottle of Jim Beam whiskey. He picked up the bottle and held it between us. "That's how much whiskey it took to get me through the elimination classes. I don't intend to have to drink the rest of it to get through the championship. I came to town to sell him; I've sold him, and now I'm going back to the ranch. Good luck with him—you're showing him."

I looked across at Dave Abel. My expression was a plea for his help. Dave shrugged, "That's the way people are up here, Monty. If you want a shot at that prize money, I guess you show the horse. We can find you a pair of chaps and a bridle." I rode Fancy Heels for an hour that evening, just to get the measure of him. The following morning, I again rode him for half an hour to warm him up. In the arena, our herd work was pretty good and Fancy Heels led going into the single cow-working phase. That part was only acceptable. After this came the dry work—stops and turns. In the end, we took second.

After a week at home working with Fancy Heels, I gained a lot of respect for Randy Bunch. The changes necessary were going to be harder to effect than I had realized. This was a mature, well-established working horse, and I could not find my way forward with him.

After a month, Fancy Heels was ten percent less effective than he had been at the Elko show; after two months, twenty percent less effective. I was, I told myself, a major trainer of Thoroughbred race-horses as well as several world champion working horses, including the legendary Johnny Tivio. I can get this job done.

After four months, I conceded defeat. I had taken Fancy Heels backward so enormously that the kindest thing was to sell him to a good ranch where he could go back to the work he enjoyed. An amateur bought him, and when I saw them compete, I saw a rider who did not notice every mistake the horse made and a horse who tried his heart out. They won often.

During the many hours I rode Fancy Heels, that old adage "You can't teach an old dog new tricks" took on new life for me. In fact, you *can* teach an old dog new tricks, but all in due time. I had been so keen to get to work on Fancy Heels that I thought I could force rapid changes on him. I pressed for a standard of excellence without taking the horse's feelings into account. It did not work.

Given the chance to work with Fancy Heels again, I would not set a time frame for making changes and demand that he stick to it. That horse taught me to respect horses and not to demand immediate perfection. I had failed him, but I did learn from the experience. In the twenty years since, the hundreds of remedial horses I have worked with have benefited from the lessons he taught me. Certain horses in my life have humbled me, and Fancy Heels was one.

———

In 1974, I got the kind of telephone call you dread.

"Crawford's taken a bad fall. He broke his neck."

My old friend Crawford Hall had been riding a young racehorse when they both fell hard to the ground. Dave Abel, a classmate of Crawford's, was with me at Flag Is Up when I got the news and we raced north to Fresno, where Crawford lay in an intensive care unit.

Crawford is the son of Clark Hall, who owned a sizable cattle operation in Shandon, not far from where James Dean was killed. In the late 1940s, Clark was a good team roper who competed in the major rodeos. I roped with him when I was ten years old, got to know him well, and went to his ranch several times. Crawford was an active boy around the ranch and would work cattle with his father. There was some devilment in him, which only made him more charming. In the early to mid-1950s, while I was at Cal Poly, only fifty miles from Crawford's home, I saw him often. He was then starting to show horses in competition and in junior rodeo. Some ten years later he took a shine to a student who was working for us at San Luis Obispo. When they married it felt like a family event.

Sadly, they drifted apart, and Crawford took a job in Tulare in the San Joaquin Valley with Greg Ward, my close friend and ex-classmate who had set up a business there training cutting horses, reined cow horses, and quarter horses for racing. Crawford was a rider assigned to all three departments.

Now he faced the reality of never riding again. I will never forget stepping into the room where Crawford was being treated for severe spinal cord damage. He had an eyebolt embedded in the top of his head and screws through his heels, and from these points he was wired to a device that looked for all the world like a barbecue spit. It provided the necessary traction and rolled his weight around, reducing damage to vital organs.

The doctor took us to one side. "Crawford can't feel anything from the shoulders down," he said calmly. "That means he is going to be a quadriplegic, with maybe five to six percent use of his arms. I'm afraid there's a long road ahead for him."

Crawford struggled with the trauma. His emotions were a tangle of hope and despair, but shock was what he felt more than anything. "If I can't be involved with horses," he told us as we stood by his bed, "I'd just as soon not live."

"I'd say the same myself," I replied. "Don't you worry, we'll find a way."

"You promise me something? If I'm good for nothing but selling pencils somewhere, you all agree to give me enough pills to put me to sleep, do you hear?"

"You won't be selling pencils, Crawford."

"Hell, I probably won't even be able to do that. I sure as hell won't be able to lift the pills to my mouth, so do it for me if I ask you."

Then hope would surge in him. "I'll do something," he said. "I'm telling you, I'm not just lying down and doing nothing. There's a spot for me somewhere."

He was a desperately unhappy sight, and our hearts went out to him. Driving back with Dave, I wondered out loud about finding a job for Crawford on our farm. The main buildings and offices are on level ground, with good surfaces between the barns, the covered riding school, the round pens, and the track.

If Crawford could learn to operate an electric wheelchair, he could be another set of eyes and oversee the operation. I scouted and found a spot on the grounds where we could locate a home specifically designed for a quadriplegic. The idea took shape: he could be employed as an observer and help me where possible. He would find his own role and cultivate his position as his abilities allowed. Crawford might have a chance, after all, to stay involved with horses and the life he loved most.

Days later I called the hospital and talked to Crawford about the potential job. Only four months after that, he and a friend came to Solvang to look the place over. By that time, they had a special van to transport him.

The transition from young and athletic to wheelchair-bound was strenuous and difficult. But Crawford would learn to operate the chair more effectively, and the future would undoubtedly bring better chairs. He was convinced that in time he would navigate the farm as well as anyone.

Doctors and therapists involved with Crawford's rehabilitation came to the farm. They cautioned us that as prospective employers, we were taking on a near-impossible task. Only with great difficulty does the human body adjust to the quadriplegic state, and we were not to underestimate the challenge Crawford faced. An initial rush of sympathy might create false hopes for him.

The prognosis looked grim. Therapists listed dozens of potential physical problems (many of which came to pass), and warned that Crawford would likely only live another three to five years—with the prospect of a more normal life expectancy if he could get past the five-year hurdle. Within a few months, Crawford was living at Flag Is Up Farms in a custom-built modular home provided by his family. He found himself a good vehicle that could get him to every corner of the farm. Crawford had a job now, and he began to shape it around horses.

"The horses themselves were therapeutic," Crawford says now, looking back on that time in his life. "When I was in rehabilitation in the hospital, there were guys there who didn't want to get up in the morning. They were looking for ways to die. I wasn't like that. I had something I wanted desperately to do—work with horses. It has never *felt* like work, though; it's always been fun. An engineer or an architect might have the same passion for building bridges or houses. Mine was for horses, and they have never stopped teaching me. The setting of the farm, the climate, being outdoors most days of the year—all that is conducive to being healthy, and I love it. But the possibility of a life with horses: that's what inspired me."

From the outset, Crawford insisted on complete cooperation from me as he commenced his education in Thoroughbred racing. A voracious reader, quick to learn, he became extremely proficient at understanding the needs of the horses. Without my realizing it, he had already taken over the operation.

After only one year, I concluded that he should manage the training operation on a daily basis; I would step back and be the overseer.

That year, 1975, I purchased a yearling I named An Act. A good horse for Crawford to begin with because he set such a high standard, An Act was a first-class prospect who went on to win the Santa Anita Derby. The next year I bought two other horses, Alleged and Super Pleasure. Super Pleasure had as much talent as any horse I have owned or trained, but he was beset by a throat problem that relegated him to being a sprinter, so we will never know how he would have turned out.

As for Alleged, Pat conceived of that name for this extraordinary horse, and we still have it as the license plate on our car. The name began as Allegiance to the Flag (his sire was Hoist the Flag) but it was later shortened to Alleged. Eventually owned by Robert Sangster and a consortium of investors, Alleged was twice the winner of the Arc de Triomphe—the most prestigious racing event in the world.

One of my favorite clippings from the *Santa Ynez Valley News* dates from October 5, 1978: "Monty and Pat Roberts of Flag Is Up Farms here in Solvang have good reason to feel proud this week as Alleged won the 57th Prix de L'Arc de Triomphe at Longchamps, France, last Sunday. Alleged, ridden by Lester Piggot, won easily by two lengths ahead of Trillion in a time of 2:36.5."

With Alleged, An Act, and Super Pleasure, Crawford had a solid foundation to build on and a standard of excellence for the horses to follow. The years have enriched his education, and he has become invaluable to the farm—as good as anyone in the racing industry. His life revolves around operating the training center, and owners take comfort in knowing that he is there, on the job, virtually all the time.

When Crawford came to me, his approach to training horses was conventional. Although a thinking horseman, he had been trained in the mainstream. Over the years, however, he has come to embrace a set of philosophies more aligned with my own.

Crawford is a character, and well known in Thoroughbred racing for his clever pranks. "I decided a long time ago," says Crawford, "that serenity is a valuable commodity and that no one should get too much of it." On the farm, an asphalt sidewalk parallel to the track opens onto a grassy area where you will often find Crawford strapped neatly into his chair, facing the track, and looking studious in his glasses and white fedora, habitually rubbing his hands as he watches a horse and jockey breeze past. You hope he is assessing the horse; you fear he is plotting mischief.

Crawford, naturally, was part of an elaborate prank pulled off in 1986. An office manager named Corky Parker—who took his job very seriously and who had a birthday coming up (a dangerous combination at the farm)—was told that an Arab sheik was coming for a barbecue, a precursor to a major horse deal. "*Don't* lose him," I instructed Corky before supposedly leaving on a trip and putting him in charge.

From my hiding place in the bushes by the house, I looked on as the theatrical conspiracy unfolded. Behind the sheik's robes, beard and sunglasses was Satish Seemar, a farm employee, whom Corky would have worked with daily. The sheik's interpreter and the suspicious, gun-toting bodyguard? Both neighbors. The stretch limousine they arrived in proved a nice touch.

While Crawford and the sheik talked horses on the terrace, rider and appointed barbecuer Sean McCarthy drank beer and feigned inebriation. "I don't give a *damn* if he's the sheik," he said too loudly, "just tell me how he likes his meat!" The increasingly distraught Corky begged Sean and pleaded with the other riders to stop imbibing. When they finally all sang Happy Birthday, the tears began to flow down Corky's face and he was hours recovering. The acting troupe spent at least that long laughing and recapping.

Crawford has also gained a reputation for the way he works with the young people who come to Flag Is Up Farms and ride for us. "Leave the horse alone," he will say to the rider. "Let him go on, let him explore a little and then correct him. He'll be all right. Let him go in the direction he wants for a few steps, and then bend him more toward what you want. Don't hammer him."

The youngster struggling with the horse will inevitably retort, "But he's going to run away." Crawford's reply is invariably laconic: "How can he do that? You have the Atlantic on your right and the Pacific on your left. Where's he going to go?"

Another Crawfordism goes: "You can't be liberated in your thinking if you're conservative in your approach." As I write this, Crawford is in his twenty-first year with us and as healthy and active as anyone in his condition could be. Hospitals and therapists have used videotape to chronicle his career. Institutions use his example as an educational tool in treating similar cases. To anyone who faces what he faced, and to anyone who meets him, Crawford Hall is an inspiration.

———

After a day at the track in 1981 I headed straight for the farm office. It was April 24. Every year on that day I feel a twinge of sadness all over again. When I walked through the door, Pat immediately stepped forward and embraced me. "Johnny Tivio," she said through tears, "is dead."

Seeing a mare being taken to the breeding barn, he had stepped up on his toes, lifted his tail, and was coming over to try to get her phone number, as usual. In the middle of the field, he dropped like a stone. Dr. Van Snow, then our veterinarian, confirmed that the old horse had suffered a heart attack. Through my sadness, I was relieved only that he had not suffered. We were just beginning to have trouble with his feet, and I had dreaded a painfully slow demise. He was sound to the last.

"We left him where he fell," said Pat, "so you could see." As I walked toward his body lying there, saw the eye empty, the life gone, all those philosophical notions about his being spared a lingering death vanished. His death hit me hard. I stayed there with Johnny Tivio, and I remembered.

By then, he had retired. He was twenty-five years old, and no one had wanted to breed to him for some time. He enjoyed the best of care, with a warm box stall of his own and a field with plenty of green grass in the daytime. He could watch everything going on from his paddock. Mares moving to and from the breeding barn had to pass by him, and every time one did Johnny Tivio acted the big, bad stallion again, calling out to them and prancing the length of the fence like a three-year-old.

Early in our life together, I showed him in Salinas in a big competition, one of the most important on the continent. Johnny Tivio was so good at everything, and so willing, that I could not decide whether to show him in the cutting division or the reined cow horse division. Pat had said, "Why not show him in both?"

It was unheard of. No one had done it before. It was impossible....

We entered him in both events, and the official response was instantaneous. "Monty, have you lost your mind?" It was our old friend, Lester Sterling, chairman of the event, calling from the grounds office. "We can't let you show Johnny Tivio in both divisions. It's just ridiculous to think he could perform that way."

"Is it against the rules?" I asked.

"Well, no. But I don't think you ought to embarrass yourself."

Eventually I persuaded Lester to agree. As I was preparing Johnny Tivio, I would fit him with one type of bit and bridle when we were training for one event, and a different one for the other. He was intelligent and read the situation perfectly: he won both divisions, a feat not attempted before nor duplicated since. In his time, Johnny Tivio was undefeated in the stallion sweepstakes—a kind of pentathlon for stallions. He was four times a world champion working cow horse. In Western riding, a form of Western dressage, he was undefeated in fourteen consecutive competitions.

More than that, though, he was a sterling character possessed of superb intelligence, uncommon pride, and an inspiring work ethic. He made it a pleasure to shrug on a coat and walk down through the early-morning mist that often blankets this valley to begin the hours of work that an establishment like this demands.

Now he lay collapsed on his side, with that heavy, final weight that only death brings. I knew where to bury him. For some time, I had it in my mind to make a special graveyard just in front of the office, where I would give each horse his own headstone. The horses' names and dates and a line or two expressing some of their qualities would be engraved in bronze plates set into the blocks of stone.

Johnny Tivio would be the first.

With some members of our staff, we went over with a low-boy trailer to where his body lay. We fitted straps underneath him and lifted him onto the trailer. Towing him across the field, I remembered eleven years earlier riding him out of the farm, down the drive in front of us, when Hastings Harcourt was casting a long shadow over our lives. Johnny Tivio had been as confident as ever, and I remembered how I took sustenance from that.

That day, when we arrived at the Gardner Ranch, a notoriously eccentric woman, Marjorie Merriweather Post Dye, had come by. She pointed at my horse in the stable and said, "Johnny Tivio."

"What about him?" I asked.

"Well, I hear you're in trouble. You need money for a legal defense. Now, I don't give money. No one gets money out of me. But I'll give you anything you want in return for that horse."

I thanked her for the offer, but it was out of the question. "No!" she corrected me, annoyed with my stupidity. "I don't mean I'd take him away from you. I'd never take him away from you. But I want to buy the ownership documents."

"The papers?"

"Yes, just for a while. For safekeeping. Just give me the papers so I can hold them, and point at them, and say I owned Johnny Tivio for a little while."

We walked up to the house and I gave her the papers, shaking my head in wonder at this courageous, strong woman who had so much her own way of doing things. In return, she made us promise to call her if we ever needed a loan toward our defense fund.

Now, as I prepared to bury the horse she so clearly adored, I hoped that Marge had enjoyed having those papers. They were all that was left of him. I dug his grave myself, using the farm's backhoe. I am not a capable hand at that machine, and it took me longer than it should have. By then it was dark, but the hole was dug and Johnny Tivio's body had to be lowered in.

This was the tough part. I knew I would never again have a friend the likes of Johnny Tivio, and I could not bring myself to cover him with earth; I had had enough. Our veterinarian volunteered to carry on while I went up to the house and crawled underneath the covers.

The plaque on his gravestone reads: "Johnny Tivio, April 24, 1956 to April 24, 1981. Known to all as the greatest all-round working horse ever to enter the arena." He died on his twenty-fifth birthday.

———

I was walking up the steep southern slope toward the house when I took, as they say in the horse world, a bad step; my lower back suddenly locked, and my legs gave out on me. I was on the ground and helpless, unable to move the lower half of my body. All sensation ceased to exist. I conjured Crawford Hall lying in traction in his hospital bed. Now, seven years later, it was my turn.

I pulled myself up the slope with my arms, in excruciating pain. Stunt riding, football, team roping, calf roping, bull riding, bulldogging: all that impact on my spinal column had ruptured the discs, and I was about to know the cost. I was forty-six years old.

A doctor declared me too critically injured to move to the hospital. He wanted to stabilize me first, and to win back the feeling in my legs. He arranged for delivery of a rack—truly an instrument of torture—and for thirty days I was strung out on this device like a rabbit on a spit. I am as strongly opposed as anyone could imagine to the indiscriminate use of mind-altering drugs. But doctor-administered morphine is truly a miracle drug for one beset by debilitating pain. I was able to function somewhat in the business-management aspect of my life while being stretched on that awful rack.

After a month, much of the sensation returned to my legs. During that time I had educated myself in the world of back woes, and settled on Dr. Bob Kerlan as the man most likely to keep me out of a wheelchair. In a friend's motor home, I was taken to Dr. Kerlan's clinic in Los Angeles. After a CAT scan (a computerized axial tomographic X ray) was taken, he and his team presented their report. They brought in a plastic model of a human spine and used it to terrify me.

Dr. Kerlan pointed to the model. "You see here, the lower back? The soft material in the core of these five discs has ruptured—due to constant heavy impacts on the spine—and leaked out, causing stalactites of invasive material. That's thirty percent of your problem. The rest is due to fractures and spurs throughout the spinal column. This is what's causing you the pain and the nerve impairment. We can get in there and clean up that stuff, and remove the spurs and you'll be left with five discs which are like doughnuts—the soft middle sections will have been sucked out of them."

I offered a hesitant "OK," but the news just got darker...

"Normally, we find just one or two gone; but all five are ruptured in your lower back. It's going to be a long operation, and we won't find out how successful we've been until it's finished."

...and darker.

"You have very extensive damage to the spine, Monty. Forget riding—don't even think of riding again. You won't be lifting a weight more than forty pounds either. You'll probably just be able to walk around under your own steam. But be happy with that, because you are on the verge of living the rest of your life in a wheelchair."

For two or three days I went through preparation. They took me off the morphine, and when the pain roared back I roared with it. I wanted to scream "Fix it!" every second of every minute. Then I went under the knife. Ten hours later, I woke up to see a smiling black woman in a perfect white uniform. She looked like an angel: had I died and gone to heaven? Or was this the other place?

"OK, Mr. Roberts," she said, "shall we visit the bathroom?"

Surely she jested. "I can't move."

"Oh yes, you can. Time to sit up now."

Was she aware I had only just come around from the anesthetic? She started to pull my feet out from the bed and sit me up. The pain shot through me; iron bolts were being driven into my back by Satan himself. She held my shoulders, but every time she let go my body would flop, as if a new hinge had been inserted somewhere in my middle.

"Wow," she said admiringly, "they must have done a good job on you." Later, they hung me in a wheeled contraption that suspended me in mid-air like a wicker chair hangs from a tree limb in a garden. I was in a sorry state.

The video of the operation was one of the more grotesque movies I have seen. The surgeons looked like a gang of carpenters with muscular forearms arriving for work; their toolboxes were filled with hammers and chisels. After cutting through and peeling back muscles and soft tissue, they went at my back like they were mending a broken house.

Following my recovery, they sent me home and told me to keep moving, to walk a minute or two more each day. I was in a wheelchair for twelve days, then on crutches for several months. I have a scar down the middle of my back from my bottom rib to my tailbone, and my lower right leg is virtually dead: you could stub a cigarette out on it. Dr. Kerlan and his gang of carpenters did a better job than he thought was possible. I can walk fine, and I can ride.

———

The horse I would ride, and still ride, is a registered quarter horse gelding, a bay. He has a white pastern on his near hind leg and a white, irregular star between the eyes with a strip that runs down to his muzzle. It forms an inverted question mark, which seems apt for this horse.

Dually was a cull from the Greg Ward Ranch, a throwaway horse whom no one would buy. He had crooked hind legs six inches shorter than they should have been, pigeon-toed feet, and was bow-legged behind. Greg and I treated him as an experiment: we tied the reins to his saddle horn and let him have his way. He *still* has his way, he's jealous and possessive of me, and he is still funny-looking, but he has also become a superb horse.

He's fourteen hands, three inches high and weighs 1,200 pounds: a solid guy, this Dually. His name refers to a type of pickup truck, called a dually (as in Dooley), with a beefed-up rear end and twin tires at the back. We use them to haul horse trailers. Such trucks look massively broad and strong if you stand behind them, and that is how Dually looks.

His rear quarters are like two small hills jammed together, and the power they give him is mind-boggling. He is a turbo-charged, twin-engined type of rocket horse, with the balance and coordination now bred into the breed. There is no way he can replace Brownie or Johnny Tivio, but Dually is a natural successor to them—both in terms of my affection for him and in his achievements. He too is a world-class, championship-winning animal in his own right.

From my first day with Dually, I felt he was at heart a near-perfect working animal.

After join-up, Dually bonded with me very strongly, and like Johnny Tivio, he will follow me around the farm without any head-gear on. I can wander up to the promontory that overlooks the farm, and he'll walk alongside as if there were an invisible thread connecting us. He has been schooled from start to finish using only the methods described in this book.

Now seven, he is in the prime of life. The understanding between us is mature and well-founded. I have not so much trained him as created an environment in which he has wanted to learn. I have never pulled at his mouth, ever; in fact, I could use cotton thread instead of leather reins. Yet, on a totally loose rein, he will slide to a blinding halt from a full gallop just hearing a single word, "Whoa," and at the same time feeling my weight settle back in the saddle. Again on a loose rein, he will spin like a top, just feeling the gossamer weight of the rein against his neck and a slight pressure applied to the inside leg.

Dually has an immense heart, which is just as well because to train him using these experimental methods takes patience and hard work from both of us. However, having learned from my experiences with Brownie and Fancy Heels, among hundreds of others, I have taken care not to dull his appetite for work by repetition or excess; it has been essential to our progress together that he remain fresh and keen.

———

The "crazy horse" is almost never born, but made. And it pains me to hear the term. If we could somehow see for ourselves all the events in a horse's life that together account for his malicious behavior, we would be astonished. Some horses will take so much, then finally take no more.

Few people still think humans are born crazy; but in the world of horses the "bad seed" myth endures. "His sire was that way, too," trainers will say of a troubled horse, and they have been saying that for 6,000 years. They are wrong: maybe two percent of horses are born bad; the rest are put on that path by people.

Stories abound about truly nasty horses. Native Dancer, who sired the fleet Northern Dancer, would pick up a groom by the teeth and toss him in the air like a stick. He would haul riders off his back by their boots. I once read that his groom, "who loved him like a son," freely admitted that had it not been for careful handling, Native Dancer would have killed someone. In his paddock, the horse would see the groom and, in his own time, come to the gate to be led away. If the groom entered the paddock before that moment, the stallion would run at him with murderous intent.

Flag Is Up Farms has also had its share of stallions requiring great vigilance, but none so dangerous as a Thoroughbred called In Tissar.

He was by Roberto out of Strip Poker, as fine a pedigree as you can imagine. It made him a half brother to the champion Landaluce. He was purchased as a yearling at Keeneland in 1979 for $250,000 by Buckram Oak Farm, and sent to France to race. He was a good winner early on, but then he was injured and offered for sale at the reduced price of $220,000.

The horse struck me as a good prospect for syndication, so along with partners Albert A. Katz and Ronald Semler, we bought him to put together a syndicate for breeding. He was a handsome, proud stallion, a "blood bay" horse — red tones with black mane and tail. In Tissar was tall, strong and muscled, especially through the neck and shoulders.

In California, we offered him at $16,000 a share, which is like arranging time-share leases on his capacity as a father. The twenty-five shares sold within two weeks, yielding the partners a gross of $400,000, which meant we were already $180,000 to the good and had kept back five shares each to be used on our own mares. This was a good piece of business.

In Tissar started covering mares in 1983 and bred without incident for the first half of the season. Then came reports that he was being aggressive with his handlers. I spent time watching him. If his handlers took him to the breeding room, he covered his mare and all was well. If, on the other hand, they turned toward his paddock instead of the breeding barn, he became aggressive.

Since the aggression seemed to be a function of his sexuality, I brought his handlers a metal noseband stallion halter to use on him, which seemed to solve the problem for a day or two. Then it recurred in the breeding room, where he had previously been willing and cooperative, if a touch overenthusiastic.

At the same time, rumors reached me that a young man on our night staff had taken it upon himself to school In Tissar. I am sure he had good intentions, but he had likely mistreated the stallion, at least in the opinion of the horse. In Tissar became dangerous, and he bit two men quite badly. I huddled with Dr. Van Snow, our resident veterinarian, and his assistant, the breeding room staff, and Darryl Skelton, who was handling the stallions.

Our solution was to create a safety zone around the stallion. Two eight-foot staves (one-and-a-half-inch-thick dowling) attached to In Tissar's halter would keep his handlers at a distance. They bred two or three mares that way. In Tissar was happy and did not object to this careful handling procedure; he even seemed proud of it.

The next time a romantic appointment was booked for him, I once again came down to observe and offer help if necessary. We brought a mare into the breeding room, cleaned under her tail with soap and water, bandaged her tail in gauze—all precautions to minimize infections and injuries to both stallion and mare—and had her standing in the center of the room.

Two men put the wooden staves on In Tissar and led him toward the breeding room where the mare waited in full heat and well "let down"—meaning that she was receptive to the stallion.

The two men led In Tissar through the large door in the center of this forty-foot-square room. Six feet into the room, he planted himself, lordly looking the situation over. In the room were seven people: two men on the staves, one man with the mare, the veterinarian, his assistant, Darryl Skelton, and myself.

I closed the door behind the stallion and Darryl and I walked over to join Dr. Snow. In Tissar stood stock-still, just looking at the mare and around the room.

Without warning, he struck out with his left front foot, reaching over the top of the stave and slapping it out of the man's hand and onto the floor. The weight of his body snapped the dowling in two. The man on that side was left holding one broken portion, while the jagged other half hung dangerously from the stallion's halter.

A second later, In Tissar reached up with his other foot and, without breaking it, slapped the stave out of the other man's hand. The horse was deadly accurate; no question, this was a calculated move.

Moving fast, he attacked the mare with his mouth wide open. He sank his teeth into her left flank, ripping at it like a wolf would a rabbit. When his shoulder struck her, she fell heavily to the floor, landing on her side. The man holding the mare fled for his life.

With a hunk of her hide in his mouth, In Tissar was now kneeling over the mare, squealing and pawing. The noise in that room was deafening, the excitement and enormous power of it overwhelming. My time in the rodeo arena with bulldogging and bronc and bull riding had given me the greatest schooling I know to cope with tense and dangerous situations, but it was little use to me now.

I moved to my right. In Tissar had knocked the mare down near the south wall, and as I moved to the corner he wheeled and took a run at me. I ran back along the wall to gain the protection of the examination chute.

Dr. Snow, who had moved along with me, held a shavings rake in his hand. His intention was to protect the mare and the rest of us by holding the stallion at bay with the rake. In Tissar went straight for him and ran into the end of the rake as if it were made of papier-mâché.

When Dr. Snow fled toward the lab in the northwest corner, he crashed into his assistant standing in the doorway, and both fell into the lab, and safety. Darryl and I both ended up in the examination chute. I never felt more vulnerable and less in charge.

The two men on the staves had sought refuge outside the north door, which was open a foot, and I am sure they were prepared to close it if the horse came that way. The man who had been holding the mare stood outside the south door, also open a foot. Having terrorized us all, In Tissar now faced the lab, weaving back and forth as if to say, "I control you all. I'm in charge now."

He turned slowly and walked on the tips of his toes with his tail stuck out and his neck arched high. It was a beautiful, terrifying sight. He went straight to the mare, who was still lying on the floor, and he stood over her flank. He pawed and squealed several times, as a stallion does when courting a mare, and the mare slowly got to her feet. Blood dripped onto the floor from the large gash on her flank.

In Tissar rooted at that flank with his nose a few times, and was fully erect. Incredibly, the mare lifted her tail to display her receptivity. He mounted her, and every one of us there stood frozen and watched in fascination: it was a primal, powerful experience.

After covering the mare, In Tissar walked slowly to the north door. He stopped there, the aggression clearly gone. The men outside slowly opened the door and walked him down the alleyway to his stall. He went quiet as a lamb.

As Dr. Snow, Darryl, and I walked along behind him, the doctor shook his head. "I'm going to carry my pistol with me from now on, and if he ever does anything like that again he'll have to die. I'm not going to risk losing somebody's life."

I agreed. Something dramatic had to be done before someone was killed. We concluded that the horse was perhaps overfed and underworked. If he was ridden in the hills, really put to work, maybe we could change his attitude. Darryl offered to ride him each day, but Dr. Snow and I insisted that one of us be around to offer help should something go wrong.

On the day set aside to try this new strategy, we took In Tissar to a place on the farm with strong corrals and cattle-handling facilities—a loading chute and a squeeze gate. Once in the gate, we would get his tack on and take him for a ride.

In the stall, Darryl managed to get a shank on In Tissar and lead him toward the corrals. Halfway there, the horse spotted a mare in a field a quarter mile away and started to play up. Darryl tried to soothe him, but the horse made a move indicating he was going to attack him. We all stood in a small half-acre area while In Tissar made some very aggressive gestures. Moments later, Darryl lost control of the shank and In Tissar was loose. We managed to avoid being attacked, but if he spotted one of us—even from a distance of 200 or 300 yards—he would go for us. He was really angry, and we ran around like Keystone Kops.

Eventually we set some gates to trap him near the heavy-duty cattle apparatus. Darryl was able to get him in the squeeze, and we swung the gate over to him until he stood in an area twelve feet long and three feet wide. When we closed the gate to move him over, he kicked it and then held his near hind leg off the ground for about twenty seconds. We held our breath, thinking he had broken his leg—the kick was that fierce. Then he put his leg down and stood on it as normal. There was just a bit of hair off, about mid-shaft on the cannon bone.

Once he was in there, Darryl tacked him up and mounted him. He took him up a hill where he could ride for about fifteen miles with no gates to open, and they were gone about three hours. When he returned, he rode him into the stallion round pen, took his saddle off, and led him to the wash rack to give him a bath. In Tissar was fine. He looked a picture of health, a fine example of a stallion in the prime of his life. You could have sold him to a schoolgirl, unless her father noticed that iron-hard, disinterested look in his eye.

We were all pleased, and Darryl started a program of riding the horse each day. On about the fifth day, Dr. Snow agreed that In Tissar was calm enough now for us to get an X ray of that still slightly sore hind leg. When this revealed a significant fracture of the cannon bone, we faced a dilemma: how long could Darryl ride him before the exercise became cruel?

Darryl cut his work right down. On the second day, when Darryl came back to the round pen and took off his saddle, In Tissar attacked him. That was the last straw. In the normal course of events, a horse with a history like this one would be destroyed. Around the world many stallions have been killed for less.

I could not bear to have him killed, however. It was dangerous even to try helping him, but we would have one last go at saving his life. In the end, I devised a complex system of gates, small enclosures and squeeze chutes that would allow In Tissar to be groomed, shod, clipped, bathed, and exercised, and to have his stable cleaned and serviced—all without having anyone in the enclosure with him.

He could also breed a mare without having anyone in the enclosure as well. He was bred in this fashion for twelve years without any injury to a mare, himself, or anyone working with him.

We now have another remedial stallion, Court Dance (by Northern Dancer) who stands in the same facility. Court Dance was owned by Robert Sangster and John Magnier when he was sent to our farm. They hoped I could sort out his problems so they could sell him, but

I quickly learned that he was another dangerous stallion beyond fixing, even beyond transporting or handling.

For the past three years, he has been breeding here under the same
system we used with In Tissar, and he is getting along very well. I always prefer to come to an understanding with a horse through communication and dialogue, but that was not possible with these two
stallions.

From the accounts I have read about violent stallions, such as Ribot
and Graustark—and even In Tissar's sire, Roberto—I have no doubt
that there exists a significant number of incurably aggressive stallions.
On a scale of 1 to 10, In Tissar was a 9.9. He was intelligent and cun-
ning and he wanted to harm people. Something in his environment
had turned him mean, and he had no intention of listening to anyone.

———

Beauty may well be in the eye of the beholder. But while conformation is, in part, subjective, there are roots of realism when assessing
the qualities of the equine athlete. And if, during an eighteen-year career buying and selling Thoroughbreds I showed that I had an eye for
a horse, that owes something to sculpture.

Early in the 1970s, when Pat took up painting and equine sculpture, she began by studying horse anatomy. You have to know the *inside* of a horse before you can begin to capture the *outside,* and I tried
to help Pat as best I could. I recall one time watching one of her
teachers sketching horses by one of the paddocks. He was using a triangle to help maintain correct proportions.

To get a sense of what I saw that day, imagine a horse seen from the
side, and over that horse lay a triangle, its apex sitting as high as the
horse's head and midway between head and tail. From that high point,
one line angled down at forty-five degrees through the shoulder; another angled down at forty-five degrees through the hip, and the baseline ran horizontally through both knees and hocks.

In a well-balanced horse, the apex is right in the middle. In a Thoroughbred racehorse, the two sides of the triangle are equal, but the
baseline is considerably longer.

Using triangles to judge conformation is so simple, yet so profound.

Pat still works in bronze and it's rare *not* to have one of her equine sculptures taking shape in our kitchen. And when I look on as she subtly molds and adjusts, I think of that day by the paddock when an artist's sketch reduced the tangled business of horse conformation to a bit of basic geometry.

From the mid-1970s until 1989, sometimes with partners, I bought yearling Thoroughbreds at one public auction, in Kentucky, say, and then sold them as two-year-olds at another public auction, perhaps in California. It's called "pinhooking"—an awful name for a demanding and risky test of horsemanship in which an eye for conformation is critical. The term *pinhooking*, it is said, comes from England, where a woman whose husband bought and sold young horses likened it to crocheting—you reach in and pinhook an animal, then put him back in.

A lot can go wrong. If you select badly, if the horse gets injured, if the market declines, the pinhooker can get pricked. The aim, of course, is to sell the horse for a lot more than you paid. My aim always was to get twice for a horse what I spent, and between 1973 and 1990, I came remarkably close: Pat and I purchased 195 yearling Thoroughbreds for $6.9 million and sold them for $13.3 million—a return on investment of forty-three percent. Every young racehorse we purchased was also sold—a rare accomplishment in a business where many operations lose five to ten percent of yearlings for one reason or another.

The numbers are impressive: eighty-two percent of the horses we sold during those eighteen years would start in races, and of that number seventy-nine percent were winners—thirteen percent of them in highly competitive stakes races. Consignors, or sellers, of horses are ranked and during our years in the business, Pat and I were ranked first ten times, second three times and third three times—for sixteen of eighteen years, then, we were in the top three.

You will likely sell well if you buy well. But that presumes an intimate knowledge of pedigrees and smart bids at the sales ring. America still uses the old tobacco auctioning system of fast chatter; it took me years to master its tricks and psychology. Shipping horses is another major challenge—for me especially since 2,500 miles separated the auction ring and my training grounds. Conditioning, foot care, nutrition, marketing, and promotion: all matter, and the trainer who falls down in just one category will suffer in the long run.

A sleek, impeccably groomed young Thoroughbred is as graceful and desirable as any animal on the planet. But letting him use his gift of speed while also keeping him sound and healthy, and starting him so he remains keen to work—there is art in that, and the record of Pat and Monty Roberts, Agents is unmatched.

In Kentucky in the mid-1970s, I bought a registered Thoroughbred yearling stallion, fourteen hands, two inches high, less than 900 pounds in weight, by Hoist The Flag out of Princess Pout. A bay horse with two rear white pasterns, he was in horrible condition and not many people gave him a second glance.

Precisely because he was so thin, I could see that he had the best skeletal balance of any Thoroughbred I had ever seen. And history would suggest I was right.

Ten years later, in 1984, I attended a Thoroughbred symposium held by Dr. Michael Osbourn, a world authority on Thoroughbred conformation. Toward the end of his lecture, he flashed a silhouette of a Thoroughbred onto the overhead projector. "This animal," he said, "is perhaps the most perfectly constructed Thoroughbred I've ever studied." He gazed out to his audience. "Can anyone name this horse, by any chance?" I raised my hand.

"Aha," said Dr. Osbourn, "how did you identify your horse in silhouette, Monty?"

I said, "You have your system of circles. You test to see if certain anatomical features meet or fail to meet the various points on the circle."

"That's correct."

"Well, I have a similar system involving a triangle." Dr. Osbourn invited me to the overhead projector to explain. My triangle, I said, seeks to discover the balance between the two major skeletal structures in a horse: the pelvis and the shoulders. These two "engines" propel the horse over the ground and their engineering determines the efficiency with which the rest of the body responds to brain signals.

Dr. Osbourn finished by saying, "For those of you still in the dark, this horse was owned by Mr. Roberts very early on in his life. That horse, twice the winner of the Arc de Triomphe, is ... Alleged."

———

My mother had not long to live, and knew it, when she set about trying to reconcile her husband and her elder son. Intuitively she hoped that through horses we might connect.

My parents' visits by this time, 1986, had become rare and short; suddenly, they were coming to the farm for an entire week. It was clear to me that my mother's cancer had gotten worse, and that this visit was both a final farewell and a peace mission.

She engineered and cajoled, pushed and prodded. She arranged for my father to watch me work with horses in the round pen, ensured he had a stool to sit on, made it so he could not wriggle free. She came close to telling him he had to sit there and take note of what I was doing and acknowledge that it was working.

On the day my father sat down, finally, to watch me start a raw horse, he was well into his seventies. I was no longer desperate for his approval, though I was still a son who would have welcomed his father's belated blessing. I was also a man in his fifties who had by this time started more than 6,500 horses. Apart from all the working horses, I had trained Thoroughbreds who had gone on to win major stakes races all over the world.

The irony of that day was not lost on me: when I began to learn the language of horses at the age of seven, my father was the one man I first wanted to impress with it. And when he turned so savagely on me, and so furiously rejected my ideas, I determined he would never see me gentle a horse. No one would.

The round corral had been a feature of European farming and Western ranching for centuries, but the one I designed was built with solid walls—partly to keep the horse's focus on me, and partly to keep out a world of disinterest and rejection. I remembered too vividly the scornful words of Ray Hackworth after seeing me gentle a horse. "That was a fluke! ... You're wrong to go against your father."

I had spent my life going against my father, and now, finally, because my mother had made it her dying wish, he would see where it had taken me. Only recently had I added to the pen the skirtlike structure that let people see me converse with horses.

This day I would start a gorgeous young chestnut filly, a horse whose character I would have to discover. I could see immediately that she was a "fast" type—quick to respond, nervous, but intelligent.

I stood in the middle of the ring and coiled my light sash line. Moving slowly, I squared my body to hers, lifting up my arms a touch and opening my fingers. I locked my eye onto her eye. The result was dramatic. She fled to the perimeter of the round pen, running counterclockwise.

"OK, Dad," I called, "I'm going to explain the sequence of events so you can understand what's happening."

I hardly needed the sash line to keep this filly going comfortably. I could control her speed by choosing where to look at her: if I kept my eyes on her eyes, I could increase the speed of her flight from me; if I moved my gaze back to her shoulder, she slowed. At all times, I kept my body squared to hers.

"The first thing I'm looking for is that inside ear to lock on to me," I called to my father, who sat still as a post on his stool. "It'll happen maybe within a minute." The words were hardly out of my mouth when the filly's ear settled on me. "Course she's going to listen out for you," my father called out.

"It's more than listening out for me. She's keeping the ear on me as a mark of respect. She's allowing me some importance here." I pitched the sash line ahead of her, causing her to turn sharply and flee in the opposite direction. Despite the switch, the ear nearest me was turned in my direction, constantly. She settled back to a steady trot.

After another revolution of the round pen, I said, "Next you'll see another mark of respect she'll want to offer me. You'll see her licking and chewing. You'll see her tongue come through her teeth, then she'll pull it back and demonstrate a chewing action."

Sure enough, she began to lick and chew. "There it is. She's saying that she's a herbivore, that if she can be allowed to eat safely, if she can be allowed to stop running away, then we can come to an agreement. We can settle our respective positions, live and let live, let's talk."

We were now five minutes into the starting procedure, and I explained to my father the final signal before join-up: "I'm looking for her to drop her head, to run along with her nose a couple of inches from the ground." Within a few minutes, the filly was trotting around blowing at the sand in front of her feet, her ear still on me.

"She's telling me it's OK, she can trust me." Turning my shoulders to a point slightly beyond the filly, I allowed my eyes to trail there, too. Immediately, the filly stopped. I waited, perfectly still, standing at an angle to her, showing my flanks and avoiding any eye contact, even out of the corner of my eye.

I sensed a reluctance in her; she found it difficult to believe I knew her language, but she was forced to acknowledge that I had responded to all her signals.

Join-up is always the most thrilling part of the process. Not because I ever doubt it will happen, but simply because it proves the possibility of communication between human and horse. A flight animal giving her trust to a fight animal, human and horse spanning the gap between them, always strikes me as miraculous. The moment it occurs is always fresh, always satisfying.

The filly took a tentative step toward me. I was not looking at her, but I knew she was weighing her next move, and deciding to join-up with me. Moments later she was standing next to me, her nose at my shoulder. I walked slowly in a circle to the right, then to the left: both times she followed me. Join-up with this filly was complete. "That's what I call join-up," I said to my father.

"How many times has that one been ridden?" my father asked doubtfully.

"Never, Dad."

"Paah."

The chestnut filly waited for what would happen next on this extraordinary day when everything would change for her. As I always try to, I reminded myself that this was possibly the most nerve-racking moment in her whole life. I called to my father, "Now I'm going to investigate the vulnerable areas, to confirm that she trusts me completely."

I walked to the center of the pen, with the filly following me. I dropped the sash line on the ground and stood at her shoulder. "The vulnerable areas are where her predators will attack," I said aloud.

Moving slowly and quietly, I ran my hands over her withers and her neck. "The big cats will jump up here, clawing into the back of a horse, biting into the top of the neck in an attempt to damage the spinal cord, paralyzing the horse or causing it to fall just from their weight.

"If the horse is paralyzed, it's easy for the cat to finish him off. If the horse isn't paralyzed, then the cat will go to the ground with him and slip his teeth around under the neck, in order to collapse the trachea and shut off his air supply. So it's important she lets me into these vulnerable areas."

Next I moved my hands slowly across her flanks and under her belly. "On every continent one type of wild dog or another preys on horses. One in the pack grabs the tail, another hangs off her nose, but the majority head for her soft flanks—another sensitive area."

She stood reasonably firm, sidestepping only once or twice. I continued until I found an absence of rejection and tension in her. Then I picked up each of her hooves, sliding my hand down from the knee or the hock over the tendon and then to the rear of the fetlock joint, before asking her to lift her feet one by one, just holding them off the ground for a second or two.

"You see, she's a flight animal and she's just allowed me to pick up her method of propulsion, her feet. She's trusting me, pretty much from top to toe, now." By this point, we were about twenty minutes into the starting procedure.

Hector Valadez now entered the round pen carrying a saddle, a saddle pad, a bridle, and a long stirrup leather as well as a second driving line. Hector had been sent to me by another trainer in 1969; then eighteen years old and weighing about eighty pounds, he looked as if he might make a jockey.

I put him on his first horse that year and he has been riding eight to twelve horses a day for me ever since, save for several short periods when he worked for friends of mine. As it turned out, he was not motivated to be a jockey: he would be a better father instead for his two sons.

Hector has spent more time with me in the round pen than any other person. While his size kept him useful on the training track, he has probably been the first rider up on about 1,500 horses during the thirty years he has been with me.

Hector positioned the equipment in the middle of the round pen, then left. The arrival of this new person in the round pen—and more alarmingly, a pile of odd-looking equipment—caused the usual consternation in the young filly. She snorted, blew at the saddle, stared hard, wandered around, and generally came to terms with it.

If anything, however, the equipment heightens join-up because the perceived danger makes the horse seek her safety zone: me. This one stood by me as I lifted the saddle onto her back, took the girth under her belly, and buckled it up the other side. "I want her to get used to the saddle for a while," I told my father, "before Hector gets on her."

I stepped back from the filly and squared up to her, driving her away again. She went into flight, cantering with an odd, skewed gait as she coped with the strange new feeling of a saddle on her back. As she cantered, then trotted around the ring, I waited for the same signals— the inside ear settling on me, the licking and chewing. This time I would not expect her to lower her head. She could not trust herself to do that with this new weight on her back. That was too much to ask so early.

"Now I'm going to try a little experiment," I announced. "You'll see she has a sweet spot just there in the ring." I had noticed a particular place where she gave me her full attention. At other points around the circle, she was distracted by something—my father, the pen door, the light above. I knew from long experience that most "babies" (young green horses) have a sweet spot and that it is best to wait until they are in it before trying the more subtle signals of Equus.

"I'm going to hold my hand across the front of my body, and when she reaches her sweet spot I'm going to do nothing more than simply open my fingers. You'll notice her pick up speed considerably."

I held my hand across in front of my chest, and when I opened my fingers she broke into a canter. "See? That's how much she's reading me. She knows she can let a cat walk right past her, but if that cat has its claws open she has to flee, and pretty quickly." I set her going in the opposite direction, allowing her to become familiar with the saddle; and after three or four revolutions, she was asking to come back in to me. I tightened her girth a notch.

"Now for the bridle. Once join-up is achieved, it's pretty much of a formality. The join-up tells me she trusts me. And with horses, that's not too big a step away from her offering to work as hard as she can for me."

She was now wearing her first bridle, standing there unconcerned, chewing at the bit that sat across her mouth for the first time. "Now that the bridle's on, we can long-line her." We were now twenty-five minutes into the procedure. I long-lined the filly in both directions; this marked the first time she had ever walked into the reins and I wanted to get her used to them before Hector got on her back, just to give him something like a steering wheel.

After the long-lining, I backed her up a step. As soon as that backward step was taken, I released the pressure on the long-lines, rewarding her immediately. Then I pulled her girth tighter by a further notch, ready for Hector to ride her. Hector came into the ring and made himself known to her. He too rubbed her vulnerable areas, until she was happy with his presence. He brushed her new saddle lightly with his hands.

Then I lifted him on to her back and he lay across her for several moments, while I turned her head this way and that to make sure she caught sight of him draped over her middle. Carefully, slowly, Hector lifted a leg over her back, and rode her for the first time.

Hector walked her around the ring, not bothering with her mouth or whether she broke into a trot or anything else. The aim was simply to let her take stock of what was happening on her back. I checked my watch. "Half an hour," I called to my father. "About average."

My father went off to quiz Hector, then returned to the viewing deck and his stool. Because my mother had so carefully chosen the day, I had started ten young horses by the time darkness fell. Each time the same process repeated itself, each time Hector was in the saddle and riding them comfortably around the ring within half an hour. No restraints, harsh words or whips.

By the end of that day, my father had seen me start more horses than he could have broken in six weeks. He came down from the viewing deck and we stood outside, hardly able to see each other's faces in the dusk.

"What do you think of that?"

"Keep doing it that way," I heard him say, "and they'll get you."

Up at the house that night, my mother seemed especially anxious to know what he thought. In her mind, much hung on this. It was a question of justice for her son and a truce between the two men she loved equally. She skirted the topic for a while, then finally she asked, "So, Marvin, how'd you enjoy what you saw today?"

"Fine."

My mother pressed. "What do you think of it all?"

My father replied, "It's suicide."

There would be no end in her lifetime (or his, for that matter) to the rift. My mother had hoped that with the passage of time, the changes in circumstances, our common interest in horses might at last help us connect. But the horse remained a towering symbol of the space between father and son.

My mother's intestinal cancer took her away from us soon afterward, and we journeyed to Salinas for her funeral. We arrived at their house, where my father had some years ago built a block of stables and created a few paddocks. Until recently he had given riding lessons and had still been involved with horses. Now, with the death of his wife, he was in a sorry state. He greeted us upon our arrival with the words, "Come on in, your mother'll be back in a while."

Pat and I looked at each other, as if to verify what we had heard him say, and then I walked inside with him. "Dad, she won't be back; she died." He waited a long while and then admitted, "Yeah, I suppose she did." Half an hour later, as we were leaving the house for the funeral service, my father stopped in his tracks and said, "Hold on, we have to wait for Marguerite. She's not back yet."

Again I jolted him back. "Dad, she's waiting for us at the funeral home. This is her funeral."

"Yeah, OK."

By a strange coincidence, the Struve and LaPorte Funeral Home was located four doors down from our old house in Salinas, 347

Church Street. It seemed to me now such a small neighborhood compared with what I remembered. The houses had shrunk, the road a thin strip of pavement.

The funeral home was operated by Jim LaPorte. In the 1940s, the whole LaPorte family, including Jim, had been our riding students at the competition grounds. Now this gray-haired man, whom I remembered as my young pupil bouncing around on the back of a horse, was greeting us. As we headed inside, my father again wondered about my mother's whereabouts. Jim told us that this often happened when elderly people long together are suddenly separated.

Only a few people attended my mother's funeral service at the local Catholic church. Her life had been spent entirely in the service of her husband and her children.

Larry and I were concerned about how fast our father was now declining and whether he could cope. Any suggestion that he move in with us was firmly rejected. Even his doctor advised against it. My father, the doctor said, was healthy as a mule, with no desire to move anywhere. The doctor had someone to check on him regularly and to ensure that he was eating well. Larry and I set up a program of regular calls and visits. If I asked my father on the phone how he was, he would say, "Fine. Got that filly going nicely now, you know, and the palomino colt is a good horse."

"Dad, you're not doing anything with those horses."

"I certainly am!"

"Well, OK."

After one visit, Larry called us to say that my father had stopped eating and was fading fast. I agreed to come the following day, but next morning—forty-two days after my mother's death—Larry found him dead.

On a hunch, Jim LaPorte politely called me to say that my father's body was lying in a room at the funeral home. Did I want to see him? Jim ushered me into a small room, clean and bare but for a stand of flowers and a trestle at one end holding the coffin. The only light in the room, a soft glow, was aimed directly on my father.

Jim left me alone and I walked forward to look into the coffin. Larry's words came back to me: "He's shrinking to nothing in front of my eyes." My father seemed only five feet tall, and the flesh had almost disappeared from his bones. I had waited for this moment most of my life. When I was ten, I knew that one day there would be a funeral, and then I could touch him. Only then. I could finally shake his hand.

For most of my life I had longed for the moment when I would stand over my dead father. This was precisely the picture I had had: he in a wooden box, me looking down on him. Through his punishments and beatings, that image had sustained me. Cowering under his blows as a child, I knew that one day he would not be able to hurt me anymore.

It was a cathartic moment, and though I have shed many tears in my life, I did not shed one as I gazed into that coffin. The anger lived on, as if he had thrashed me yesterday, not more than forty years earlier.

He, at least, was relieved of whatever made him like he was. I will not forget the triggers that set him off—when I forgot one of his orders, or defied him. Once he had for many hours tied up a horse's hind leg, and I could bear the horse's pain no longer. I released him, intending to retie the ropes later, but when my father returned home earlier than I expected and saw what I had done, he chased me around the barn and flung me from a haystack. Another bloodied skull, another trip to Dr. Murphy.

I knew the triggers that led to violence. I, too, have felt that anger rise in me, felt the urge to strike out at someone in my family. But I put my grip on that anger. I swore that this man in the box would be the last link in the chain of violence and anger aimed as much at humans as at horses.

What stopped me, what still stops me, was the man my father killed. At that moment in the Golden Dragon saloon, I had sworn I would not be cast in my father's image. My father's death put a final seal on that pact with myself.

———

After leaving the funeral home, I was moved to drive to Chinatown and find the bar where all those years ago I had watched my father's cruel arrest of the black man. It was still a downtrodden area and now there were drug addicts lying around as well, which was not the case in 1943.

The Golden Dragon was not where it should have been. As I searched, a police car swung by and parked right behind me. My Lincoln looked out of place in this area. The officer carefully approached the passenger-side window carefully, and I lowered it so he could speak.

"You're lost, right?"

"No, I'm not lost. I'm back here to visit. It's more than forty years since I last sat in this spot." Because I had not immediately asked for his help in navigating my way out of this dangerous neighborhood, he perhaps suspected I had come to buy drugs and his manner became more guarded.

"Oh yeah?"

I went on, "There used to be a saloon here called the Golden Dragon. You know what happened to it?"

"It was torn down a year ago maybe."

"My father made an arrest in there forty years ago. It was a bad night. I came by just to remember it."

The officer brightened. "Your father was a policeman?"

"For twelve years, as it turned out. He retired from the force quite a few years ago now, though."

"What was his name?"

"Marvin Roberts."

"Oh yeah. There's a big funeral for him tomorrow. A lot of officers are going to that."

He was right. At my father's service the following day, an enormous contingent of Salinas policemen added to an already packed church. At my mother's funeral only six weeks earlier, the church had been virtually empty.

———

One day a ghost called me on the phone.

"It's Lyman Fowler here."

I could do no more than echo his own name back to him, but with an exclamation mark at the end of it. "I wonder if you remember, but I used to teach you in high school?"

"Of course I do."

"You might also remember, I had you do a paper?"

"I remember it distinctly."

"I'm retired now as you can imagine. But I have a favor to ask of you. I'm the social director of my church group and every year we try to go somewhere pretty. Somewhere civilized. No muggings or any of that, because we're quite a geriatric group as you might expect."

"What can I do for you?"

"I thought it might be possible to bring them out to have a look at your place. We wouldn't be any trouble; we'd only take up an hour or two of your time, but we've read about you in the papers, of course, and it occurred to me that it might be possible."

After agreeing on a time for the tour, I put the phone down and shook my head in disbelief. I remembered Mr. Fowler all right, and that "life's ambition" project with the big red F written across it. He was coming to visit the establishment that bore quite a resemblance to the plans I had submitted in that paper, plans he had initially rejected as impossibly extravagant.

On that perfect summer's day when the bus arrived at Flag Is Up Farms, Mr. Fowler—he would always be *Mr.* Fowler to me—was the first to step out. Despite his age, he did not stoop. He was still very tall, still smartly dressed, and with the same olive complexion and prominent eyes that I remembered. His hair had turned completely white, and his face was lined; otherwise, it was the same man.

He offered me a long, graceful hand and spoke in his precise way. "Monty, hello." Then he kept coming and gave me a heartfelt embrace—which seemed unlike him. People were filing off the bus and now stood in a semicircle; fifty seniors looking expectantly at me.

Lyman Fowler made his introductory speech. "Ladies and gentlemen, this is Monty Roberts, whom I've told you about, and he's kindly offered to show us his establishment, Flag Is Up Farms." Given the advanced years of many of these people, much of the tour had to be conducted from the bus. Like a proper tour guide, I used the bus's microphone to explain the sights as we drove around.

My guests had all lived in agricultural communities, so were genuinely interested in the planning of the farm. I had arranged for some horses to be on the training track; parked alongside, we could watch the Thoroughbreds breeze by. Lastly, we drove up the slope to the house, where everyone came inside to look around. Out on the terrace, refreshments in hand, they could see the whole farm spread out below.

Mr. Fowler then gave a speech I will always remember. We stood side by side as he began, "As you all know, I taught Monty when he was a young man. However, he taught me something, and it's possibly the most valuable lesson I ever learned."

He paused, then articulated a notion—almost word for word—that my mother had voiced to me almost four decades ago and that I had written down in a brave little note appended to the paper I returned to him. "A teacher does not have the right to put a cap on the aspirations of his students, no matter how unreal those aspirations might seem." He held out his long arm, indicating the buildings and paddocks below us. "There was a time when I told Monty that this was unattainable. Now we've all had a good look around, and seen how he proved me wrong."

Lyman Fowler clearly enjoyed telling this story, and I felt a great warmth toward him.

CHAPTER 6

Deer Friends

One cloudy day in November 1977, I was riding Johnny Tivio around the farm as I often did to check on pastures, fences, and horses. I would ride over the farm itself and then up a hill north of the property. From that vantage I could see much of the valley.

I was on one of those high trails in a canyon when I noticed activity on the face of the hill. A group of coyotes was frantically darting in and out of the brush. When I got closer, I saw that they had a deer down and were in a feeding frenzy, ripping at her hide with their sharp incisors. I ran at them with Johnny Tivio and used a rope I happened to have on the saddle to drive them off.

The coyotes ran to a higher position on the hill before turning to look back. I chased them further still before returning to have a look at the deer. She was an old doe, thin and toothless, and probably only half her normal body weight. She had severe lacerations from the coyotes' attack. Scouting around for offspring, I spotted two half-grown fawns, obviously hers. I hoped they would fare all right; they were old enough to survive once they found their way back to the herd.

The task now was to save the life of this old doe. I cantered down the hill to the shop area where I got my pickup truck, woven fencing, and steel posts.

With several farm-hands, I drove as close as I could to the doe. The coyotes, meanwhile, had inched back down the hill toward her. I started up the hill yelling at them, rope in hand and slapping my leg to divert their attention from the doe while the farmhands unloaded the fencing and posts.

Eventually, the three of us built a coyote-proof cage over the doe about fifteen feet in diameter and closed at the top. I put some grain and alfalfa hay in there and a bucket of water. As we worked around her, the weak doe struggled vainly to rise. I was certain that she would be dead the next day, but I had to give her a chance.

When I arrived the following morning, she was up on her keel and had eaten and taken some water. This itself was amazing; wild deer rarely allow themselves to eat or drink in captivity. I disturbed her as little as possible, and for the next four or five days I returned only long enough to ensure she had food and water.

By the fifth day she was standing and taking a few steps around her enclosure. Fortunately, she lacked enough strength to run at the fencing and bash into it as a healthy wild deer would. Before she recovered and began doing just that, I decided the best course of action was to try to accustom her to my presence so she would not panic at the sight of me.

I started by entering the cage, bending over, and working gently with her, making the same subtle and nonthreatening movements I used in starting horses. Amazingly, I was to find that the two languages are almost identical. Saving the doe launched me on an adventure that has spanned nearly twenty years. It has been one of the most gratifying experiences of my life.

———

Grandma, as I called her, was only two or three weeks in the cage before she was strong enough to take a chance on going outside. When I opened the cage, she walked off in that stately fashion that deer have, but you could tell she had no desire to put much distance between herself and me.

Next morning, I found her a hundred yards or so away from the cage. I put more grain and alfalfa inside and fashioned a watering device. Each day I worked with her, using the concepts of Advance and Retreat. Whenever she acted as though she preferred not to be with me, I would deliberately push her away and walk behind her for up to three miles. When I saw her circling and showing me her flanks, thinking about renegotiating with me, I would turn and walk away in the opposite direction.

I was squaring up, looking her in the eye, driving her away, then dropping off and turning from her, just as I did with horses. I could coax her back toward me. But join-up with Grandma seemed more tentative, not as solid. In fact, it would be several years before I could entice her from the herd and have her stand as close to me as I was accustomed to with horses.

Finally, one day, it happened. I had been pressing her away from me for some time, watching for the signals that said she was seeking relief from this disciplinary action. She showed me her flanks, locked an ear onto me; she mouthed at me, a silent whisper that she was a herbivore and wanted to try trusting me. Then she dropped her head and walked along like that, with her mouth inches above the rough terrain.

I backed off, turned at an angle and no longer looked her in the eye. We were in a beautiful spot on a promontory overlooking the farm, so I lay on the ground and turned my face to the sun. I watched as Grandma came closer and closer. I realized my dream of join-up with a deer. She trusted me. The warm sun seemed to bless that moment: the deer chewing her cud, the man with the grin, the eagle overhead catching the updrafts from the valley floor.

I learned a great deal from Grandma. I discovered that the flight mechanism of a deer is many times more sensitive than that of a horse. When I made a mistake in one of my movements, I would pay, sometimes for weeks or even months. This hypersensitive flight mechanism taught me subtle lessons that proved invaluable as I continued to refine my understanding of Equus, the language of the horse.

Consider this example. On one occasion, I was encouraging Grandma to come to me: I had my shoulders at a forty-five degree angle to her, looking away. However, I wanted to see what she was doing, so I glanced at her out of the corner of my eye too quickly. Grandma saw that I had broken the rules, and she walked 500 yards away and would not let me close to her for three days.

I realized I had been making the same mistake with horses; I quite often glanced quickly at them out of the corner of my eye when I was not meant to. In the round pen, I started working with a horse, experimenting with the speed with which I moved my eyes. I also tried different ways of reading the image of the horse out of the corner of my eye without actually looking at the horse.

By moving my eyes more slowly, I found I could temper the flight impulse. As soon as I understood that, Grandma was much easier to work with. I also found that spreading my fingers, moving my arms or going too quickly from retreat to advance all set her off, slowing the process of communication.

Again, I experimented with the horses I was starting. When I held out my arms as part of squaring to send the horse away, open fingers set the horse going quicker and faster. To the horse, the opening fingers were like a cat opening its claws, a clear sign of aggression.

Without Grandma's help, I would never have learned this more refined aspect of the language. It was as though this frail old lady was giving me advanced lessons in Equus; she was fine-tuning my responses and taking my qualification to a higher degree. Perhaps it was to repay me for saving her life back in the canyon. When Grandma died of natural causes on December 2, 1995, we buried her on the hill near the house.

While I worked with Grandma, I was thinking how fruitful it would be to start with a young deer, one with a malleable mind and not yet traumatized by life. I wanted to see if such a deer would respond faster than Grandma, who carried her life's baggage with her.

There were not many deer to be seen when I came to the farm in 1966. By the time I encountered Grandma, I had lived on the farm for eleven years, and throughout that time I never saw more than three or four deer in a group. But during the first four or five years I worked with Grandma, the number of deer making their home on the farm increased markedly.

I picked out a young male and began to work with him. Later on I called him Yoplait, from the brand of yogurt he enjoyed. He was a better student than Grandma; but then, by this time, so was I. Within six months, his behavior had changed significantly. I could draw him from the other deer, give him a rub around the neck and head, and stroke him. He always seemed a rather indifferent character, and I assumed that in general deer were like that. I later came to understand that they all have different personalities.

Yoplait would ignore me for long periods of time, staring in the other direction. I assumed I was making mistakes, and no doubt I was, to some degree.

Ours was not always a perfect relationship, but it did endure for twelve years. During his life, Yoplait came to believe that Flag Is Up Farms was his property. He would often go to the highest point north of the farm and lie there regally, as if surveying it. He would become aggressive with people and other animals who he thought were intruders. When strangers came, he would jealously position himself between them and me, brushing them away. Yoplait's indifference was unique to him; his possessiveness, however, is a trait I now know to be pervasive in his species. My employees told me that when I left the farm he became uneasy; he would look for me, and at night he would lie outside my bedroom.

Later, I tried an experiment. On the day of my departure, I put one of my worn undershirts near a tree. Instructed to watch for his reactions, staff later reported that he would lie near the undershirt for inordinate periods until I returned.

Later still, I put undershirts in plastic bags and tied them in knots to hold my scent, leaving them with my employees to set near a tree and change every three or four days. I was conditioning Yoplait to think that I was still there. This seemed to work. Without the undershirts he would get restless, often leaving the farm. When I was away for extended periods, Yoplait would walk into nearby Solvang, which posed a danger to him and created a minor brouhaha in the town.

It remains a part of my routine to organize some dirty undershirts for the deer. On extended trips, I mail used clothing back to the ranch, to keep my deer friends happy.

During his formative years, Yoplait took a dislike to both Pat and her dog, Jay. He regarded them as competition and made this much abundantly clear: the dog was to stay in the house, and Pat was to stay away from me, at least while he was around. Yoplait had the dog, a Queensland Heeler, completely intimidated. At the slightest provocation, the deer would lower his head and drive the dog back into the house.

Once, when I was away for an extended period, Pat decided to plant some flowers in the back garden. By now the deer had increased to sixty or seventy in the family group; several of them spent most of their lives close to the house, and there were only a few plants they would not eat.

Pat, however, had discovered that the deer declined blue flowers. Working on hands and knees, outside the kitchen and laundry room, Pat was planting blue flowers when she discovered that Yoplait was coming along behind her, uprooting each plant and dropping it uneaten. Pat picked up a broom and waved it at him, driving him off the hill and down toward the farm.

But Yoplait was not finished. Pat warmed up her Jaguar, opening the garage door to let the exhaust fumes escape. She then went into the house to get some things to take to the office and returned to find Yoplait in the garage and on top of the car. Pat had only recently bought the car and was proud of it, naturally. Yoplait had danced on the trunk and hood and used his antlers to rake the sides. The whole car had to be repainted.

I am sure the following is *just* coincidence, but Yoplait had also knocked down a photograph of Pat and Jay that hung on the garage wall. The garage is a kind of gallery, with some fifty photographs hanging there. Yoplait had seemingly chosen his target carefully, if not vengefully, and the glass in the frame was shattered. Crowning the photo now was a neat little pile of deer dung. There was no need to probe the pile for yogurt traces. The culprit was abundantly clear.

Pat telephoned me that evening and recounted all this, and just before she broke off she said that for dinner she might be having... venison.

Yoplait's gypsy ways would cost him. One time he crossed the highway in front of the farm and got hit by a car. He broke his right hip, and his right hind leg swung like a flag in the breeze. I found him on the front lawn of the house, as though begging for help. With assistance, I lifted him into the bed of my pickup truck, then took him to one of the stables and put him in a box stall. If I could put the leg in a cast, perhaps I could save his life. The vet tried, but Yoplait would abide no one other than me working on him. Because of his resistance, the cast would have done more harm than good.

With no other choice, I continued alone. He settled enough to lie on a very deep bed of straw with his broken leg propped in place. I put grain, hay, and water within reach. He lay there for two weeks before I finally saw him stand, and I noticed that the leg had started to mend and was fairly rigid.

He put no weight on it for another two or three weeks, and it healed. Ultimately Yoplait walked without even a noticeable limp. The healing properties of deer are astonishing; many times Yoplait and other deer have overcome injuries that would have been fatal to any horse.

Another time, Yoplait broke his jaw in many places and had several teeth knocked out in another altercation with a car. That time, I had to feed him hot gruel to keep him alive. His jaw healed, and while he had a funny smile on his face thereafter, he was able to live comfortably and eat normally. Yoplait finally succumbed to a third highway accident.

By then, I had begun to work on another male deer, Bambo. He was a dramatic success and joined up strongly. He is so tame now that I can run at him, slapping my thighs, and all he does is ignore me and come closer. Now twelve years of age, he has displayed the same jealousy I saw in Yoplait and other deer I have worked with, but to a lesser degree.

More kindly disposed than Yoplait and less inclined to take offense with strangers, he is still possessive. He frequents our house and is diligent about greeting me in the morning and coming around at dinnertime when he knows I am home. Were I to walk, say, five miles up into the hills, I could literally take Bambo with me and bring him back to the house again, controlling his movements by using communication skills.

It was only in 1990 that I started to work with a young female we call Patricia. Like Yoplait in character, she is distant and cold and will ignore me for long periods of time. She is also virtually expressionless in her communication. But unlike Yoplait, she is in no way surly. She bears no ill will to anyone; strangers are simply ignored. Patricia is by far my greatest challenge: she tests my ability to communicate each time I work with her.

Some years later, I took on another female called Feline (pronounced Fa-*lean*). She is one of the sweetest, kindest, most attentive deer I have come across. She never ignores me, and her responses are dramatic. When I ask her to go away, she expresses great displeasure at this horrid discipline. She shakes her head and will actually balk, round her back, and jump up in front. A horse who roots his nose out in a circle is making a very different motion but saying precisely the same thing: "I don't want to go away. I didn't mean that. I'm sorry for what I did." When you invite her back, you can almost see her smile. She returns fast, full of reaction.

One morning I noticed that Feline's muzzle and the bridge of her nose were swollen to almost double their normal size, the result, perhaps, of an insect bite. Almost all the deer I have chosen as subjects have come to the house quickly when injured and presented themselves on the lawn, as if to say, "I need your help and attention."

Feline's swelling subsided in a few days. She has been a joy to work with; her responses are keen and more sensitive than any horse I have dealt with. It is hard to compare animals, but the intelligence of horses and deer seems on a par. Both share a highly developed flight mechanism. But if you were to release horses and deer and mountain lions in Santa Barbara County—devoid of human interference—I think the horses would be wiped out before the deer. We have too long underestimated the intelligence and acuity of deer.

As commonly happens, a doe on the farm once gave birth to twins, one male and one female. She then proceeded to walk away from them and not return. I saw the twins several times on the hill 300 yards from the house. The first time they were still wet, newborn, and unable to stand. Four hours later, the doe was still nowhere to be found. And though up and walking around a bit, the twins were still weak and hungry.

Around sunset that day, the twins had moved down the hill and were starting to bump into one another looking for a way to nurse. Still no mother. If I were to touch the newborns, the mother might permanently reject them. And none of the deer I had joined up with were domesticated—they were wild when I started working with them, and remained able to function in the wild. I was concerned that these little ones would "imprint" on us as parents, and would lose their ability to live as deer in the wild. I decided to let them go, hoping that the doe would return and suckle them during the night. The following morning, they looked pretty sad. Though loath to intervene, I finally did take action.

I gave them each three ounces of goat's milk. A farm goat had just given birth, so I got the first milk and the colostrum that comes with it. Then I left the twin fawns where they were. By sundown the next day the mother still had not returned, so we took out adoption papers. We brought the two babies to the breeding barn and started to feed them with the goat's milk at four-hour intervals for about three days. A Thoroughbred breeding farm makes this easy; our night foaling attendant is trained for this kind of work. Then I brought in a female goat who was fresh with milk and fostered them onto her, and they began nursing.

Cyrus and Reba, as we called them, were successfully established into the wild at about three months of age. A joy to have about, they spend most of their time a few hundred yards from the house, and are acutely responsive to the communication process. Both are extremely friendly with the people around us as well as with strangers. I can take them with me as I wander the ranch or leave them at home at will. They will eat out of my hand and, if I am not careful, follow me through the door into the house.

I have learned a great deal from my communication with the deer, but it is important to keep in mind that, in one sense, these deer I have chosen to work with have received no great favors from me. Living in the wild is a challenge for them once they lose their full desire to flee from danger. Because I have assumed responsibility for their protection, I have also learned to keep things as natural as I can, except for the communication work.

When I speak with equestrian groups around the world and mention working with deer in the wild, the response is usually disbelief: The deer will run away, there is no way to communicate with them. Yes, the deer will flee, but if you follow and then read the curve they make, you will see that they often circle around to stay within a given area. They do not continue on.

If I create in my mind's eye a round pen several miles in diameter, and if I think about the deer as horses in a round pen, I do, in fact, communicate with them effectively. It has worked for me virtually without fail. I have to be twice as tenacious and twice as delicate in my responses with deer as I do with horses, but it does work.

Working with deer is a time-consuming activity, which few people have the inclination to pursue. If I have been silly enough to accumulate this knowledge, others can learn from me and avoid having to walk about on a hillside for weeks at a time.

I like to think of myself as multilingual: I speak English (quite well actually), desperately poor Spanish, a better than passable Horse, and I can get along quite nicely in Deer.

CHAPTER 7

The Invitation That Changed My Life

One December evening in 1988, when I was fifty-three years old, my longtime friend and neighbor, John Bowles, called me. "Monty," he said in his unmistakable southern accent, "guess what? The Queen of England wants to meet you." Her Majesty, he said, was intrigued by my claims of being able to communicate with horses.

John Bowles is not above playing a practical joke or two. I asked why he, plain John Bowles, was carrying royal messages.

He replied that an English friend of his, a certain Sir John Miller, the Queen's former equerry—her horse manager—had instructed him to locate me. Her Majesty had noticed articles in *The Blood Horse* and *Florida Horse* (she is an avid reader of these and many other equestrian magazines) about demonstrations I had given.

Not long afterward, Sir John Miller came to the farm for a demonstration and was excited by what he saw. On the way back to the house, he listed particular dates during the following year—Her Majesty's itinerary. It began to sink in that he was fitting me into the royal schedule. Some weeks later, I received a formal letter of invitation from Buckingham Palace: in April 1989 I was to spend a week at Windsor Castle.

"I wonder," Sir John had asked me in his upper-class accent, giving every syllable its due, "if a demonstration such as I've just seen could be accomplished for Her Majesty in the mews?"

I had no idea what a mews was, but I nevertheless assured him that we could make it work somehow. If the Queen was convinced that my work was worthwhile, said Sir John, she would arrange for me to tour several British towns and cities. Most important, she would want Newmarket (home of the largest racing community in Britain) and Gleneagles (site of a large equestrian center) to be part of that itinerary.

After the better part of a lifetime concealing from the world what I knew about horses, the interest of the Queen offered the prospect of a door opening wide. If I could prove to Her Majesty's satisfaction that my work was credible and important, I could bring my methods to the broadest possible audience.

On April 5, 1989, I was met at Heathrow Airport by Sir John. We drove directly to Windsor Castle, a distance of only ten or fifteen miles. Parked there were vehicles that looked more like Sherman tanks than passenger cars. I was told the Queen was having lunch with Russian president Mikhail Gorbachev and his wife, Raisa, and they had shipped in their own cars for the occasion.

The interior of the castle was a revelation. Behind these doorways and in these corridors, great affairs of state had been conducted for hundreds of years. The royal family had owned racehorses for hundreds more years than my own country had existed. Walking past tapestries and huge paintings, I had the feeling that a country boy from California was going as far up in the world as it was possible to go.

Sir John took me down to a meadow in front of the castle, where he showed me fifteen horses of all colors, shapes and sizes. In a separate paddock was a Thoroughbred filly, making a total of sixteen horses, none of which had been ridden. All green and raw but halter-broken, these were the horses I would communicate with during my week-long series of demonstrations here.

Then Sir John took me to the stable area on one side of the castle. This, I understood at last, was the mews. Next we toured the indoor riding school. It had the look of a chapel, with Gothic-style windows and a high, vaulted ceiling. At one end, fronted with glass and wood, was a balcony—a soundproof viewing stand for the royal family. In the center of the riding school was a fifty-foot wire-mesh round pen that Sir John and I had arranged to be delivered and set up.

I had never demonstrated my techniques in such a pen before, and I was unsure how the horses would react. They would be able to see through the wire to the outside, which would reduce their focus on me. There was, however, no other option.

The Queen had apparently invited up to 200 people to watch me during the coming week. She herself would spend only an hour with me on the Monday morning—prior commitments would allow no more time than that—but she would probably watch the days' events on video in the evenings.

After our tour, Sir John and I walked back to Windsor Castle. The Gorbachevs were set to leave. It was an eerie feeling watching the Russian guards mingling with British security officers, men carrying machine guns around the ramparts of the castle. Some small upset occurred between the two factions and, as I watched, a senior British officer—clearly a master grudge holder—turned away muttering loudly, "By God, we stopped them in the Crimea and we'll stop them at Windsor Castle."

At nine o'clock the next morning, we were back at the castle so I could introduce the horses to the round pen. Experience has taught me that my demonstrations work more effectively when the horse is not overly distracted by his surroundings. When I arrived, I immediately sensed a cold feeling from the grooms; the head groom, in particular, seemed to think I was treading on his toes.

I had asked several times for assistance in shepherding these horses, one at time, into the pen. While I tried to muster aid, a lady dressed in impeccable riding clothes walked through the riding hall and started talking to Sir John. She was an erect, obviously self-assured woman with a commanding walk and demeanor. His transformation was remarkable: suddenly his stance, even the tone of his voice, changed.

He was talking with the Queen of England.

For some days I had pondered the proper salutation to use, should I meet her. And should I bow, or was a handshake the order of the day?

Now she was coming toward me. Far from home, the guest of a foreign nation, I wanted to do the right thing. But the Queen made it
easy for me by offering her hand. I shook it and said, "Your Majesty,"
and let it go at that. She was quick to put me at my ease. "Come, Mr.
Roberts," she said, "and show me this lions' cage in the center of the
riding hall. I want you to tell me about it."

Together we walked into the riding hall and looked at the wire-
mesh round pen. "It appears," she said, "to be the sort of thing you
should enter with a whip and a chair." I agreed with her, although the
similarity only then occurred to me, and I worried that it would strike
the horses as equally forbidding. I gave her a summary of what I intended to do the following morning. I was pleased that she wanted to
know as much as possible beforehand. Then she was gone.

I hoped I had at least made a good start. The relationship between
us was now relatively informal, and I had the impression of a straight-
forward woman who was making happen what she wanted to happen.

At midday on the Sunday, reinforcements arrived: Pat, my son,
Marty, and my rider Sean McCarthy, came directly to Windsor Castle. Working with me in the round pen for nine years, Sean has been
that first rider for more than 1,400 horses. Now, he and I went over
our equipment in the round pen; then I showed him the horses in the
field. He was surprised at the diverse range of animals. Standing in
the separate paddock were two or three mostly Thoroughbred horses;
the one filly was a registered Thoroughbred. There were two large
Shire Piebalds who would go on to be drum horses in the ceremonial
division of the royal stables, a few warm-blood crosses, a few other
large horses, and some smaller types right down to the Fell and
Haflinger ponies. I was reasonably confident that none would kill me.

Our preparation done, we spent the evening at Sir John's home,
Shotover House, near Oxford, which has been in his family for more
than a century. Together with Major Dick Hearn—who was Her
Majesty's racehorse trainer for many years—and his wife, Sheila, we
enjoyed a fine dinner that evening that went a long way toward
steadying my nerves for the following day. The next morning, at nine
o'clock, we were due to meet the Queen, Prince Philip, and Queen
Elizabeth, the Queen Mother, at the riding hall.

Once they arrived, the event took on official, even ceremonial, overtones. The woman in riding clothes was now the Queen of England attending an engagement. She and her party were surrounded by security personnel and subject to rules of protocol. Sir John Miller introduced us as though she and I had not spoken the day before, and he again pointed to the glassed-in viewing gallery from which the royal party would view the demonstration, as if no discussion of all of this had taken place. The event began to take on a life of its own.

I was, I admit, nervous. As a rule I am a relaxed person; my work requires it. How disconcerting, then, to feel my pulse rate soar and my concentration falter. The royal family, accompanied by Pat and Marty, moved to the gallery and took their seats.

I was charged first of all with "breaking in" the young Thoroughbred filly—owned by the Queen Mother herself, who would be watching intently. As I entered the round pen, it occurred to me that unless I relaxed I would not be able to communicate with the horse as I normally do. The filly would then not be receptive and this could become the most embarrassing and humiliating day of my life. As I closed the gate, a sense of terror engulfed me.

The filly—adolescent, skittish, and wide-eyed with fear—was brought in by her handler and released. I recognized a raw young creature more frightened than I was and needing my comfort and assistance. The instant I saw this, my nerves settled and I got down to work.

In minutes, I could feel things come right. The filly gave me the signals I was looking for and behaved exactly as I would have predicted. She was following me around the ring within seven minutes. In her predicament, she trusted me. I was her comfort.

Within fifteen minutes, this high-strung Thoroughbred stood steady as a rock while I fixed her first saddle on her. After just twenty-five minutes, she quietly accepted the bridle and snaffle bit, and Sean was on her back riding around the ring. It was as if she had been looking forward to this all her life. Finally, Sean dismounted and she was led away.

As I left the round pen, the Queen, Prince Philip, and the Queen Mother rose from their seats to come down and join me. The Queen was the first to emerge from the door of the viewing gallery. With a smile on her face, she put out her hand to shake mine and said, "That was beautiful." She told me she was amazed how the filly had responded, that I should feel proud of the work I was doing.

How long I had waited to hear someone say just that. For most of my life, my ideas on schooling horses had been scorned and rejected, my work done in virtual seclusion because no one was ready to see it. To have no less a person than the Queen of England, a woman who knows and cares for horses and is herself a leading expert on horses, praise my work in such warm and genuine language marked a profound and deeply satisfying turnaround, and I cherish it to this day.

Shortly afterward, Prince Philip shook hands and asked me if I could work with the young men who were "breaking in" some of his Fell ponies that week. I was delighted by these responses to my demonstration, but I confess I was waiting especially for a reaction from the filly's owner, the Queen Mother. Then she too appeared, and I was bowled over by the warmest appreciation I could have hoped for. With tears in her eyes, she quietly and firmly said, "That was one of the most wonderful things I've ever seen in my life." She was visibly moved by what she had seen her filly do, and by witnessing what communication is possible between human and horse.

Seeing her emotional reaction, I was caught up in the moment and I forgot who she was and where we were. It felt right to put my arms out and give her a gentle hug. The security guards stiffened with surprise and stepped forward. It hit me that no one was supposed to touch the royal family in this intimate way: I dropped my arms and stepped back a full stride.

However, the Queen Mother did not seem in the least offended. Still talking in a soft voice, she told me she hoped I would continue my work and bring about a different, more humane relationship between humans and horses. I think back on her reaction as being the one that would satisfy me for the rest of my life.

Imagine the impact of all this. It was as though I was finally allowed out into the daylight, blinking a bit in the fierce glare of publicity, but with my work recognized as valid and genuine. The Queen, one of the most important figures in the horse world, would actively promote public demonstrations of my work. But if I needed the royal seal of approval, so did some other doubting Thomases still need convincing.

After the first demonstration, we went with Sir John and twelve others, most of them journalists, to the Savile Gardens Restaurant in Windsor Park. During lunch, Sir John changed positions several times in order to have conversations on his radio phone. On the way back to the castle to continue our demonstrations, he mentioned to me that the stable staff were making an unscheduled stop to pick up two new horses.

Much later, I would learn that some members of the Queen's staff had suggested to her that I had done something underhanded with the horses as I took them through the ring to acclimatize them. In short, they suspected skulduggery. The Queen had not agreed with their judgment. What, she asked them, would convince them? They had suggested a stiffer test, one they doubted I would pass. A truck would be sent over to Hampton Court to pick up two large, three-year-old piebald stallions that were very raw and had barely been handled.

Sir John wanted me to start these horses without acclimatizing them to the ring. Because my working methods were new to him, it did not strike him as much of a request. It meant that the horses, however, faced a double and coincidental threat: the most traumatic experience of their lives to that point in a frightening new environment.

This new plan concerned me; there was enough pressure on the event, and on the horses, already. Back at the Windsor mews, a small van was parked with the two piebald stallions shoehorned into it. They were sweating and banging around. When the first was taken off, the other screamed fiercely and the first one called loudly back. They had been kept together in a field at Hampton Court, and were obviously deeply attached.

Meanwhile, a hundred guests had come to see the demonstration that afternoon. The stable staff were lined up against the wall, some of them smiling, there to watch me fail and my work be judged as fraudulent. Sir John took the microphone and stepped into the round pen to introduce me. The huge colt came charging toward him and slapped his big front feet on the ground, displaying his anger. Sir John stepped quickly back outside the gate and made the introduction from there. One could hardly blame him.

I was not happy about these new circumstances, which were both unfair and dangerous. The aggressive colt was still distracted by the other horse calling him from just outside the building. Suddenly, everyone stood up; the Queen had walked in. She was not scheduled to be here, but she obviously wanted to see the outcome of this new test. From an area behind the seats, she gestured to everyone that they might sit down. Sir John continued with his introduction and explained what they were about to see.

I stepped through the gate into the round pen, picked up my line and began. The colt circled me, acting with an all-male arrogance. I pressed him a touch harder to go away, and he did just that. As he left me and went to work, cantering a good circle against the fence, he forgot about his partner outside and tuned in to my presence and what I was doing. He was working hard for me. After three or four circles of the round pen, I was getting a good response from him and my voice rose a few decibels in volume.

"I'm looking to have the same conversation with him as I'm having with you. And I can assure you, he will talk to me. Watch out for the inside ear. The licking and chewing. The head down, skating a couple of inches above the ground. Great! There he goes...."

I wanted to drive it home—to the stable crew especially—that this was a legitimate process, that this horse was communicating with me. Indeed, I felt a good deal more comfortable conversing with this horse than I did with the skeptics in the royal stable. This unruly colt, after all, believed me within two minutes and trusted me after seven.

Sean rode him without difficulty and well before the thirty-minute mark. It was a perfect demonstration, and the Queen's reaction was one of pleasure and satisfaction. Her confidence in my work had been well-founded. As I waited for the big colt's companion, the stable hands started to filter back to their work areas. I politely asked them to come back and watch me start both horses from Hampton Court, not just one.

They returned to their old positions against the wall, but perhaps with slightly more open minds now. I started the second horse, and the demonstration went equally smoothly. For the rest of the week, I continued with demonstrations before different audiences. The doubt I had originally encountered was either gone, or had at least dissipated.

The Queen and others, most of them involved with royal horses, continued to ask guests to come to see what I could do. Each day brought audiences of 200 people. On the Tuesday morning, the Queen again arrived unexpectedly to watch the horses work. She returned on Tuesday afternoon, Wednesday morning, Wednesday afternoon, all day Thursday and Friday morning. It was an exhilarating feeling to have won her commitment to the extent that she changed her itinerary.

We share a genuine fascination with horses and it was a great pleasure to talk with her about them. As her support continued, my respect and feelings of warmth for her grew steadily.

At one point, my neighbor John Bowles arrived from California. When he entered the stable area, I was speaking with the Queen. John walked up behind her, off to one side and stuck his hand out with a big smile, ready to greet me. When he realized I was conversing with the Queen, a look of consternation fell across his face.

I had spent so much time with so many Sir Johns and Lady Annes by this point that when along came plain John Bowles, a good old boy from the deep South if ever there was one, I shook his hand and confidently said, "Your Majesty, this is Sir John Bowles." I had bestowed instant knighthood on an old friend for services rendered.

That week we started sixteen of the Queen's horses, four ponies for Prince Philip, the Queen Mother's filly and one show-jumping prospect owned by a friend of the Queen's—a total of twenty-two horses during the five days.

In addition, we decided to ride the Queen Mother's Thoroughbred filly each day and bring her on a bit, so that before we left the Queen Mother could watch her ridden in the open parkland surrounding Windsor Castle. There was the risk of embarrassment because a young horse going outside for the first time can do silly things, no matter how well started. I would take the risk.

That Friday in mid-April 1989 must be written in the record books as one of the most glorious, sunny days that England ever experienced. Only occasionally did billowy white clouds sail across those brilliant skies. Windsor, and England, looked as beautiful and civilized as only England can.

The Queen Mother was chauffeured in, and I stepped to an area near the car to greet her. Before the car had even stopped rolling, she opened the rear door with a big smile on her face and greeted me as though she had known me all her life. She gave her filly a rub on the nose and spoke with Sean, then greeted head groom Roger Oliver, Sir John and Pat.

With Roger leading on an experienced horse, Sean followed into the magnificent gardens on the filly and elegantly put her through her paces. On that day, in that setting, man and horse together seemed a thing of rare beauty, a scene that might have been taken straight from a fairy tale.

The Queen herself had an important engagement but she had asked to be informed when the filly was ridden in case she could slip away to see her. As we walked back up the hill toward the castle, we saw the Queen coming out of her apartments, dressed for her engagement. She greeted us with a warm smile and was generous in her praise of the filly on her first outdoor ride. Thanking me for spending the week at Windsor Castle, she went on to outline the plans she had for the countrywide tour on which I was due to embark. This day, this week, had been among the most rewarding in my life. The pressure had vanished, and our visit had been a success. For myself, my family, and for Sean, it had been a storybook week.

That afternoon, we went back to Shotover House to stay the night. Sean was looking forward to seeing Sir John's butler again, a man who went by the name of Horseman. Sir John called Horseman's wife, who also worked at Shotover House, Horsewoman. If Shotover House— that gracious, square-built manor—was as I expected, so was the English butler who came with it.

Horseman was probably no more than sixty, but he looked eighty-five. Stooped and gray, he had a sad, droopy face with big watery eyes. He was dressed properly, but his collars and cuffs had seen a lot of wear. His method was to move quickly, wobbling on his feet as if his joints were suspect. With each step he mumbled, and occasionally the mumbles got louder and took on a strangled quality. At first, I worried that he was about to die; then he would revert to his regular mumbling as if nothing had happened. He neither explained these outbursts nor sought any response.

When I arrived at the manor house, he trotted as fast as he could across the gravel and attempted to lift up my heavy suitcase, muttering away, "Oh-oh-oh-oh, I'll get that." It seemed unfair to ask him to carry anything, but he would not hear otherwise. While Horseman's arms were being pulled out of their sockets, Sir John introduced him: "Ah, this is my butler Horseman; he'll show you to your room. The Canopy Room, Horseman."

The shallow stone steps into the house were trouble enough, but now we faced several flights of stairs as well. Horseman soldiered on. Several times he had to stop and rest, clutching his chest and muttering. He settled me into my room and showed me the bathroom, made four more trips to fetch towels, and returned yet again with a pitcher of water and a glass. I feared each trip might be his last.

During dinner we saw his wife. Like Horseman but less disheveled, Horsewoman was apparently in charge of the kitchen; she helped him bring out the food and lay it on the sideboard.

When Sean arrived later in the week he came straight to me with disbelief written all over his face. "Did you see that butler guy?" He was entranced by this unique figure. Sean's room was a flight farther up than ours, so heaven knows how long it must have taken for him to be shown to his room.

One evening Sir John was expecting important company for dinner and he asked Horseman, "Can we have the sitting room in tip-top condition, please, for tonight? Give the room a thorough going-over." By day's end, Horseman had yet to reach this item on his list of duties, and we happened to see his version of "a thorough going-over." Conversing as usual with himself and carrying a feather duster, he batted anything that got in his way. Then he took the fifteen-foot-high curtains and flapped them against the walls, pushed a pile of newspapers to one side—and the sitting room was ready.

Before dinner, with all of us in the now tip-top sitting room, Sir

John got involved in a long telephone conversation. Horseman took orders for drinks, then disappeared.

Sir John remained on the phone and fifteen minutes ticked by. Still no Horseman. Fearing the worst, Sean volunteered to reconnoiter and found him leaning against a sideboard in the hall. Mumbling as ever, he was lifting each heavy glass decanter to his lips and taking long pulls, then shifting the decanters around as if they were pieces on a chessboard. Sean picked out enough words to understand that the butler was drinking from each decanter to determine its contents.

By the end of that evening, Horseman was flying. His manner became imperious; he played to the hilt the part of an English butler and announced new arrivals as though shouting over hundreds of people. He was magnificent. Sean followed him around like a puppy; a smile never left his face. Horseman and Horsewoman are both dead now, but they gave us much pleasure and many laughs, and I know Sir John must miss them. Sean and I were genuinely fond of that old man.

For our nationwide tour, Sean, Pat, and I had the use of a car loaned to us by the Queen—a rock-solid, bullet-proof Ford Scorpio. The response I got on the tour was remarkable. In Newmarket we faced five extraordinarily wild two- and three-year-olds. They were just a shade quieter than mustangs, extremely raw and green, but they were healthy and well-fed. The weather was hostile, with driving wind and rain on the second day, and I could not imagine that people would come. But 200 or 300 people braved that weather and the horses went well. One of them was filmed by Channel 4, which televised the event all over the British Isles. Sheik Mohammed and a contingent of people from the United Arab Emirates also came, and I am told they liked what they saw.

We stayed at Sandringham, on the Queen's property, with Michael Osborne and his wife. They arranged a wonderful dinner party where I answered many questions. Later we stopped at the Yorkshire Riding Centre, then pressed on to the impressive Gleneagles hotel and leisure facility in Scotland. Between 400 and 500 people attended and asked countless questions in Scottish accents so rich I really needed an interpreter.

In Scotland, Sean had just ridden a four-year-old stallion—an aggressive, well-fed animal, I remember, sixteen hands, two inches high and more than 1,200 pounds in weight. When the horse relaxed and forgot about being a stallion, he went beautifully. Up on his back for the first time, Sean could relax, and he called to me in a loud voice, "Fifty-first fluke in a row!"

I had to explain my laughter to the audience. "You know," I said, "every place we go, there's always someone who says that what they're watching must be a fluke. It's become a standing joke. New audience, new fluke! Well, as Sean mentioned, this is our fifty-first fluke in a row in this country, and I'm not even counting the many thousands of horses I've started before I landed at Heathrow."

We then flew to the Isle of Man, where we had perhaps our oddest experience. We were picked up at the airport by a woman in her late sixties who had seen much wind and sun and who went by the curious name of Dizzy Wriggle. Warmly gracious and hospitable, she told us en route that she and her husband lived in the cobbled stable block now; their old house was too big for them. Billy Wriggle got around in a wheelchair.

Pat, Sean, and I followed her into the most ancient house I have ever seen; it was close to a thousand years old. We would spend the night here. The smell in one room was deathly foul, and as I approached the fireplace I saw the source: a horse's foot on the mantel. After a favorite horse had died, Dizzy had someone saw off one foot and prop it there without curing it.

The mansion had not been lived in for a long time. Huge old toilets, their cracked wooden seats dating from the dark ages, sheltered spiders. Taps produced leaves and twigs. Dizzy disappeared into a bedroom and started shouting: she was throwing a tribe of dogs off our bed. Whippets and spaniels and setters tumbled past us, and we wondered if the mastiffs had the house to themselves.

That night, we dined in the main house—its kitchen kick started for the occasion—with the most stimulating company. They were far removed from our experience of life, yet they received us with much hospitality and genuine interest. Though the plates were chipped and the glasses leaked, everything was done properly. Billy Wriggle, his white hair greased back, sat at the end of the table, stoic in his demeanor, talking in a voice as loud as a bugle. He spilled generous quantities of food and wine down his canary-yellow sweater.

The lady to my right enlightened me on the history of personal hygiene. "Washing yourself," she began, "is unhealthy. All this soap—destructive to your skin. And our ancestors knew that. In former times, they didn't do all this silly washing. When they went to the loo, they merely dipped their hands in a bowl of potpourri and emerged fragrant and refreshed."

Following tradition, the ladies were then asked to leave the room. Billy Wriggle produced a box of Havanas that may have predated the house, and everyone proceeded to try to light the things. Port was served. There followed more questions, disagreements, discussions, and more to drink. We toasted the Queen. One by one, each man stood to deliver his own recitation—amusing or solemn, about Mother England and the Crown. After each pronouncement came another toast: "God Save the Queen."

When the ladies returned, the party began to break up. I helped Dizzy load Billy into the car to drive the short distance to the stable block. Convinced she would have to flee something in the night—spiders, ghosts, dogs—Pat went to bed fully dressed.

The next morning the three of us walked down to the stable block where the same pack of dogs all gathered in a circle, noses to the ground, tails wagging. They were lapping at a large pool of blood. It seems that Dizzy, while transferring Billy from the car to his wheelchair, had dropped him, and he had bled profusely onto the cobbles from a deep cut on his leg. He was at the hospital now, recovering. So this was old-fashioned, upper-class English life!

After the Isle of Man we went to Chichester, a country town in the south of England, and started some New Forest ponies and wild horses, mostly for people involved in the Pony Club and the horse-show circuit. Various other dates brought the head-count to ninety-eight horses and ponies. On average, each horse accepted saddle, bridle, and rider in twenty-seven minutes. Returning to Shotover House, we spent a day with Sir John and gave him an account of our tour. I also wrote a report for the Queen and left it with him to deliver personally.

When we flew home to California, I had the feeling that life would never be the same again. As the plane lifted off that beautiful, crowded island—"this sceptered isle . . . this blessed plot," as the bard called it—I imagined all the horses down there whose lives we had briefly touched and I wanted to continue. I believed I would return to Britain many times in the future, and I was right.

It also looked as if my association with the Royal Family's horses would continue. The Queen had asked if she could send people to California to study my techniques and to start her young horses accordingly. Victor Blackman from Dick Hearn's yard, and later from Lord Huntington's yard, would do just that, and returned to take charge of starting the Queen's yearlings.

Corporal Major Terry Pendry, who oversaw the starting of horses for the Household Cavalry, and Richard Maxwell, also in the Household Cavalry, would also study extensively with me. These were new opportunities, and I was glad to accept them.

When Ireland beckoned in 1990, for example, I went. I found the Irish people down-to-earth and interested in testing me to the hilt. They brought me tough horses and demanded honesty and openness in my dealings with them.

My Irish contact was Hugh McCusker, who is famous for his hunter show horses. It put a different spin on my visit there and opened up a new world for me. Hugh is known on the English show-horse scene as "the flamboyant Irishman," and I would go along with that description.

Hugh had scheduled a demonstration in the town of Kill, near Dublin. The property we were to use had just been bought by the president of the Irish Draft Horse Association, Fenton Flannely and he was keen to use the demonstration as a launch for his facility. He asked me to start a pair of fillies and said there would possibly be a third horse.

As was routine by now, we arrived beforehand to introduce the horses to the round pen.

One of the horses, a flashy three-year-old Irish draft colt called Stanley, had feet the size of dinner plates and a neck you would have trouble encircling with your arms. This was the mysterious "third horse."

Shown the pen, Stanley seemed quite alert—an "all-boy" sort, aggressive and uncooperative. Hugh knew nothing of the colt's history, only that he was completely green. When it was time for Stanley to return to his stall, two boys came for him. This did not seem out of line at the time, but all came clear later.

That evening, before a near-capacity crowd of about 500 people, both fillies went extremely well, and we were, if anything, ahead of schedule. Hugh said the owner wanted to break for refreshments but would I then start the big colt, Stanley? Fair enough, I said.

When it was announced over the public address system that I would soon be in the pen with Stanley, a ripple of interest ran through the crowd. My experience in match racing and rodeos in small towns told me there was something in the wind. By ten P.M. there were more people in the building than *before* the break: every seat was filled, and many people were standing. Hugh McCusker explained: When people heard that Stanley was going to be started without a lead rope on his head, many in the audience had telephoned their friends to come and see this cowboy get eaten alive.

When Stanley was brought into the building, he was cautiously led by the two lads, each with a lead rope on either side. They kept their distance from him, and a third groom kept him moving from behind. When he was inside, they gently released the two lead ropes.

With the adrenaline surging in his body from being under the lights and having hundreds of people watching him, Stanley marched around the pen and appeared very much in charge. This was a colt with a well-earned reputation. I switched on my lapel microphone and announced to the crowd that I was ready to go ahead. As I walked toward the gate leading into the round pen, you could have heard a pin drop.

I opened the gate and stepped into the pen. At that time Stanley was on the far side, about fifty feet from me. As I closed the gate behind me and stepped away from the fence, he arched his neck and marched about three steps toward me. Then he pinned his ears back, bared his teeth, and came at me, full-speed. The audience gasped. I tripped the latch on the gate and stepped outside. The colt slammed to a halt inches from the fence and turned away to show off his supremacy.

"Wow!" I exclaimed to the crowd. "What are you trying to do to me here?" I shook my head and put my hands on my hips, looking around at the banks of people sitting and staring. "Surely the nice people of Ireland wouldn't set me up for something like this, would they?"

Not a word was spoken, not a sound could be heard. I stood there for a while; then I sat down on a chair near my gate and gave the impression that I was very worried about going into the pen and dealing with this horse. I addressed the audience again. "On this trip I've met a lot of skeptical Irish horsemen who feel that some of my work is less than believable. Now, I know that Ireland is filled with good horsemen—in fact, I'm sure there are a lot of them in the building right now. And since I'm a fifty-six-year-old man who's completely out of shape and has had half his backbone surgically removed, I'd very much like to ask for a volunteer to come and deal with this horse. It would be interesting to see what an Irish horseman could do with a horse as aggressive as this."

I sat there for a few seconds and listened to this deep silence. In truth, I wanted to see a few red faces. And then I said in a surprised voice, "No volunteers? Come on, think about it. Let's get some young kid down here who's in good shape, and he can go ahead and do this horse. I'll make some suggestions from outside the ring."

The silence endured. The only sound was of the colt's breath and his giant foot pawing at the floor of the round pen. Then I said, "Well, I guess I'm going to have to go ahead and do him." From my equipment bag I took my nylon rope, entered the pen and immediately started to swing a loop.

This young Irish draft horse had never seen a cowboy before, so he stood off and moved around the perimeter of the pen and looked me over. He was confused enough by this loop whirling around my head; he wasn't going to try to charge through it.

We circled one another for a few seconds and I started to close in on him. He went into a high-stepping trot near the fence. I continued to close on him, and he picked up speed. When the time was right, I threw the loop, which caught him around the neck. This was real western stuff I had been doing all my life.

The colt went crazy. He bawled and bucked and did everything he could do to shed this rope. Now he had a new concern: I was not the problem, the rope was. I would just give him a little tug now and then, and he would go into renewed orbit, expressing all the rage he had locked up in him. This went on for thirty or forty seconds; then he settled down and came to a stop.

At that point I slipped in near him, and I wound the rope around his head in a come-along—a way, remember, to apply pressure to nerves on the horse's head.

And then I started to school Stanley on the come-along. His aggressive tendencies were clearly obvious for about five minutes. Then he began to settle and respond to me; he started giving me the early signs of "join-up"; he opened up an ear to me, according me that much respect anyway. Then I observed his tongue come out from between his teeth, and he was licking and chewing. I was communicating with him pretty well within five to eight minutes.

Rather than go through the normal loose-horse or free-horse join-up, I continued to work with the come-along on him. He would have been a very dangerous horse to work with had I released him in the pen.

When he was comfortable, I put the saddle on his back and he had a few complaints about that, but not too many. He started to calm down a bit and have confidence in me. I put on the bridle, then long-lines, and I long-lined him pretty hard for about ten or twelve minutes. I brought in my rider, who was a game lad to climb on such a monster animal with the power of two normal horses. But the colt was acting well, and I was giving him plenty of encouragement. Once the rider was up and he was working in a controlled circle, we gave him about fifteen minutes of trotting and cantering. The colt performed well in what I still consider one of the best demonstrations I have ever done. The Irish crowd was amazed and full of questions. I could have stayed there for hours talking with them about what they had seen, but I was ushered away to a party at the owner's house.

There I finally learned the story. Stanley had been the champion in-hand Irish draft at the Dublin Horse Show the year before as a two-year-old, but he had become very aggressive and had been kept in a dark stall ever since. I was, more than anything, pleased to have plucked him from the darkness. With proper handling, he could now shrug off his reputation and put the trauma behind him.

In 1996, I returned to the same venue. They had put up some show-jumping fences in one corner of the arena, but I thought nothing of it. But after my demonstration, the organizers unveiled their surprise for me. "Monty," said one, "this is Stanley, and he's now Ireland's finest show-jumping Irish draft horse." They brought him in and a young rider put Stanley through his paces. All his power and grace were now controlled and fluid. The big colt was wonderful to behold as he jumped those fences.

Another trip to Ireland took me to the Irish National Stallion Show at Ballinasloe, in the very center of Ireland. The stallion festival was a large event held in the bowl of a valley, but the bowl seemed to be rapidly filling with water. It was a quagmire. We have drops of rain in California—sometimes big drops during a storm—but I had never witnessed these curtains of water that were now drifting across the countryside.

Why not cancel the event? Hugh McCusker pointed out that if they started canceling events in Ireland because of rain, there would be none left to go to. The brave Irish turned up and stayed. By the time we had rented a four-wheel drive vehicle and made our way into the grounds, there must have been 3,000 people there. The place looked like Woodstock, except that everyone was in oilskins.

The two stallions we would start were in a truck on a nearby promontory, so we slogged our way up there. They were squeezed into a tiny van where they banged and kicked; steam rolled from air vents set into the top. A young Irish fellow, soaked to the skin, was in charge. We agreed not to unload the horses to show them the round pen—the return swim to the trailer would have been treacherous. This was going to be a once-only effort. When the time came, the round pen was a mudhole with me in the middle of it.

In the absence of a lapel microphone, someone gave me a remote microphone the size of a cucumber. How to attach it to me so I had both hands free was a problem. They took my coat and shirt off, taped the cucumber to my chest, then squeezed the water out of my clothes and allowed me to put them back on.

The first stallion was sliding down the hill, towing the lad behind him like a dinghy behind a sailboat. The horse's neighbor in the trailer was screaming, and he was screaming back. When the stallion stepped into the round pen, his feet were sucked into mud a foot deep. He probably could not have run from me had he wanted to.

I started my usual introduction. "Ladies and gentlemen…" But with a fizz and a crackle, the cucumber died. By this time, I was too drenched to care. I was just going to go on, try to rescue some sort of demonstration and get out of there.

Hugh ran to the announcer's stand. Seconds later I heard his voice come over the public address system, loud and clear: "Monty Roberts's microphone has been drowned out, so I'm going to take over, and I know he would have said something along the following lines: "Good afternoon, ladies and gentlemen, my name is Monty Roberts and we're here today to…" Hugh McCusker was my voice that day, and he did fine.

Perhaps the horses wanted out of the rain as much as we did: they were begging to join up with me. They seemed to understand how important it was that they cooperate. Together, they were two of the best demonstrations of the language of Equus that I have ever undertaken.

Afterward, Hugh McCusker and I headed straight for the nearest supply of best Irish malt whisky.

CHAPTER 8

When a Racehorse's Worst Nightmare Is a Starting Gate

I look back on my life and clearly see that certain events were more than just points on a calendar: some actually changed the pattern of my life altogether.

The first of these occurred in 1943 when my father killed the black man; my conversation with Brownie in 1948 also looms large. In 1956 I married Pat, and I now know how fortunate I was to find her, how essential is her support and tolerance for my shortcomings and maniacal approach to work. The births of our children—Debbie in 1957, Laurel in 1959, and Marty in 1961—also profoundly influenced my life.

There is the Monty Roberts before 1989, when I spent my first week with the Queen and her family, and the Monty Roberts who came afterward.

With horses, there was my life before and after Johnny Tivio: I have never gotten close to another horse with a brain like his; he trained me, not I him.

My experience with a horse called Lomitas in 1991 must be counted as the most recent landmark event in my life.

Owned by Walther J. Jacobs of Bremen, Germany, and placed in training there with the gifted Andreas Wohler, Lomitas was a good-looking chestnut colt that would race in the colors of Gestut Fahrhof, the Jacobs stud farm. Lomitas's sire is Nininski and his dam is La Colorada, by Surumu.

By early 1990 Lomitas began to show potential by turning in speedy workout times, and by early that summer he looked to be a fine prospect. Lomitas won both of his starts in 1990, and that year was the highest-rated two-year-old in Germany. Gestut Fahrhof was no stranger to top horses, but it is always an honor to have a champion two-year-old. The Kentucky Derby and other classic races for three-year-olds present themselves as exciting targets. This was the kind of horse Lomitas was.

The first sign of trouble came in April 1991. Lomitas was prepped and ready for his debut as a three-year-old, but he initially balked at loading in the van to go to the race. At the track, there was a bigger problem: the starting gate. The horse repeatedly refused to go inside, threw his head up, sidestepped, and pulled back. Other horses and their jockeys were in their stalls, awaiting Lomitas. No one likes this situation, least of all the jockeys, for whom sitting in the starting gate is always a nerve-racking time.

After close to twenty minutes of struggle, the race began and Lomitas won. But imagine the apprehension in the Gestut Fahrhof camp when their champion came so close to being disqualified. After two weeks of more schooling and tests before race stewards—who warned that a similar episode would result in a life ban—Lomitas was entered in a race on a turf course in Cologne. Once more it proved difficult to load him into the van—but what happened on the track that day defies belief.

Lomitas was the last horse brought to the starting gate, and again he refused to enter. As they had on the previous occasion, the other horses stood and waited for twenty minutes while track officials literally wrestled with Lomitas. They put a hood on to blindfold him, they yanked his tail up over his back and even the jockey's shoulder. (Perhaps they thought the tail was a lever they could use to pry him into the gate.) A dozen men, some in front, some behind, alternately pulled and pushed the horse, trying to force him forward and into the gate.

At that point, Lomitas became vicious, attacked the men, and caused injuries. He ended up lying on the ground, exhausted from the fight. The race finally started, but without Lomitas. He lay behind the starting gate like a fallen athlete, immobile, on his side. Immediately after the race, the stewards carried through with their threat. The owners, the Jacobses, left the track in despair. Their young champion horse was not only a nonperformer, but a convicted criminal who would never race again.

By this time, I had a reputation for successfully treating remedial Thoroughbred racehorses. Andreas Wohler, Lomitas's trainer, asked me if I would set the horse straight. So on June 12, 1991, I put my life aside and left for Germany.

At the airport, I saw a young man in riding breeches, perhaps a Wohler stable hand sent to meet me. "Do you know Andreas Wohler?" I asked him. He smiled. "I am Andreas Wohler."

We drove immediately to the Bremen Racecourse (where Andreas and others lease facilities for training and stabling their strings of horses). There I met the superstar, Lomitas. When I entered his box stall, he turned his head to look at me. Out loud, and full of awe, I said the single word "Gorgeous!" He was a registered Thoroughbred stallion, sixteen hands high, 1,150 pounds, chestnut in color. He had a white pastern on the off-hind leg and a star between his eyes with an elongated strip that widened and ended between his nostrils. I could see every point of his skeletal frame hitting its mark: he had a near-perfect Thoroughbred racehorse conformation. "Correct of limb, in every way," I said.

I walked over to where he was munching hay, standing against the back of his stall, and greeted him with a stroke on his neck. "Hello, Lomitas, you're a fine man, eh?" I proceeded to move my hands back along his body, and I felt that he wanted to move into my hands, away from the wall. I held out against the pressure, and he immediately kicked out behind. I logged this as a possible response to any number of things, and continued making his acquaintance. He struck me as a breathtaking animal, with a look in his eye that spoke of very high intelligence. I had traveled a long way to be standing here, and suddenly I was pleased to have made the journey.

My task was specific: cure this horse of his starting-gate terror. After discussing it on the phone beforehand, Andreas had constructed for our mission a solid-wall, permanent training gate, which was much safer than the conventional kind. I would work with Lomitas in the center of a riding hall on the Bremen Racecourse where the footing was secure and the facilities are first-class.

I would need an assistant, someone who could speak English and who knew horses as well. With remedial horses, the people are as important to the success of the project as the horse. Andreas introduced me to a young man by the name of Simon Stokes. Talented and courteous, Simon Stokes is a former champion jump jockey from Chichester whose nose had been broken many times from pushing fences over with his head. He also rode on the flat and helped Andreas train horses; after living in Germany for eleven years, he spoke fluent German. With Simon and Andreas I had expert help.

On June 13, I set about trying to get to know Lomitas a little better. I took him into the covered riding hall—a small track 200 yards in circumference and sixteen feet wide. Standing there with him, I moved to the end of the rope and asked him to step toward me. He seemed reluctant to step into my space. I raised one arm sharply above my head, then the other. He did not seem unduly alarmed, which told me that he had not been abused by punishments that come from a raised hand. I stood next to him and lifted my knee and leg under his keel. Again, there was no discernible tightening of the abdominal muscles, no sudden grunt or lifting of the thorax. Plainly, he had not been abused in that area either. Then I took a short length of rope and swung it near his head. He paused and looked at me, then moved sideways and paused again. In his own intelligent fashion, he was struggling to understand me, but his lack of panic told me he had not been whipped.

Finally, I led him closer to the wall and placed my hands along his side, as if to hold him closer against the wall. Immediately, he kicked out and plunged forward, showing classic signs of claustrophobia.

This much was clear: Although his relationship with humans was obviously a good one, he was prepared to blame us for placing him inside enclosed structures such as starting gates and vans. And he was perfectly happy to express that discomfort to his handlers. As Lomitas saw it, people were treating him unfairly.

I stopped to allow the pair of us a breather. Looking at his fine build and marking the extraordinary intelligence in his eye, I thought, I am in the presence of greatness. I had better do my job with patience, diligence, and competence.

If I tested Lomitas for signs of abuse, it was not because I distrusted Andreas and Simon. I always accord my horses the respect of asking them to speak for themselves. I have been lied to by humans but never by a horse; it's not within his scope. And unlike a green horse (who is more like a blank slate), any horse ever handled by humans comes with stories, perhaps baggage and sometimes terrible events etched on their psyches. Lomitas was telling me, "I have been treated unfairly and I fear it's going to get worse."

When Andreas and Simon returned to the stable from their other duties, I was back near Lomitas's stall, leading him around. I asked, "Can we use a round pen or lunging ring somewhere nearby, so I can work him?"

"Hmmm...that might be difficult," said Andreas.

"I need to turn him loose, to let him go on his own and win his trust."

I felt that if I could join up with Lomitas he might accept the confined positions we asked him to walk into. "Well," said Andreas after giving the matter some thought, "there's a show-jumping ring about ten miles away, but we'd need to get him into a transport truck to take him there, which counts that out."

"No," I replied, "hang on, we can do the van, I'm sure we can." Andreas and Simon were both nervous about this, but clearly it had to be done. So they ordered a van. When it arrived, Andreas suggested backing the van into the barn: with the ramp in the center aisle, Lomitas would be less able to slip around the side.

"He's going to have to learn to enter the van like a gentleman one day," I replied, "and we might as well start as we mean to go on. Let's deal with this in the middle of the yard and do it properly from the outset."

With the van parked there, the ramp down and waiting, I attached a long lead rope to his halter (a come-along) and schooled him for about half an hour. During the schooling process he was obedient, hard-working and well-mannered. Until he showed me a problem, I was going to treat him like a normal horse, and that meant loading him into the van.

I walked up the ramp and he willingly followed me into the van. The instant he was inside, the helpers standing by ran to lift the ramp. "No," I told them, "leave the ramp down. I'm going to walk him off and on several times." The Irish exercise riders who were there warned me: "If you bring him off, you'll never get him back on again."

Have a little faith, I suggested. I walked Lomitas off and on the van without incident fifteen to twenty times before we closed it up and made our trip to the show-jumping yard. The building offered good footing, but it was too big: 150 feet long and 100 feet wide. Ideally I needed a fifty-foot round pen.

With jump poles and standards, I fashioned a round pen, built it, in fact, around Lomitas while he stood there watching me. Then I went to work.

Free of any rope on his head, he went into flight immediately when I pressed him away from me. He cantered steadily around the perimeter, with one ear already locked on to me. Within a minute or two, he understood what I was doing and I began to observe some licking and chewing. He was such an intelligent horse that in less than fifteen minutes he was in full conversation with me. I quickly had a good join-up; he trusted me.

Now I wanted to take this trust a bit further. I dismantled the jump poles, so that we now occupied the main arena. It took a few minutes. He ran away from me for a while and thought he was going to take charge, but as soon as I told him to go away, farther away, he was pressing to come back. I would go anywhere in the building, and he was right there with me, his nose to my shoulder.

When that happened, I felt confident we could work through the problems with the starting gate. Going home, he entered the van like an old horse who had never had a problem with vans. Back at the stables in Bremen, we put him away, fed him, and left him to have a good night's rest.

On June 15, 1991, I started to work Lomitas in the permanent training gate. I was banking on his trust, on taking it one step at a time, and on creating within him a desire to enter the gate. Within a short period, he was going in and out with no problems. Later that morning, Simon put some tack on him and sat on his back while I led him in and out. We were able to close the gate behind him and initiate the process of letting him walk out in a very relaxed manner. This took us through the morning.

In the afternoon, Andreas had invited the head starter from the Bremen Racecourse to watch Lomitas walking in and out of the training gate. He spent about an hour with me that day and was impressed by what he saw. The starter would recommend that the stewards reassess the situation and give Lomitas another chance—if he could pass all the necessary tests.

During the first test the next morning in proper racing gates at the Bremen Racecourse, Lomitas was troubled and a bit difficult at times, but he was trying hard for me, and before the morning was over he was going in and out of the gates easily. The stewards then set up another test on June 18. They would want to see Lomitas exhibit the same steady behavior, but this time with other horses in the starting gate. Lomitas passed that test with flying colors, but it was still not the way I wanted it. He was a little tentative entering and a little nervous while in there.

Andreas wanted to run Lomitas at Bremen on June 23. The stewards, though, would require yet another test—and this time they would want him to be nearly perfect. Only then would they consider reinstating him.

On the morning of June 20 we all assembled in front of the Bremen grandstand. With three horses for company in the starting gate, Lomitas was close to perfect. The stewards said they would reinstate the horse for one race and then reassess. They added a proviso that I come with him, and that nobody from the track handle him. To avoid him standing in there for a long period, it was also suggested that Lomitas be the last horse to enter the starting gate.

The morning of the race I was tense. I felt the gaze of all 20,000 people in the stands. Lomitas had become something of a legend among German racing fans. A national hero with an immense following, he was the gifted horse who had fought with his trainers and refused to race. As I walked Lomitas around behind the starting gates, parents were holding little children over the fence and calling out, "Oh, Lomi, Lomi, Lomi."

We walked around behind those stalls for what seemed an interminable length of time. Finally, I realized that something was wrong. All the other horses in the race were gathered to one side of the track and the jockeys were deep in conversation. Andreas was huddling with the head starter and other officials.

Finally, Andreas came to me with the news that the jockeys would boycott the race unless Lomitas entered the gate first. They said they were tired of being put in the gates and waiting for Lomitas to have it out with the starting-gate crew.

I said it made no difference to me. I walked Lomitas right in: he was good as gold. As I stood there with him, thanking him for giving us a good result on this important occasion, a starting-gate attendant opened the gate in front of us, then—with me directly in Lomitas's path—he went around behind and closed the back gate. Normally this is never done: I could have been severely trampled.

Then it hit me: perhaps the starting-gate crew did not *want* this to work. With their straps and ropes and blindfolds, they would brush Lomitas as they went behind him. Accidental or intentional, I cannot say, but the horse never did misbehave. If they were surly then, the crew would have been more so later: the burden of the coverage in the sports pages that evening was that the German starting-gate attendants had been put to shame by a Californian.

Lomitas stood there calmly while they loaded the other horses. And, in a delicious bit of irony, track officials had considerable difficulties with some of the *other* horses. Finally, all were loaded. Lomitas broke well. He stayed in third or fourth position for much of the race and, with his great talent, simply overwhelmed the field in the last quarter mile. It was an undiluted pleasure to see that horse take his rightful place in the winner's enclosure.

This triumph was the first in a series of victories for Lomitas. Later that year, he would be named Germany's champion three-year-old and Horse of the Year. His earnings climbed to 1,600,000 deutsch marks ($1.1 million U.S.).

Such an experience with a horse of this quality bonds man and beast in a way not easy to describe. In just a short time, I felt the same degree of love for Lomitas as I had for Johnny Tivio, Brownie, and Ginger. Lomitas finished his year with three Group I victories in succession, the highest-rated German racehorse in the history of the country.

Andreas gave Lomitas an easy time through the winter of 1991 in order to prepare for the 1992 racing season. Hopes were high for another outstanding year, but then the story took a strange, dark twist. Lomitas was owned by Walther Jacobs, a man I came to know and admire, and one of the finest owners in the racing industry. In 1991, he was eighty-four years old, and his courage and determination would be tested as the Lomitas story unfolded.

Early in 1992, before the racing season began, Mr. Jacobs received a blackmail letter demanding 400,000 deutsch marks, or Lomitas would be harmed or killed. He told me they were taking special precautions with security, and naturally he was concerned. It occurred to me that Mr. Jacobs might simply want to back away from the whole situation and retire Lomitas from racing. He was, however, determined to meet it head on.

I went to Hamburg in June 1992 and watched Simon, who was now handling Lomitas in the starting gate. Lomitas had no problems and won the race. Everything seemed fine. But blackmail letters were still coming and still threatening harm to the horse if the extortionist was not paid. To signal his intent, the letter-writer burned down a hay barn on the Gestut Fahrhof stud farm.

Guards with dogs were deployed around the clock, and additional security was arranged. In late July 1992 Lomitas made the trip to Düsseldorf. He entered the gate without incident and ran in the race, but his performance was lackluster and he finished fifth. He was clearly not himself, and a new letter from the blackmailer pointed to the reason: "We only gave him enough to make him sick," it read. This was simply a warning shot across the bow—to demonstrate that someone had access to the horse and the will to harm him.

Now events took on a new momentum: Lomitas would go into hiding when he was well enough to travel. He would be quarantined in England, then travel to the United States, where he would race in California. I was amazed at the strength and tenacity of Mr. Jacobs through all of this. Another owner might have hidden from the blackmailer, but Mr. Jacobs, in essence, said, "This man will not stop me from racing my horse if I want to race him."

We had to wait fifteen days before moving Lomitas because he became very ill. The letter indicated he had been given a heavy metals poison, which affected his liver and other vital organs. He was a cruel sight. The beautiful horse hung his head, and his eye was dull; he was turned in on himself, concentrating on the illness and the pain. We all felt great anger and incomprehension that anyone could be capable of doing this.

Lomitas fought off the poison within ten days. His head came up, he began to eat a little. A measure of interest returned to his expression. As quickly as possible, he was shipped in secret to Newmarket. Only an inner circle of high-ranking police officers, Lufthansa officials, and people in Mr. Jacobs's office knew of the plan. Simon had once ridden a horse called Pirelli, and that was the name we gave him. In England, we hid him in Susan Piggot's yard.

During the four-week quarantine period, Simon gradually put Lomitas back to work. In mid-September, he was placed in training with Ron McAnally at Santa Anita, California. Lomitas trained well through October and November, and looked to be ready to start racing at Santa Anita after Christmas.

But unexpectedly, in mid-December, Lomitas developed a quarter crack on the off-fore foot. This was a blow to me, for Lomitas never had a foot problem the whole time he trained and raced in Germany. A patch was applied to the crack and training continued. Soon other cracks showed up, on a rear foot, then on the near-fore foot. All this within a three-week period.

Ron McAnally knew of a good quarter-crack specialist in New York by the name of Ian McKinley. We had him flown out and at a roundtable discussion at the track with the veterinarians and other farriers, McKinley asked, "What happened to this horse about five months ago?" At that moment the connection became clear. "He was poisoned," I replied.

McKinley showed me a band of disconnected foot wall about half an inch wide right around all four feet on Lomitas. I had not made the connection until Ian asked the question. The band of tissue had darkened around the entire foot, and the foot had grown down, this separated area had been taxed and the cracks resulted.

McKinley used a substance called Equilox on each foot, whether it had cracks or not. He was strengthening the wall artificially by laying this space-age polymer over the top. We were then able to train Lomitas without further cracks developing, but it was February before he could race.

In his first race, the horse who crossed the line before Lomitas had interfered with him, and Lomitas was named the winner. His next race was in April at Hollywood Park. Distracted just as the gates opened, he got off to a terrible start and began nine lengths behind the leader. Even as the field turned for home, he was probably twelve to fifteen lengths behind.

Then he made a blinding run at the leaders. He ran the fastest last quarter ever undertaken at Hollywood Park. As far as we could tell, had he broken with the pack at the beginning he would have been only two-fifths of a second off the world record for that distance.

But his feet continued to plague him, and it was decided to retire him to stud. He left the United States in 1994 to stand at Gestut Fahrhof for the breeding season of 1995. While his American initiative fell short of my goals, Lomitas earned approximately $100,000 and served notice that he was a formidable competitor on the American race scene.

The German breeders have responded strongly to Lomitas as a breeding prospect, and he was booked to sixty mares in 1996 and sixty more in 1997. Like a true champion, he does this job well, too. He has a conception rate in the ninety-percentile range. It will be interesting to see if Lomitas can pass along his talents to the next generation. My hope is that his story is just beginning.

As for the extortion attempt, no one was ever arrested, but the police did confront a likely suspect and the letters ceased.

———

Plainly, horses and starting gates sometimes mix like oil and water, and if Lomitas presented a great challenge in that regard, so did a horse with the imposing name, Prince of Darkness.

In 1990, I was staying in an English country house. It was the dead of night, but sleep would not come. Prince of Darkness was the source of my insomnia, and I could not stop thinking about him. Getting out of bed, I began to pace up and down the upstairs landing. What could I do with this horse? Where was the gap in my understanding of this big, highly charged animal?

Then I heard footsteps. A door opened and my host, Sir Mark Prescott, appeared, likewise in his robe. The two of us blinked at each other.

"I'm sorry if I disturbed you," I said "but I couldn't sleep. I can't seem to get my brain to stop working."

Sympathizing, Sir Mark took up a position at the window, his face cast in moonlight. Suddenly, his expression sharpened. "Well, I'll be," he muttered softly. "Come and see."

I went and stood next to him. From the window, we could see over the sloping roof of the house to the stable yard. In the moonlight we could clearly make out Prince of Darkness, his head appearing first at the window of his stall and then at the door as he walked around. He was as awake as we were.

Sir Mark sighed. "That's three of us trying to work out what's wrong, then."

Prince of Darkness had been trained by Sir Mark in Newmarket, and was owned by Pin Oak Stables of Kentucky, along with English partners. He was a large-framed dark bay standing about 16.3 hands high, very muscular and long in the body.

He must have weighed 1,400 pounds, but he was no big clod of a horse: he was bright in his eyes, with alert ears, well-balanced and well-proportioned. They called him Prince of Darkness because he had once killed a steer in the paddock, perhaps not viciously but after rough play. He would have been like a cat playing with a mouse. This horse was on fire all the time but nothing set him off more than starting gates.

Starting gates were not built for a horse his size: he was so long that his nose touched the front gate and his hindquarters pressed into the rear gate, and so broad that the rails touched him on either side.

Typically of horses who learn to hate starting gates, his first few entries had been trouble-free. Then one day they were loading him during a training session on the heath in Newmarket, and he failed to step in fully. An attendant slapped him on the outer thigh with his hand and the horse kicked out, hitting the side of the starting gate. He subsequently developed a negative attitude toward all gates—while walking toward them, entering them, or standing inside.

I had come to England to work with him once already and thought the job had been done, but I was not back in California three days before I got a call from Sir Mark. I was disappointed, but I also stand behind my work and I returned immediately on a no-fee basis.

What had happened was this: They had apparently gone to the gates on the heath and Prince of Darkness had been upset from the time he arrived. They got him in, but once there he had tried to kick the gate to pieces. Now he would go nowhere near one.

What had changed him so much? I had had him going in and out of starting gates like a dream. And now the three of us—the horse, Sir Mark, and me—were bedeviled by it all and sleepless to boot.

That night, over dinner, I asked Sir Mark what it was like to transport Prince of Darkness in a van. The horse was no problem, he said, whether the stalls were narrow or wide. This was hard to believe, given what I had been through all that day in the starting gates. Sir Mark suggested that we book a van with adjustable partitions so I could see for myself.

My plan was to load the horse and give him a wide stall while we drove slowly around. Then we would narrow the partition and subsequently increase the van's speed. I would stand inside the van at the horse's head so I could both observe him and instruct the driver. The aim was to identify the source of the horse's deep-seated claustrophobia.

We loaded Prince of Darkness and started a tour of Newmarket, driving slowly and making careful turns. He was completely at ease in his stall, so we stopped and narrowed the partition. Still, he seemed comfortable. When I asked the driver to increase his speed and make more aggressive turns, the engine note rose an octave. In front of me, Prince of Darkness seemed unconcerned. He braced himself against the corners and took no notice when any part of the van touched his body. Now we were sailing around the town. Anyone following us must have thought crooks had stolen the van as we squealed around corners and took roundabouts at stomach-turning speed. The horse and I were rolling around like a ship's cargo in a storm.

Prince of Darkness was in the narrowest possible stall and the driver was risking his license to give us all the ride of a lifetime. For all that, the horse did not kick or lean, and offered not the slightest resistance or anger. A far cry from what I had seen the previous day in the starting gate.

What distinguished the stall in the van (which he abided agreeably), and the starting gate (which he kicked to bits)? Back at the yard, I stared hard at both of them. Where was this horse's fear coming from? Clearly it was not claustrophobia, because he had been content in the van. Something about the starting gate spooked him. But what?

That night, after three days of futility, I wanted to quit and offer Sir Mark a refund, but those words just would not come. All my life I had found ways to win, and I could not bear the thought of losing this contest. I decided to give it one more try.

The following day was the toughest of them all: nine demanding and dangerous hours. Geraldine Rees, a friend of Sir Mark's, came along and patiently watched the proceedings. As Prince of Darkness was led riderless into the starting gate, I stood in front of him, just as I had in the van. I wanted to observe every nuance of behavior as he went in.

He walked in, crashing and banging. No sooner was he in than he lunged forward, charging from that gate as if men with lances were arranged along the sides and poking him. He had no concern for me being in his way at all and galloped right through me, knocking me to the ground.

I stood up and wiped the dust off. This was a problem, because I needed to get even closer. The next time he blasted from the stall in a flurry, he knocked me down again, and still I was no wiser about his terror. This was no game for a man of my age and with part of his spinal column missing, but I was determined to go in yet a little closer.

Once again he jumped forward and bowled me over, stepping on my leg, side, and ear. Then he ran to the end of my come-along, turned, and stood there looking at me from twenty feet away. I was hurting badly, but in a flash, it came to me. Though my brain was muddled by this time, I had noticed something: just before he jumped up and ran over the top of me, Prince of Darkness had rolled his eye back to look at his off flank and his attention seemed to be focused on the off-side rail.

I stood there, bruised, battered, with a trickle of blood running into my collar, but I had found the source of his fear. The rail itself, of course! A van has smooth sides whereas starting gates have rails on each side. I could have kicked myself for not realizing sooner, but I felt a surge of excitement. After a few tests, I knew I was right.

That evening, Sir Mark and I discussed the situation. With mounting anticipation, he phoned various racing officials to investigate the possibility of removing the rails from inside a given starting gate. No luck: because of the way they are constructed, when you remove the rail from one horse's stall, you also remove it from the next.

Early next morning, I outlined another idea. If we could create something similar to what a picador's horse wears in the bull ring—a drape made of heavy leather to go over his rear quarters—perhaps we could convince Prince of Darkness that he had enough protection from those evil rails.

It was a wild thought, and I had grave doubts about its practicality. Many years beforehand, I had draped a leather cape over a horse's rear quarters and attached it to my Western saddle. When I then asked the horse to make a sliding stop from extreme speed, it encouraged him to drop his hips. He had to in order to hold his rear feet in the ground and support the weight of the cape.

If I could use something like this to protect Prince of Darkness's sides from those rails, he might accept the starting gate.

"What if we used carpet?" asked Geraldine Rees. *Yes.* We drove to Newmarket and bought a roll of remnant carpet. Then we went to Gibson's Saddlery, and I started to design the kind of thing I thought might work. The prototype, no more than carpet sewn onto both sides of a stable blanket, was finished in just a few hours and we raced back to the stables to try it out.

When I put the Prince in the starting stalls with his special blanket on, I immediately knew we were on the right track. I gave Geraldine Rees a congratulatory pat on the back. "Look, he's still frightened and not very confident, but he's staying in there, isn't he?"

It felt good to stand in front of that huge animal and know that I might at last stay on my feet. The more he rubbed against the sides of the stall, stepping backward and forward, the more Prince of Darkness realized that he had protection from the rails. He relaxed and calmed down. We were making progress.

We raced back to Gibson's Saddlery, fearful that the shop would be closed. The next day was Good Friday, with the Easter holiday period to follow. But Gibson's staff were good enough to work that evening and the next morning to further develop the prototype.

The blanket would fit only the horse's hindquarters and would be held in place by straps. A ring sewn onto the blanket near the tail offered a place where a rope could be fastened: the idea was that the horse would actually break from the stall and run out from under the blanket. The horse races on, the blanket stays behind.

Sunday afternoon we tried it. We took Prince of Darkness, with other horses for company, to the starting gates. I did my routine of letting him break slowly, using the blanket for protection. He responded very well. We schooled him again the following day, and that evening I told Sir Mark—then in France on business—that I thought the horse would make a good start at Warwick on the following day.

George Duffield, the jockey, was game to try this invention, but a little embarrassed.

"Carpet? He's wearing a carpet?"

"That's what it's made of, sure."

"Is it patterned carpet or plain?"

"It has a slight pattern, I suppose you'd say."

"Oh no," he groaned.

"Don't you like patterned carpet?"

He held his hands up in the air in mock surrender. "No—it's fine, I don't mind looking like an idiot. Maybe I ought to wear the same pattern. The same color. Let's go for it. Trade in the silks. Can we stop at the carpet store on the way and measure me up for a tufted Wilton?"

I assured him that Prince of Darkness had to have his magic carpet or he would refuse to start. The head starter was similarly apprehensive about the blanket, but he had given Sir Mark permission to use this unconventional apparatus and he could not back down now.

When I put the contraption up behind George in the starting gate, it drew a lot of comments from the other jockeys. In truth, it was a touch ignoble to have someone holding on to the rear of your horse with a piece of rope when you were hoping to run a race in a few seconds' time. I hoped the invention would work the first time. Inventions seldom do.

Now they were under starter's orders. I dug my heel in, grasped the rope firmly, ready to take the strain as Prince of Darkness left the stall. "And they're off!" the announcer called. There was a terrific kick on the rope and then it went dead as Prince of Darkness broke from underneath his blanket with perfect timing. The carpet lay there on the bottom of the gate. Success!

There were eighteen horses in the race, and at Warwick they run about seven furlongs and make a hard left. When they made the turn, Prince of Darkness was the clear leader. He did not win that day, but he made the best start and he went on to be a winner.

Since that time, Gibson's Saddlery has gone on to make many more blankets like the one that Prince of Darkness wore. On Thoroughbred racetracks all over the world, they call horses who need the security of such a device "blanket horses," and more than 1,000 such horses have used it successfully.

I'll take some credit for the invention, but it was Prince of Darkness who made me see the light.

———

To understand how Greg Ward became the best breeder and trainer of cow horses in North America, you must know something of his first horse—a fat little creature called Blackie. He was bought for

$350, saddle included. When I met Greg and heard the story, I thought the saddle was worth more than the horse.

Greg was born in 1935, the same year I was, in Bakersfield, California, and we were to become good friends. He seemed destined for a brilliant career in sports, but at the age of seventeen those dreams ended. To earn money to buy a horse, Greg was on a neighbor's farm driving a tractor when it rolled on a hillside; metal driven into his head left him unconscious and blind. After numerous operations, one to insert a plate in his head, his sight returned—but his peripheral vision was all but gone, and with it his future in athletics.

His parents later helped him to buy his first horse, the eight-year-old Blackie. When Greg went to California Polytechnic State University, San Luis Obispo, he took Blackie with him. Ahead of me by two years, he had been asking questions and watching riders in competition: all in an attempt to make the college rodeo team. He did make it, and contributed to national championships we won in 1958 and 1959.

I recall watching Greg ride Blackie and thinking, "Why is he wasting his time? What will that horse ever be?" I was young, wore championship buckles, and had no time for an ordinary horse like Blackie. I now realize how wrong, how pompous I was to laugh at that horse. Blackie gave Greg everything he had and forgave him his mistakes. A classier, more sensitive horse might have been less sympathetic to him. Blackie, it turns out, mattered a great deal to the Western horse industry—because he was teaching one of the greatest horsemen who ever lived. I should have known better about Blackie, because my Brownie had been important to me.

Greg later bought forty-three acres near Tulare, California, where he built the training establishment he still owns. It now includes two covered arenas and a half-mile track. Horses trained at the Ward Ranch, either by Greg or his son John, have for the past thirty or more years amassed an enviable record. Their horses have won twelve world championships in cutting and reined cow-horse events, along with millions of dollars in prize money. Young horses bred on the Ward Ranch—including Dual Pep, the most popular stallion in their industry—have sold for millions of dollars and won that amount in the showring. Valued at $2 million, Dual Pep has won more than

$300,000 in prize money and has a breeding income of $500,000 per year. Where cow horses are concerned, the Ward Ranch is the class of the continent.

Economics alone requires that his horses perform extremely well in competition to earn back their high value. His training methods, plainly, are not the result of vague notions about kindness to animals—though Greg would never be anything but kind and respectful of them. As proven against the toughest competition, his methods are both the best *and* the kindest.

I once saw something at his ranch that thrilled me. "Monty," he said, "come and have a look at my new babies." Five handlers led the young horses in from the field without so much as pulling on their lead ropes. The horses were then saddled up and the riders carefully mounted. Out on the track, the gates were closed but the horses were otherwise free to wander. A sixth person on an experienced saddle horse carried a long wand with a plastic flag at the end—used if needed to keep horses from endangering one another. "During the first twenty days of riding," said Greg, "we allow them to do whatever they want. There's no tension on the reins whatsoever."

If a horse wanted to graze along the fence line, to canter, simply stand, or even lie down and roll, that was all fine: to grant this last wish, the rider dismounted and watched, unconcerned. I marveled at the correct thinking behind this approach. The horses were learning to carry the riders' weight and had no suspicion that they might ever be punished for anything. There was no chance to cultivate resentment or aggressive tendencies toward their human partners.

The success of these methods and others outlined in this book point to a new beginning in the relationship between man and horse, and it has been my privilege to make a contribution to this spirit of understanding.

———

In England recently, I received an invitation to meet with the Queen to bring her up to date on my work and to discuss views on the world of horses in general. Corporal Major Terry Pendry drove me through the now-familiar grounds of Windsor Castle. "You'll be meeting Her

Majesty outside," he said, as he briefed me for the upcoming meeting. Outside? Were we going to stroll around the grounds together, or meet in the mews and look over some of her horses? Terry parked to one side of the lawn that sweeps down in front of the castle.

In the middle of this huge expanse of perfectly manicured green lawn sat a figure at a small table. A white cable snaked from the table to the castle and disappeared inside. I began the long trek over the lawn, and as I drew near I recognized Her Majesty sitting there. The corners of the snowy-white tablecloth flapped idly in the breeze. The bone china and silverware stood ready for our tea.

The Queen greeted me in a very informal way, and I sat down at the table. She poured tea from a pot attached to that long white cord. We enjoyed finger sandwiches and tea as we began to talk. It was a perfect occasion in a perfect setting. We talked about horses, and once again she proved to be an interesting and informed owner. I felt thoroughly privileged to have met this woman whom history has placed in a unique position.

I brought her up to date on the course offered at West Oxfordshire College under the directorship of Kelly Marks. The course offers my training methods—the first time that a course of this nature has been specifically designed and built into the curriculum. I told her of my recent experiences over starting gates. I said I looked forward to the future, when students of my methodology would advance to such an extent that my current practices would be dismissed as archaic. Even as I write *The Man Who Listens to Horses,* veterinarians are developing the ability to "listen" to horses to determine which part of the animal's gut hurts—the duodenum loop, the small or the large intestine.

Long after the tea party was scheduled to end, the Queen and I rose to our feet. Our parting was genuinely warm. I had a vision of what this scene would look like from the ramparts of the castle: the white square of the table amid the green expanse of lawn, the remains of our tea, the chairs askew, the Queen of England strolling in the direction of the castle, and heading toward a parked car, the California cowboy, shaking his head in disbelief at the curious circumstances in which he found himself.

Nearly 800 years ago, a very different ruler, a conqueror named

Temujin, had a very different attitude to horses. His Mongol empire grew to encompass the shores of the Pacific and the northern stretches of the Black Sea. Standing astride a quarter of the world's surface, he changed his name to Genghis Khan, meaning "master of all." Deservedly, that name now conjures unimaginable cruelty, an iron will, and an inflexible resolve.

His chief ally in the remarkable expansion of his power and influence was the horse. Using ropes and whips, Genghis Khan harnessed the horse's strength, stamina, and speed. Like many who profess to love the horse and *do* love the horse, the Mongols broke their young horses in the cruel, conventional way. They cherished the string of horses they took to war, but inevitably some were ridden to death.

Horses had no answer to the Khan's cruelty, had no voice. But they did have a language. No one saw it, no one tried to see it, but that language has probably existed for 45 million years, virtually unchanged. We should put this into perspective: Humankind has been on this planet for only a few hundred thousand years, and already human language has fragmented into thousands of different tongues.

The absence of communication between human and horse has led to a disastrous history of cruelty and abuse. As a result, we did not gain the willing cooperation of the horse nearly as much as we might have done. Our loss has been considerable—the emotional connection with the horse has been diminished, but so has the performance and work we might have gained.

It is a balance I have tried to redress during a lifetime's work with horses. Happily, that work continues.

Appendix

Join-up: A Step-by-Step Guide

The Man Who Listens to Horses sets out to tell the reader something of my life and how my ideas on starting horses were shaped. This appendix constitutes the how-to section of the book.

It should be plain that starting horses gently is easy, efficient, and systematic: it is freely available to anyone with a positive attitude who is not frightened of horses. The first requirement is that you discard all preconceived notions about starting the young horse. Do retain, however, all your experiences with the horse that have taught you not to fear him and that enable you to move around him safely and effectively.

Hold in your mind the idea that the horse can do no wrong; that any action taken by the horse—especially the young unstarted horse—was most likely influenced by you. We can do little to teach the horse; we can only create an environment in which he can learn. Likewise with people: the student who has knowledge pushed into his brain learns little, but he can absorb a great deal when he chooses to learn.

Actions speak louder than words. We say it but too rarely live by it. The horse uses a predictable, discernible, and effective language, one that requires no interpreters. Like any form of communication, Equus, as I call it, requires some effort to master. If we refuse to believe that the horse can communicate, pain can be used to train him somewhat effectively. But pain is needless and terribly limiting.

What if, on your first day of school, your teacher put a chain through your mouth or over your nose, gave it a jerk, and then took a whip to you when you tried to get away. What would your relationship with that teacher be like? How would you view school from that point on? While the horse's brain is not as complex as the human's, our response to cruelty is similar. The point of my method is to create a relationship based on trust and confidence.

Most conventionally started horses form an adversarial relationship with the humans who employ them. If they agree to perform, it is with a reluctant attitude. The first rule of starting a fresh horse, then, is *no pain.* You the trainer will not hit, kick, jerk, pull, tie, or restrain. If you are forced to use some restraint, it should be of the mildest nature and without the feeling of *you must* communicated to the horse. Suggest to the horse that *you would rather he did* but not that *he must.*

The horse is the quintessential flight animal. When pressure is applied to the relationship, he will almost always choose to leave rather than fight. The phenomenon that I call Advance and Retreat is evident throughout the animal kingdom—between animals of the same and different species and even between humans. Consider, for example, the fourteen-year-old boy in high school who is attracted to a girl in his class and follows her incessantly. She wants nothing to do with him. He may persist for several months, and then give up. Only at this point does she show interest. Advance. Retreat. It's a useful tool in both human and equine psychology.

In starting the young horse—I never use the term *breaking*—the intention is to cause this animal to accept without trauma the saddle, bridle, and rider. In my demonstrations we accomplish that in about thirty minutes. I am suggesting, however, that with completely green horses it is best before the starting procedure to take a few days to accustom them to the bit and to a small measure of communication through long-lines and the mouth of the horse.

In starting the horse, the aim is to achieve a number of related aims: you want to join up with the horse and convince the horse to follow you. You want to be able to touch his vulnerable areas and pick up his feet. You want to put on him saddle pad, saddle, bit, and bridle. Attach long-lines. Get the rider on. Move a full circle right, one step back, a full circle left and, again, one step back.

You will need the following equipment:

- two long lines thirty feet long
- one snaffle bit, fully equipped
- one saddle (your preference)
- one saddle pad
- one stirrup leather
- a halter on the horse

I use a round pen in my operation, and while not absolutely necessary, it does make the job easier. My pen is fifty feet in diameter (16 meters) with a solid wall eight feet high (2.4 meters) and roofed over. Its sand surface has a two-inch cushion. I have, however, started horses in the wild with no fences, riding a horse to aid in travel. A square pen can be used, but it is much better if you can panel the corners out. Fifty feet in diameter is optimum for mid sized horses. Good footing is important for the safety of horses and people.

Bring the horse, with his halter on, into the pen and have with you one long-line, preferably a light sash thirty feet long (nine meters). Stand near the center of the pen and introduce yourself by rubbing with the flat of your hand (no patting) the horse's forehead, even if you are already acquainted. Now move away and toward the rear of the horse, staying out of the kick zone.

When you are behind the animal or when he flees—whichever comes first—pitch the line toward his rear quarters. This light sash (long-line) cannot hurt him in any way. At this point, almost all young horses will take flight and proceed around the pen. The horse is retreating so you must advance. Keep the pressure on. Pitch the line about two times per revolution or whatever it takes to keep your subject retreating.

Maintain an aggressive mode: Your eyes drilled on his eyes, your shoulder axis square with his head. Maintain forward movement as much as possible, but do not enter his kick zone. Try to get the horse to canter five or six revolutions one way; then reverse and repeat, except that this time you are readying the horse for a message: Would he like to stop all this work?

Particularly watch the inside ear (the ear, that is, closest to you in the center of the pen). That ear will slow up its movement or stop moving altogether, while the outside ear will continue to monitor his surroundings. The head will begin to tip, ears to inside, and the neck will bend slightly to bring the head closer to the center of the circle. He will probably lick and chew, running his tongue outside the mouth.

Finally, he should crane his head down near the ground. The ear gives you respect. Coming closer means just that. Licking and chewing says, "I am a flight animal, and I'm eating so I can't fear you." Craning the head down means, "If we could have a meeting to renegotiate, I would let you be the chairman." Experience will sharpen your senses to this communication, but essentially when you observe the horse in this mode, he is asking you to take the pressure off. He wants to stop.

Now coil the line and assume a submissive mode, with your eyes down. Do not look at his eyes. Bring your shoulder axis to a forty-five degree position. This is an invitation for him to come to you, or at least look your way and stop retreating. If he will come to you, this is good! If he stands and faces you but does not move forward, then start to move closer to him, but do it in arcs or semicircles, not straight at him.

If he leaves you, put him back to work for a few more laps. Then repeat the process. As you move closer, do it with your shoulder axis at forty-five degree angles to his body axis. For the most part, show your back to him. He should voluntarily move toward you and reach out with his nose to your shoulders. This is *join-up*.

When you can approach his head, give him a good rub between the eyes and then walk away, moving in circles. I like to start by circling on the right hand about ten feet in diameter. After the right is accomplished, circle left and repeat several times. He should follow you or at least move to maintain his head in your direction. This I call *follow up*. If he does not follow you, then you will find yourself facing his rear and you should put him back to work. Again, stay clear of the kick zone.

Once *follow up* is evident, the horse should follow you to the center of the pen and stand comfortably for the next step, which is to enter his vulnerable areas. Starting on the near side (the side you mount and dismount on), use both hands to massage neck, withers, back, hips, fore flanks, and rear flanks. Once you have done the same on the off side, you are ready to pick up the feet. Do this using the normal safe procedures.

You are now ready to bring the balance of your equipment into the pen and place it on the ground near the center. Allow the horse time to look the equipment over. Move between the equipment and the horse several times in both directions until your subject prefers to follow you instead of examining the tack. Once you have his attention, snap one line to the halter, placing the line over your left arm about three feet from the snap.

Gently place the saddle pad on his back, first ahead of the withers and then sliding it back in place. If he walks away, do not punish him; just ease him around, cause him to *join up*, and repeat the process (though you should not have to). Once the pad is in place, pick up the saddle (with the irons up and the girth over the seat). Slide your body along the near side of the neck to the point of the shoulder.

With the saddle resting on your right hip, gently place the saddle on his back and move past his head giving him a rub on the off side. Without hesitation, take the girth down slowly and smoothly, adjust the girth to reach approximately to the mid-fetlock joint and move smoothly back to the near side, giving the head a rub on the way by.

Stand near the fore leg and bring the girth up and place the front buckle on the front billot, draw it snug, reading your horse all the way. Do not make it too tight, but tight enough that it will not turn if he bucks. Next, place the back buckle on the back billot and snug it up a bit tighter than the front one.

Go back to the front one and level the two up. Unsnap the line and step back cautiously, line in hand, moving backward away from your horse. Favor the rear portion, staying out of the kick zone. Send him away with the line and be careful not to encourage joining up and bucking at the same time.

Above all, *stay calm*. Your horse must believe that he is the only one bothered by this saddle, or he will be more inclined to buck. Watch for signs that he once again wants to *join up* but only allow it when he is traveling comfortably with the saddle.

As soon as he is back with you, put the bridle on and place the reins under the rear of the saddle or some other place of safe attachment. Leave plenty of slack in the reins. Now, take your extra stirrup leather and drop it through the off-stirrup iron so that it hangs halfway through. Then move to the near side and carefully pick up both ends of the leather and buckle it through the near iron. The stirrups are thus buckled together under the horse.

Take both lines at the snap end and place one over the seat of the saddle, allowing the snap to just reach the ground on the off side. Then place the second snap through the near iron (back to front) and snap it on the near-side bit ring. Move to the off side and repeat.

Move back to the near side. Pick up the two lines at the side of the horse and move backward and laterally—outside the kick zone— toward the rear of the horse. You are now justified in moving him forward and swinging the right rein over his hips to the long-lines.

If you are not experienced with long-lines, move slowly. You want to accomplish a little communication through the mouth, but do it cautiously. Practice this process with older, more experienced horses for a significant period of time before you try it with a first-timer. You could hurt your horse or yourself.

If you are experienced with lines, ask your horse to circle at the canter and then trot both ways. Ask him to negotiate turns and stops. Finally, stop him, facing away from the center and ask him to rein back one step.

At this point, most horses I start are ready to be ridden. You may elect to ride him yourself or have another person do so; either way is fine. Make sure the saddle is adjusted properly and the girth is tight enough to prevent the saddle from turning. If you are using a rider, bring in that rider (wearing, of course, all proper safety equipment).

Snap a line on the near-side bit ring. Give your rider a minute or two to get acquainted with the horse. Have the rider rub both sides of the horse and treat him as you have. I then leg my rider up. First, I ask the rider to just "belly over," so that the rider's belt buckle lies against the pommel.

Then I move the horse carefully, first in two or three left circles and then to the right two or three times. If the horse is happy and accepting the rider lying over him, guide the rider's foot into the near iron as he mounts. Repeat the circles.

If your horse is relaxed and accepting the seated rider, make larger circles that lead the horse nearer the perimeter. Carefully unsnap the line and help the rider accomplish a circle of the pen in each direction. No cantering; walk and trot will suffice. After each revolution, I like my rider to rein back one step.

Do not rush matters. If your horse is not ready to be mounted, do it another day. Remember that my demonstrations must be done in one session so that viewers can see the entire procedure. This does not mean that you must do the same.

This system of starting horses will save so much time that even moving slowly and cautiously, you will still be well ahead. It is the quality of your work that matters, not how fast you accomplish it. We all want the well-behaved, happy, and willing horse at the conclusion. It is on this result that you will be judged.

When the horse has accepted saddle, bridle, and rider, he should *not* be traumatized and should elect to stay with you rather than go away. Remember, let your animal be free. *Do not restrict.* Make it pleasant for him to be near you, and put him to work if he wants to be away from you. *No pain.*

If you can accomplish this process, then you have helped to make the world a better place for the horse.

Afterword

Monty Roberts is sometimes the horseman of last resort. Horses under death sentence are brought to him for one final attempt at solving their phobias; if he fails, the horse boards a trailer and is never seen again.

During some time I spent with Monty early in 1997, I watched on successive evenings as he worked in the round pen with a bright-eyed brown mare named Robin. I remember how she looked right at me when I lit my pipe, how keen her interest, how alert her gaze. I had wanted this sweet and gentle Thoroughbred to succeed in any case, but from that moment I wanted it a little more.

Rehabilitation for this horse had been a roller coaster. Tuesday was a nightmare; Wednesday was a dream; this evening, Thursday, offered a little of both. Monty had until Sunday to undo the terrible damage that a human had done to the horse. Otherwise, she was a dangerous horse who would have to be put down.

Robin's conundrum was this: She was terrified of standing tied. Perhaps someone had whacked her one time when she balked a little at a rope; perhaps that person had continued to hit her, escalating matters until he or she had inflicted on the horse a full-blown, deep-seated phobia.

When Monty tied Robin to a post on the rim of the round pen where the good doctor typically attends his equine patients, all hell broke loose. To see what transpired there was to be reminded that a horse is two animals: There is the horse amiably led on a halter rope or grazing in his paddock or snoozing in his stall, the horse we think we know. The one we instinctively want to stroke and pat on the nose and spoil with carrots. But this mare at the end of the rope was another creature entirely. Monty had led her to the post, quietly tied her there, then gingerly backed away—as if he had just lit a stick of dynamite and sought cover behind a rock. Monty was the mare's comfort and within seconds she realized her plight and began to thrash like a marlin, diving and leaping to spit the hated hook. From my vantage on the elevated walkway around the pen, I winced every time she hit the turf, rolling like a felled tree in a storm. She tore up the ground and when her hooves hammered the wall of the pen I silently pleaded with her.

Please don't break a leg. *Please* stop. *Please.*

Finally she lay there, grounded, chest heaving, the taut rope around her neck straining at the dead weight of her, her eyes wide and circling. As wrenching and pitiful a sight as I had ever seen.

"It's like heroin," Monty said aloud to the gallery, where four of his students had gathered to watch their professor. He was staring at the mare as he spoke, his look, like his voice, at once compassionate and detached. "She's addicted to pulling."

In previous days at the farm the mare had broken all manner of ropes and halters, including some guaranteed by their manufacturers. But Monty now had her attached to a device that he hoped would endure her manic pulling and awesome strength. "Pound for pound," said Monty, "this is the strongest horse I have ever seen."

A thick rope circled one of the massive round wooden pillars set outside the pen to support the roof: this rope then led to a buckle, more rope, then a three-foot length of tough inner tube. The rubber—perhaps—had enough give and strength to take pressure off the rope, and the mare might thus be spared yet a little more trauma and the danger of injury that a snapped rope could bring. But now she rose, dug in with her hooves, squared herself to face the pillar and, with every fiber in her body, began to pull. She seemed to grow in stature as a fierce and mostly silent battle ensued. The inner tube lengthened ominously, the rope slowly twisted under the strain. I watched and waited for something to give: the rope, the buckle, the rubber—the horse.

Robin went on pulling, seemingly oblivious to the pain that the nooselike rope must have inflicted on her neck. I hated what I saw but could not look away. All eyes were on the bright-eyed mare. Monty warned away a student near the pillar, worried that if a link in the chain of rope-rubber-rope snapped, the mare would be catapulted backward and the buckle might go the other way, like a missile from a lethal slingshot. But the apparatus held, and the mare eased up a little. The war of tugging had taken a toll on her. Monty approached her carefully, looking to the ground as he always does with unfamiliar horses before patting her on the head, soothing her with his hands, talking to her, encouraging her. How sweet the calm in the tempest's wake.

Monty was wary—a life with horses had taught him that, but at his age, his body battered by all he has been through, he is nowhere near as nimble as he once was. There is no doubting that to touch that mare at that moment required courage, no doubting that Monty Roberts has deep wells of it.

At times the tethered mare seemed ready to flap again, like that hooked marlin, and to stand too close to the wall within range of her was to risk being crushed or kicked. The horse had learned that pulling would liberate her, end her rope-induced agony. Now she would learn a new and hard truth—that pulling got her nowhere. Monty understood that she had to see that for herself. The heroin addict, he would say, must be allowed to hit bottom before rehabilitation can begin. The mare seemed to possess the intelligence to grasp that, but did she possess the will?

Monty took her off the apparatus and moved her into the center of the ring. He used the halter rope to lead her forward, then laid the rope against her chest to urge her backward. She responded freely and willingly, never once hesitating. Good girl, Robin. Good girl. Then he attached her once more to the rope and rubber, and though she seemed discomfited, she managed. The addict said no to the needle. Now a student led the mare away to another post in a big covered arena, and again she passed the test. Flying colors this time. I lit my pipe as they led her to the gate where I stood, and there they paused while Monty talked to a student. The mare seemed enchanted with my pipe and the smoke, and I wondered where the other creature, the phobic one, had gone. This mare seemed almost tiny; that other one had grown tall in her terror.

Weeks later, when I returned to the farm, the mare was still there. The owner was no longer willing to spend money on her rehabilitation but neither was he insisting that she be shot. It would take time to heal her, but Monty believed it was possible. So he had simply taken her under his wing, as he had so many other outcasts—troubled children, wounded deer, reject horses—determined that he succeed, determined that she have a good and decent life.

Of course, I want that mare in her stall, not in some trailer bound for an abattoir. Monty Roberts wants that, too. But he wants a lot—a better world for horses (and indeed all animals), a better world for humans.

———

What has Monty learned about horses that might prove useful to the way that humans deal with one another? Horses, he says, have been his best teachers, but surely the round pen and the rodeo ring are one thing, the human arena quite another?

Not at all, argues Monty. "It's the same psychology." If Monty Roberts would recast humankind's contract with horses, he is equally passionate about rethinking our contract with each other—in our working relationships and business dealings, and especially between parents and children.

Monty often calls himself "a horse psychologist," but when he was a student at Cal Poly he was drawn to human psychology, too. By the time he and Pat were themselves parents of three children, he had had extensive experience working with street kids damaged by drugs, physical abuse, indifferent care, and a host of other social disorders.

While Monty's world of horses was taking its many varied, and sometimes tortured, turns, the idiosyncratic Roberts household was also taking shape. Over time, Pat and Monty took in forty-seven children, some staying for years and living like brothers and sisters to Deborah and Laurel and Marty.

By Monty's reckoning, every one of those forty-seven children had cause to falter. Typically twelve to fourteen years of age, some had tangled with school authorities or the law, some had been dismissed as backward, some were hooked on hard drugs or suffered from eating disorders. Most came from dysfunctional families. Here were nestlings with broken wings, but—again by Monty's own reckoning—forty of them learned to fly, many of them well. The rest landed in jail or returned to the streets and died there. Their fates were, of course, distressing blows to Monty and Pat, but he argues that given the baggage these children came with, their overall outcome reflects well on his approach. And it is his approach that Monty wants the world to consider.

Monty tells the story of a boy and a horse and water, and it encapsulates the spirit of his thinking. The story is perhaps too neat, too close to parable, but I found myself dwelling on it later.

At one point in their lives, Pat and Monty took in a nine-year-old child. Let us call him, for the sake of the story, Matt. The boy had an interest in horses, wanted one particular horse to ride and work with on his own. Fine, said Monty, but you must respect the horse; you will be responsible for keeping that horse brushed and fed and watered. Matt agreed. A few weeks later Monty noticed that the horse lacked water on a hot day and was pawing at his bucket; Monty watered him. When Matt got home from school he was upset at his forgetfulness. At this point, he and Monty entered into a written contract in which a four-ounce water glass figured prominently. If Matt neglected to water the horse, he would have to fill the horse's bucket by degrees, using that glass and water from a faucet fifty feet from the stall until the horse was satisfied and the bucket was full.

The glass would sit on a shelf in the tack room, and need never be used, only serve as a useful reminder. But three weeks later Matt forgot again. Glass in hand, he set about his task. Each time he returned with the tumbler and emptied it into the bucket the parched horse would drink it in one swallow. By midnight Matt was still at it.

Pat had gone down to check on him (the stalls are some distance from the farmhouse), and she worried aloud to Monty about how exhausted he seemed. "Should I let you stop before the bucket is full?" Monty asked Matt. The boy shook his head. By the time the bucket was nearly full and the horse was clearly sated, the boy had probably moved seven to ten gallons of water, a glass at a time. It was two A.M. when Monty put his arm around Matt's shoulder. "I'm very proud of you," he said. "You accepted responsibility for your actions." Together they walked up the winding road to the house.

That day, says Monty, was a turning point in Matt's life. "The change was remarkable. His schoolwork had been on the bottom, and he went to straight A's. His self-confidence went from a one to a nine. He had been a meek, withdrawn boy who had been urinating on the playground and labeled by his teachers as severely learning-impaired. Eventually his gift for mathematics was discovered, and before leaving grammar school he was tackling university-level math." Matt later graduated from college and started a successful business. While living at the Roberts's farm, he never again had occasion to use the glass.

If parents and their children sometimes need to renegotiate—to learn the nature of respect and self-respect—so too, says Monty, do corporations and employees. "We used to have whips on ships, it used to be OK to beat a child or for a husband to beat a wife, and we still possess a strong thread of that in our corporate structure. It's wrong, and it's not effective either."

Since 1990, thousands of corporate officers, educators, physicians, and others—the list to date includes more than 240 firms and organizations from around the world—have come to Flag Is Up Farms to hear what a man known for his horse skills has to teach about people skills. Monty's philosophy is rooted in respect and ends with expectations clearly defined: People must be allowed to fail, he says, but do not protect the lazy or incompetent; above all, people must be allowed to succeed and be rewarded if they meet or exceed the terms of the contract.

"For centuries," says Monty, "humans have said to horses *you do what I tell you or I'll hurt you.* Humans still say that to each other, still threaten and force and intimidate. I am convinced that my discoveries with horses also have value in the workplace, in the educational and penal systems, in the raising of children. At heart I am saying that no one has the right to say *you must* to an animal—or to an another human." It is a great leap, of course, from a contract written on a tack-room blackboard about watering a horse, to the complex interplay between an individual employee and a multinational corporate entity. And Monty is the first to recognize that point. But just as trust has to be won with a horse, so must it be won between people and the organizations that employ them. Monty Roberts hopes that his pioneering work in the human-to-horse field has so opened up the potential for communication that decades hence the relationship will evolve and change beyond recognition. Similarly, our understanding of human-to-human interactions might also take great leaps forward. That, too, is his hope.

Meanwhile, Monty Roberts goes around the world working with horses and spreading the word: inflicting pain does not work. The occasional public demonstrations, especially those involving abused horses, have stirred deeply buried emotions in some onlookers. For any in the audience who have themselves been abused, the horse in the ring becomes an almost too-potent metaphor. During one demonstration at Flag Is Up Farms, five women—all of them, as it turned out, victims of violence—fainted. On another occasion, Monty was doing a demonstration in England when a young girl approached him during the intermission. "I knew instinctively she had been abused," he said. "I invited her back later, and then I took her and her father aside and told him we had to talk about his daughter, and that I had as much sympathy for the abuser as for the victim." The man began to weep. Subsequently, Monty helped him get counseling.

But the most compelling incident took place in Dublin. Monty was working in a round pen with a so-called mad horse before a throng of people. The horse's owner, a handsome, agitated woman, had previously explained how impossible it was even to catch the horse in the paddock. "My husband," she told Monty, "is a good horseman, a tough horseman, and he says this horse is a maniac."

In the ring, Monty used hand motions to prove to his satisfaction that the horse had been beaten. "I am going to tell you what the horse is saying," he told the audience through his lapel microphone.

"Maybe I'm misinterpreting; maybe he's lying. So we'll take it with a grain of salt, but let's listen." A few minutes later he went on: "He's saying he's been kicked in the belly and head, and had a whip across the hocks. This horse is full of stories."

At that point Monty looked over to the woman, who was frozen in her aspect, her mouth open. Her face betrayed her sudden doubts about the wisdom of letting this man tell all about her horse—and more. "She was looking across the ring to her husband, and when I spotted him I knew the horse was telling the truth. Horses, in fact, never lie, and this horse was no exception. The horse comes to me, I saddle him and get a rider on, and the horse is moving around like a million dollars. By now both the man and his wife are extremely distraught."

"Someone," Monty said into the microphone, "has to apologize to this horse."

The demonstration over, the crowd began to leave the arena. The woman approached Monty in the ring.

"You're in danger," he told her.

"I can't talk about that," she replied. "I'd rather give up my life."

When her husband joined them, Monty told them that their lives would be a shambles until they got a handle on the violence. Monty had cut to the quick, and the response was immediate and emotional. The man threw his arms around Monty, and pleaded, "I need help, I need help." It must have been a riveting scene: in the ring where a mad horse had been proven sane, three people, their arms entwined, linked by a common history of pain.

The man did get the help he needed and now conducts seminars for other men who use their fists on the people they say they love. And so the man who listens to horses, and bids us to do the same, has an added task: imploring humans to listen to each other.

———

Late in March of 1997, Monty Roberts set out to complete a circle: Almost fifty years after first watching wild horses in the high desert, he would return to that terrain and try to get close to a fiery little mustang. As Monty the boy had done, Monty the man packed his saddle bags with beef jerky, tied a red bandanna round his neck, and set out on his quest.

The mustang project, as I came to call it, sought to answer this imposing question: Could Monty Roberts gentle a wild horse virtually *in the wild?* No round pen. No light cotton line. No half-hour join-up. Just a sixty-one-year-old man with a suspect back, riding long and hard, day and night, in pursuit of a wild animal more prone to flee than to stop for a chat.

Monty Roberts had joined up with mustangs as a boy in 1952, but because he kept that experience and even his ideas on horses to himself—we now see why—no one knew other than a few confidants such as Bill Dorrance (brother of Tom Dorrance, a notable horse gentler). Who would believe him anyway? Forty-five years later, the BBC decided to document the event; this film would allow Monty to say two things: "I *did,* and I *still can.*"

All that time working in the virtual dark can give a man a craving for the light. The mustang film was inherently somewhat contrived, as all films are, but, at the end of it, Monty's message about the wisdom of gentling horses would be clearly seen. First you show the world, then you change the world.

The mustang project started when someone at Flag Is Up Farms noticed an upcoming sale of mustangs. The Bureau of Land Management, which oversees America's wild horses and regulates their numbers, periodically offers mustangs for adoption—an alternative to culling their numbers by killing them. Monty drew the fifty-second and final card. He had his eye on a 13.2-hand three-year-old bay, and when it came Monty's time, the horse was still there.

The BBC immediately warmed to the mustang project when it was proposed to them. The British edition of *The Man Who Listens to Horses* had sold extremely well and, no doubt helped by the royal imprimatur, stirred interest both in Monty's life and in his ideas about horses. When I arrived at the farm on Good Friday, March 28, 1997, the six-person film crew was there.

Monty and I had talked about the project weeks beforehand, and he seemed intense about the mountain of detail: hired wranglers, RVs and scissor lifts, BBC bureaucrats. He had the air of a commodore impatient that the fleet keep up as he plowed forward with his dream. He saw this as a kind of last hurrah, or at least a last hurrah in the saddle, and he was determined that it go well.

Monty felt confident, as ever, in his ability to get through to the horse. But he was also acutely aware that this was an extraordinary and difficult undertaking and that, if things went wrong, he would have egg on his face and the British Broadcasting Corporation to mollify. What if the mustang got hung up on a barbed-wire fence? Would Monty's surgically buttressed back endure such a ride? Would the cameras spook the wild horse? Would the weather hold?

Saturday, March 29. With its Western facade, the Maverick Saloon in Santa Ynez is more like a Montana hangout than anything I ever imagined for California. The film crew is gathering sound and color: line-dancing (a choreographed human dressage that requires hours of schooling beforehand), Art Green's band, wind-blown cowboys, exquisitely tall cowgirls, black string ties, straight-leg blue jeans, fancy red boots.

The conceit of the film is to be established here, so three horsemen opine on the porch. They tip up their felt hats, shake their heads, pronounce Monty out of his cotton-pickin'... But old-time roper Dutch Wilson says that while trying to gentle a mustang in the wild is a ludicrous proposition, Monty Roberts can do it if anyone can.

That night the tension in Monty is all gone. He is ready. At nine P.M. he leaves the saloon and heads off alone in his truck, hauling a trailer and three horses—The Cadet, Big Red Fox, and, of course, Dually. By now it's cold outside. The high desert of the Cuyuma Valley will be colder still.

A woman seated beside me assures me in a friendly way that line-dancing is much easier than it looks and threatens to take me out on the dance floor. Time to go.

Sunday, March 30. Wilderness-bound at dawn with Pat Roberts in her van. Northeast of Solvang, the land gradually rises, then turns harsh as you leave the coast. On each trip to this wild valley I have admired a massive fist-shaped rock formation. This way, the standing rock seems to point, this way to the mustang project.

I know, thanks to John McPhee's *Assembling California,* that a rock mass caught between fault lines is what geologists call a *horse*. I cannot be sure that my fist-shaped rock is a true horse, but I like the notion that it is. Geologists, wrote McPhee, are like dermatologists crawling "like fleas on the world's tough hide." The high desert's seismic skin astonishes with its range of color: ochre, burnt orange, slate gray, myriad chalk and cream colors, the granite carved and layered and fractured.

Sycamores line the dry river beds in the Cuyuma Valley, hoping for a drink that this year might not come. The white oaks are leafing out; the live oaks are ever green. Sage, yucca, and cactus grow from dust here in "the Quee-*yama*" as they call it. I like the names: Lower China Creek, Green Canyon, Wasioja Creek, the Caliente Mountains.

Up and down the valley I notice the white boxed hives, the bees foraging on the sage and sometimes hitting the van windshield like hail. Monty has said that tarantulas occasionally darken the roads with their numbers. Higher up the valley I see the odd oil rig, one lone hang glider riding the updrafts, and quite a few cattle in pastures that stretch all the way to the mountains: what there is not, in this wide and desolate valley, is people.

Down a half-mile-long dust road, through two cattle gates and over one river is Pat Russell's ranch—shoot headquarters. The film crew is active, the sound man gleefully checking his equipment and alternately singing and humming: "Rollin' rollin' rollin', keep them dogies rollin', keep them dogies rollin', Rawhide..." Perhaps he records what he now hears—horses nickering, cattle complaining, birds beckoning, the wind rising, the hum of man and nature gearing up.

A young wrangler named Scott Silvera—he will ride the mustang if the mustang is agreeable—mounts his own stallion who gives him a loud ninety second imitation of a bucking bronc. "Is the film crew getting all this?" laughs Scott, as he hangs on to his pink-eyed, skewbald, and very wired horse.

Pat Russell, as beefy as Monty but taller, will head up the wranglers and work behind the scenes. He knows the ropes: a lot of film crews have been out here over the years, he tells me. Countless Marlboro Man cigarette ads were shot here for television, magazines, and billboards. The creators like "the big feeling," how the pine forest, the ocean, the craggy hills and the high desert all intersect here where the ranches are as big as forty thousand acres.

Only later do I learn that Pat Russell was, and is, a Marlboro Man himself, and ever since the early 1970s has featured in countless ads riding the range or sitting by a fire and a chuck wagon. Truth is, I never once saw this cowboy icon light up. Like many cowboys, he does not smoke, but chews, his tobacco.

Pat warns us about the snakes now emerging from their dark winter dens. Blind, hungry, and cranky, they strike out at body heat. The film crew is disconcerted to hear about the fifty-six-inch rattler killed on Pat's ranch the week before. For the next four days, those without cowboy boots think *snake* with every step.

Monty, chaps over his blue jeans and wearing his usual straw hat and brown oilskin jacket, tacks up The Cadet. Nearby, on a sorrel quarter horse mare named Sharon, is Caleb Twisselman. A fresh-faced sixteen-year-old from nearby Carissa Plains, he will help Monty physically accomplish his task, and he listens as Monty explains to him, and thus to the film audience, what he is doing and why.

Caleb's presence drives home the point that Monty is going back to his youth. But the circle resonates another way: Caleb's mother, Cathy, a wrangler on the set, learned how to ride in San Luis Obispo decades beforehand. Her teacher: Pat Roberts.

Monty tells me that sleeping in the truck the night before brought back memories of cold nights in the Nevada desert. That morning he rose into the saddle at seven-thirty to help the wranglers—Pat Russell, Cathy and Caleb Twisselman, Barney Skelton, and Scott Silvera—evict cattle from a flatland chosen for this portion of the filming. The wild horse had been corralled at Pat Russell's ranch for a month, with one horse to keep him company (a corral mate), before being released into a herd of semiferal horses. The film would now record the drama of the two horses (still together for company) being cut out of that herd. Monty would then begin the long process of join-up with the wild mustang.

Here in the high meadow the wind through the oaks is a constant, like rapids. Riffling through the long grass, the wind makes mesmerizing patterns, turns knolls kinetic. California is never what it seems.

The distant mountains can look baked brown, the meadows a monotonous green. But get low to the ground (checking first for snakes, of course) and the modest but prolific wildflowers begin to impress. Pat's wife Claudia says that people come from all over the country to see the 185 varieties—purple lupines, Johnny-jump-ups, Indian hyacinths, fiddlenecks shaped like violas, owl's clover with their little yellow "eyes," strawberry clover, hog's fennel, gold-colored California poppies.

Suddenly, the director's walkie-talkie comes alive. The herd is coming. It is, as I imagined it would be, a magnificent sight—twenty-five horses galloping across the plain. Horses on the run are still an emblem of freedom, still (and maybe more than ever) exhilarating to see.

The herd settles around a solitary oak on an otherwise treeless flat. Scouted thoroughly, this place has been carefully chosen: the riverbed on one side, steep hills on another, and a barbed-wire fence line behind. The place offers the wranglers a space to maneuver yet one with borders. At first I have trouble picking out the mustang with my binoculars. But soon more than his small size and one white hind sock distinguish him: it is his guardedness. The other horses, some of them rodeo broncs, have all had some human contact. While the wranglers encircle the herd, the horses graze. The mustang, though, misses nothing. His head is up almost constantly, his body tense, his ears tilting like radar beacons. The wranglers try to cut the two horses out of the herd. The mustang and the corral mate he has clearly bonded with share the same natural desire: to be with the herd. The mustang and his pal are scooting, raising little puffs of dust as they try dashes and feints and circles to rejoin the herd. Here is a reminder of the powerful herd instinct, the one that Monty must harness.

I join three members of the film crew down on the flat. The director wants close-ups of the horses, so the wranglers drive them at our huddled human island. It's a thrill to be within feet of those pounding hoofs and flying manes and the "hyaass" of the wranglers, but you hope the horses remember to go around, like water round a rock, not spill over the top.

Later, I see a snake on the road. We back up and catch his form heading into a gulley, see the white stripes, the four-foot black body, the diamond-shaped head, the creamy rattle. "Did you kill it?" Pat's wife, Claudia, wants to know back at the barn, and is disappointed we did not. The snakes bite cattle and horses and menace ranch families from spring to fall.

Monty and Caleb, meanwhile, using the corral mate as lure, draw the mustang several miles farther up the valley to a 1,200-acre pasture where Monty in days to come will join up with this horse—or not. Monty wears an earpiece so the director can issue instructions by radio, and it has worked passably well all day. But now, to enable dramatic overhead shots, a helicopter enters the equation. Monty stuffs a white T-shirt in his jacket; waving it is the signal for the chopper to back off.

But as he gallops to keep the mustang in sight, the chopper misses that signal and now it's too late. "That was the hardest part of the whole four days," Monty would say later. "I couldn't hear them because of the engine and they couldn't see my signal, and they kept the horse running at thirty or forty miles an hour. It was killing me to stay in a gallop for the better part of an hour and a half; I had to be up out of the saddle to spare the horse's back. I was unsure of the ground, and one stumble at that speed could have ended the film, and it could have killed me. I was just praying for the sun to go down."

Darkness sends the chopper packing, but then comes the cold. I put on every sweater I have under my jean jacket and huddle around the campfire. Set deep into the meadow, our camp is a great circle of horse trailers and tethered horses, cars and trucks, and recreational vehicles as big as bungalows. Overhead, Comet Hale-Bopp trails its ghostly luminescence and the stars sparkle, but there is little moon to cast light. The pasture is utterly silent, enveloped in dark like some black fog that hides even my hand in front of me.

Monty is now riding Big Red Fox, a rugged looking Thoroughbred, cutting a swath through the wind and the dark. He has to stay now with the horse until they join up, however long that may take. This had been an early source of puzzlement for me: surely the night would swallow up a wild horse, flashlight or no? "Your own horse can tell you which way the mustang went," Monty said. "If you can listen to your own horse, he can be your compass and your guide."

By nine P.M. everyone—film crew, wranglers, kids, and dogs—has gone home or to the Buckhorn motel in New Cuyama. Claudia settles into a huge white teepee near the fire and Pat Russell and I sit there awhile discussing E. Annie Proulx's *The Shipping News*, a novel of Newfoundland we both admire and one in which knots loom large. One minute this cowboy says in a slow drawl something like "I ain't cussin' him", the next minute he's talking literature. And cowboys love ropes and knots almost as much as sailors do; that day Pat taught me the bowline for tethering horses.

I borrow Pat Roberts's van and head for the Buckhorn. As I drive down the dirt road, the heater on high, I keep thinking of Monty somewhere out there. He switched horses at six P.M. and I heard him mutter—to the horse, maybe to himself—"*You* can do it, *you* can do it." On I drive, mystified by how the darkness has made the vast pasture bigger, the gate farther. Then the more likely prospect dawns: I am lost.

The carcass of a steer I noticed on the way in that morning, its ribs arcing and white, finally gives me back my bearings. Monty's compass is a live horse; mine is a dead cow. Someone has closed the crude gate, but I do finally find it. Back at the Buckhorn, I am glad of my modest bed and the long hot shower that warms my chilled bones. While I sink into sleep, Monty and Big Red Fox and a nameless mustang ride on.

Monday, March 31. Morning brings cold rain. The temperature is dropping fast and the wind, after dying, is back. "It was cold all right and uncomfortable," Monty would say of the all-night ride. Three jackets did not keep out the cold and the damp. "The mustang took me for a long ride, maybe a hundred miles. Mostly trots, but he would take off on long gallops, too. He tested every aspect of the perimeter, and I kept thinking if [wrangler] Barney Skelton had not ridden every inch of that fence line and fixed every weak point, that mustang could have been hurt."

Despite his night in the saddle, Monty looks surprisingly fresh. Says he has a second wind. During the trek, Big Red Fox grew attached to the mustang and though fatigued did not want to stop. But he is wet and shivering, and Pat Roberts rubs him down, feeds and waters him, and puts a double blanket on him. The Cadet, meanwhile, still has swollen legs from yesterday's gallop; he, too, had come in Sunday at dusk wet and trembling, his legs crying out for linament and leg wraps. For the moment, Monty is down to one horse: Dually. The wild horse, meanwhile, is a half mile away on the other side of a high knoll and shows no sign of slowing down.

All morning Caleb and Monty try to get close to him. He begins to tolerate them to some extent. But only on the near side, the horse's left side; approaches from the off side, the horse's right, are met with flight or anger.

Now, the film crew gone for the moment, Monty and Caleb are alone with the mustang; only Cathy, as back-up wrangler, looks on. On a high knoll overlooking the flat a quarter-mile away, I lean against an old log and, with my binoculars, wait and see.

Patiently, slowly, Monty and Caleb edge closer to the horse between them. An hour passes. Then one, now both, reach down and touch the mustang. He does not at first welcome human hands on his withers and long black mane, but he learns to abide it and what I feel on seeing that first contact is a sense of privilege. You want to mark the moment when a wild animal trusts humans enough to allow touch. In the distance, ridged mountains the color of sandpaper cast elegant black shadows and form a fittingly dramatic backdrop for boy and man and horse. The wind is bitter but the sun is its counter. I understand why some tribes chose to leave their dead on raised wooden structures atop windswept crests like this one. In my mind is Chief Dan George's line, "It is a good day to die." This is a good place to die.

Caleb touches the mustang for longer periods now, but then Monty breaks off, as if to leave. The contract between Monty and mustang is clear: you let me touch you, I will ride away as reward. Each time he rides a little farther, comes back a little faster. The mustang understands.

Later that afternoon, Monty, on Dually ("I can get a quarter of an inch out of Dually," says Monty), neatly parks next to the mustang and slowly slips on a halter. With the film crew up close to record all this, I, too, listen in. "These horses need patience," Monty tells Caleb in that voice fathers use when passing wisdom on to a son. "If you act like you've only got fifteen minutes, it'll take all day. Act like you've got all day and it'll only take fifteen minutes."

The mustang is only thirty feet from me as I lean my elbows on a truck bed, but I cannot stop watching him through the binoculars. The detail is intoxicating; this, I know, is what so engaged Monty as a boy in Nevada watching wild horses. I marvel at how the wind plays with the mustang's long forelocks, how lively his large eyes are, how the fetlocks are so rich in feathery white hair, how explosive he can be when he feels his space invaded. I have yet to hear him make a sound, though he has plenty to say.

"Do you want to ride my horse?" Cathy asks me during a lull. She has seen me walking The Cadet beyond the camp and helping with grooming, so of course I am delighted to ride. Down the fence line about a quarter mile, it happens: I hear the rattle first, far louder and more menacing than even the movies make it sound, then see the pale angry snake slither off. The horse has come within a foot of stepping on it; he has no doubt seen snakes before. There is no scream of alarm, no pawing of the air, just my beating eastern heart.

When I report this second sighting to the wranglers lying in a circle on their elbows, the first question from Barney is, "Did you kill it?" If, Scott tells me, I see a *third* snake and similarly fail to dispatch it, I owe them twenty-four beers. Cowboy math.

Monty, meanwhile, is asking the mustang about putting on a surcingle—a wide girth used to accustom him to the tight cinch and a precursor to a saddle. First, he delicately lays the belt across the mustang's back. But the sound of its metal buckles spooks him, and Monty stops to tape them. Cinching the surcingle with Monty and Caleb in the saddle requires the use of a four-foot metal hook: it looks like a tool to pluck keys from inside a locked car. Monty slowly lowers the hook blindly below the horse's belly, and, with Caleb directing from the other side of the horse, catches the dangling belt, draws it up delicately, and finally cinches the surcingle.

Depending on who Monty is riding, the mustang is either submissively "snapping"—stretching out his neck with his mouth open like a

foal, or flattening his ears and striking out with his hooves. A borrowed horse called George gets the rude treatment; big Dually gets
the sweetness and light.

When Monty rides into camp that evening around supper time—
after thirty-five hours in the saddle, stopping only to relieve himself
and switch horses—his stance is a little wider than I remember, but so
is his smile.

In the bar that night at the Buckhorn, while far too many oversized
and stuffed stags look on, we all celebrate. The end, it seems, is in
sight. The mustang will get a good night's sleep in an enclosure at
camp; but then again, so will Monty in the Buckhorn.

April 1, 1997. While I, with regret, head home, Monty continues
schooling the horse he will call Shy Boy. The weather has become
more California-like, sunny and warm. The wind has stopped howling.

Driving west to Santa Maria and the airport, I have the voices of
the English film director, John Groom, and that of the head wrangler,
Pat Russell, in my head from days of listening to the crackle of the
walkie-talkie.

"*Maun*-tee," John would begin. "Say again?"

"*Maw*-nee," Pat would say, "Ya want that other horse o' yours?"

April 2, 1997. This is day four, and by now Monty has learned a few
things about Shy Boy. "He's intelligent," says Monty, "and tolerant to
a degree. He does not, however, like to be outside his language." In the
morning, Monty decides the time has come for the mustang to be ridden. And while the horse now tolerates being touched, haltered and
even saddled, what the film audience may see is how dangerous he remains. Scott Silvera, who had been chosen as the first person to ride
the mustang, is extremely capable in the saddle, and even rides broncs
at the rodeo, but he cannot speak the language of the horse as Monty
can; that puts him, as Monty says, outside the mustang's language.
When Scott gets close for the first time, the horse jumps back then
lands a blow with one front foot.

Later in the day, as Monty releases Shy Boy, he moves too quickly
to untie a knot and the horse strikes him hard on the hand. "It was my
fault," says Monty, "and the horse came right back up licking and
chewing. It was reactive on his part."

Finally, Scott does get on. The mustang was reluctant during the mounting but once Scott was on, calmly accepted the rider. "When Scott's bottom touched the saddle," says Monty, "that was a very emotional moment for me." Two days afterward, Monty called me. "It's just sinking in," he said. "The desire to do what I did must have been buried deep because right now I'm exploding." He had the proof he wanted, for all to see.

Shy Boy now resides at Flag Is Up Farms, where Monty joined up with him once more on Thursday of that week, but this time in a fifty-foot round pen. A far cry from days before when a man six weeks short of sixty-two made fast and epic circles in a vast and epic pasture and politely asked a wild horse for a word, or two.

———

This book has been very much about looking back on an extraordinary life with horses. But Monty Roberts, never one to aim low in terms of ambition, has set his sights on what might be called a World Learning Center. Based at his farm near Solvang, California, it would ensure that his methods would go on being taught to new generations of gentlers. His son, Marty, whose law practice specializes in equine matters, may well administer the center if it comes to pass. Meanwhile, Monty has been lobbying certain people who are impressed with his work and who might be willing to bankroll a trust fund and launch the school.

Ambitions change as you go," says Monty. At one time I might have said that my goal was to win three Kentucky Derbies in a row. Now I feel a higher calling. I've got to hurry. If I've got ten years left I'll be fortunate. But if I die tomorrow, I don't die. Enough of what I've taught will go on for the next few generations at least."

Monty's dreams are lofty, but he is in the habit of realizing them. The vision now is for Flag Is Up Farms, already a world-class Thoroughbred racehorse facility, to become a mecca for horse gentlers. Trainers from every land, or at least every land where horses matter, would learn to work harmoniously with horses and take back with them a body of knowledge to pass on to others. With luck and diligence, Monty Roberts's way would become the way of the future.

The whips and spurs and crops and bits as fierce as weapons would all be tossed, maybe this time for good. A few might reside in the glass cases of museums, where people of a more enlightened future may examine them and shake their heads in wonder and dismay. Whatever possessed our ancestors, those people may ask, to use such barbaric instruments on an animal so noble, so sweetly disposed, as the horse?

—Lawrence Scanlan

Lawrence Scanlan is the author of Riding High, *co-authored with Ian Millar, and* Big Ben. *He lives near Kingston, Ontario.*

For More Information

My goal is to leave the world a better place, for horses and people, than I found it.

In that effort I invite you to call for further information regarding clinics, conferences, educational videos, or other educational material at:

toll free	1-888-U2-MONTY
	1-888-826-6689
on-line	www.MontyRoberts.com
E-mail	admin@MontyRoberts.com

Thank you,
Monty Roberts

ABOUT THE TYPE

The text of this book was set in Janson, a misnamed type-face designed in about 1690 by Nicholas Kis, a Hungarian in Amsterdam. In 1919 the matrices became the property of the Stempel Foundry in Frankfurt. It is an old-style book face of excellent clarity and sharpness. Janson serifs are concave and splayed; the contrast beween thick and thin strokes is marked.

GAMES OF
MANY NATIONS

GAMES OF
MANY NATIONS

E. O. Harbin

ABINGDON PRESS

New York
Nashville

GAMES OF MANY NATIONS

Copyright MCMLIV by Pierce & Washabaugh

Library of Congress Catalog Card Number: 54-8238

B

SET UP, PRINTED, AND BOUND BY THE
PARTHENON PRESS, AT NASHVILLE,
TENNESSEE, UNITED STATES OF AMERICA

DEDICATED TO the "goodly fellowship" of missionaries and other workers the world around who give their lives to the cause of world brotherhood

INTRODUCTION

THIS IS A COLLECTION of games that are played the world around. They may be played by all age groups—children, youth, and adults. Boy Scouts, Girl Scouts, and similar organizations; church groups; and other organizations interested in developing the spirit of world brotherhood will find them helpful. They might be used successfully in various programs such as "A World Playday," "A Trip Around the World," and so on. Folk dances have not been included because there are many source books containing them.

As you play these games, try to come to a friendly appreciation of the people from whom they come. In these days of world tension it is well to remind ourselves of the kinship of men everywhere. This kinship is apparent as you note the similarities in games played in different nations.

"Blindman's Buff" is a universal favorite. In Russia and Greece it is played exactly as it is in the United States. In China there is a slight variation, the players stooping to avoid being caught. In Africa there is another variation, two players being blindfolded, with the runner indicating his position by striking two sticks together.

"Drop the Handkerchief" is played in Italy, Greece, Japan, and Russia. In Japan it is called "Hankachiotoshi."

"Hide and Seek" under various names is played in most European countries. In France it is called "Cache Cache." "How Do You Like Your Neighbor?" is played in the Balkans and in Turkey, and there is mention of its being played in Constantinople as early as 1649. "Jintori" in Japan is the same as "Prisoner's Base" in the United States. "Going to Jerusalem," or "Musical Chairs," is played in Germany under the name of "Mauer Blumchen" (wallflower). "Sonca" (emphasis on the last syllable) means "toss." It is a Philippine Island version of "Jacks." Six hard fruits, stones, or marbles are used for the jacks. In India this game is called "Guttak" (emphasis on the last syllable), and five hard, round beans are used. "Pum-Pum-Pulloi," as played in the Philippines, is the same as our "Pom-Pom-Pullaway." "Last Couple Out," a game we play in the United States, is played in Russia under the name of "Gorelki," in Scotland as "Widower," and in Africa, where it is called "Kholo Eveawo." "Quatre Coins," literally "four corners," is the French name for "Pussy Wants a Corner." The French also play "Saute-Mouton" ("Leapfrog"), "Colin-Maillard" ("Blindman's Buff"), and "Pigeon Voli" ("Birds Fly").

It is interesting to note the origins of many games. "Prisoner's Base" and "Stealing Sticks" date back to the first Olympics. "Croquet" originated in France, where it was known as "Pall-Mall"; and from there it went to England, where it gave its name to the famous street in London called "Pall Mall." "Hide and Seek" grew out of an early custom in which people went out in the spring to find birds, flowers, or insects to bring back as evidence of the coming of the season. In some European countries the hiders imitate birds to tip off the hunters, thus reflecting the background of the game. I had always thought "Chinese

Checkers" was an adaptation of the old Swedish game "Helma." However, Dr. Liu I Hsin insists that it has an authentic Chinese background. He says he played it as a child and that his grandfather and his grandfather's grandfather played it before him. He says that in China the game is played with fifteen marbles in each corner, while "Helma" is played with ten marbles and there are only two players in the game at a time.

"Badminton" is the ancient game of "Poona" from India. More than two thousand years ago it was played in the Orient. An English army officer introduced it to his friends on his estate in England. The estate happened to bear the title "Badminton," so from then on that's what the game was called. Tennis was born in France. Bowling was introduced into the United States by the Dutch settlers. Plato credits football to the Egyptians, and Holland and Scotland both claim credit for golf. Basketball, volleyball, and modern baseball originated in the United States, although baseball is a close relative of the old English game of "Rounders."

I am deeply grateful for the help in the preparation of this material that I received from many persons around the world. Miss Alberta Tarr, of Hiroshima, Japan, is responsible for most of the games from Japan. The Rev. Asa W. Mellinger, of Chicopee, Massachusetts, is a minister who follows anthropology as a hobby and in doing so has discovered a number of games from many countries, of which he has contributed to this book the following: "African Simon Says," "African Game Trap," "Jarabadach," "Spear the Whale," "Leopards and Cattle," and a variation of "Scissors Chess." Miss Helen Johnson, of New York City, has contributed much also and has been most helpful in suggesting missionaries to contact for contributions. For the games they contributed to the collection my appreciation is here expressed to others, as follows: William M. Holt, of

9

Cochabamba, Bolivia, for "Juego del Panuelo," "Paloma y Gavilan," and "La Palma"; Lois Davidson, of Iquique, Chile, for "The King's Messenger," "Va El Tren," "La Canasta," and "Cambio de Instrumentos"; J. W. Dyson for "Fist Slinging" and "Pick-Up Race"; H. L. Li, of Taiwan, China, for "Throwing the Square," "Clasping for Seven," "Catching Seven Pieces," and "Spreading the Fist"; Gene Hibbard, of Windham, Ohio, for "Da Err," "Chinese Hopscotch," and "Chinese Stick Rhythms"; Christine Evans, of Holguin, Cuba, for "The Fans," "The Dogs and the Chickens," "Doña Ana," "Cuba and Spain," "Asi Jugaba Porque Jugue," and "Matandile"; Christine Evans and Ione Clay, of Cuba, for "La Marisola"; Peter Olsen, of Minneapolis, Minn., for "Stykes"; Marcelle Mancuit for "La-Marelle"; Patricia McHugh, of Honolulu, Hawaii, for "Pahee," "Noa," "Puhenehene," and "Loulou"; Arthur W. Howard, of Lucknow, India, for "Kho-Kho," "Sia Mar Danda," and "Gooli Danda"; Kuribashi, a Japanese student, for a variation of "Scissors Chess" and "Five Eyes"; Fujino Atsuko and Tomito Mayumi, of Hiroshima, Japan, for "Big Lantern, Little Lantern" and "Rakansan"; S. Truda, of Hiroshima, for "Foreigner"; Hiroko Yagi and Shimako Hashimoto, of Hiroshima, for "Karutatori"; Seiko Ashiwa, of Hiroshima, for "Poem Card Playing"; Yuriko Sakai and Miyoka Morimoto, of Hiroshima, for "Sugoroku"; Yoko Animoto, of Hiroshima, for "Kagome-Kagome"; Takako Twane and Chizue Suga, of Hiroshima, for "Takaratori"; Fuijiko Yamada, of Hiroshima, for "Otedama"; Junko Masumoto, of Hiroshima, for "Hanakago"; Leonor Arce for "Little Clown" and "The Little Ball"; Carol Moe, of Bayombong, P. I., for "San Pedro and San Pablo"; Violeta Cavallero, of Montevideo, Uruguay, for "The Color Market," "The Blind Hen," and "The Wolf."

E. O. HARBIN

CONTENTS

GAMES OF
MANY NATIONS

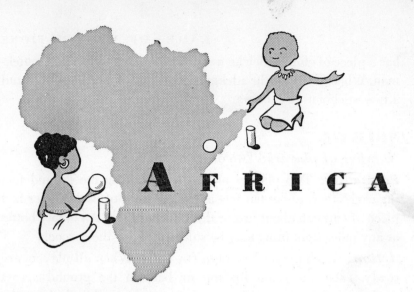

AFRICA

MULAMBILWA

Number of players: Two teams of five to nine each.

Formation and equipment: Teams kneel facing each other about fifteen or twenty feet apart. In front of each player is a tenpin or pop bottle. Each player has a ball.

Action: At the signal to start, each player throws or rolls his ball at the pin of some opponent. When all pins are down for one team, the members of that team must get up and run to their goal, a line about twenty or thirty feet away. If caught, they must pay forfeits or receive roughing from their captors.

AFRICAN BLINDMAN'S BUFF

Number of players: Five or more.

Formation: Circle, with two blindfolded players inside.

Action: One of the blindfolded players has two sticks which he must hit together often to indicate where he is. Instruct him to keep his sticks low so the other blindfolded player, who is "It," will not be stuck in the face if he runs into them. Usually "It"

15

has a piece of cloth which he waves in the effort to locate the stick-man. When "It" tags the stickman, that person becomes "It" and a new stickman is chosen.

NSIKWI

Number of players: Two or more.

Formation: Two players or two teams sit on the ground facing each other, about ten feet apart. In front of each player is a piece of corncob about two or three inches high. An empty bottle or any other light thing may be substituted for the corncob.

Action: Each player has a top (or ball). When all players are ready, each one sends his top or ball on the ground across the intervening space with great force, trying to knock down the corncob of his opponent. Each hit registers a point.

HEN AND WILDCAT

Number of players: Five or more.

Formation and action: One player is chosen as the hen and another as the wildcat. The rest of the players are the chickens. The hen leads the chickens around and warns them of any approaching danger. The wildcat hides himself. At unexpected times and places he springs out and tries to catch any foolish chicken who fails to drop to the ground at the mother hen's warning. This may continue until all chickens are caught, or a new hen and a new wildcat may be chosen whenever a chicken is caught.

CATTLE STOCKADE

This game is very similar to our "Bull in the Ring."

Number of players: Twelve or more.

Formation and action: Players form a circle, hands clasped,

16

around one or more players. These inside players represent the cattle. They hold up their hands and rush against the "stockade," trying to break through. If they succeed, the players responsible for the break-through become the cattle.

LION AND DEER TAG

Number of players: Five or more.

Formation and action: This is played just like tag except that "It" is the lion and the rest of the players are deer.

AFRICAN HANDBALL

Number of players: Six or more.

Action: Players are divided into two equal teams. The game is started by a member of one team tossing a ball to one of his own side. The object of the game is for a team to keep possession of the ball as long as possible. The other team tries to intercept it and gain possession of it.

Every time the ball is caught, the members of that team, except the player catching the ball, clap their hands and stamp their feet.

AFRICAN SIMON SAYS

Number of players: Four or more.

Formation: A leader faces the other players, who stand in a straight line in front of him.

Action: This game may be played in two ways:

1. The leader faces one player in the line. Each of them raises his arms above his head and claps his hands together. Suddenly the leader thrusts one of his arms out in front of him as if striking a blow. The other player must respond immediately by bringing forward his corresponding arm—right

17

must match right; left must match left. If he brings forward the wrong arm, the leader wins. On an agreed number of wins the leader becomes a chief and retires from the game.

2. The leader stands before the entire group. All players follow him in what he does. A player who makes a mistake takes the leader's place, and the leader joins the group. If several players make mistakes, the leader points out the one to take his place.

AFRICAN GAME TRAP

This is similar to the game of "Arches," in which the players march to music, the bridge falling when the music stops.

Number of players: Fifteen to one hundred.

Formation: Players form a single circle. Two players take hold of hands and form a bridge or "trap" under which the other players must march.

Action: The marchers sing or chant as they clap their hands rhythmically:

> Lions and leopards, lions and leopards,
>   Hunting at night;
> Lions and leopards, lions and leopards,
>   Catch the game!

The "trap" falls upon the word "game."

Players caught form additional "traps." The game continues until all players have been caught. Players must move in rhythm, not pausing or dashing through to keep from getting caught.

JARABADACH

This game is somewhat similar to "Ticktacktoe."

Number of players: Two.

Equipment: One player has three white stones or markers, and the other has three black ones. The game is played on a diagram marked on the ground or on paper. This diagram is in the form of a large square divided into four small squares by two lines. The plays are made on the nine points of this large square.

Action: Players take turns in placing their markers, one at a time, on any of the nine points of the square. The purpose is to get three in a row before the opponent can. After the six pieces are placed, players take turns in moving along the lines, a space at a time, until one of the players wins.

SPEAR THE WHALE,
OR ESKIMO ESCAPADES

Number of players: Two.

Equipment: A diamond-shaped piece of plywood four inches wide and six inches long. In the center of this piece is a hole one inch in diameter. In the Arctic this piece is cut from whalebone and the block at the end from walrus tusk. This block is rectangular and may be made of a piece of pine. If of pine, then it should be two inches by three inches by four inches, to be the proper weight. Thus the block would vary in size, depending on the kind of material used. Strings are attached to the ends of the diamond as indicated in the diagram. One string connects the block with the diamond. The other string is suspended from a doorway, bar, or tree limb, so that the hole in the diamond-shaped piece is waist high.

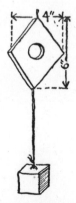

Two wands, each twenty inches long, must be made. The ends should be blunt and rounded, and small enough to slip easily into the hole in the diamond. Sandpaper the wands so they will be smooth to handle.

Draw two parallel lines five feet apart, with the diamond-shaped piece suspended midway between the lines. For children the parallel lines may be closer together. However, see that they are far enough apart so that there will be no danger of players striking each other with their wands.

Action: Each player attempts to thrust his wand through the hole, and at the same time he tries to keep his opponent from doing likewise. Sounds easy, does it? Just try it! Play for the best two out of three or the best three out of five points.

BALL RACE

Equipment: A ball for each player. The Indians use a five- or six-inch ball of wood or stone covered with mesquite gum. A volleyball or play ball may be used.

Action: Players engage in a foot race in which they kick the ball ahead of them. A player has not finished the course until both he and the ball are over the goal line. Touching the ball with the hands disqualifies a player.

Variation: Use a football. This will make it harder to keep the ball in the course.

WHERE IS THE STICK?

Number of players: Six or more.

Equipment: Two small sticks about the size and shape of a piece of chalk. One of these sticks is marked by a white or black stripe, a notch, or some other mark so as to distinguish it from the other.

Formation: Players are divided into two equal sides. They

22

sit facing one another about two feet apart. The leader on one side holds the two sticks. He changes them from one hand to the other, putting his hands back of him once in a while and trying to keep the sticks from being seen.

Action: When the leader indicates he is ready, the players on the opposing team try to guess which hand holds the marked stick. One player at a time guesses. If he guesses correctly, he becomes the leader and the other side guesses. If he guesses incorrectly, the game continues with the same leader manipulating the sticks. When three wrong guesses have been made, the sticks change sides.

PIMA STICKS
Number of players: Two or more.

Equipment: A set of four sticks six to nine inches long and one to two inches wide and two slender marking sticks about a foot long. The four Pima sticks are flat on one side and rounded on the other like yoot sticks (see page 122). On the flat side they are marked by carved lines filled with black paint (see diagram). The other side is rounded and painted red. A space ten feet square is enclosed by holes as in diagram.

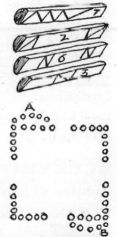

Action: A player (or team) places his marking stick in the corner hole at *A*. The opponent (or opposing team) puts his marking stick in the corner hole at *B*. The object of the game is to move the marking stick around the square, hole by hole. The first one around wins. The moving is determined by tossing the four Pima sticks up in the air, all at one time. They indicate the score as follows: Four round sides up count 10; four flat sides up count 5; only one flat side up counts whatever its marking indicates—7, 6, 3, or 2 (see diagram). The player moves his marking stick accordingly. *A* moves to the right around the arch, then returns to the first hole at the top of the square and moves all around the square. *B* moves to the left around the arch and then to the right around the square. Whenever the count brings the marking stick to a hole occupied by the stick of an opponent, that opponent is sent back to the starting point. Passing an opponent does not send him "home."

ARROW GAME

Number of players: Six or more.

Formation: Two teams of equal numbers line up about forty feet from a target. This target is an arrow standing upright against a hillside.

Action: Players from the two teams alternate in shooting with bow and arrow at the arrow on the hill. The one who hits the target or who comes closest to it scores a point for his team.

Variations: Substitute a slingshot for the bow and arrow, or use a ball, with a stick, piece of cardboard, or other marker for the target.

BUCKSKIN BALL

Number of players: Ten or more.

Equipment: The ball may be a large buckskin ball, a volleyball, or a softball. Each player has a branch four or five feet long, containing a knot or bend at one end.

Formation: Two teams of equal numbers arrange themselves over the playing field as players do for the game of hockey. The two captains stand at center on the dividing line between the two goals. These goals are about one hundred feet on each

24

side of the dividing line. They are indicated by buffalo robes, one at each end, or by some other appropriate marker.

Action: The ball is thrown between the captains on the dividing line. Each team tries to get it over the opponent's buffalo robe by the use of the sticks.

PAPAGO

Number of players: Two to twenty.

Equipment: Four cups or cones and a small object such as a bean or a marble.

Action: If there are more than two players, they divide into two teams. One of the players takes the four cones, conceals the bean or marble in one of them, and then fills them all with sand. He gives the filled cups to his opponent or to the opposing team. The opponent hands them back one at a time. If the first one handed back contains the hidden bean, the player who filled the cups scores ten points. If the bean is in the second cup, he scores six points. The third one counts four points, and the fourth counts nothing. The opponent or other team then hides the bean, and the game continues. Fifty points is out.

TOKINAWAS, OR RING AND ARROW

Number of players: Four.

Equipment: A ring seven inches in diameter made of dry corn husks, wrapped half with white and half with red cord. Four darts made of corncobs, each with two feathers in one end and a wooden point ten inches long in the other.

Action: Two players face each other, six to ten feet apart. They roll the ring back and forth. The other two players on opposite sides throw their darts, one at a time, at the moving ring. The player who hits the ring or shoots through it oftenest in ten trials wins.

BATTLEDORE AND SHUTTLECOCK

This is somewhat similar to "Badminton."

Number of players: Five or more.

Equipment: A battledore for each player. This is a circular piece of wood about nine inches in diameter, with a wooden handle. A ping-pong paddle will do. The shuttlecock could be a badminton bird or a large cork with three feathers stuck in it.

Formation: Circle, with players about six to ten feet apart.

Action: A player starts by batting the shuttlecock to his neighbor to the right. That player must keep it going by batting it to the next player to his right. When a player fails to hit a fair serve, he is out. The game continues until only one man is left. If a player knocks the shuttlecock over the head of another player, he drops out and not the player who was unable to reach it.

KICK THE STICK RELAY

Number of players: Six or more.

Formation and action: Two teams line up in relay formation at a starting line. In front of each team is a crooked stick about twelve inches long. The first player kicks the stick to the goal and back. The stick must be kicked along the ground, not in the air. The first player leaves the stick in front of the next player on his team. That player repeats the performance. The first team to have all its runners complete the course wins.

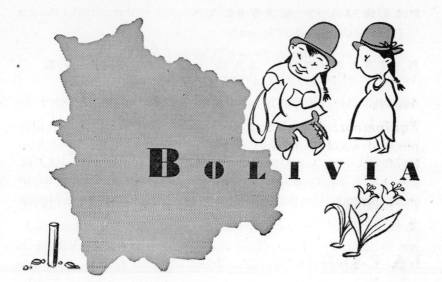

JUEGO DEL PANUELO
(Handkerchief Game)

Number of players: Sixteen to thirty-two.

Formation: Cross.

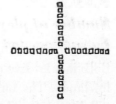

Action: The players are seated in two lines forming a cross (see diagram). One person is elected to be "It." This person circles the group and drops the handkerchief behind the person seated at the end of one of the lines. When the handkerchief is dropped, everyone in that particular line (eight in the above diagram) must circle the group and return to his seat. In the meantime "It" takes one of the vacated seats. Of course, when players return to their seats, the last person arriving is without a seat, and he becomes "It." The game is continued as long as desired.

PALOMA Y GAVILAN

(The Eagle and the Pigeon)

This game is similar to our "Cat and Rat."

Number of players: Eight or more.

Action: One person is chosen to be the eagle. Another is chosen to be the pigeon. All the others form a circle and join hands. The eagle chases the pigeon about the circle. Those who make up the circle are on the side of the pigeon and let him pass under their clasped hands. They try not to let the eagle come through. The game lasts until the eagle catches the pigeon or gives up trying.

LA PALMA

Number of players: Two or more.

Equipment: This game is very popular with the Indians of Bolivia who live either on the Altiplano or down in the tropical lowlands. The only equipment needed (or used by them) is a tail bone of a donkey or a llama (a stick may be used) and several rocks. The bone is stuck in the ground for a target. A line is made in the ground about three yards from the bone. Other lines are made, each about three yards farther from the bone than the preceding line. There are about six lines in all, with the last being eighteen yards from the bone.

Action: The players (usually boys) take turns, standing first at line number one, with their slings and try to hit the bone with a rock. In case they do not have slings, they merely throw rocks. If the person is successful in hitting the bone at line number one, he moves on to line number two. The first person to hit the bone from all six lines wins the game. When the players are very good with their slings, they sometimes double the distance between lines.

CAT AND RAT

This is similar to our "Cat and Rat."

Number of players: Ten or more.

Formation: The other players form a circle, hands clasped. Two players represent the cat and rat. The cat stands outside the circle and the rat inside.

Action: The Brazilian game, however, adds a very interesting feature. The cat knocks on the back of one of the players in the circle. That player asks, "What do you want?"

"I want to see the rat," replies the cat.

"You cannot see him now," says the circle player.

"When can I see him?" asks the cat.

"At ten o'clock," comes the reply. (The player can call out any time he desires.)

Immediately the circle begins moving around in rhythm as they count off the hours. All the players may call off the hours. Thus they call, "One o'clock, ticktock! Two o'clock, ticktock!

Three o'clock, ticktock!" and so on, until they reach the announced time, which in this case is ten o'clock. At this point the circle stops moving. The cat steps up again to the player whose back he tapped. He knocks again. This time the dialogue is as follows: "What do you want?"

"I want to see the rat."

"What time is it?"

"Ten o'clock!" answers the cat.

"All right; come in!"

The cat ducks in, and the rat tries to elude him by getting outside. From there on it is played just as the American game.

In moving around, while counting off the hours, players should make an effort to get good rhythm. By taking two steps between each call and two steps while making the call, they can do this.

HIT THE PENNY

(Also many other South American countries)

Number of players: Two or more.

Equipment: A bamboo stick, twelve to eighteen inches long, is set up in the ground. A piece of broomstick may be substituted, if bamboo is not available. On top of the bamboo is placed a penny or other coin, or a metal washer. The stick is in the center of a circle about three feet in diameter. This circle is marked on the ground. If the game is played indoors, the coin may be placed on a stool and the circle may be indicated by a string.

Action: Players stand at a distance of four to six feet and take turns trying to knock the coin off the bamboo by throwing a penny at it. If they knock it off and outside the three-foot circle, they score one point. If it drops inside the circle or if they miss it, they score nothing.

MORRAL, OR GRAB BAG
(Also many other South American countries)

Number of players: Any number.

Equipment: A large sack or container filled with enough gifts for everyone in the group. These gifts may be comical or otherwise.

Action: Players, in turn, reach into the grab bag and take out a present. Sometimes mottoes, fortunes, or verses are used instead of presents. In this case they are read by those who draw them, for the amusement of the crowd.

Variation: If desired, suggestions for stunts to be performed may be placed on slips of paper, perhaps in small envelopes. (See section on forfeits, page 148, for ideas for stunts.) The persons drawing them must perform, as directed, for the entertainment of the group.

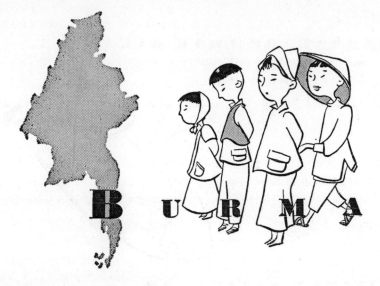

LOO K'BAH ZEE

Number of players: Six or more.

Formation: Players form a straight line, holding their hands open behind them. One player is back of the line.

Action: The player back of the line holds a stone or other small object (a marble perhaps) in his hand. He walks up and down pretending to put the object in a player's hands. Finally he does drop it into a player's hands. That player darts out of the line, trying to avoid being tagged by those on either side of him. The taggers may not move out of their places, but must catch him as he leaves his place. If the runner is not caught, he goes back to his own place and the game continues. If he is caught, he exchanges places with the player behind the line.

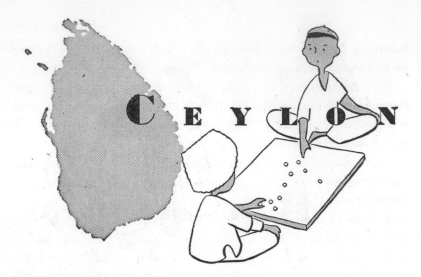

C E Y L O N

DIVIYAN KELIYA, OR LEOPARDS AND CATTLE

This is somewhat similar to "Fox and Geese."

Number of players: Two.

Equipment: A board ten to twelve inches square marked as indicated in the diagram. Care should be taken to see that all lines are properly placed. If desired, holes may be drilled at the forty-nine points of intersection, and marbles may be used for the cattle and leopards. Otherwise use twenty-four counters (checkers) for the cattle and two of contrasting color for the leopards.

Action: One player takes the twenty-four cattle. His opponent uses the two leopards. The object of the game is for the cattle to pen the leopards so they cannot be moved or for the leopards to "eat up" (jump) the cattle.

To start the game, a leopard is placed at the center intersection. One of the cattle is then placed anywhere on the board,

34

followed by the second leopard, which also may be placed on any vacant spot on the board.

Play alternates, the cattle being placed one at a time. Between each placement the leopard may either jump, if a jump is possible, or else move along one of the marked lines from the spot occupied to an adjacent empty spot.

Cattle cannot be moved until they have all been placed. They may then move one space at a time along the lines to an adjacent empty space.

A leopard may "eat up" one of the cattle by jumping over it from an adjacent space to an empty space beyond, along one of the lines. Double or triple jumps, as in checkers, are permitted. A jump cannot be refused. Cattle cannot jump. Leopards may jump backward, forward, or sideways along the lines.

Cattle win if both leopards are completely cornered. Leopards win if they "eat up" enough cattle (usually ten) so that they cannot be cornered.[1]

---

[1] This is an ancient game, handed down through the centuries from one generation to the next. The fact that it is still played is some indication of its worth.

CHILE

LA BARRA

Number of players: Eight or more.

Formation: Two teams of players line up in one straight line. In front of them, about twenty feet away, stands "It," one player of one of the teams.

Action: The opposing team to "It's" team shouts the question "Barra?" When someone from the other team answers, "Dicha la Barra!" a player runs out from the team that shouted the question and tries to tag "It." At the same time a player runs out from the opposing team and tries to tag the runner before he touches "It." If the runner succeeds in touching "It" before being tagged himself, "It" becomes a prisoner. If the runner is tagged himself, however, before he reaches "It," he becomes prisoner.

The other team then sends one of its men out to stand twenty feet away, and the game continues. The game ends when one team has only one player left.

THE KING'S MESSENGER

Number of players: Eight to twelve.

Formation: Circle or line.

Action: Each player is given the name of a color—Red, Blue, Yellow, and so forth—and one player is the king's messenger. The king's messenger enters and says that the king has been robbed and one of the players is the guilty person. There is a pattern to the dialogue, and a forfeit has to be paid for each mistake made. A mistake is made when any player answers out of turn or when a player hesitates too long before answering the king's messenger. The dialogue goes thus:

> *K. M.:* I have come to say that the king has lost a gold ring and that Red has it.
>
> *Red:* I, my Lord?
>
> *K. M.:* Yes, my Lord.
>
> *Red:* No, my Lord.
>
> *K. M.:* Then who has it?
>
> *Red:* Yellow has it.

The dialogue is repeated until all the players have been asked for the gold ring, after which players retrieve the objects they forfeited by doing some kind of stunt (see section on forfeits, page 148).

VA EL TREN

Number of players: Eight to twenty.

Formation: The players are seated in a circle on the ground or floor.

Action: A small stone is passed from hand to hand as they sing the song *Va El Tren*. When they get to the word *chiquichiquicha* (pronounced "chicky-chicky-chaw"), the player who has the stone in his hand retains it until the word is finished. Keeping time to the music and to the three parts of the word (as indicated in the pronunciation above), he touches the ground three times with the stone, first directly in front of himself, then a little way forward, and then back to the original spot. If any player forgets to touch the stone to the ground three times, in time to the music and the word, he has to drop out of the game. The game continues until all are out.[2]

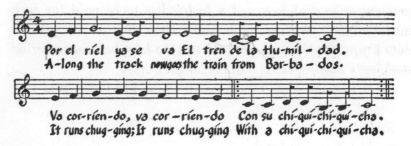

Por el riel ya se va El tren de la Hu-mil - dad.
A-long the track now goes the train from Bar-ba - dos.

Va cor-rien-do, va cor-rien-do Con su chi-qui-chi-qui-cha.
It runs chug-ging; It runs chug-ging With a chi-qui-chi-qui-cha.

LA CANASTA

Number of players: Ten or more.

Formation: Circle.

Action: This game is like our game "Fruit Basket" except that "It" begins by saying, "I have just been to the fruit market, and I bought limes, oranges," and so on. In Chile the "market" is really a market, a whole square block of stalls, so the connotation of the word "market" is considerably different there. When "It" calls out the fruits he has bought, the players bearing these names must immediately change places, or chairs if they are used. "It" tries to get one of the places, and if he succeeds, the player left without a place automatically becomes "It."

---

[2] A game similar to this may be found in my *Fun Encyclopedia*, pp. 491-92. It is entitled "You Must Pass This Spoon." A game like it is played in the Netherlands, except that there each player takes off his shoe and passes it to his neighbor to the right. On the words "do just what I do" the player taps the floor with the shoe to the right, to the left, and back to the right, and then on to the next player in the circle.

CAMBIO DE INSTRUMENTOS

Number of players: Eight or more.

Formation: Circle.

Action: "It" leaves the room. Each player is given the name of a musical instrument, and when "It" returns to the room, the players begin to make the motion required for any one of the instruments. One player gives the signal for changing the motions to that of some other instrument as often as he likes provided "It" does not see him give the signal. If "It" catches him giving the signal for the change, then he must become "It" and leave the room.

CHINESE CHECKERS

Number of players: Two to six.

Equipment: The board for this game can easily be made of beaver board, cardboard, three-ply, or, if desired, out of walnut, cherry, or pine. The game is played on a six-point star. Paint each point of the star a different color and then shellac the entire board. When six play, each has ten "men" in his point of the star. Men may be discs cut from old mop handles or half-inch dowels, sandpapered to a smooth finish and 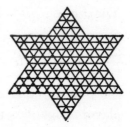 painted in the colors corresponding to those on the board. Or holes may be bored at the intersections and marbles or pegs used instead of discs.

Action: The men are placed on the intersections, beginning with the point, so that they are placed 1, 2, 3, 4, and so on. Each player tries to get his men across to the opposite star point. He may move in any direction except backward. Jumps may be

40

made of one man at a time as in checkers, but no man is removed from the board. Series of jumps may be made, of course. Often a player gets a "ladder" set up by which he jumps all the way across the board. No jumps or moves may be made back into an opponent's star point.

Three players can play the game using alternating star points for starting points. In this case fifteen men may be used.

FINGERS OUT

Number of players: Two.

Formation and action: The two players face each other. They count, "One, two, three!" On "three" they put out their right hands, either closed or with one or more fingers extended. At the same time they shout some number. The player who guesses the correct number of the sum total of fingers extended, or the nearest to it, scores a point. Five points may constitute a game.

TSOO! TSOO!

Number of players: Four or more.

Formation and action: One player is blindfolded. The remaining players are chickens. The blindfolded player says, "Tsoo! Tsoo!" meaning, "Come and seek your mother." The chickens run up and try to touch him without being caught. The player caught becomes the blindman.

FORCING THE CITY GATES
(Also the Philippines)

Number of players: Ten or more.

Formation: Two lines each with an equal number of players, ten to fifteen feet apart. Each team has a captain. Players in each line hold hands.

Action: A player runs out from one side and dashes with all his force against the hands of his opponents. If he breaks through, he takes back to his side the two players whose clasped hands he separated. If he fails to break through, he has to join his opponents. Then a player from the other side attempts to "force the gates." This continues until one side has no one left.

CAT AND MOUSE

Number of players: Ten to thirty.

Formation: Circle, with all but two players holding hands. One of those players is the cat, who stands outside the circle. The other is the mouse, who stands inside the circle.

Action: The circle of players revolves about the mouse. When it stops, the cat darts in at one side and the mouse goes out the other. The cat pursues the mouse, but he must follow exactly the path the mouse has taken, with no short cuts. The two wind in and out of the circle until the mouse is caught. Then two more players are chosen, or the cat may become the mouse and a new cat may be chosen.

LAME CHICKEN

Number of players: Two or more.

Equipment: Each of two players or of two teams has ten sticks, ten or twelve inches long. These sticks are arranged in a row about ten inches apart like rungs on a ladder, one row for each team.

Action: The player (lame chicken) must hop over these sticks without touching any of them. Touching a stick disqualifies him. After hopping over the last stick, still on one foot, he reaches down and picks up the stick. He then hops back over the remaining sticks. Dropping the stick, he hops over the nine re-maining sticks, picks up the ninth stick, again hopping over the remaining sticks. This continues until all the sticks have been picked up. A player is disqualified if he touches both feet to the ground or if he touches a stick with his foot.

Variations: 1. The game may be run as a race. A player who fouls must start over.

2. It may be used as a relay. The first player hops over ten sticks, returning with the tenth. The second man hops over nine, the third hops over eight, and so on.

3. The lame chicken may change by hopping on the other foot every other round. The winner is the team with most players finishing without mistakes.

SHUTTLECOCK

This is an interesting game for all age groups. Many of the Chinese develop considerable skill in playing it.

Number of players: One to twenty.

Equipment: Shuttlecock, which may be made of four chicken feathers and a piece of thick cardboard. Cut out a circular piece of cardboard about an inch and a quarter in diameter. Paint it with cardboard or tempera paint. Attach the four feathers at the top center of the cardboard disc. Hold the feathers in place with a piece of cellophane glued to the cardboard disc.

Action: The player tosses the shuttlecock into the air and then kicks it with his foot back into the air. He continues this as long as he can do it without missing. When a player gets fairly skillful, he kicks the shuttlecock not only with his instep but with his heel, sometimes alternating the heel and the instep kicks.

FIST SLINGING, OR FIST MATCHING[3]

Number of players: Two or more.

Action: One player acts as "caller." He wins or loses accordingly. He may take as many tries as has been determined, or the players may simply take turns. The caller calls out a number from zero to ten if two are playing. This call is made just as each player "throws his fist," holding up any number of fingers he desires. If the sum of the fingers on the two fists is the amount called, the caller wins. If it is not, he loses. Scores may be kept or penalties or awards made as agreed upon.

If three persons play, there will be three fists and therefore a possible total of fifteen fingers; for four, twenty fingers; and so on. The caller must call a number that will come within the total number of fingers that may be held up.

The caller may use names or other substitutes for actual numbers. For example, he may shout, "Tom, Dick, and Harry," meaning three; or "Romeo and Juliet," meaning two; or "double quartet" (eight); or "one week" (seven). The Chinese often call the names of places, lines of poetry, famous persons in history, and the like. This adds great subtlety and humor to the game, and calls for quick and witty thinking.

All calls must be made to synchronize exactly with the throwing of the fingers, so that no player can adjust his fingers in order to win.

Note the similarity of this game to "Spreading the Fist," page 47.

THROWING THE SQUARE

Number of players: Two or more, or two teams.

Equipment: Draw a rectangle, approximately twelve by twenty-

[3] The Chinese name means literally "throwing fists."

four inches, on the ground or floor. Divide it into two equal squares. Each player has a disc (a coin, a flat rock, or a washer).

Action: One player places his disc in one of the squares. The other player stands on a line about eight to ten feet away from the rectangle. From this point he tosses his disc at the squares. If it lands in the square with the other player's disc in it, he scores two points. If it lands in the vacant square, he scores one point. If it lands outside the rectangle, he scores nothing. Players take turns in tossing.

PICKUP RACE

Number of players: Two to eight. The game may be played by teams.

Equipment: One pair of chopsticks and two bowls for each player. These bowls are placed on tables or chairs eight to ten feet apart. Four or five marbles for each player. These marbles are placed in the bowls at one side of the room. For inexperienced players substitute marshmallows, popcorn, or nuts for the marbles.

Action: At the signal to go, players try to pick up the marbles and carry them to the other bowl. The one who first completes the four or five trips wins.

Rules: 1. The players must pick up the marbles one at a time.

2. Hands are not allowed to touch the marbles.

3. If a player drops a marble, he must pick it up, put it in the original bowl, and start again.

CLASPING FOR SEVEN

This game is so similar to "Buzz," "Counting to Thirty," and other such games that one wonders about its original source.

Number of players: Twenty to forty.

Formation: Players are seated in a circle.

Action: Players in the circle call out successive numbers, beginning with one. When it is the turn of one whose number is seven, or seventeen, or twenty-seven, or any number containing the digit seven, he clasps his hands instead of calling the number. These are called "bright" or "conspicuous" sevens.

Similarly on multiples of seven (fourteen, twenty-one, twenty-eight, and so on) the player should clasp his hands instead of calling the number. These multiples are called "dark" or "inconspicuous" sevens.

Whoever makes a mistake drops out of the game, and the numbering is begun again at one.

Other numbers, such as four, six, eight, nine, and so on, may be used instead of seven.

A more complicated version of the game requires the player to clasp his hands on sevens and multiples, smile at eights and multiples, and nod at nines and multiples.

CATCHING SEVEN PIECES

This is similar to our game of "Jacks."

Number of players: Two or more.

Formation: Players stand at a table or are seated on the ground or floor.

Equipment: Seven small cloth bags about one inch square. Fill with sand or rice.

Action: Players take turns. A player holds all seven pieces in his right hand. He drops them on the table (or ground), being careful to spread them out so that no two are touching. He picks one of the pieces up, tosses it in the air, quickly grabs another piece from the table, and then catches the one tossed into the air before it falls to the table. Similarly he grabs another from the table, until he holds all seven in his palm. He should retain the previous ones in his hand while throwing one up and grabbing the next one.

Letting the piece tossed into the air drop to the table or touching or moving the other pieces on the table except the one being grabbed forfeits the player's turn.

SPREADING THE FIST

Number of players: Six or more.

Formation: Players are grouped in teams of three each. Two of the three players form a horse thus:  *A* stands erect. *B* bends his back, holding the hands of *A*, thus forming the horse. *C* is the "rider." Two teams face each other. Four players could play the game. In this case there would be just one horse. *D*, the extra player, would stand in front of *A* and contend with *C*.

Action: The two "riders" engage in the game of spreading the fist. Each holds up his right fist simultaneously. As he does so, he calls a number. At the same time he holds up from one to five fingers. Whichever gets the correct total wins. If neither gets the right number, they try again immediately. This continues until one of them calls the correct total.

The winner takes *A*'s place in forming the horse. The loser takes *B*'s place, with bended back.

Arrange it so that each player gets an opportunity to be the "rider."

DA ERR

Number of players: Two or more.

Equipment: A stick about six inches long, sharpened at both ends so that, when it is hit on one end, it bounces into the air. Another stick, twenty-four to thirty-six inches long, is used as a club. A sawed-off broomstick makes ideal equipment because of its smoothness and durability.

A three-foot square is outlined on the ground. If teams are to play the game, the square should be smaller.

Action: The batter knocks the short stick into the air by hitting on one of its sharpened ends. While it is in the air, he hits it as far as possible with a swinging stroke. From the point where it stops the opposing player tries to toss the short stick into the three-foot square. If successful he becomes the batter.

Often the game is played with three or four players on a side. Each player on a side gets to hit the short stick. The first player hits from the square. The second hits from the point where it rests after the first player's smash. And so on until all the players on the team have hit it. Thus it is often far from the square after the last player has hit it. However, the team in the field gets one throw for each man on its team. By thus relaying it the last man is often close enough simply to drop the short stick in the square. That's the reason for making the square smaller when more than two play the game.

CHINESE HOPSCOTCH
Number of players: Two or more.

Equipment: Make a rectangle eight by four feet. Mark it into eight squares as indicated in the diagram. Each player supplies himself with a small, flat stone.

Action: Standing a few feet away from the rectangle, the first player tosses his stone, trying to land it in square number one. If successful he hops into square one and kicks the stone out of the rectangle. He then tries for square two. From there he must

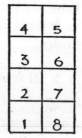

48

kick his stone into square one and then out of the rectangle. So it goes until he has completed all eight squares.

If a player misses his throw by rolling or sliding out, or if the stone touches a line, or if he touches a line with his foot or lets the other foot down, he loses his turn.

If his throw is successful but he misses in kicking the stone out or he touches the other foot to the ground, he is privileged to put his stone in that square without tossing for it on his next turn.

CHINESE STICK RHYTHMS
Number of players: Two.

Equipment: Each has a stick six feet long (broomstick).

Action: Standing, facing, they make rhythm by striking sticks on ground, then striking them together. Positions: (A) On ground. (B) Sticks crossed high. (C) Crossed low. Right foot is forward, right hand in forward grasping position. Possible rhythms: AB, ABCB, AB, ABCB, and so on. Or go up to ten or twenty and back to two, as: AB, ABCB, ABCBCB, ABCBCBCB, and so forth.

BEACH LAME CHICKEN
This game is a good one for a sandy beach. In fact it is so used in China. Or it may be played in the yard or even in the parlor. It is very similar to "Lame Chicken."

Number of players: Two or more—or even one can have a lot of fun trying his skill.

Equipment: Usually bathing slippers are used. However, it may be played with bean bags, strips of seaweed, shells, or whatever is handy.

Formation and Action: Place five to ten bathing slippers in a straight row and about ten to twelve inches apart. There should be a row for each group playing. Each player in turn becomes a "lame chicken." He hops on one foot over each slipper. On hopping over the last slipper, he kicks it with the foot he's hopping on, picks it up, and hops back over the other slippers. After hopping over slipper number one, he kicks it, picks it up, and hops back over the remaining slippers. This process is continued without stopping until all the slippers have been picked up. During all this time he must never let the "lame foot" touch the ground. Nor must he touch a shoe except in regular turn when he is supposed to kick it and pick it up.

Players who fall, touch the "lame foot" to the ground, or touch any of the shoes out of turn drop out of the contest.

IAU CHHUNG

Number of players: Two to eight.

Equipment: Four sticks are needed for this ancient Chinese game. Two of these are of equal length and fat. The other two are light, usually of bamboo. They are about one foot and six inches long, respectively. The longer stick is the "club," while the shorter six-inch stick is the "twig."

Action: Lots are drawn to determine who will be first batter, second batter, third, and so on. The batter places the twig across the two parallel fat sticks so that it protrudes beyond them on one side. He sharply strikes this protruding end with a downward blow so that the twig rises in the air. The other players try to catch it as it comes down. If it is caught, the batter must take the field and the next batter comes up to strike. If it is not caught, the batter is ready for the next test.

This time the twig is laid crosswise on the two fat sticks, while one of the fielders throws the club at it. He has three tries from a position at least five yards away. If he hits the twig, the batter is out. If he misses, the batter takes the third test.

The fielder takes the twig and tosses it to the batter, who tries to hit it with the club. He is allowed three trials. If he hits the twig, it is allowed to fall to the ground unimpeded. The batter then measures the distance from where he is standing to the twig, using the club as a measuring rod.

A batter continues to bat until he is put out. Each time he goes through the three tests.

The scoring is by club measures. Each club measure is a point.

Fifty to one hundred points constitute a game, as decided by the players before beginning. The last player out is loser.

There are two penalties for losing—the "hmmmmmm" penalty and the hopping penalty. Before beginning the game the players decide how many times the loser shall pay the penalty— that is, whether it will be two, or three, or four times. The same number of times is given to each penalty.

To impose the "hmmmmmm" penalty, the winner tosses the twig as far as he can. The loser must run after it and bring it back, all the way saying "hmmmmmm." If he should stop saying "hmmmmmm" before returning, three more such penalties are levied.

In the hopping penalty the winner throws the twig and the loser hops after it, picks it up, and hops back without touching his foot to the ground. If he fails, three more hopping penalties are inflicted.

CATCHING THE DRAGON'S TAIL

Number of players: Ten or more.

Formation: All players stand in a line, their hands on one another's shoulders. The first person in line is the head of the dragon, and the last is the tail.

Action: The head tries to catch the tail by maneuvering the line around so that he can tag the end player. The line must not break. All the other players do their best to keep the head from catching the dragon's tail. When the head catches the tail, the end player becomes the head and the player who was in front of him becomes the tail.

FAN MIEN, OR REVERSES

Number of players: Two.

Equipment: A checkerboard. Sixty-four discs, each three fourths of an inch wide. These may be cut out of cardboard. They are one color on one side and another color on the other. Use paint or crayons.

Action: The play always starts at the center of the board, with the players alternating in placing the first discs on the four center squares. Then there will be two green and two red discs at the center, if green and red are used. After that each player places his discs so as to capture some of the discs of his opponent. This is done by getting one or more of his discs between one's own. When this is done, all the discs in between are turned over  to show the other color. Plays cannot be made just anywhere on the board, but must be made next to a disc already played. One loses his turn unless he can turn over one or more of an opponent's discs on his play.

The four corners are strategic points. Therefore skillful players try to maneuver opponents into making plays which give them the corners.

At the end of the game the player having the most of his color up wins. Placing a disc between two of an opponent's does not turn it over. Thus a player may place a green between two reds without penalty. But if a green is on one side of a row of reds and a player plays another green on the other side of the row, all the red discs in between the two greens are turned over with the green up.

If a player gets an opponent's man between his own men in more than one direction, diagonally, vertically, or horizontally, he turns over all men so caught.

WATER SPRITE

Number of players: Ten to thirty.

Formation: Two lines of players face one another twenty to sixty feet apart. Between the two lines stands the "Water Sprite," who is "It." The intervening space represents the river.

Action: The Water Sprite beckons to one of the players to leave the "bank" and cross the "river." Immediately the Water Sprite must close his eyes and count to ten. The player signaled in turn signals to a player on the opposite bank while the Water Sprite has his eyes covered. These two players try to exchange positions while the Water Sprite tries to tag one of them. If he succeeds, the person tagged takes his place.

KICK THE MARBLES

Number of players: Two, or more if desired.

Equipment: Two large marbles, an inch and a half in diameter, are needed. Two old golf balls or two tennis balls may be substituted for the marbles.

Action: One player begins the game by putting a marble on the ground and giving it a shove with his shoe. He then puts down the other marble and shoves it in the same way, trying to hit the first marble. If his opponent desires, he may call for him to kick the marble in a certain direction by ordering, "Kick east of the other marble." Or he may require that he kick west, or south, or north. If the kicker succeeds, he kicks again, trying to hit the marble. One point is scored if the kicker lands his marble east, west, south, or north of the other marble, as directed. A point is also scored for every hit. If he kicks in the direction ordered and hits in the same shot, he scores double the number of points.

FRYING VEGETABLES

This is a Chinese version of "Fruit Basket."

Number of players: Ten or more.

Formation: Players are seated in a circle, with "It" standing at center.

Action: All the players are given the names of vegetables— corn, cabbage, carrots, cauliflower, beans, beets, turnips, and so on. "It" calls the names of two vegetables. The players representing those vegetables must exchange seats. In the mix-up "It" tries to get a seat. The player left out is "It," and the game continues. If "It" calls, "Frying pan turn over!" all players must change seats.

CUBA

CHOCOLONGA

Number of players: Five or more.

Action: A player is selected from the crowd. He stands at arm's length before a circle or other marker on the wall. He is told to touch the circle as near the center as possible, while he is blindfolded. During the time he is being blindfolded and turned around three times, someone stands in front of the circle so that the player's finger goes into his mouth instead of touching the circle. This player catches the finger between his teeth and bites it gently. If preferred, some sort of pinching instrument may be used.

THE FLOWER GARDEN

Number of players: Ten or more.

Formation: Players are seated in a circle.

Action: The leader gives the name of a flower to each of the players. Then he says, "In a garden of flowers that I saw, nothing but the rose was lacking." Then he asks, "What was it that was lacking?" The rose answers immediately, "The violet was lacking." The violet must then respond, "The violet was there because I saw it. It was the pansy that was lacking." The game proceeds thus rapidly until some player fails to respond. This player must pay a forfeit.

THE NUTS

Number of players: Ten or more.

Formation: Players are seated in a circle.

Action: The leader gives such phrases as the following to certain of the players: "How many?" and "How expensive?" To the other players he gives numbers, five and multiples of five (ten, fifteen, twenty, twenty-five, thirty, and so on).

The leader begins by saying, "How many?" The person with that phrase must answer immediately, "Sir?" Then the leader says, "How many nuts did they give you at the store for a dime?" "How many" must answer with the number five or a multiple of five. The leader may either repeat the number or say, "How expensive?" or, "How cheap?" or any of the other phrases given the various players. Players must listen attentively and respond accordingly or pay a forfeit.

THE DOGS AND THE CHICKENS

Number of players: Eight or more.

Formation: Players are seated in a circle.

Action: Each player is given the name of a city or town. The leader starts the game by saying, "In ———— the dogs crow and the chickens bark." The player who has the name of the city called must reply quickly, "No, sir, in ———— the dogs do not crow and the chickens do not bark. Where the dogs crow and the chickens bark is in ————." The player bearing that name replies immediately in the same fashion. When a player fails to respond quickly or makes a mistake in responding, he must pay a forfeit.

THE PRIEST'S HAT

This is a Cuban version of "The Prince of Paris."

Number of players: Eight or more.

Formation: Players are seated in a circle. The person acting as leader stands at center.

Action: The leader says, "The priest has lost his hat, and they tell me that someone in this room found it and hid it. I do not know who it is, but I think it is ————." At the same time he points at someone in the circle. This player must not speak or smile, but with vigorous motions of the head must deny the charge, point out someone else, who in turn denies it and points to another person. The point of the game is to make some player laugh or smile, or to catch him off guard so that he fails to respond immediately. Guilty players must pay a forfeit. The looks of mock surprise on the faces of players charged with the offense and their solemn protests in pantomime are exceedingly funny. Before long a number of forfeits will be surrendered. When a player is guilty, the forfeit is paid and the leader starts the game again.

THE FANS, OR LOS ABANICOS

Formation: The players sit or stand in a circle.

Action: The first player says to the one on his right (in Cuba all plays are made to the right instead of the left), "My husband has come home from a journey." The second player asks, "What did he bring you?" The reply is, "A fan." The first player starts fanning with his left hand. The second player turns to the one on his right and repeats, "My husband has come home from a journey." The game proceeds this way until all the players are fanning with their left hands. On the second round each player continues to move his left hand in the motion of fanning and also his right hand, for the husband has brought two fans. If three and four fans are desired, both feet must be put into action. The last time around the circle the reply to the question "What did he bring you?" is "an image of St. Teresa," and the player bobs his head while both hands and both feet are going in fanning motion.

MY FRIEND HAS RETURNED FROM THE ORIENT

Action: Players divide into two groups. A line is drawn between them. One group decides on some object to represent in pantomime and then goes up to the other group and says, "My friend has returned from the Orient." The other group asks, "What did he bring with him?" The first group shows by pantomime. If one of the other group guesses what the object is, the entire group start running to catch as many of the first group as possible before they reach the "safe" line. Those captured they take to their side. The object is to get all the players on one side.

DONA ANA NO ESTA AQUI

The following song is sung by the players, in a circle, walking around slowly, holding hands, with one player in the center, representing Doña Ana.

Doña An-a is not here; she's out a-mong her flow'rs; She's o-pen-ing the rose-buds And clos-ing up the pinks.

Let's go a-round her house And see what we can see; They say that Doña An-a Eats par-sley and green peas.

Then Doña Ana sings alone:

> Who are these funny people
> That in my house do peep
> And neither night nor day
> Allow me to sleep?

The circle sings back:

> We are the jolly students
> Who've come to go to school
> And live here very near you
> In the chapel on the hill.

The circle stops, and the players ask, "How are you, Doña Ana?" Doña Ana replies that she has fever. The circle starts again, singing the first part, and then stops and asks again, "How is Doña Ana?" This time she replies that she has died, and her ghost rushes out and catches the fleeing players. The one she touches first becomes Doña Ana in the center of the circle, and the game is repeated as many times as desired.[4]

[4] Spanish text and melody and game directions from *Canciones Populares* by Allena Luce, copyright 1921, 1949, by Silver Burdett Company, New York. Used with

CUBA AND SPAIN

This is a tag game the children love to play.

Formation: Players form two lines, opposite one another, about ten feet apart, or more if they want to run farther. One side is called Spain and the other side Cuba.

Action: A player from Spain is chosen to go to Cuba. All the Cuban players hold out their left hands, palms up. The Spanish representative rubs his right hand once over the palm of each player until he comes to the one he wants to run after him. Instead of rubbing, he strikes this player's palm; and the player chases him to his side. If he catches him before he gets "home," he takes him to Cuba's side and goes to Spain to repeat the performance. The object is to get all Spain's players on Cuba's side or vice versa.

SAN SERENI, OR ASI JUGABA PORQUE JUGUE

There are two variations of this game—the boys' and the girls'. In the boys' game there should be a leader, San Serení, who suggests the motions. At the words "And this is how they made them" all imitate the shoemaker or whatever other occupation has been chosen.

San Se-re-ní who lived a good life taught the boys to Make good shoes And this is how they made them Tap tap-a tap-a tap.

permission. In Cuba almost all children's games are played with music, and this book has a number of them. The author calls them the Puerto Rican equivalent of Mother Goose rhymes. "Doña Ana No Está Aquí" is one of the more popular ones. It's similar to "Miss Jennia Jones," with different music. As the book is in Spanish, I have translated the words to fit the music as it is in the book.

Other occupations and their corresponding motions might
be as follows:

Taught the boys to drive a car,
And this is how they drove it (imitate turning steering wheel).
Taught the boys to paint a house (imitate painting with a brush).
Taught the boys to sing a song (sing tra-la-la-la-la-la).

The Spanish words are as follows:

> San Serení
> de la buena, buena vida,
> hacen así, así los zapateros
> así, así, así (Los imitan)
> así me gusta a mí.

The girls' game consists of seven divisions of two stanzas
each. In the first stanza the participants, forming a circle, sing
their explanation of the fact that the child who is the subject
of their story was unable to go out for a good time ("pasear").
The group act out each duty as it is mentioned.

> Monday morning early
> A little girl went out to play,
> But she could not play because
> She had to wash the clothes.
> And this is how she washed the clothes;
> I saw her wash them so.
>
> Tuesday morning early
> A little girl went out to play,
> But she could not play because
> She had to starch the clothes.

And this is how she starched the clothes;
I saw her starch them so.

Wednesday morning early
A little girl went out to play,
But she could not play because
She had to hang the clothes.
And this is how she hung the clothes;
I saw her hang them so.

Thursday morning early
A little girl went out to play,
But she could not play because
She had to sprinkle the clothes.
And this is how she sprinkled the clothes;
I saw her sprinkle them so.

Friday morning early
A little girl went out to play,
But she could not play because
She had to iron the clothes.
And this is how she ironed the clothes;
I saw her iron them so.

Saturday morning early
A little girl went out to play,
But she could not play because
She had to clean the house.
And this is how she cleaned the house;
I saw her clean it so.

Sunday morning early
A little girl went out to play,
But she could not play because
She had to go to church.
And this is how she went to church;
I saw her go this way.

The Spanish words are as follows:
She had to wash on Monday:

>Lunes antes de almorzar
>una niña fué a pasear;
>ella no podía pasear
>porque tenía que lavar.
>
>Así lavaba así, así . . ,
>Así lavaba así, así . . .
>Así lavaba así, así . . .
>Así lavaba que yo la vi.

Starch on Tuesday:

>Martes antes de almorzar
>una niña fué a pasear;
>ella no podía pasear
>porque tenía que almidonar
>
>Así almidonaba así, así . . .
>Así almidonaba así, así . . .
>Así almidonaba así, así . . .
>Así almidonaba que yo la vi.

Hang out the clothes on Wednesday:

>Miércoles antes de almorzar
>una niña fué a pasear;

ella no podía pasear
porque tenía que tender.

Así tendía así, así . . .
Así tendía así, así . . .
Así tendía así, así . . .
Así tendía que yo la vi.

Sprinkle clothes on Thursday:

Jueves antes de almorzar
una niña fué a pasear;
ella no podía pasear
porque tenía que rociar.

Así rociaba, así, así . . .
Así rociaba, así, así . . .
Así rociaba, así, así . . .
Así rociaba que yo la vi.

Iron on Friday:

Viernes antes de almorzar
una niña fué a pasear
ella no podía pasear
porque tenía que planchar.

Así planchaba así, así . . .
Así planchaba así, así . . .
Así planchaba así, así . . .
Así planchaba que yo la vi.

Clean on Saturday:

Sábado antes de almorzar
una niña fué a pasear

ella no podía pasear
porque tenía que limpiar.

Así limpiaba así, así . . .
Así limpiaba así, así . . .
Así limpiaba así, así . . .
Así limpiaba que yo la vi.

Pray on Sunday or go to church:

Domingo antes de almorzar
una niña fué a pasear
ella no quiso pasear,
porque ella quera orar.

Así oraba así, así . . .
Así oraba así, así . . .
Así oraba así, así . . .
Así oraba que yo la vi.[5]

LA MARISOLA

Formation: This game is played by a group of children in a circle, with Marisola in the center and one child outside the circle.

Action: The children in the circle walk around Marisola and sing:

Marí-sol-a was sitting In her flow-er gar-den Op-en-ing the rose-buds, clos-ing the car-na-tions.

With the last words each child in the circle catches hold of

[5] Spanish text and melody and game directions from *Canciones Populares* by Allena Luce, copyright, 1921, 1949, by Silver Burdett Company, New York. Used with permission.

Marisola's skirt. She protests in the singing of the second stanza:

> Who are all these people
> Passing by my garden,
> Making so much noise
> That I cannot sleep?

Then the child who remains outside the circle sings:

> We are jolly students
> Come to spend our time
> In the little chapel
> Of our saint Pilar.

He walks around the circle, touching the head of each child in the circle and singing:

> Handkerchief of pure gold,
> Handkerchief of silver,
> Come outside the circle
> When this touches you.

With the last word, "you," the child whose head he has just touched leaves the circle. This process is repeated until Marisola is left alone.

The Spanish words are as follows:

> Estaba la Marisola
> Sentad a en su vergel,
> Abriendo la rosa
> Y cerrando el clavel.
>
> ¿Quien son esa gente
> Que pasa por aqui?

Que de dia ni de noche
Me dejan dormir.

Somos los estudiantes
Que venimos a estudiar
A la capillita
De nuestra Pilar.

Panuelo de oro,
Panuelo de plata,
Que se quite, quite,
Esta prenda falsa.

MATANDILE, OR MATARILE, OR AMBOS A DOS

The words "Matandile" and "Mambroche" are nonsensical and cannot be translated.

In this game the player who represents Matandile stands facing the remainder of the group, at a distance of eight or ten feet, and sings:

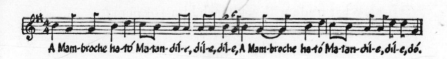

A Mam-broche ha-tó Ma-tan-díl-e, díl-e, díl-e, A Mam-broche ha-tó Ma-tan-díl-e, díl-e, dó.

The others, in chorus, ask what he wishes:

What do you wish?
Matandile, dile, dile,
What do you wish?
Matandile, dile, dó.

Matandile replies that he is looking for a page:

> I wish a valet (or page),
> Matandile, dile, dile,
> I wish a valet (or page),
> Matandile, dile, dó.

The chorus asks what page he wishes:

> Which page do you wish?
> Matandile, dile, dile,
> Which page do you wish?
> Matandile, dile, dó.

Matandile in reply names one of the chorus:

> I wish ———— (name of player chosen),
> Matandile, dile, dile,
> I wish ———— (name of player chosen),
> Matandile, dile, dó.

The chorus asks what will be the trade of the child chosen:

> What trade will you teach him (or her)?
> Matandile, dile, dile,
> What trade will you teach him (or her)?
> Matandile, dile, dó.

In reply Matandile names a trade or a profession, such as laundress, cook, pianist, and so on:

> I shall make him (or her) ———— (the trade),
> Matandile, dile, dile,
> I shall make him (or her) ———— (the trade),
> Matandile, dile, dó.

The chorus replies that this trade or profession is or is not agreeable to the child chosen:

That trade suits him (or her) fine,

or

That trade does not suit him (or her),
Matandile, dile, dile,
That trade suits him (or her) fine,

or

That trade does not suit him (or her),
Matandile, dile, dó.

If the chorus says the trade is agreeable to the player chosen, he goes to the side of Matandile; and the above process is repeated in the selection of each of the other members of the chorus. If, on the other hand, the trade is not agreeable, Matandile suggests other trades, until the chorus says one is agreeable, and the player chosen goes to his side.

After the whole chorus has gone over to Matandile, they form a circle and sing:

Let's go have a good time
Jumping up and down.

The Spanish words to the song are as follows:

A Mambroche ható
Matandile, dile, dile
A Mambroche ható
Matandile, dile, dó.

Qué quería usted?
Matandile, dile, dile
Qué quería usted?
Matandile, dile, dó.

69

Yo quería un paje,
Matandile, dile, dile,
Yo quería un paje,
Matandile, dile, dó.

¿Que paje quería usted?
Matandile, dile, dile,
¿Que paje quería usted?
Matandile, dile, dó.

Yo quería a ———— (name of player chosen),
Matandile, dile, dile,
Yo quería a ———— (name of player chosen),
Matandile, dile, dó.

¿Qué oficio le va a poner?
Matandile, dile, dile,
¿Qué oficio le va a poner?
Matandile, dile, dó.

Le pondremos ———— (the trade),
Matandile, dile, dile,
Le pondremos ———— (the trade),
Matandile, dile, dó.

Ese oficio sí (no) le agrada,
Matandile, dile, dile,
Ese oficio sí (no) le agrada,
Matandile, dile, dó.

Celebremos la fiesta real
Dando vueltas en general.[6]

---

[6] Spanish text and melody and game directions from *Canciones Populares* by Allena Luce, copyright, 1921, 1949, by Silver Burdett Company, New York. Used with permission.

DENMARK

BIRD'S ALIVE

This game is similar to our "Jack's Alive."

Number of players: Six to thirty.

Formation: Players are seated in a circle.

Action: The players pass a lighted paper or stick from one to another. The player in whose hand the fire goes out must pay a forfeit, which he must redeem. (See section on forfeits, page 148.) Players may blow on the paper or stick to keep alive any spark of fire. As they pass the fire, they say, "Bird's alive!" [7]

BASTE THE BEAR
(Also Germany)

Number of players: Ten to thirty.

Formation: The players form a circle. The bear is seated on a stool at the center. With him is a keeper. These two hold to

---

[7] This game grew out of an old Danish tale of a nobleman who left a pet bird with a peasant while he was off to war. The bird died, and the peasant was punished for his negligence. As Danish children play the game, they say, "Lad ikke min Herre Fugl doee" ("Let not my Lord's bird die.")

either end of a piece of rope, about two feet in length and knotted at both ends to make it easier for them to hold onto it.

Action: Players move in to center and try to "baste" the bear (tag or push him) without being tagged in turn by the keeper or the bear. When a player is tagged, he must take the bear's place. The bear then becomes the keeper, and the keeper joins the group in the circle. At no time while the attack is being made may the keeper and the bear let go of the short rope. That means their range of activity is limited. In lieu of a rope they may be required to clasp hands, or a circle four or five feet in diameter may be drawn around them and the keeper must keep within those limits.

FISHING GAME

This is a Danish game, and tradition has it that it is played only at the Christmas season and that every child six years or under has a set of his own fishing poles.

Equipment: The poles are made from a thirty-six-inch dowel pin, cut in four lengths, making each pole about nine inches long. A small screw eye is placed in one end of the pin, a silken or heavy thread about seven inches long is tied into the screw eye, and on the other end of the thread a dress hook is tied. This makes the fishing pole. The poles may all be painted the same color or different colors, to add beauty to the game. The fish are

made from corks about an inch high or from rounds, about three fourths of an inch high, cut from broom or mop handles. Staples are driven into the top of the fish, and the fish are numbered from one to twenty on the bottoms, each fish bearing a number. The fish should be painted or varnished. They are placed on a table or on the floor for the game, not floated on water.

Action: Four players fish at once. The fishing is done by catching the dress hook on the end of the fishing pole into the staple on the fish. As soon as one fish is caught, he is unhooked and another is gone after. At the close of the game the player catching the *most pounds of fish* (as computed by the numbers on the bottoms) wins the game. The number of fish caught does not count. The fun comes when all players are after the last fish on the table.

STYKES
(Sticks)

This is similar to the Chinese game of "Iau Chhung."

Number of players: Five to ten.

Equipment: Two bricks or stones, a stick six to eight inches long, a stick thirty to thirty-six inches long.

Action: One player is batter. The other players locate themselves wherever they think he might possibly knock the stick. The two bricks or stones are placed about four or five inches apart, and the short stick is laid on top of them. The batter puts the long stick under the short one and gives it a boost into the air. The other players try to catch the short stick before it touches the ground. If they do so, the batter must place the long stick across the two bricks. The player who caught the stick then tosses it at the long stick trying to knock it off the bricks. If he does so, the batter loses his turn. If the short stick misses and hits the ground, the batter then defends the space between the two bricks with the long stick while one of the fielders tries to toss the short stick in between the two bricks. If the fielder is able to throw the short stick between the two bricks, the batter loses his turn. If, however, the batter fends off the short stick, he continues his play by placing the short stick across the two bricks. He then hoists it in the air with his batting stick and hits it as far as he can. Using his bat, he measures with his long stick to the point where the small stick landed. The number of stick lengths indicates his score. Then another batter takes his turn. This continues until all players have had a chance to bat. The game is played for two or three rounds, and the player with the highest score wins.

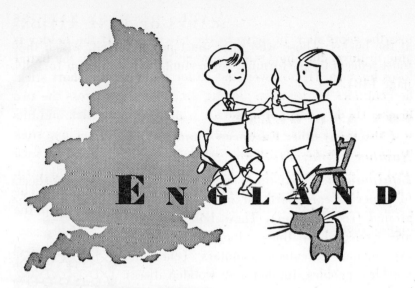

ENGLAND

FOX IN THE HOLE

Number of players: Ten to twenty.

Formation: Players are seated in a circle.

Action: A lighted candle is passed around the circle. The player in whose hand it goes out must pay a forfeit for each offense. When enough forfeits have been collected, players must redeem them by performing certain stunts for the group (see section on forfeits, page 148). The candle should be in a candleholder to protect the clothes of the players from drippings.

HIT THE BUCKET
(Also Spain, Italy, Germany)

Number of players: Five or more.

Formation: Players form a semicircle around a bucket, standing at a distance of eight to twelve feet. Each player has a pebble, beanbag, or some other object to throw. Often a basketball or volleyball is used instead of a bucket.

Action: At the signal to throw, each player tosses his missile at the bucket. Those who miss must pay a forfeit, which they must redeem by performing some stunt (see section on forfeits, page 148).[8]

FOX AND GEESE
(Also many other European countries)

Number of players: Two.

Equipment: Thirty-three spots or holes are marked on sheets of paper or cardboard, or made in a wooden base or in the ground (see diagram). These holes or spots are connected by lines, along which moves are made. Seventeen counters (checkers, marbles, pebbles, linoleum or wooden discs) represent the geese, and the fox is represented by a counter distinguished from the geese by color, size, or material.

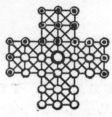

Formation: The geese are placed on every spot or hole in the three top rows and at the end of the fourth and fifth rows. The fox is placed on the center spot or hole.

Action: One player moves the fox and the other the geese. The fox has the first move. He tries to maneuver into such a position as to make it possible to jump the geese, as in checkers. Whenever he jumps a goose, he captures it and takes it off the board. He may jump forward and backward, up, down, and across. A jump is made possible when the fox is on a spot adjacent to a goose and the space next beyond the goose is vacant. The fox does not have to jump, but jumps only when he desires to do so.

---

[8] This game originated in ancient Europe. It grew out of a cruel game in which a pot with a hole in the bottom was placed over a chicken. The chicken's head protruded through the hole. A blindfolded player was given a stick, with which he tried to hit the chicken. Later it was played with a pot on a stick, which the blindfolded player tried to hit. It was called "Hit the Pot."

Players alternate moves, and each is forced to move each time. In other words, a player may not waive a move because it is not advantageous. The moves are made from one space to an adjacent vacant space on the line and in any direction desired.

The geese try to pen the fox so that he cannot move. The geese cannot jump. Only the fox has that privilege.

NINE MEN'S MORRIS

This ancient game is common to a number of countries. The French call it "Merilles"; the Germans call it "Muhl"; the English call it "Five-Penny Morris," "Nine-Men's or Nine-Penny Morris," depending on the number of counters used. It is mentioned in A Midsummer Night's Dream.

Number of players: Two.

Equipment: A board ten or twelve inches square. Three concentric squares are marked on this board, crossed by lines connecting the corners and in the middle of each side (see diagram). This makes twenty-four points or stations. These points may be drilled with a countersink. In this case marbles could be used for counters. 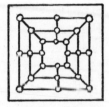 Each player has nine counters of contrasting color. These counters may be pegs (golf tees, for instance, marbles, pebbles, cardboard, wood, or buttons).

Action: The players place their nine counters, one at a time, alternately, trying to get three in a row. This is achieved by getting three consecutive counters on any line, except that the corner diagonal lines are not regarded as making a legitimate three-in-a-row.

When a player gets three in a row, he is privileged to take one of his opponent's counters off the board, except that he may not disturb an opponent's three-in-a-row.

After the counters are all placed, the players move their men, trying to set up a three-in-a-row. Each player takes his turn. Moves may be made only on the lines and for only one space. When a player is trimmed down to three men, he is privileged to move anywhere on the board, as he desires. Thus he may jump across the board to block his opponent and then move back to three-in-a-row on the next move.

The game is won when one's opponent has only two men left.

FRANCE

FRENCH BLINDMAN'S BUFF

This is played the same as our "Blindman's Buff" except that "It" has his hands tied behind his back instead of being blindfolded. This lessens the risk of accident and is great fun.

LAMARELLE

This game is played much the same as "Hopscotch." However, the French have some variations that make it a bit more difficult than the game we usually play. Note the diagrams of two of these variations.

Equipment: In addition to the diagram is a small flat stone or a disc made from linoleum or wood.

Action: The player tosses the disc toward Space 1. If it lands outside that space or on the line, he loses his turn. Spaces must be taken in their regular turn, except a penalty space, which he tries to avoid by skipping to the next

space in order. The penalty spaces are "Start Over" in Variation One and Space 13 in Variation Two. In Variation One, when he lands at "Home," he can rest by putting both feet to the ground. Of course each time he finishes a turn, he can rest by putting both feet to the  ground before starting on a new turn. In Variation Two, if he lands on Space 13, he has to go back and start over. When he lands on Space 13, he rests before proceeding. He also rests before hopping over the remaining spaces.

GERMANY

DOG COLLAR

Number of players: Two or even teams.

Formation: Two players, on all fours, face each other. Their heads are in a loop of strong cloth. In some cases a belt is used for the loop. A line or marker separates the two players. Teams of players may be paired.

Action: At the signal to go opponents try to pull each other across the line separating them. At the end of one minute the winner is the one who has pulled his opponent on his side of the line.

BASTE THE BEAR
(Also Denmark)

Number of players: Ten to thirty.

Formation: The players form a circle around two of their number. One of these is the bear, who sits in the center of the circle. The other is the keeper, who guards the bear. These two hold onto a piece of rope about two feet in length, knotted at both

81

ends to make it easier to hold. If no rope is available, the bear and the keeper may be required to clasp hands, the bear's right hand in the keeper's left. Or a small circle may be drawn around the two behind which the keeper may not go.

Action: When the keeper is ready he shouts, "The bear is free!" Then, and not until then, the other players may "baste" the bear. That is, they may tap him, strike him, push him. However, if anyone does this before the keeper announces that the bear is free, he takes the bear's place. He also takes the bear's place when the keeper or the bear tags him as he tries to baste the bear. The bear then becomes the keeper, and the former keeper takes his place in the circle.

GREECE

PEBBLE CHASE

Number of players: Four to ten.

Formation: Players form in a line, facing a leader. They stand side by side, with their hands extended, palms together.

Action: The leader has a pebble or marble. He passes it down the line and pretends to drop it into each player's hands. He actually gives it to one of the players. That player dashes to a previously named spot and back, in order to return the pebble to the leader. The other players chase him. The one who catches him before he can return the pebble becomes the next leader. If the runner succeeds in getting back without being tagged, he becomes the next leader.

RIDER BALL

Number of players: Eight or more.

Equipment: A basketball, volleyball, or softball.

Formation: Players pair off in circle formation. One player in each pair sits on the shoulders of his teammate.

Action: One of the mounted players begins the game by tossing the ball to another mounted player in the circle. The ball is thrown from one to the other, no particular order being observed. If a mounted player drops the ball, he dismounts and changes places with the player on whose shoulders he has been seated.

ODD OR EVEN

This game was a favorite in ancient Greece and Rome.

Number of players: Two or more. If more, pair off. After each contest move on to a new opponent.

Equipment: A small number of beans (ten perhaps) for each player.

Action: One player puts some of his beans in one hand, closes it, and holds it out toward his opponent. "Odd or even?" he asks. The opponent looks at the clenched fist and guesses, "Even!" It happens to be odd as the player shows by opening his hand. "Give me one to make it even," he says; and the mistaken guesser hands over one bean. Now the other player guesses. On a correct guess the guesser is given one bean. This continues until one of the players has no more beans.

In a large group players go from one player to another. At the end of five minutes all players stop and count beans, and the one who has the most is the winner.

Variation: On a correct guess the guesser gets all the beans in the extended hand. On an incorrect guess the guesser surrenders as many beans as are in the extended hand.

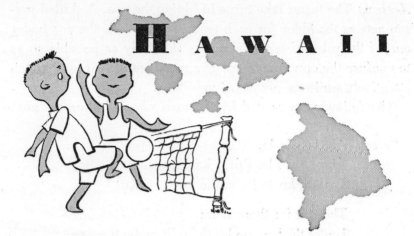

HAWAII

PAHEE

Number of players: Two or more.

Equipment: A short javelin, made of the hard wood of the "ulei" or "kauilor," is used. It is made thick at the forward end, or head, tapering off toward the tail end.

Action: The pahee, or javelin, is cast on the roadway or sward in such a way as to slide or skip along on the ground. One point is earned each time a player casts the pahee the farthest. Ten points win the game.

NOA

Number of players: Ten or more.

Formation: Two teams of equal number sit facing one another. Five piles of tapa (a bark cloth) are placed on a mat between the two teams. The piles of tapa are named in this order: Kihipuka, Pilimoe, Kau, Phihiluka, and Kihimoe. Under these piles the noa is hidden, beginning with the Kihipuka. The noa is a small piece of wood or stone.

Action: The teams take turns in hiding the noa. A skilled person acts as the hider for each team. He conceals the noa under one of the piles of tapa, faking as skillfully as possible so as to confuse the opposing team. The members of that team watch attentively while the noa is being hidden.

The following is recited by the man who is hiding the noa:

> Aia la, aia la,
> I ke Kau, i ke Pili, i ka Moe,
> Ilaila e ku ai ka noa a kaua, e Ku! [9]

> There it is; there it is;
> Under the kau, under the pili, under the moe,
> There is lodged our noa. It is lodged.

Now the watching side tries to guess under which pile of tapa the noa is hidden. If they guess correctly, they score one point.

The first team to score ten points wins.

PUHENEHENE, OR PA-POHENE

Number of players: Twelve to thirty.

Equipment: A long piece of tapa (a kind of bark cloth), made by stitching several pieces together. Sometimes it is called "Kapa," which means "beaten cloth." [10] The other piece of equipment is a pebble, which is called a "noa."

Formation: Two teams of equal number sit in lines facing one another.

---

[9] In pronouncing Hawaiian words each vowel is given its full value. In other words, it is pronounced as written.

[10] Patricia McHugh, of Honolulu, says she and her friends often use a substitute for tapa. They take regular brown wrapping paper and put an over-all Indian-looking design on it in shades of orange and brown. Then the paper is twisted and crushed until it is soft and wrinkled.

Action: One team has possession of the noa. A leader calls out, "Puheoheo!" and all the players answer, "Puheoheo!" [11] Then three players lift up the long tapa so as to make a curtain between the two teams. One player on the team who has the noa hides it on one of his teammates. The tapa is removed. All the players on the team with the noa lean forward and look down, to hide their expressions so they won't give away who has the noa. The other team guesses where it is, and if they guess correctly, they score one point. If they miss, the team with the noa scores a point. The first team to score ten points is victor. The teams take turns hiding the noa.

This game is usually played at night. In ancient times it was a favorite with adults.

LOULOU

Number of players: Two.

Action: The two players hook their right forefingers together. Then they pull. The player who holds on the longest without letting go or straightening his finger is winner.

---

[11] In ancient times the leader whistled the call on an instrument known as a "puheoheo." Then a player stood forth and chanted a gay and pleasing song. What this ceremony had to do with the playing of the game isn't clear.

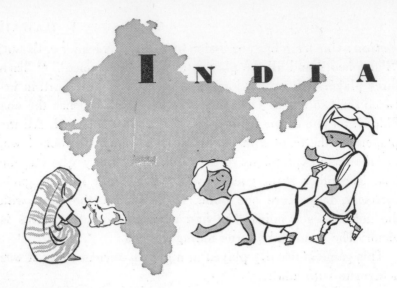

KABADDI[12]   (Number 1)

This game is commonly known as "Hututo" in Bombay and in the central provinces. In Madras it is known as "Chedugudu."

Number of players: Ten or more.

Formation: Two equal teams stand on either side of a dividing line and twenty to thirty feet from that line. The line may be indicated by a rope or rocks or a lime marker.

Action: A player from Team One approaches and crosses the dividing line into Team Two's territory, calling out, "Kabaddi! Kabaddi! Kabaddi!" He goes as close as he can to the members of Team Two, trying to touch anyone of them with his hand or his foot and at the same time avoid being seized by him. If he succeeds in touching an opponent and in getting back across the dividing line without being seized, the player he has touched must drop out of the game. However, he must continue to call, "Kabaddi!" all the time he is trying to tag an opponent. To make it more difficult, this must all be

[12] This is pronounced "Kabad dee," with the accent on the last syllable.

done in one breath. If he is unsuccessful in his efforts and finds he is running out of breath, he must run back to his side of the line. If his opponents should seize him, he may struggle to get back to the dividing line. If he is successful in reaching it with either his hand or his foot, he is safe and the opponent who first seized him drops out of the game.

After a player on Team One has gone over into Team Two's territory and returns to his side or has been captured, a player from Team Two ventures into Team One's territory. The game continues until one side has no players left.

KABADDI (Number 2)

The Madras Olympic Association has worked out rules somewhat different and a bit more involved than the above simplified version. Some of these rules follow. They provide that the game be played by two teams of seven players each. A field fourteen by eleven yards is marked off (see diagram).

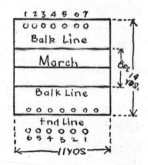

Players who are eliminated take their places behind the end line in the order in which they are eliminated and await substitution.

The attacking team is dubbed the "Raiders." The defending team is known as the "Antis." Teams take turn in attacking and defending.

The "Kabaddi" is known as the "Cant." In other words, the Raiders must keep saying, "Kabaddi," in one breath.

Scoring: If a Raider reaches home with Cant after touching one or more Antis, he scores one point for each Anti touched. The Antis touched are automatically out. They go into the end zone and await their turn for revival.

Each Raider must cross the Balk Line of the opposite team at least once during a raid. But in case of a pursuit the Raider pursuing and touching an Anti immediately following his raid need not cross the Balk Line and the Anti so touched is out. However, the Raiders must keep saying, "Kabaddi," until he reaches home.

An Anti, or intruder, if touched by one of his opponents with Cant, is out and the opposite team scores one point.

If a Raider is warned against any danger by one of his own team, the Antis score one point.

A Raider is not to be held by any part of his body other than his trunk or limbs. For any violation of this rule the opponent scores one point.

If a Raider succeeds in touching the March with any part of his body in spite of a struggle with the Antis, all those of the Antis who come in contact with him are put out and the raiding team scores as many points as the number of players put out.

When a team manages to put out the entire opposing team, they score two points in addition to the number of points scored by putting out individual players.

When only one or two players are left during any game and the captain of the team "declares" them out in order to bring in the full team, the opponents score as many points as there are players left before "declaring" as well as two points for putting out the entire team.

The whole side, when put out during play, is revived automatically and the opposite team scores two more points in addition to the usual points scored for putting out the individual members of the opposite team.

If a Raider who has been touched or held by one of the Antis does not reach his home with Cant (that is, by continuing to say, "Kabaddi," in one breath), the Raider is out and the defending team scores one point.

Fouls: A player must not attempt to stifle a Raider's Cant by shutting his mouth, throttling, or any other way. The referee may disqualify a player for using such tactics.

Violent tackling leading to injuries to the body is forbidden. A player may be disqualified for breaking this rule.

In cases where a player is disqualified, a substitute may take his place. Each team is allowed a maximum of two substitutes. A team must not take over five seconds to send a Raider when asked to do so by the referee. Failure to do so is considered as delaying the game, and one point is conceded to the opponents.

Duration of game: The game consists of two thirty-minute periods with a five-minute rest between halves.

For junior and women's matches there are two twenty-minute periods with a five-minute rest between.

Other regulations: The team which wins the toss has the right to choose its home. The other team sends a Raider. Teams change homes for the second half of the game.

If the score is a tie at the end of the game, the game continues for periods of ten minutes each until the tie is broken.

"Time out" may be called by the captain of a team once during the first half and once during the second half of a game for rest or for substitution. Such "time-out" periods shall not exceed two minutes.

The Madras regulations require that all players be suitably numbered and all teams appear in distinctive uniforms. The numbers shall be six inches high and in bold type. Sleeveless jerseys with distinctive colors are suggested.

A Raider may become an intruder and may be put out by any Anti taking Cant when one or more intruders are in the raiding field. The team that puts him out scores one point.

By an intruder is meant:

1. A player found on the March or in the opponent's home when a raid is on.

2. A Raider who has left the March but is without a Cant, or a Raider who has lost his Cant before reaching home.

Exceptions: No Anti in a struggle will be deemed an intruder while the struggle is on. By a struggle is meant the holding of a Raider by one or more Antis to prevent him from reaching home with Cant.

SCORPION'S STING

Number of players: Four or more.

Formation: Players gather closely about one player, the scorpion, who walks on all fours. However, he is supposed to raise one leg, which represent's his stinger.

Action: The scorpion tries to touch a player with his raised leg. If he does, that player becomes the scorpion. The players tease the scorpion by touching his head, his shoulders, his hands, or even his stinger, being careful to prevent his stinging them.

KAE DANDA

Number of players: Five or more.

Formation: All but one player climb a low-branched tree, easily climbed. A stick two feet in length is placed on the ground against the tree. One player is the watchman. He stands at a distance of thirty yards or so from the tree.

Action: Anyone of the players may get down out of the tree.

The watchman tries to touch this player before he can get possession of the stick and toss it away. The player throws the stick as far as possible under his leg. When the stick is tossed away, the watchman must retrieve it, place it under the tree, and then try to tag the daring player before he can climb back into the tree. If a player is tagged before he can get rid of the stick or before he can ascend the tree, he becomes the new watchman.

If the watchman calls, "All jump!" all players must come down out of the tree. This means plenty of action.

KHO-KHO

Number of players: Eighteen.

Field: This is a team-tag game with nine members on each team. The Kho-kho court is laid out as indicated in the diagram. It

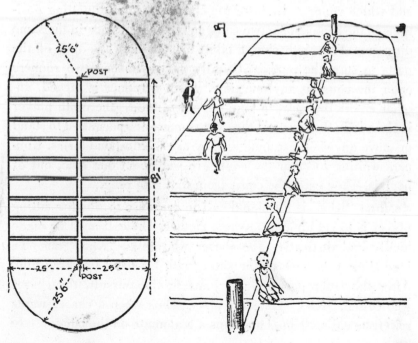

consists of a rectangular area eighty-one by fifty-one feet. At either end of the rectangle there is a semicircle with a radius of twenty-five feet, six inches. The rectangle is divided into halves by a central lane eighty-one feet long and one foot wide and in nine rectangular areas by marking eight lanes which are fifty-one feet long and one foot wide. These lanes are eight feet apart.

The one-foot squares in the middle of these lanes formed across the central lane are called "squares." In these the eight nonactive chasers squat (see diagram).

There are two posts at the ends of the rectangle, located in the middle, one at each end. These posts are made of wood and rise four feet above the ground. Their circumference should be from twelve to sixteen inches.

Formation: By toss it is decided which team shall be chasers and which runners. Eight of the chasers assume squatting positions in the squares. No two consecutive chasers face in the same direction. The ninth chaser takes his position at either of the posts to start the pursuit. Usually not more than two runners enter the court at any one time. When a runner is tagged, another enters the court to take his place, unless the ninth player is already in the court. At the start runners are permitted to stand or move anywhere, so long as they are within boundaries. Runners waiting to enter the court are seated on one side, out of bounds. They enter the court from that side only.

Action: "Kho" is the signal call in response to which a sitting player is to get up and pursue a runner. The call must be made loudly and distinctly. The chaser who calls, "Kho," must be immediately in back of the sitter, with his hand touching him. After the sitter gets up and joins in the pursuit, the chaser who called, "Kho," takes his place. Thus when a chaser wants relief, he calls, "Kho," and taps a teammate on the back.

No chaser is allowed to cross the lengthwise middle strip, although he is permitted to reach across the strip to touch a runner on the other side.

Other rules: Once a chaser starts in one direction, he may not turn to go back except at the turn post.

A runner is out in the following cases:

1. If he is touched by an active chaser with the hand.
2. If he touches any of the sitting chasers.
3. If he goes completely out of bounds. A player is not out of bounds if one foot is inside the boundary.
4. A runner is not out if a chaser committed a foul prior to his being touched.

A foul shall be called on a chaser if:

1. He changes the direction of his running.
2. He turns his shoulder line through more than a right angle.
3. He cries, "Kho," incorrectly.
4. He crosses the middle strip.

Each team alternates in chasing and being chased.

The maximum time allowed for each chase is seven minutes. There is a five-minute rest period before the other team takes the field as chasers.

Scoring: The chasers score ten times as many points as the number of runners put out. If all nine runners are knocked out before the expiration of seven minutes, thirty extra points are added to the score of the chasers and the game continues until the expiration of seven minutes. All extra players tagged in this additional time count ten points each.

SIA MAR DANDA
(Jackal Hit Wood)

Number of players: Three or more.

Formation: This game is played among trees easy to climb. Draw a small circle, eight to ten inches in diameter, under a tree. Place a short stick (danda) inside the circle. One player is selected to be "It."

Action: Start the game by having one of the players throw the stick under his leg as far as he can. This is the signal for all players to scramble. They climb the trees. "It" runs to get the stick. He brings it back and places it inside the circle. He then tries to tag one of the players. However, he can only tag when the stick is in the circle. Any player may get the stick and re-throw it, if he can do so without being tagged. The tagged player becomes "It," and the game continues.

GOOLI DANDA

This is similar to two Chinese games: Iau Chhung" and "Da Err."

Number of players: Ten to twenty.

Equipment: A gooli, which is a short stick about six inches long, sharpened at both ends. A danda, a stick about two feet long, used for hitting.

Formation: Players are divided into two teams. One team takes the field. The opposing team sends one player up to bat.

Action: The batter places the gooli crosswise over a narrow trench, made by digging a hole in the ground or by placing two bricks or stones an inch or so apart. He then hoists the gooli by placing the end of the danda underneath it and heaving it as far as possible. The field team tries to catch the gooli before it touches the ground. If it is caught, the batter is out. The field team then gets its chance to bat.

If the gooli is not caught, the batter lays the danda crossways near the trench. The fielder nearest the spot where the gooli landed tries to hit the danda by throwing the gooli at it. If he hits it or if the gooli lands within one danda length of the trench, the batter is out.

Otherwise the batter spins the gooli into the air by striking it on one of the sharpened ends with the danda. He then tries to hit it while it is in the air, knocking it as far as possible. He gets three such chances to knock the gooli as far from the trench as he can. After the final blow he estimates the number of danda lengths the gooli is from the trench. This is called the number of "lals." If not challenged, this is his score. If he is challenged, there is a measurement made. If his guess was too high, he gets no runs and is out.

Note: When I was a boy, in Louisville, Kentucky, we played a game we called "Dainty." It was very similar to "Gooli Danda." The game was very popular in the neighborhood where I lived. Boys up through the teen ages would find it a good game of skill today.

We used a broomstick to make the knocker and the "dainty." The knocker is from three to four feet in length. The dainty is about five inches long, sharpened like a pencil at both ends. The batter tips the dainty into the air by striking one end of it sharply. Then he tries to hit it before it touches the ground, knocking it as far as possible. When he hits it well, there is the same feeling of thrill that comes to a baseball player who hits a ball right "on the nose."

In "Dainty" a circle about ten inches in diameter is drawn. An opponent stands behind a line eight to ten feet from the circle. With an underhand toss he pitches the dainty at the circle. If he gets it completely in the circle, the batter is out and loses his turn. If any part of the dainty touches the circle, the batter gets one hit. If it lands outside the circle, the batter gets three hits. He then estimates the distance and calls the number of jumps he will give his opponent. If the opponent concedes, the batter scores as many points as the number of jumps called. If, however, the opponent accepts the challenge and jumps over the dainty in the number of jumps called or in less than the number called, the batter scores nothing.

Usually a score of 100 or 150 points is set before the game begins. The first player to make that number of points wins.

I have often wondered if the name "dainty" did not come from the Indian word "danda."

ITALY

FOLLOW THROUGH TAG

Number of players: Ten to twenty.

Formation: Players form a circle, clasping hands and holding up arms to make arches. One player, the runner, stands inside the circle; and another, the chaser, stands outside.

Action: The chaser tries to catch the runner, but he must follow the exact route of the runner, going under the same arms. When he catches him or gives up, two more players are selected to be runner and chaser.

CHICKEN MARKET

Number of players: Six or more.

Formation: One player has charge of the market. Another is the buyer. The rest of the players are lined up in a row. They are the chickens. They stoop down and clasp their hands under their knees.

Action: The buyer comes up and asks, "Have you any

chickens?" "Yes, I have very nice chickens," answers the marketman. "Would you like to try them?" "If you please," responds the buyer. Then he goes behind the row of chickens. He places his hand on the first chicken's head and says, "This one is too tough." Then he puts his hand on the second chicken's head, saying, "This one is too old." He tries the third, saying, "This one is too skinny." At last he says, "This one is just right."

Then the buyer and the marketman take hold of this chicken, one by each arm, and swing it. "One, two, three!" they count as they swing. "You are a good little chicken. You kept your hands clasped, and you didn't laugh."

If a chicken unclasps his hands or laughs or smiles, he is put out of the game.

BALITO, OR LE BOCCE
(Also Croatia.)

Number of players: Two to six.

Equipment: Eight wooden balls, preferably of lignum vitae, four and one-half inches in diameter. Four of these balls should be marked with two rings so as to distinguish them from the other four.

An extra ball, three inches in diameter, is painted white. It is called the pallino or jack.

Field: The court or alley should measure sixty feet in length and eight feet in width. It should be walled by boards, two inches by twelve inches by ten or twelve feet in length. Joints of the board ends should be smooth on the inside of the alley. The backboards at the ends should be of the same construction but two and one-half feet high, with braced corners. All inside joints should be smooth. On the inside walls twelve feet from each backboard a foul line is painted. A regulator peg is driven flush to the ground midway of the backboards and midway of the side walls.

The grounds should be as well built as a tennis court. At each end the ground should rise for two feet to a point two inches above the general level, at the backboard itself. This keeps the balls from hugging the backboards. Along the length the ground should have a slight pitch to the middle, so that rain water will drain off easily. The ground should be smooth and as hard-packed as possible.

Action: The object of the game is for each player to throw his ball closest to the pallino and also to scatter from the pallino the balls of his opponent.

One of the players, selected by tossing a coin, begins the game by throwing the pallino, thus determining the bowling distance. (The player to throw the pallino first may be determined by having each player roll the pallino toward the regulator peg. The one who lands nearest starts the game.)

When there are two players, each has four balls. The position of the bowler is back of the twelve-foot foul line. The one who is to throw the pallino bowls it any length he pleases. He then rolls one of his balls, trying to land it near the pallino. His opponent then trys to land one of his balls even closer. If he does not succeed with his first ball, he rolls his second, third, or fourth ball until he has the better position or until all his balls are used. Then the first player takes a second turn and continues until he has the better position or all his balls have been rolled.

The player having one or more balls nearest the pallino scores as many points as he has balls closer than any of his opponent's balls. If all four of his balls are closer to the pallino than any of his opponent's balls, his score of four is doubled to eight.

When each side has a ball touching the pallino, or there is a tie, neither player scores and the pallino is thrown again by the player who threw it for that play.

The player who scores is the one to throw the pallino for the next play.

Twenty-one points constitute a game.

When more than two are playing, the players divide into teams. Each player plays his own ball or two balls apiece as the team may agree among themselves.

When three are playing, each throws one ball at the pallino. The one nearest plays alone and uses four balls. The other two take two balls each and are partners.

When five are playing, the two who comes nearest the pallino are teamed against the other three. The three decide among themselves who throws the extra ball.

Teams for match games number three each.

To dislodge an opponent, a player may toss the ball through the air in the effort to strike the opponent's ball on the fly.

It is legitimate also to hit the pallino and move it away from an opponent's ball.

Players may carom their shots off the side or backboards to get a favored position.

Variation: Use croquet balls on a smooth lawn with a golf ball or a toy wooden bowling ball for the pallino.

MORRA

This game is similar to the Chinese game "Fingers Out." It calls for the use of the fingers, vocal chords, and strategy.

Number of players: Two or more—no required number.

Action: Players pair off. There is no signal to start the game— just a simultaneous outstretching of the fingers of one hand.

Before the fingers are quite out, both players call a number between two and ten. If the number called by one of the contestants corresponds to the sum of the number of fingers extended by both contestants, a point is scored by the correct caller.

The game may be played by teams, with the players paired against one another. If there are four or less on a team, six points may constitute a game. With more than four players to a team, twelve points may decide the tilt.

JAPANESE TAG

Number of players: Four or more.

Action: The one who is "It" tries to tag a player. However, the tagged player must put one hand on the spot touched by the chaser, whether the back, the shoulder, the elbow, the knee, or other part of the body. In this position he must chase the other players. He is relieved of his position only when he tags another player.

When there is a large number of players, several taggers may be used at the same time.

HANETSUKI

This game is played a great deal at New Year's with gay battledore and shuttlecock. It is similar to "Badminton."

Number of players: Ten or more.

Equipment: Two shuttlecocks, which may be made of large

corks and chicken feathers. A tennis or badminton racket for each player.

Formation and action: Divide players into two equal groups. Each group forms a circle and is provided with a shuttlecock. At the signal to start, the shuttlecock is batted into the air in each circle. The group keeping its shuttlecock in the air the longest wins a point. The best three out of five may be declared champion.

Variation: Use a large toy balloon. In this case each side may have a balloon and proceed as with the shuttlecock, hitting the balloon with the open hand. Or a row of chairs may divide the two teams, and one balloon may be batted back and forth over the barrier. When the balloon touches the floor on one side, a point is scored by their opponents.

HANA, HANA, HANA, KUCHI

This game is similar to "Scrambled Anatomy."

Number of players: Two or more.

Formation and action: Divide into two sides, which sit facing one another. The captain for one side stands up and says, "Hana, hana, hana, kuchi," which means "nose, nose, nose, mouth." On the first three words he taps his nose, while on the fourth, instead of tapping his mouth, he touches some other feature, such as his ear, for instance. The idea of the game is for the players of the opposing side to do what the captain says and not what he does. All players who make mistakes may drop out or, as the Japanese play it, submit to being daubed on the cheek with flour and water.

The other captain now takes his turn. If the idea of eliminating is followed, the side with the player who stays in the game the longest wins. If the other plan is followed, the fun will consist in artistically daubing the cheeks of the opposing players with flour paste.

The names of other features are "mimi" (ear) and "me" (eye).

It may be decided to play the game using only English. Thus the captain might say, "Nose, nose, nose, eye," at the same time touching his ear or mouth, to confuse the opponents.

Variation: The game may also be used as a circle game with no sides. In this case all players would follow the commands of the leader.

YEMARI, OR BOUNCE THE BALL

The word "Yemari" means "Handball," although the game is different from handball as we play it.

Number of players: Four or more.

Equipment: The ball is usually about two inches in diameter, or about the size of a tennis ball. Or a large rubber ball may be used, if desired.

Formation and action: The players stand in a circle. One player tosses the ball to the floor so that it will bounce straight up to him. As it rebounds, he strikes it back with his open hand. He continues this as long as the ball is within reach. However, he must not move from his place in the circle. When the ball moves near another player, then that player must bounce it and continue to do so as did the first player. The game continues until some player fails to hit the ball on the rebound. If a player misses, he drops out and the circle draws closer. This continues until only one player is left.

Variation: Each player bounces the ball until he misses, being allowed to move to any position to keep up with it. Count

106

the number of times the ball is hit on the rebound. The highest score wins.

TAKARA-SAGASHI, OR HUNTING THE TREASURE

Number of players: Ten to twenty.

Formation: Two teams of equal numbers sit facing one another.

Action: One team has a coin (or other small article). They pass this coin from one teammate to the other (or pretend to do so) while the other team watches intently. The coin moves from fist to fist, with many gestures made to deceive the opponents. At a signal from the watchers all passing ceases, and the passers drop their clenched fists on their knees. The watchers ask the passers to open their fists, one at a time. The idea is to leave the fist holding the coin until all other fists have been opened. When the coin is uncovered, all fists closed at the time are counted and scored against the guessers.

Then the other side hides the coin, and the game continues. The side with the lowest score wins.

SCISSORS CHESS, OR HASAMI SHOGI

Number of players: Two.

Equipment: A board with 8, 9, or 10 squares on each side, thus making 64, 81, or 100 squares on the entire board (see diagram). The traditional board has nine on each side. A checkerboard may be used. Checkers may be used for counters, or marbles may be used if holes are countersunk in the board.

107

Counters should be of two contrasting colors. Thus one player uses red and the other yellow.

Action: The game may be played in either of two ways.

1. Each player has two rows of men at his end of the board. The object is to move his men so as to get five in a row not counting the two rows at his end of the board. Players move in turn. They may move as far as they like in a straight unimpeded line either horizontally or vertically. No diagonal moves are allowed. A player may not land on a spot already occupied, nor can he jump over intervening men, except that he can move up to an intervening man and then jump over him to the next space on the next move, if he desires.

When a player sandwiches one or more of his opponent's men between two of his own men, he has scissored him and he takes the opponent's men off the board. If he voluntarily moves a man between two of his opponent's men, that is not considered a scissors and the man remains on the board.

When a player gets five in a row, horizontally, vertically, or diagonally, he wins the game.

Men may be moved back and forth or sideways at any time to prevent capture or to set up a play, except that a player moves only on his regular turn.

2. Each player has one row of men at his end of the board. The object of the game is to capture and remove from the board his opponent's men.

Players move as in Game 1, no diagonal moves being allowed. They maneuver, trying to pinch an opponent between two of their men. No effort is made to get five in a row as in Game 1.

A man in a corner may be captured by blocking his movement. Occupying the two adjacent horizontal and vertical spaces accomplishes this.

FIVE EYES

Number of players: Two.

Equipment: Same as for "Scissors Chess" (page 107).

Action: Players hold counters in their hands and take turn about placing them on the board. The object of the game is to get five men in a row either vertically, horizontally, or diagonally. At the same time each player tries to prevent his opponent from getting five in a row. The first player to succeed is winner.

OKI CHOCHIN, CHRISSI CHOCHIA, OR BIG LANTERN, LITTLE LANTERN

Number of players: Three or more.

Formation: Players stand or sit in a circle.

Action: The leader calls, "Big lantern!" and at the same time indicates a small lantern by holding his outstretched hands close together. All the rest of the players must form a big lantern by holding their hands far apart. When the leader calls, "Little lantern!" he holds his hands far apart, thus forming a big lantern. The others must do exactly the opposite to what the leader does by forming a little lantern. Players who make mistakes may be required to pay a forfeit or may drop out until only one player is left. The leader tries to confuse players by always doing the opposite to the command.

KICK THE CAN

Number of players: Four or more.

Formation: A circle about four feet in diameter is drawn with chalk or lime. In the center of this circle is an empty can.

Action: One player is "It." The can is kicked out of the circle. "It" must retrieve it and place it back in the center of the circle. As soon as the can is kicked, all the other players run and hide.

"It" tries to find them. When he spies a player, he calls his name and dashes for the can. If he beats the hider to it, that person becomes a prisoner. If he does not, that player kicks the can and runs and hides again. Any hider may rush in and kick the can if he can beat "It" to it. The game continues until "It" has caught all the hiders. Then it may be replayed with the first player caught being "It."

SLAP HAND
(Also Korea)
Number of players: Two.

Action: This is a game requiring speed and alertness. The two players stand facing each other. One of the players extends one hand, palm up. The other player extends his hand, palm down, and gently strokes the extended palm of his opponent. Suddenly he makes a swift, sharp strike at the opponent's palm. The opponent endeavors to withdraw his hand so that the striker misses. If the striker slaps the extended palm, he scores a point. The players alternate in striking. A striker may feint at striking to keep his opponent guessing. However, if he makes a downward motion of striking, he is considered to have used up his turn.

JANKENPON, OR STONE, PAPER, SCISSORS

This game is like our "Eeny, Meeny, Miny, Mo." It is often used as a counting-out game to decide who is to be "It."

Number of players: Two or more.

Action: This game may be played in several ways.

1. Two players face each other with hands behind them. Together they say, "Jan-ken-pon!" On the syllable *pon* both players bring their hands forward to represent stone, paper,

or scissors. The stone is represented by a clenched fist; the paper by the open hand; the scissors by extending the index and middle fingers. The stone beats the scissors because it will dull them. The scissors beat the paper because they can cut it. The paper beats the stone because it can wrap it up. When a player loses, he extends one arm toward the winner, who "burns" the loser's wrist by hitting it a glancing blow with the first two fingers of his hand.

2. The game may be played by teams. They face one another in pairs. The leader counts, "One, two, three!" and on "three" the pairs contest, and one point is awarded for each win.

3. Teams decide on what they will do. All players represent the same thing. A mistake by any one player disqualifies his team and scores a point for the other side. Ten points is the game.

4. "Jankenpon Relay." The Japanese have a relay race built on this game. The course is square or rectangular in shape. It can be marked off by stones, sticks, trees, or chairs. Runners line up at opposite corners at the same end of the field. On the signal to go the first man on each team starts running around the square. When the two runners meet, they stop, put one hand behind them, and shout "Jankenpon!" On "pon" they hold out their hands, representing stone, paper, or scissors. The winner continues on his way. The loser drops out, shouting to his next teammate to start. The new man rushes out to meet the victorious opponent. Each time two runners meet, they stop to do "Jankenpon," the winner always proceeding around the square. The first team to get a runner to the opponent's corner wins.

RAKANSAN

Number of players: Six to thirty.
Formation: Circle, with players standing or seated.

Action: Players sing "Rakansan."

Ra-kan san ga so-ro-ta-ra ma-wa-so-ja-na-í-ka yoí-ya-sa, yoí-ya-sa, yoí-ya-sa.

As this song is sung, players assume poses of various sorts—hands up, finger on nose, hands held up in rabbit position, finger pointing, hands to sides of head, and so on. During the singing each player quickly assumes the pose of the player immediately to the right of him. A player who makes a mistake drops out of the circle for the next round. This continues until only one player is left. A player must be alert to note the original pose of the player to his right before the change is made.

FOREIGNER

This game is evidently an adaptation of "Sugar Loaf Town" or "What's Your Trade" as played in the United States.

Number of players: Any number.

Formation: Divide into two equal groups. These groups face one another, about twenty feet apart. The acting side is always the "foreign" group.

Action: The foreign group approaches to within five feet of the other group. "Here we come!" they call. "Where from?" asks the other line of players. A leader of the foreigners then replies, "America" (or Italy, England, India, China, Russia, Germany, or any other foreign country).

A leader from the home group asks, "What's your occupation?" The foreigners pantomime their occupation. They do it by wearing a cap and apron, kneading dough, baking bread, and so forth.

The home team tries to guess what the occupation is. When they guess correctly, the foreigners turn and run back to their

112

country (indicated by a line or some markers). The home team chases them, and all foreigners who are captured must join the home team.

Then the home team becomes the foreigners, and the game continues. At the close of the game the side with the most players wins.

KARUTATORI

Number of players: Any number.

Equipment: Ninety-two cards. Forty-six of them have selected poems on them; the other forty-six have pictures suggested by the poems. These picture cards are displayed on the floor or table.

Formation: Players are seated in a circle.

Action: A leader reads aloud the poem on one of the cards. The players listen carefully. At the same time they look over the picture cards. As soon as a player thinks he has located the right picture for the particular poem being read, he snaps up the card. If he is right, he keeps the card. The player with the most cards at the end of the game wins.

If a player snaps up the wrong card, he may be penalized one point. This will prevent wild grabbing for cards.

Naturally the Japanese use Japanese poems. For English-speaking groups *Songs from the Land of Dawn,* by Kagawa and others (Friendship Press, 1949), and *Songs from the Slums,* by Kagawa (Abingdon Press, 1935), will offer a number of usable poems for this game. In the first book such poems by Kagawa as "O Skylarks, Teach Japan to Sing," "One with the Universe," "The Simple Life," and "I Call the Swallows" could be used. This book also has a section of selected classical Japanese poems. In *Songs from the Slums* poems like "Only a Flower," "If Only There Are Stars," "Autumn Sunshine," and "Discovery" could

113

be used. English and American poems like Leigh Hunt's "Abou Ben Adhem," Frank Stanton's "The World," Longfellow's "A Psalm of Life," Markham's "Outwitted" and "The Man with the Hoe," Kipling's "When Earth's Last Picture Is Painted," Browning's "Pippa Passes," are possibilities. Any good collection of poems will reveal others.

This is an excellent game for a youth or adult group. It can be adapted for children by using nursery rhymes and other children's poems.

POEM CARD PLAYING

Number of players: Four to eight.

Equipment: Two hundred cards. The poems used by the Japanese are those of "waka," or Japanese poems of thirty-one syllables. They are mostly lyrical poetry composed more than one thousand years ago. Each poem is divided into two parts by a pause. The first part consists of seventeen syllables and the second part fourteen. The first part is written on the first one hundred cards. The second part, or doublet, appears on the other one hundred.

Formation: Players sit on a mat, teams of an equal number facing one another.

Action: The doublet cards are dealt evenly to the two teams. The leader, or reciter, holds the other cards. Each team arranges its doublet cards on the mat where they can be seen by all the players.

The leader reads or recites the first part of one of the poems. The players, on hearing it, try to pick up the appropriate double card. A good player, on hearing the first few words or syllables of the poem calls to mind the second part. He locates the doublet. As soon as the first part is finished, his hand comes down swiftly with his forefinger touching the correct card. The first player to succeed gets the doublet card. At the end the team or individual with the most cards is declared winner.

This is a time-honored game among the literate classes. It is played by grownups as well as by teen-age boys and girls. It is played most often at the New Year season, at which time parties are given in the various homes. Besides being a good pastime it has done much toward popularizing poetry.

An English-speaking group would use poems or excerpts familiar to its people, such as Markham's "Outwitted," Kipling's "If —" Longfellow's "The Arrow and the Song," Holmes' "The Chambered Nautilus" (perhaps the last stanza, "Build thee more stately mansions"), Kilmer's "Trees," Carruth's "Each in His Own Tongue" (one stanza), Field's "Little Boy Blue." Any good collection of poems will furnish plenty of material.

Adapt the game to the ages and capacity of your group. With small children Mother Goose rhymes may be used. The number of poems and cards used can be cut to twenty or thirty. The player who gets the doublet reads it aloud to the others.

SUGOROKU

Number of players: Two to four.

Equipment: A cardboard or paper the size of a checkerboard and marked as indicated in diagram. The squares on the board lead to the center square or home. A wooden cube, one half to five eighths of an inch square, with numbers one to six on sides. Or a cardboard indicator with spinner. This can be made easily. Divide cardboard into six equal sections numbered one to six. Pin a cardboard arrow or metal spinner at center

115

and flip it with the finger. Where it stops indicates the number of spaces to move. A small disc or marker for each player. A button will do. There should be a different color for each player. A flat space on the floor, ground, or table for the board.

Action: Players do "Jankenpon" (page 110) to decide who is to start the game. The winner tosses the cube or spins the indicator. The number he gets indicates the number of spaces he is to move his marker. If he lands on a square marked "sing a song," or "skip turn," or "move four," or some other direction, he acts accordingly. If he lands on "go back," he must begin all over again. If his throw takes him past "stop," he must stop there anyway. To land on "stop," however, means simply that he rests there until his next turn.

The first player to get his marker "home" wins.

KAGOME-KAGOME

Number of players: Three or more.

Formation: Circle with one player at center, who is the bird.

Action: The bird stands with his eyes closed. The others march around him intoning the following:

> The bird, the bird,
> The bird in a cage,
> When do you come
> Out of your cage?

After circling around the bird several times, they stop and ask, "Who is behind you?"

The bird answers, "Hanako," or some other name. If he is right, the person whose name he called becomes the bird and the game continues.

116

TAKARATORI

Number of players: Six to twenty, in two equal teams.

Formation: Draw a large letter *S* (see diagram) with a stick or line outdoors; indoors or on a concrete court use chalk. Place some heavy object, such as a stone, at either end of the *S*. This is the treasure or takara. Draw several islands around the *S*. Players of the two teams locate themselves about the letter.

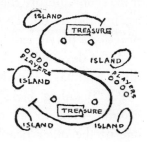

One or more of the players for each team stand inside the *S* to protect the treasure and their team's end of the *S*.

Action: Other players locate themselves outside the *S* and venture in to try to capture the treasure belonging to their opponents. However, only when they are inside an island may they put both feet down. At all other times they must hop on one foot.

When a player tries to capture the treasure, he is tagged by an opposing player guarding the treasure. These two players then do "Jankenpon" (page 110). The loser is considered dead. He drops out of the game. All this time the players must stand or hop on one foot and can rest only by returning to one of the islands.

The first team to capture the treasure wins.

OTEDAMA

Number of players: Two or more, or one player can play alone just for the fun of developing his skill at the game.

Equipment: From three to six otedama (or beanbags). The Japanese make these out of colorful cloth.

Action: The game may be played two ways:

117

1. "Beanbag juggling": The player has two beanbags in his right hand. He tosses one of them in the air. Before it comes down, he tosses up the second beanbag, catching the first one as it descends. Before the second comes down, he tosses up the first again, and so on. This is repeated until the player misses. By practice a player can become rather skillful.

After developing skill in juggling two with one hand, add a third beanbag. Try the same thing by using both hands.

2. "Beanbag jacks": Drop five beanbags on the floor or ground. Pick up one of them, toss it into the air, and pick up one of the other beanbags before catching the one tossed into the air. Play just as in the game of "Jacks."

HANAKAGO

(The Flower Basket)

This is similar to "Fruit Basket."

Number of players: Ten to thirty.

Formation: Players are seated in a circle with one player, who is "It," standing at center. Cushions or chairs are used for seats. There must be a seat for each player except "It."

Action: Each player is given the name of a flower—cherry blossom, aster, and so on. "It" calls the names of any two flowers. The players representing those flowers must change seats. In the scramble "It" tries to get a seat. The player left out becomes "It," and the game continues. If "It" calls, "Hanakago!" all the players must change seats.

MAN, GUN, TIGER

This is an adaptation of the Japanese game "Jankenpon."

Number of players: Two or more.

Formation and action: Two sides line up facing one another. Each side decides which it will represent— either man, gun, or tiger. If man, the players hold their two forefingers up to their lips to represent a flowing mustache. If gun, the players aim, as if shooting, and yell, "Bang!" If tiger, they hold their hands up, claw fashion, and snarl, showing their teeth. The man beats the gun, because he shoots the gun. The gun beats the tiger, and the tiger beats the man. Score points.

WELL KONO

Number of players: Two.

Equipment: A board or paper about six or eight inches square marked as in the diagram. Countersink the five holes as in other marble games, such as "Chinese Checkers." Use four marbles, two of one color and two of another. Or mark the diagram on paper or cardboard, using a cork bottle stopper, the end dipped in ink, for the five spots. Make the lines with ink, pencil, or crayon. Instead of using marbles, use checkers or cardboard discs, again two of one color and two of another.

Action: One player's men are placed in the two top spaces and the other's in the two bottom ones. The center spot is vacant. The player who has his men in the top spaces plays first by moving one of his men to the center. His opponent moves a man to the space vacated. Players move alternately. No jumping is allowed, and all moves must be along one of the marked lines from one space to the adjacent empty space. A player wins when he corners his opponent's men so that neither can be moved.

FOUR FIELD KONO

Number of players: Two.

Equipment: A board about seven inches by five inches with sixteen holes as indicated in the diagram. Or use cardboard and sixteen spots made with a cork stopper dipped in ink. If a board is used and the game is played with marbles, use molding around the outside of the board and provide a space at either end for captured marbles. Sixteen counters (marbles or checkers) in two contrasting colors will be needed, eight for each player.

Action: Each player arranges his eight counters in the two rows at his end of the board. The object of the game is to capture all the opponent's men.

One player starts the game by jumping one of his own men so as to land in the next space beyond occupied by an opponent's man. By so doing he captures that man. Players take turns in moving vertically or horizontally, but never diagonally. After the initial moves of the game players move their men forward, or backward, or sideways, from one spot to an adjacent empty spot to get two men in such a position as to make a jump possible. A jump can be made only when a player has two of his own men together in adjacent spots, in which case he may jump one over the other to land in the adjacent space beyond, thus capturing the opponent's man in that space. A player does not have to jump unless he wishes to do so, nor can a jump be made except when it captures an opponent's man.

A man can be captured if he can be surrounded by his opponent's men so that he cannot move either horizontally or vertically. This is usually done by getting a man in a corner space with two opponents in adjacent spaces. Such a man is captured even though other moves on the board are possible.

YOOT

A missionary says this game is a great favorite in Korea, particularly at New Year's time. Adults as well as children play it.

Number of players: Two or more.

Equipment: A cardboard or paper diagram about eight by eight inches. The diagram is a circle or square of twenty spots. A cross of nine spots divides the circle into four equal segments. This cross is made by a center spot and two extra spots on each arm to complete 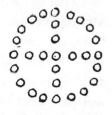 the cross (see diagram). These spots may be made by dipping a cork in ink and printing on the cardboard or paper.

Four small discs, three fourths of an inch in diameter, for each player. These may be made of linoleum or heavy cardboard. Each player should have a set in a particular color—four reds, four greens, four blues, or four yellows, and so on.

Four yoot sticks, one set for each diagram in use. Since not more than four players can play on one diagram, it may be necessary to have several diagrams and thus several games going on at the same time. The yoot sticks are twigs split into two pieces, so that there is a flat side and a round side to each stick (see diagram). A convenient size would be two inches long by three fourths of an inch wide. The Koreans use twigs usually about a foot in length. Smooth the sticks by trimming and sandpapering. Paint or varnish  them. This will add to the satisfaction of handling them. Excellent yoot sticks may be made of broomsticks.

Action: A player starts the game by tossing the four sticks up in the air. When they land on the table or floor, their meaning is as follows:

1. One flat side up, called "pig," move one spot.
2. Two flat sides up, called "dog," move two spots.
3. Three flat sides up, called "kuel," move three spots.
4. Four flat sides up, called "yoot," move five spots and get an extra throw.
5. No flat sides up, called "mo," move four spots and get an extra throw.

Players toss in turn and move a disc to the spot indicated. The object of the game is to get around the board and back to the starting point.

If a player lands a disc exactly on an intersection, he may move down that intersection, thus making it unnecessary to travel all the way around the board.

If a player lands on a spot occupied by an opponent, he captures that opponent and sends him back home.

Each player has four men to move around. He may exercise his own judgment about which one to move on a throw. The idea is to get all four men around. The one who does this first is winner.

MALAYA

CALAH PANJANG, OR BAMBOO LONG

Number of players: Twelve.

Formation: Players are divided into two teams of six each. One team runs while the other tries to catch them. The catchers must run only on the lines assigned them (see diagram). In other words, Number One protects his line, Number Two his, and so on. Number Six is in charge of the main line through the middle. The five lines are about twenty yards long and ten yards apart.

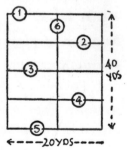

Action: At a given signal the players start running. The runners must watch their chance, keeping clear of lines where they may be caught. Chasers can run up and down only the lines assigned them.

If a player is tagged, the whole side is out and their opponents become the runners.

124

If anyone in the running group can run across the five lines and back again, he shouts, "Toe," to let the others know they have won.

BLIND GUESSER

Number of players: Six to twenty.

Action: One of the players is blindfolded. The other players pass by, performing some action. As they do so, the leader tells the blindfolded player what action each player is performing without naming the player. When every player has performed, the leader takes off the blindfold, names some action that has been performed, and asks that the guesser point to the player who performed it. If the guesser points to the right person, that person is blindfolded and the game continues. Otherwise he has to be blindfolded again.

TURTLE'S NEST

Number of players: Any number.

Formation: One player is the turtle, guarding the turtle's nest. The other players stand where they wish.

Action: Four or five pebbles become the turtle eggs. They are placed in a small circle, which represents the turtle's nest. The turtle stoops over the eggs, watching carefully. The other players slip up and try to take away the eggs. If a player is touched by the turtle as he tries to take the eggs, he becomes the turtle to guard the remaining eggs. This is continued until all the eggs have been taken. They are now hidden in several places. The last player who is the turtle has to search for the eggs. If he does not succeed in finding them all, he must pay a forfeit.

GRINDING STONE

Number of players: Any number.

Formation: One player stands beside the leader. The others stand about at random, but only a little way from the leader.

Action: The leader begins by saying, "Grinding stone! Grinding stone!" He then commands the other players to perform some action, such as, "Hop on one foot!" "Imitate a bird flying!" "Sing a song!" "Be the traffic cop at a busy corner!" The player standing beside the leader lunges after the other players trying to tag one of them before he can obey the leader's command. If he succeeds in catching someone, the player caught takes his place beside the leader.

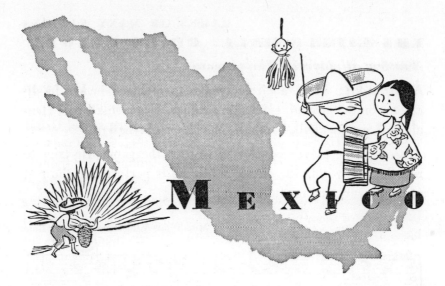

LITTLE CLOWN

(El Lindo Payasito)

Number of players: Any number.

Action: The player chosen as Little Clown goes through some action of his own choosing, such as clapping his hands, stamping his feet, flopping his arms, and so on. The rest of the players mimic him as they sing or hum the following song:

Mrs. Temis Valderrana de Perez Rojo

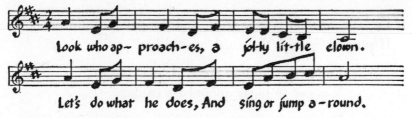

Look who ap-proach-es, a jol-ly lit-tle clown.

Let's do what he does, And sing or jump a-round.

Then another Little Clown is chosen, and the game continues.

127

THE LITTLE BALL, OR LA PELOTA

Number of players: Two or more.

Equipment: Mark a circle twelve to eighteen inches in diameter on the ground, sidewalk, or floor. Use a small ball (tennis ball, croquet ball, baseball, or rubber playball).

Action: One player is selected to start the game. He tries to roll the ball within the circle. While he is performing, the rest of the players sing the following song:

Mrs. Temis Valderrana de Perez Rojo

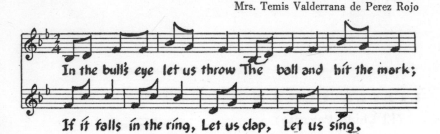

In the bull's eye let us throw The ball and hit the mark;
If it falls in the ring, Let us clap, Let us sing.

If the player is successful, the others sing:

> It has fallen in the ring;
> Let us clap, let us sing.
>
> Let us clap, let us sing;
> It has fallen in the ring.

If he fails, another player tries, and the game continues.
If sung in Spanish the words would be:

> En la rueda quiere yo, la pelota colocar
> Y si cae su lugar aplaudir y cantar.
>
> En la ruedo ya cayo aplaudir y cantar,
> Aplaudir y cantar en la ruedo ya cayo.

FRUITS

Number of players: Ten to twenty.

Formation: Players sit in a circle.

Action: One player is designated as master, another as servant, and the rest are given names of fruits—apples, apricots, bananas, blackberries, blueberries, currants, cantaloupes, dates, figs, grapes, guavas, lemons, loganberries, melons, oranges, peaches, pears, plums, raspberries, strawberries, and so on.

The game starts with the master asking the servant, "Where wert thou?" and continues as follows:

Servant: "In the house of the apple."
Apple: "It is not so."
Servant: "Then where wert thou?"
Apple: "In the house of the master."
Master: "It is not so."
Apple: "Then where were you?"
Master: "In the house of the plum."

So the questions and answers go. All players must use the words "thou" and "thee" except when addressing the master, when they use "you." Anyone breaking this rule or failing to answer immediately must pay a forfeit. The game is played until there are as many forfeits as desired.

COYOTE AND SHEEP

Number of players: Eight to twelve. One player is the shepherd, one the coyote, and the rest are sheep.

Formation: The sheep and shepherd form in a line, one behind the other, each with hands clasped around the waist of the player in front of him. The shepherd is at the head of the line.

129

Action: The coyote approaches, and the shepherd asks, "What does the coyote want?" The coyote answers, "I want fat meat!" The shepherd calls, "Then go to the end of the line where the fattest lambs are."

When the shepherd says this, the coyote breaks for the end of the line to tag one of the lambs. The shepherd defends his flock by extending his arms and running this way and that thus endeavoring to prevent the coyote from getting to the last sheep. The sheep and shepherd must not break their line. If they do, the shepherd becomes the next coyote, and the next man in line becomes the shepherd. The same thing is true when the coyote tags the last player in line.

ROMPIENDO LA PINATA

This is a popular game in Mexico, particularly at Christmastime.

Number of players: Ten or more.

Equipment: A large paper bag, the pinata, is filled with nuts and candy wrapped in wax paper. The mouth of the bag is tied, and the bag is hung from the ceiling (or a tree limb or door sill) with a cord. The bag is dressed and marked to represent a boy or a girl, using crepe or tissue paper or clothes.

Action: The players, each in turn, are given a stick; and with eyes blindfolded they try to break the pinata. They are turned around several times to make the feat more difficult. Only one stroke is allowed each player, and he is not permitted to grope for the bag. When someone finally breaks the pinata and the contents are scattered, all the players scramble for them.

Sometimes a bit of novelty is introduced into the game by preparing three pinatas—the first filled with flour and rice, the second with a pair of old shoes, the third with sweets, "dulces."

130

SOLEMN ACTION

Number of players: Six or more.

Formation: Players sit in a circle.

Action: One player is designated to start the game. He makes some motion, such as pinching the nose of the player to his right or tickling him under the chin. Each player, in turn, repeats this motion with the next player to the right. Thus it goes around the circle. No player must laugh or speak. If anyone does, he drops out of the game. The last one left is winner.

"HELP!"

Number of players: Four to ten.

Action: This is a tag game. The player who is to be "It" is determined in an interesting manner. One player stands with hand extended, palm down. The others place their index or forefinger on this extended palm. The player with the extended hand suddenly closes his fist. The player whose finger is caught becomes "It" and chases the others. If more than one player has his finger caught, the process is repeated with those caught until only one remains.

Those who are being chased may call for "Help!" any time. On such a call any other player may take hold of the hand of the calling player, thus saving him from being tagged. A player who is caught becomes "It," and the game proceeds.

CALABAZA

This game is similar to "Pussy Wants a Corner."

Number of players: Four or more.

132

Formation: Markers are placed about the room or yard, there being one less marker than the number of players. The markers may be made by chalk crosses or paper or flat stones. Players form a circle.

Action: Players sing in the same tone the word "Calabaza" ("everyone to his house") eight times. After the eighth Calabaza is sung, all players run for a marker. The player left out is "It." He then goes to one of the players and asks, "Are there any eggs?" "In the other corner," replies the player questioned. Meanwhile the other players are changing places while "It" tries to get a place. If he succeeds, the player left without a place must ask the question and seek to get a home.

BLIND HEN

Number of players: Ten or more.

Formation: Players stand in a circle, with one blindfolded player, representing the blind hen, at center.

Action: A player standing in the circle asks, "What have you lost?" The hen answers, "A thimble and a needle." The one in the circle then asks, "Where?" The hen replies, "In the hay stack." The circle player then steps to the center and says, "Kneel down." He then turns the hen around several times. When he has finished, the players in the circle start running around shouting, "Blind hen!" until the hen tags one of them. The player tagged becomes the hen. Players may tease the hen by coming in close and shouting, "Blind hen!"

WOLF

Number of players: Six or more.

Formation: Circle, with one player at center.

Action: The player at center is the wolf. The other players call to him, "Wolf, Wolf, are you ready?" The wolf answers, "No, I've got to put my stockings on!" Again they call, and he answers, "No, I've got to put on my shoes." Each time he goes through the motions of putting on the piece of wearing apparel he names. It may be his hat, his coat, his pants, his shirt, skirt, or gloves, or whatever he chooses to name. Suddenly he answers, "Yes, I'm ready and here I come!" Immediately all players scatter and rush to a designated safety zone. It may be the bounds of the yard or the walls of the room. The wolf tries to tag a player before he reaches safety. If he does, that person becomes the wolf and the game continues. The wolf may get ready on any call that suits him.

PHILIPPINES

SAN PEDRO AND SAN PABLO

Number of players: Four or more.

Field: Outline a square at least ten by ten feet. Divide it into four equal squares by bisecting lines (see diagram). When more than four players are involved, enlarge the field accordingly.

Formation: One player is captain for each team. On the defensive team the captain stands at center where the lines cross. He must always keep at least one foot in contact with this central spot. Four other defending players guard each of the four intersecting lines. No defending player may leave his line to tag an opponent. The attacking team scatters into the four squares.

Action: Attacking players try to cross the lines inside the field without being tagged. Each time an attacking player crosses an intersecting line, he scores a point for his team. When a player is tagged, he pays a forfeit or is declared out of the game

135

until the teams change sides. Teams take turns being defenders and attackers. A defender must not step out of the outside line of the square. If he does, he is considered out.[13]

STOOP TAG

Number of players: Five or more.

Formation: Players scatter over the playing area with one player being "It."

Action: "It" chases the others, trying to tag one of them. A player may escape being tagged by stooping or squatting. However, each player may stoop only three times. After that he may escape being tagged only by running. Any player tagged becomes "It." In a large group there should be several taggers.

POTATO JOUST

Number of players: Two or more.

Formation: Two players face each other, about three feet apart. Each player must kneel and lift one leg from the floor. This leg he holds up with one of his hands. In the other hand he has a potato firmly jabbed on the prongs of a fork. A cushion may be provided each combatant.

Action: Each player tries to knock his opponent's potato off the fork, at the same time protecting his own. Players often develop quite a bit of skill in handling the fork—a slight turn of the wrist, a quick push, and a potato is flying.

A player is defeated if:

1. He loses his potato.

2. He topples over three times. (If he is obliged to let go of his foot in order to keep his balance, it is considered a fall.)

[13] Says Carol Moe, of Bayombong, P. I. "This game I saw first when children had marked out the lines with water on the dry beach at Aparri in bright moonlight. They were having a riot of a good time at it. I've seen it many other places since. . . . There are two teams of from two to five players each."

3. He stumbles against his opponent and causes him to fall.

Each time a fall occurs, each contestant is allowed to change the knee upon which he is resting.

LAME DUCK

Number of players: Four or more.

Formation: Players scatter about the playing space, with one player being the lame duck. Limits of the playing area should be determined before the game begins.

Action: The lame duck hops on one foot and tries to tag one of the other players. If he succeeds, the player caught becomes the lame duck and the game continues.

PUSS IN THE CIRCLE

Number of players: Four or more.

Formation: A circle four to six feet in diameter is marked on the ground or floor. A white string may be used to make this circle. One player, who is puss, stands in the center of the circle. The other players stand outside the circle, surrounding it.

Action: The object is for puss to tag the other players. They may be tagged whenever they put a foot inside the circle. They tease puss by stepping in and out of the circle or by feigning such action. Anyone whom puss touches becomes a prisoner and helps tag the others.

SIPA SIPA

(Also Hawaii)

Number of players: Ten or more.

Equipment: A hand-woven wicker ball, six inches in diameter. The court is twenty-five by fifty feet. There is a net three feet high

137

across the middle of the court, dividing it into two twenty-five-foot areas.

Action: The rules reverse our volleyball rules in that the ball may not legally touch any part of the body above the waist. The ball must be batted with the knees or feet. In this fashion players try to bat it over the net into the opponent's court.

R U S S I A

GORELKI, WIDOWER, OR LAST COUPLE OUT

(Also Scotland, Sweden)

Number of players: Nine or more.

Formation: Players line up by couples. An extra player, who is "It," stands from six to ten feet in front of the head couple, face forward.

Action: When "It" shouts, "Last couple out!" that couple must leave the rear and move forward with the idea of passing "It" and taking hold of hands in front of him. They must come up on either side of the line of players and not on the same side. They may come swiftly or slowly as they desire. "It" may not turn his head to see them coming. He must look straight ahead. Only when they get even with him can he leave his place. When they do get even with him, he dashes after one of them, trying

139

to tag him before they can join hands in front of him. If he succeeds, the player tagged take his place as "It" and he and the other member of the couple become the head couple. If the couple succeeds in getting together, they become the head couple and "It" tries again.

SCOTLAND

WEE BOLOGNA MAN

Number of players: Six or more.

Formation: A leader stands in front of the group of players, or he may stand in the center with the others forming a circle around him.

Action: The leader repeats:

> I'm the Wee Bologna Man;
> Always do the best you can
> To follow the Wee Bologna Man.

He then goes through the motions of playing some instrument in the band—a fife, a drum, a trombone, a violin, a piano, a trumpet, cymbals, a bass fiddle. Or he imitates an orchestra leader, a drum major, or goes through some other motion, as he chooses. The rest of the players follow suit.

A good leader puts the group through at a brisk pace. Each time he changes to another movement, he must repeat the rhyme.

Leaders may be changed often by the simple process of pointing or by calling the name of another player. The action should be fast.

HOW MANY MILES TO BABYLON?

This game originated from the practice of the toll charge that had to be paid when one entered a city.

Number of players: Eight or more.

Formation: Players stand, by couples, in two lines facing one another, with eight to ten feet between the lines. Couples hold hands.

Action: A dialogue takes place between the two lines, the players of each chanting their lines in unison. The tempo is fast. They sway back and forth in rhythm, swinging clasped hands by couples, as they sway and repeat the words.

First line: "How many miles to Babylon?"
Second line: "Only a bare threescore and ten."
First line: "Will we be there by candlelight?"
Second line: "Yes, you will, and back again."
First line: "Open your gates and let us through."
Second line: "Not without a beck and boo (bow),
        Not without a side and sou."
First line: "Here's a beck and here's a boo,
        Here's a side and here's a sou.
        Open your gates and let us through."
Second line: "We'll open the gates and let them through."

At the words "Here's a beck and here's a boo" the players of the first line suit the action to the words by placing the hands on the hips for a "beck" and making a bow for a "boo." On "Here's

142

a side and here's a sou" they stand erect and turn the head to the right and then to the left.

Then the partners clasp hands and run forward eight steps in rhythm. Each couple of the first line passes under the up-raised arms of the opposite couple of the second line. Having taken the eight steps, the running couple turns around in four running steps, facing the "city gates" from the other side. The couples in the second line, the "gates," also turn in four running steps. Now the group is in position to repeat the game with the first line representing the "gates."

The game may be played to the music of "Country Gardens," if desired.

SMUGGLE THE GEG

Number of players: Eight or more.

Equipment: The "geg" may be a marble, a pebble, a knife, a key, or anything of the sort.

Field: A den four by six feet is marked off at the center of the playing space. Boundaries are decided.

Formation and action: Players are divided into two teams, the "Ins" and the "Outs." The Outs get the geg. They get into a huddle and hide the geg on one of their players. Or they stand in a line and pass it from hand to hand behind their backs, leaving it finally in the possession of one of their players.

The Ins stand by the den while the Outs, or "smugglers," run and hide themselves. Before they are finally hidden, the Outs must shout, "Smugglers!" The Ins then try to find and tag them. The object of the Ins is to find the player who has the geg. Since they probably do not know which player that is, they will have to challenge every player tagged.

If the custodian of the geg can return to the den without being tagged, the Outs win and they remain in possession of the geg for the next game.

When an In catches an Out, the latter is not a prisoner until the In takes off the Out's cap (if he is wearing one) and places the palm of his hand on the prisoner's head. When this is done, the Out must cease struggling. Then the In demands, "Deliver up the geg!" If the captured player has it, he must surrender it at once. The fact is then shouted aloud, and all players return to the den. If the player caught does not have the geg, he goes free. When the geg is found, the two teams change places.

URUGUAY

THE COLOR MARKET

Number of players: Ten to twenty-five.

Formation: Circle, with leader and two or three other players at center. The extra players at center represent artists, weavers, and/or decorators.

Action: Each player in the circle has been given the name of some color—red, yellow, blue, green, purple, orange, violet, black, white, brown, crimson, beige, chartreuse, tan, cream, gold, silver, gray, olive, pink, cerise, maroon, ebony, lilac, rose, and so on.

The players at center take turns in "visiting" the market. There is a knock. The leader or manager of the market asks, "Who is there?" The knocker answers, "Artist," or, "Weaver," or, "Decorator," according to whose turn it is. "What color do you want?" asks the leader. If he calls a color that is in the circle, the player representing that color leaves the circle and stands behind the buyer.

At the end the side having the most players wins.

THE BLIND HEN

Number of players: Ten or more.

Formation: Players form a circle with a blindfolded player, who is the blind hen, at the center.

Action: Players move in toward the blind hen, asking, "What have you lost, Little Hen?" The blind hen answers, "I lost my pencil and pen." The other players tease the blind hen, saying, "We know where they are, but we will not tell." The blind hen tries to tag someone before he can get back to the circle. The one who is caught becomes the blind hen, and the game continues.

THE WOLF

Number of players: Ten or more.

Formation: One player is chosen to be the wolf. He lives by himself, apart from the other players. Boundaries of the field are determined beforehand, and the "home" line is designated. The other players occupy this space between the home line and the wolf.

Action: The players frolic around the field (the space between the wolf and home base). They chant:

> In the fields let us play,
> While the wolf is away.

They then approach the wolf and ask, "Are you ready, Wolf?" The wolf answers, "I am getting up." So the others play in the field again. Each time they near the wolf and ask if he is ready. He continues to answer that he is getting ready. All of a sudden,

146

however, he shouts, "I am starting to get you." With that he starts in pursuit. The player who is caught becomes the wolf, and the game is played again.

Note the similarity of this game to the "Wolf" game from Peru.

F O R F E I T S

In many games, particularly from Latin countries, forfeits are required of those players who commit some fault. In a small crowd effort is made to get at least one forfeit from each player. In a large group a game is continued until the desired number of persons have been caught.

The usual procedure in redeeming forfeits is as follows: A player is seated in a chair behind which is another person, who holds up the forfeits one at a time. The judge, or person seated, is not allowed to see the forfeits, although everyone else in the room does. The following dialogue takes place:

Forfeit holder: "Heavy, Heavy, hangs over your poor head." (He displays the article—a knife, for instance—over the head of the judge.)
Judge: "Fine or superfine?"
Forfeit holder: "Fine. What shall the owner do to redeem it?"

Then the judge pronounces the sentence by naming something the owner must do for the entertainment of the group.

148

If the forfeit holder answers, "Fine," the judge knows the article belongs to a boy. If he answers, "Superfine," he knows it belongs to a girl.

A list of forfeit stunts follows:

1. Repeat "Mary Had a Little Lamb" backward. The performer may be required to repeat all four lines or the first line in this fashion.

2. Imitate a fat man tying his shoelace.

3. Imitate a fat woman wearing a big hat getting on a crowded elevator.

4. Dance around the room three times with a broom for a partner.

5. Imitate a fat man getting off a crowded bus.

6. Bend your head as low as you can toward the floor.

7. Sing a popular song, with the crowd joining in on the chorus.

8. Repeat, "blue bread," rapidly five times.

9. Make faces in three different ways at three different people.

10. Smile three different ways at three different people.

11. Repeat rapidly three times, "Six sickly songsters sipping cider."

12. Imitate a girl on the phone talking to her best boy friend. Pantomime only.

13. Enter the room in three different manners.

14. Crow like a rooster.

15. Imitate the noise made by a cat in a midnight row.

16. Bark first like a small dog and then like a large one.

17. Quack like a duck.

18. Say rapidly three times, "Big black bear bit a big blue bug."

19. Balance a tennis ball on your nose. ("Three cheers for a good try.")

20. Imitate a cat lapping up a saucer of milk.

21. Be Sir Sad Sack, the knight of a rueful countenance. Select someone to serve as your squire. The two of you go to each girl in the room. The squire solemnly kisses the hand of each girl and then wipes the mouth of Sir Sad Sack with a handkerchief. The knight must look sad and forlorn throughout the ceremony.

22. Say three nice things about yourself while standing on one leg.

23. Imitate a gum-chewing, gossiping, primping typist in pantomime.

24. Spell your own last name backward.

25. Sing a lullaby to a sofa cushion.

26. Laugh five different ways.

27. Shake hands with five different people in five different kinds of handshakes.

28. Pantomime a saleslady trying to sell a hat to a hard-to-please lady customer.

29. Pantomime a baseball pitcher in the act of pitching to a batter and then catching the pop fly which the batter hits near the pitcher's box.

30. Pantomime a baby sitter taking care of a squalling baby.

31. Say rapidly three times, "Shoes and socks shocked Susan."

32. Say rapidly three times, "Sam sawed six slick, slim, slender saplings."

33. Put one hand where the other hand cannot touch it. This is done by putting one hand on the elbow, back of the wrist, or forearm of the other arm. (Let the victim try to work it out for himself.)

34. Place an object in the room on the floor so that no one can jump over it. This is done by placing the object in a corner against the wall.

35. Imitate a girl dressing her hair before a mirror.

36. Repeat dramatically Hamlet's line, "To be, or not to be: that is the question."

37. Hold an imaginary conversation with some noted historical character (Christopher Columbus, George Washington, Abraham Lincoln, and so on).

38. Pose as the Statue of Liberty.

39. Pantomime the teaching of a class in geography.

40. Deliver a half-minute Fourth-of-July oration.

41. Pantomime anger, grief, remorse, joy, hatred, love, ecstasy.

42. Imitate a farmer calling hogs.

43. Pantomime a person driving a jeep over a very rough road.

44. Pantomime both the photographer and the person whose picture is being taken. Try to get the subject to smile. As the subject do your best to display your "ivories."

45. Pantomime a rooter at a football game. An important goal after touchdown is being kicked. You want it to be good. The ball is snapped. It is kicked. It is in the air. It just goes over the crossbar for a successful kick. Whew!

46. Repeat in dramatic manner, "Give me liberty, or give me death!"

47. Pick three other people in the room to help you sing a quartet selection.

48. Give three reasons why we ought to let you go on living.

49. Pantomime a boy (girl) ordering an ice-cream soda and consuming it on a hot summer day. Place your order, receive it, get a straw, and go to work.

50. Deliver a dramatic speech, repeating only the letters of the alphabet.

51. Pantomime "Little Miss Muffet" when the spider sat down beside her.

52. Pantomime "Little Jack Horner."

53. Pantomime a basketball player shooting a foul.

54. Pantomime a boy flying a kite.

55. Pantomime a dentist who is pulling a tooth hard to get. Use someone in the group as your patient.

56. Pantomime someone with a bad case of mumps.

57. Pantomime a girl unwillingly washing dishes.

58. Repeat three times the following, "Seven simple sleepy sailors slipping sideways in sleet and slush."

GAME INDEX

CLASSIFIED INDEX

Games Requiring Forfeits

Guessing Games

Pantomime

Racing Games

Rhythm Games

Singing Games

Games of Skill

Lowering the Boom

THE BOBBY BAUN STORY

Bobby Baun

with Anne Logan

Stoddart

Published in 2000 by Stoddart Publishing Co. Limited
34 Lesmill Road, Toronto, Canada M3B 2T6
180 Varick Street, 9th Floor, New York, New York 10014

Distributed in Canada by:
General Distribution Services Ltd.
325 Humber College Blvd.,
Toronto, Ontario M9W 7C3
Tel. (416) 213-1919
Fax (416) 213-1917
Email cservice@genpub.com

Distributed in the United States by:
General Distribution Services Inc.
PMB 128, 4500 Witmer Industrial Estates,
Niagara Falls, New York 14305-1386
Toll-free Tel. 1-800-805-1083
Toll-free Fax 1-800-481-6207
Email gdsinc@genpub.com

04 03 02 01 00   1 2 3 4 5

Canadian Cataloguing in Publication Data

Baun, Bobby
Lowering the boom: the Bobby Baun story
Includes index.
ISBN 0-7737-3259-4
1. Baun, Bobby. 2. Hockey players — Canada — Biography. I. Logan, Anne M. II. Title.
GV848.5.B38A3 2000   796.962'092   C00-931359-1

U.S. Cataloging-in-Publication Data
(Library of Congress Standards)

Baun, Bobby, 1936–
Lowering the boom: the Bobby Baun story / Bobby Baun, Anne Logan. — 1st ed.
[240]p. : ill.; cm.
ISBN 0-7737-3259-4
1. Baun, Bobby, 1936– . 2. Hockey players — Biography.
3. National Hockey League — Biography. I. Logan, Anne. II. Title.
796.962 /64/ 092   21   2000   CIP

Jacket design: Bill Douglas @ The Bang
Text design: Joseph Gisini / Andrew Smith Graphics Inc.

THE CANADA COUNCIL | LE CONSEIL DES ARTS
FOR THE ARTS | DU CANADA
SINCE 1957 | DEPUIS 1957

*We acknowledge for their financial support of our publishing program the
Canada Council for the Arts, the Ontario Arts Council, and the Government of Canada
through the Book Publishing Industry Development Program (BPIDP).*

Printed and bound in Canada

To the little person who dares to
dream about becoming a somebody,
and not just a hockey player

Contents

Acknowledgments

I WOULD LIKE TO MAKE MENTION OF THE MANY PEOPLE WHO encouraged and helped me to write this book.

First, of course, I would like to thank my family. Every member spoke freely and honestly to my co-author, Anne Logan, as much about my weaknesses as my strengths. I would particularly like to thank my wife Sallie; my children, Jeff, Greg, Brian, Michelle, and Patti; and my two sisters, Joyce and Marlene. I also include some of my extended family, especially my cousins Minnie and Patti Giffin.

I would like to thank all my friends outside the world of hockey: Don James, Ron Joyce, Harry Rosen, Doug Cole, Ken Girard, Senator Keith Davey, Roy Main, Del Page, John and Bill Cawker, and Cicely and Phil Brownlee.

Anne and I spoke to prior members of the board of Maple Leaf Gardens, and the Silver Seven: Jack Amell, George Mara, Doug Roxborough, and the late Paul McNamara. Tom Smythe, an exceptionally brave man, was also helpful.

From the world of hockey, I thank Red Kelly, Frank Mahovlich,

Carl Brewer, Eddie Shack, Billy Harris, Dick Duff, Allan Stanley, Darryl Sittler, Jim Gregory, Bobby Haggert (who was particularly helpful), and my first coach, George Kitchen. David Keon, Bert Olmstead, and Mike Nykoluk all helped out via lengthy long-distance interviews.

I give honourable mention to the reporters who, though we did not talk to them directly, provided a wealth of clippings in their words of the time: Red Burnett, Scott Young, George Gross, Red MacLeod, and Milt Dunnell.

More than helpful were our editors, Don Bastian and Jim Gifford. Whenever we needed a slap on the wrist, they managed to do it in such a way that it felt more like a pat on the back; our enthusiasm was never dampened. They feel this is a great book. We agree, and we hope you feel the same way.

PART I

Before
the Fame

CHAPTER 1

From Saskatchewan to Scarborough

As I sit in my office, contemplating how to tackle my memoirs, one little thing I did in 1964 always comes to mind: the "broken-leg" goal in game six of that season's Stanley Cup finals. Everywhere I go, whenever I meet new hockey fans, the same subject always comes up: "You scored the Stanley Cup–winning goal with a broken ankle!" Well, that's not exactly true, as you'll see later in this book. However, I usually don't correct people — sometimes I do, but mostly, out of politeness, I just agree with them.

I'm not normally the dramatic type, but the goal in 1964 certainly was a dramatic moment, one that has had a significant effect on my life. For "The Goal," I will always be grateful. Andy Warhol said that everyone would get fifteen minutes of fame. Looking back, my fifteen minutes came and went in a flash, apparently caused by a fluke, but I believe "The Goal" was the high point of twenty-eight years of determination, dedication, and desire. Since then I've had over thirty-five years of dreams and disappointments, fuelled by the same determination and dedication.

I have always believed strongly that we are the product of our roots, and my background has always been very important to me. My grandparents came all the way from Germany to the Saskatchewan prairie, where they were homesteaders. They were true pioneers, and I think people today — especially young people — would appreciate what they have so much more if they could travel back in time and experience my grandparents' lifestyle firsthand. They'd followed their dreams, and there was no one to back them up if they failed. I think this is the source of that self-reliance and perseverance that has served me so well.

My father decided when I was quite young that his future lay in and around the east end of Toronto, and before too long he went into business for himself, showing that same determination and self-sufficiency. His decision put me in a position where, through my own hard work and desire, I'd be noticed by a scout for the Toronto Maple Leafs and end up on the road to the National Hockey League.

I entered this world on the plains of Saskatchewan at a hefty ten pounds plus. My mother once said it felt as if I were born fully grown. Carl Brewer, my defence partner of many years, has told people that he feels I have always been "larger than life." Yet deep inside, I sometimes still feel like a little boy as I continue to skate my way through life.

I was born on September 9, 1936, in the small town of Lanigan, Saskatchewan, to Ethel and Ted Baun. I was the first of three children, and the only son; two sisters, Joyce and Marlene, arrived after the family moved east to Toronto. My given names are Robert Neil, although people tend to call me Bob or, even more often, Bobby.

My grandfather was German, and had been given his plot of land in northern Saskatchewan upon arriving in Canada. He cleared the land with a three-furrow plough, pulled by a team of twelve horses. Besides farming, he also worked as a blacksmith, a trade that was very much in demand considering how dependent everybody was on horsepower. At first, my grandparents lived in a tent — a very big tent, I imagine, since there were eventually thirteen children. Straw was the only insulation available, other than body heat.

Big families seemed to be the norm in those days: Aunt Mary, one of my mother's sisters, lived in Hubbert, Saskatchewan, and gave birth to seventeen children, fifteen of whom survived.

This part of the country was also the stomping ground of a famous politician, John Diefenbaker, of whom my father was a devout follower. Diefenbaker has always been thought of as a Westerner, but he was born in Ontario and moved West with his family at a very young age. It quite horrified Dad, a true blue Tory, in later years when, thanks to my close friend Senator Keith Davey, I became a Liberal supporter.

Saskatchewan has also produced an entire All-Star team of hockey players: Johnny Bower, Gordie Howe (my nemesis at first, later my friend), Wendel Clark, Max Bentley (the "Dipsy-Doodle Dandy from Delisle"), Elmer Lach, and my close friend, Bert Olmstead.

By the time I was three, my family had moved to Toronto, but each summer we would drive back to Saskatchewan to visit. Occasionally I was even left to spend the summer there. Those visits are among my most vivid and pleasant childhood memories.

The summer of 1941 is a trip I particularly like to recall, probably because I remember the cars so vividly. My cousin Minnie, her husband, Frank Strugnell, and her brother Joe Cherish, often travelled with us — adults in the front, children in the back, spread out between two vehicles. This particular year Dad had taken two 1941 Chevrolet coupes and made cushioned seats out of the jump seat in the back so we children would be comfortable during the long drive. The adults were all smoking cigarettes like mad in the front seat, probably to relieve their own boredom, and they didn't realize that the smoke was billowing into the back. In self-defence, I kept my head out the window most of the way.

Music was an important part of those trips. Both my parents had guitars, and we would all sing our way across Canada.

Minnie found the drive a bit of a trial, as of course, did I, and I apparently made it that much worse for her. I would constantly ask, "Where is Minnesota?" or "Have we reached Minnesota yet?" I don't know where I'd got it into my head that we'd travel through Minnesota — maybe I just heard the name somewhere and thought it sounded exotic. Minnie claims I was such a pest that she could have killed me. And now, she adds, whenever she hears my name the first thing she thinks of is Minnesota. In spite of this, we became the best of friends once I reached adulthood.

For some reason, my father had no affinity for Americans, and so refused to travel through the United States, even though it would have made for a much shorter drive. Maybe my constant repetition of "Minnesota" got to him, too! Gasoline was being rationed in those days, but because Dad worked in a service station he always had lots of extra coupons — so that was one less reason to opt for the shorter route.

The Trans-Canada Highway hadn't even been dreamed of yet, and many of the roads were still made of gravel. We had our share of flat tires as a result, and we would end up needing to be towed. It seemed like we were towed halfway across Northern Ontario.

On the road, Dad would take hotel rooms for the ladies, but he and I would sleep in the car. The mosquitoes were beyond control and that just gave him another excuse to smoke.

While we were on the farm, I would sleep in a tent, and hang around with Grandpa by day, sometimes spending hours on the plough. He only spoke German, so I didn't understand a word he said, but I would quietly observe what he was doing and then try to pitch in and help. The ability to sit and watch would serve me well during my hockey career, when I would spend many hours in hotel lobbies, train stations, and, later, in airports, and people-watching would provide all the diversion I needed.

Joe Cherish was usually on the farm whenever I was, and we would hunt and play together. He was a few years older, and one time even wanted me to call him "Uncle." I wouldn't have any of that, so he twisted the skin on my arm in an attempt to make me give in or scream, but I refused to do either. This may have been an early indication of my physical strength and my pain threshold.

From the age of six I always had a rifle and each day I'd be allocated one shell, with the expectation that I'd bring something home for dinner. I had to be pretty selective because I was never allowed more than that one shell. I'd shoot rabbits, gophers, and sometimes even coyotes.

Meat was stored down a well, where the temperature remained within a constant range between 37 and 40 degrees Fahrenheit. Meat kept for up to forty days down there. The farm "refrigerator" was really an ice house filled with blocks of ice covered in sawdust. Vegetables were stored in a root cellar, along with huge quantities of preserves. It seemed to me there was enough food to last a lifetime. And because my grandmother was German, there was always enough sauerkraut put away to last for at least two years.

I remember returning to visit my granny, in 1987, when she was about ninety-two years old. She still lived in her original homestead, chopped her own firewood, and baked in an open outdoor fireplace, which is still standing there today. I loved to help her to knead the dough, and then churn the butter while the bread was baking. I remember that smell as if it were yesterday. My grandmother also taught me how to catch chickens (with a loop of binder twine that had been baited with grain) behead them, and pluck them. I also helped to scrub the laundry on an old washboard, like the ones people collect as antique ornaments today. My grandparents made their own soap and, equally important, their own whiskey.

Every meal was a banquet. This may have been the source of my lifelong passion for food — not just eating it, but more importantly preparing it. It's no secret that one of my off-ice hobbies has always been gourmet cooking.

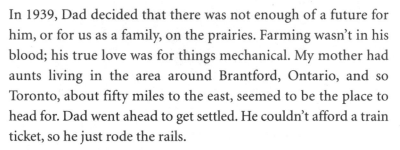

In 1939, Dad decided that there was not enough of a future for him, or for us as a family, on the prairies. Farming wasn't in his blood; his true love was for things mechanical. My mother had aunts living in the area around Brantford, Ontario, and so Toronto, about fifty miles to the east, seemed to be the place to head for. Dad went ahead to get settled. He couldn't afford a train ticket, so he just rode the rails.

His first job was at Robinette's gas station, in the east end of Toronto, at the corner of Kingston Road and Woodbine Avenue. He struck up what would become a lifelong friendship with a co-worker, Ed Langfield. He even boarded with Ed and his wife, Dorothy, for a time. The Langfields had a son, Russ, who conveniently happened to be about my age. Their house on Kenilworth Avenue would become the scene of much of my childhood mischief.

After eight or nine months, Dad had enough money to mail out tickets for mom and me to take the train east. Within a year of the move, my mom was pregnant and my sister Joyce was born. And I soon started in at Norway Public School, where I got the best marks of my academic career.

For some reason, which none of us are too certain about now, Dad thought his mechanical abilities would be better developed at General Motors, so he got a job on the assembly line. He also bought a piece of land in Pickering, on Kingston Road near Rougemount Drive, with seven hundred feet of frontage on what was then a gravel road. Dad and his friends built a house for the family and subdivided the remainder of the plot into two lots. The Morgans built next door and later became our babysitters.

It's hard to believe today, when Highway 401 carries twelve lanes of traffic through the area, that this was considered the country, but it was. I can remember hunting with my pals for rabbits. We'd send a ferret down one end of the rabbit's hole, and it would chase the occupant out the other end. If we were having a good weekend, we'd catch a dozen rabbits. The Rouge River was nearby and we could fish and swim in it, and skate on it in the winter.

When the time came for my first pair of skates, I'm sure no one could have anticipated what it would lead to! Trouble was, they were far too big, and even the usual cures of stuffing them with newspapers or extra socks failed to help. I just could not stand up in them. Dad finally relented, put that first pair away for later on, and bought me another, smaller pair. However, all my life my skating socks were wet, either from perspiration or the snow I just couldn't seem to keep out of them.

When I wasn't skating, I was romping on the fields of the Strouds' farm in what is now known as the town of Pickering. It was here that, one day, I cut my hand very badly on an old cross-cut saw and ran home to Mom — dripping blood, but not crying. She bandaged me up and I went right back out to play. It was the second time I can remember displaying unusual tolerance for pain.

One experience from those days on the Rouge River valley still gives me the occasional nightmare. My father had caught a pig, either for the neighbours or for ourselves. First he tied up the legs, then he stuck a sharp knife in the pig's throat to kill it and drain out the blood. The next step was to hang it by hooks from a tree. When it was well dead, he would drop it in a vat of boiling water to scald off the hair. This sounds grotesque, but it was a common practice in those days.

I remember one day when a huge truck, loaded with canned

goods, missed the bridge across the Rouge, turned upside-down, caught on fire, and slid into the valley. The driver was killed, but that didn't deter folks from greedily grabbing as many tins as they could carry home.

While we lived in Pickering, I was enrolled in a school called Rouge Hills Public School (it's now known as E.B. Fenn), which was built by the grandfather of a family friend, Bob Burrow.

After about six months on the assembly line, Dad felt his entrepreneurial urges were being stifled. In 1940 he bought his first garage; he was now on the road he had mapped out for himself back in Saskatchewan. He was also still on Kingston Road, but now he was in Scarborough.

He was so pleased after his first year in business that on Christmas Eve he and his cousin Joe Cherish celebrated with a few drinks, which led to a few too many drinks. A policeman walking the beat, by the name of Harold Adamson — he later became chief of police for Metropolitan Toronto — found him sitting on the floor of the garage. Mr. Adamson picked him up and took him home. The incident must have made quite an impression on Dad, because he vowed he would never again drink alcohol — and to his credit, he never did. Not that he wouldn't be tempted: the family regularly went to visit the aunts, uncles, and cousins on farms near Burford and Brantford, and these would turn into all-day outings that always ended with a huge feast. The adults, particularly the men, would imbibe throughout the day, but Dad kept to his word and remained cold sober throughout.

Once Dad had his own service station, it seemed to make more sense to move the family into Scarborough, closer to the job. We moved to a house at 24 Avalon Boulevard, where I spent the rest of my youth. It also meant a much bigger school for me: Birch Cliff Public School, which I attended from Grade 2 right through to graduation in Grade 8. It was quite an adjustment for me. I would run and hide behind the Alpine Hotel, which is still standing and in those days adjoined Dad's station. Again, Harold Adamson would come to the rescue: he'd find me there and deliver me to Dad, who would return me to school — usually after what might be called a spanking. The school finally demoted me to Grade 1 to see if I could fit in better there. Ironically, the school's principal was our next-door neighbour on Avalon. I think I was in his office so often there could have been a chair there with my name on it.

I don't think I was a particularly bad kid — it's just that I could never resist a good prank. One of my favourites was to hide behind the coats after everyone arrived. Unbeknownst to anyone, I was rearranging all the children's coats and boots so that no one could find their things when they needed them for recess. I would put the smelliest boots with the cleanest kid's coat, then muddle all of their mittens, and if I still hadn't been caught, I'd mix up their socks!

I remember two teachers fondly: Mrs. Sutter in Grade 5 and Lorne Wideman in Grade 8, who went on to become the principal. Mr. Wideman stood six foot four and weighed about 220 pounds, and in his youth he'd been approached to play semi-pro baseball. In addition to teaching the eighth grade, he also taught Physical Education — needless to say, my favourite subject — and he coached the school's soccer, hockey, and fastball teams. The Birch Cliff teams were always at the top of their league.

During recess, Mr. Wideman would hit a baseball and promise a nickel or dime to whoever caught it. It was one of my favourite games, and even in my early years, I would invariably catch the ball, which annoyed the older kids no end. As I advanced a few grades, I must have decided I was being unfair, because I would divert the ball to the little kids — and I still wouldn't let the older ones catch it! Mr. Wideman also organized running races and barrel jumping, both of which I always excelled at. The competitive spirit was surfacing already.

Mr. Wideman was an inspiration to many students over the

years — he had such a big heart. His hands were also quite big — I speak from experience: you did not want to see that hand in action! He was tough, but always fair. He was also a keen outdoorsman, right up to eighty years of age. I am proud to say he followed my hockey career, and later my business career, right up until his death.

Some of my memories of Birch Cliff are not related to athletics. It was there that the basic disciplines were instilled: manners, saying please and thank you, common courtesy. My report cards were beginning to slip, but there was one major exception: memory work. My grade for this was always above 90 per cent and stood out rather conspicuously from the 60s and 70s. I am truly blessed to still have a strong memory: it's sure proven helpful for putting together this book.

The devil in me was also starting to surface; and where there was mischief, I was usually nearby. At a very early age, when I'd get a bit bored, I would throw stones at cars. Admittedly, many children do this without realizing there could be disastrous consequences. On one occasion, I hurled a stone at a car window, narrowly missing the driver and a mother holding a baby, and it came out the other side of the car. When Dad heard about this, and managed to find me, I was hiding under the front porch, where I'd stayed for about twelve hours. When I finally emerged, I experienced what I'd been trying to avoid: Dad's strong hand, and a very sore backside.

I've had a lifelong love affair with cars, which I must have inherited from my father, although he was drawn to the mechanical aspect, while I was more interested in how they looked and how fast they could go. And this attraction started very early for me: one day — I figure I was about four — I got in the driver's seat just after Dad had returned home from work and gone inside for dinner. I put the car in gear and it took off down Kenilworth Avenue, which was on a very steep hill. I stood on the driver's seat, trying to steer. The only way I could think of to stop the car was to drive it into the veranda of a house at the bottom of the hill. So I did. Not surprisingly, I had another encounter with Dad's strong hand.

I also knew that cars ran on gasoline, so Russ Langfield and I decided to top up the tank of Dad's car. Except we tried a different form of fuel. First we put sand into the tank, then we peed on top of it. The end result was, of course, a badly damaged engine and another sore bottom.

One of the stunts I liked to pull with the older boys was to jump on a streetcar as it passed, and then hop off before the conductor could catch us. We weren't really going anywhere, we just wanted to see what was going on and what we could get away with. I also remember stealing an apple or two from the fruit store owned by the family of Steve Stavro, who now controls the Toronto Maple Leafs.

Another time I decided that Joyce and I should sit at the top of the stairs and wait for Santa Claus to arrive. Our parents were shattered when they caught us there as they began their Christmas Eve chores.

Dogs have also been a special part of my life for as long as I can remember. The first one was called Bunty, and she was a cross between a St. Bernard and a Labrador. We bought her from an Ontario Provincial Police officer, a Mr. Trinell, who lived across the street when we were by the Rouge River. When we moved into Scarborough, Bunty was too big, so we had to send her to one of my aunt's farms where we could still go and visit her. Sadly, she lost one front leg and I can still remember her running along with the children — hopping, really — on her three legs. She was replaced later on by Ricky, who was part collie and part St. Bernard. Unfortunately, he only lasted a few years; he was hit by a bus when Joyce was walking him.

As I supposedly matured, and Joyce tried to catch up to "big brother," our parents came to rely on me to take her everywhere. I was always going off somewhere, usually skating, and Joyce was used to tagging along. One day I went to a show and, in typical brotherly fashion, refused to take her along. I just plain left without her. She decided to go skating on her own with two other little girls. As they crossed the street, one of her friends got across in time, the other one waited, but Joyce was hit by a car and suffered compound fractures to both legs. She was in the Hospital for Sick Children for almost a year, and spent much of that time in a body cast.

To this day I have never really forgiven myself for that, yet Joyce says she remembers me reading to her hour after hour during her recuperation. We were fortunate to have Dr. Black, the leading orthopedic surgeon at the time, caring for Joyce. Happily, she made a complete recovery, caught up with her schooling, matured, and married Paul Manos. They have two grown children, Michael and Melanie.

I remember many of the neighbours on Avalon Boulevard as being great athletes. In those days the street was a dead end, so it was a safe place to play. Some of the boys were Jim Henderson, John Lickley, and the Baird brothers — David, Douglas, and the much younger Duncan. I was myself much younger, but I tended to tag along with — or chase, in an attempt to play with — the older children. I was probably a royal pain.

If we weren't playing road hockey, you could usually find us at the old Toronto brickyards on Gerrard Street, just east of Victoria Park Avenue. It was a used-up quarry that always had water in it because it had been dug so deep. It was a wonderful place to swim in the summertime, and to play pickup hockey or shinny in the wintertime. It has been filled in now, but there's still a vacant field there by the railway tracks.

The first organized hockey I can remember was with Birchmount Baptist Church, although I was by no means a regular attendee at the church or Sunday school. One of our neighbours, Mrs. Beveridge, was the Sunday school teacher. Whenever I did attend she would reward me, in the hope that I might continue to do so, by giving me those pastel-coloured candies called "conversation candy" — the ones with little sayings on them.

The Baptist Church had a team in a league that played on an outdoor rink that the Scarborough Lions Club used to build at the corner of Kingston Road and Birchmount — they'd flood the baseball diamond to make a place for us to play. George Kitchen, my first coach, had organized the league, drawn up the schedules, and made sure we all had team sweaters and socks.

There were a couple of teams from Baptist churches in the area, one from the United Church — and a team from St. Nicholas Anglican Church, which was coached by Rev. Lewis Garnsworthy, who later went on to become the Anglican archbishop of Toronto. Some years later he would perform the ceremony when Sallie and I got married.

George followed my career for years afterward. When I asked him recently what he thought about me as a young hockey player, he said, "You were never a particularly good skater, but you were determined. I could see that you were a natural defenceman. I'll never forget that first year — I could actually see sparks fly as your blades touched the ice along the boards."

George's own son Fred was much faster, and very aggressive, but just did not have that drive to make hockey his career. He graduated with degrees from three American colleges, playing on championship hockey teams for all of them, and then put the game aside and went on to become a heart surgeon.

I'd always get to the rink early because I lived the closest. Of course there weren't any Zambonis in those days, so we had to scrape and flood the ice ourselves with a hose. We'd clear the snow off the ice with homemade scrapers, which consisted of a big piece of plywood with a strip of tin along the bottom that served as a blade. I was one of the few little guys who could handle one of them, and I've always said that's what helped me become a powerful skater, because I pushed more snow than anybody.

Eventually the Lions built the Scarborough Arena Gardens, which in its day was the largest and best facility outside of Toronto. It still stands at the corner of Kingston Road and Birchmount, and although it's part of the city of Toronto now, in those days it was east of the magical dividing line — Victoria Park Avenue — where Toronto ended and Scarborough began. The location was significant because Conn Smythe, who owned Maple Leaf Gardens, would not permit another new indoor arena within the old Toronto city limits. In one of my earliest investments, I cashed in $100 worth of World War II saving stamps I had saved up and bought myself a share in the new rink.

While the new arena was being built, our games moved west along Kingston Road to Victoria Park Avenue. There was an outdoor rink at the St. John's Training School that had what was probably the best outdoor ice in the city. And because there were lots of trees around to protect it from the sun, that rink lasted longer than any of the others in the neighbourhood.

At this stage in my life I began making some close friendships that have lasted to this day. Most of these began around good old-fashioned street hockey. Some chums, like Mike Nykoluk, also went on to careers in hockey. Others, like Don James, became successful in business. The Cawker brothers pursued careers in construction. I look back on those early years and think of them as such a wonderful way to grow up. All the people around me were so very different, but they all had one thing in common: a positive attitude.

CHAPTER 2

The Budding Blueliner

AT ABOUT THE AGE OF TEN, A LOT OF CHANGES WERE HAPPENING in my life. To begin with, there was a third and final addition to the Baun family: another baby girl, Marlene. Because of the age difference between us, Marlene and I did not become as close as Joyce and I did, but we made up for it later in life. I do remember one occasion when she tried to play with me, but I wanted to play with my buddies. So we all got annoyed with her and tied her to a tree.

Also around that time, hockey began to take a bigger chunk of my time. It was around 1946, when I was ten, that I got my first Toronto Hockey League card. I also tore the cartilage in both my knees at this age. A trainer for the Balmy Beach senior football team, Gord Ford, taped them up and he must have done a good job, because I never had any problems with them again until recently. When you consider the abuse those knees took over my many years of playing hockey, that's nothing short of amazing.

Neither of my parents had a husky build, nor did they show a particular inclination for sports. But there are other traits of theirs I do see in myself as I look back.

My father certainly was a very dedicated, hard worker, always trying to provide the best for his wife and family. In the 1940s and '50s he was bringing home at least $500 a week in cash for Mom to cover the household expenses. That was very good money back then. He also seemed to carry a large amount of cash in his wallet all the time.

As soon as he could afford to do so, he bought Mom a mink stole. Mom always had a liking for the finer things, which may account for my expensive tastes in clothes, food, and wine.

Dad was also an original thinker. At his service station, he employed attractive ladies to pump the gas. They'd smile at you as they put gas in the tank, they'd clean the windshield, and they'd brush out the interior of your car with a whisk broom. In summer they wore short skirts or shorts, while in the winter they'd switch to neatly tailored slacks. Dad's approach to the business was completely unheard of in those days, but it worked: I can remember cars lining up for a quarter of a mile down the road just to get their gas. Looking back now, I guess this was an illustration of what I sometimes refer to as "the Baun weakness."

In the winter of 1944, when Toronto experienced a major blizzard, Dad had me help him clear a path along Avalon Boulevard, all the way — and slightly uphill — to Kingston Road.

Dad had such an acute sensitivity to motors that he could recognize an engine just by the sound it made. He'd also wanted to go to aeronautical school, and this interest seemed to rub off on me; I had an air force uniform when I was a little boy, and I loved to play with planes. And in my adult years I took flying lessons.

Mom was certainly no shrinking violet. I am obviously prejudiced, but everyone who remembers her thinks of her as being absolutely gorgeous. But she didn't let it go to her head: she was also known for being a friend to all, whether rich or poor.

According to her cousin Minnie, Mom "absolutely idolized" me. I always felt that Mom strove to be a somebody, and I felt fortunate to be able to provide her with some measure of importance. We always understood that she was the first woman ever to drink champagne from the Stanley Cup. Some may dispute this, since Marguerite Norris was president of the Detroit Red Wings when they won the Cup in 1954, but it still makes for a nice memory.

As I say, around the age of ten my thoughts became taken over by hockey. To learn about hockey, or any game, you have to prepare yourself both physically and mentally. You have to know your own strengths and weaknesses as much as those of the opposition. I wanted to learn anything I could about how to become a better player.

When I was in Grade 5, I would doodle game plays in my workbooks, plotting manoeuvres I might try to perform on the ice. We did not have television at the time, so I and the other boys from my neighbourhood, many of whom were older than me, would listen to Foster Hewitt and try to visualize what the NHL players were doing. That was how it started for me: trying to re-create the players' moves and styles as they were being described to me over the radio.

I found it exciting just to prepare and care for my equipment, especially my skates. Nobody dared touch my skates. Bert Stalworthy would sharpen them every Friday night, using a long, wide grinder that gave a smoother edge to the blade and a hollow ground to the middle. I learned to use a coin to check the level of my skates' hollow, and I would do this every day to check for nicks or rounded edges. I still do it today when I go skating.

Around this point, Don James entered my life. He would become my closest friend, advisor, confidant, and sometimes — although I hate to admit it — even my stabilizing influence. We both seemed to enjoy the same activities, primarily sports. We played hockey together, went swimming together, just generally hung out together, along with another friend, Sammy Kane.

One of our favourite swimming holes was that quarry at the old Toronto brickyard. Don, Sammy, and Art were swimming there one day, and Don dove into a spot that wasn't deep enough. He broke his neck and he has been a quadriplegic ever since. Yet this remarkable man continued his schooling, got a job with a cable company, worked his way up, and eventually bought the company. He got married, he and June have three grown children, and he still does a considerable amount of charity work. Above all, he has one of the sharpest and most endearing senses of humour imaginable.

The tragedies for us did not end there. In the summer of 1952, when I was fifteen years old, one of our friends, Art Insul, was hit and killed by a train; not long after that, Sammy was also killed in a car accident. Sammy's mom says now that what got her through the first Christmas after Sammy's death was the fact that Don and I came to spend some time with her. To us it just seemed the logical thing to do.

Still, the number one interest, above and beyond my friends, was hockey. It seemed I was always playing with the older kids, and because my birthday was in September I was always a grade level behind my chums. Once I graduated from the church league, I played on a Midget team sponsored by Burton Roofers. Somehow I ended up as the coach, manager, and defenceman. We'd play all over the Toronto area, travelling by bus and streetcar and playing at arenas — many of them outdoor — with names like Ravina Gardens, Icelandia, Unionville, and Stouffville.

The Burton Roofers team always had a small roster, and quite often only six players would show up. On those occasions the six of us would have to play the whole game, and as a result the better organized teams, like the Marlboros and Toronto Red Wings, would beat the shit out of us. But we'd always make them pay the price, and we quickly became known as the renegades from Scarborough that everyone hated to play. We were just having too much fun to worry about winning, and all that extra ice time sure helped me develop as a player.

One regular opponent of ours was Bobby Haggert, who played for the Toronto Red Wings. He claims that I was "always hooking the hell out of everyone." I have a vivid memory of landing on Haggert's arm and breaking it. Haggert went on to become the Marlies' trainer at about the same time that I played for them, after which he was the Leafs' trainer for many years. He's now well respected as a player representative, and along the way we became good friends.

Dad, perhaps inspired by my sports-mindedness, sponsored various teams through his service station — everything from little tykes to intermediate fastball, in both Blantyre Park and the Beaches neighbourhood in Toronto.

When I wasn't playing for the Burton Roofers, I'd also do a little pleasure skating on the weekends. A favourite spot was Little Switzerland, on Murkham Road, north of Eglinton Avenue. There was a large oval, about half a mile around, that backed onto the Scarborough Golf Club, of which I would be a member for many years later on. There was a change house built to resemble a Swiss chalet and it had an enormous pot-bellied stove, which we'd sit in front of while we relaxed with hot dogs, pop, and hot chocolate.

By the time I reached high school, I was well into a growth spurt. Within a year I went from about 109 pounds to 155. This was certainly helpful for another sport I really enjoyed, football. I played quarterback at the bantam level, then switched to fullback. Danny Nykoluk, my friend Mike's brother, was the centre, and a couple of other players that come to mind were Bart and Nalan Mall. We were a tough team — I remember that the team from Leaside High School was especially terrified of playing the rougher team from Scarborough.

Danny couldn't play hockey worth a damn, but he was a big tough goon who was made to play football. He turned pro and was eventually elected to the Canadian Football Hall of Fame. I only went as far as the Balmy Beach junior and senior tryouts. When I signed with the Marlboros, that put an end to my football career. It was a tough choice for me to make, because I always thought I was better at football than I was at hockey.

I was still going to school, and this is where the outlook was not as good. All my marks had dropped to the 50s and 60s, and math in particular was not a favourite of mine. I remember getting one grade as low as 28, and my teachers would make comments like "disappointing," and "a more concentrated effort is needed." The funny thing was, when it came to hockey I never had any problem summoning the "concentrated effort" I needed to move ahead of the others.

One time, when my mom signed the report card, she added a request: "Would you give Bob extra help after school in mathematics?" Another year she admitted: "I am sure if Bob would do more work at home he could do much better at school." There was a space on the report card where the parent was to fill in the amount of time the child spent on homework or studying. For Grade 9, this was shown as "one half hour." By the second term in Grade 10, Mom was honest, and she filled in "zero" hours with the comment that "Bob concentrated too much on hockey instead of his school work."

As a result I was not promoted to Grade 11, but was allowed to attend eleventh-grade classes on trial. It was a short-lived trial and I was soon back in Grade 10, although the marks did improve considerably the second time around.

I guess by that time I had outgrown my attraction to the cute little girl in class. Along with my tendency to hang out with older boys, I was now quite attracted to an "older woman." When you are only thirteen or fourteen, even a one-year difference in age seems considerable, and I love a challenge.

Sallie Krohn was a petite English girl whose parents had

moved to Canada a few years before, when she was eleven. She was an only child, lived not that far from us in the Scarborough area, and also attended Scarborough Collegiate (now known as the R.H. King Academy). She caught my eye after I noticed her attending a few events with Don James. If you ask her all these years later what attracted her, she'll hesitate to admit that it was my other friends — and Sammy Kane in particular — and skating. I'd like to think that after one date I made sure that changed.

I was not always on skates. I was equally keen about finding little jobs to earn extra money. Dick Duff once said, "Bob always has a finger on different ideas and business projects — always two or three things on the go at one time." Even today, in the year 2000, I am always keen to hear about a business venture.

Back when I was nine, I was already begging to help my dad around the garage. He'd let me jockey the cars — once my feet could reach the pedals — and help him out with minor grease jobs, and even oil changes. Within a couple of years I'd learned to remove mufflers and tail pipes and replace springs. Somewhere along the way I figured out that Dad was deliberately giving me the worst jobs in order to discourage me from becoming a mechanic.

I also branched out to work for others. I delivered groceries on my bicycle and helped out in a fish and chips store, making french fries and deliveries.

At the age of fourteen I got a job with Consumers Gas, digging ditches on Davenport Road in Toronto's west end. The ditch had to be six feet deep and two feet wide, and we had to meet those specifications exactly. It wouldn't do if they were, for instance, two and a quarter feet wide, or one foot eleven inches. A foreman stood over me constantly to make sure I did the job correctly. It wasn't long before I was fired for talking back to him.

From there I went on to do construction work for Yolles &
Rotenberg, a company that was a leading real estate developer in
Toronto in the early 1950s. They built factories and car dealerships
on what was then a vast expanse of land along Eglinton Avenue
between Victoria Park and Warden, a stretch that would become
known as the Golden Mile.

Yolles & Rotenberg also built one of the first modern apartment buildings in the city, on the brow of a hill on Avenue Road,
called the Benvenuto. Here I worked with the maintenance
department to keep the building clean. To this day I still consider
them to be among the nicest people I ever worked for.

In my early hockey-playing days, in the church and school
leagues, I met a pair of brothers by the name of Cawker. Bill
Cawker remembers how we would all fire pucks at the back wall
of the Loblaws store at Kingston Road and Warden Avenue.
Invariably I would be the last one there, still shooting pucks hours
after everyone else had gone home. "It wasn't that Bob was that
good," Bill says, "he just would never give up." John Cawker
worked with me on a project to build the gas pipeline to Sarnia,
and he noticed that, along with my determination, I possessed
"impatience to get the job done." On the ice, he said, "You could
skate around Bob but you could never get past him."

The three of us used to spend quite a bit of spare time
together building things. We even restored a couple of cars — a
Model T Ford, and a 1938 Plymouth. John and I also tried to build
a boat. We all used to "shell out" together at Halloween, and on
one occasion we weren't too pleased with a man who'd given us a
rotten apple, so we pitched it through his window. I also remember that the three of us tried to smoke a cigar for the first time,
behind the Baptist church. We were all sick as dogs. However, I've
since come to thoroughly enjoy a good cigar.

When I began my career in pro hockey, I still had to work
during the summers. There wasn't an NHLer in those days who

could live on his hockey salary alone. Like many of the Leafs, I did some work for Smythe Sand and Gravel, and I'd also worked on some jobs with Bill and John, so we decided to form our own company, Baun & Cawker Construction.

We had two specialties when we started out: building trout ponds, and repairing roofs. John likes to say, "Someone hiring us had to have deep pockets, because we were expensive, but they knew they were getting a good job." The biggest pond we ever built was for a man who needed one large enough to land his float plane. We dug the pond; the plane landed. There was one small hitch: the pond wasn't big enough for the plane to take off again!

The three of us were charter members of the new Hot Stove Club at Maple Leaf Gardens. The club had a restaurant with a bar where we could entertain clients — who were suitably impressed because you couldn't get in without a membership. John had a weakness for martinis in those days, so he'd wine and dine prospective customers over lunch, and from there he'd go and climb up ladders and inspect roofs. It's a wonder we avoided a serious accident!

The company thrived for some years, and did well enough for us all to be dressed by Harry Rosen and for John to buy Allan Stanley's Cadillac — Stanley would treat himself to a new one at the end of each season. But eventually, times changed, and the company got into different fields, such as bridge construction, where we became sub-contractors.

Our ultimate downfall was a bad contract in Oshawa, one in which we were the innocent victims. My initial reaction when things started to turn sour was, "Don't quit working and don't sell out." But around the same time we discovered that we had lost money due to someone pocketing cash to the extent that we could no longer remain in business. The company was dissolved amicably and the creditors were paid off — which does seem unusual by today's standards.

My continuing friendship with the Cawkers has defied the theory that having friends as business partners spells trouble for both relationships. Sallie and I still visit Bill and Cicely Cawker in Florida each winter, and we play golf together near Fenelon Falls in the summer. In Florida, the Cawkers live in a mobile home, so the kitchen is not gigantic, but Cicely likes to tease me, saying that "Bob can whip up some fantastic meals in it, if only he could clean up as well!" We three, plus wives and other friends, have rung in the New Year together for many years, including the millennium.

About the time I was playing with the Burton Roofers team, I was also in a league called the Big Six. This was sort of an outlaw operation that played all its games at the Scarborough Arena Gardens. All the teams were local, and we'd consistently draw 800 to 1,000 fans to see us play on Saturday nights. Most of the fellows I played football or high school sports with, particularly my pal Mike Nykoluk, were also in the Big Six.

It was a very competitive league, with a high calibre of play; although it was intended to be an under-20 circuit, everybody knew that all the clubs had ringers who were twenty-two, twenty-three, and twenty-four years old, and who were playing under fake birth certificates. Once you turned twenty, unless you'd turned pro, you were all washed up as far as hockey was concerned. There was no other place for these guys to play — Toronto didn't have any Senior teams anymore, and the recreational leagues that are so common today were unheard of.

I was one of the younger players in the Big Six, so I think it was a very good training ground for me, having to match wits with such experienced players. This, combined with all the ice time I got with Burton Roofers, played an important role in my development as a hockey player.

Bob Davidson was the head scout in the Maple Leafs organization, and around this time he'd identified Mike Nykoluk as a good prospect for their Junior affiliate, the Marlboros. But Mike refused to go to the Weston Dukes Junior B tryout camp unless his buddy, that awkward little kid Bobby Baun, came along, too.

I suppose Davidson must have had a few misgivings about this arrangement, but a lot of other teams had their eye on Mike, and Toronto was doubly determined to sign him. When Nykoluk failed to show up for a practice of the Junior B's, the team was so anxious that they sent a car to pick him up. But he was holding firm: he would not go unless I came along. They finally relented, realizing there was no other way to sign their top prospect.

Mike was assigned to the Weston Dukes, the Marlies' Junior B team, and the organization wanted me to try for the Marlboro Minor Midget team. I was hesitant because the team was already fully stacked with players, many of whom went on to become good friends — Ken Girard, Bob Nevin, Bill Kennedy, Harry Neale, and Ron Casey. Plus, it felt like I was taking a step backward. Here I'd been playing with grown men, and they wanted me to play against fifteen- and sixteen-year-olds. In the end, I agreed to play for them.

By January of 1953 I was promoted to the Junior B team, the Weston Dukes, where I stayed for only three games before I was called up to the Junior A Marlies. I trotted off to Maple Leaf Gardens one afternoon, all revved up for one of those doubleheader games, and when I got to the door they wouldn't let me in. Imagine: the best-dressed man in Canada for two years running during the 1960s was almost turned away because he was not dressed in proper Gardens attire: I wasn't wearing a suit and tie! Somehow, I talked my way in and played. I think I caught a break when the Leafs called Eric Nesterenko up to the big team, which opened a roster spot on the Marlies. One of the Toronto papers said that I "did not look a bit out of place." I also earned a mention in the

Leaf program, which used to contain an update column about the Junior prospects. I was described as "built like a combination of Leo Boivin and Bill Juzda. Sure he makes mistakes, but wait 'til he grows up." Heady stuff for a sixteen-year-old defenceman!

In September 1951 I made my debut as a member of the Toronto Marlboros Midget team. For the first time, Harold Ballard and Stafford Smythe entered my life. Ballard was the president of the Toronto Marlboros, and Stafford, the son of Maple Leafs owner Conn Smythe, was general manager. They were offering me what was called a C Form, and signing it meant that I would not only become a member of the Marlies, but the Toronto Maple Leafs would also own my playing rights should I decide to turn pro.

Since I wasn't old enough to sign a contract, I thought I should bring my dad along to hear what Harold and Stafford had to say. Along the way, I told Dad that I really believed I could one day be a hockey player for the Maple Leafs and that this was where it would all have to begin. We sat in Stafford's car to discuss terms — I remember my father was quite impressed with the car and climbed into the front seat. I sat behind him.

They offered $50 a week for me to play, $25 a week for room and board, and a $100 bonus to sign the form. My father couldn't believe that they would actually pay me for playing hockey — all he knew about hockey was that I kept pestering him for the two dollars I needed to buy a new stick. It looked like he was ready to sign on the line that minute, so I kicked the back of the seat to signal that I thought we should shut up, go home, and talk it over. Incredibly, he was starstruck and I was the one who thought cooler heads should prevail.

On the way home I told Dad, "You know, sometimes if they *really* want you they'll give you more." The next day I went back to the Gardens, screwed up my nerve, and told them, "My Dad thinks I should get $75 a week, plus $35 room and board, and a $200 bonus." They grumbled a bit, but eventually gave in. It was my first experience acting as my own agent, but it wouldn't be the only time I'd get more out of the Leafs than they wanted to pay me. And so, a career began, along with lifelong friendships with the Ballard and Smythe families.

My first defence partner was Jack Bionda. That first year he looked after me like a little brother — he was like the Pied Piper, everyone followed him. I could start any ruckus I wanted on the ice and Bionda was always there to take over. He was from Huntsville, Ontario, but he'd lived away from home since a very young age. He was very streetwise, and helped me along in that department. His NHL career was brief — only 93 games — but he went on to become one of the greatest lacrosse players ever, and was inducted into the Canadian Sports Hall of Fame for that sport. Sadly, he died in November 1999 after complications resulting from knee surgery. I was one of the eulogists at his funeral.

Another friend I made in those days was Lou Bendo, who came from Timmins but now has many business interests in Windsor. Although he did not go on to the big league, I would still classify him as a wonderful hockey player.

In my third year I also encountered one of the players who would later become my nemesis — or one of them: Bobby Hull, who was playing for Galt.

We lost out in the 1954 playoffs to the St. Catharines Tee Pees. They had a great team, including the Cullen boys, Brian and Barry, who were the Gretzkys of their day. The announcer for the game was a man named Rex Stimers, and he was a real character. Over the years he turned into a loyal Bobby Baun fan, which might have been helped by the fact that his sister lived across the street from our family. As I recall, he always had a little liquid refreshment to keep him warm and excited while he announced the games.

My coach that year was Reg Hamilton, an ex-Leaf, and he made an impression in more ways than one. In the hockey arena, I would assess him as a tough coach, but what really stood out about him was that he was always dressed to the nines. At the time, Hamilton was quoted as saying about me, "He's just turned seventeen and he's terrific, improving all the time. Tell him what to do and he does it."

The 1953–54 Marlies were a free-thinking team with a lot of character. Some of the names from the lineup are ones that crop up again and again throughout my career: Bobby Pulford, Billy Harris, Ken Girard, Gerry James, and my defence partner Al Mac-Neil. The trainer was none other than Bobby Haggert.

Gerry James is someone I would describe as one of Canada's best athletes. He went on to great success in other sports, including football and track and field. He starred in the Canadian Football League, most notably with the Winnipeg Blue Bombers, for over a dozen years. Not only was he talented, he was one of the toughest athletes I can name. And he was probably one of the best fighters I ever saw on the ice.

The Marlboros weren't the Leafs' only supply of talent. They sponsored another team, the St. Michael's Majors, against whom the Marlies played in the Ontario Hockey Association's Junior A league. This team was largely made up of boys from out of town who'd signed a Maple Leaf C Form. Most came from mining towns in Northern Ontario — Dick and Les Duff from Kirkland Lake; Frank Mahovlich from Schumacher; and goalie Gerry McNamara from Sturgeon Falls. A few years before, it had been Tim Horton from Copper Cliff, while other greats, including Dave Keon from Rouyn-Noranda, Quebec, made a similar move in subsequent years.

For the 1954–55 season, Turk Broda took over as coach of the Marlies. Turk had been a Hall-of-Fame goaltender for the Leafs, but his personality didn't fit the goalie stereotype: he had a jovial, gregarious manner. I suspect that the fact he was so much fun to be with was the reason why his teams gave their best effort for him. Turk was a winner in all that he played: hockey, golf, even cards.

In the spring of 1955 we had a rematch with St. Catharines in the OHA championship series. Billy Harris scored the goal that won the Marlies' first Junior A title in twenty-three years. Winning the OHA championship earned us the right to go on to play the Quebec Frontenacs for the Eastern Canadian Championship.

The press was starting to play up my abilities. One story carried the headline, "Baun Marlie Key." Broda was quoted as saying, "If he keeps on playing the way he did against St. Catharines, we'll be that much tougher to beat. He was the big reason Toronto beat St. Catharines. His defensive play was the best by a junior in a long time."

Before we met the Frontenacs, we had to contend with an unexpected opponent: the measles. Several members of the team came down with a nasty bout of the childhood disease. Then, a few of the players who'd managed to avoid the measles came down with the flu. It was a weakened bunch of hockey players that got off the train in Quebec City.

Even though our dressing room must have looked like a hospital ward at times, we were just strong enough to beat out Quebec and win the Richardson Cup for the championship of Eastern Canada. This entitled us to go on to "the Big One" — the finals for the coveted Memorial Cup — against the Regina Pats in Saskatchewan.

We boarded the train in Toronto, and Bobby Haggert remembers our train had an added bonus on this trip — the first dome car. The boys were crisply attired in their ties and jackets; Turk stood out because he favoured a bow tie. I remember my mom had come along to be part of the Marlie cheering section.

Our leading scorer, Billy Harris, was in the middle of final exams at the University of Toronto, and naturally did not want to miss them, so U of T arranged for him to write the exams out West at Regina College.

It took some effort to adjust to the prairie climate. Even I, a

Saskatchewan native, found it easy to get out of breath at times. Broda insisted his boys were "in top shape, as long as they don't get the idea the series is a pushover."

There's one off-ice incident that I recall vividly. Some of the players, including me, were innocently walking down the street in Regina, and we spotted a gorgeous girl across the road. One of the guys whistled in appreciation. A few yards ahead, the girl met her husband, and he didn't look the least bit pleased about his wife being whistled at. I immediately recognized the man as Reggie White, a lineman with the Saskatchewan Roughriders.

Reggie crossed the street and elbowed me so hard that I fell to one knee. When I regained my feet, I was ready for a fight. I looked back for my buddies, only to discover that they'd all disappeared — except for one, Billy Harris. Billy somehow managed to convince this very aggravated football player that it was all just innocent fun and that we should depart as friends.

We won the best-of-seven series 4 games to 1. Two of the games went into overtime — we won both. It was the first Memorial Cup victory by a Marlie team in twenty-six years. On our return to Toronto, each of us wore a Stetson hat to crown our standard jackets and ties. Most important of all, captain Mike Nykoluk carried the Memorial Cup. We were met at Union Station by a line of convertibles, and we were escorted to City Hall by the Queen's Own Rifles. The ticker-tape parade was followed by a reception in our honour, hosted by Mayor Nathan Phillips. Then it was on to Maple Leaf Gardens, where we were joined by friends and family for a "tea party." Finally, we were all invited to Stafford Smythe's house for a private celebration.

For me, this would be the first of a number of parties at the Smythe home, and I treasure my memories of all of them. Stafford and Dorothea always made me feel like a son. I remember workers at the Smythe gravel pit telling me stories of how Stafford had had to fight every inch of the way, how he'd had the tar beaten out of him many times, simply because he was Conn's son. I always felt that Stafford, who was a trained engineer, preferred the sand and gravel business to hockey, even though his great insight into people was worth more to the hockey and arena operations.

Finally, there was a Memorial Cup dinner, which was promoted as something that would become an annual event. The Marlies, of course, were all there, and so were some of the St. Mike's Majors. Toe Blake and a pair of Junior Canadiens graduates, Ernie Roach and Bobby Frampton, were flown in from Montreal. The best quip of the evening belonged to Conn Smythe, who said he thought hockey players were supposed to be poor, but he couldn't ever find room to park his Cadillac at Maple Leaf Gardens unless Bobby Baun was out of town with his.

CHAPTER 3

The Road to the Big League

WITH OUR FIRST MEMORIAL CUP UNDER OUR BELTS, A NUMBER of us on the Marlies were starting to believe there was a real chance of making it into the National Hockey League. In mid-August, I received a registered letter from Maple Leaf Gardens:

Dear Bob:

Arrangements have been made for the Leafs to have their pre-season training in St. Catharines, Ontario, and we would very much like to have you attend. All players will report at the Welland House before 3 P.M. on Tuesday, September 13th, 1955, to pick out equipment and have physical examinations.

Trainers will be available to supply your equipment from 2 P.M. on, and doctors will be on hand for physical examinations from 3 P.M.

Players must not make other commitments and must attend training dinner at 6 p. m.

Would you kindly make your own arrangements to

get to St. Catharines, and you will be reimbursed on arrival. It would be advisable to bring along your own skates.

Kindly advise at your earliest convenience that you will be in attendance at camp.

> Yours very truly,
> King Clancy
> Coach

You can just imagine the frantic phone calls amongst the Marlies — "Did you get a letter?" — and the shattering disappointment among those who didn't.

On the first day of the 1955 training camp, general manager Hap Day said he was adopting a new philosophy for the Leafs: "Guts, Goals, and Glamour." He told the press that the "Leafs will not be pushed around; they will strike terror into the hearts of goalkeepers and while accomplishing same they will exude a type of rabble-rousing glamour that will incite stampedes at the box office."

Because they wanted to keep me with my Marlies defence partner, Al MacNeil, they sent another prime prospect, Marc Reaume — who'd already been with the Leafs during the previous spring's playoffs — down the road to Niagara Falls, where the Leafs' American league affiliate, the Pittsburgh Hornets, had their training camp. "MacNeil and Baun are terrific bodycheckers," said Day, "and all players are transferable anyway."

The closeness of the minor-league training camp kept you on your toes. It also provided ample opportunity for the Leaf coach and manager to keep a watchful eye on both teams. And it was well known that Conn Smythe, the owner of the Leafs and Maple Leaf Gardens, also had a tendency to pop in unexpectedly and check things out for himself.

George Mara, who'd been a member of Canada's 1948

Olympic team, told me a story about a Leaf camp he attended as a young hopeful. He was getting something out of the trunk of his car, a blue Mercury convertible, when out of nowhere he heard a gruff, gravelly voice call out, "Whose car is that?" Meekly, George answered, "It's mine, sir."

"Well," Smythe retorted, "what is it doing here?"

Mara suddenly got up a burst of courage and answered, "I'm here at training camp, Major Smythe. As a matter of fact, I'm even the leading scorer."

Still not satisfied, Smythe grumbled, "With a car like that, you're not hungry enough to be here."

Nothing more ever came of that incident, but George eventually decided he didn't need hockey. His family owned the William Mara wine and distilling concern, and he eventually became a member of the "Silver Seven" committee that took over the Gardens when Conn stepped down. Ultimately he became chairman of the board at Maple Leaf Gardens.

For those of us Marlies in camp, there was the novelty of skating with real NHLers, but there was something else that took even more getting used to: the presence of a number of St. Michael's Majors. We'd played against them in the OHA as if they were our mortal enemies, now we would have to get along as teammates. The same went for the Cullen boys, who'd been bitter playoff rivals as members of the St. Catharines Tee Pees.

During this training camp I played for the first time with someone who would become a lifelong close friend: Tim Horton. At twenty-five, he was already the veteran of three full NHL seasons. The previous March, he'd been on the receiving end of a devastating open-ice hip check by New York Rangers defenceman Bill Gadsby. His leg was fractured in two places, and his jaw and cheekbone were broken. They had to pull out one of his teeth and wire his jaw shut. He was in hospital about six weeks and it looked like he'd never play again.

One of the reasons his leg was injured so badly was that his skate got caught in a rut. Gadsby's check would have sent him flying, but instead his one foot stayed planted. In those days, the ice at Maple Leaf Gardens was dreadful. We'd play Wednesday night, and on Thursday morning they'd completely remove the ice for the wrestling matches. We'd go back in for practice on Friday afternoon — you couldn't practice in the morning because they were still busy putting the ice back in — and there wouldn't be much ice between you and the dirt floor. The ice-making equipment came from the stone age, and they had a hard time regulating the temperature. So the ice would freeze too quickly and get brittle. During Saturday night's game, it wouldn't be unusual for a player's skates to carve out a huge rut in the ice.

During the summer of 1955, Tim and I both worked at Conn Smythe's sand and gravel pit. Tim ran the scales, because it was a job where he could sit with his leg fully extended, and I was his "gofer." The Leafs also recruited me to help work him back into playing shape. At first he couldn't move much at all, but eventually we were running together around the track at the old Central YMCA in downtown Toronto, and playing basketball. To fix his leg was really a sonofabitch. They had to put pins in his leg to hold everything in place. What an inspiration it was to see him come back from that for a fourth season.

In later years, Sallie and I would babysit for the Horton girls (eventually there were four daughters) so that Tim and Lori could get a break.

I also briefly had the chance to play with goaltender Harry Lumley. I always found it important to work with the goalies, because they could see the entire ice surface from their vantage point, especially the defensive zone. Harry was tough on rookies — you didn't want to get too close to him because he'd just as soon use that big goal stick on his teammates as he would the opponents. But he taught me an important lesson: always give the goaltender a chance to see the puck. The biggest mistake a defenceman can make is to crowd the crease or screen the goalie. Harry's downfall was his attitude that he never made a mistake: a goal was always someone else's fault. He was just very intense, and it was what made him a great goalie.

Hardly a day had gone by before Marc Reaume had worked his way back from Niagara Falls up to the Leaf camp, and in our first exhibition game he scored two goals — a rare enough feat in those days, but especially difficult for a defenceman.

The man who caught everyone's eye was Billy Harris. Red Burnett of the *Toronto Star* said that Harris "fits between Sid Smith and Eric Nesterenko like corned beef with rye."

Day cautioned that it was a bit "too early to place the stamp of approval on rookies, but Harris could be the best rookie centre to hit camp since Ted Kennedy, the man he is billed to replace." Coach Clancy added, "The kid looked good."

Clancy was also asked about me. "I think we've got a real big leaguer in Baun. He's one of the best junior defence prospects I've ever seen. He has speed, courage, a good shot, knows how to take a man out and is a nice boy with it — willing to learn."

On the first day of camp I somehow managed to outsmart American league tough guy Bill Burega. We collided near centre ice, and you could hear the crash through the whole arena. Burega was knocked cold and had to be taken off on a stretcher. He ended up getting four stitches where a tooth had protruded through his lip. I may have been the winner, but I too was left woozy and I needed eight stitches where Burega's teeth had cut my cheek open.

Clancy was actually pleased with all the Junior talent in camp on just the opening day. "If Hap Day asked me to select my squad off this one workout," he said, "there'd be a heck of a lot of last season's team missing from the lineup. These kids weren't just good, they were great, and this was the most rugged opening practice I've seen since Charlie Conacher was chasing me around."

In spite of all the praise and glory, the time was not quite ripe for me to make the jump. Instead, I was sent packing, returned to the Marlies. As a nineteen-year-old I still had a year of Junior eligibility. I took some comfort from Red Burnett's column in the *Star*: "Baun was the most pleasant surprise. His speed, effective checking and punishing body work were more outstanding than most of the veterans."

Still, I was shattered to be the first one asked to go home. All the positive press had gone to my head and I was confident I'd make the team. But the experience taught me that you can't eat good press.

Hockey was not the only thing filling my days and nights, although school had by now become pretty much a lost cause. I struggled into Grade 11, taking several attempts to do so. My teacher, Mr. Edwards, and I never really got along, and finally I'd had enough. He made an untrue accusation about my girlfriend Sallie and I told the principal that either Mr. Edwards would have to apologize or I would leave. As you can guess, I ended up quitting school. It's not a path I would ever recommend to a boy or girl today, since I have the utmost respect — envy, even — for those who do achieve a higher education, but my future in major-league hockey seemed assured and at the time it seemed a risk worth taking.

I started working for the Smythe Sand and Gravel Company, in the pit on Jane Street, between Eglinton and St. Clair avenues, as well as the one on 14th Avenue between Markham Road and Woodbine Avenue. Working the pit was a great way for an athlete to keep in shape while I earned much-needed money, which I would spend — in order — on my car, my wardrobe, and my dates with Sallie. (I think she was well aware of my priorities in those days, and just tried not to let it bother her.)

Right next door to the Jane Street pit was Primeau Block, owned by "Gentleman Joe" Primeau, who'd been a star centreman with the Toronto Maple Leafs from 1929–30 until 1935–36, and coach of the Leafs from 1950–51 until 1952–53. He coached the Leafs to a Stanley Cup win in 1951, after winning a couple of Memorial Cups behind the St. Mike's Majors' bench. He also led a Senior team to an Allan Cup championship in 1950. Joe helped out at Marlie practices and games, and I have to admit that I thought more about the game after he'd finished with me than at any other time. He was total class.

The Smythe pit was managed by Hap Day, the same man who managed his hockey team. Every morning at 7 o'clock sharp, Day would arrive for work. I was as terrified of him as I was of Smythe. It may have all gone back to my school days when I did not do too well with authority.

I've always been a student of people and their habits, and I did take note that Smythe would drive out of his garage every day at noon — either for lunch or to check on his race horses at the stable. He was always gone for well over an hour. I also noticed that the garage was fully equipped to wash a car. One day I figured I'd have enough time to slip in there and give my prized Cadillac a good cleaning before the old man got back. Of course, on this of all days, Smythe returned early. In his inimitable gravel voice, he called out, "Whose goddamned Cadillac is in my spot? And if it's that Baun guy, no player of mine should be driving a Cadillac anyway! Get that thing out of there!" Sheepishly, I got in the car and drove it to the back lot where it belonged.

The home opener for the 1955–56 season was a rematch of the previous spring's OHA final, as we faced St. Catharines, whose lineup now featured Bobby Hull. We lost that game, but it didn't set the tone for the season. In fact we would end up defeating the Tee Pees in the semifinals en route to an appointment with the Barrie Flyers in the championship series. We made short work of the Flyers, taking the series four games to one and winning our second consecutive John Ross Robertson Cup.

Sportswriter Gordon Campbell's column ran under the headline "A Pair of Bobs Take OHA Junior 'A' Pot for Marlboros." Campbell compared our team to the Leafs in the days when they had a pair of Bills, Ezinicki and Barilko: "Baun laid Flyers around like nine pins throughout the contest while Pulford was a one-man scoring gang." Even Hap Emms, the Barrie manager said, "There isn't a better player in the league than Baun. He's rough, but I like 'em rough. I think he's the best pro prospect you've got." Awfully generous of Emms, considering one of my checks had landed George Raneiri with a fractured ankle, while another one cost Jack Kane a shoulder separation.

This year we met the Montreal Junior Canadiens in the Eastern Canadian finals. Their lineup boasted such future NHLers as Ralph Backstrom, Eddie Johnston, and André Pronovost. It was a close eight-game series, but we did it again, winning the final game, 2–0. Our goalie, Len Broderick, rang up three shutouts in the series.

Good as Broderick was, I think the hero of the series was Charlie Burns. He'd suffered a serious head injury during practice the year before, and it was doubtful if he would ever play again. He underwent delicate surgery that left him with a plate in his skull. He felt he was ready for action, but Smythe would not take the risk of letting him play, fearing a re-injury. Burns played himself back into shape with baseball and then industrial-league hockey until he was able to convince Smythe to give him a chance. He eventually made it to the NHL, and he's known as one of the first pros to wear a helmet.

I was not forgotten in all of this. According to the Toronto *Telegram*, "Sharing the spotlight with Burns were the rock 'n' roll twins of MacNeil and Baun."

And an important person had noticed my efforts, along with

41

those of my defence partner Al MacNeil. Conn Smythe pointed out to writer Wilf Smith that we "were on the ice for only four Canadiens goals in the whole series." Smith took this to indicate that Conn was singling us out as the most likely prospects for the Leafs defence the next season.

This year the Memorial Cup series would be played in Toronto. We had a lot to prove. Our opponents would again be the Regina Pats.

We played — and won — our final game on May 6, 1956. In my scrapbook, Mom wrote (and this is exactly as she wrote it):

> May 14th, 1956. Monday 10 o'clock.
> This is the end of Bob's junior hockey.
> He turn pro. May 14. He is 19 years old.
> Best of luck, Bob.

On the same page she'd stuck in a clipping from a Bob Hesketh column where he refers to me as "the Scarboro stalwart, the real find of the season from a Leaf standpoint … Baun has the guts of a burglar." He neglected to go on to say that the only things I ever stole in my life were goals.

Having been to the Leafs' training camp in 1955, and having done rather well, I guessed it was a sure bet I would be invited back in 1956. Nonetheless, it was a great relief when that registered letter arrived. There were a few changes this year: first, the letter came from the new Leafs coach, Howie Meeker; second, training camp had been moved from St. Catharines to Sudbury, Ontario — players were to report to the Nickel Range Hotel on Tuesday, September 18. There was one other difference from the year before: "In view of the fact that nearly all players have cars," Meeker wrote, "I am assuming you will not need railway transportation."

I certainly did have a car! All my life, automobiles have been one of my most treasured possessions, and one of my weaknesses. At this time I was still driving my first car, a 1951 Cadillac I'd purchased from Addison's on Bay Street, where I would later work. Percy Link sold it to me, and it was a surprise to discover it had been previously owned by Dr. Black — the man who'd operated on my sister Joyce. I'd put $2,500 down for it and paid down the remaining $1,000 at $100 a month.

Hockey players, both then and now, have always driven the finest cars, but for some reason mine always seemed to stand out as the best of them all. We had a laugh in 1955, when Billy Harris, Jack Caffery, and Dick Duff all bought the exact same car, right down to the colour: they were Chevrolet Bel Air two-door hardtops, and all three were blue and white. They looked like triplets in the parking lot.

Unlike today's hockey players, we all had summer jobs. Not because we wanted to fill in the time — although with the much shorter season we certainly had a lot more of it — but simply because we had to. The salaries we earned in those years were not enough to feed a family.

Some of the bachelors — Harris, Duff, and Bob Pulford among them — took the summer months to continue working toward their university degrees. The majority, however, had to work. I wasn't alone in doing construction or working in a sand and gravel pit. Frank Mahovlich was headed in that direction as well. Tim Horton had worked in the Toronto *Telegram*'s classified advertising department, but went into Smythe Sand and Gravel later on. The Cullen boys leased a soft ice-cream business, then switched to selling cars. George Armstrong worked in a mine near his home in Falconbridge, and both Ron Stewart and Tod Sloan worked for breweries. And of course Gerry James played professional football for his hometown Winnipeg Blue Bombers.

Towards the end of the summer, some of the guys got together and we rented the Lakeshore Arena to get our skating muscles back in shape and maybe get an edge on the pros when training camp rolled around. I also discovered that Teeder Kennedy was skating at Ted Reeve Arena to get back in shape. He was trying to come back after having sat out the entire 1955–56 season. I skated with him every day for an hour and a half to two hours, and found it a wonderful learning experience.

I didn't know Teeder all that well, but I became a big fan of his during that time we worked out together. My first reaction was, "What's this sonofabitch doing, trying to come back?" His work ethic was incredible, and at his age, and having been away a year, you can believe it was hard work. He was just punishing himself, and I couldn't figure out why anyone would want to hurt that much on purpose. His determination to come back really inspired me, in much the same way as Tim Horton had the year before.

And working with him made me a better skater. I'd start out setting a pace for him, and at first it was a breeze, but then he'd catch up to me and I'd have to take it up a notch. I think that if I hadn't worked out with Teeder Kennedy, I'd never have been able to keep up with Carl Brewer when the Leafs teamed me up with him a couple of years later.

The Leaf braintrust decided that Hap Day's slogan of the year before — "Guts, Goals, and Glamour" — needed to be replaced. The general opinion was that the team hadn't shown much in the way of guts, hadn't scored many goals, and there was certainly no glamour in a record of 24 wins, 33 losses, and 13 ties.

Now it was time for a new regime. Day stayed on as general manager, but King Clancy was named as his assistant, while Howie Meeker took King's place as coach. The new slogan for this year was "Rock and Roll with Howie Meeker and the Crew Cuts." Clancy said it referred to the second phase of the Leafs' youth movement.

The new blood at this training camp included Gary Collins, Pat Hannigan, Al MacNeil, Bob Pulford, Gary Aldcorn, Barry

Cullen, Mike Nykoluk, Dick Duff, Billy Harris, Ron Hurst, and Marc Reaume. And me. Jim Proudfoot dubbed it "Operation Peach Fuzz."

My buddy Jack Bionda had moved on, having been traded to Boston. The Bruins felt his style of play would fit in better there.

MacNeil and I were now being touted as the "Dynamite Twins." I was hopeful that MacNeil and I could stay together as defence partners. We'd had the time of our lives in Junior and we had developed a knack for bodychecking. During that camp, Al hit the Howell brothers harder than I have ever seen anyone hit since — but they were always clean hits in open ice. The Howell brothers did survive; Harry Howell went on to a twenty-one-year NHL career, most notably with the New York Rangers, while Ron played professional football.

I always stuck close to MacNeil at contract time. The veterans were never going to help the rookies, would never help you establish what you were worth, so we had to figure it out for ourselves. Al would go in and talk with Hap Day, then I'd do the same separately. Afterwards we'd get together and compare notes, decide on our "demands," then we'd each go in and sign. As a result, we were able to get much better deals than most young defencemen at the time.

Looking back now, I'd say we got the best deal for our first two years — $8,000 a year, plus a $4,000 signing bonus. After that it was $20,000 for two years plus a bonus. The problem in those days was that the stars like Gordie Howe and Rocket Richard had no idea what they were worth, and that held everybody back. The rest of us fell in line behind. And unlike MacNeil and me, hardly anyone talked about their salary, and that cost us all, too. It blew me away in 1964 when I found out that Terry Sawchuk, a real legend of the game, was only making $18,000, because that was less than I was getting!

We travelled around Northern Ontario by bus a lot that fall, playing exhibition games against American Hockey League teams. In Noranda, the Cleveland Barons held us to a tie, and Meeker wasn't happy with that. The next day, he made us skate for two hours, and we never put a puck on the ice. There were 4,000 kids in the arena watching us practice, and I'm sure they went home shocked at what they'd seen. The punishment of the drill caused some players, like Barry Cullen, to be sick over the boards. The old pros just plain wilted. Even the youngsters — like Pulford and me — who'd been keeping in shape, almost dropped.

There was a teenager in the stands that day who'd just signed up to play for St. Michael's. If that's what hockey was going to be like, he told his mother, he didn't want to go to Toronto after all! Somehow the boy's mom convinced him it wouldn't be that bad. Had she not been so persuasive, Toronto would have missed out on one of its best, and best-loved, hockey stars, because that boy, Dave Keon, would win four Stanley Cups, two Lady Byng Trophies (as the league's most gentlemanly player), a Calder Trophy as rookie of the year, and the Conn Smythe Trophy as most valuable player in the Stanley Cup playoffs. He played in the NHL for eighteen years, plus four more in the World Hockey Association.

All was not misery at training camp: we got the odd night out, and on one occasion we met a real hillbilly singer who was performing in our hotel. His name was Stompin' Tom Connors. He's had a career full of highs and lows, but he's probably more famous now than ever; his early-1970s recording of "The Hockey Song" is an anthem that's played in hockey arenas all across Canada.

As training camp progressed, everyone knew that Hap Day would have to cut seven players and send them to the Leafs' American league farm club, which was now located in Rochester, New York. Red Burnett wrote that MacNeil and I were "one of the most effective units in camp, and it is doubtful if they will be broken up." But in the end, Al made the big team while I was sent down to Rochester.

I was devastated. I felt like I'd hit the bottom of the barrel. What frightened me was the thought that I might end up as one of the members of the "awkward squad." Every team in those days had five or six players who were constantly shuttling back and forth between the big club and the American league. Most of these guys had had a good shot at the NHL, but they were never going to have a steady job, even as a journeyman. So they'd embrace the minor-league lifestyle, living out of a suitcase, sharing some dingy little apartment for half the year, then packing everything up and going home for the summer.

That just wasn't for me. I'd been fortunate so far to have always played in my hometown, enjoying my mom's home-cooked meals, sleeping in my own bed. And being close to Sallie, to whom I was engaged by this time. So I was reluctant about going to Rochester.

While I looked around for a suitable place to live, I stayed in the Strathcona Hotel, where I became good friends with the manager, Joe Stanway. Like me, he was a connoisseur of gourmet food and fine wine. He spoiled me rotten.

In an attempt to create some sense of a "home base," I rented a huge, furnished house. It became the place where everyone gathered, especially for meals. Even though the kitchen was tiny, I really got into gear with my cooking. Unfortunately, while everyone from the team loved to drop in, no one was doing anything about keeping the house clean.

Rochester was playing in a brand new arena, which should have been a plus. Unfortunately, it wasn't quite finished yet. There were no lights in the dressing room, and not even so much as a hook to hang our clothes on. The guys on the team started to hammer in a few hooks and put up a few lights, but when the unions caught wind of our efforts they threatened to close the place down if we didn't stop.

The Leafs shared the Rochester farm team with the Montreal

Canadiens, so half of the players were Leafs and half were Habs. I'd played against a few of the Montreal guys in the Junior playoffs the year before.

The other cities in the league were Springfield (Massachusetts), Providence, Hershey, Cleveland, and Buffalo. We travelled to our road games on buses, which we called "Iron Lungs" because the older guys would spend the entire trip puffing away on cigarettes or cigars. The air would be so cloudy you could hardly see. I rode with my head out the window half the time, just like I did on the family trips back to Saskatchewan.

I didn't hang out with the other players all that often. I'd always look for a nice place to go for dinner, while most of the guys would head for a White Castle for hamburgers, hot dogs, and fries. Then if they were lucky, they had enough left over for a beer. Well, in those days I didn't drink, so I found myself wandering around a lot by myself or with Billy Harris.

Everyone on the team was a bachelor, except for Earl Balfour and Ron Hurst. The three of us used to sneak off in my Cadillac to Toronto so that they could see their wives and I could see Sallie. We'd leave right after a game or practice — I'd do all the driving while Hursty and Balfour split a case of beer in the back seat. The next morning we'd shove off at about 5 o'clock or 5:30, hoping to get back in time for practice and before our coach, Billy Reay, noticed we were gone. I'd drive again while the other two turkeys, hung over and worn out from a night with their wives, snoozed.

Hurst and Balfour were a couple of characters straight out of the movie *Slap Shot*. I used to room with Benny Woit, and in Springfield one night, Hursty was in our room. Before long he started throwing beer bottles out the window and listening for the sound of shattering glass when they hit the pavement below. The next thing I know, he'd thrown a lamp out the window. Then he got it into his head to throw out one of the chairs!

By this time Woit had sobered up enough to stop him. You

have to understand, I couldn't do anything because I was a rookie — that was the protocol. Somebody had called the police and they knocked on Hursty's door. When he answered it, he was dressed neatly in his suit, dress shirt, and tie, acting as if nothing had been going on. But they had him dead to rights and the next thing we knew we were back on the bus and the cops were escorting us out of Springfield. That was vintage Hursty.

The most horrifying moment I remember from those days came during a game in Hershey. Larry Zeidel cracked Gord Hannigan on the back of the head, opening a cut that would require twenty-three stitches. Hannigan was helped off the ice, taken to the dressing room, stitched up, and returned to the bench. The first chance he got, he jumped over the boards, went right for Zeidel, and cross-checked him across the face for thirty stitches. After the game I headed straight for a phone, called my mother, and said, "I'm coming home. I don't know what I'm doing here." She convinced me to stick it out a while longer.

My coach in Rochester, Billy Reay, was a real godsend. He took an interest in me when I was at my lowest point, at a time when I was having no fun, was surrounded by players who were either renegades or just screwing around and wasting their talent, and when all I could do was try to think of ways to get back home to Toronto.

There was one lasting, pleasant memory of that time: an event called the Hitchcock Awards Dinner. All sorts of prominent athletes attended. The head table guests were Mickey Mantle, Yogi Berra, Billy Martin, and Whitey Ford from the New York Yankees; boxers Floyd Patterson and Rocky Marciano; and Bill Russell of basketball's Boston Celtics. All of them had a bottle of Canadian Club in front of them, and at the end of the evening, every bottle of Canadian Club was empty. But there was one man at the head table who stole the show, with his good looks, impeccable manners, and wonderful speech: Jean Béliveau of the Montreal Canadiens.

I also noticed that *his* bottle of Canadian Club was untouched. I was never so proud to be a Canadian.

Finally, the call came. Billy Reay had been instructed to tell me to report to Montreal, where the Leafs were playing the next night, in plenty of time for the game. The only problem was, Reay couldn't find me. I'd driven to Toronto to see Sallie! When word reached me, I figured I'd just drive straight to Montreal. In fact it was even easier to get there from Toronto than from Rochester. Except I remembered one important detail: my skates were still in Rochester! I worried that I'd blown it; a mistake like this would sentence me to the minor leagues forever. My career would be over before it had even begun.

I drove back to Rochester, got my skates, took the train — via New York — to Montreal, and finally took a cab to the Forum. I was so excited and so relieved to be there, and on time, that I tipped the cabby $100 U.S. by mistake. My roommate, Benny Woit, told me as I left that I would never be back in the minors, and I vowed I never would.

PART II

Ready for Prime Time

CHAPTER 4

Blue and White Forever

I PLAYED IN MY FIRST GAME AS A TORONTO MAPLE LEAF ON November 29, 1956. The Leafs were enduring a rash of injuries and were constantly dipping into Rochester for reinforcements. On the blue line, Jim Thomson, Jim Morrison, and Hugh Bolton were all sidelined at this point in the season. Rex MacLeod wrote that the Toronto lineup was "more patched up than a hobo's trousers." Now, the Montreal Canadiens also relied on Rochester for players, and one paper reported that coach Billy Reay "could be excused for developing a 'tennis neck' as he viewed the player traffic flowing through his dressing room door."

That first game was at the Montreal Forum against the Habs, and I quickly zeroed in on a player who would become a favourite target of mine: Henri "Pocket Rocket" Richard. We'd played each other when he was with Junior Canadiens and I was a Marlboro. It was always fun to play against him and to try to outwit him. I never dared look at Henri and call him a "frog"; instead, I used to call him "gorf" — frog spelled backwards. In some games, Richard would claim he'd been hit so often he thought he was in a war!

But although we had constant run-ins, we have always liked and respected each other off the ice.

I also made sure that Habs centre Jean Béliveau — who was leading the league in scoring — knew who I was. According to Hal Walker of the *Telegram*, "Baun gave big Jean Béliveau a rough time and accepted no sass from the big guy." A couple of days later he noted that, "Baun doesn't back off from anyone, and rival forwards have learned to keep their eyes peeled for the sturdy little blocker."

You'd think, after reviews like that, that I'd truly arrived. But it wasn't so. It was back down to Rochester for me, though I'd return the following Wednesday to make my Maple Leaf Gardens debut against the same Canadiens. With all the injuries among the Leaf defence corps, I would split my time almost evenly between the National and American leagues for the rest of the season.

My Marlie defence partner, Al MacNeil, was getting a longer look with the parent club than I was. The Rochester newspaper had done a piece on the two of us, saying, "The deadly duo could make the step to the National Hockey League next season and certainly rate among the most prized rookies in hockey today."

Nothing really stands out about my first few NHL games. For someone in my situation, it was easy to make the transition to the big team. I always felt that the young Leafs had the important advantage over most other Junior players that we grew up playing at Maple Leaf Gardens. Even today, so many young players entering the NHL have never played in the big cities and they don't know what it's like to have the adulation — or the attention paid to every move you make — that comes with playing in the NHL. But we Marlies — and the St. Mike's Majors and Montreal Junior Canadiens, too — had grown up playing in front of 14,000 fans. We were initiated into the whole idea of being on show and having to conduct ourselves as professionals. It was even easier for the Marlies than the Majors because most of us were local boys.

One of the Canadiens who had all of us fit to be tied was

Dickie Moore. By the first week of December he had scored 14 goals, and half of them were against the Toronto Maple Leafs.

Prior to my second game, Hap Day's big announcement was that, in the wake of all the injuries, the Leafs had acquired a portable X-ray machine for the Gardens infirmary. He'd be able to tell within ten minutes whether an injured player had a broken bone, or was "merely" badly bruised and therefore able to keep playing.

Moving between the NHL and American League, I was able to compare the two, and one of the biggest pluses I observed about the major league was the train travel. It was a breath of fresh air — literally! — to ride the train. The slower pace meant that you really learned a lot more about your fellow players, whether through the card games that always seemed to be in progress or by just chatting. On some occasions, particularly the Toronto-to-Montreal run, you'd often be on the same train as an opposing team. But you were forbidden to speak to any of them, and if you did it was likely you'd be demoted to the minors. After my playing days, I missed the camaraderie of train travel.

In a *Globe and Mail* article, I talked about another difference between the majors and the bus leagues: "I used to think it was enough that you knocked your man down, but you have to be a two-way player in [the NHL] game. You have to lug that puck, too."

I also told that reporter that the most important thing was to keep in shape at all times — winter and summer. When I wasn't working at the sand and gravel pit, I used to water-ski for ten miles at a time, and swim four or five lengths of a pool underwater — on one breath. I got this idea after reading about the breathing techniques of famous singers like Frank Sinatra. I would also snorkel in long underwear rather than a wet suit.

One of my closest friends in those days made his NHL debut at the same time as me. Ken Girard and I had more or less grown up together, but he was three months younger, so he was still with the Marlboros when I was assigned to Rochester in 1956. He was called up straight from the Marlies for a few games when George Armstrong got hurt. The next year he was in the American league, but by then I'd made the NHL to stay. He didn't mind his tenure in Rochester as much as I did because he felt it would prepare him better for the pressures of the big league.

Our friendship led me to my love of golf. Ken was the assistant pro, under Jack McLaughlin, at the Cedarbrae Golf and Country Club in Scarborough, and he got me a summer job managing the pro shop. Jack kept me on the practice fairway all summer. It was a tough summer — I worked ten to twelve hours a day — but I really gained a passion for the game. Ken went on to have a very successful career as a golf pro at the London (Ontario) Hunt Club, and he and I still try to get together for at least one or two games a year.

A major milestone in my life came in the spring of 1957. At 6:30 P.M. on Friday, May 10, at St. Nicholas Anglican Church, I married my childhood sweetheart, Sallie Krohn. The Rev. Lewis Garnsworthy, by now a friend of ours, married us. Ken Girard was my best man.

Margaret Knowlton described the event in one of the society columns: "The beautiful English bride will wear a long white satin and lace bridal gown with finger tip veil. Her maid of honour, Bob's sister Joyce Baun, will wear a dress of baby blue silk organza. Bridesmaids Pat Millen and Jane Edwards, friends of the bride, will also be dressed in baby blue silk organza, and flower girl Marlene Baun, youngest sister of the groom, will wear pink silk organza."

There was a strangely sad note to the occasion. For some unknown reason, my mother had never liked Sallie. She used to stall me whenever I was going to visit her, and make it clear she did not approve. Sometimes I'd have to walk for miles along Kingston Road to get to Sallie's house because no one would lend me a car. My sisters Joyce and Marlene, and Sallie herself, all feel the problem was that Sallie was one year older than me.

The girls say the dress my mother chose for the wedding was

the darkest shade of navy blue. So dark in fact, it was as close as you could get to wearing black. They all look back and laugh about it now, because almost immediately after the wedding, Mom turned around 180 degrees and Sallie became her closest friend and confidante. The two of them attended every Leaf home game together, and they even travelled to some road games together during the playoffs.

The reception was at the Coach House of Fantasy Farm, and I still look back fondly upon the occasion. According to my sister Joyce, I amazed them all when I took to the dance floor as if that, and not hockey, were my profession. When I was a child, my mother had been quite insistent that I take dance classes, and she would drop me off at the studio's front door; but, being rebellious and stubborn, I had better ideas, and I'd sneak directly out the back door as soon she'd driven off.

Just before the wedding, I got quite a shock when I got the bills for cleaning up and repairing all the damage done to that great house I'd rented in Rochester. I had to deal with this at the same time as we purchased and moved into our first home at 77 Mason Road in Scarborough, near Eglinton Avenue and Markham Road. The house was conveniently located directly across from a public school, but I can't take any credit for planning ahead. I was so young and excited that I probably never even noticed the school until years later!

We left for a honeymoon in Florida, and our son Jeff arrived a little over nine months later. He was the first of five children born over the next eight years. As a parent I am proud to say that we must have done something right because people from all walks of life have commented on what lovely people all five have become. Allan Stanley had the boys at his hockey camp and said they were the most polite boys he'd ever had there; he adds that they were always the first to pitch in where help was needed. Don James, undoubtedly my closest friend, says, "Without being prejudiced by our friendship, all five are totally different, but they are all well-disciplined, fine people. Sallie and Bob both have done an excellent job."

A few months after the wedding, Sallie was interviewed by Margaret Scott, who for many years wrote a column for the Leaf's program about some of the more personal aspects of the players' lives. Sallie was asked to describe me. "I don't blame people for thinking Bob is tough," she said, "but it's just his style. A lot of people get a great surprise when they meet him, because he's entirely different once he's off the ice. He's kind of quiet, very easy to get along with, and grand company. I truly wish all the fans could meet him.

"When he's on the ice, he's all competitor. He thinks only of hockey and winning games." She went on to say that I was "the biggest eater on the team, shuns liquor and gets pretty tense on game days."

Sallie also spoke very endearingly about her new mother-in-law: "I've never seen a fan like her; she's the Leafs' most faithful fan. When Bob was with Marlboros she attended every home and away game, even going as far as Ottawa, Montreal, and Regina for the Memorial Cup finals. Last season we travelled to Rochester to see every Sunday game, and she's a honey of a companion, very youthful and full of fun."

———— ● ————

The summer of 1957 was time for more changes in the Maple Leaf's front office. First of all, Billy Reay, my coach in Rochester, would be behind the Leafs' bench. Meanwhile, Conn Smythe had fired general manager Hap Day and replaced him with last year's coach, Howie Meeker.

When Day left, it was a shock all over the hockey world, because he'd also been running things at Smythe Sand and Gravel — he even owned a piece of that business. He and Conn had worked together many years. But there were rumblings that the players were trying to organize — which we were — and Smythe was already unhappy about the unionization of the sand and gravel business. Rather than deal with the unions there, he ultimately chose to close down the company, even though he'd just purchased new equipment. His son Stafford, along with Buck Houle and Jesse James, bought the tractor and trailers and tried to make a go of it on their own, and never made any money.

But I was looking forward to playing for Billy Reay. I had a lot of respect for Billy and truly liked him, and I believe those feelings were mutual. He used the "soft sell" to get his ideas across, in much the way that Toe Blake or Joe Primeau did. Meeker had been at the other end of the scale, a real taskmaster. If you have ever seen him as a television commentator, he was exactly the same as a coach. He wanted to bring in a whole lot of new ideas, and if they'd gotten rid of all the old guys his plan might have worked. But the veterans just didn't want to hear any of what he had to say. He'd try to tell Jimmy Thomson, who'd been in the NHL for ten years, to hold his stick this way, or turn that way to take out a forward. You can imagine how far he got.

Gord Walker wrote a piece describing one of Howie's practices, after a loss to Montreal, that really defined his coaching style: "Howie Meeker lashed the Leafs with his whistle and GM Hap Day compounded the torture by lashing Meeker's lash. Meeker had them sprinting from end to end, from blue line to blue line, and interrupted the torture only briefly to allow them a shot or so at Ed Chadwick. If they live, they might be rough for the Rangers tomorrow."

On another front, Smythe was hot because Jimmy Thomson, the team captain, had been the Leafs' representative on the players' association board. In August 1957 he sold Thomson to the Chicago Black Hawks, the same punishment that had been handed out to Detroit's Ted Lindsay. In the '50s, getting sent to Chicago was the worst thing that could happen to an NHLer.

I know Lindsay still regrets that the players' association of 1957 didn't succeed. At the NHL All-Star Game in Toronto in February 2000, he said, "It's just a shame it wasn't successful right then, because it would have meant that that thief, Alan Eagleson, would never have got off the ground."

But things still hadn't settled down at the Gardens. Before anybody had even given him the key to the filing cabinets, Howie Meeker was gassed as general manager. Conn had been withdrawing from the Gardens and turning things over to Stafford, who set up a seven-man board called the Hockey Committee to make all the decisions. It quickly became known as the "Silver Seven": Stafford Smythe; R.J. "Jack" Amell, vice president of Robert Amell & Company, a large jewellery manufacturer that would later design the Leafs' Stanley Cup championship rings; John W. Bassett, owner and publisher of the Toronto *Telegram*; George R. Gardiner, president of a stock-brokerage firm; W.M. "Bill" Hatch, vice president of McLaren's Food Products; Ian Johnson, lawyer for Conn Smythe and Maple Leaf Gardens; and finally, George Mara, owner of the William Mara wine importing company — the same George Mara whose run-in with Conn I talked about earlier. Harold Ballard and Paul McNamara would later sit on this committee as well.

My teammate Billy Harris had a clever way of describing the chaos at this time. In his book *The Glory Years*, he wrote, "When the dust settled, the Leafs did not have a general manager, and King Clancy was his assistant."

By the fall of 1957, I was expecting I would start training camp off with a bang and everything would fall into place for me as planned. But in my life nothing's ever gone exactly according to plan. There have been many peaks and valleys. I guess the "secret to my success" is my uncanny ability to avoid staying down for very long. My attitude is best described by a line from Frank Sinatra's song "High Hopes" — I always try to "pick myself up, dust myself off, and start all over again." Of course, it could also be said I've always had to have things "My Way"!

I arrived at the '57 training camp with "high hopes," but soon after the workouts began my muscles seized right up. I kept getting cramps and muscle spasms whenever I'd start skating. I don't have to tell you how afraid I was. Jim Thomson's departure meant there was a vacancy for a defenceman, and I intended to fill it. With a new bride, a new house, and a baby on the way, a trip back to the minor leagues was *not* in my plans!

The Leafs *did* demote me to Rochester, where ex-Leaf Bucko McDonald, from Sundridge, Ontario, was the coach. I was really feeling low when I met him. I wasn't sure I had the stomach to go on playing. But Bucko asked me to have lunch with him. He was famous for his appetite, so I knew we'd get along just fine — and we each ate two steaks. Luckily, he paid. He also clued me in about the game plan he had in store for me.

Bucko felt I needed to play to get my confidence back, so in the exhibition game that night he played me for 25 minutes. For our next game, he upped my ice time to 35 minutes, and in the third I played for 45 minutes. The other fellows on the roster didn't mind my hogging the ice like that: most of the guys were older and glad to get the rest. They also seemed to get a warped kind of pleasure out of watching me get battered back into shape. I think Bucko gave me the power boost I needed — I cracked the Leaf lineup that autumn and never looked back.

The exhibition games we played against Montreal that season gave me an unbeatable opportunity to really study the Canadiens and the way they played. I noticed that each club in that six-team league had its own unique methods, systems, and approach to the game. If you were a Leaf, it was because you were Conn Smythe's kind of player. If you didn't fit into the mould, it didn't matter if you were a 50-goal scorer, you weren't going to be around for very long. They'd quickly banish you to the Acapulco No-Sweats.

Comparing Toronto to Montreal in 1957, Toronto had a very defensive system, whereas Montreal favoured an explosive, fast-paced offence. Their lineup featured the great Doug Harvey, Dickie Moore, and in those days both Richard brothers — Maurice "The Rocket," and Henri, the "Pocket Rocket." Maurice was one of my heroes in my youth, and now I was playing against him! But the player I admired most was Jean Béliveau — but I must say, that admiration never prevented me from giving the big guy a good, clean bodycheck every now and again.

There was someone else who inspired me during this period, and that was Tim Horton. All I had to do was remember how he'd recovered from what the doctors thought were a career-ending series of injuries. Timmy's comeback was a real lesson for me, to be as strong and loose as possible. Later in his career, Timmy earned the "Iron Man" nickname, because he suited up for 486 consecutive games between 1961 and 1968. It's still a Leaf record. Until that sad day in 1974 when he died, we thought of him as being nearly invincible.

When I returned to the Leafs, we were still struggling. My buddy Al MacNeil hadn't been playing as well as they thought he would, and Billy Reay was having a tough time finding defence pairs that really clicked. Another thing I noticed was a real animosity between the St. Michael's graduates and the players who'd come up from the Marlboros. It wasn't unexpected — we'd been taught to see each other as the enemy through four years of OHA action, and now we were suddenly supposed to be comrades. We fought frequently and viciously, to the point that our practices were tougher than most games. I always had a running battle with Dick Duff, and I know I took my chances with his brother Les. I may have even mixed it up with both of them at the same time!

Milt Dunnell of the *Toronto Star* did a column about me and seemed to notice I'd matured and started to play a much steadier game. According to Milt, my coach, Billy Reay, "fingered Baun as the Leaf whose improvement had been the most impressive."

Red Burnett, also from the *Star*, wrote: "Baun is the kind of player who packs them in at the box office, and Smythe rates him high in Leaf plans. Yesterday he talked of Bob the Bomb as the best thing to come along since Bill Barilko was lost on a fishing trip. Leafs have never been able to fill Barilko's shoes. Baun could be the answer."

Strangely enough, like Barilko, I've always loved to fish, and my favourite summer pastime is to fly into some remote spot in the north, far removed from the real world, and pursue this hobby with a few close friends. Those who know me well, and particularly my daughter Patti, feel that this is the real Bob Baun: relaxing, far from civilization, fishing with my friends. I also love to spend time with my family at Charleston Lake, at the cottage of my friends, the Giffins.

Burnett also said our goalie, Ed Chadwick, "was one of the best net-minders in the league last season, and should be better this term." He added that "Our young defencemen will blossom out once they find out Reay won't bench them for every mistake."

Ed was a good-natured guy, about the same age as most of us defencemen. But our inexperience on the blue line did him in. Our goals-against in 1957–58 was the worst by far in the league, and Ed was shell-shocked. He never got to be the goalie I think he could have been. I think he would have done very well if the two-goalie system had been in place in those days.

Another player the Leafs had pinned a lot of their hopes on was nineteen-year-old Frank Mahovlich. With his size (six feet, 205 pounds) and scoring punch (52 goals in his last year of Junior), it's little wonder King Clancy started calling him "Moses."

The *Star*'s Milt Dunnell asked me how I prepared for a game. I told him I'd start by concentrating on the centremen, the ones who got the plays going. Then I'd think about the wingers, who could give you a lot of trouble. Dunnell went on to describe how I built up my morale by telling myself I must be as good as the other guys, or else I wouldn't be drawing an NHL salary.

Looking back now, I was never really a fancy skater, but a power skater. I could keep going all day. At practices, I was always the last one off the ice, working especially hard on skating backwards.

To me, each game was a chess match. I learned early that you had to move the puck quickly, and to make things happen by taking away your opponents' strength. I heard about a technique Jack Nicklaus used, called visualization. After a round of golf was over, he'd visualize the shots he hadn't made. Then he'd move over to the practice tee and work on those shots. I'd do the same thing: I believe you have to practice every bit as intensely as you play the games if you want to get it right.

As the season progressed, I settled in well with my new defence partner, Marc Reaume. In December, coach Reay was quoted as saying: "I wouldn't trade Reaume for any defenceman in this league, and Baun has developed into our best defenceman, making the opposition take notice more and more in every game. You have to count him as one of the most improved players in the league." Reaume said I had "come a long way in a short time. I never have to look around or even think about his side because he never leaves his position."

I credited the maturity of my play to that time I'd spent in Rochester. I watched Benny Woit and Tommy Williams and noticed that they hit far more people than I did, but without charging all over the place like a bull. I woke up to the fact that I was never going to make it to the NHL unless I stopped charging out of position in a futile effort to knock the other fellow cold. And Junior Langlois stayed with me for an extra half hour after every practice; thanks to him, I improved my other skills: carrying the puck, shooting from the point, and passing.

Around Christmas we seemed headed for the .500 mark, but as the New Year began, we were slipping in the standings. Reay was particularly displeased with his earlier favourites: Bob Pulford, Barry Cullen, Marc Reaume, and, last but not least, Bob Baun. "We gave them taffy when they went well," Reay complained, "so I think it's only fair to remind them when they are not." The only thing that spared us all a trip to Rochester was the fact that there wasn't anyone better on the farm team.

We ended the 1957–58 season with a record of 21 wins, 38 losses, and 11 ties. Even the lowly Black Hawks were ahead of us. It was the first time a Toronto team had finished in last place since 1927. We missed the playoffs, but many of us younger players got a wonderful opportunity to go to the semifinal games between the Montreal Canadiens and Detroit Red Wings. Of course, I focused on the defencemen I admired: Doug Harvey for Montreal, and Detroit's Red Kelly and Marcel Pronovost, both of whom would become Leaf teammates in later years.

I also marvelled at the great Gordie Howe. I couldn't believe his reflexes, or the way he manoeuvred. He was also a master at ragging the puck to kill a penalty. He'd just dare opponents to try to take the puck away from him.

My play had improved enough that year that I had a chance of winning the Calder Trophy, awarded to the NHL's rookie of the year. I probably wasn't as interested in the trophy as the $1,000 bonus that came with it. In 1958 that was a fair amount of cash.

Even the Leaf program had a little plug: "Toughest rookie in the league? It could be Bobby Baun. He's rough, he's tough, and he's mean enough."

But I'd been left off the ballot. Stafford Smythe, ever protective of his charges, sent a telegram to the NHL offices to protest the oversight. The league responded that I was ineligible — the award was only given to players who hadn't played more than 20 games in any previous season. Smythe made the case that I had played exactly 20 games in 1956–57 — *not more than* 20! He also pointed out that the Leafs had deliberately benched me in the last couple of weeks that season in order to protect my future Calder chances.

Stafford made a valiant effort, but it was all in vain. The real Calder race was between Frank Mahovlich and Bobby Hull, and it was a tight one. In the end, Mahovlich was named the Calder winner as rookie of the year with 120 votes to Hull's 116. I managed to garner 10 votes.

Although Frank had done well, the team had not, and Smythe was not pleased. We all knew that there would be significant changes made before next season.

During the off-season I landed a summer job that was quite different from the gravel pit. Foster Hewitt, the Leafs' play-by-play announcer, also owned a Toronto radio station, CKFH. His sales manager was Keith Davey, and he suggested to Foster that they hire a hockey player to sell advertising. Foster went along with the idea, and after some brainstorming they hit upon my name.

Keith and I had never met, but we've since become the best of friends. In later years he was appointed to the Senate, and his skill in the political backrooms led the press to dub him the Liberal Party's "rainmaker." I'd talked with Foster many times on the Leafs' overnight train trips because he always had the bunk across the aisle from mine. At the radio station, Foster started needling me about the sales work I'd been doing for Herb Kearney's car dealership, Hearn Pontiac Buick. I couldn't ignore Foster's ribbing, so I made sure the very first advertising contract I brought into CKFH was for Hearn to sponsor the 6 o'clock news.

Then, perhaps inspired by my love of fine clothing, I headed off to Parliament Street, where a fellow by the name of Harry

Rosen had just opened a new men's wear shop. I sold the radio air time, Harry Rosen got a lifelong customer, and the two of us have been friends ever since. And to give you an idea of how small a town Toronto can be, a few years down the road I became friends with Red Kelly, who was also a Rosen customer, and who also knew Keith Davey through his Liberal Party connections.

Speaking of Harry, I was glad to be able to do him a good turn when he opened his next store, in the Richmond-Adelaide Centre. Red and I spent a full day chatting with customers and signing autographs. He remains appreciative of that personal appearance.

In all my years of dealing with Harry Rosen, I have always worked with the same man, Steve Pollack. What makes Steve so great is that he always lets me think I am actually choosing my own wardrobe. Someone asked Harry if I had a natural flair for dressing, or whether he had imposed it on me over the years. His diplomatic reply. "Bob had the natural flair, but I tried to mature it over the years."

He was amused when asked about my reputation for frequently going over budget, and whether I paid my bills. "Well yes," he replied, "eventually — with the emphasis on eventually!" Frank Mahovlich once remarked that Bob Baun invented Harry Rosen. Asked if he was offended by that assessment, Harry said, "Not at all. Actually, I am quite flattered."

Mahovlich has admired my clothing and grooming for some years, but he used to scoff at the fact that I got manicures, writing off the whole idea as frivolous. One day in Philadelphia at the Warwick hotel, he walked by the shop where I was enjoying one, and he decided, "If he can do that, then I can, too!" I understand that he, too, has been getting manicures ever since.

CHAPTER 5

Punch
Takes Charge

BY 1958 THE LEAFS HAD FALLEN TO LAST PLACE. IN THE PREVIOUS four seasons we'd finished third, fourth, fifth, then sixth. Defence had always been Toronto's strong suit, but in 1957–58 we allowed 226 goals, the most by far of any Leaf team to date. There were a lot of good young players in the lineup — that summer, Ron Stewart was twenty-six; Barry and Brian Cullen were twenty-three and twenty-four; Dick Duff, Bob Pulford, and I were twenty-two; Frank Mahovlich was twenty; Horton and Armstrong were the old men at twenty-eight — but that also shows there was a lack of experience. And there was a lack of leadership coming from the front office. It was clear that changes were needed.

In most situations like this, the team will opt for a change of coaches. But not Stafford Smythe: in his opinion, the time had come to hand the Silver Seven's management powers over to one man: George "Punch" Imlach. Most of us didn't know this guy from Adam, as all his hockey experience had come in the minor leagues. Most recently he'd been coach and general manager of Boston's American league farm team, the Springfield Indians. Prior to that, he'd been with the Quebec Aces of the Quebec Senior Hockey League, where at various times he'd been a player, coach, manager, and even owner. It was there that he coached a young Jean Béliveau.

Punch was originally hired in June 1958 to be the "assistant general manager," but he wasn't very keen to be the "assistant" anything. He wanted the official title of general manager, and was assured he would get it eventually. But he seemed to be making the player moves even then.

There were a number of roster changes during the off-season. Billy Reay, before Imlach took over, sensed that the Leafs' youth movement needed to be balanced with experience, and so he grabbed a couple of veterans, via the Intra-League Draft, that other teams had given up on: Johnny Bower, a thirty-three-year-old goalie who'd been buried in the Rangers' farm system, and Bert Olmstead, a thirty-one-year-old left winger who'd won four Stanley Cups with the Montreal Canadiens. A few days later, Tod Sloan — who'd taken over from Jim Thomson as the Leafs' rep on the players' association — was sold to the Chicago Black Hawks.

Finally, just days before the season began, Imlach, now in charge, traded Jim Morrison to the Boston Bruins for a thirty-two-year-old defenceman, Allan Stanley. At six foot two, he was bigger than most of the other Leaf defenceman, and while he couldn't skate all that well, he'd shown over the last two years in Boston that he could move the puck a bit.

Bower was something special, too, like fine wine aging to perfection. He'd spent twelve of the last thirteen years in the minors — he still holds the American league record for career shutouts. He got a shot at the big league in 1953–54, when the Rangers decided for some reason to send Gump Worsley to the minors. Now, Gump had just won the Calder Trophy! John played about as well as you could with the Rangers in the early '50s, but after only one season, just as mysteriously, they decided to bring Gump back up and send Johnny back down.

The remarkable thing about John was that he had a book on every forward in the league. He knew how hard everyone shot, whether they liked to put it high or low, what part of the ice they'd be likely to take a shot from. He left very little to chance, and whenever he did gamble, the odds always seemed to be on his side.

He was one of the most even-tempered goalies I ever knew. You could rarely see the highs or lows, but you could bet he'd go to hell and back to stop a puck. He practised all-out, and he would never leave a puck in his net after practice.

Johnny wanted nothing more than to get his ten years in the NHL and collect a pension. In later years, Punch would use that against him to keep his salary down.

Our training camp that year was in Peterborough, and the rules were strict. If you had your car with you, it was to be left at the hotel and you were to walk to the arena for practices. Management checked the parking lot to be sure no one cheated on that rule.

One bright spot was Rompin' Ronnie Hawkins, who usually performed there and befriended most of us. He still lives in the area, running a bed and breakfast.

Stafford Smythe was there on opening day to greet everyone with a handshake. Now, you might think he was being civil, but the rumour was that he was checking to make sure everyone's hands were calloused from hard work over the summer months.

Our training camp was once again marked by fighting among the players — an area in which Dick Duff and I were particularly enthusiastic. Bower had never seen anything like it. "It sure has been rugged," he said. "The first time I saw Dick take dead aim at Bobby Baun, I figured he'd wind up on the ice like a scrambled egg. Instead, he knocked Bob back five feet and kept right on coming for a shot on goal. I passed it off as a fluke until he rattled Baun on a few other occasions and gave the same treatment to others just as big." Staff Smythe, whom I always considered an acute judge of hockey talent, left training camp for his other business interests, but first expressed displeasure with his defence: "I never thought I would see the day when anyone would push Baun around like that."

Rex MacLeod reported that, "The thud of colliding bodies would have sounded like a symphony to a sanguine fellow like King Clancy."

Another thing that surprised John was the pace of our practices. "At Cleveland we'd take it easy for about six or seven days and then start the heavy work. Here we've been at it hammer and tong since the first time the coach dropped the puck." Billy Reay was still coach, but it was clear that Punch was beginning to influence the way practices were run. Our afternoon rounds of golf had been replaced with a second gruelling workout.

Stafford also wanted to reintroduce a scheme his father had used with some success. Imlach would be dispatched to the upper seats of the arena — which in Peterborough were called the "passionate purples" — to watch for mistakes and blow his whistle to alert Reay in case he missed an error at ice level.

Staff was never one to mince words, and he told reporter Stan Houston, "I'm certainly not trying to prove myself wrong in hiring these guys [Imlach and Reay], but they are two minor leaguers going into a major league game. If their duties are not done I am not answering for it. They are."

The season got off to a dreadful start. By the third week of November we'd won 5, lost 10, and tied one. It was as if Reay and Imlach each had one hand on the steering wheel but neither of them had been given a road map. By the 22nd of November Smythe, backed by his Silver Seven committee, gave Punch free rein to hire, fire, trade, buy, or sell, and he accepted the responsibility willingly: "I'd rather be shot as a lion than a lamb. This team can make the playoffs, but some changes will have to be made. Now that I'm responsible, I intend to make them." Stafford made it clear that Punch would also be responsible for the coaching, "either by advising, directing, or replacing the incumbent."

One change that coach Reay made was to split up the Baun-Reaume tandem and put me on Tim Horton's right defence. "The only way Baun knows how to play hockey is to belt everybody in sight," Billy explained, "but Baun won't be the only Leaf out there hitting."

We'd added a lot of experience to our lineup, but there was still room on the roster for another talented ex-Marlie. Carl Brewer, a twenty-year-old defenceman, came streaking out of nowhere. I remembered him only vaguely from my last year with the Marlboros, and he could hardly skate then. Now he just blew past everybody; he had the same stride that Bobby Orr would display ten years later. He was a wonderfully gifted athlete with a perfect body size. Between Horton, Stanley, Brewer, Reaume, and me, the Leafs had all the necessary pieces to create a dominating defence corps. But no one had figured out yet where to fit those pieces into the puzzle.

A week passed with Punch in full charge as general manager. We tied the Rangers and Black Hawks, and we lost back-to-back games against Detroit. No wins. Punch had seen enough, so he went to the top and asked Smythe's permission to fire Reay. Smythe wasn't thrilled, but he agreed. A promise is a promise, and he'd pledged to give Imlach complete control over hiring and firing.

But who was there to hire? King Clancy was one possibility, as he'd been a winning coach for the Leafs in the past. But Punch chose a different route, as he usually did, and hired himself as coach, while retaining the general manager's post. Clancy would assist him with both jobs.

Then Punch did something even more unusual. He went around the dressing room and asked each of us, in turn, if we would play for him. To a man, we said we would. Even Frank Mahovlich, who would later have tremendous problems dealing with Punch, said at the time, "He instilled a lot of confidence in a lot of players." Billy Harris expressed some concern about the lack of stability — he was now going to play for his fourth coach in four NHL seasons — but Smythe managed to reassure him, saying that, with the crop of young talent the Leafs had, they would go on to be the best in the league.

Another concern was how Bert Olmstead — the senior player in terms of NHL experience, and a friend of Reay's — would feel. But Bert was a sensible man, and was willing to go along — to a point. Bert was really the key to our future success. He was a real student of the game, and while he wasn't alone on our team in this regard — Stanley and Horton, and later, Red Kelly, really knew their hockey, too — Bert was the only one who'd stand up to Punch. Bert would watch Imlach at the chalkboard and just shake his head; finally he couldn't contain himself any longer and said something like, "No, that's not the fuckin' way!" And to Punch's credit, he looked right at Olmstead and said, "Well, then, you show us the way." And Bert would walk up to the board and go through the sequence of what was going to happen on the ice, especially in the offensive zone.

Hockey was the only thing on Bert's mind. He would start by asking us questions, to see how much we really knew about the game. He'd forgotten more than most of us knew. He'd teach us for hours on the train, or at mealtime, or whenever there was time for a talk. That's what really set him apart: not only did he know how to win, but he could show us and tell us how to win. When Red Kelly came over from Detroit, he'd won four Stanley Cups, so he knew about winning, but he was less a teacher and more the type to lead by example. Timmy Horton knew the game, but he couldn't tell you the game. The same went for George Armstrong; he had a hard time conveying what he knew to the younger players.

Bert never let up on us. He was determined to keep us honest. If you thought you'd played a great game, he would tell you how you could improve. His theory was that you had to want to win more than the other guy. I saw eye to eye with him on this point: my theory was that they didn't pay us to lose.

Looking back today, Bert says he felt Imlach was a great coach behind the bench, but no good in the other areas of coaching, perhaps because he had an ego the size of the Empire State Building. I always saw Imlach as a motivator — and in today's NHL he'd be a negative motivator. You couldn't manage today the way he did in those days. And Punch was certainly not a teacher, and that's where Bert Olmstead backed him up so well.

Now, Punch had pretty much given control of the forwards to Bert Olmstead, but he still dictated what was going on in the defensive zone. And somewhere along the line during the 1958–59 season he stumbled upon the magic combination. He paired Tim Horton with Allan Stanley, and teamed me up with Carl Brewer. Marc Reaume became our spare defenceman. Tim and Allan complemented each other because Tim could really move around, while Allan played the angles. And Brewer was just a bit faster than me, and better at handling the puck, but we both liked to knock the opponents around, so we were a great team.

You might think it took a stroke of genius to build a defence like that, but I'm not so sure. Imlach was still feeling his way around, just learning what to do. Everything he did was premeditated, and I never saw him push the panic button, but I think most of his decisions were the result of a hunch he'd had. I think in those early days he'd make a decision and never really be able to tell you why. He'd just live and die by his hunches, even though sometimes they seemed to come right out of left field. I became very close with Punch just before he died, and we'd often go out for lunch with friends. They'd all sit back and laugh as the two of us invariably argued about his coaching prowess.

Off the ice, a unique and somewhat eccentric individual entered my life around this time, and it wouldn't be too long before everyone on the team got to know him. Doug Cole had begun life as an orphan, and he eventually became a policeman. He and a business partner, Chuck Penstone, decided to buy an old hotel at the corner of Dundas and Sherbourne streets in downtown Toronto and turn it into a restaurant. I knew about Penstone because he had worked at my father's service station next to the Alpine Hotel on Kingston Road; in fact, that's where Doug and Chuck got the idea.

Well, when I heard about the new restaurant, I just couldn't resist checking it out. I headed over to their place, which they'd called George's Spaghetti House, and it quickly became a second home. During the Leafs' so-called glory years, George's was the unofficial team hangout. Doug became another lifelong friend.

When it came to food, George's took the lead over other Toronto restaurants. It was one of the first places in Toronto to serve pizza, and, with some input from me, Doug began to order king crab legs from New York and steaks from Boston. But he also stayed true to the "spaghetti house" theme. His lunch specialties included Italian meatball sandwiches, as well as veal and Italian sausage sandwiches. They became real hits.

The Leafs would drop by after every home game, unless we had a flight out that night, and we'd also drop in regularly for lunch. At first, the public wasn't aware we were there, so it was practically a private club. By the time the press let the secret out, well, the place would be so full of hockey players there was little room for anyone else.

George's became part of a Baun Christmas tradition. I used to arrange for a limo to pick up me and the boys on Christmas Eve morning, and our first stop would be to get haircuts. Then it was on to George's for lunch, and finally downtown to pick out a Christmas present for Sallie. It brings back years of happy memories. Anytime I was feeling low, I could go in there and always leave feeling like a new person, just because of the friendly, cheerful attitude of the staff.

Jazz was George's calling card, and it just so happened that most of the Leafs were jazz buffs. We heard some of Toronto's most famous performers there when they were just starting out. George's was the first home of Moe Koffman, Ed Bickard, Ray Brown, and Rob McConnell. It was the starting place for Malka and Joso — Joso now runs one of Toronto's unique and very "in" restaurants, specializing in fish and decorated with life-size nude statues and paintings.

Moe Koffman eventually moved on to the Towne Tavern, but it was at George's that he introduced his biggest hit, "Swinging Shepherd Blues." Rob McConnell went on to found a very successful group, The Boss Brass. I also remember Alf Coward, a pianist who performed there for five years, and Val Pringle, a songstress who must have stood about six foot six, was also a regular in later years. Alf's ex-wife would handle my banking, and still later she'd become a lady friend of mine.

At first, to make ends meet, Doug continued to operate the hotel. You wouldn't find this place listed in the Michelin guide — it was a long way from being the Royal York! There were twenty-six rooms, and they turned over quickly. I wouldn't say they rented by the hour, because I doubt many patrons stayed the full hour. I used to help Doug out, and we both can remember one night when business was quite brisk: we had to change sheets 159 times.

Eventually, George's became successful enough that they added another room, which they called Castle George. This was a great hideout for the players, once people started hanging around George's looking for us. It's not that we hockey players were antisocial, but as we became more and more successful, the spotlight grew harder and harder to avoid, and after a game we really just wanted to wind down together, out of the public eye.

For the opening night of Castle George, I greeted everyone at the door and Bob Cole of CKFH made the introductions. Al Boliska of radio station CHUM was there, and he nearly expired after putting on the suit of armour that was part of the room's décor. The first summer it was open, I also worked there, in the evenings, greeting guests and studying the cooks in the kitchen. I'd progressed from changing sheets.

Doug, like me, was also very interested in art and in this department he also had a keen eye for undiscovered talent. Gerald Gladstone painted the murals on the walls, and he did it just for the food and refreshment. Years later his paintings are quite valuable, but of course the murals will always remain with the building. A couple of others from the art community "in" crowd who frequented George's were Dennis Burton, who often wore a real Davy Crockett style racoon hat, and Clive Peacock. Doug describes him as "a goer, a doer, a looker, and an artist."

Even though it was still Toronto the Good, Doug would always make sure that there was a case of beer under the table so we could keep on drinking after hours. He always tried to make sure there was enough to last until we were ready to go home, but if we ran out, we'd put Timmy Horton to work. We always called him Clark Kent, but he was really Superman — he'd pry open the iron bars and bust the lock across the liquor cabinet, and the bar would reopen.

There are a lot of wild stories that involve George's and the Toronto Maple Leafs. The guys used to play a card game called Bullshit Poker. One night, Dick Duff seemed to be beating everyone else, and then for some reason he decided to take a swipe at Timmy. Well, Timmy reciprocated by literally hanging him out an office window upstairs. On another occasion, Timmy liked a new rug in one of the rooms, so he just rolled it up and took it home. No one challenged him — no one was that crazy! Doug didn't mind, because we all knew that whenever Timmy got the bright idea to "steal" something, he'd always return it the next day. And he'd be full of remorse.

I would often take the day's receipts home with me. It wasn't unusual for there to be $10,000 in cash, and, hard as it is to believe today, I used to just carry it home in paper bags.

Doug would often entertain at his home, and I was a regular guest. He'd also have the whole team over from time to time. He had a trampoline — they weren't common in those days — and I loved to use it as a tool for getting in shape after an injury or after the summer.

Bert Olmstead attended one of Doug's parties, and here's how Doug describes him: "He was a windmill in the corner. He lambasted the whole team, said they'd never win the Stanley Cup — and they won the next year!" Doug wasn't exactly a Punch Imlach fan, but he did say, "He was trying to get a job done, and he did it, and he won four Stanley Cups."

In later years, Doug went on to invest in another restaurant, and this one was also the first of its kind in Toronto. It was called the Underground Railroad, and it specialized in soul food. There were four original investors: Doug; John Henry Jackson and Dave Mann of the Toronto Argonauts; and a man who went on to considerable fame elsewhere, by the name of Bill Cosby. It was a success, particularly in the beginning, but it never took off quite the way George's did.

For the 1958–59 season, we began to fly to other cities, though we still spent a lot of time on the road. The league made it a rule that the visiting team must arrive either the day or night before a game. If back-to-back games were scheduled over a weekend, it meant we'd have to scramble to the airport after the Saturday night game, so we could be in the other team's city that same night.

I have painful memories of one of those home-and-home weekends. We were playing Detroit at the Gardens on Saturday night, and at the beginning of the third period I caught Gordie Howe with his head down. I dealt him a good clean bodycheck that left me really quite proud of myself. About ten minutes later I caught him again, and he went down and was very slow to get back up. I was named third star of the game for my efforts.

We went to Detroit, this time by train, and while we were shooting the breeze in the smoker, the guys warned me to be careful of Howe. The big guy has a memory like an elephant, they assured me. I was still feeling pretty cocky, and I told them there was no problem, I could handle Gordie!

In Sunday's game, we were heading into the third period and I got a half-assed breakaway down the right side. I was moving pretty quickly, thinking I should probably make a play to one of my forwards, but nobody was open. And who should be back on the Wings blue line but Gordie Howe. He forced me around the back of the net — where I probably should have stopped, à la Gretzky, but in my "wisdom" I kept going. Howe nuzzled in beside me and gave my head a rap with his elbow, pushing my head against the glass. I fell down, but picked myself up and started to chase Gordie back down the ice. With the blood gushing out the top of my head, I must have looked like a sperm whale. I caught him at the Leaf blue line and gave him a two-hander with my stick across the seat of his pants. I lifted him at least a foot off the ice, breaking my stick, but I was smart enough to skate like hell off the ice before he could catch up with me again. Gordie never forgot that incident. He told the story at a sports celebrity dinner in Brampton, Ontario, and he said he needed a rubber ring for his sore ass after that game.

With Imlach pulling the strings, we became a .500 hockey team. We weren't world-beaters yet, but we were basically holding our own. Around Christmastime, Punch completed his overhaul of the lineup by adding a right winger from the Hershey Bears by the name of Gerry Ehman, as well as Larry Regan in January.

Ehman had been in the minor leagues for six years, and he'd developed a reputation as a goal scorer. He was from Cudworth,

Saskatchewan, and he looked like a square-jawed gunslinger, so we nicknamed him Tex. He had a knack for shooting the puck with a quick flick of his wrists. He wasn't the greatest skater, which is probably why he had been a career minor leaguer, but he had a great attitude and good hockey sense; you could always count on him to be on his wing. He was a good journeyman hockey player who really racked up some points when he became a fixture of the Rochester lineup during the 1960s. Punch put him on a line with Billy Harris and Frank Mahovlich, and it was called the HEM Line.

Speaking of Christmas, it was one of the toughest times of the year for a hockey player. Looking back at my seventeen years in the NHL, I can count on one hand the number of times I was actually home on Christmas Day. Even if you were the home team, it played havoc with your holiday plans. But if you were one of the unlucky three clubs that had to play an away game on December 24, 25, or 26, it could be unbearable. Unfortunately they didn't abolish this ridiculous scheduling quirk until the year I retired.

The players didn't care for playing at Christmas, but it was worse on our kids. They'd always be confused whenever Santa Claus came a few days early, and explaining that it was the same at the Hortons' house, or the Keons' or the Kellys' didn't make it any easier. For the players, it meant we'd miss out on seeing our kids' smiling faces as they opened their presents.

Christmas also made us players even more aware that we were missing out on seeing our children grow up. Between September and April, we'd never be home on the weekends. We'd always be away for a couple of days during the week, and on the day of home games it was time for the kids to be quiet while you napped. You were rarely available for skating lessons, minor hockey games, piano recitals, or school plays. We all missed first steps or the first tooth falling out or, more importantly, the first day of school, which always overlapped training camp.

King Clancy used to say that Christmas was the saddest day of the year for him, and I concur. I remember — just barely — one year I was in Boston on Christmas Eve. I was staying with friends, and I got so drunk that I couldn't make the table for Christmas dinner.

For some reason, the Christmas of 1959 was one of those occasions when I was home. So we held a party at my house, and invited all the players as well as wives and girlfriends. My mother decided to dress up as Santa, only to discover when she arrived that Bobby Haggert had done the same. So, with a few adjustments to her costume, she became Mrs. Claus. This party began a tradition of celebrating Christmas and the end of the season at the Baun residence. As had happened in Rochester, I had become the team's social director.

If Punch Imlach was getting comfortable in his new dual role, he certainly didn't let up on us players. The practices got tougher and tougher. In February, Imlach came up with another new wrinkle: before each game he'd show us movie clips of the previous game, pointing out both good and bad moves we'd made. It's now commonplace for coaches to use videotape as a teaching aid, and Roger Neilson gets much of the credit for this innovation, but Punch was doing it in the '50s.

We'd been continuing along at a fairly even pace, winning a couple, losing a couple, but never really catching fire. On March 9, 1959, with about two weeks to go in the season, the NHL standings looked like this:

	GP	W	L	T	PTS
Montreal	63	36	15	12	84
Chicago	64	26	25	13	65
Boston	64	27	28	9	63
New York	63	25	26	12	62
Toronto	**64**	**22**	**31**	**11**	**55**
Detroit	64	23	34	7	53

It wasn't technically impossible for us to overtake New York, but it was as close to hopeless as you could get. We had to hope for a Ranger collapse, and that wasn't likely because they had a pretty good team: Gump Worsley in net; Bill Gadsby and Harry Howell on defence; and guys like Andy Bathgate, Dean Prentice, and Camille Henry up front. The good news was we still had to play the Rangers twice in our final six games.

On Wednesday, March 11, we were at home against the Montreal Canadiens, and they beat us badly, 6–2. But we shook it off, and Johnny Bower stopped everything the Rangers threw at him that Saturday as we won, 5–0.

The next night, it was the Rangers again, this time at Madison Square Garden. Getting into the old Garden used to be an adventure, because kids with pea shooters would always line up by the entrance on 50th Street, and they'd just let fly with these little blobs of paper, pelting you on the side of the head. They were just murder on the visiting team. It was a wild game, but we came out on top, 6–5.

The following Thursday we were at the Forum to play the Canadiens. We caught a break because it was one of the rare occasions that season that Jacques Plante wasn't in net for Montreal. They'd called up a goalie from the Quebec Senior league by the name of Claude Pronovost, and we unloaded on him, emerging with a 6–3 win.

Our last home game was Saturday night against Chicago. They were struggling at this point, and we beat them, 5–1.

The next day, Sunday, March 22, we were in Detroit. We trailed the Rangers by just one point, and we each had one game left to play. We had to win, and of course New York had to lose its game against Montreal. Punch left nothing to chance; he sent a telegram to his old pupil, Jean Béliveau, asking him to score a couple of goals. Big Jean came through, and the Canadiens won, 4–2.

The Red Wings, who were already out of the playoffs, weren't going to be as obliging. They cruised to a 2–0 lead on first-period goals from Norm Ullman and Marcel Pronovost.

The second period was a real showcase for another of Punch's mid-season acquisitions. Larry Regan had won the Calder Trophy as a Boston Bruin a couple of years before, but in January 1959 they'd put him on waivers. The Leafs grabbed him, and he was a productive part of our offence in the second half. Larry put us on the scoreboard at 2:41 of the second period, after which I got a rare goal at 4:15 to tie it up.

Ullman scored again just after the 15-minute mark to put Detroit back in front, but at 17:08 my defence partner, Carl Brewer, tied it up, assisted by Mahovlich and Regan. Larry was having a hot night: 21 seconds later he scored his second goal, and for the first time in the game the Leafs were leading, 4–3. There was no time to pat ourselves on the back, though, because Pronovost scored again with a little over a minute left in the second period and we went to the intermission deadlocked at 4–4.

Bower was unbeatable in the third period, stopping all ten Detroit shots, while Regan (again!) set up Dick Duff's game-winning goal at 2:51. Just before the 15-minute mark, I assisted on Billy Harris's insurance marker, and we were in the playoffs!

Here are the final standings for 1958–59:

	GP	W	L	T	PTS
Montreal	70	39	18	13	91
Boston	70	32	29	9	73
Chicago	70	28	29	13	69
Toronto	**70**	**27**	**32**	**11**	**65**
New York	70	26	32	12	64
Detroit	70	25	37	8	58

The Rangers had lost six of their last seven games, and they only won five of their last twenty games. Their tough guy, Lou Fontinato, had been badly beaten in a fight with Gordie Howe, and I think they lost a lot of their heart after that incident.

They also had quite a challenge playing in New York, with the night life and all the other distractions of the big city. And the Garden was always booked for the circus, or a convention, or something. Their only practice rink was the pits! It was upstairs at the former Madison Square Garden, and it was just a dinky half-size sheet of ice, surrounded by tin boards. You'd shoot the puck against the boards and it would start your head ringing. The Leafs practised there a couple of times and I just thought, "My God, how did people ever play here?"

Meanwhile, we'd finished with a five-game winning streak. We didn't have time to stop and think about what we were doing down that stretch — we just went on automatic pilot, played and practised as hard as ever, and ground out the wins one by one. I know that Duff and I were having our usual fights every day in practice, and that was always a good sign. And I guess during those two weeks we just really came together as a cohesive unit.

Imlach was elated, telling the reporters at the Detroit Olympia, "We're the hungriest team in the world, and we're just getting started. We've been so hungry for something like this that we could taste it."

Our hunger was satisfied in another way as well: the victory entitled each player to a fourth-place bonus of $900 from the National Hockey League.

The Toronto *Telegram* brought back a bit of the Hap Day era in the headline, "An Old Slogan Is Recalled — Guts, Goals and Glamour."

CHAPTER 6

Moving on Up

GOING INTO THE PLAYOFFS FOR THE FIRST TIME SINCE MY JUNIOR days was pretty heady stuff. But we didn't get time to rest on our laurels. After the game in Detroit, it was straight onto a chartered plane to Boston, which would be the site of our first two playoff games.

The Bruins had a solid team with lots of experienced players — guys like Vic Stasiuk, Doug Mohns, Leo Boivin, Fernie Flaman, Bronco Horvath, and former Leaf goalie Harry Lumley. The team also featured a young John Bucyk.

Everyone in the league knew Flaman as a dirty sonofabitch. He was a defenceman, and he'd wander into the offensive zone while you were following the play in the corner, and the next thing you know you'd be on your ass because he'd kicked your feet out from under you. You'd turn around, and he was gone. There was no way to get back at him because the puck was already going the other way — in fact, he'd usually wait until the referee was following the play out of the zone before he'd get you. His timing was always impeccable. There wasn't anybody in the league he wouldn't try that trick on.

It seemed strange to be playing in the spring, and it was especially warm in Boston that year. The old Boston Garden felt like a steam bath. Players today, playing in facilities like the Air Canada Centre, have no idea what those old arenas were like. And Boston's was one of the worst. The visitors' dressing room was miserable and cramped — it couldn't have been bigger than twelve feet square. There was one tiny window, and it looked into an alley. As a result, the room smelled dreadful, and it always felt dirty.

Worst of all, the visitors' room was at the other end of the rink from our bench, so you had to walk past all those crazy railbirds. I could have retired early if I had a dollar for every time I heard them call out, "Hey, Bahhhhhn! Hey, Bahhhhhn!" in their Boston accents. As you can probably imagine, they drove Al Arbour of Chicago to distraction, yelling "Ahhhhh-bah! Ahhhhh-bah!"

One night in Boston, during the warm-up, one of these guys was calling "Ahhhhh-bah! Hey, Ahhhhh-bah!" and giving Al the high sign and pointing to his eye. This went on quite a few times as we skated around, and finally Al couldn't contain himself any longer. He skated over to the fan and said, "What the hell do you mean by this?" And the fan leaned forward and said, "Fuck ahhh-hhf, Ahhhhh-bah!"

The tone for that series was set early on: it was going to be a very physical battle. Between the heat, the tough play, Harry Lumley's great goaltending, and our inexperience, we got whipped pretty good in those first two games, 5–1 and 4–2.

These days, teams change their whole style during the play-offs. All of a sudden everyone remembers how to backcheck, the goalies step up, and the scoring drops off. I never noticed those kinds of changes when I played. And during that stretch in 1959, every game during the last two weeks of the regular season had been like a playoff game anyway.

The series shifted back to Toronto, and Gerry Ehman was the hero in game three. He tied the game, 2–2, late in the third period,

Long before I first stepped out onto the ice for the Toronto Maple Leafs, I skated for neighbourhood teams, including the Birchcliff Baptist church.

With sisters Joyce (left) and Marlene in 1949. Later, in the NHL, I was rarely known to be a Boy Scout.

The 1952–53 Marlies (I'm in the back row, second from the right). That's my good friend Jack Bionda in the middle row, fourth from the right. Jack was a great hockey player and was a lacrosse star.

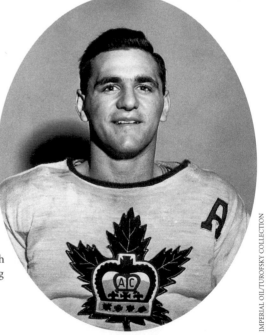

As an assistant captain with the Memorial Cup–winning Marlies in 1956.

With Sallie in 1953 at my high school prom at Scarborough Collegiate (now R.H. King).

Leaning against my 1951 Cadillac in 1954. I've always been fond of expensive cars.

With my family, about 1954, after the first Memorial Cup win.
From the left: me, my sister Joyce, Mom, Dad, and my sister Marlene.

With Leaf trainer Tim Daly in 1956. Daly was a character. He would do a shadow box routine before every game to loosen us up.

Having a good time with some of my teammates. From the left: Barry Cullen, Dick Duff, me, Billy Harris, and Frank Mahovlich.

Here I help out goalie Ed Chadwick, taking a puck in the chest in action against the Hawks on December 14, 1957.

Passing out cigars after the birth of my son Jeff in February 1958 with Tim Horton (left), Jimmy Morrison, and Paul Masnick.

I always tried to be in the middle of the action. Here I'm helping George Armstrong take care of Eric Nesterenko while Gary Aldcorn (centre), referee George Hayes, and Marc Reaume look on.

Staff Smythe (left), Harold Ballard, and I celebrate the birth of my son Brian on St. Patrick's Day, 1961.

Tim Daly, as Santa, hands my son Brian a Christmas gift while Sallie looks on.
Every Christmas Tim would scare the jumpin's out of the children.

On the parade route through the streets of Toronto after our 1961–62 Stanley Cup win.

FRANK M. LENNON

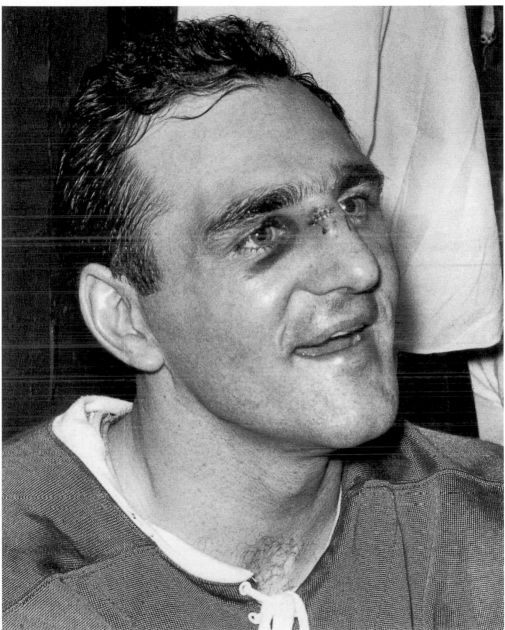

Hockey's a tough game. I often wore battle scars during the Original Six era.

Brian sits in my lap as I sign a ledger after our 1963 Cup win, while Eddie Shack and David Keon (over Eddie's right shoulder) look on.

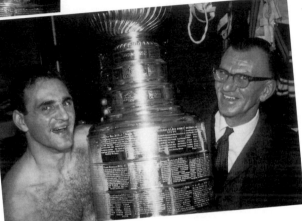

Dad and I posing with the Cup in 1963. That was probably the last time Dad ever attended one of my games at the rink. He'd watch the games at home while eating candies.

TORONTO SUN SYNDICATE

I was in a lot of pain when they carried me off the ice during the third period of game six of the 1964 finals against the Red Wings. I came back to score the game-winning goal in overtime on what I would later find out to be a broken leg. The win gave the Leafs a boost, and we went on to defeat the Wings in game seven to take the Cup.

then scored the winner in overtime. The fourth game was also a 3–2 overtime victory; this time Frank Mahovlich broke the tie with a power-play goal while Boston's Jean-Guy Gendron was in the penalty box. (Today, you don't see many penalties called during overtime in a playoff game.)

We won game five, in Boston, 4–1, putting us ahead, three games to two. Back in Toronto, the Bruins showed that they still had some life in them as they squeaked past us, 5–4. The seventh and deciding game was at the Boston Garden, and once again it was Ehman with the series-winning goal with about two minutes left to play.

After one of the wins in Boston, we were treated to a rare example of Punch Imlach's sense of humour. Punch was led into the dressing room after the game, and a club official announced, "I'm sorry to announce to you that we have just employed a new coach." We all looked a bit startled as Imlach walked in, wearing a bushy wig under his trademark fedora. He shook hands with each player, then took off the wig to reveal his usual shiny bald pate. He confessed that the wig had been given to him by some Bruin fans who told him they'd had enough of his "crystal ball" head.

The victory over the Bruins meant we were headed for the Stanley Cup finals. Without any further ado, we were off to Montreal, where just two days later we were to meet the Canadiens, who'd already put together a string of three Cup championships. Going into that series, we had all the confidence we'd ever need, but we were sorely lacking playoff experience. Aside from Bert Olmstead — this was his ninth consecutive trip to the finals — nobody really knew what to expect.

The Canadiens had the most explosive offence the league had ever seen — their 258 goals that year were more than any NHL team had ever scored. They were led by Dickie Moore — who set a league record for points, with 96 — and Jean Béliveau, whose 91 points were the most ever by a centreman. You had to look a long way down the scoring leaders to find our top guy, Dick Duff, with his 29 goals and 53 points! We defencemen had our work cut out for us. Punch planned to use Horton and Stanley against the Béliveau line, while Carl and I would face Henri Richard's. We would average between 28 and 32 minutes a game during the series.

For a team that wasn't supposed to be in the playoffs that year, we made a series of it. In games one, two, and four, we took tie scores into the second intermission, only to lose all three in the third period by scores of 5–3, 3–1, and 3–2. We were also encouraged by our showing in game three, which we won 3–2 on Dick Duff's goal at 10:06 of overtime. But in the fifth game, at the Forum, the Habs scored three goals in just over sixteen minutes and they never looked back. They won the game, 5–3, and sipped champagne from the Stanley Cup for the fourth time in a row.

Most of us felt that what we'd accomplished that year was far beyond anyone's expectations — except, perhaps, Punch Imlach's.

During the off-season I was busy with countless charitable appearances, such as kids softball games. The summer of 1959 also brought another son, Gregory, into the Baun family. And that led to the usual, inevitable, hustling for a few extra bucks. That year the makers of Bee Hive Corn Syrup came to the rescue, and sponsored some players to speak at banquets and other public appearances.

Since that time I've probably made more than 5,000 speaking engagements, and in recent years the majority have been for charitable causes. I'll never forget my first appearance — as much as I wish I could!

It was back in 1956, and Rev. Lewis Garnsworthy asked me to address his former Cub and Scout troop — Number 152. I stood up in front of the boys, opened my mouth wide — and not a word would come out. Finally, I gave up and sat down, feeling quite ashamed. About fifteen minutes later I fielded some questions, and I handled those much more successfully. My fee that day was ten dollars, plus a few cents for mileage. By the next year, I was considered more experienced, so my rate went up to $20 plus 30 cents a mile. I'd get called upon two or three times a week, so it grew to be quite worthwhile, once I got the hang of it.

Those of us who were getting into hockey in the late 1950s were a new breed. We were men who planned ahead, thinking beyond our playing days and preparing for whatever the future might hold. Traditionally, a player nearing the end of his career would move into farming, construction, sales — the same kind of job he'd probably been doing in the summers. A very lucky few, like Joe Primeau, would build their own business. A few others would go into coaching or managing a hockey team, but there were few opportunities to do that at the top level.

A group of us younger Leafs decided that wasn't for us. Some of us had been dabbling in the stock market, so we decided to get together on a regular basis and discuss our investments. In 1959, four of us — Carl Brewer, Billy Harris, Bob Pulford, and me — formed what we called the Blue and White Investment Club. When Bob Nevin broke in with the Leafs in 1960, he joined us. We'd get together, often over lunch, three or four times a week, and naturally in the course of these discussions we'd drift off to other topics. And one subject that seemed to come up more and more often was the need for a National Hockey League Players' Association.

Ted Lindsay had tried to establish a players' association back in 1956, and it never got off the ground. The Leafs had hung together back then, and even filed an anti-trust suit against the NHL, but the owners in Montreal and Detroit managed to intimidate the players and suddenly there was no support.

One of the big issues we started talking about was contracts. As I've mentioned, the age-old problem in hockey was that the veterans would never help the rookies in this area. They always thought we should just keep our mouths shut and do as we were told. When it came to salaries, we never knew if we were getting a raw deal or not, never knew whether we were up or down. In later years, around 1966 or 1967, a lot of young guys were being added to the lineup, and I didn't mind helping them out. Punch really blew his stack when he caught the kids lined up outside my hotel room to discuss their contracts with me.

It's been well documented that Bob Pulford had a lawyer friend he'd gone to school with — Alan Eagleson, who was a partner in a firm called Blaney, Pasternak, Luck, and Smela. The other partners in the firm were Jim Blaney, Ted Luck, Erwin Pasternak, Ray Smela, and Bob Watson. Eagleson was young, aggressive, and dying to make a mark for himself. He saw our situation as the opportunity he'd been looking for. Jim Blaney was a small-c conservative who was the Eagle's stabilizing influence — as much as he could be — and someone I still consider to be a good friend after all these years.

It would be nearly ten years before a players' association was in fact a reality, but in the meantime Eagleson was laying the groundwork by taking on clients, acting as a player agent. One of his first, whom he met through the Blue and White Group, was Carl Brewer. A couple of years later, he'd hooked up with his most famous client, Bobby Orr. To the betterment of hockey, both of these men, and many thousands more, would eventually become Eagleson's bitter enemies.

—•—

I'd like to take a few moments here to talk about a key person in any hockey player's success: the player's wife. In my day she really could not hold a full-time job — the players were constantly going on road trips, and given our salaries in those days, the cost of a nanny was not within reach. As my second son, Greg, says: "We hardly saw my father when we were little." In the summer, unless they took a holiday together — which was also expensive if you had a large family like the Bauns — the kids didn't see Dad, either, because he was working at his summer job. And it usually ran from dawn to dusk. (As tough as the players had it, we can't forget the referees and linesmen, for whom there was never any such thing as a home game.)

To keep their sanity, the wives and girlfriends would often make friends with each other. They would attend games together, usually in pairs — or groups of four at the most — spread out throughout the blue seats at Maple Leaf Gardens. They would also visit with each other between periods in a dingy room by the underground parking garage.

Ever the organizer, Sallie decided to form a bridge club with a few of the other spouses. After all, they figured, the husbands would always be on hand to babysit on the same nights. The club is still going strong, and it consists of Marilyn (Brewer) Patterson, Barb Tushingham, Bibs Ullman, Gayle Litzenberger, Norma Shack, Anne Whipper, Mary Cairns, Marg Tolton, and Terry Conboy. Two members no longer live in Toronto, but they've never been excluded — Karen Pappin and Roz Pulford. Sadly, they've lost one member, the late Sylvia Harris. The club serves as a women's group as well, so members have never been disqualified due to divorce or breakups.

By the training camp of 1959, Punch Imlach had taken full control. He even had the seal of approval from the top dog, Conn Smythe: "He's the best coach this team has had since Hap Day. I've watched him behind the bench, handling those youngsters, and I liked what I saw. This team needs Imlach. He's got them to the playoffs, the office upstairs is running smoothly. We've got Clancy and Bob Davidson and the rest. The Committee of Seven is there to make the trades and deals. When Imlach finally has this team moulded into a team, with all the holes plugged, it will once more be a great team."

Smythe, of course, was right, but there was a lot of hard work ahead. Training camp this year felt even more like boot camp than ever. Just like last year, we were to leave our cars at the hotel lot and walk to and from the arena, a good two miles every day. Not only would they be checking the arena lot, but Punch was likely to have Clancy, his favourite gofer, checking up and down the side streets for expensive vehicles that might have magically moved themselves from the hotel lot. We were to be up at 6:45 every morning and on the ice by 8 o'clock.

For the first day of practice, they let Tim Daly take charge, in honour of his seventy-fifth birthday. The trainers are often the forgotten men on any sports team, yet they are vital to a team's success. Today's trainers are highly skilled and qualified. In the old days, they just stumbled into it, or, as Daly put it, they "learned it gradually over a period of years."

Daly had been a boxer, and even then he'd started out carrying his brother's equipment until one day they were short a competitor and he stepped into the ring for the first time. In time he'd connected with the Toronto St. Patricks hockey team, and stayed on when they became the Maple Leafs. Decades later, he was still with them. He had coached baseball as well, and his greatest achievement was the time he massaged the leg of Ty Cobb for an entire night: it was not until the next day, when they took Cobb to hospital, they discovered the leg was broken. Among the Leafs he was known equally for his sense of humour and his inabilities with the English language.

In later years Tommy Naylor joined the staff as an assistant to Tim Daly. He was a much more studious man and he'd started out as an Olympic speed skater. He'd also worked for CCM, the leading skate and equipment manufacturer for many decades. As a hobby he tinkered with sporting equipment, trying to make it safer. There was a close bond between the two of us, and Naylor's daughter, Marg, married my childhood buddy Russ Langfield.

Some of Naylor's inventions were a result of injuries I had experienced. Up until Tommy Naylor, you pretty much improvised when it came to protecting your ankles inside your skates. Guys would stuff their skate boots with newspapers, bulky socks, or whatever was handy. Tommy developed a plastic insert. He also noticed that a sharp skate blade could cut through the leather boot and sever the tendons, so he invented a device to protect them. On several occasions my toes had been injured when a skate blade cut through that part of the boot. Naylor invented a steel toe guard. He is also credited with designing the plastic tips on the ends of the old skate blades, as well as wraparound ankle guards. Once, I broke a thumb, and the injury would have kept me out of action for weeks. Naylor came up with a special fibre "cast," built into the thumb of my glove, that enabled me to return much sooner.

The next person to take over as trainer was young Bobby Haggert, and Naylor stayed on to assist him. Bob had grown up playing with — or rather, against — me and some of my team-mates. When he didn't pan out as a player, he stuck with the team as a trainer. After that he seemed to follow me through each step. He claims he acted as clubhouse boy for the Marlie Seniors when they won the Allan Cup in 1950. He worked as an actual trainer, as an after-school job, from 1950 until 1955. As Bobby remembers it, "In those days you learned firsthand from the guy before you." Dr. Jim Murray, the team doctor, took Bobby under his wing, and brought him along to seminars as well.

Besides acting as trainer for all the Leafs' Stanley Cup–winning teams of the '60s, Haggert also founded the Canadian Athletic Trainers Association. It began with twenty-five members, now has 1,000, and the word "Trainer" has been changed to "Therapist." He also belonged to an American group called the National Athletic

Trainers Association, which held lectures and conferences every year in a different U.S. city.

A Toronto sportswriter by the name of George Dulmage did a very realistic summation of Imlach as we headed into a new season. "In a world where everything is crazy and mixed-up and dreadfully serious, there is a constant that keeps us poor Canadians from going out of our minds. It is the eternal confidence of George Imlach. Mr. Imlach, as you know, has the cold effrontery and the IBM brain of a riverboat gambler. Mixed with a little of Billy Graham, the evangelist. He makes you believe."

One oddity that we encountered during this training camp was fog. It happened during an exhibition game against Cleveland in St. Thomas, Ontario. Players would lose the puck totally in the dense haze; the Cleveland goalie tried unsuccessfully to poke holes in it by waving his stick; and finally the referee ordered all the players to get off the bench to skate around in hopes that it would dissipate for a while. The final result was a 6–1 Leafs win in a game where "no one, including the referee, had the foggiest notion of what was happening!" The fans couldn't have been blamed if they wanted their money back. We prayed it wasn't an omen of things to come!

As the season neared, we managed to avoid the wholesale changes of the year before. Brian Cullen became a New York Ranger via the Intra-League Draft, while his brother Barry was traded to Detroit for Johnny Wilson. We were a much stronger team than the year before. There'd be no sneaking into the playoffs this time.

One thing that stands out about 1959–60 is that the defencemen created a lot more offence than usual. Allan Stanley led all NHL blueliners with 10 goals, while Tim Horton's 29 assists were more than any other Leaf — even the forwards. I know these aren't exactly Bobby Orr–type numbers I'm throwing around, but it'll show you just how drastically Orr changed the way we all thought about the defenceman's job.

They must have been putting something into the defencemen's pre-game meals, because I scored 8 goals that year, a career high for me. This was truly extraordinary because in over seventeen years I only averaged about two a year. But this season I got off to an incredible start, and I think I already had 5 or 6 by the first of November. I even had Frank Mahovlich and Bobby Hull beat!

I didn't have much of a shot, because I'd hurt both my elbows quite early on. I fell and cut them, split them, from the inside. Both of them have been operated on, and I always had to have them taped up to play. They made a special set of elbow pads for me, but they didn't provide full flexibility, so I was never able to shoot the puck that well. I always just tried to keep the puck low — I always worked at that, and was pretty good at it.

You'd think a guy with forty career NHL goals would remember every last one of them, but that's not the case. The only two that really come to mind are the one in game six of the 1964 finals — no one will let me forget that one! — and the one I scored in the semifinals against Montreal that same year, when I had a breakaway right after getting out of the penalty box. I know I scored some pretty ones, and it would never fail to shock everyone when I'd make a spectacular rush and beat the goaltender. I'd always leave them saying, "Where the hell did *he* come from?"

But let's face it, my defence partner Carl Brewer was the guy whose job it was to move the puck. I always seemed to get paired off with one of the offensive-minded guys, so it was never in my game plan to join the rush. And in Punch's system, defence came first. If we didn't let you score, we only needed one goal to win. Still, when you consider I was averaging thirty minutes of ice time a game, it's amazing how few goals, or even assists, I was getting.

Something else that happened was that I got pigeonholed as a defenceman from the very beginning, from those days in the church league, and I never moved around much to the other positions. That's one thing I like about what they're doing with the kids today: they move around a little bit more, forwards playing on the off wing and so on.

Anyway, I was getting a lot of good publicity as the season went on. My name was showing up in the headlines: "Sparked by Baun, Leafs Come Alive"; "NHL Gives Baun Top Mark Among Leafs"; and "Baun and Angels Save Leaf Tie." In that last story, about a game against the Black Hawks, the reporter said I was "everywhere and a second goaltender." In the same game, Chicago forward Kenny Wharram suffered a broken jaw after a run-in with me. He told the papers that "Bobby Baun hit me a solid check and I felt it right down to my skates."

Another pleasant surprise down the stretch in 1960 was the acquisition of thirty-two-year-old Leonard "Red" Kelly from Detroit. On February 5, the Wings traded him to the Rangers, along with a forward by the name of Billy McNeill. Bill Gadsby and Eddie Shack were supposed to go the other way. The trade was unexpected. As Red's wife, Andra, put it, "[Detroit manager] Jack Adams gave me away at our wedding, and now seven months later he gave Red away." Kelly declared he would retire rather than go to New York, and McNeill announced his retirement as well. The deal was cancelled.

When the Leafs got wind of the situation, they asked permission to approach Kelly and find out whether he'd play for Toronto. The man chosen to make the sales pitch was none other than the loquacious King Clancy. Red said he was "enchanted and amused by the Clancy charm," and a deal was made. The Kellys would later confirm their allegiance to the Leafs by nicknaming one of their children Clancy. Red later admitted that his decision to retire had been an impulse, stemming from hurt feelings — he felt unwanted when the Wings dealt him after twelve and a half solid seasons.

The Leafs had Kelly, while Detroit got my former defence partner, Marc Reaume, who'd been spending a lot of time on the bench since I'd clicked with Carl Brewer. I thought it was a good opportunity for Marc, because they liked his freewheeling style and it looked like he'd finally be getting some ice time. Detroit offered him that chance. One thing I'll never forget about Marc is that trainer Tim Daly could never pronounce his name. He always called him "Rizoom."

For nearly thirteen years, Kelly had been a first-rate defence-man, earning multiple nominations to the First All-Star Team and winning the Norris Trophy as the league's top blueliner. He'd always been one of the best at moving the puck, and Imlach had another one of his hunches, gambling that Red could help us up front. For the rest of his career, he'd be a centreman with the Toronto Maple Leafs.

As luck would have it, we played back-to-back games against Detroit that very weekend, and we whipped them, 7–1 and 3–1. In the Saturday game at the Gardens, we scored all seven goals in the third period. I guess we were all just pumped up on Red's behalf. As Fred Cederberg wrote in his column, "Last weekend, the Detroit Red Wings lost Red Kelly to Leafs. This weekend, the Wings lost the weekend to the same club."

We finished the regular season with 79 points, which left us comfortably in second place behind Montreal. It was the Leafs' best season since 1950–51. Our first-round playoff opponent would be Detroit, whom we'd beaten 3–2 in the final game of the regular season, and they hadn't given us much trouble all year. Plus, the series would open at Maple Leaf Gardens. We had good reason to feel confident heading into these playoffs.

We lost the first game, 2–1, but came back to take the second one, 4–2. The action shifted to the Olympia, and we gave the fans their money's worth. At the end of regulation time, we were tied at 4–4. We played one twenty-minute overtime period, then a second. Still no one could break the deadlock. Finally, three minutes into the third overtime period, Frank Mahovlich put the puck behind Terry Sawchuk and we could all go home. Frank had just finished serving a major penalty, so it's a safe bet he had the freshest legs on the ice at that moment.

Two nights later, we were again tied at the end of regular play — this time it was 1–1. And this time it was the Wings' Gerry Melnyk who broke the tie, mercifully after only 1:54 of extra time. Fortunately, we had two nights off before game five in Toronto. It was a close one, but we managed to come out on top, 5–4. The next night it was back to the Olympia, and there was no way we were going to overtime on this night in Detroit. We won the game, and the series, 4–2.

The Stanley Cup finals would be a rematch of the 1959 series, as we again faced the Canadiens. They were well-rested, having done away with their semifinal opponent, the Chicago Black Hawks, in just four games. Jacques Plante really kicked into high gear during that series, recording shutouts in games three and four.

In game one of the finals, the Habs scored three goals in the first twelve minutes, and the Pocket Rocket, Henri Richard, set up all three goals. This established a pattern that would repeat throughout the series, with the Canadiens taking the early lead and the Leafs trying desperately to catch up. We closed the gap in the first game to 3–2, but Henri scored a minute and a half into the third period to put a 4–2 Montreal victory on ice.

In game two, Dickie Moore and Jean Béliveau put the Habs ahead 2–0. Larry Regan got one back for us late in the first, and Bower and Plante turned aside every last shot the rest of the way. In the third game, we spotted the Canadiens a 3–0 lead. We got one from Johnny Wilson late in the second period, but Montreal came back with two more goals in the third. Maurice Richard scored the goal that made it 5–1, and immediately skated to Bower's net and retrieved the puck. That gesture got everyone buzzing that he was thinking seriously about retiring after this series. It was the Rocket's 34th goal in the Stanley Cup finals, and to this day no one's ever scored more.

In game four, Béliveau and Harvey scored within twenty-eight seconds of each other, and Plante just stoned us, as the Habs rolled to a 4–0 win. The Canadiens had won the Cup in what was then the minimum of eight games, duplicating the feat of the 1952 Detroit Red Wings. Plante's goals-against average in those playoffs was 1.35. Worst of all, NHL officials rolled the Cup out onto the ice at Maple Leaf Gardens, and it wasn't for us.

I always felt much of the credit for our early success belonged to the older pros — Allan Stanley, Johnny Bower, and particularly Bert Olmstead. And, last but not least, team captain George Armstrong. He could handle Punch in a way that no one else could, before, or after. He was a great buffer between Punch and the players. We'd be complaining something or other, and he'd say, "I'll talk to Punch about it." He'd come back to us a few days later and say, "Well, I talked to Punch about it and things are really gonna change." Now, you could bet dollars to donuts he hadn't said a word to Imlach, but by then we'd usually forgotten what we were so angry about in the first place.

PART III

The Very Good Years

CHAPTER 7

Dawn of the Glory Years

AS THE TORONTO MAPLE LEAFS ENTERED THE 1960s IT FELT LIKE we had really jelled, and that good feeling was translating into measurable success in the standings. We had come together from all over the country, from all walks of life, a mixture of young and old players, but we all seemed to bring the same two qualities to the table: a zest for life combined with an intense desire to win. We were a close-knit bunch; we all knew each other's families as well as we knew each other's strengths and weaknesses on the ice. As George Mara, one of the Silver Seven, said, "You couldn't buy what that team had, or what they gave."

Looking back on the personalities of that team, I have to start with the captain, George (Army) Armstrong. He took over as captain in 1957, succeeding Teeder Kennedy, and he held the position longer than anyone before or since. As I've mentioned, he was the much-needed buffer between Imlach and the players, and his razor-sharp sense of humour helped him perform this part of the job tremendously well. He may not have been the best skater, but he had a keen sense of the game, played his position as well as anyone, and you could often count on him to score a key goal. No one played in more seasons — 21 — or more games — 1,187 — as a Leaf.

Next in line is Johnny Bower, the goalie extraordinaire. He and Army were the two big smokers on the team, so they always roomed together. Every day, John would swear off cigarettes, and by the intermission or the end of practice you'd catch him taking a smoke break in the washroom. Bower was notoriously thrifty. On the road, he'd always pocket his per diem money instead of going out for breakfast. Instead, he'd mix up a glass of Tang and a cup of instant coffee in his hotel room. He had good reason to be so frugal: Punch paid him next to nothing. When he first joined us, I think John was making as much at age thirty-four as I was earning as a twenty-two-year-old defenceman.

On the ice, Bower played as if he had a sixth sense. Sometimes you'd see him set up where he thought the puck *should* be, rather than where it actually was. He'd just have a gut feeling about the way the play was developing, and he'd move to that spot. And I have to admit, his gambles almost always paid off.

Now, to give John his due, he wasn't the only Leaf who was tight with a dollar. Bob Pulford had the same reputation. The authors of the book *Net Worth*, David Cruise and Alison Griffiths, said that Pully appreciates a nickel more than most people do a $20 bill. One time in New York, Pulford was with his roommate, Brian Cullen, when Cullen spotted a quarter in the bedroom. Pully insisted they "share" the quarter, but Brian refused. Later that morning, after Cullen had gone to sleep, Pully grabbed the quarter, went downstairs, and bought a newspaper. Cullen was awake when he returned, and Pully announced, "I have bought *us* a newspaper."

My defence partner, Carl Brewer, was a superb athlete, and from day one he was very intense. When he first came to training camp, he was so fast it was as if he had a rocket in his ass; he seemed to have an extra gear that the rest of us lacked. He also had lightning-quick reflexes and he was smart as a whip. In fact, he was *too* smart to be a hockey player in that day and age, and that led to many a run-in with Punch.

Carl was also deathly afraid of flying; he was a real white-knuckler. On one occasion, we were returning from New York on a Vanguard turbo-prop plane, and an engine blew. The flames shot about twelve feet into the air. Naturally, it had to be Brewer and I who were seated right by that engine! The plane shuddered as if it had hit a wall, and Carl bolted to the back of the cabin and stayed there. Of course, he wasn't the only one who thought he was done for. King Clancy, ever the devout Catholic, pulled out his rosary beads and started working them like there was no tomorrow. Punch Imlach started jabbering away at a mile a minute.

The pilot came back into the cabin, inspected the engine through my window, and said he was going to try to put out the fire. The next thing I saw was foam pouring out the top of the engine, extinguishing the flames. Back in the cockpit, the pilot announced that we would have no problem making it to Toronto on three engines, adding we could even fly on one if we had to. Well, three I could handle, but I wasn't anxious to try out his theory about one. And I don't think anyone was happier when we touched down at the old Malton airport than Carl Brewer.

Tim Horton was one of my dearest friends, off the ice as well as on. He had great reflexes, but he had terrible eyesight. Off the ice he wore glasses as thick as Coke bottles. But he'd never wear his glasses in a game or in practice, even though Al Arbour did.

Whenever we went to New York, Timmy would always go to the Marble Collegiate Church to hear Norman Vincent Peale, the author of *The Power of Positive Thinking*, speak. Timmy was a true convert, and he'd usually bring Billy Harris and me along. Peale's writings would serve as my Bible and help me many times in my life.

Tim couldn't fight, but he could squeeze you to death with one of his bear hugs. He didn't know his own strength, and I think he was a bit frightened of what he could do. We'd heard some wild stories about Tim from his early years in Pittsburgh, but he seemed to settle down when he moved to Toronto. A lot of the time he'd be the most mild-mannered, almost shy, fellow you'd ever meet. Still, you could sense that a storm was always brewing just beneath the calm veneer.

After a couple of beers, Clark Kent would turn into Superman. On the road, Timmy always wanted to keep the party going, and it didn't matter if you wanted to get to sleep. It didn't do any good to lock your door, either, because he'd just break it down. On one trip to Boston, we were staying at the Sheraton-Plaza Hotel, on the top floor. The hallways were exceptionally narrow, so we figured Tim wouldn't be able to break down any doors.

That night he decided to drop in on Frank Mahovlich and Davey Keon. Not only did he manage to unhinge the door, but the transom came crashing down with it! Frank didn't know where to go, so he cowered behind the TV set, while Davey hid behind the bed. Horton picked up the bed, turned it upside-down, and dropped it back on the floor. After a few minutes, he disappeared.

Dave and Frank tried to put the door back in place, so it would look like nothing had happened, but the hotel security guards knew better and called Punch. Punch walked into the room, looked at the two of them, and barked, "Who did this?" Davey was about five-eight, 160 pounds, and he looked Punch right in the eye and said, meekly, "Do you think *I* could've done this?" Nevertheless, Punch made Keon and Mahovlich pay the $2,500 repair bill.

One day we decided that Horton had never been properly initiated. It took about four or five of us to hold him down. We proceeded to shave his entire genital area, and then, to prevent infection — or so we said — we massaged in some liniment. It stung for at least three days! Vaseline was the only cure, which of course made a greasy mess.

Allan Stanley was another older player I sought out as a confidant. I always felt he was there for me. He visited me frequently in 1974, when I went into hospital for a series of operations. I wanted to get everything fixed, and I'd scheduled knee and elbow surgery for Monday, neck surgery on Wednesday, and, later in the week, a nose job. One day Allan came in for a visit and produced a bottle of vodka. One of the doctors happened by, looked at Allan sternly, and said, "Surely you're not giving that to the patient, are you?" Stanley hadn't expected to get caught, but he quickly covered his tracks. "No, just one little shot for him and the rest is for me." Away went the doctor, and, as the afternoon passed, away went the vodka. And, by the end of the week, away went the idea of getting my nose fixed!

Even if Allan hadn't brought the bottle of vodka, I was fully prepared. I'd secretly set up a bar in my room, fully stocked with Scotch, rye, gin, vodka, red and white wine, and even a little Grand Marnier and cognac — all with the appropriate glasses, of course. Dick Horkins delivered my favourite lobster bisque from La Scala restaurant on four of the seven days I was there. And the gang from George's Spaghetti House were delivering anything else I needed. I'd never had it so good — I nearly didn't want to go home.

But back to the team. I don't think there was ever a better defence corps than the pairings of Stanley and Horton, and Brewer and Baun. Montreal had Doug Harvey and Tom Johnson, but they didn't have another defenceman who could touch us. Today's NHL rosters carry six or seven defencemen, but I don't think there's a team in the league that could come up with four as good as we were.

On the forward lines, behind Armstrong we had Bobby Nevin and Ron Stewart on the right side. Stewie was a great skater and backchecker. Nevin wasn't quite as quick, but he thought each play through. Each were excellent checkers, and they were both capable of 20-goal years. And I'd say 20 goals in the original six-team league would be worth 40 today.

On the left wing, we were led by Dickie Duff, a wonderful, hard-nosed player, a good scorer who always got the big goals when we needed them. He was always quick with the one-liners, always needling somebody. We used to fight daily in practice, for better or worse. Our feud lasted for years, and had its roots in Junior hockey, when I played for Marlboros and he was a St. Mike's Major. Sportswriter Red Burnett asked me about it, and my answer at the time was, "My wife Sallie started it all. Even when she was my girlfriend she kept telling me how cute Dickie was. She still thinks he's cute. Being the jealous type, I decided to muss the cute little kid up just to annoy Sallie. He doesn't muss without a fuss, so that's how it all began."

Frank Mahovlich was also on the left wing, and he was one of those guys who sometimes seemed as if he was in another world. And opposing teams probably wished he was. There was nobody better to watch when Frank had it in high gear and was all riled up. It was something to behold.

Bert Olmstead, the windmill, was a good playmaker who never left anything to chance. Everything was premeditated with him, he always had a plan. And he was as tough as they come, giving no quarter and not asking for any. He had a wonderful expression in the dressing room: "Sow the canary seed and see how it grows," meaning, tell a fib and see how it grows — a great lesson for children.

Bob Pulford was a disciple of Bert's and another student of the game. He never changed; always gave his all, day in and day out. He was never flashy, but he could do it all, reminding me of Teeder Kennedy.

Down the middle, Dave Keon was like a tiny whippet, small but quick. He was truly a great two-way player, and a friend. When he first arrived in training camp we knew he could skate, but we had no idea how focused he was. I loved how he would stick his jaw out — you were never certain whether he was mad, or if it was just the kind of determination you see in a dog that won't let go of a bone. Whenever we returned from a road trip, we would go to his house, and his wife, Lola, would make us a huge breakfast in the wee hours of the morning, while he and I rehashed the previous night's game.

Dave and I were neighbours in Scarborough, and we played a lot of golf together at the Scarborough Golf Club. He was a far superior player to me, probably because he practised more diligently. He was then, and has always remained, a very private person. And frugal — the only time I remember him treating himself to a luxury was when he bought an Aston Martin.

Billy Harris was always there, from childhood on up. He was a studious player, a quality he showed in all his pursuits. Billy and I shared an interest in jazz — there's a story told that he wouldn't sign his C Form unless the Leafs threw in some tickets to a Nat King Cole concert. On road trips we'd usually go off to hear someone perform, and Billy had a real eye for scouting out talent that no one had heard of yet. In Boston we'd go to Blinstrom's to hear Louis Armstrong — whom we were lucky enough to meet — and the Pink Panther for Peggy Lee.

It was always interesting to watch players and singers like these, because you could see that the ones who'd been around a while were always giving 100 per cent. That's how I tried to be on the ice. I approached every game as if it was the last one I'd ever play. I rarely had time for anything but the best.

Last but not least was Eddie Shack, the hustler from Sudbury, the late arrival who brought a whole new dimension to the team from 1960 onward. He'd grown up under some tough coaches, the worst being Phil Watson in New York. But Eddie was a born entertainer, and a kind and wonderful friend. Sometimes you wouldn't want to be on the ice at the same time as Eddie because he'd get into trouble with his mouth — he had a limitless inventory of four-letter words.

It took me some time to realize that he could neither read nor write. He was often teased about it, but I never paid much attention, until one occasion when we were sharing a hospital room. People would come in to get his autograph, and they'd want him to personalize it with a message like "Get Well" or "Good Luck." Shackie would hand the paper to me to fill in that part, then he'd take it back and just sign his name. What an obstacle it must have been for him throughout his life.

A vital part of our team was our physiotherapist, Carl Elieff. He came to the Leafs from an American college, and he'd set up an office on Parliament Street where the players went for treatments after practice. It became a great meeting spot, and Van Petroff, who catered many Baun family parties, would bring over beer and sandwiches. We called Elieff the real healer because he could work miracles on a charley horse or any kind of sprain. He also had a smile or joke to perk you up if injuries were getting you down. You could also tell him anything and be certain it wasn't going beyond the walls of his office. Everyone loved Carl and his wife, Lilly. Along with Dr. Jim Murray and his wife, Shirley, we considered them part of the team — much to Punch's chagrin.

Dr. Murray was considered the best stitcher in the league. On the road, when a player was cut he could wait until he got back to Toronto to be stitched up by Murray, and you can be sure that's what the player did. He was another confidant to the players, and he'd always take our side over management's. We were lucky in Toronto to have such people caring for us.

As the '60s began, it was also time for a bigger home for the growing Baun family. We were on the move before we'd even got a chance to check out that school across the street on Mason

Road! I fell in love with one house, as much for its location as for any other reason: it was just off the first fairway of Scarborough Golf Club.

I was a member there, thanks to a couple of former Leafs, Jimmy Thomson and Teeder Kennedy, who sponsored me. I was always sneaking over to the club to practice or play. It was the hey-day of Arnold Palmer, Gene Littler, Sam Snead, and Ben Hogan, and I followed their careers fanatically. The pro at Scarborough, Bob Gray, was considered one of the great short-iron players, and he was assisted by Phil Brownlee, who's remained another friend and fishing companion of mine. Phil was only five feet tall, and looked more like a jockey than a golfer. Everyone liked him, and some of the members helped him out so he could attend college in Houston. One year, Brownlee played in the Masters and was runner-up to Jack Nicklaus as top amateur.

Phil also shared my interest in cars, another expensive hobby. He would scout out the car he thought I should have each year, and these varied from Corvettes to a wide-track Pontiac Bonneville.

Meanwhile, the purchase of our new house at 24 Cromwell Road was running into complications. My father-in-law, Eric Krohn, was now in real estate, and he hadn't been able to sell the Mason Road house before we moved. I didn't know how I was going to carry two houses at the same time, so I went to my bank manager at the Toronto-Dominion Bank to see if he could extend my loan. The answer was "no go." When I showed up for work at my summer job at CKFH, I must have been visibly dejected or crestfallen, because Foster Hewitt's secretary asked me what was wrong. I told her the story, and she insisted on mentioning it to Foster. She knew he liked me, and thought he might be able to help. Sure enough, I was called in to Foster's office and told that arrange-ments had been made at the Royal Bank branch downstairs, and all I had to do was sign the papers. Needless to say, my strong opinions about the two banks were shaped by this experience.

Still, I've always gotten along well personally with Sam Payton (former COB of the TD bank).

While we moved in at Cromwell Road, Mr. Krohn saw a story in the paper, just before Christmas, about a couple whose house had been destroyed by fire. They had two children. I agreed with Sallie's father that it would be a nice idea, a real Christian gesture, to offer them the use of our old house for a month while they found other accommodations. A number of other individuals and organizations had helped in other ways, and the woman said at the time that "Things were so bleak after the fire, but now we can begin to plan again." I came to regret my largess after the family moved out, when I found out it would cost $6,000 — a hefty sum in 1960 — just to repair the damage they had done.

At the end of 1960 training camp, we'd added two new rookies: Bob Nevin from the Marlies, and Dave Keon from St. Mike's. We also had a new fifth defenceman, Larry Hillman, whom we'd picked up from Boston in the Intra-League Draft. He was only 23, but he was already entering his sixth season as a pro.

Punch put Nevin together with Frank Mahovlich and Red Kelly, and suddenly we had as good a first line as anyone in the league. We were a bit slow getting out of the starting gate, and in the first week of November, Punch sent Johnny Wilson and Pat Hannigan to the Rangers for Eddie Shack. When Shack arrived it was like adding a pinch of spice to the stew, but I'm sure there were times when Imlach sorely regretted making that trade.

Here's a typical story about Punch and Shackie. Punch was annoyed at Eddie for taunting Bob Pulford during practice. As the rest of us skated off the ice, Imlach told Shack to skate laps of the ice at Maple Leaf Gardens until he was told to stop. The coach trotted off to his office, forgetting all about poor Shackie, who continued to do as he was told, probably for several hours, fortunate to have the stamina to do so. It was enough to make the Maple Leaf Gardens employees dizzy. Not until Imlach walked back through the arena to get his car did he realize Eddie was still skating around in circles. Pretending he hadn't forgotten, Imlach huffed, "It's okay, Shackie, you can go home now."

Mahovlich and Kelly were a magical combination that season, and about halfway through the year it started to look as if Frank had a real shot at scoring 50 goals. Red Kelly got injured, and Frank's pace slowed down a bit, but by the beginning of February he'd become the first Leaf to score 40 goals in a season.

By now he was really under the microscope from the press and the fans, and if he didn't score they were all over him, calling him a bum. He skated with that big, effortless stride, and they'd complain he wasn't working hard enough. He got in a fight one night with Bill Gadsby of the Rangers, and the papers carried a picture of it. Frank got hate mail for weeks over that one.

Near the end of the season, on March 16, we were in Montreal. The Leafs and Canadiens were battling for first place, and each of us had a potential 50-goal scorer: Frank had 48 goals, and Boom Boom Geoffrion had 49. Frank couldn't buy a scoring chance that night, or in the other two games left in the regular season, and he ended up with 48. Boom Boom scored against us that night, and became the second player to reach 50 goals. (Rocket Richard was the first.) The Habs ended the season on a hot streak, and nudged us out of first place, 92 points to 90.

The next day, March 17, 1961, our third son, Brian Kelly, was born. But you didn't get to pause for a milestone like that in those days, and two nights later I was with the team in New York for our last game of the season. During a pile-up in front of the Leaf net, I fell directly onto Camille Henry's skate. In those days there was no guard on the tip of the blade, and some players kept their blade so sharp the end was like a dagger. The blade sliced into my throat, narrowly missing my jugular vein, and came out under my tongue.

I got up, skated to the bench, put a towel to my throat, and walked to the Madison Square Garden's hospital room under my own steam.

The MSG hospital was notorious among hockey players as a place to avoid if at all possible. It was a room, no more than eight feet by eight, with a 25-watt light bulb and a green shade. The doctor sat there throughout the game, playing gin rummy and smoking cigars, so that the air in the room was a blue fog of smoke. I was stitched up by the Rangers' team doctor, Kazuo Yanagisawa, a true character, who always wore a holster with a gun in it, then returned to the Leafs' dressing room. Trainer Bobby Haggert took one look at me and said, "I presume you're going to pack it in for the night?" Not me, I wanted to play again in the third period, and I did.

I remember going to the bench midway into the third period because I wasn't feeling very well. We had barely piled onto the bus to the airport when Harold Ballard noticed that I was gasping for air and unable to speak. Ballard and Bobby Haggert both realized how serious this could be. Tim Horton and King Clancy tried to rush me to the Polyclinic, which was fortunately just across the street. In the middle of the road I fell, pretty well unconscious. I couldn't breathe because my tongue was being pushed down my throat by the hemorrhaging. I was transferred from the Polyclinic to St. Clare's Hospital, where a doctor had to operate twice to drain the blood that had engorged my tongue. At least there was proper lighting and no cloud of smoke.

The doctors called it lacerations of the chin, and hematoma. This caused my mouth to swell under my tongue, forcing the tongue down my throat, and preventing me from breathing or talking. Dr. Yanagisawa insisted that this would never have happened had I obeyed doctor's orders and not gone back to play that night. While in hospital, I scribbled a note to Harold in which I told him I thought I was going to die. Ballard stayed behind in New York so he could fly home with me.

I was sent home and admitted immediately to Toronto East General Hospital, where Sallie and Brian were still patients. When mother, father, and baby were all released from hospital a few days later, the Leafs sent a car and driver to bring us home. The press were waiting by that car, and there was such a commotion as they asked me about my bandaged neck and the newborn baby in my arms that we drove off, leaving Sallie, who was in tears by now, sitting by the curb in the wheelchair!

I missed the first two playoff games against the Detroit Red Wings, but true to Punch's adage — "If they can walk, they can skate" — I was back in action a week later at the Olympia.

Trainer Bobby Haggert loves to recall another more pleasant anecdote about New York. My penchant for clothes was well known among my teammates. I came to Haggert and told him I had an opportunity to shop at the Izod golf shirt warehouse (this was long before warehouse outlets became so popular) and was glad to bring along my teammates. I asked Haggert for an extra equipment bag so we could "smuggle" our purchases home on the train. For his efforts, I would reward him with a free shirt.

Haggert was rendered speechless by the sight of a true clotheshorse in action. When I'd come upon a shirt or sweater I liked, I would never say, "I'll take that in blue, please." Instead, I'd say, "I'll take one in blue, one in yellow, one in green, one in red, one in pink, and one in black." The ultimate challenge for me was to hide them all from Sallie.

Mission accomplished, but the team decided to play a major prank on me. First, they removed every piece of clothing except for an item in size XXXL — which I'd joked was probably for sportswriter Red Burnett. When I looked in the bag, nothing else was left for me. Of course, the bill *was* sent to me and I took it with me to the Gardens so my teammates could pay me for their purchases. But none would own up to having bought anything. They kept up this front for some time, and eventually I was getting a little desperate — and short of money. I asked Punch to solve the problem, and he did. He announced that the players would be fined a very substantial sum if they did not pay up, and eventually they all did.

The Leafs had been expected to beat fourth-place Detroit in the 1961 semifinals. We'd finished 24 points ahead of them in the standings, and had posted a 7–2–5 record against the Wings in our fourteen regular-season games. We outlasted them, 3–2 in game one, as George Armstrong scored at 4:51 of the second overtime period. After that, we didn't even get a sniff. Detroit took the next four in a row, by scores of 4–2, 2–0, 4–1, and 3–2.

Meanwhile, in the other series, Chicago upset the first-place Canadiens. It wasn't as much of an upset as Detroit's win, because the Hawks and Habs had been evenly matched throughout the season.

A number of Leaf standouts were remembered when the league handed out its awards in 1961: Johnny Bower won the Vezina Trophy as top goaltender, Dave Keon was named rookie of the year — Bob Nevin was runner-up in the voting — and Red Kelly picked up his fourth Lady Byng Trophy. We placed two players on the First All-Star Team: Bower in goal and Mahovlich at left wing. Allan Stanley was again named to the Second Team as a defenceman.

But for me, it was disappointing not to win the Stanley Cup. I really thought we were ready that year, and I'm sure that with the proper handling we would have won it. It all comes back to the way Punch Imlach handled us. A true hockey grandmaster, a tactician like Anatoli Tarasov, probably would look at the talent on our roster, and compare it with our record and the number of Stanley Cups we won, and just laugh. With the players and resources we had at our disposal, no one should have been close to the Toronto Maple Leafs during that twelve-year span from 1955 to 1967. And so much of that, it seems to me, was Punch Imlach's inability to control his ego. The old saying goes that there's no *I* in "team," but there certainly was an *I* in Imlach.

There's a story about Punch that illustrates how he never really changed. In the late 1970s, Harold Ballard had brought him back to run the team, and as he was walking into the rink, he was greeted by Paul McNamara — who'd been a member of the Silver Seven and was now chairman of the board of Maple Leaf Gardens Ltd. McNamara suggested they get together for lunch some time and catch up on old times. Imlach replied, "I'm busy for the next six weeks." What a cruel and ungracious way to treat a man who'd helped him out of many a tight jam over the years.

When I look back on the Leaf teams I played on, we were far too slow in getting to the top, and success disappeared so quickly. I think we underachieved, and if a strategist like Toe Blake had been behind the bench, they'd be talking about the Toronto Maple Leafs the way they talk about the Montreal Canadiens of the 1950s and 1960s. If there'd been a coach who'd been able to keep the players in the right frame of mind, the way Toe did, there'd have been no limit.

I thought we were there in 1961, and I know Bert Olmstead thought we were there, too. He gave everybody shit after that season because he wanted to retire a champion, and we hadn't won anything yet.

CHAPTER 8

Winning

As THE 1961–62 SEASON APPROACHED, PUNCH IMLACH CHOSE TO stand pat, making no major changes to the Maple Leaf lineup. He had, however, been concerned about the lack of a reliable backup for Johnny Bower, who'd played 66 and 58 games over the last two seasons. So back in January he dealt Ed Chadwick to the Bruins for Don Simmons.

In June, Punch also dipped into the Intra-League Draft and came up with Al Arbour, whom the Chicago Black Hawks had given up on. Al became our spare defenceman when injuries caused Larry Hillman to miss most of the season.

We entered the season with a new sense of determination, losing only once in our first six games. I felt I had my defence moves down pat by now. When a hockey game is in progress, it looks like chaos. But so much of what we did was premeditated. In the six-team league, we played each of the other teams fourteen times. That gave ample opportunity to learn the other players' habits, strengths, and weaknesses. It certainly did not just happen: every move was premeditated.

We defencemen relied on our wingers to watch their checks. And if I missed the man I was trying to hit, I expected my defence partner to provide some backup. Carl and I had it worked out pretty well: one of us would stay a little in front of the other. I played on the right side, so if the puck carrier was coming down Carl's wing, I'd be about six feet to his right, and a little bit behind him. If the puck carrier was on my wing, Carl would move a bit to the left, and back me up. If the puck was coming down the middle, I moved forward and took him out, either straight up and down, or sometimes with my hip, like a cross-body block in football. With any luck, that would send the puck carrier airborne. I would say I learned to play this way from having played football.

The keys were timing and moving across the ice to meet the opposing forward at the correct angle. I would try and make it very difficult for the player to cut back, then I'd get out of the way. This also kept me in the play if I happened to miss him. To me, it boiled down to keeping centre ice away from the opposition, as well as trying to force the play, or the puck, to the weaker players.

By the New Year, I was being given some of the credit for the Leafs' surge. The headline over Red Burnett's column on January 5, 1962, read, "In the Most Improved Leaf Category, Bobby Baun Deserves a Big Mention." When asked my opinion on why I was playing better, I answered that my wife had had serious surgery, and I'd been somewhat preoccupied until she had been given a clean bill of health. I was also recovering from a broken big toe, so I wasn't in as much pain when I played. Finally, I said, I felt I'd always been a slow starter. Harold Ballard, who'd just become a partner in Maple Leaf Gardens — Stafford, Harold, and John Bassett had taken over the Gardens and the Leafs from the Silver Seven — gave me his endorsement: "Baun made the NHL through hard work and hard work is keeping him on the team."

Around Christmas, Red Kelly injured his knee, and he'd be out for a few weeks. Punch Imlach noticed that the Black Hawks had put Ed Litzenberger, a three-time 30-goal scorer, on waivers. We'd now added two members of last year's Stanley Cup–winning squad to our ranks.

Around this time another forward, Johnny MacMillan, had joined the team *and* moved in with my parents. Johnny was a fellow Westerner, hailing from Lethbridge, Alberta. He'd also played U.S. college hockey for the University of Denver, which made him a rarity in the NHL in those days. Johnny added a lot of speed to our lineup and he was a good team player.

We played hard throughout the season, and finished second to the Canadiens for the third year in a row. We met the New York Rangers in the first round of the playoffs, and won the first two games, 4–2 and 2–1. The Rangers took the next two at Madison Square Garden, 5–4 and 4–2. The star of game four was a twenty-year-old right winger who'd only just been called up from Junior A. His name was Rod Gilbert and he scored two goals against us that night.

Back in Toronto, Red Kelly took a pass from Frank Mahovlich at 4:23 of the second overtime period to win game five for us, 3–2. Gump Worsley stopped more than 50 shots in that game, and the crowd got up and gave him a standing ovation when it was over. Normally, the series would have moved to New York for the sixth game, but the turkeys who ran Madison Square Garden always booked the circus into their rink every April. I guess they just assumed the hockey team wasn't going to make the playoffs, and most years they were right. So we played game six in Toronto, and by that point the Rangers were just plain out of gas. Meanwhile our confidence had kicked into high gear, and we won in a 7–1 cakewalk.

We knew it was only a matter of time before we won that series with the Rangers, because our style of hockey was designed to wear down the opponents. Their lineup also had quite a few guys who were gun-shy. The breaking point came in that last game, and we just blew them away.

Meanwhile, the Black Hawks had lost the first two games of their playoff series against the Canadiens. But they came back to win the next four, and Glenn Hall put the icing on the cake by shutting out the Habs in game six. I'm sure the Hawks thought we were going to be a pushover in the finals. After all, they were the defending champs, and I think they expected us to be the same team that had caved in against Detroit the year before. But we *weren't* the same team — we'd grown up in the space of that one year, and we had no doubt in our minds that we were going to win.

Bobby Hull and I used to run at each other like two bull moose in rut. This was fine with me; I could stand anything as long as he didn't shoot the puck at my big toe or instep — that caused me more pain than anything else. I didn't mind blocking his shots, as long as he hit me on the body. I used to practice shot-blocking. As I'd learned from Harry Lumley, the key was to do it in such a way that I could give the goaltender something to see. But at the same time, you had to prevent the puck carrier from getting a decent angle to shoot from. I would always try and keep my body compact and go down on one knee. I tried to avoid sprawling across the ice, because if the puck carrier faked a shot I wanted to be able to get back to full stride in an instant. I also tried to bring the player in as close as possible before he let go of his shot, thereby cutting down his chance for success. When players started using the curved sticks, this became considerably harder, because the shot would rise so fast.

In game one against Chicago, we just kept getting Eric Nesterenko's goat. We succeeded in making him take a bunch of foolish penalties. This was a problem for the Black Hawks because Nesterenko was the Hawks' best checker, and coach Rudy Pilous was counting on him to neutralize our big gun, Frank Mahovlich. Punch played the hell out of Mahovlich, because he knew that if Nesterenko was on the ice, it meant Bobby Hull wasn't out there. The first two games were at Maple Leaf Gardens, giving Punch the advantage of the last line change, so we pretty much controlled the games, which we won, 4–1 and 3–2.

We went into Chicago for game three, and Glenn Hall just stoned us. We lost that one, 3–0, and the Hawks took the fourth game, 4–1, and even worse, Johnny Bower reinjured his groin. For game five, Punch had no choice but to play Don Simmons. Don hadn't played much that year — he'd only been in nine games all season — so we didn't take any chances. We opened it up all the way. Bob Pulford scored a hat trick, and the Big M chipped in a couple more, and we won, 8–4. We were ahead three games to two, but game six would be played in front of those crazy fans at Chicago Stadium.

Simmons was in the net for us, but because we were on the road we switched back to the close-checking style that was our calling card. After two periods, there was no score. We'd outshot the Black Hawks 27–12, but Glenn Hall wasn't letting anything get past him, and Don Simmons was doing a pretty good job of holding down the fort in our end. Something had to give, and at 8:56 of the third period, Bobby Hull scored to put Chicago ahead, 1–0. Well, the fans in the Stadium went wild. Debris poured down from the stands and onto the ice: beer cups, bottles, and even red ink. It took at least fifteen minutes before the ice was cleared and we were given the go-ahead to resume play.

Well, that delay just destroyed any momentum the Hawks might have built up, and at the same time it gave us time to catch our breath and regain our bearings. Frank Mahovlich carried the puck into the Chicago zone, and he noticed Bobby Nevin pulling up alongside him. He shovelled it over to Nevin, who instantly fired it past Glenn Hall at 10:29 of the third period. Toronto 1, Chicago 1.

About four minutes later, Eric Nesterenko was in the penalty box — again. On the power play, Tim Horton picked up the puck behind the Leafs' net, and broke out of the zone the way he did so well. He passed it to George Armstrong, who crossed the blue line and dished it back to Timmy. Meanwhile, Davey Keon was jostling around in front of the Chicago net, tying up Reggie Fleming and screening Glenn Hall so he couldn't see what was going on. Someone closed in on Horton and he looked for an open man. Dickie Duff was right there and he was looking at a wide-open net. Time of the goal, 14:14.

You could have heard a pin drop in the Chicago Stadium when Duff scored to put us ahead. We went into our defensive mode for the last five minutes, and I don't think they had a single scoring chance the rest of the way. The clock seemed to take forever to wind its way down to zero, and it was murder just sitting on the bench — Punch played Tim and Allan for the closing minutes. Finally the game ended, and the Toronto Maple Leafs had won their first Stanley Cup championship since Bill Barilko's memorable goal back in 1951.

When Bower, who was still injured, walked out onto the ice for the Cup presentation, the Chicago Stadium organist played "Old Soldiers Never Die." By then, the Chicago fans were graciously applauding us. Sportswriter Scott Young described the scene when we returned to the dressing room: "The Leafs waded around in sweaty equipment, yelling and shaking hands with one another, and drinking champagne out of the Stanley Cup."

Bert Olmstead, the "windmill," sat quietly in his chair. Of course, he'd been here before: this was his fifth Stanley Cup victory. He was shaking his head, as if he thought we could have done better. That image left an impression on me — and, I believe, all of us — for the rest of our lives. A reporter congratulated him, and Bert replied, "When you win the last game you play, you'll never go wrong." He was asked if this was really his last game. "I'm pretty sure it is," he said. He'd had enough, and he felt it was time to go home, back out West.

When Bert came to us from Montreal, he was disillusioned with the system. "Hockey players in those days were nothing but white slave labour," he says today. At the end of the 1958 season, the Habs had won their third Stanley Cup in a row. By this point, Bert had been named to the All-Star Team twice. He had also played on torn ligaments during the last game of the Stanley Cup finals. He wrote Frank Selke, Sr., asking for a $2,000 raise. Selke replied that Bert knew he hated corresponding by mail, that he would see him in the fall, and hoped he would have a good summer. Oh, and by the way, forget the raise, Bert.

At that point Bert wanted to retire and become a coach, but the Canadiens offered him every job under the sun *except* a coaching position. When they refused to accommodate him, he asked for a trade, specifically to Toronto. Instead, the Canadiens exposed him in the Intra-League Draft — and as luck would have it, the Leafs drafted him. We were a much better team because of him.

———— ●————

We didn't get much time to celebrate before we had to catch our flight back to Toronto, and most of us were too exhausted to really appreciate what we'd done. We arrived at the airport in Malton at 3:30 A.M., but the early hour hadn't deterred the crowd of 2,000 or so who greeted us as we stepped off the plane. That was only a taste of what was to come. I can't remember such excitement in the city of Toronto, before or since.

Mayor Nathan Phillips announced that a civic reception would be held to honour the team on Wednesday. No one, especially us Leafs, could have anticipated the crowds that would turn out on that balmy (72 degrees Fahrenheit) spring afternoon. The official estimate was that 50,000 people were waiting for us on or around the City Hall steps, while another 50,000 or more lined the parade of nineteen convertibles — led by the Queen's Own Rifles — up Bay Street. The ticker tape and confetti was thick as fog as the cars passed. Some compared the scene to Charles Lindbergh's reception in New York in the 1920s, and it was generally agreed that this was a bigger event than the Royal visit to Toronto back in 1939.

Eddie Shack danced the twist in his car during the many stops along the parade route. The police did their best, but it was clear they weren't prepared for such a large, frenzied crowd. Fifty children were separated from their parents that day. Each and every member of the team was mobbed as we alighted from our vehicles. Some of the players almost lost their watches as people tried to grab them off their wrists, and many did lose their handkerchiefs. I was almost choked by someone trying to steal my tie, and Brewer was just a bit nervous because his wallet contained a large amount of cash he'd drawn out for a trip to Florida he'd be taking later in the day. But not one of us was the least bit annoyed — except maybe for one policeman, who, when it was all over, was overheard muttering, "I wish now they'd lost that friggin' Cup."

Once we reached the steps of City Hall, the Mayor attempted to welcome and congratulate us. His task was rendered impossible by the raucous euphoric crowd. He finally moved the ceremonies indoors, taking us to the council chamber, where he presented us all — even management — with gold-plated City of Toronto cuff links. Captain George "The Chief" Armstrong had perhaps one of the best lines of the day when he said, "For once, the Indians came out on top!" Then we piled into the convertibles and sped off to Maple Leaf Gardens, where a buffet luncheon was waiting for us. Stafford Smythe took aside the Maple Leaf Gardens employees, thanked them for their help, and rewarded each of them with a bonus of an extra week's holiday, with pay.

Each of us was given time for family photographs with the Stanley Cup, and as my son, Brian, was our youngest, we put him inside the Cup's basin. Almost on cue, he peed in it. My father was much better behaved, dressed in a suit and tie, but when I saw his photo after, with mechanic's grease in his fingernails, I felt humble once again.

Over the summer, Smythe worked with Jack Amell, a jeweller and a member of the Silver Seven, to design a Stanley Cup ring.

Birks made the rings, and the Gardens would present one to each player, coach, trainers, and executive. It is a gold ring, centred by a silver maple leaf with a diamond in the middle. The words "Stanley Cup Champions" surround the leaf. On one shank is a Stanley Cup, with two more maple leaves to fill out the space at the top; on the other shank is the image of the new (as yet, then, incomplete) City Hall, with "Toronto" inscribed above, and again two leaves to balance things. Unlike many championship rings, this one is as distinguished and tasteful in the year 2000 as it was in 1962.

No matter what we Leaf players did from that day on, our lives would be changed forever. Torontonians are mad about hockey, and that made us their ultimate heroes. We'd won a place in their hearts above and beyond any other athletes in town, or for that matter from any other walk of life. Even now, nearly forty years later, most of us are still recognized almost everywhere we go in the city. But in Punch Imlach's esteem, we hadn't changed a bit. He was never one to savour the triumph, and as far as he was concerned it was merely the end of one season and time to prepare for the next. He would accept no less than a return to the winners' circle in 1963, and he didn't let up on us one iota.

The threat of a trade or demotion was always in the papers. The league was so small, and so competitive, that you always had to be ready to answer the question, "What have you done for me lately?" So what if Johnny Bower was runner-up for the Vezina Trophy? Why didn't he win it? Frank Mahovlich made the Second All-Star Team? Well, he was a First Team All-Star the year before — he must be slipping. Imlach used to hold these things over the players' heads all the time, gambling — and quite often correctly — that a player's desire to be a hockey player would exceed his desire to be paid a decent salary.

As the 1962 training camp began, Frank Mahovlich's contract

was up, and he thought he was in line for a substantial pay hike — after all, he'd scored 81 goals over the past two years, and he was now a key member of the Stanley Cup champions. He went into a meeting with the Leaf brass, and they offered him the usual $1,000 raise, and told him he could take it or leave it. Frank chose to leave it. He walked out of the hotel room, and walked out of training camp. He eventually returned, but he still didn't have a contract signed.

In those days, we used to play the All-Star Game just before the regular season began. A team of All-Stars from the rest of the league would play the Stanley Cup champions on their home rink. The night before the game there'd be a big banquet where they'd hand out the awards from the year before. All the league brass would be there, and of course there was an unlimited supply of refreshment. The Leafs still hadn't signed Frank, so Jim Norris walked up to Harold Ballard and offered to buy Mahovlich for a million dollars.

No one could believe it when it came out in the papers the next morning, and it seemed like it was all a publicity stunt, but Hawks GM Tommy Ivan showed up at the Gardens the next morning with a cheque for $1 million. And Norris's reaction when he found out the Leafs had reneged suggests it was no joke.

It seems the only man in Toronto who *didn't* know about the deal was Frank Mahovlich. Imlach called him in, put a contract in front of him — for the amount Frank had been asking for in the first place — and Frank signed, no questions asked. You can bet if he'd known what all the ruckus was about, the pot would have been sweetened a little bit more.

Every year during training camp, the Toronto Maple Leafs would head out on a barnstorming tour. We'd play a heavy schedule of exhibition games, mostly against minor-league competition. In the fall of 1963, we headed to Quebec City to play a game at the Colisée, and afterward we got into the beer. That's when Timmy

Horton decided to barricade the main intersection of the city with barrels of cement, which only he was strong enough to move. As a result, traffic was backed up for miles. When the police arrived, he tried to buy his way out of the mess! Because of his great strength, it took three policemen to wrestle him into a squad car.

Meanwhile, back at our hotel, Ron Stewart got it into his head to take over the switchboard. He started putting together these massive conference calls with Punch, the mayor of Quebec, and the players. What a night. The next morning there was a picture of Timmy, in his Clark Kent glasses, on the front page of the *Toronto Star*. We counted ourselves lucky that the tour wouldn't pass through Toronto — the press, and probably Timmy's wife, would have been all over us.

Our next stop was Saskatoon, and when we arrived I was invited to go duck hunting with Alf Pike. Alf was the coach of the team we were scheduled to play, the Los Angeles Blades, and he provided the equipment. All I needed was an excuse to get me out of the morning practice, and I thought I had that one covered. I went to Punch and asked him if it would be okay if I went to visit my grandmother, who lived nearby. Imlach gave me permission.

I thought I'd gotten away with the perfect crime, but some of the reporters got wind of what I was really up to, and they wrote it up. The next morning, Imlach was reading the paper over breakfast and he saw the headline, "Baun Goes Duck Hunting." He was so angry he spilled scalding-hot coffee in his lap. When I breezed into the hotel lobby with a dozen ducks under my arm, Punch was waiting for me and he promptly fined me a hundred bucks. George Gross's column the next day ran under the most memorable headline of my playing career: "Baun's 'Grandma' Goes Quack." Punch must have realized the humour of the situation, because he excused the whole team from practice two days later. The headline over Gross's column this time: "Bob Baun Goes Duck Hunting … Legally!"

After Saskatoon, it was on to Portland. We lost a game against the local team, the Buckaroos, and Punch slapped us with a midnight curfew. Carl Brewer, Billy Harris, and I headed off to the Kon Tiki Room for several rounds of mai tais. We spotted Imlach and King Clancy in the corner, so we made a point of bidding them good night at 11:55 P.M. We had to pass the pool on the way to our rooms, and we just couldn't resist — we dove into the hotel pool, fully clothed, me in my Harry Rosen's and $500 shoes, Carl Brewer in his Hawaiian underwear, and Billy Harris in his more conservative undergarments. Before we turned in, we knocked on George Armstrong and Johnny Bower's door and chatted with them awhile - - and the whole time our dripping-wet clothes were leaving huge puddles in the hotel corridor.

The management was furious, and they told Punch that some of his players had been in the pool and were dripping water all over the place. "Impossible," he insisted. "They all met their curfew." They told him he might want to check out the huge puddle outside Armstrong and Bower's room. He knocked on their door, and they insisted they'd been asleep and knew nothing about the water damage. Punch never did find out who the culprits were.

The last stop on the tour was Vancouver. About eight members of the team — myself included, of course — chartered a boat and went out for the day. Each of us consumed a fair quantity of liquor. When we returned, we attended a B.C. Lions football game. We got back to the hotel, and we knew that Stafford, Harold Ballard, and their friend Coley Hall would have arranged for some ladies of the night. So a bunch of us decided to break out the fire hose and spray it through the keyhole into the owners' suite. Four of us disguised ourselves by wearing pillowcases over our heads: Armstrong unwound the hose, Dick Duff took the middle, and Tim Horton and I positioned ourselves nearest the door. We prepared for the barrage of water, but it never came. Armstrong ran off and left us standing there looking like fools, with a limp hose pointed at the doorway.

I got off to a flying start in 1962–63, scoring three goals in my first five games, which exceeded my average of about a goal a year. At that point I was tied with Mahovlich for the team scoring lead. Fortunately for me, I didn't start entertaining any notions of earning a Mahovlich-size salary, because I'd only score one goal over the rest of the season. By November, the injury jinx had struck me yet again. It started as the flu, turned into pneumonia, and I lost ten pounds. But both the team and I would regain our momentum during the second half of the season.

My absence provided a chance for Kent Douglas, whom we'd acquired during the off-season, to get more ice time. Although Kent was a "rookie" — and he would win the 1963 Calder Trophy as rookie of the year — he was actually seven months older than me. He'd bounced around the minor leagues for a few years before landing a spot on the Springfield Indians of the American league. I remembered Kent from his days as a Junior in Kitchener, and he hadn't changed a bit. He had a hair-trigger temper that could explode at any time, combined with nerves of steel. As a result, you never knew what he'd do next.

One night Kent had his stick on Gordie Howe's throat and told him not to move. Gordie didn't even dare draw a breath. Kent had a stick that had to weigh ten ounces more than anyone else's, and he could pick the eye off a fly from anywhere. He had perfect balance, and he could shoot and pass the puck with the best of them. But he had a real weakness for the ladies — I think he had a pair of silk pyjamas in every city in the league! — and he also had trouble keeping his weight under control. He spent much of the time in a battle of wills with Punch Imlach — and I think Kent won.

The Baun billeting service was in full swing in 1962–63. My mom had taken in Rod Seiling, a forward from Kitchener who was playing for Neil McNeil — a Catholic high school that had taken over operation of the St. Michael's Junior team that year. Rod later told his second Mom, "I think you take these games more seriously than the players." That left no room for Johnny MacMillan, so he moved in with Sallie and me. As a result, I was totally neglected by my three sons while they waited on Johnny hand and foot.

Meanwhile, with a little help from his pal Keith Davey, Red Kelly had decided to seek election as a federal Member of Parliament for the Liberals. He ran, he won, and he managed to keep up both jobs at once. He would be re-elected in 1963, when his Tory opponent would be none other than Alan Eagleson.

There'd also been some talk about my entering politics, which emanated from my close connection to Keith Davey. When Keith was the national organizer for the Liberal Party, he'd given me an important job: keeping Lester B. Pearson, the prime minister, out of his hair during strategy meetings at the Royal York Hotel. I found Pearson to be a very interesting guy. Although he was a scholar, and I certainly wasn't, I was pleased to discover he was also a jock. He loved to talk hockey and baseball, and he was a great fan of the New York Yankees.

Toward the end of February 1963, the first-place Chicago Black Hawks started a downward slide that enabled us to grab top spot for the first time since 1948. The four playoff teams — Toronto, Chicago, Montreal, and Detroit — were in a virtual dead heat, as only five points separated us. It was the closest finish anyone could remember.

Frank Mahovlich was the only Leaf scorer among the league's top ten, and I'm sure it was tempting for our opponents to zero in on him and try to shut him — and our offence — down. And that's exactly what happened during the 1963 playoffs: Frank had no goals and only two assists to show for his efforts. But we won the Cup that year because we had such a tremendously balanced attack. In any given game, we could count on some combination of Kelly, Keon, Pulford, Armstrong, Duff, Nevin, Stewart, or Shack to step up and pull the trigger.

We drew the Montreal Canadiens in the semifinals, and

Bower really was the China Wall for us, recording a pair of shutouts and allowing only six goals in five games. The key to that series came in game three, when the Canadiens' legendary power-play unit was on the ice for five minutes and couldn't score. The fifth and final game was a study in contrasts, as Johnny Bower, our oldest player, backed us to a 5–0 shutout, while one of our youngest players, Dave Keon, scored twice.

I've said it many times: there has never been a rivalry in the National Hockey League to equal that of Toronto and Montreal. In the playoffs, we met them in seven series in nine years.

The Canadiens were loaded with great players, beginning with Jacques Plante in goal. Always an innovator, he was one of the first to move behind his net and play the puck. And of course he made the face mask a mandatory part of the goalie's equipment. It was a real pleasure when I got the chance to play on the same team as him in 1970–71 and 1971–72.

In front of Plante in the 1960s, Doug Harvey could change the pace of a game in a split second with one of his feather-light passes. He was an athlete's athlete: he had perfect eye-hand coordination, and was hardly ever caught out of position. He could also be mean as a polecat when the mood struck him. A couple of other Hab defencemen — Dollard St. Laurent and Tom Johnson — were good players, but not among my favourites.

Butch Bouchard was a big man, and in my first NHL game, I went through his legs and came out the other side — not because of a good move, just by chance!

Dickie Moore was another left winger, and he won the scoring championship twice. He drove most defencemen crazy, as you never knew what he was going to do next. He could run you over one minute, then fake you out and go around you the next. I'll never forget his blue eyes, which would redden as he grew more determined.

Most important of all, of course, were Henri Richard and Jean Béliveau. As I've already mentioned, I could really get under

Henri's skin with a verbal jab. When I first entered the league, Henri was centring a line with Moore on his left side and his older brother, Maurice, on the right wing. No weaknesses there! I rode the Rocket in from the blue line in one game and his look was so intense that it scared the shit out of me.

Jean Béliveau was a real long drink of water, and those tall players were forever getting their sticks or elbows in my face. Between Béliveau, Moore, and Olmstead, I must have taken at least a hundred stitches in my head. Once Jean set up in front of the net, it was tough to move him away; all you could see were arms and legs. His shot was hard and heavy, and goaltenders did not like the feel of it in their catching gloves.

Not to be forgotten in the pack is Bernie "Boom Boom" Geoffrion, who was noted for his quick and flashy shot, a very strong right winger.

Going into the City of Montreal was always a treat for me. I loved the French cooking, and the way the ladies always dressed to the nines. And trying to speak French was always fun. We enjoyed the fans and their enthusiasm — even though it was always directed against us — and the many people we met in the province. Quebec doesn't seem as welcoming to me as it used to be, and that's a real shame.

In the other semifinal series, Detroit spotted the Black Hawks to a 2–0 lead in games, but then they dropped the hammer. They outshot Chicago 93–38 in games three and four, and cruised to a 4–2 series win. The Red Wings had given us a bit more trouble than the Black Hawks during the regular season, but at this point we were on such a roll that I don't think it would have mattered whom we played.

The Leafs and Red Wings both played a similar, close-checking style, but you'd never have known it from the way game one opened. Dick Duff exploded for two goals in the first 68 seconds — it's still an NHL record for the fastest two goals from the start of a playoff game. Bob Nevin chipped in a pair of his own, and we won easily, 4–2. Two nights later, Ron Stewart was our big gun, beating Terry Sawchuk twice to lead us to another 4–2 victory.

We split a pair of tight games in Detroit. The Wings took game three 3–2, to which we responded with a 4–2 win in a game that was tied at 2 after two periods. Game five was played at Maple Leaf Gardens, and we limited the Wings to just five shots in the first twenty minutes. Meanwhile, with about two minutes to go, Davey Keon beat Sawchuk for a shorthanded goal. Alex Delvecchio tied it up shortly after the intermission, and it stayed 1–1 until 13:28 of the third frame, when Shackie scored what would be the Cup-winning goal. Victory still wasn't assured, though. At 19:00, Bob Pulford drew a penalty, and Sid Abel pulled Sawchuk out of the Detroit net for a sixth attacker. For the last minute, they had six skaters to our four. With Gordie Howe on top of Bower, Norm Ullman missed the empty net. We killed off the penalty, and Armstrong found Keon in the clear with five seconds on the clock and Davey cashed in for a short-handed, empty-net goal.

This time we'd won the Cup on home ice, and that was a special treat. It meant we didn't have to hurry to catch a plane, so we could celebrate even before we left the dressing room. We threw Stafford Smythe and Harold Ballard into the showers, fully clothed, while Punch wrote a message on the blackboard: "No Practice Tomorrow!"

The Cup win was somewhat of an anticlimax. There was another celebration, complete with ticker-tape parade, and another meeting on the steps of City Hall — this time, it was a new mayor, David Somerville, who gave us each yet another set of cuff links. But there was a sense of "been there, done that." The Toronto Maple Leaf board of directors decided not to order new Stanley Cup rings that year. Instead, they gave us a larger diamond for our 1962 rings!

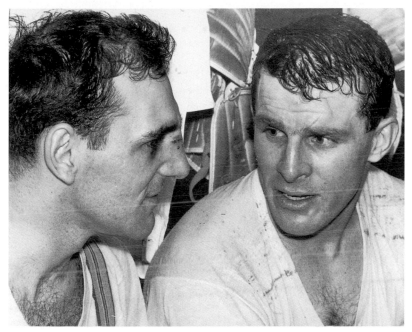

Carl Brewer was a smart hockey player and a smart man. Carl did more for hockey and hockey players of all ages than anyone I know. He was tenacious in going up against the NHL pension society.

Tim Horton (left), Eddie Shack, and I share a big meal.

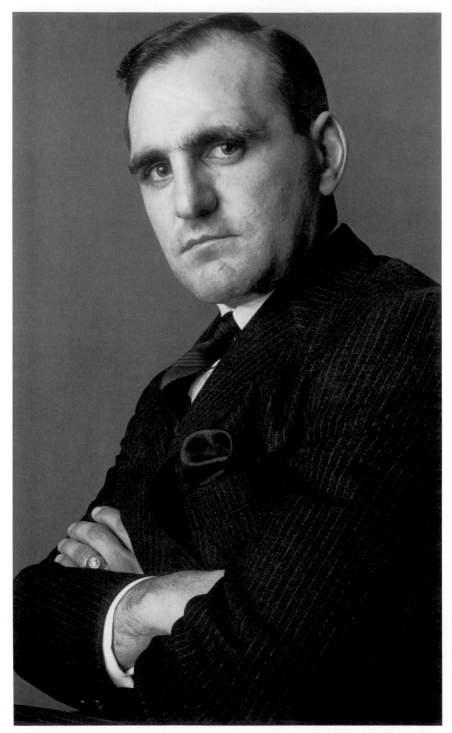

Posing for a 1965 Brut ad, which won the National Advertising Award for newspapers.

I played against some of the strongest players ever, including Bobby Hull and Gordie Howe, but I always found the "Pocket Rocket," Henri Richard, to be one of the toughest smaller players on the ice.

I always kept my head on defence, though it wasn't always easy when checking the likes of Bert Marshall.

Carl Brewer and I wrestle with Claude Larose (#23) in front of Johnny Bower.

Though Gordie Howe and I were enemies on the ice when I played against him, we became close friends. Here I try to take him out of the play behind Terry Sawchuk's net while Peter Stemkowski and referee Bill Friday look on.

Soon after we won the Cup in 1967, I moved on to the Oakland Seals. I have great memories of that team, the last Leaf team to win the Cup. Tim Horton (second row, third from right), for one, was a great friend.

Bobby Hull (#9) was a tough character. Here Lou Angotti tries to get my attention, but I've got my eyes set on Hull.

Frank Mahovlich (centre), Carl Brewer, and I became teammates once again with the Red Wings.

King Clancy presents me with the J.P. Bickell Award for 1971. This award is only given out every few years.

Gordie Howe presents me with a gift from Bruce Norris of the Detroit Red Wings.

At a newsstand in 1971 in my Pierre Cardin attire from Harry Rosen after winning the Golden Hanger Award as best dressed man of 1971.

Walking along the feed lot at the
farm in 1973. Life as a businessman
was often more difficult than life on
the Leaf blueline.

Ready to fish at the Caughnawana
Hunting and Fishing Camp in 1990.

With some NHL greats, including Norm Ullman (middle row, far left), Harry Pidhirny (on Ullman's right), Wally Stanowski (on Pidhirny's right), Peter Conacher (middle row, third from left), Ike Hildebrand (to my right), Andy Bathgate (back right), and Eddie Shack (front left) and Jackie Hamilton (front right).

Remembering some great times with our old friend Stanley. From back left (clockwise): Punch Imlach, Johnny Bower, me, Harold Ballard, King Clancy, Mike Walton, Red Kelly, Allan Stanley, and Ron Ellis. I still think we should have won even more Cups with the talent we had.

After the 1963 Cup win, the Leafs were delayed at La Guardia airport during some bad weather, and noticed future president Richard Nixon, who was also waiting for the weather to clear. The boys teased Eddie Shack, and dared him to go talk to Nixon. Eddie went up to Nixon and said, "How do you do, I'm Eddie Shack. I play for the Toronto Maple Leafs."

Nixon said, "Yes, I know who you are, and I know you won the Stanley Cup last year, and I recognize some of the rest of the guys."

Shack turned to Red Kelly and said, "By the way, Red, who the hell did you say this guy is, anyway?"

After the laughter stopped, we spent some time talking to the president.

In the summer I took Sallie to Augusta, Georgia, to play golf. Through Dick Duff, I had cultivated a friendship with prominent Torontonian Dick Horkins. Mr. Horkins took me to the Masters golf tournament in Augusta on several occasion, and we also visited his aunt, Adelaide, in the town of Aiken, South Carolina. You might not have heard of Aiken, but it's well known in the South, and until recently was the polo capital of the world. And many of the wealthier horse breeders, such as the Whitneys, the Vanderbilts, and Prince Charles, have farms there.

Aunt Adelaide was quite a character. She kept a "house," more of an estate, that required a full-time staff of four to maintain. After graduating from Radcliffe, Aunt Adelaide and a friend set up a soup kitchen in Boston that fed two thousand people a day.

While visiting with Aunt Adelaide, Sallie, who was pregnant, was more nauseous than usual. Huge pots of shrimp plants seemed to be the culprits, so Aunt Adelaide had them removed.

On the way home from Aunt Adelaide's, after having had a few drinks with dinner, I drove right through a stop sign and ran into a pickup truck carrying a load of firewood. The driver of the truck, a black man covered in blood, was in a panic. There was firewood everywhere. I was trying to help the driver wipe off the blood and Sallie was trying to calm him down when the police arrived. The police, noticing my out-of-state plates, asked where we had come from, and I told them we had been houseguests of Adelaide McLelland. The police called Aunt Adelaide while she was still at the dinner table — she was never to be disturbed at dinner. The chief of police suggested she might want to be interrupted; there had been an accident and her guests were involved.

Keep in mind that we were in the South, and it was a different era. The chief wanted to know if Aunt Adelaide wished to press charges against the black truck driver, and wanted to arrange repairs to our car.

Aunt Adelaide replied "no," she did not wish to press charges. She also offered to buy the driver's firewood. She bought firewood from that man every year for the rest of her life in Aiken.

Back in the hockey world, Punch must have been starting to hear criticism of his coaching ability, because he took the opportunity to defend himself in a newspaper column. "This is a sound hockey club," he wrote, "real champions, just the right blending of age and youth. The experts said my old players — Johnny Bower, Red Kelly and Allan Stanley — were over the hill. I knew [the experts] were wrong. They're a special breed of athlete."

He ended by saying, "I have tried to teach my men that you don't wait for things to happen; you go out and make them happen. That's what they did this season, and this is why we are the league and Stanley Cup champions."

CHAPTER 9

The Year of "The Goal"

DURING THE 1963–64 SEASON WE STARTED TO SEE SOME CRACKS forming in the Toronto Maple Leafs. My defence partner Carl Brewer was on a collision course with Punch Imlach, and one of the early battles came during training camp. Carl had been named a First Team All-Star the year before, and he was after a lot more money. Imlach balked, and Carl decided to hold out. He left training camp, enrolled at McMaster University, and announced he was trading NHL hockey for college football. Imlach got wind of this via the papers and sent King Clancy down the Queen Elizabeth Way to get Carl's name on a contract.

In an early-season game at the Montreal Forum, Bobby Pulford got into a fight with the Canadiens' rookie defenceman, Terry Harper, and the two of them were sent off to cool their jets. In those days NHL rinks only had one penalty box, and they skated into the box together and just kept right on fighting! Stafford Smythe saw this and immediately ordered the crew at Maple Leaf Gardens to build separate penalty boxes for the home and visiting teams.

It was my turn to stir things up on December 7, when we played the Chicago Black Hawks. I started a bench-clearing brawl. Reggie Fleming had pitchforked Eddie Shack, who fell to the ice in agony. Fleming went directly to the penalty box, where Stan Mikita was already sitting out some earlier infraction. The two of them tried to pull me into the penalty box, and I tried to pull both of them out. Both teams came pouring off their benches, and it was the worst donnybrook in hockey history. In Ross Brewitt's book *Clear the Track*, Mikita remembers spectators, including Dick Shatto of the Argonauts, coming down from the seats and getting into the melee. The NHL fined me $2,800 — the largest fine to that date. To put that fine into perspective, my salary that year was $12,500.

That Christmas, Sallie received a letter with an enclosure from Conn Smythe that I would like to reprint here, as it has remained a treasured possession:

Conn Smythe
Maple Leaf Gardens
Toronto
December 19th, 1963

Dear Mrs. Baun:
Your husband has filled me with very fine feeling, so that I can enjoy this Christmas. I was so proud to see him prove to everybody that he believed in "one for all and all for one," which is the spirit that has made the Maple Leaf name a proud one for more than thirty years.

I don't believe in dirty play, but in this day and age, men must stand up and be counted if the future is going to be safe for our children.

I would appreciate it if you would spend this money on something you were going to buy for the house, and as

I am not allowed to pay Bobby's fine, perhaps this will have a softening effect.

My best wishes to you and Bobby and your family for a lovely Christmas and a most happy and prosperous New Year.

Yours very truly,

Conn Smythe

Enclosed was a cheque for $2,800.

Despite this incident, I really wasn't a fighter. Everyone said I covered my own, but I was more like Timmy Horton — if I got in trouble, I'd usually try to get in close. I wasn't about to try to stand toe-to-toe with a good fighter like John Ferguson; I'd just get inside and hold on until they wore themselves out. But I wasn't what they'd call a cementhead.

On December 17, the team had just arrived in Montreal when I got word that our first daughter, whom we'd been planning to call Mary, had been born. A group of us celebrated in the Panorama Room at the Queen Elizabeth Hotel, and needless to say, the drinks were on me. I called Sallie in her hospital room and managed to convince her that, since I was in the province of Quebec, the baby should have a French name. Sallie isn't usually that easily swayed, but she agreed, and so Mary became Michelle.

I was seated on one side of the table with Horton and Dave Keon, while Frank Mahovlich was on the other side, bragging to Allan Stanley about how well he'd been playing. I was pretty full of myself, and for some reason I decided to start in on Frank, who was one of the more loyal husbands on the team. "If you think you're playing that well, can you tell me if you would cheat on your wife?"

Frank ignored me, so I resumed my conversation with Dave and Tim. But a few minutes later I turned toward Frank and asked the same question. "If you ask me that one more time," he replied,

"I'll hit you." I've never been one to back down from a challenge, so I repeated my question a third time. Frank was true to his word — he popped me! Stanley and Horton had to step in and break it up.

The next night we played the Canadiens, and the score was tied 3–3 going into the third period. We ended up losing the game, 7–3, and Punch was not the least bit pleased. "I don't know what you guys were doing last night," he said, "but you're all fined $100." Ever since, Michelle has been reminded that she is the $2,500 baby because that was close to the total of the fines, the phone calls, and the bar bill.

— ⬤ —

Hockey players always have some routine or ritual to help prepare themselves for a game. Mine began by heading down to the Gardens in the morning for a skate and a meeting. First we'd all doctor our skates and sticks. In Toronto, our sticks were as big and heavy as two-by-fours. Players today choose their own make and model of stick — in fact, they're often paid to endorse a particular brand — but when I played, the Maple Leafs dealt with one supplier, and the team would order the biggest, heaviest sticks. I guess they figured they'd last longer. But the players would all sneak into Tommy Naylor's room and sand down the blades and shave the handles, so that the sticks would be lighter and easier to grip. Our skates were sharpened for every game, and some of the guys would take the edge off by rubbing their stick on the blades.

On the morning of a game, I would always drive to the Gardens along the same route. I'd drop my car off to be washed, go to the meeting, and then go to Harry Barberian's to pick up my steak. I'd drive home, have my steak about one o'clock, then do some yard work or listen to music till about three. Then it was time to come inside and have a prairie dog — a nap. At four thirty I'd shave and shower, then drive back to the Gardens. For an eight o'clock game, we'd want to be at the rink by six.

By this time my stomach would be working overtime to digest the steak, baked potato, and salad I'd had for dinner. And now I must reveal the real reason for my nickname "The Boomer" — and it had nothing whatsoever to do with a booming shot. Before every game, I got nervous gas, and if I *didn't* have it before a game I knew I wasn't going to play well.

Everybody in the league ate a pre-game steak, and looking back I'd say we were crazy. After a dinner like that you'd feel like a walrus by the time you walked into the dressing room. Around this time I became one of the first Leafs to eat lighter meals. A lot of players today like to eat pasta on game day, but of course I was already getting enough of that at George's Spaghetti House, so I'd always sit down to a plate of scrambled eggs instead. On road trips, I used to drive Punch to distraction because I wouldn't eat a steak like the other players.

Whenever I was in New York, spending money was part of my ritual. And golf equipment was one of my favourite purchases. On one occasion I'd bought a new golf club, and I decided to try it out right there, in my hotel room on the twelfth floor of the Commodore Hotel. I closed the venetian blinds to make sure the golf ball didn't break the window. But when I hit the ball, it went through the blinds, out the window, and right down onto 42nd Street. Fortunately, it didn't hit anyone, because I'm sure it picked up a fair bit of speed as it fell.

I was with Carl Brewer the night he tasted his first beer, at the Pentagon Bar behind that same Commodore Hotel. Brewer was notorious for how quickly he could down his regular drink, a Coke. He'd literally gulp it down in one swallow. On this night, it was Allan Stanley's round, and he left the table for just a few minutes. When he returned, Carl's glass was already empty. He'd downed the beer as quickly as if it were a Coke, and I was the only one to witness the event.

In those days, the NHL selected All-Star Teams twice a year: at the midway point and at the end of the regular season. When the All-Star selections were released for the first half, I was pleased to find I'd been named to the Second Team. Unfortunately, a charley horse started acting up on me, and I missed the last week of January and all of February 1964. I didn't turn up on either of the post-season All-Star Teams.

There was one game I didn't miss, but I wish I could have. It was January 18, 1964, and we were hosting the Boston Bruins. They beat us 11–0, and it was perhaps the most embarrassing loss in the history of the Toronto Maple Leafs. As the game wore on, and it became clear we were getting shellacked, it seemed as if no one wanted to step on the ice. And once we were on, it was a race to get back on the bench. Allan and Tim took the worst of the beating; they were on the ice for six or seven goals. Carl and I fared a little better, as we were only on the ice for four goals.

Punch fined everybody $100, but the one we all felt badly for was Don Simmons. That number of pucks never got past our goalies in a practice, let alone a game. The funny thing is he went out the very next night and shut out the Black Hawks, 2–0. We all earned our $100 back with that win, and the flight home from Chicago was much more pleasant than the trip down.

That year a number of us were heavily invested in the stock market. There was one mining stock, Texas Gulf, that we all seemed to be into. At one point I was up thirty or forty thousand dollars — and in those days my salary was only $12,500, with a $5,000 bonus for making the playoffs. We were hardly paying any attention to hockey because we were too busy talking to our brokers. We had a phone glued to each ear and at times it seemed like one in our ass. Allan Stanley stayed in that Texas Gulf stock for the longest, and he made thousands of dollars from that investment.

If our minds were wandering, Punch Imlach delivered the wake-up call we needed on February 22, when he made a shocking, blockbuster trade. Dick Duff and Bob Nevin, both of whom were hometown favourites, were sent to the New York Rangers along with prospects Rod Seiling, Arnie Brown, and Bill Collins. In return, we got New York captain Andy Bathgate and Don McKenney. We were scheduled to play the Rangers that very night, and the deal was announced an hour and a half before game time. But that was Punch: he'd make a decision, pull the string, and it didn't matter who he hurt. He wouldn't bat an eye.

He sure shook up the team — we were not one bit pleased. I think everyone on that team would agree that Duff and Nevin should never have been let go. Dick had carried the team on his back during the lean years of the late '50s, and when it came to checking, Nevvie was the number-one right winger in the league. I didn't care what Andy could do, and Don McKenney was a nice guy, but he was nowhere near the calibre of the two players we'd lost.

With Duffy gone, I had no one to fight with during the practices. It worked out well for him in the end, though: just before Christmas 1964, he was traded to the Canadiens, where he went on to win four more Stanley Cups. He ended up with six championships to my four.

When McKenney and Bathgate arrived, they were greeted with stony silence. Andy came on quite gregariously, and Timmy Horton took it upon himself to welcome him to the Leafs: "Well, Alice, you can shut up and go sit down in the corner!"

The two ex-Rangers were very productive for us down the stretch, and the record book says that we posted a record of 9–4–2 after the trade. If the trade was what made the difference for us that year, then so be it — it was another of Punch's gambles and it paid off. I just don't think we should have made the trade.

The Leafs finished third, which set us up to play the Montreal Canadiens in the semifinals. The series opened at the Forum, and we split the first two games. In game two, I scored one of the goals in our 2–1 victory. I wasn't used to being the centre of attention, but I'd have to get used to it before the playoffs were over. The Habs took a 3–2 lead in games, but Johnny Bower slammed the door on them in games six and seven. First he shut them out, 3–0, then he made 38 saves en route to a 3–1 win. Dave Keon scored all three goals in game seven — one shorthanded, one even-strength, and one into an empty net.

The finals were a rematch of the 1963 series: Leafs versus Red Wings. Detroit had followed the same tough path to the finals as we had, falling behind 3–2 in their series against Chicago, then rebounding to win the last two. Even though we'd won our regular-season series quite handily — 8–3 with 3 ties — we had a sense this would be a tough series. There were a couple of veterans in the Detroit lineup, Bill Gadsby and Norm Ullman, who'd missed out on the Wings' glory years of the early 1950s, and we knew they were especially hungry for a championship. And of course the older guys like Gordie Howe, Terry Sawchuk, and Marcel Pronovost hadn't sipped champagne from the Cup since 1955.

The 1964 finals opened at Maple Leaf Gardens, and Detroit took a 2–1 lead into the second intermission of game one. Then, four minutes into the third period, George Armstrong got a power-play goal to tie the score. With less than a minute left in regulation time, Ullman was carrying the puck on a Detroit power play. He tried to pass to one of his wingers, but Bob Pulford intercepted the pass and beat Sawchuk for a shorthanded goal with only two seconds on the clock.

The Wings took the lead again in game two. This time it was 3–1 after two periods. Kelly got us back in the game about twelve minutes into the third period, and Gerry Ehman tied it with 43 seconds left, to send the game into overtime. We'd pushed our luck as far as it would go, however, and the Wings seemed to catch their second wind in the extra period, outshooting us 8–1. Near the 8-minute mark, Ullman passed to Howe, and Allan Stanley and Timmy Horton both locked in on Gordie. They prevented him from getting a decent shot away, but they'd left Larry Jeffrey in the clear on the other side of the goal crease, where he was perfectly positioned for the tip-in.

The next two games were at the Olympia, and whenever we played in Detroit during the playoffs we'd stay at the Dearborn Inn. It was outside the city, and the place was so quiet you could hear the grass grow. Punch thought he could keep an eagle eye on us that way, and there were few opportunities to get into mischief.

In game three, we let them get ahead 3–0 before we struggled back. Don McKenney scored the tying goal for us at 18:47 of the third period, but it wasn't enough. Less than a minute later, Howe found Alex Delvecchio, who beat Bower with only 17 seconds on the clock. Two nights later we fell behind *again*. This time it was 2–1, but Dave Keon, Andy Bathgate, and Frank Mahovlich scored a trio of unanswered goals to give us a 4–2 win and even up the series at two games each.

Back at the Gardens on April 21, Terry Sawchuk was as brilliant as ever, stopping 33 of 34 Toronto shots. We were never really in that game, and we lost 2–1. At that point, with the series returning to the Olympia for game six, it started to look as if the Cup was firmly within the Red Wings' grasp. How could anyone have guessed that the turning point for the Maple Leafs, and for Bob Baun in particular, would come in that game.

For once, we would open the scoring, and Bob Pulford got a shorthanded goal — I was in the penalty box — at 17:01 of the first period. We took that lead into the intermission, but Paul Henderson tied it about four minutes into the second period, and the Wings went ahead on Pit Martin's power-play goal — yup, that was me in the penalty box again! — at 10:56. Pully tied it with his second goal at 14:36, but Gordie put the Wings back in front about a minute and a half later. With about two minutes left in the second period, I assisted on Billy Harris's game-tying goal, and we went to the dressing rooms with a 3–3 tie.

During the third period, Detroit had the best chance to win the game. Bruce MacGregor hit the post about six minutes into the period. The Red Wings should have won it there and then, but somehow we got a reprieve. About seven and a half minutes into the period, I was killing a penalty to Carl Brewer, when I was struck on the right ankle by a shot by Gordie Howe that bounced off Larry Jeffrey's stick. It wasn't even a shot on goal — they were on the power play and he was just shooting it into our zone. I felt a sharp pain. Play was stopped at 7:42 of the third period. I skated two more shifts. At 12:35 I went into the corner very hard with Detroit's Andre Pronovost, and the injury to my right leg was aggravated further. The puck was frozen for a face-off in our zone, and in those days defencemen took all the face-offs in the defensive zone, so I lined up at the circle, and it was none other than Gordie staring back at me. I gave him a couple of winks to try and distract him, hoping he would do something nasty and draw a penalty, but no such luck. I won the draw, spun on my right leg, and tried to interfere with Gord's progress. That's when I heard something pop and my leg just caved in underneath me. There was, I'm told, 13:15 left on the clock.

I tried to get back up, but I couldn't. My teammates tried to help me to my feet, but it was no good. I was carried from the ice on a stretcher, which was definitely not a spot I liked to be in — especially in a game with so much at stake. I was examined by our team doctor, Jim Murray, and an orthopedic surgeon from Chicago by the name of Dr. Stromberg. They suggested taping and freezing it, determining that it was unlikely I would hurt it further. I agreed, because the adrenaline was running high and I just wanted to get back out on the ice and help my team — the sooner the better.

Red Kelly was later brought in with an injury. With only 16 seconds left in regulation time, he'd taken an elbow from Wings' defenceman Bill Gadsby, which sent him spinning to the ground. The ligaments in his knee were torn. He was injured too badly to return.

As the shot of anaesthetic took effect, I was able to put full weight on my right ankle, and I returned to the Leaf bench.

The overtime period began, and Allan and Tim were on the ice. It was time for a line change, and Punch was calling for Carl and Larry Hillman. I told Larry to stay put — I was going out on the ice.

The puck was in the Detroit end, and Junior Langlois fired it blindly up the boards. I was at the point position, and the puck was rolling a bit as it came to me. I didn't bother to stop it, I just slapped it toward the net. It fluttered like a Phil Niekro knuckle-ball, and it was headed straight at Gadsby, and it deflected off his stick, up and into the net behind Sawchuk. At 1:43 of overtime, I'd scored the game-winning goal.

I couldn't believe this was all happening — everything looked like it was in slow motion for me. Sawchuk would later claim he had it covered until it hit Gadsby's stick. I didn't really care how it went in; all I knew was that Detroit was not going to win the Cup that night and that we would have another shot at it back home.

Some years later, I would hear of a woman who had been about to go into labour that night, but she refused to be taken to hospital until the game was decided. As soon as I scored, the woman gave birth to a daughter, Heather Melvin. Coincidentally, Heather's first child was born on the same date!

When the game was over, the dressing room looked like a hospital ward, with Kelly and his leg taking up one bench and me and mine occupying another. But I've always found that everything hurts less when you're winning, and while the experts listed Kelly and me as doubtful starters in game seven, I knew better. When we arrived in Toronto, Kelly was transferred to East General Hospital, and Jim Murray tried to convince me to get the leg X-rayed. I refused. I was afraid they might find out something that I didn't want to know; besides, after the seventh game I'd have all summer to recover!

Dr. Murray suspected that I'd sustained a hairline fracture of the fibula, the outer bone in the lower leg. The rumour was that I'd broken my ankle, but if that had been the case I probably wouldn't have been able to stand up, as a broken ankle leaves your foot dangling uncontrollably. Murray assured me there would be no risk of injuring the leg more seriously — or damaging it permanently — if I played in game seven, as long as it was taped and frozen. That was all I needed to know. I was determined to play in that game, and as far as I was concerned Saturday night couldn't come quickly enough.

I couldn't settle down at home, and there were too many distractions anyway, so I drove to Ray Smela's farm, enjoyed the fresh country air, and stayed overnight. I spent the evening with my leg submerged in a bucket of ice water. On the day of the game I drove home for my traditional pre-game steak and nap, then it was down to the Gardens.

By the evening of the game, Kelly and I were in the Leafs dressing room at Maple Leaf Gardens, unbeknownst to the press or the Detroit Red Wings. We were pumped full of Novocaine and ready to play. Imlach had a bit of the showman in him, and he sent all the players out for the warm-up — all except for Kelly and me. The Leafs took to the ice to a great ovation, and it was only after the applause had died down that Punch called for Kelly to skate out. Another roar of approval from the crowd. Finally Punch sent me out, and the place went wild. Imlach knew that the crowd reaction would leave the Leafs energized and positive, while at the same time taking all the wind out of the Red Wings' sails.

Imlach wasn't certain that Red and I would last through the

entire game, so he dressed Al Arbour and Kent Douglas just in case. I remember thinking during the game that this was the worst handicap I had ever played under. I had the full use of the ankle and knee, but the part in between was braced and taped.

Three minutes into the game, Andy Bathgate closed in on Sawchuk and picked out the top corner on his short side. Much to Terry's disbelief, it went in. We sat on that lead for the rest of the period, and during the intermission Red and I took additional injections of Novocaine. The two of us took our regular shifts throughout the second period, which was scoreless, after which it was time for yet another injection.

In the third period, Dave Keon's shot just missed Sawchuk's catching glove, and we were ahead 2–0. When the siren sounded we'd won the game, 4–0, and won our third Stanley Cup in as many years. I'm proud to say I was named one of the three stars of the game.

Afterwards, Kelly and I were both in agony. Red was in such bad shape that they carried him out of the dressing room on a stretcher and took him back to hospital. But I wasn't about to miss a party, so I attended the one at the Smythes' home. Tommy Smythe, who was then in his teens, has a clear recollection of me sitting with my leg again in a bucket of ice water as the team whooped it up. From there I went to Bob Pulford's place, and we were still at it at six o'clock on Sunday morning.

The city gave another ticker-tape reception, but the weather was damp and dreary, and folks were getting a bit blasé by now, so only 5,000 fans greeted us along the parade route. I still hadn't had my leg X-rayed, but I thought it best not to attend the parade. I knew that the main bone in my leg wasn't broken, but there were no assurances beyond that, and I did not want to jeopardize it further. When I finally did get the leg looked at, I found out that I'd broken a small bone on the outside of my leg, just above the ankle.

The broken bone may have been a small one, but it still meant

I'd have to wear a full cast. You can imagine how much I loved lugging that thing around. After a few days, it was replaced with a lighter one, but it still weighed a ton compared to today's fibreglass casts. By June, I'd had enough of the heat and weight of the cast, to say nothing of the crutches, and I decided to take matters into my own hands. I was in a hotel room in Vancouver and I had a few free hours, so I soaked my leg in the bathtub until the cast came off. I have to admit my leg was pretty sore after that.

I've often been asked how I managed to play on a broken leg. Part of the answer is that I've always had an uncommonly high pain threshold. Pain specialists have studied me, and other athletes like me, to figure out why we can carry on after suffering injuries that would completely flatten others. I don't know what they learned, but I would suggest that a large part of it comes from my ability to put mind over matter, what Norman Vincent Peale called the power of positive thinking. When I'm in pain, I've always been able to just block it out.

Sports Illustrated lists "the goal" as the seventeenth best sports achievement in the twentieth century, and the Canadian edition lists it as the sixteenth.

I will say that I continue to be amazed at how this one incident has given me more mileage than any other in my entire life. The story of my goal in game six seems to have become one of those tales from Toronto's sports history that will never be forgotten. I know I'll never live it down. It was also sort of a turning point in my life. My life has followed many new and different courses over the years, but I've never reached as high a peak as I did that night in April 1964.

CHAPTER 10

Downfall of the Leafs

Y OU WOULD PROBABLY EXPECT THAT THE MEMBERS OF A THREE-time Stanley Cup championship team were just drowning in lucrative offers to trade in on that fame and achievement by promoting this event or endorsing that product. Well, there certainly were opportunities, but they always seemed to be filtered through Punch Imlach's office. It became just one more way for Punch to control the players: if you weren't in his good books, you didn't get the chances to earn extra money.

Marketing had always been an area that interested me, and I'd had experience with CKFH, Harry Rosen, and General Motors, for whom I'd already racked up years of sales experience — Dave Keon and I had worked at Alex Irvine Chevrolet in Scarborough, and before that I'd been with Harry Addison of Addison on Bay and Herb Kearney's Hearn Pontiac Buick.

I had my spies out there hunting out opportunities for me. One of them was Keith Davey, of course, and another was my new neighbour on Ruden Crescent in Don Mills, Morley Arnason. Morley was a fellow Saskatchewan native and an ardent hockey fan. Most important of all, he was an executive with the Ogilvy & Mather advertising firm.

Keith had made arrangements for me to visit Canadian troops in Germany during the 1964 off-season. At the same time, the principal sponsor of *Hockey Night In Canada*, Imperial Oil — makers of Esso gasoline — wanted a player to tour Canada with a special timing mechanism to test the speed of people's shots. Punch wanted the Germany trip to be sent George Armstrong's way, so I agreed, as long as I got the "Tiger in the Tank" promotion for Esso. I made a series of appearances with Murray Westgate of *Hockey Night in Canada*, starting in Toronto and then travelling to dealers across the country. It was during the Esso trip that I got sick of hobbling around on my cast, and took it off in Vancouver.

During the summer holidays, I chartered a large Chris Craft boat to cruise Georgian Bay, and we took along two other couples — the Bill Cawkers and the Warners, Lorraine and Joe. We set out from Keswick, Ontario, on the southern tip of Lake Simcoe, and followed the Trent-Severn waterway. I remember we encountered some terrible storms north of Parry Sound. During the night we could hear something banging so I ran up on deck in the nude and grabbed the boat rail. Because of my strength, it broke off and left me flat on the deck, naked and feeling useless. The weather did let up, however, and I got the chance to take part in my favourite training exercise, a ten-mile water ski on Georgian Bay.

That September, Sallie decided to give me a puppy for my birthday. I'd been completely in the dark about this, and when I was out late the night she brought the little sausage-dog home, Sallie just went to bed and put the puppy in my place. That was my introduction to Christy. The name would present a problem, because we'd decided if we had another daughter we'd call her Christine. Shortly afterward, we discovered that Sallie was pregnant again, and sure enough, we had a girl. (For Michelle's sake, and with three boys already in the family, we were hoping that there'd be another girl.) So we changed our plans and named our new daughter after one of our closest friends, Patti Giffin.

This summer, it was Timmy Horton's turn to help me get back into shape. We worked out together a lot, and I spent hours in my new pool — not just swimming underwater, but also flutter kicking and diving from the one-metre board. There was also Doug Cole's trampoline, and it helped build up strength in the leg.

In 1964, the Blue and White Investment Group was in full swing, demanding a greater and greater amount of our attention. For one thing, talk among the members about organizing a players' association was really getting serious. And we even found some time to discuss the stock trades around which the group had been founded in the first place. We'd been dabbling enthusiastically in the penny stock market, feeling it was quite harmless. But Charlie Burns, a Gardens director, got wind of some of our holdings, such as Texas Gulf, and decided to have a talk with me and lawyer Ray Smela. He spent about three hours with us, and basically explained the financial facts of life to us. He also sold our stock, netting each member a profit of about $10,000.

This fascination with the stock market had almost cost us the Stanley Cup in 1964. Our minds just weren't on hockey. And I know from experience that an athlete cannot afford to have too many concerns at one time. You really need a disciplined, focused mind to play a sport, and this was especially true for me, as a defenceman who depended heavily on his wits to get the job done.

Training camp was a time to put these distractions behind us. During those six weeks we prepared mentally, as well as physically, to play hockey. In past years, at least, this had been the case. Times were changing, and not for the better.

For some reason, the Toronto Maple Leafs always chose this time of year to negotiate player contracts. And, as the Imlach era wore on, this became a more and more frustrating aspect of the pre-season. In 1962, it had been Frank Mahovlich's turn to hold out. In 1963, Carl Brewer had walked out briefly. I was in the second year of a two-year contract, and I thought I'd ask Punch if I could renegotiate. He said no, so I resigned myself to having as good a year as I could, and strengthen my bargaining position.

As tough as Punch and the owners could be, you at least had the sense for many years that we were all working toward the same goal — to win the Stanley Cup. But it became quite clear during the fall of 1964 that we were losing sight of that shared vision. Imlach and Stafford Smythe had started to squabble, and their disagreements were being aired in the newspapers. When Imlach traded Duff and Nevin to the Rangers, he'd really driven a wedge into the team. Then we discovered that Punch had a lady friend he would see when we were out West for our pre-season games, and there was another one who'd sit behind the bench in New York. We lost a lot of respect for him, and it was never the same again. We also suspected that the heavy slate of exhibition games — as many as twenty — were bringing in enough cash on their own to pay the entire team's salaries, and we resented that because we were generating all this money.

To be fair to Punch, I don't think he was getting the big raises he felt he deserved as coach and general manager of such a successful hockey team. He started looking around for ways to turn a buck, and one thing he did was to buy into the Leafs' farm club in Rochester, along with his buddy Joe Crozier. It seemed to me that Punch was taking advantage of his position with the Leafs to pad Rochester's lineup with full-time minor leaguers. Guys like Larry Hillman and Al Arbour had originally been brought in to help the Maple Leafs, and now they were fixtures in Rochester. It was a game Punch played with Staff Smythe and Harold Ballard, shuffling around players who belonged to them as if they were his own. In 1965 he sent down Eddie Shack for two weeks to boost the gate receipts. In fact, Shackie never really left Toronto, because the Americans set up a deal to play their home games during that stretch at Maple Leaf Gardens. Eventually Imlach and Crozier realized quite a windfall when he sold the Americans to Vancouver for a million and a half dollars.

Smythe and Ballard were getting greedy, too. When I played my first game there, Maple Leaf Gardens seated 12,500. By the time I left in 1967, there were 15,500 seats. And the building hadn't gotten any bigger! Meanwhile, we started to hear stories about Smythe and Ballard having vast amounts of construction done at their cottages and charging it to Maple Leaf Gardens Ltd. The other directors should have known what was going on. After all, they were all lifelong friends. I should add that they were all very fine men who happened to be caught in a difficult situation. And when they realized their reputations were on the line, John Bassett pulled the plug on Stafford and Harold, and they all, except for Paul McNamara, resigned from the board.

Every fall, NHL president Clarence Campbell used to hold a meeting on behalf of the league's pension society. Most of the players used to sleep through it, but I was always sitting front row centre, raising my hand and asking questions. More often than not, Campbell would dismiss my queries with a curt "Sit down, Mr. Baun. What do *you* know about this?" This attitude, more than any other factor, is what I believe led to the formation of the NHL Players' Association.

The Blue and White Group were meeting even more frequently by now, and one of the more vocal participants was lawyer Alan Eagleson. He'd hear us air our grievances about Punch — the way he ran the practices, the contract negotiations, and the endorsement deals. He'd become privy to a lot of what hockey players were really thinking, and before we knew it he was starting to jockey for the position of top dog within the as-yet unborn players' association.

Eagleson was as tenacious as a bulldog. He also had the ability to surround himself with successful, solid people, be they hockey players, politicians, or businessmen. He was very active in the Progressive Conservative Party, and always made sure he introduced us to all the right politicians, like Ontario premier John Robarts, or his successor, Bill Davis. Of course, these introductions also served to help him build up his own alliances in both camps, as well as his own ego. The only man who seemed able to control Alan was Jim Blaney, who is my idea of a man's man and a lawyer's lawyer. He's also a wonderful friend.

Eagleson just happened to be in the right place at the right time. The whole world of hockey and hockey players was changing. We were tired of the way the establishment treated us, and we were ready to do something about it. Agents were just beginning to enter the picture, and with expansion in the works, player salaries were set to rise.

Alan's big opportunity came along in the person of Bobby Orr. Orr came from Parry Sound, Ontario, and had been signed by the Boston Bruins organization. He was playing Junior for the Oshawa Generals, and he needed an agent. Alan could not have found a higher-profile player on which to build an empire as a player agent. Orr is probably the Stan Musial of hockey, a super-nice person who lives and breathes hockey. A solid friendship was formed, only to unravel a decade later. In all the discussion and coverage of Eagleson and his manipulation of the NHLPA, no one has ever faulted Bobby Orr, nor should they. Through it all, he has remained a gentleman, and an honest one.

The writing seemed to be on the wall for expansion in 1967, although at this point we all had no concept of what that would really mean to hockey — or to us.

On the ice, it was as if there was a shadow over us between 1964 and 1966. For three years, the Toronto Maple Leafs had been a proud championship hockey team, and all we players really wanted to do was play some hockey, have a little fun, and get a pat on the back occasionally for our efforts. But the team's leadership had broken down, and their message wasn't coming through as clearly, if at all.

Every June, it seemed that Punch Imlach could be counted on to reach into the league's "discard pile," the Intra-League Draft, and draw a couple of aces. This year he picked up Dickie Moore, the ex-Canadien scoring star who'd been retired for a year, and goaltending legend Terry Sawchuk from Detroit.

Moore had a bad knee when he arrived — it was actually the reason he'd retired. I was hopeful that his arrival would be like the return of Bert Olmstead. He was a wonderful hockey talent, both in mind and body — he was tough, yet brainy. And just a little more volatile than Bert had been. Dickie was one of the best ever to play in the NHL; his record speaks for itself.

Timmy and I got along really well with Dickie. When we played against him, he was one of those players who gave you the puck, then took it back from you, just for fun. He was always doing this to Timmy, and then saying, "We got Tim!" I don't think there was anybody who had more fun, on or off the ice, than the three of us — we were probably the last of the great pranksters in the NHL. Dickie told us the story of how he'd tried to shave Junior Langlois, the same way we'd done with Timmy. Langlois hid in the train's washroom, so Dickie tried to smoke him out. Instead, the train car caught on fire!

Terry Sawchuk was a real loner who seldom socialized with the rest of us. But he was an amazing goalie. I'd been playing against him for eight years and knew what amazing hands he had — probably the best eye-hand coordination of any goalie I encountered. And what reflexes! He wouldn't practise when

Shackie was on the ice; instead he'd head for the corner or side of the rink — anywhere he could be out of the line of fire. It was interesting to watch Terry warm up. He would just stand like a mannequin or scarecrow between the pipes, and just wave his arms at the puck. All he wanted was to feel the puck hit his blocking or catching hand — he'd almost never move his body. Apparently he had a terrible drinking problem, but I never saw any evidence of that while I played with him — that's probably what he was doing when he was off by himself.

We hadn't been adding many rookies lately, but the Marlboros system was still cranking them out, and this year's model was a nineteen-year-old right winger by the name of Ron Ellis. There was also Peter Stemkowski, a centreman who would be called up from Rochester in the second half of the season. A few years later we would end up as teammates — and roommates — on the Detroit Red Wings.

By November, Frank Mahovlich had had enough of it all — Punch, the press, the boo birds. He was depressed and exhausted, and he checked himself into hospital for a month. Three of our top players — Andy Bathgate, Allan Stanley, and George Armstrong — lost big chunks of the season to injuries. Dickie Moore was nowhere near 100 per cent healthy that year, either, and he ended up retiring again when the season ended. Ironically, Red Kelly and I were among the most durable players on the team that year; neither one of us missed a game in 1964–65.

One bright spot that year was the play of our goaltenders — Bower and Sawchuk split the duties down the middle, and ended up sharing the Vezina Trophy. I had what I consider to be my best year personally: I played in all 70 games, had one of my best years offensively with 18 points, and rung up 160 penalty minutes. The fact that my contract was expiring must have been a good motivator.

We crawled across the finish line that year with a record of 30–26–14, good for fourth place and a spot in the semifinals against Montreal. The Habs defence shut us down in the first two games, which we lost, 3–2 and 3–1. We got an overtime goal from Dave Keon in game three, which gave us just enough momentum to beat the Canadiens again in game four, 4–2. But we lost the next two, 3–1 and 4–3. There would be no champagne this year.

NHL players had always been brainwashed to view their opponents as the enemy. Every game had been like a war, whether it was Montreal or Detroit or Chicago we were playing against. The back-to-back games, where you'd play a Saturday night game in Toronto and a Sunday evening in, for instance, Chicago, reinforced this idea. This was another attitude that would die during the 1960s. And the reason was, believe it or not, the introduction of hockey schools or hockey camps. We had the opportunity to meet and work with players from other teams, something we had never been allowed to do before, and discovered that they weren't such bad guys. We were finding out — and it's amazing how surprised we were to discover this — that those guys were human, too. It was a valuable lesson, one that would make it easier to finally get the NHLPA going.

The season had barely ended before Punch Imlach started cleaning house. On May 20, 1965, he sent Andy Bathgate, Billy Harris, and minor-leaguer Gary Jarrett to Detroit. In return we got Marcel Pronovost and a boatload of players who were soon ticketed for our farm clubs in Rochester, Victoria, or Tulsa: Larry Jeffrey, Aut Erickson, Ed Joyal, and Lowell MacDonald. Three weeks later, Ron Stewart was dealt to the Bruins. We got centre Orland Kurtenbach, plus Pat Stapleton — who would be snapped up by the Chicago Black Hawks the very next day in the Intra-League Draft — and Andy Hebenton, who'd play the entire season in Victoria.

Bower and Sawchuk were playing as well as ever, but as the 1965–66 season approached, they were nearing their forty-first and thirty-sixth birthdays, respectively. The question was how durable they would be. So in September, Punch traded a couple of minor leaguers to Springfield of the American league to get Bruce Gamble, and for the next couple of years we made use of three goalies. In fact there was one game, at the end of the '65–66 season, when Punch used all three goalies — Bower, Sawchuk, and Gamble each played a period. It was one of those showboat moves Punch would come up with once in a while, like putting a lineup of five defencemen on the ice.

In the fall of 1965, it was contract time again, and I asked for a raise of $10,000. Punch only offered $2,000. Those figures seem like pocket change in today's multimillion-dollar contract negotiations, but in those days a $2,000 annual raise was the norm, and a hike of ten grand was reserved for the Béliveaus, Howes, Hulls, and maybe the Mahovliches of the league. To Punch, such a request, coming from a defenceman, was unconscionable. By this time, Carl Brewer's contract was also up, and he'd grown disillusioned with the whole system.

Carl and I decided to become holdouts. The team went to New York for an exhibition game, and I elected to stay at home. The papers started reporting the inevitable trade rumours: I was supposedly going to New York, along with Shackie, in exchange for Bob Nevin and Vic Hadfield. Imlach was quoted as saying that the proposition "sounds interesting." You can bet that didn't help my confidence. While the Leafs were busy losing their next three exhibition games, I was enjoying a Thanksgiving weekend with my family — an unexpected, and unheard-of, pleasure for an NHL player.

In the end, it all worked out quite well for me. I got a raise of $8,000, and was reinstated just in time for the All-Star Game in Montreal, in which I'd been invited to play. As I said at the time, I had to give a little, but they gave a lot. Carl, on the other hand, decided that money wasn't the only issue after all. His morale had hit rock bottom, and he concluded that he didn't need the Toronto Maple Leafs. Just shy of his twenty-seventh birthday, he retired from hockey and enrolled at the University of Toronto.

Shortly after my contract dispute with Punch was resolved, I had meetings with player agent Bob Woolf in New York and Boston. I'd come a long way from comparing notes with Al MacNeil! Years later, Woolf would become notorious when he negotiated Derek Sanderson's deal with the Philadelphia Blazers of the World Hockey Association. At the time, it was the richest contract any hockey player had ever signed.

The year 1965 was one in which I'd have many awakenings. Some were pleasant and some were not. Shortly before Christmas of 1965, I heard about a young man in Toronto's Princess Margaret Hospital, which specializes in the treatment of cancer patients. He was apparently a big fan of mine and had asked to see me. I went in before Christmas and gave him my sweater as a present. I went back Christmas week to discover that he had died. I also learned that he'd asked to be buried in my sweater. This was a real shock. It made me fully aware of how short life can be. Sallie and I started to talk about moving our family away from the suburbs and into the country, to give them a better perspective on life.

As a result of Timmy Horton dragging me along to Norman Vincent Peale's church in New York, I had become a real follower of his advocacy of the power of positive thinking. I was also starting to combine this with psychocybernetics, which basically means to steer oneself in the right direction. We have many weak moments in our lives (in my case it could be wine, women, and song) and we need a strong base to give us the strength and confidence to go ahead, to do the right thing.

During the off-season I'd attended the General Motors management school. I went to Detroit, where I was part of a group of thirty-two men from all over the world: Taiwan, Brazil, South Africa, England, and Germany. There were two other Canadians as well, Brian Rowntree of Toronto and Ted Brooks of Calgary. It was a six-week course, and classes ran from 7 A.M. until 7 P.M. for six days a week. Each night I'd spend three or four hours studying. What a rude awakening for a hockey player — in all his endless workouts, Punch had never really encouraged us to exercise our brains! Many of my classmates had MBAs, and one was a university professor, and here I was, a Grade 10 dropout.

For the first three days, they pumped reams of information into our heads, then they tested us to see where we all ranked — and I was at the bottom of the list. I was embarrassed and deflated, and I wanted to go home. I phoned Sallie and told her of my plight, and she suggested that this was not a good time to give up. She convinced me to stick it out for a few more weeks. I stuck with it, and I was rewarded for my diligence: I ended up in the top five per cent of the class, and I was appointed back-up valedictorian to give the speech to the chairman of the board of General Motors, Mr. Estes.

By this time, after two Memorial Cups and three Stanley Cups, I was also finally coming to the conclusion that I really understood the game of hockey. My entire game plan was premeditated. In my mind's eye, I would try to picture ways of taking away from the opposing team's strengths and try to force them to resort to their weaknesses. And it boiled down to this: keep the ice directly in front of your net clear, and force the shooters to the side. The puck should never go in on your goaltender's short side. Johnny Bower was a master at keeping the ice in front of him clear: he would use his stick whenever a player tried to come across in front of the net. I must say that this understanding was helped considerably by playing with Allan Stanley and being coached by King Clancy. They were two masters of the defensive zone — I used to think either of them could have played in a rocking chair.

Unfortunately, I'd get few opportunities to really put my hockey knowledge into practice over the next few years. The departure of Carl Brewer left me without a steady defence partner and, just before Christmas 1965, I had trouble with my knee ligaments that kept me out till Valentine's Day. (Giving me another rare opportunity to spend Christmas with my family.) Combined with the friction between me and Punch, I found myself demoted to the fifth defence spot on the roster. Kent Douglas and Marcel Pronovost would form the second defence pair behind Horton and Stanley at first, and 1966–67, it was Pronovost and Larry Hillman.

The 1965–66 season was just as forgettable as the year before. We started out on the receiving end of back-to-back shutouts against Chicago and Detroit, and we'd be shut out twice more by the time we'd played 11 games. Over that stretch, we posted a record of 3–6–2. I didn't have to worry about being traded to New York — the Leafs were playing as badly as the Rangers ever did in that era! We finally found second gear, and we recovered well enough the rest of the way to finish in third place. Frank Mahovlich had his first 30-goal season in three years, and Shackie came back from his exile in Rochester to score 26 goals in 63 games. Johnny Bower's goals-against average, 2.25, was the best in the league, and left-winger Brit Selby was rookie of the year. But we weren't enough for the Montreal Canadiens, who swept us out of the semifinals in four games.

To me, the years from 1964 to 1966 represent lost opportunities, both on and off the ice. Even with the losses of Duff, Brewer, and Harris, our roster hadn't changed much from that of the three Stanley Cup years. And we'd added talented youngsters like Ron Ellis and Jim Pappin. But the turmoil of those years kept us out of the winners' circle. Part of the blame, as I've shown, belongs to the owners and Punch Imlach. But the players' focus had turned away from hockey, too, and that's partly because we Leafs were spending so much time trying to get the players' association off the ground. And with the aid of hindsight, it's possible to see that we were making mistakes on that front that would prevent us from realizing our goals for the association.

Alan Eagleson aggressively promoted himself as the leader of any new players' association. He'd really charmed us, but once he became executive director of the NHL Players' Association when it was founded in May 1967, he proved to be just as dictatorial as Imlach. And on one level, he was coming from the same mindset: that we were just a bunch of dumb hockey players who should let him do all the thinking. When you think of it, it didn't make sense to put a player agent in charge of the association. The NHLPA was supposed to represent all the players' interests, but how could Eagleson do that when he would naturally give preferential treatment to a Bobby Orr or one of his other clients? Bob Woolf, the agent I'd had some discussions with earlier, raised this very issue. Teams were refusing to even meet with him and some other agents; the agents asked the NHLPA to intervene, and they were told that it was every man for himself. In one case, the Rangers suggested that Clarence Campbell and Alan Eagleson act as arbitrators. The fact that an NHL boss would be so comfortable with Eagleson should have rung some alarm bells among the players.

Billy Harris and I later came to the realization that we players should have patterned our organization after the Major League Baseball Players' Association, which was reconfiguring itself into a very effective unit just as we were getting started. The ballplayers had brought in Marvin Miller from the steelworkers' union to act as their executive director. When he took over, the players' complaints had been about such trivia as the condition of the field or the size of the locker room. They had been more worried about getting paid for the extra eight games, when the schedule went from 154 games to 162, than they were about the fact that television revenues were growing by leaps and bounds and heading straight into the owners' pockets.

Player pensions were a major issue, and Miller felt they weren't being handled properly. As he put it in his book, "Every player, it seemed, knew of a former big leaguer who was out of the game, with nothing to show for a career of training, playing ball and travelling, except some memories." As many of the Blue and White Group were closer to retirement age than not, this was something we could relate to. Miller pointed out that, like the NHL's system, Major League Baseball's pension system was a "contributory plan," which meant that the players and owners each paid into it. But in the real world, employers were footing the full cost of pension plans, and that's what Miller instituted in baseball.

Another ingredient that baseball had, and which hockey lacked, was the presence of a man like Joe Cronin, the president of the American League. He'd been a player, as well as a manager and executive, and during negotiations for a pension increase he told the player representatives, "Remember, I'm one of the men you are negotiating a pension increase for!" He also made an excellent point when he said that "the players come and the players go, but the owners stay on forever." How right he was! Well, hockey didn't have a Joe Cronin, we had a Clarence Campbell, who just kept telling us how wonderful our pension plan was. This is the same man who was accused of running afoul of the law when he was fingered in the Sky Shops scandal.

Even though our situations were similar in the mid 1960s, the baseball players' association became a powerful voice for the players, while we paddled our own canoe. Marvin Miller had his players' best financial interests at heart, while Eagleson did what was good for him and his favourite high-profile clients. All the while we'd keep hearing about how the Team Canada Summit Series and the All-Star Games were pouring millions into this gold-plated pension fund, but when it came time to draw that pension, players of my generation, who founded the association, would be bitterly disappointed.

Of course, it was only after the fact that we discovered the inroads the baseball players were making. In 1967, lined up behind Alan Eagleson, we really thought we were onto something. Bob Pulford of the Leafs was elected as the first president of the NHLPA, in large part because Toronto was the association's base of operations. Pully would get tremendous heat from Punch Imlach, who was determined to hang tough. He'd lose the "A," which signified he was an alternate captain, from his sweater. The management of the other clubs was making it just as difficult for their teams' player representatives.

The story of the veterans' fight to get to the bottom of the pension mess has been well documented in books like *Net Worth* and *Game Misconduct*. But the fight isn't over yet. As bad as Eagleson was, Bob Goodenow has not achieved much for the old-timers. And the NHLPA really is in a position to help us: today's NHLPA rakes in millions from licensing the players' names and images for hockey cards, product endorsements, television shows, sweaters, and tournaments like the World Cup. The NHLPA and the current NHL players should be ashamed at what the players of my generation — and the players who tried to get the NHLPA up and running in 1957 — are getting for a pension. Johnny Bower's contribution to hockey is worth far more than $6,000 a year.

CHAPTER 11

A Last Drink from the Cup

As the 1966–67 season opened, they were starting to call the Toronto Maple Leafs the "Over the Hill Gang." Here's a look at our regulars from that year, along with their ages on opening day:

GOALIES
Johnny Bower, 41
Terry Sawchuk, 36

DEFENCEMEN
Allan Stanley, 40
Tim Horton, 36
Marcel Pronovost, 36
Bob Baun, 30
Kent Douglas, 30

FORWARDS
Red Kelly, 39
George Armstrong, 36
Bob Pulford, 30
Eddie Shack, 29
Frank Mahovlich, 28
Jim Pappin, 27
Larry Jeffrey, 26
Dave Keon, 26
Brian Conacher, 25
Peter Stemkowski, 23
Ron Ellis, 21

And although he was the youngest, Ellis was no greenhorn: at twenty-one he already had two full NHL seasons under his belt.

Reporters were picking us to finish as low as fifth, but I didn't share their pessimism. I've always felt that the great team players, the ones with the greatest pride in their jobs and respect for the game, were the veterans.

This year it was Frank Mahovlich's turn to hold out, and he didn't join the team until the regular season was three games old. There was also the usual rash of injuries that we always suffered in training camp because ours was so tough (I broke my nose during the pre-season that year), so for the first couple of weeks there you were more likely to find a John Brenneman, Wayne Carleton, Bruce Gamble, or Larry Hillman in the lineup than Mahovlich, Pulford, Ellis, Bower, or Baun. But it didn't seem to matter who was in or out of the lineup; we were off to a flying start. Through October and November, we battled Chicago and New York — who were surprising everyone — for first place. Just when things couldn't be better for the Over the Hill Gang, Sawchuk's back flared up after a 6–3 loss to the Canadiens, and he would be sidelined for two months.

A few days later, we were in Detroit, and we were behind 3–1 with about three minutes to go. Punch decided to pull Bower and go with six skaters for the full three minutes. It's either a miracle — or a prime example of the Leafs defence in action — that the Red Wings only scored one goal during that time. Bower hurt his shoulder in that game, so we called up a kid from Rochester, Gary "Suitcase" Smith. He played for us in a game on December 21 at the Forum. It was about five minutes into the game, and Montreal's tough guy, John Ferguson, was dealing out his usual brand of mayhem. Smith started heckling Fergie from the bench, so Punch walked up behind him and said, "You want him, go get him," and put Smith into the game. At the 13-minute mark, he made a glove save, looked up the ice, and saw a clear path to the

Canadiens goal. So he just started skating down the ice like there was no tomorrow. He got past the blue line, put the puck on the ice, and started stickhandling. He got a little past centre ice, and J.C. Tremblay knocked him into next week. We lost the game, 6–2, Suitcase Smith got sent down to Victoria the next day, and the NHL eventually made a rule that the goalie couldn't skate past centre ice.

As Canada's Centennial year began, the Leafs and Canadiens were third and fourth in the NHL standings. The All-Star Game was being played at mid-season for the first time ever in 1966–67, and the Leafs had been playing well heading into the break, but the Black Hawks and Rangers were on fire and had opened up a lead on us. The Habs, meanwhile, were hovering around the .500 mark after an early slump.

Just before the All-Star Game, we lost 4–0 to the Chicago Black Hawks. We didn't know it at the time, but we were about to go nearly a month without a win. Right after the All-Star Game, we lost back-to-back games against Detroit, by a combined score of 11–6. Punch responded by sending Jim Pappin to the minors. The Bruins beat us, then the Canadiens — who beat us at the Gardens for the first time that season. In back-to-back games against the Black Hawks, we were shellacked both times, 5–2 and 5–1. In the first game, Bobby Hull blasted a slap shot off the toe of my skate, and I briefly joined Terry Sawchuk, Red Kelly, and Johnny Bower on the sidelines.

We'd lost seven in a row by February 1, when we went into Montreal. Kelly, Bower, and I were back in the lineup, and I opened the scoring. But if we thought we'd seen the light at the end of the tunnel, it was the headlight of an express train. Montreal pasted us 7–1, and the streak was up to eight losses. We were better against the Rangers — we only lost 4–1. The Leafs had not only lost nine in a row, we'd managed to lose against every team in the league in the process. On February 8 we had Detroit at home, and we lost 5–2 to them. Nothing Punch tried — and he was all over the place, playing Timmy Horton on right wing, going with four lines instead of three — seemed to work. And now we were in fifth place.

Something had to give, and on Saturday, February 11, we finally got a point when we tied Chicago, 4–4. The next night we went into Boston and beat them, 2–1, and on Wednesday, Bower shut out the New York Rangers, 6–0. Just when we thought things couldn't get any weirder, Punch Imlach saw one of the team doctors the morning of our next game, complaining that he wasn't feeling well. The doctor took one look at him and diagnosed him as suffering from exhaustion. Although Imlach protested, he was admitted to hospital immediately.

That night, Saturday, February 18, King Clancy took over behind the Leaf bench, and we beat the Boston Bruins, 5–3. The win put us back into fourth place, back into the playoff race, and just two points behind the Canadiens, who were still ambling along around the .500 mark. Four nights later we faced the Canadiens, and beat them, 5–2. That weekend we beat Detroit back-to-back, and as suddenly as it had begun, we were now the owners of a six-game winning streak.

Now we were back to having fun! King was laughing, cracking jokes, patting us on the back. He always said, "You can slide further on shit than you can on sandpaper," and we were living proof. His strategies didn't make much more sense than Punch's — at one point he had a line with three centres: Pulford, Keon, and Stemkowski — but he was doing something right because we only lost once during that ten-game session where he was behind the bench.

On Sunday, March 12, Punch rejoined us for an afternoon game in Chicago, and we proceeded to lose, 5–0. It had nothing to do with Punch. After the run we'd had, it was only natural that there'd be a letdown. With nine games left to play, the Black

Hawks had clinched first place in front of a national CBS television audience. While they celebrated, we were glad to be back in the playoff hunt. And there was a real dogfight for second through fourth place at this point in the season: New York had 65 points, we were in third with 63, and Montreal had 60.

Over the next three weeks, it was Montreal's turn to switch on the afterburners. They finished the season on an eleven-game unbeaten streak to claim second place. We closed with a couple of decisive wins, 5–1 over the Rangers and 5–2 over Boston, to maintain our hold on third. The New Yorkers had slumped a bit down the stretch, and came in fourth.

After Sunday night's game against Boston, Punch flew us to Trenton, Ontario, where we got on a bus for Peterborough. We'd remain there until it was time to fly to Chicago for Thursday's playoff opener. It was as if we were back in training camp. I guess Punch didn't want us to leave our game in the bars on Rush Street.

By this point, I wasn't playing much, a fact I wasn't very happy about. I figured that at the age of thirty I was still in my prime. But as far as Punch was concerned, I'd become one of the black aces. After one of the last practices in Peterborough, I stayed out to do more stops and starts after everyone else had left the ice. Punch was watching with a bunch of reporters, and he made a smart-assed remark that didn't go over very well with me. So I went right up to him and told him to stick the team right up his ass. It probably wasn't a very clever move on my part, and I'm sure it came back to haunt me. The NHL would add six expansion teams in 1967–68, and when the Toronto Maple Leafs drew up their list of players to be made available in the expansion draft, my name was on it.

We opened the playoffs in Chicago on Thursday, April 6, 1967. In honour of Canada's centennial year, the Toronto Maple Leafs were wearing newly designed hockey sweaters that featured a modernized maple leaf similar to the one on the new Canadian flag. Prior to game one, the experts couldn't be blamed for picking Chicago to beat us. They seemed to have it all in 1966–67: an offence that had scored an NHL-record 264 goals and a Vezina-winning goaltending tandem of Denis DeJordy and Glenn Hall. Our top scorer, Davey Keon, was twelfth in the league. Five of the players ahead of him in the scoring race were Black Hawks. And they'd won the regular-season series with us, 8–4 with a couple of ties. We concluded that we weren't going to outgun them; the key would be to get tough with Stan Mikita's line.

In game one, we got *too* tough, and we were focusing more on hitting than on checking and playing our game. We lost that one 5–2. I'd been paired with Horton in that game, but Punch decided to bench me for Sunday's game. Immediately after the game we were on the plane to Toronto for more practices. Despite all the flying around and skating, we were in better shape than the Black Hawks for game two, and the Keon-Armstrong line powered us to a 3–1 win.

The crazy thing about this series was that the Wirtzes, the owners of the Black Hawks, had booked the Ice Capades into the Chicago Stadium at the same time as our playoff series. So on the nights there wasn't a game, there was an ice show. The owners knew when the playoffs were, and they knew their team was good enough to make the playoffs, so I can only guess that they didn't care. It was the same story in New York with the circus every April. The league seemed to be easily split in those days between three clubs that were committed to hockey — Detroit, Toronto, and Montreal — and three that just didn't give a fig — Boston, New York, and Chicago. The attitude made its way down to the players, too. The Red Wings, Leafs, and Canadiens mostly owned homes in the town they played in, and were raising families or going to university, while the Rangers, Bruins, and Black Hawks were living the same gypsy lifestyle I'd seen in the minor leagues.

Back in Toronto, in the pre-game warm-up for game three at

the Gardens, Bobby Hull ripped a slap shot that rose up, over the glass, and into Harold Ballard's bunker that was built into the end of the rink. The puck smacked Harold right on the nose, breaking his glasses and blackening his eyes. Ballard would later try to get a photo with Bobby, but Hawks coach Billy Reay put the kibosh on that idea. In game three, Terry Sawchuk stopped more than his share of those slap shots, making thirty-five saves in a 3–1 Leaf win. It was the young pups — Ellis, Walton, Pappin, and Stemkowski — whose names were all over the score sheet.

Game four was a 2–2 tie after two periods, but ex-Leaf Eric Nesterenko beat Sawchuk early in the third, and Bobby Hull got an insurance goal. Mike Walton put us back in the game with a little over two minutes left, and Punch pulled out all the stops, yanking Sawchuk and playing a lineup of Mahovlich, Keon, Ellis, Pappin, Pulford, and Hillman. We kept the pressure on Denis Dejordy, but we just couldn't get the tying goal. The final score was Chicago 4, Toronto 3.

The series returned to Chicago Stadium for the fifth game, and Sawchuk had run out of gas. Johnny Bower got the start. It was a Saturday afternoon game, and it was unusually warm inside the Stadium. Both teams looked sluggish early on, but Walton put us ahead, 1–0. At the 9-minute mark, we were playing four on four, and Bower left his net to clear the puck. But he didn't put enough on it and it headed straight for the stick of Pierre Pilote, who handed it to Lou Angotti, who had a wide-open net to shoot at. John suddenly looked shaky, and a minute later he gave up a rebound that Bobby Hull knocked in just under the crossbar. Chicago 2, Toronto 1.

Punch looked at Sawchuk, who said he'd rather wait till the start of the second period to go in. A few minutes later, Chicago's Bill Hay took a hooking penalty, and Mahovlich tipped in a Keon pass on the power play. We went into the intermission with a 2–2 tie.

During the intermission, Bower admitted he just didn't have

it that day, and Sawchuk took over. About three minutes into the second period, Chicago was on the power play, and a Hull slap shot caught Sawchuk on the shoulder and dropped him to the ice. Terry didn't wear a lot of padding under his jersey — few goalies did. As Sawchuk lay on the ice, the Hawks could hardly contain themselves. You could just see how badly they were hoping that Bower would have to return to the game. But all they did was get Sawchuk properly pissed off. For the next two periods the Leaf net was like a shooting gallery as the Hawks tried to knock Terry out of the game. He faced 37 shots over the next two periods, and stopped every one of them. Meanwhile, Stemkowski and Pappin each beat Dejordy in the third period and we won, 4–2.

When we next saw the Hawks, three nights later at Maple Leaf Gardens, you could see that the wind had been taken out of their sails. Sawchuk turned in another stunning performance, stopping 34 of 35 shots, and we won 3–1. But the Leafs were already think-ing about the Montreal Canadiens, our opponents in the finals, who'd made easy work of the New York Rangers, sweeping them in four games.

Heading into the finals, the Canadiens were full of confidence. They'd just gone fifteen games without a loss, and the word was out that they'd even reserved a spot for the Stanley Cup in the Quebec pavilion at Expo 67. But Punch Imlach was a master at pushing people's buttons, and this year he zeroed in on Rogatien Vachon, the Canadiens' twenty-one-year-old rookie goaltender. "There is no way that they can beat us with a Junior B goaltender," Punch said. He dismissed the Habs' opposition during their unbeaten streak as a bunch of "peashooters."

It looked like Punch might have to eat his words. Sawchuk didn't look like himself in game one. He gave up five goals in the first 45 minutes and Johnny Bower had to go in and mop up for him. The game was hopeless enough that Imlach actually gave me some ice time in the last fifteen minutes! We lost that one 6–2.

Bower looked better than Sawchuk in the workout on Saturday morning, so Punch started him in game two. Playing his hunch paid off for Imlach, as John stopped everything thrown his way, even though the Habs were crashing the crease at every opportunity. Instead of intimidating Bower, they just got him angry. Meanwhile, Stemkowski and Walton scored power-play goals — which were a rare commodity on the Toronto Maple Leafs, because we almost never practised the power play — and we won 3–0.

Game three went back and forth, and we were tied 2–2 after the second period. There was no score in the third period, or in the first overtime session. Finally, at 8:26 of the second overtime, Bob Pulford was in heavy traffic in front of the Habs' net and redirected Jim Pappin's shot into the net to break the deadlock. Bower had stopped 60 shots that night, while Vachon saved 51. That performance prompted Imlach to promote Vachon to Junior A status.

Bower was supposed to start game four, but during the pre-game warmup he pulled a groin muscle and Sawchuk had to play. In the middle of the first period, Ralph Backstrom and Jean Béliveau scored within forty seconds of each other, and the Habs took a 2–0 lead into the first intermission. In the second period, Punch put me into the game in Allan Stanley's place, and he put Shack in the game to try to get something going. By the middle of the second, we'd made a game of it — the score was 3–2 for Montreal — but that was all we had in the tank. Montreal scored three unanswered goals to leave with a 6–2 win. The series was tied at two games each.

In Montreal, Sawchuk got a telegram from a guy in Newfoundland who wanted to know how much he'd been bribed to throw game four. Feeling like he had that much more to prove, he went out and stood on his head in game five. Léon Rochefort waved at a pass from my old sparring partner, Dick Duff, and scored a fluky goal to put the Canadiens ahead, 1–0. Terry slammed the door on the Habs the rest of the way, stopping 37 of 38 shots. The puck was in our end most of the time, but the Canadiens were uncharacteristically making mistakes, and we capitalized, building up a 4–1 lead after two periods. Toe Blake yanked Vachon and replaced him with Gump Worsley for the third period, and he shut us down. But we managed to force the Habs to play dump-and-chase hockey, which was not their style at all, and they couldn't get anything going either.

Before game six at Maple Leaf Gardens, Imlach gave a speech. He told us that game six was a must-win. If he lost, we reasoned, we'd have to go back to Montreal, and he couldn't see any way the Canadiens would let us win a seventh game in the Forum. He made it clear to some of his "old pappies" that it might be their last game — and, with expansion on the horizon, certainly their last game as Toronto Maple Leafs.

Part of me hoped desperately that Punch would tap me on the shoulder, and tell me to take a regular shift. But part of me felt rusty from the lack of action. I didn't want to let the team down or embarrass myself. Shackie had been benched as well, but unlike him I didn't have the ability to see any humour in the situation.

The Canadiens must have gotten a pep talk from Toe Blake as well, because they came out firing. They fired seventeen shots at Terry Sawchuk in the first period. But Terry looked as if he had an extra pair of arms, because nothing got past him. We only managed 11 shots at Gump Worsley, and if he was rusty it didn't show. The first period ended in a scoreless draw.

About six minutes into the second, Habs defenceman Jacques Laperrière took a slap shot that bounced off Allan Stanley's leg and ended up on Red Kelly's stick. There was only one man back as Kelly and Ellis took off down the ice. Worsley saved Red's shot, but Ellis was in perfect position to drive home the rebound. Montreal turned up the heat, but Sawchuk stoned them. Then, in the last minute of play, we caught another break. Jim Pappin's shot went in off a skate to put us ahead 2–0. Dick Duff scored for the Canadiens at 5:28 of the third, but we'd taken control of the game. Our wingers and defencemen tied up their wingers, which left their playmakers, Béliveau and Backstrom, with nobody to pass to.

In the last minute of play, with the score 2–1 for Toronto, there was a face-off in our end and Toe Blake pulled Gump for a sixth attacker. Ever the showman, Punch put out a lineup made up completely of his old pappies: Stanley and Horton on defence, with a forward line of Kelly, Armstrong, and Pulford. No room for black aces like me and Shack.

Imlach told Stanley to take the face-off. He wasn't sure at first that he'd heard Punch correctly — apparently he hadn't taken a face-off in years. Defencemen used to take the face-offs in their own zone all the time, and it made perfect sense for two reasons. First of all, the way they line up now, the defenceman at the back of the circle is rather useless — he doesn't have anything to do. And the other thing was, the defenceman would always take the other team's top centreman out of the play. Timmy Horton won more than his share of face-offs because he was so strong. His reflexes and eyesight were weak, but when you're in that close, who gives a shit — all you have to do is lay on the muscle, neutralize the centreman. And he did that extremely well. But in 1964–65 they started calling an interference penalty for this kind of jostling around.

So Stanley lined up across from Béliveau, and they dropped the puck. Stanley didn't know what else to do, so he reverted to his old habit — he took a run right at big Jean, caught him off-balance. The puck went back to Red Kelly, and he shovelled it forward to Pully. Pulford carried it across the blue line, saw Armstrong across the ice, and passed it. Armstrong crossed the red line so there'd be no icing call if he missed the net, and he wristed it into the empty goal. Toronto 3, Montreal 1.

It was the NHL's fiftieth season, Canada's centennial year, and the twenty-fifth and final year of the "Original Six," and the Toronto Maple Leafs were the Stanley Cup champions. Dave Keon was named the most valuable player in the playoffs, and became the first — and to this date, the only — Maple Leaf presented with the Conn Smythe Trophy. But something was missing. I felt I couldn't enjoy the team's success as much as I would have liked to. It was great for the team, but Larry Hillman was on the ice when I thought I should have been. I felt like an outcast, even though I was among friends with whom I'd lived, travelled, and played hockey for eleven years — and with some of the ex-Marlies, fifteen years counting Junior. I felt like I was losing the brothers I'd never had.

The only bright spot to that final evening came during the television show *Sports Hot Seat*, when Bobby Hull was asked to name the toughest defender he had encountered in his playing career. His reply: Bobby Baun. "When Baun is out there, that right side is like an obstacle course." My ego desperately needed that confirmation.

Bob Pennington of the Toronto *Telegram* caught up with me after the last practice before that final game. "Nobody seemed to notice that Baun came in long after the rest," he wrote, "sweating and stone-faced to sit alone in the bleak private world of the also-ran. Three years ago he would have been the one they all wanted to interview. Now they barely gave a nod."

On May 5, 1967, the city of Toronto held its customary parade of convertibles up Bay Street, this time to Nathan Phillips Square in front of New City Hall, directly across the street from the scene of our other three celebrations. There was only one team member absent from the festivities: the spare defenceman, Bobby Baun. I would have felt like a fraud if I'd shown up. My absence didn't go unnoticed. I'm told that there was a chant all along the parade route from the loyal fans: "Where is Baun? Where is Baun?"

Eventually one of the reporters got hold of Sallie and asked that same question. "He just wanted to get away," she said. "I guess his pride was hurt. He took our sons up to Charleston Lake and went fishing. He thought it would be better to go away for a few days."

PART IV

The Long Road Home

CHAPTER 12

Oakland

WITHIN A MONTH OF OUR STANLEY CUP WIN, THE NATIONAL Hockey League sat down to attend to the business of expansion. Six new teams were to be added: the Los Angeles Kings, Minnesota North Stars, Philadelphia Flyers, Pittsburgh Penguins, St. Louis Blues, and the California Seals. The league would be split into two divisions — the six new teams would all play in the "West" Division, while the established clubs made up the "East." The only question that remained was where the expansion teams would get their players from.

The NHL answered that question by announcing that on June 6, 1967, it would hold an expansion draft. The six established teams could withhold their eleven top skaters and one goaltender, but the rest would be pretty much up for grabs. It represented a tremendous opportunity for minor-leaguers to gain major-league recognition — and income. As well, the oldtimers would be able to extend their careers a few years, and black aces such as myself stood to land a steady job. But no one could predict how good the hockey would be in 1967–68, and fans, players, reporters, and owners were all concerned. Adding to the players' uncertainty, it was anybody's guess which dozen would be protected, and who would be sacrificed to the upstart teams.

However, I tried not to worry too much about what was beyond my control, and I went fishing. Part of me actually wanted to get drafted by one of the new teams, so I could storm back into the Gardens and prove that Punch had been wrong about me. A few days before the draft, I heard that I was not going to be protected, and I wasn't surprised, but I was still bitterly disappointed. The phone was ringing off the hook, with people asking me how I felt about the situation. One of those phone calls came from an old friend, Bert Olmstead, who'd been hired as coach and general manager of the California Seals.

"Sit tight," Bert said, "you're going to be our number-one draft choice." Well, I put down the phone and probably belted out a few bars of "California, Here I Come." My heart was set on rejoining Bert, and I even had my lawyer, Jim Blaney, draft a retirement announcement in case I was chosen by any other team.

Olmstead proved to be true to his word, choosing me in the first round. The Seals also selected my old teammates, Billy Harris and Kent Douglas. Wally Boyer, Terry Clancy, Aut Erickson, and goaltender Gary Smith had also been in the Leafs system. Other names who were familiar to me — if not to the hockey fans of northern California — included goalie Charlie Hodge from the Canadiens, and Larry Cahan and Bill Hicke, from the Rangers' system. There was even some local content: my old Marlie teammate, Charlie Burns, and Gerry Odrowski had been regulars for several years with the San Francisco Seals when they played in the Western league. There was a lot of experience, and even a few Stanley Cups in that lineup. On paper, we looked to be the team to beat in the West Division.

The one unanswered question for me has always been who really decided to leave me unprotected — was it Punch Imlach or the owner, Stafford Smythe? I suspected it was Imlach, but for over thirty years I have never been sure. I spoke to Stafford's only son, Tom, and he said, "I was really too young at the time to know what went on behind the scenes, but as you had always been considered almost like part of our family, I doubt very much if it was my father's doing."

I asked George Mara, a member of the Gardens board in those days, and he answered without hesitation that it was indeed Imlach who left me unprotected. Even Stafford Smythe was upset about it, George says, but by the time he found out it was too late to change anything.

Meanwhile, members of the 1967 Stanley Cup-winning Toronto Maple Leafs were being cast to the wind. Los Angeles got goalie Terry Sawchuk. The Kings also had an all–Maple Leaf front office: Larry Regan was general manager, while Red Kelly, who'd retired, was the Kings' first coach. And not two weeks after the Stanley Cup parade, the Leafs sent Eddie Shack to the Boston Bruins. And in March 1968, Frank Mahovlich and Pete Stemkowski would be dealt to Detroit.

There were all sorts of rumours flying around about retired players who might return to active duty now that the league had doubled in size. I started one about Carl Brewer joining me in Oakland. I was giving a speech in Orillia, Ontario, during the off-season, and I actually said that Brewer would play for the Seals if he decided to return to the NHL. The press contacted Brewer, and he replied, "I know nothing about this." Since leaving the Leaf training camp in 1965, he'd spent a year away from the game, then been reinstated as an amateur hockey player and joined the Canadian National Team. He admitted that four or five clubs — and not just expansion teams — had expressed interest in him. But he would not return to the NHL until the 1969–70 season. In 1967–68, he would play with the Muskegon Mohawks of the International Hockey League.

Carl was also asked around that time if he agreed that I'd lost my effectiveness since losing him as a defence partner. "I'd argue that," he said. "Bobby is a talented hockey player. You know how hard he plays. When you play like that, you're bound to be injured a lot. The trouble is, where most people wouldn't play, Bobby does despite those injuries. And that hurts his play."

There was another rumour circulating that Jacques Plante was going to join the team. This one was half-correct: he was joining us, but not to play; instead he was working with the goalies. There was some concern that Charlie Hodge might not sign, and by having Plante in camp the team was hoping that one of the other goalies would be ready to take over. The Seals did sign Plante to a tryout contract, but then it was discovered that his rights still belonged to the New York Rangers. The Seals would have had to make a trade to acquire his goaltending services. I believe they still had to make a cash payment to the Rangers just to have him around as a consultant. Plante would return to the NHL the following season, with the St. Louis Blues, where he and Glenn Hall would form a Vezina Trophy–winning duo.

One important change that expansion brought with it was that there was a new batch of owners who hadn't been part of the old boys' network. The original six had been a tight-knit little unit. For years there'd really only been three influential voices: Conn Smythe in Toronto; Frank Selke in Montreal; and the Norrises, who owned the Black Hawks and Red Wings, were major shareholders in the Madison Square Garden corporation, and were quietly financing the Boston Bruins. It was said at one time that NHL stood for "Norris House League."

Well, some of these new owners had never even seen a hockey puck; they had their own way of doing things; and they weren't about to be bullied by the old guard. One of the byproducts was that suddenly hockey players were getting a hell of a lot more money than ever before. The president of the Seals, Frank Selke, Jr., contacted me and offered a three-year, no-cut contract worth $37,500 a year. That was one-third more than I'd been getting from the Maple Leafs! Selke told me it was the best contract that had ever been offered to any defenceman playing in the NHL.

The owner of the Seals, Barry Van Gerbig, was a twenty-eight-year-old who'd played goal for Princeton University. His godfather was Bing Crosby, and his father-in-law was Douglas Fairbanks, Jr. He was one of those owners who just loved being around the players. He was young for an owner of an NHL team, and had movie star good looks.

Initially, I told the Seals I'd have to consider their offer carefully. I had a lot of business interests to take care of. I'd been working on selling a machine that tested the speed of a hockey player's shot. It had so far clocked Mahovlich at 110 miles per hour, Bobby Hull at 105, and my own shot at 84. I had also been working toward getting my own car dealership, and if I moved away I'd be putting that opportunity in jeopardy. I'd also just purchased a farm, Ballybawn, and I couldn't just leave it behind. I promised California I would make a decision by the middle of July. Sallie and I ended up in Vancouver on a business trip that summer and we decided there to fly down to Oakland and sign with the Seals. We also bought a gorgeous home overlooking the San Francisco Bay — we'd always been the social hub for the team in Toronto, so we figured we may as well keep up the tradition.

We returned to Toronto and sold our house on Ruden Crescent — which, needless to say, was a stone's throw from the Donalda Golf & Country Club. We spent part of the summer at a cottage on Lake Simcoe, near Alan Eagleson's place. Then we lived briefly in an apartment, then to a motel in Oakland while we waited for our furniture to arrive. That's a lot of moving around for anyone, but imagine what it was like for a family of seven! Along the way, I was also doing some promotional work for Esso and for the Oakland Seals. It was one busy summer.

Another familiar face from back home was joining us on the West coast. Tim Ryan, the former CFTO television sportscaster, had joined the Seals as director of publicity. He'd also be the play-by-play announcer. He was eager for the new season to begin, and he started to describe the new arena, the Oakland-Alameda Coliseum, as the "Jewel Box."

Training camp was held in Port Huron, Michigan, just across the river from Sarnia, Ontario. But before NHL camps opened, something happened that would throw a monkey wrench into my plans: Bob Pulford resigned as president of the NHL Players' Association. It was fairly obvious to me that he'd been under pressure from Imlach to do so. The player chosen to replace Pully as interim president? None other than Bobby Baun. Even on an interim basis, that meant that I'd have to attend NHLPA meetings, most of which were held in Toronto. That wouldn't be a problem during training camp, but could prove inconvenient on an ongoing basis as I was based a whole continent away.

The team saw it this way, too: before I flew east, Bert Olmstead warned me not to show up in camp as president of the association. "I'd duck that headache if I were him," he told the press. "He'll have enough problems just concentrating on hockey this winter." To show they weren't fooling, the Seals told me they'd fine me $1,000 a day until I resigned. I stewed about this for almost two weeks, during which I felt like Casper the ghost — no one wanted to be near me or my family. Finally, I made an impetuous decision: I bought seven plane tickets for Toronto.

Our furniture was, at that very moment, being flown to California. That didn't matter, it would have to be shipped back. The kids had been having a wonderful time living in the motel, playing in the swimming pool every day, and dreaming of living by a real ocean. They'd be disappointed, but they'd get over it.

Olmstead met me at the airport. He managed to convince me to come back, and he waived the fine, which by now had reached $13,000. The next six months would be hectic, as I flew back to Toronto whenever my schedule allowed so that we could get the NHLPA underway. It was a relief to turn things over to Norm Ullman, who took over when he was traded to the Maple Leafs in March 1968.

During training camp, I was asked about all the bones I'd broken over the years, and whether I felt I was brittle. "I don't think I'm what you would call brittle," I said, "Furthermore, I've never babied myself! I'll play with an injury if I can help the club. But I do use my body, and you have to take punishment every time you dish it out." I concluded by saying, "I feel better this year than I have in a long time, and I figure that I can play another ten years if I have to."

It was a big adjustment to wear the kelly-green-and-blue Seals sweater after all those years in Leaf and Marlboro blue and white. And what an honour it was on opening night, when I discovered that sweater also had a "C" stitched to it, indicating that I'd been named the first captain of the California Seals. Olmstead was quoted as saying, "I wish I had 16 like him. I don't know of a more honest hockey player. He has tremendous pride, the kind of a guy you can build a team around. Any young kid coming into this league looks at the way Bobby comes off the ice with his sweater stuck to his skin with perspiration, and he soon realizes what you have to do to play in this league. We want Bobby to be our leader."

The season got off to a flying start as the Seals beat the Philadelphia Flyers 5–1 in our opening game. According to the Oakland paper, I was "handing out bodychecks like a Tahoe blackjack dealer," while the Seals "hit, hustled and hammered" the Flyers. I was really pleased with the way we'd gone at them. Much of the credit belonged to fellow ex-Leaf Kent Douglas. We put together three pretty good periods of hockey: unfortunately we didn't have too many more.

Olmstead told George Gross, "I've seen Billy Harris play better." As the year went on, it seemed Olmstead was always criticizing Harris, egged on by his assistant coach, Gord Fashoway. Bert and Fashoway had been friends before they teamed up in Oakland, and seemed to really respect each other. The constant criticism strained, for a while, the very close friendship I'd enjoyed with Bert, although it has since been repaired.

Fashoway was not averse to berating the players, taking a not-so-gentle swipe at Kent Douglas: "If Kent doesn't pare a little suet off his hide, we'll take a slice out of his pocket. He's overweight, and it shows in his play." The reference to Douglas did not offend me as much as those to Harris, which seemed to be constant. Although Kent and I had been roommates, and defence partners on various occasions, in those days we were never particularly close friends, whereas Billy and I have long been good friends.

Team owner Barry Van Gerbig was more than pleased with the season start: "I think it is unbelievable to have this kind of game played by a new team. It's the best coached team for this early in the season that I've ever seen. A team that works this hard has got to win, and that's Bert's kind of hockey." Van Gerbig was optimistic about the team's defence corps: "If we've got to be beaten this first season, it is believed the victors' trainers, team doctors and dentists will be the only real winners." He called me "the most fearless man in hockey today."

You just had to love Barry, but he had no idea what he was taking on, other than he loved to be a jock. Bert and Frank had their hands full trying to give him a line to go on.

Also impressed with the opening game was a minor shareholder by the name of Bing Crosby, Barry's godfather. "Oh I'm just a very, very small owner," he said, "but I'm a very big fan. I'll be here a lot. This is my team. That was a marvellous defence by Oakland, I mean California. The class of play has stepped up a lot over last year. And what a place to play."

It's interesting to note that even one of the owners had trouble keeping track of the team name. The new team was originally called the California Seals, the name it had gone by in its final season in the Western Hockey League, after crossing the Bay from San Francisco. But by mid-December, they had become the Oakland Seals. (The Coliseum in Oakland was much better suited to hockey than the old Cow Palace in San Francisco, which would become home ice for the San Jose Sharks during its first couple of seasons in the NHL. Unfortunately, the sophisticated San Franciscans would never cross the Bay Bridge in sufficient numbers to keep the Seals afloat.) In 1970 they would change yet again, this time to the California Golden Seals.

One of our most avid fans was Charles Schulz, creator of the "Peanuts" cartoon strip. We had some nice visits with him in the dressing room after the games. He also built his own private arena and invited me to skate there with him.

As the season wore on, I found it hard to believe we were playing hockey in such a mild climate. I used to try to put myself into the "hockey" mindset by drawing all the blinds, lighting the fireplace, and staring like an idiot at a big painting of a winter scene. After about fifteen minutes I'd say, "Who the hell am I trying to kid?" and I'd go outside and sit on the patio.

Although the opening-night reviews were positive, the Seals were a franchise in trouble. It was originally thought that owning an NHL franchise was like a licence to print money, and in the original six cities this was certainly still the case. But the "second six" weren't exactly packing them into the rinks. We drew a crowd of 6,886 to our home opener, but only 4,155 came to our second game, and the third game was witnessed by only 3,419. Brian O'Neill, an NHL executive, said at the time, "There is no doubt that a lot of people figured we'd do better than what we have. But I think it will pick up." Stafford Smythe's reaction was guarded: "I'll start worrying when a team, say California, wins six or seven games and is on top but isn't drawing." It's true we weren't exactly the second coming of the Canadiens.

Tim Ryan, the Seals' publicity director, admitted the team was disappointed, but he was hopeful that an upcoming three-game set against the established clubs would be a bigger draw than the Flyers. He also pointed out that the San Francisco media didn't pay much attention to Oakland sports, and that this was an obstacle. "If we had to rely on the city for fans, we'd die. So what we have to do is maybe go 75 miles in all directions — except into the ocean — to places like Sacramento, Berkeley, San Jose, Stockton and dozens of others."

On the ice, expansion was starting off much better than I'd thought it would. The calibre of play among the new teams was better than I'd anticipated. There was a lot of enthusiasm and spirit among the new teams, and it was going a long way. But the Seals just weren't winning enough games. We started out well enough, with two wins and a tie at home before setting out on our first road trip. But by the time we reached Toronto, on October 28, we'd lost four in a row.

We were operating at a distinct disadvantage, playing on the West coast. Only the Los Angeles Kings were really close by; all the other teams were clumped between the Midwest and the Eastern seaboard. And the road trips were incredible. In the six-team league, you could pretty well count on playing home games on Wednesday and Saturday. Road games were usually Thursday (Montreal) or Sunday (New York, Detroit, Chicago, or Boston.) But with the Seals, they were scheduling five- or six-game road trips as if it was nothing. During one stretch, between December

23 and January 4, we played seven road games in a row. We were home just long enough to wash our socks and underwear, then it was on the road for six more games between January 24 and February 4.

On our first trip east, Olmstead expressed this concern, suggesting we might be jet-lagged, then added, "Every time I figure out what is wrong with us, something happens. Last night in Detroit [an 8–2 Seals loss] we skated better than in any game this year. But you've never seen the Wings play better, they were flying."

With the all the Leaf alumni on the Seals, you can bet we were looking forward to our first stop at Maple Leaf Gardens. It was also special for King Clancy, who would see his son Terry play in the NHL for the first time. "All I want is to see him do well. But dammit, I want to win. I don't know if he has been playing that much lately but if he isn't good enough, then he isn't good enough!"

Louis Cauz did a whimsical piece on the former Leafs and was one of the few to mention Billy Harris: "He's a lot greyer on top but he can still skate with the best of them. I have an idea the place will rock if old Hinky whips a shot past Johnny Bower."

We held our own for the first two periods, with the Seals ahead 2–1, but disaster struck in the third period and the final score was 5–2. "This is the fifth game in a row we've blown in the third period," Bert Olmstead said afterward. "Something always happens between the eighth and twelfth minute of the third period and we go to pieces. I can't explain it. We just can't do a thing right around that time."

Olmstead had praised me the night before, saying that I always gave 100 per cent, but this time I felt I had lost the game for us: "On Pappin's goal I should have gone into our end to play the puck, not reach for it at the blue line. It hopped over my stick, and Pappin knocked it down, then went in to score. On his second goal I should have played the puck, not tried to stickhandle. I didn't cover my man on the fifth goal."

Olmstead and I tended on many occasions to speak freely, usually in a complimentary fashion, about each other. I told Dick Beddoes, "He's right, like he always is about hockey. If you make fundamental mistakes you lose. If you don't make mistakes and you're anywhere even in talent, you win. Olmstead is the Lombardi of hockey. Under Olmstead, skating is the first commandment. Some days it is skating for two hours at a stretch without stopping." Olmstead's frank reply to that was: "It is boring as hell, but we skate a lot to build up stamina."

I experienced a fair number of injuries while playing for Oakland. The local newspaper reported that "The Seals' injury report usually includes a reference to Bobby to the effect that he's pretty banged up but he'll play."

There was one injury in particular that may have been more significant than I first realized. I was breaking in a new pair of skates, and I tripped trying to make a check. I hadn't been hit by anyone; my feet just slipped out from under me when I tried to check Jean Béliveau. When I fell, I twisted my neck, causing numbness in my right hand. The doctors said I had suffered a contusion to the nerves of my right hand, but the fact I was under the care of a neurosurgeon, and kept over in Montreal, probably says more than the doctors were letting me know at the time. Looking back, both Sallie and I wonder if that wasn't the first time I broke my neck. I had to live on 222s for years after that event.

By mid-December, there was already talk of moving the team out of Oakland. This was really encouraging for the players to read in the paper! One rumour was that we were headed to Vancouver, which had been in the running for an expansion team but lacked an NHL-calibre arena. (Harold Ballard and Stafford Smythe had been planning to build one, but mothballed that idea when the government wouldn't donate the land.) A move north would have suited Olmstead just fine; he had come to Oakland after coaching the Vancouver Canucks of the Western Hockey League. The Baun children were also starting to get a bit homesick, and a move to Vancouver would at least be back to Canada.

I was one who hoped we'd stay put. The sunrises and sunsets we could see every day at our new home were spectacular. The views overlooking San Francisco Bay to the Golden Gate Bridge and the Bay Bridge were quite incredible. We backed onto the Sequoia Hills golf course, so the air was permeated with a wonderful mixture of scents — the sequoia trees, the flowers, and the salt air of the ocean — that never ceased to amaze us.

The fondest memory shared by all our children is of their trips to Fisherman's Wharf on a Friday night to pick out crab legs for dinner. The two older boys also remember that they decided to run away from home one day, only to end up in a patch of poison oak, which meant they had to abandon their plan and run home to mom for first-aid.

At mid-season I got a thrill when I was asked to play in the All-Star Game, which was played in Toronto on January 16, 1968. It was the last year of the old format in which a team of NHL All-Stars would take on the previous season's Stanley Cup champion, in this case the Toronto Maple Leafs. It was another chance to play in Toronto, and this time my coach would be Toe Blake of the Montreal Canadiens.

While I was in Toronto for the festivities, the Oakland Seals were involved in one of the most tragic events in hockey history. On January 13, they were playing in Minnesota, and North Stars centreman Bill Masterton was checked, almost simultaneously, by Oakland forwards Ron Harris and Larry Cahan. The hit caused Masterton to fall backwards and land headfirst on the ice. He passed away two days later, never having regained consciousness.

I didn't know Bill, nor did many of us in the league, because he'd only just arrived in the NHL. He'd been a teammate of

Johnny MacMillan's at the University of Denver, and was one of those fellows — and there were many like him — who bounced around the minor leagues. His big break had come at the age of twenty-nine, when he made the Minnesota lineup. His death was a key motivator in the move to make helmets mandatory in the NHL, which finally happened eleven years later in 1979. The team also donated an award, the Bill Masterton Memorial Trophy, for the player who displays the greatest perseverance and dedication to hockey.

The weather in Toronto had been horrendous, and it delayed the arrival of some of the All-Stars. Blake thought I was one of them. He was sure that he'd missed a phone call from Bert Olmstead telling him I wouldn't be able to make it. An hour later, he bumped into me in the lobby of the Royal York Hotel. You better believe I was determined to play in the All-Star Game — I'd travelled nearly twenty hours to get there, and I hadn't played a game since my injury in Montreal.

After the All-Star break, it became a long season indeed for the Oakland Seals. With all the hockey brains and ability we had at our disposal, we should have had it all figured out, but try as we might, we simply couldn't bring that team together. I felt so badly for Bert; it was disheartening to watch so much pride become shattered. We'd all let ourselves down. Bert finally gave up his coaching duties to Gord Fashoway for the final ten games.

Our record of 15 wins, 42 losses, and 17 ties left us deep in sixth place in the West, 20 points behind fifth-place Pittsburgh. Looking at our record, it seems our defence, so often a problem for expansion clubs, wasn't that bad. Our goals against were around the middle of the pack. Where we really fell down was in scoring: only 153 goals for, the lowest total in the NHL since 1955–56.

In spite of it all, Sallie and I loved California. We had had the best year of our marriage, and the best year as a family to that date. We were truly on our own that season, because in Toronto we'd always been surrounded by close friends or extended family. We made wonderful friends there, who we're still close with today, particularly Bonnie and Bill Hubbard, whom we met through our boys.

We also became very close to Lee and Tim Ryan — he's now with CBS Sports. Like us, they enjoyed the fine wine and food available in San Francisco's world-renowned restaurants, so we would venture out together to places like The Blue Fox, Shadows, The Glad Hand in Sausalito, The Blue Dolphin in Carmel, Nepenthe at Big Sur, and Chez Madelaine at Stinson Beach.

The topless rage was also taking flight in San Francisco during this era, particularly at the Peppermint Lounge. The owner, Ted Levinson, was quite a character, and he wanted Tim Ryan and me to help him put together a show for Las Vegas called "Nudes on Ice." Our wives were not amused, and Tim and I regretfully had to turn down this once-in-a-lifetime opportunity.

Tim was very adventurous, so the two of us would love to hop on a cable car, see what was happening, and jump off where and when we felt like it. After my experience at Wayne State University and the General Motors management school, my mind had been opened to all new horizons. So I would spend a lot of time in art galleries — not just in the Bay Area, but all over North America. I also became a voracious reader, as I am to this day.

———

As the end of the 1967–68 season drew near, the atmosphere around the Seals got more and more discouraging. Attendance for our games in Oakland had been poor. Van Gerbig's pockets weren't as deep as the hockey world had been led to believe. The owners voted decisively (8–4) against the move to Vancouver that Labatt's Breweries had proposed. Van Gerbig promised a new-look front office: Fred Glover of the AHL's Cleveland Barons would take over as coach, while Frank Selke, Jr., would assume the GM's role.

The disorganization and lack of hockey interest got to me, and I asked Selke to trade me — and, if possible, to one of the established clubs. On May 27, 1968, he obliged me. I was traded to the Detroit Red Wings, along with defenceman Ron Harris. In return, the Seals got defenceman Howie Young, left-winger Gary Jarrett, right-winger Doug Roberts, and a twenty-year-old goal-tending prospect from the Flin Flon Bombers, Chris Worthy. I found out about the trade over the radio as my family and I drove back east to the farm. Fortunately, we were close to home, near London, Ontario, when the shocking announcement came.

Detroit general manager Sid Abel said, "We were looking for a rugged, experienced defenceman and I think we have one in Baun. His record as a defenceman speaks for him and we are looking for him to fit into our team." Selke expressed regret at losing me: "I hated to give up a guy like Baun. If we'd had eighteen Bobby Bauns, we'd have had no problems. He's just a super guy who always gives 110 per cent effort. He was our leader and I feel we gave up an awful lot, but our principal need was for a left winger and we feel in Jarrett we got a good one." For me, going to the Red Wings was like getting back in the majors.

CHAPTER 13

Back East

IN JUNE 1968 THE DETROIT RED WINGS INVITED ME TO THE DRAFT meetings in Montreal to meet my new bosses: Bruce Norris, the owner; Sid Abel, the general manager; and the coach, Bill Gadsby. Their veteran stars, Gordie Howe and Alex Delvecchio, would also be there. I was more than a little apprehensive about the meeting, because I didn't feel I had much in common with this bunch. Part of me was still feeling the effects of twelve years of training to see the Red Wings as the enemy.

I was to meet them in the bar of the Queen Elizabeth Hotel at about eight o'clock, so I decided to try and relax while I enjoyed a fine dinner at one of my favourite spots, the Beaver Club, located in the same hotel. I really treated myself: lobster soufflé, fresh asparagus, and a bottle of Pouilly Fuisse. I was all set to tuck in when Lefty Wilson, the Detroit trainer, came in to tell me that Mr. Norris was waiting to meet me in the bar. "I'll meet with him after," I replied.

No sooner had I said this than Norris, accompanied by Howe and Delvecchio, came over to my table and said he just wanted to see how tough I was. At six foot five, Norris was a big bear of a man, and he clearly had a few drinks under his belt. Before I really knew what was happening, he started to fight me. Tables and food started flying, and Norris soon fell ass over tea kettle on the floor. Everything and everyone went quiet, until Mr. Norris got up, looked at me, and said, "You're tough enough!"

What a way to meet your new boss. In the end I became quite fond of him, and he gave me quite an insight into the cattle business when I decided to get into that line. And eventually I came to enjoy being a Red Wing.

Detroit is a great city for a professional athlete. It's a blue-collar town, a union town, and the fans are tremendously knowledgeable. And they really get behind the teams. I mean, Toronto was a great place to be a hockey player, but in Detroit you'd go to a restaurant, and somebody would pick up the tab. There was always some organization or another giving a sports banquet. And in those days the Tigers were winning the World Series, and it was fun to go to the ballpark. In fact, the guys from all three teams — Red Wings, Tigers, and Lions — were very close. And the Red Wings have the strongest alumni association. If I were to come back as a player again, Detroit would be high on my list of cities to play in.

Sid Abel had been collecting ex-Leafs. He already had Frank Mahovlich, Peter Stemkowski, Kent Douglas, and Garry Unger. He also owned the NHL rights to Carl Brewer, and I think he was relishing the idea of reuniting the old defence pair. But Brewer was not prepared to discuss such a move yet. He later admitted he had talked to Abel on several occasions, and may even have convinced Sid to trade for me. But in 1968 he was committed to coaching the Finnish National Team, and if things worked out right, he'd be playing and coaching in Finland. Carl did come to play in Detroit, during the 1969–70 season.

Detroit seemed to harbour a lot of Baun fans, perhaps

because of — or in spite of! — the 1964 broken-leg goal. After I'd been a Wing for a few months, sportswriter Bill Brennan of the Detroit *Free Press* wrote an article about me that was unlike any I'd seen before: "On the ice Bob Baun looks, sometimes acts like an alley fighter. Off the ice, Baun talks softly and intelligently and sounds sometimes like an English squire. But his clothes, they are mod … and mad. Bell bottoms. Wide lapels. Big stripes. Jackets with an Edwardian flair." (I hope Harry Rosen doesn't read this!)

"To the spectators who crowd into the Olympia," he concluded, "Baun is the symbol of courage. Quite frequently he is given an ovation when he skates off the ice. This happens to no other National Hockey League defenceman." What a way to make me feel welcome.

One fellow who might have been a little concerned to see me again was Garry Unger. I'd taught the younger rookie an expensive lesson when he first came to Toronto. As Unger left the Toronto dressing room for the first time, I told him the team's dress code was very strict. It was mandatory to wear a jacket and tie whenever you were travelling or going to and from the Gardens. Before he could utter a word of protest, I'd corralled him and taken him off to see Harry Rosen, which he couldn't really afford on a rookie's salary in those days.

Now it was *my* turn to be nervous as I entered the Detroit dressing room, because I was meeting Gordie Howe for the very first time as someone other than "the enemy." Gordie — along with Henri Richard and Bobby Hull — had always been on my list of key players to keep away from my goal. It was only the season before that I had rated him the toughest opponent of all. Give him half a step, and he'd be gone. We had played together in two All-Star Games (1965 and 1968), and against each other in three

(1962, '63, and '64) but that wasn't the same thing at all. I had always thought about how it would be to play a whole season with the big guy.

I discovered that he was an inspiration for any player. He had such a genuine love for the game. He had the perfect physique to be an athlete, along with incredible instincts and head for the game. If he'd had the advantages that the young players today enjoy, and played in the same time span as Gretzky, I'm convinced that no one would have even come close to Gord. Of course, he did play one season in the NHL at the same time as Gretzky — at age fifty-two! — and scored 15 goals. Just tremendous.

Gord was involved in the greatest play I ever remember seeing in hockey. It was in the spring of 1969 and we were playing Boston. Gord picked the puck up inside our blue line and started down the right side. Don Awrey moved in to take Gordie out, so he switched his stick to his right hand and, with his left arm stretched out, he let Awrey come to him. Awrey got close, and Gordie flung him to one side like a sack of potatoes. Immediately, Bobby Orr saw what was happening, and he tried to do the same thing as Awrey — and he ended up on his backside.

By this time, Howe was working his way in toward Cheevers, the goalie. You could see that Cheevers wanted to poke-check the puck off of Gordie's stick, but as soon as Gerry made his move, Gordie tucked the puck between his feet, switched the stick over to his left hand, and wristed the puck into the top left-hand corner of the net. It was a display of amazing puck control, along with soft hands.

From playing together, Gordie and I became friends, and one summer the Bauns — all seven of us — were invited to the Howes' cottage. Greg remembers it rather well, as he took off by himself in one of the boats — he was only ten, so it must have been a smaller fishing boat. When I found him I was cross, but I said, "You're too old now for a spanking." And so Greg was spared.

The question remains: was it that Greg really was too old, or was it that I wasn't about to spank him in front of the great Gordie Howe? Either way, Greg never did get another spanking.

Later that same summer, Michelle, who was much younger, was about to get a spanking as well. I told her to go upstairs and pull down her pants, which she did. Just as I raised my hand, she peed all over me. That was definitely the last spanking she ever got.

That first year with the Red Wings, the Bauns lived in Tecumseh, a town near Windsor, Ontario. Sallie and I felt more comfortable living on the Canadian side of the border until we really knew our way around. Both the Mahovlich brothers, Peter and Frank, were living there as well, and Sallie and Frank's wife, Marie, were good company for each other.

I also had an opportunity to renew my friendship with Lou Bendo, Windsor's "Mr. Hockey," whom I'd played with in my first year of Junior. Lou got me back to my two favourite outdoor passions: fly fishing and hunting for ducks and pheasants. He is still one of the greatest outdoors people I know, and I know a few. And his wife, Sally, was another good friend for Sallie.

The season really got off to a flying start for me. My coach, Bill Gadsby, had been a defenceman in his playing days, and he seemed more than pleased with my play. "Baun is playing All-Star hockey," he said. "In one game at the Olympia, Baun drew three ovations when he left the ice after his turn, a mighty rare compliment for a defenceman."

Gadsby added, "You'll notice Baun, for all his roughness, doesn't go in for rampages, like John Ferguson, Reg Fleming, or Ted Green, or knock down drag 'em out fights." It's true that I've always thought playing that way is hardly worthwhile. It takes more out of you than it does a guy like Green or Ferguson. My only regret was that, being only five foot nine, I got a lot of elbows in the face. I wish I could've been three or four inches taller.

Detroit was the youngest team I had played on since breaking into the league with the Leafs. I also found myself playing a different style — I was passing the puck far more effectively than I'd done in Toronto. With the Leafs, I'd make the one pass to Brewer, and that was the extent of my puck-handling. Now I was moving it up to the forwards more often.

When I first heard about the trade to Detroit, I wasn't sure if it would be good for me. But the organization treated me tremendously and my morale was way up. I was also playing some of my finest hockey. I played in all 76 games and I was named the team's top defenceman for 1968–69, an honour that came with a pair of first-class tickets to anywhere in the world that Air Canada flew. Sallie and I figured we would go for the long haul and use them to go to Moscow.

I also noticed a change for the better in the other ex-Leafs, many of whom had felt repressed under Imlach's control. Imlach was a winner, but he had no concept of how to handle people. Frank Mahovlich was a perfect example. One day in March of 1969, he and I were chatting on the Red Wings bus, when I asked the driver to stop the bus so I could get off and buy coffee and donuts for everyone. As I stepped off the bus, I turned to reporter Paul Dulmage and said, "Listen to him. In eleven years in Toronto I don't think I ever said more than twenty-two words to Mahovlich. I've spent the last year finding out what a great guy he is."

Frank was on a Detroit radio talk show and he spoke exceptionally freely about the Imlach era and how his life had changed since. "I could take it for the first four or five years in Toronto, but the last few years I shouldn't have been there. They've made me feel wanted here in Detroit. Gordie Howe wouldn't let me be a loner. There's more fellowship here than there was on the Leafs."

In fact, Howe had said some years before: "If they don't want him there, we'd be glad to take him."

Frank went on: "Everything was so regimented in Toronto. You had to skate all the time — stops and starts, that stuff. Skating never did me any good. I haven't practised half as much [in Detroit] and I'm a lot stronger." The Wings' public relations director, Ron Cantera, expressed the team's attitude toward Frank: "When he's good, he's the Big M, and when he's great we call him the Very Large M!" While everyone's stick had their surname stamped on it, Frank's were stamped "The Big M."

In Detroit, I also came to feel vindicated against Punch. After Brewer retired from the Leafs, the conventional wisdom was that my play had diminished. But in Oakland, and especially this first year in Detroit, I'd been able to prove myself without Carl. I'd also proven, despite Punch's opinion to the contrary, that I was capable of playing a full season and being a regular contributor to an NHL team.

The 1968–69 season was a year of great individual achievements for the Red Wings. While Bobby Hull set a new goal-scoring record with 58, Frank Mahovlich scored a career-high 49. Phil Esposito became the first 100-point man in history, with 126, and he was followed quickly by Hull (107) and our own Gordie Howe, with 44 goals and 59 assists for 103 points. Not bad for a forty-one-year-old! The unit of Howe, Delvecchio, and Mahovlich, which had been dubbed The Production Line II, scored a record number of goals for a forward line.

Unfortunately, we would miss the playoffs that year. The NHL's system let the top four teams in each division into the post-season playoffs. So while we'd posted a winning record of 33–31–12, we'd come in fifth in the East, seven points behind Toronto. Meanwhile, in the West, lesser teams such as the L.A. Kings (58 points to our 78) qualified. In a nasty bit of irony, the Oakland Seals came in second in the West, improving from 47 points to 69, and made the playoffs.

But the system shouldn't take all of the blame. Fact is, from my point of view, Sid Abel was running a country club, not a hockey team. At least not the kind of hockey team I was used to. You'd walk into the dressing room, and you'd see Sid on the massage table, getting a rubdown. Here's the general manager of an NHL team, but he's still trying to be one of the boys. This made it difficult for Bill Gadsby to overrule him. And the Wings' practices were a bowl of cherries compared to Punch's two-a-days. I'm not saying the Red Wings should have run things the way Punch did, but it was alarming that no one seemed too concerned that all these great individual performances weren't jelling into a cohesive unit.

As the 1968–69 season wound down, there was talk about whether Brewer would be joining us the following year. When the Wings had acquired Carl's rights in March 1968, they were given a window of opportunity, which expired on April 1, 1969, in which to sign him. After that date, Detroit would have to pay $15,000 compensation to the Leafs. Speaking on the radio just before the deadline, Mahovlich said, "I think Carl Brewer would like it here." One Detroit paper also pointed to my improved play and said, "Carl will find Baun a much improved defenceman. In four seasons he has become accomplished, polished, more skilful and self-reliant, and an all-star in his own right."

So it looked as if for the 1969–70 season, the Detroit Red Wings would have five players who Imlach, in his own manner, had cast aside.

The off-season of 1969 did not start off very well for me. Doctors had discovered that my mother had bowel cancer. Typical of the old school of thought, everyone chose to ignore it, no one discussed it, and my dad just kept his worries to himself, as he always did.

Sallie and I decided Moscow was a bit far to go under the circumstances, so we opted instead for London, England. We wandered around the English countryside, and I totally fell in love with the farms, and the small towns, especially Devon, Sherbourne, and Torquay. We ended up staying for three or four days in Torquay at a wonderful old hotel called the Imperial.

We were having a romantic dinner, overlooking the English Channel, when I felt a tap on my shoulder. Three young boys — Chris, Tim, and Peter Vernon — were standing there and asking for my autograph. What a small world.

The boys' parents, Sally and Tom Vernon, remained friends of ours for over thirty years. Tom had sold his company, Parker Brothers, to General Mills, and was running the company in Europe for a few years. They took us on a fishing trip on a chartered boat, and the water was so rough that even the captain got seasick. The next year, Tom invited me — boys only! — to Camp Caughnawana, in northern Quebec, for fly fishing, and we continued to go there until Tom's death. "Caug" is a very exclusive private fishing club — its members include the Eaton family — and the easiest access is to fly in by turbo Beavers. I now take my sons, and grandsons.

The summer of 1969 did bring with it one other fun and memorable event: the first annual American Airlines golf tournament. This was an elaborate event that ran over five days. When Sallie found out I was taking part, she was not impressed: "You're supposed to be farming, not golfing!" What I hadn't told her was that I had already gone to Harry Rosen's to outfit myself for the occasion — to the tune of $3,000, quite a bundle in 1969! But it was necessary, I told myself: I wouldn't just be golfing, there were also breakfasts, formal dinners, and other events, and I had a certain sartorial reputation to live up to.

On the second-last night I decided to have a party in my room, and I had pizzas sent all the way from George's Spaghetti House. That last morning I had to hustle to clean up the room, which was a royal mess, before Sallie arrived for the final dinner.

I was paired in the tournament with Gump Worsley, who was such a nervous flyer that he drove from Montreal to attend. I guess it wasn't very good publicity for the sponsor when we won. The prize money almost covered the cost of the clothes from Rosen's — actually, neither of us pocketed all of our winnings; we each gave half to the charity chosen to benefit from the proceeds of the tournament, the Big Brothers of Metropolitan Toronto.

We also got the good news that summer that the house in Oakland had finally sold, giving us an opportunity to buy in the Detroit area. We settled for Bloomfield, which was a very upscale suburb on the north end of the city. Our neighbours were mostly people who worked at "the motors" — GM, Ford, or Chrysler — and the schools were excellent. Greg decided to get a paper route, and we were somewhat anxious, to put it mildly, when we found out a boy who had a route in the next suburb had been shot by an angry customer.

In my spare time — something a hockey player has lots of, and perhaps sometimes too much — I would browse the art galleries and antique stores. Our house was a lovely English Tudor with a slate roof, a style we had fallen in love with on our trip to England. We had a neighbour who was a decorator, so she would send me to all the "right" places. I purchased a beautiful Jacobean dining-room suite, as well as a mahogany desk with gargoyles carved on the legs, which I found in a barn. I also picked up some light fixtures, which had been in the homes of members of the Ford family.

My favourite artist was, and still is, Andrew Wyeth. Even in those days I could only afford prints, but I remain fascinated by his work, as well as by his life. Sallie is not as enthusiastic about my taste in art, so my collection today remains packed in storage.

Carl did make his comeback in the 1969–70 season. Sid appointed me his "caretaker." He didn't know what to do with Carl, just couldn't figure him out and was frightened by some of the tales he'd heard, and Carl always ended up getting his own way. It started at contract time — Carl ended up making more than Gordie Howe. But hell, *I* was making more than Gordie Howe, and was Gordie ever upset when I told him so.

Sid wanted me to make sure of two things: that Carl got to bed on time, and that I kept him out of Gordie's hair, because the two of them got along like oil and water. Gordie wanted to punch Brewer's lights out almost every day — Carl doesn't know how many times he came just that close to dying! I was also supposed to make sure Brewer's famous fear of flying didn't get out of hand. He was such a white-knuckler, he'd need a bottle of whiskey in him just to get on the plane. By the time the plane landed, he'd be three-quarters shot. I think I asked Sid for an extra ten grand just to look after Carl because it was nearly a full-time job.

Carl's talent was incredible, and that season he'd have a career year with 39 points, but what did him in was that he was just too deep a thinker. I know that when I started to think it always got me in trouble!

In the fall of 1969 we were being touted as strong contenders for the Stanley Cup. Then, after two games, both of which we won, Abel fired Gadsby and took over as coach. I mean, you've got to wonder about a team that fires its coach for having a perfect record.

We had a great year, finishing third in the East with a record of 40–21–15. Now, we clinched our playoff spot on Saturday night in Detroit, and we still had a game the next afternoon in New York, but when we got to the dressing room, we found there was champagne everywhere. The management was celebrating because we'd made the playoffs! In Toronto you sometimes didn't even celebrate after winning the Stanley Cup.

The Sunday game was meaningless to us, but it was very significant to the Rangers. They were two points behind with the Canadiens for fourth place. If they beat us, they had a chance to be in the playoffs and put Montreal out. We all stank in that game, myself included, and the Rangers beat us, 9–5. After the game I gave everyone in the dressing room hell, *including* Sid Abel and Bruce Norris. I guess I should have known then that my tenure in Detroit would not last much longer.

In 1970, Sid Abel hired a new coach, Ned Harkness, who'd built championship college teams at RPI and Cornell. He'd be assisted by Jim Bishop from Oshawa. Ned was the first coach from the U.S. college ranks ever to coach in the NHL. I'd heard a bit about him, and knew that he was a disciple of Vince Lombardi's style of coaching. His motivational approach was right up my alley, and his thinking about the game of hockey was sound. But his arrival in the Wings training camp would make for some stormy times.

The other guys weren't sure what to expect, and Harkness didn't make a good first impression on the veterans — Mahovlich, Howe, Delvecchio, Stemkowski, and Gary Bergman. Harkness was a very emotional man, and he and Bishop came in like a couple of evangelists. You could see they thought they were going to change the world with their approach to the game. And they were looking for the players to share their enthusiasm. Except these were grown men, not college kids, and they weren't the "rah-rah" type, and they were never going to be because they were professionals.

Some of the players thought Harkness was from another planet, and Ned didn't improve matters when he started trading away players he suspected of not seeing things his way. I don't know if it was a coincidence but, when he cleaned house, he started with the ex-Leafs. Carl Brewer, a Second Team All-Star in his comeback year, didn't even show up for training camp, and ten games into the season Peter Stemkowski was dealt to the New York Rangers.

Stemmer, my roommate, had been in Ned's bad book since training camp. One night, about five minutes after he came back to the hotel room, there was a knock at the door, and when I opened it I saw a girl, naked as a newborn and high as a kite, lying on the floor in the hallway, pretending to be swimming. I turned to Peter and said, "Who's this?" He said, "I can't get rid of her!" A couple of minutes later, Ned came walking down the hall to our room for some reason or another, and without batting an eye just stepped right over her and into our room. Then he turned around and said, "What's that?" One of the great moments in sport.

I knew that my high salary — $45,000 — combined with my feud with Sid Abel, meant I wouldn't be around long. I told a reporter so: "I am not the most popular guy in Harkness' family. Early this season I had to take a stand or sit on the fence, and I am not a fence sitter. I won't enlarge on the problem, but I'd be surprised if I finish the season here."

On Tuesday, November 3, 1970, the Red Wings put me on waivers. I'd heard through my friend Don Giffin that Maple Leafs GM Jim Gregory was interested in bringing me back to Toronto — he had a carload of young defenceman and he desperately needed an experienced blueliner. And my salary wouldn't be a problem. But it didn't appear likely I'd end up in Toronto; under the waiver system, the last-place team had the first chance to put in a claim, then the second-last team, and so on up the standings. Toronto was third in line behind the California Golden Seals and Punch Imlach's Buffalo Sabres.

The minute my name hit the waiver wire he put in a claim, but before I even had time to think about it, Punch had traded my rights to the St. Louis Blues.

While all this was going on, nobody from the Red Wings organization talked to me. We'd just settled into the house in Bloomfield, and the children were enrolled in school and had just started their year. Realizing this would be my third move in four seasons, I even considered retiring and staying in Detroit. It was hardest on my kids — they kept asking, "What's going to happen to us, Daddy?" and it really hurt that I didn't have a good answer for them. George Gross got hold of me, and I was rather bitter when I talked to him. "You know, the steers on the farm are better off; at least they know what's waiting for them," I said.

Finally, Punch called and told me about the trade to St. Louis. Later, Scotty Bowman, the Blues' GM, called to say he was very enthusiastic, and was anxious for me to come to St. Louis. I felt I needed a few days to think about it.

I went to St. Louis to look around, and found that it had a few things going for it. I'd played with the coach, Al Arbour, and had enjoyed chatting with him now. I was also thrilled about the opportunity to play in front of Glenn Hall, one of the only great goaltenders I had missed playing with. But my meeting with Scotty Bowman did not go well. I found him to be another Punch: arrogant and pompous with an ego to match. I left my skates there to be painted, but I came home with many questions still unanswered. I was given permission to miss the Blues' two upcoming games.

I phoned Don Giffin to see if he could get me back to Toronto. He suggested I stay close to the phone. I also called Clarence Campbell and told him that I felt like a side of beef the way I was being traded around, after fourteen years in the NHL.

By Thursday the 12th, I still hadn't made up my mind, and the Blues suspended me for failing to report. The next day I had lunch at a friend's restaurant and stayed longer than I should have, without phoning Sallie to let her know my whereabouts. So I decided to bring home a peace offering of some fresh lobsters and my favourite white wine, Pouilly Fuisse. She was not impressed with me that day. Just as we were about to sit down to supper at 6:58 P.M. — and I can remember the time as clearly as if it were yesterday — I got a call from Jim Gregory. I had been traded back to Toronto. The deal was finalized on Friday the 13th.

In exchange for me, the Blues got Brit Selby, who was ending his second tour of duty as a Leaf. A Marlie graduate, he'd been rookie of the year in 1965–66, but spent most of the next season injured in the minors. Philadelphia picked him up in the 1967 expansion draft, only to trade him back in March 1969. He was a nice guy, but just one of those players who never lived up to the team's early expectations.

After I left Detroit, the housecleaning continued. In January 1971, Frank Mahovlich was traded to the Montreal Canadiens, where he would get the chance to win two more Stanley Cups, and in February it was Garry Unger's turn to walk the plank.

Mahovlich later told me a story about the cruel ending to my tenure in Detroit. I played for the Wings on November 1, and the next morning when the guys came in to practise they noticed that there was no sweater in my place in the dressing room. To add insult to injury, my number 4 had already been given to Larry Brown, the player who was coming over from New York in the Stemkowski trade. Frank thought this was one of the most hurtful situations he ever witnessed in professional hockey.

By mid-season, the Red Wings had a record of 12 wins, 22 losses, and 4 ties, and the team was about ready to revolt. So Bruce Norris fired the general manager, Sid Abel, and promoted Harkness to the GM's office. Detroit would finish seventh in the East Division — behind everyone, even the expansion teams in Buffalo and Vancouver. The team was in a real mess all year, and it was unfortunate for Ned. I really felt the college coaches had something to offer, and in later years, when my son Jeff played under Tom Watt at the University of Toronto (and after I'd finished coaching the Toros), I would become a real advocate of the college system. Tom was a real student of the game.

When the Leafs re-acquired me, it was a relief. Mid-season trades are always disruptive, but the blow was softened by the knowledge I was coming home rather than going to another city I knew nothing about. NHL president Clarence Campbell had apparently helped broker the deal when I made it clear that I would definitely not play for St. Louis, but I always felt a lot of the credit for the trade should go to Don Giffin.

We had been very close since the early 1960s, when the Giffins bought their cottage on Charleston Lake. The Bauns, Brewers, and Mahovliches used the cottage for two or three weeks every summer. They also had a property in Muskoka, and this is where they came to know the Smythes: Dot Smythe and Patti Giffin remain extremely close friends.

The Gardens' board of directors had become anxious about all the extracurricular expenses incurred by Stafford and Ballard. John Bassett tipped off the Bank of Commerce, which called Harold and Stafford's $4.5 million loan, and the two had forty-eight hours to cough up the money. Staff called Don for help, and he went to Sam Payton at the Toronto-Dominion Bank, and arrangements were made to help bail out the owners.

"Giff" had the financial wherewithal to do that. He'd built up a company called Giffin Sheet Metal. He was basically self-taught, and he had a tremendous knowledge of engineering. He could pick apart the most complex jobs. Until the day he died, he carried his union card for sheet metal. I felt he had the strongest ideals of any man I ever met.

In 1970 "Giff" became a member of the Gardens board and became a strong presence around the organization, and a major shareholder. At one point he had more Gardens stock than anyone except Ballard. He loved hockey, and he loved the Maple Leaf tradition. His company sponsored many kids' teams in Mississauga. Mostly, he just loved being around the Gardens. When Ballard died, Giffin handled the Gardens' affairs; there was a lot of squabbling and turmoil, and I think this led to his early death from cancer — he was just too worn out from fighting the Gardens' battles to fight his illness. One of his greatest achievements was bringing in Cliff Fletcher as general manager and restoring the winning tradition to the Toronto Maple Leafs.

CHAPTER 14

Back Home

The night after my trade to Toronto, the Maple Leafs had a home game against the Boston Bruins. I was eager to play right away, but there was still one minor hitch: my skates were now bright blue and gold, and they were still in St. Louis. It was a tight squeeze, but Gregory managed to fly them in by game time. I played more than thirty minutes that night and was chosen the first star of the game. It was so good to be back that I could have played for two days solid.

The move was just the boost I needed as a player, but it was also good for my family. We could finally settle back into Bally-bawn, which I had been longing to do, and the children could return to their old schools and old friends. And if the weather was bad, I could always just zip down to the Gardens by GO train.

And, believe it or not, we ended up doing just that one night in February, when the snow was so deep that Sallie and I rode our snowmobiles to the GO station. It snowed the entire evening, and when we returned not even our snowmobiles were up to the task of the eight-mile trip back to the farm. At 2 A.M. we stopped at a local service station run by a friend, Gerry Fisher, so we could phone home and check in. We'd left our oldest, Jeff, by then thirteen, to babysit the others for the first time. We felt we didn't have to worry about anyone getting into the farm or harming the children, because no one could get near it for the snow. They were all fine, and to our relief, they'd gone to sleep at the proper hour! Sallie and I ended up spending what was left of that night at the gas station. At dawn, Fisher got us back to the farm, and I only had about an hour's sleep before I had to hop back on the snowmobile, to the GO train, for a rare Sunday afternoon game.

It was clear as soon as I arrived in Toronto why the Leafs needed me. I was to be the senior citizen to lend stability and guidance to a very young defence squad. Rick Ley (currently a Leaf assistant coach) and Brad Selwood were 22; Jim Dorey, Jim McKenny, and Mike Pelyk were 23; and Brian Glennie was 24. All except the rookie Selwood were in their second or third full seasons in the NHL. One newspaper referred to them as the "Pablum defence." I welcomed the challenge. One of the first things I did was to take the defencemen and goalies out to lunch and go over strategy. I even picked up the cheque.

These sessions were not meant to be like a classroom, where I was the old professor and they were the students. There's a limit to how much you can do by just sitting there lecturing. Besides, there wasn't much these players needed to be told; they were bright guys who knew what had to be done. But the get-togethers were a valuable way for us to iron out a plan on how to work with our goalies, Jacques Plante and Bruce Gamble — or as we called them, "Jake and Bates."

Plante, who was no slouch when it came to directing a defence, explained my contribution to *The Hockey News*: "Baun talks to them all the time on the ice, telling them where to go and what to do. He is a leader and the best kind of leader because he goes ahead and does what he's talking about. What he tells the players isn't something abstract. They can see the correctness of it because that's what he does and he's successful."

It was a real treat playing with Jacques Plante. He was notorious as a loner and an eccentric, but no one could fault his hockey knowledge. One night in 1962, Jacques was playing for the Canadiens in Chicago, and he told the referee that the nets weren't big enough. Everyone thought it was another of his nutty ideas, but they decided to humour him by measuring the net. When they did, they found the crossbar was indeed two inches too low. It turned out the Black Hawks' equipment supplier misunderstood the standards, and thought the net was supposed to be four feet to the top of the crossbar, not the bottom.

Everyone knows Plante was the first goalie to wear a face mask on a regular basis, but it's not as well known that he was an innovator in the design and development of goalie equipment. He had a factory that made goalie masks, and he made enough off that operation that he could afford not to draw a dollar of his Leafs salary — he deferred his pay till years later.

He turned 42 during the 1970–71 season, and he put up the best goals-against average in the league. In February 1971 we dealt Bruce Gamble and Mike Walton to Philadelphia for Bernie Parent. Bernie was a character's character, and he just idolized Jacques. The two years they played together in Toronto made Bernie into a Hall of Famer.

Jim Gregory asked me if I would mind taking Jim McKenny, who was known to have a drinking problem — which he has since conquered, more than admirably — out to dinner and try and tell him to cut back a bit. I had no problem with this request because I really liked McKenny, as most everyone did. We settled on the Westbury Hotel, just behind Maple Leaf Gardens, a place that had one of Toronto's best dining rooms. We had a very pleasant evening, and we enjoyed more than a few drinks, more than a little wine, and even some dinner. By the time we got up to leave, it had snowed considerably. We each got into our cars, and in those days I was driving a Corvette. I backed up right into a huge snowbank, and got stuck. The two of us got out of our cars and tried to dislodge mine from the snowbank, and who should walk by but Jim Gregory. He kept right on walking, offering no help whatsoever, chuckling to himself. I'm sure he was wondering if his brilliant idea of sending the two of us to dinner was really so brilliant after all.

The Leafs had finished last in the East in 1969–70, and when I arrived in mid-November it looked like that's where they were headed again, as they'd put up a record of 3 wins and 10 losses. By mid-December we were about to embark upon a remarkable hot streak of 13 wins, 1 loss, and 2 ties. Where we'd been losing 5–1 and 7–2, we were now winning decisively. On January 2, 1971, we played the Detroit Red Wings, and they must have been slow in recovering from New Year's celebrations because we beat them 13–0.

Sportswriter Red Burnett noticed the improvement: "Pelyk has been working for a month, improving with every game, looking good even when his mates looked bad. The big reasons? Skating ability and a willingness to mix it." Pelyk, himself, said: "I'm not a holler guy and I need someone like the 'Boomer' around to keep me on my toes. He'll get on me if I don't jump for the puck or take a man in the corners."

Jim Dorey said he found it tough to play with me at first, because I would stand up at the blue line and seldom retreat. Then he admitted that he wasn't playing aggressively enough. "I got here because I was aggressive, played the man more than the puck. That's the way I have to play."

Paul Dulmage of the *Telegram* listed off the factors that contributed to our success. "Item One was the return of George Armstrong from an injury. [George was always an underrated part of the club.] Item Two was the return of Bob Baun. His body-checking, his experience, and his proof of the fact that he has always belonged in a Maple Leaf sweater have been an inspiration to the defence."

Skipping down the list, Dulmage cited the suspension of Mike Walton as Item Five. Walton was under the heavy influence of his agent, Alan Eagleson, who seemed bent on adding fuel to the fire rather than smoothing things over. His situation was also complicated by the fact that he'd married Conn Smythe's granddaughter, Candy. Red Kelly, who was now the coach and general manager of the Pittsburgh Penguins, said, "They seem to be getting on all right without what's-his-name." Walton was eventually part of a three-way deal that sent him to Boston via Philadelphia.

At around this same time, the Leafs called up a fiery young left winger from our Tulsa farm club: Brian "Spinner" Spencer. He'd played nine games for the Leafs the year before, but this time he felt he had the opportunity to really make an impression. He'd phoned his parents in Fort St. James, British Columbia, to let them know he'd be on *Hockey Night in Canada* that Saturday, as well as to tell them about the birth of his daughter. They were thrilled; it had been his father's dream to see Brian play in the NHL. Adding to the excitement was the fact that Brian was going to be interviewed on TV during the intermission.

Unfortunately, the Vancouver Canucks were playing at home that night, and it was their game that would be broadcast throughout British Columbia. When Spencer's father tuned in to see the Canucks instead of the Maple Leafs, he was livid. He drove to the nearest CBC affiliate, in Prince George, and raised hell, demanding that the station switch to the Toronto game. He ended up in a shootout with the Royal Canadian Mounted Police and lost his life.

We had a game the next night in Buffalo, and by the time the team bus left the Gardens, Brian had been told the sad news. He insisted on carrying on — he said playing for the Leafs was the opportunity of a lifetime, and he felt his father would want him to do so. He sat quietly with me at the front of the bus, and I tried to talk him into flying home right away, but he refused to change his mind. He played in Buffalo — we won 4–0 and he was named the game's third star — and took the bus back to Toronto with the team. Again he sat with me and talked a lot about his dad. When we got back to Toronto he took the long, sad flight home to bury his father.

At Christmastime I hosted one of my famous parties, this time at Ballybawn. I'd rented and borrowed enough snowmobiles for the whole team to have some fun. They had fun all right — half the snowmobiles were wrecked by the end of the evening. Darryl Sittler, who was just breaking into the league that year, said I was the one person who would try and get the team together, although not always on such a wild note.

Darryl was also shocked by my ability to spend money. We were in Vancouver for a game, and I wandered down to an art gallery and bought a piece of Eskimo sculpture worth four or five thousand dollars. Well, that represented Darryl's signing bonus, so his eyes were big as saucers when he found out how much it was worth.

I also liked to give Sittler a rough time in practice. I'd put my stick between his legs to pull him down, and that would annoy him no end. He'd always get his revenge when he got back to his feet, though, by rubbing my bald head. That was just as hard for me to bear.

In the second half of the season, I suffered a couple of injuries. One was a broken toe, but the other was more serious. During a March game in Philadelphia, I felt like I had a stiff neck, and the early diagnosis was whiplash. I made the trip to Oakland with the team a few nights later, but I was examined there and they decided to send me back home for therapy. The injury was described as a charley horse in my neck. Paul Dulmage's column was titled, "Baun So Sore, Even His Hair Hurts."

Rex MacLeod reiterated my strongest trait: "He is amazingly durable and seemingly indifferent to pain." What I liked about Rex was that he was one of those sportswriters who did not come into the dressing room just to bug you. Scott Young was another. Both of them only sought you out if they had in-depth questions, and they would only take up your time for a good reason. In my early years, Scott even brought along his young son Neil, and he would sit on my lap while we chatted. Who would have expected that Neil would go on to be a world-famous rock singer?

The Leafs ended the season in fourth place in the East Division, with a record of 37–33–8, good enough to get us into the playoffs for only the second time since 1967. In the playoffs we met the league's second-best team, the New York Rangers. They had a powerful lineup: the Vezina-winning duo of Ed Giacomin and Gilles Villemure in net, a defence led by Brad Park, and the famous GAG (Goal-a-Game) Line of Jean Ratelle, Rod Gilbert, and Vic Hadfield up front. We were eliminated in six games, the last of which was decided by an overtime goal scored by former Leaf Bob Nevin.

There was a wild moment during game two at Madison Square Garden. Somehow, Vic Hadfield got hold of Bernie Parent's mask and threw it into the stands. Naturally, it was a pro-Ranger crowd, so there was no way we were getting the mask back. We finished the game — which we won, 4–1 — with Jacques Plante in net.

Defeat is always demoralizing, but the coverage of that playoff series eased the pain somewhat for me. The headlines read, "Rangers Take Toll On Aching Bob Baun," "Baun Made 'Em Respectable," and "Baun Wilts, So Do The Leafs." At one point, Ranger left-winger Ted Irvine said, "He's the guy we've got to go after, he's the key to their defence.... As a matter of fact, although

I hate to admit it, you have to kind of admire the man the way he keeps coming back for more … As Baun weakens, you can see the Leafs whole game go to pieces."

Dick Beddoes of the *Globe and Mail* wrote: "Rangers kept knocking Baun down and he kept getting up, and his squat frame seemed an inch or two shorter every time."

As summer rolled around, the Leafs announced that I was to be the 1971 winner of the J.P. Bickell Memorial Cup. The trophy was awarded by the board of directors to an outstanding Leaf player. It wasn't handed out every year, and Tim Horton had been the last recipient, in 1969. It was a touching way to cap my homecoming.

The trophy is unusual in that it is gold rather than silver, and the player receives a small replica to keep. It was announced that I would be presented with the trophy during a pre-game ceremony at the Leafs' first home game of 1971–72. But fate would intervene to prevent this from happening.

In July 1971, the Leafs' owners, Stafford Smythe and Harold Ballard, were charged with tax evasion, theft and fraud. They'd been accused of using Gardens funds for their own purposes: paving cottage driveways, giving lavish weddings for daughters, making expensive improvements to their homes. These things aren't uncommon in business, and if they'd been the only two owners, no one would have blinked. But Maple Leaf Gardens Ltd. was a public corporation with many shareholders who felt it was wrong that the profits weren't being distributed properly. So Smythe and Ballard got caught. Many secrets were revealed about the two, and the most sensational was that they kept an apartment in a high-rise next door to the Gardens, under the name S.H. Marlie, which they used primarily to entertain lady friends. The Gardens was paying for that apartment, too.

The Mounties, the federal tax department, and the Attorney

222

General of Ontario's office were all investigating the Gardens' files, but still Harold didn't stop his monkey business. Right under their noses, Ballard loaded up the trunk of his car with steaks from the Hot Stove Lounge to fill his cottage freezer. Another director, George Mara, came upon this scene and advised Harold to think twice about what he was doing.

Stafford, on the other hand, was far more serious and took the charges very much to heart. He vowed he would never go to jail, and he never did. He was a heavy drinker, and in the fall of 1971 he had to be operated on for a perforated ulcer. In October, while still in hospital, he bled to death at the age of 50. He died twelve days before he and Ballard were scheduled to stand trial. Stafford's father, Conn, could only watch as all this went on. He disliked Ballard intensely, and it must have been painful for him to see his creation come under Harold's control.

I will never forget the fiasco of Stafford's funeral. Staff's casket had been set up at home, and Harold, who was beside himself, tried to pull Stafford out of the coffin. Someone else smashed the flowerpots on the front walk. Stafford's widow, Dorothea, always a lady, retired to her bedroom, and Don Giffin tried in vain to maintain some semblance of order. Meanwhile, investors hoping to buy Stafford's MLG shares were buzzing all over the house having discussions.

In the end, Ballard, as executor of Stafford's estate, bought all his shares. The following October, he was sentenced to three years at Millhaven Penitentiary, having been convicted of forty-seven counts of fraud and theft. It's a story in itself, and much has been written about it.

Stafford's death came at the beginning of the 1971–72 season. Our home opener had been scheduled for October 13, but that game was postponed until November 1. We were on the ice for our next scheduled home game, October 16, against the New York Rangers, and the players wore black armbands in Stafford's memory. A moment of silence was also observed. The Bickell ceremony was scratched, but I didn't mind. I was truly saddened by Stafford's death, and my main concern was obviously respect and sympathy for the Smythe family.

The Leafs again finished fourth in 1971–72. Those were the years when the Bruins, Rangers, Canadiens, and Black Hawks were dominating the league, and they were showing no sign of letting up. The Leafs had excellent goaltending, and our defence had solidified greatly during the past two years — if I don't say so myself. We were also solid up the middle, with Keon, Norm Ullman, Darryl Sittler, and Jim Harrison. The club's weak spot was on the wings. There was no depth beyond Ron Ellis and Paul Henderson.

We faced Boston in the 1972 playoffs, a team that was on its way to its second Cup win in three years. Gerry Cheevers, one of the best big-game goalies around, and Ed Johnston each shut us out as the Bruins eliminated us easily in five games. They had a big three of Bobby Orr, Ted Green, and Carol Vadnais on defence, and tremendous depth on the forward lines: Phil Esposito, John Bucyk, Ken Hodge, Wayne Cashman, Fred Stanfield, Johnny McKenzie, Eddie Westfall, and Mike Walton.

The 1972–73 season began routinely enough, with training camp and the usual exhibition games. One of these was in Detroit, against my old team, the Red Wings. While I was gone, my sisters, Joyce and Marlene, decided that the time had come to break the news to our father that Mom's cancer was spreading. The doctors felt there was nothing more they could do, and she only had a matter of months to live. By this point, Dad was busying himself by inventing things. He'd bought himself a little garage in Milliken — not a service station, but a sort of glorified shed — to use as a workshop.

His inventions were ahead of their time, and Dad probably could have done quite well with them if he'd pursued them further. One was a carburetor that, if installed in a car, would deliver 46 miles per gallon of gas. He buried it on the property. He couldn't swim, so he invented pontoons with fins, so he could walk on water. He had such confidence in them he'd go back and forth in the water, trusting them implicitly.

The other inventions were smaller, but they're in use today. One was a pipe cutter; another was a snipper for a car's water hose. And this particular day he was working on a plastic snip-off lid for an oil tin, similar to the ones they have inside orange-juice cartons nowadays.

Marlene knew where this little shed was, and she drove up to invite him back for dinner. When she arrived, the place was surrounded by police and fire vehicles. One of the policemen approached her, and when she said she'd come to speak to her father, he looked at her and said, quite matter-of-factly, "I'm sorry, miss, but your daddy is dead."

She was stunned, and she didn't really absorb the news. "Oh, but that can't be," she replied. "It's our mother who's dying." Unfortunately, the news was true. He had suffered a massive heart attack and died immediately, on September 27, 1972.

Marlene returned to Joyce's place, and they reached me with the sad and shocking news before the game in Detroit. I said I'd get home as fast as I could, and I told them to make sure they got hold of our father's wallet. I had two things in mind: Dad always carried a large amount of cash, and I didn't want anyone to steal it; secondly, and this was a reason I didn't outline to my sisters, I didn't want our mom to see any papers that might be in the wallet.

I was in shock when I caught a plane out of Detroit that night. I ate nothing on the plane, but I did have a few drinks. As the only son, there would be a lot for me to deal with as soon as I landed. First of all, given Mother's Ukrainian background and large family, most of whom had moved east, I knew a huge visitation would have to be planned. Then there was the funeral to arrange and get through. Given Mom's own precarious health, we wanted to spare her as much as possible. Finally, there was the usual reception for friends and family after the funeral, which we held back at our parents' home, which they had built on a lovely piece of property by the shore of Lake Ontario.

When all this was over, I went upstairs to lie down. In due course, I got up to go to the bathroom, and relatives noticed I was in there a long time. Sallie went up to check on me, and she found that I had become hysterical. I'd lost all control, and I was thrashing at the walls. No one could even begin to calm me down. My family all say that they were terrified — they'd never seen me like this before. I'm glad and fortunate to be able to say that they never have since. It was out of character for me; I'd always been considered the strong one with the broad shoulders that everyone could always lean on. It was what was expected of a professional athlete. In recent years, much of that has changed; when an athlete announces his retirement, no one is ever surprised or critical if he sheds a few tears.

Sallie called Dave Keon, a very close friend who also happened to live nearby. He wasn't strong enough to overpower me — this was one time when my physical strength was a detriment rather than an asset. Dave called Tim Horton, one of the strongest people he could think of, and who had come into town for the funeral. Finally, an ambulance was called.

It took both hockey players to hold me down while the ambulance attendants tried to sedate me and get me to the hospital. Once there, I was put into a straitjacket and shackled to the hospital bed. When Keon came in to speak to me, I stood up, bed and all! The doctors gave me some sedatives, but they didn't seem to have much effect. Still, they refused to give me a stronger dose. Dave and Timmy called the Leafs' medical expert, Dr. Hastings, and he rushed right over. He was able to convince the doctors that — having had considerable experience with me, and knowing my pain threshold — I would require at least double the normal amount of medication for a man of my size. This finally calmed me down.

Sallie says she still remembers the sight of me strapped into the straitjacket while Dave Keon looked up at me, trying to reassure me. If it weren't for the tragedy of the situation, it would have been comical. Joyce and Marlene say they will never forget seeing me in that state.

Immediately after I was released from hospital, Sallie took me, alone, to our cottage at Charleston Lake. It has always been one of my favourite places. My sisters were proud of Sallie for coming up with the idea, yet at the same time they were concerned that it was an awfully remote place to be if anything happened again. But it was as if Sallie knew what I really needed; rest, and time to recover and prepare for what lay ahead. My mother was living out a terminal illness, so there would still be much sadness yet to face.

After a week at Charleston Lake, I rejoined the Leafs and played in five of the team's first six games. Then, on October 21, I suffered an injury in a game against Detroit that would ultimately end my career.

As much as I can remember about the game, Mike Pelyk had the puck and I'd lost my stick. I shouted for him to freeze the puck, but he probably didn't hear me because he threw it behind the net. I tried to kick at it as Mickey Redmond closed in. I'd hit Mickey pretty hard in the first period and now, as I was off-balance from trying to kick the puck, Mickey knocked me to the ice.

I realized immediately that I would land on my head unless I went into a tuck position. I knew this from my off-ice activities such as trampolining and diving. Thanks to the tuck position I landed on my neck instead of my head. But I knew right away that something awful had happened to my neck.

Originally I thought, and hoped, it was a recurrence of that neck injury I'd suffered in Montreal when I was playing for Oakland. In retrospect, Sallie and I both feel that incident contributed to this injury. This time the doctors told me that, if I got hurt again, there was a 95 per cent chance I would wind up in a wheelchair. I didn't like those odds, so I decided to retire. All I had to do was remember my childhood friend Don James's accident, and his subsequent life in a wheelchair, to know the risks I'd run by continuing to play.

I went into seclusion on my farm for twenty-four hours. I had absolutely no idea what I would do with the rest of my life. I hadn't given much thought to retiring; I knew, of course, that the day would come, and maybe even in the next year or two, but I hadn't planned on it being right now. I talked with Jim Gregory, who was assuring. "Don't worry," he said, "we'll look after you." And to the Leafs' credit, they did. I was paid my full contract, which ran through the end of the 1973–74 season. Gregory, King Clancy, and coach Johnny McLellan were all very supportive; McLellan even asked me to come and help him out with the coaching.

I've never been the type of person to just sit around, and even with my contract paid up, I frankly couldn't afford to retire. George Gross visited me at the farm, and so did Trent Frayne. Gross asked me what I planned to do next, and I tried to give him a reasonable answer to a very difficult, yet logical question. "There are several possibilities," I told him. "Hockey is one. Cars are another, and the restaurant business is still another. I've always been interested in cars. I've worked for General Motors for most of the time since I turned pro. Maybe I'll want to own a car dealership. I still have to do a lot of thinking."

There was also the farm to take care of, especially once spring rolled around. "That's what I'll be," I finally told Gross, "a full-time farmer. But don't call me a gentleman farmer, because I like manure on my boots!" I've always tried to be positive, so I mentioned one thing I would be able to do now that I hadn't been able to before, certainly not while under contract: I thought I might take up skiing.

On December 16, my Mom, to whom I'd been so devoted, succumbed to cancer. Mom had been interviewed on many occasions, and her constant presence at Leaf games was well documented. "I simply couldn't bear to miss a game," she said once. "Sure I worry, and I'm probably the loudest shouter in the blues. I don't like fights nor wild scrambles but I'd rather be there than watching on TV." Mom regretted that she'd been unable to babysit more often because "I am never available on a hockey night. I go to the games regardless of weather or health and if the team loses, it takes me a day or two to recover from the disappointment."

In one article, Mom mentioned that my dad would watch the games on television. "Actually he's a very critical observer and though he'll compliment Bob on a good game, he's quick to bring up his bad plays, but I think it's just his gruff way of showing fatherly pride." This was a source of the trouble I'd had in dealing with my father's sudden death: Dad, as far as I could remember, had never really praised me as a hockey player.

In another interview, Mom lamented how she regretted ignoring me after a football game. I was thirteen, and I'd come home late for dinner. She told me to sit down and get eating, only to have me interrupt to say I needed to go to the hospital. When she finally looked at me, she realized that my nose was pushed over to one side, obviously broken, and I really was suffering. She felt terrible!

And now I would have to carry on without the most humane, caring person I'd ever known. No one could ever take her place. I loved and respected both my parents, accepting their few weaknesses in amongst their many strengths.

Friends and family came to Ballybawn for a reception. It was a slippery winter day, and by the time Don and Patti Giffin, who'd stayed for dinner, left for home, the weather conditions had deteriorated considerably. Their car slid through a stop sign and they were broadsided by another vehicle. Patti got the worst of it; she suffered broken ribs and a broken collarbone. When I heard about the crash, I jumped into my car and drove directly to Ajax-Pickering Hospital, where I stayed with Patti all night.

We'd become close friends with the Giffins around the time that Stafford Smythe died. I already knew Don's brother Harold, who was a United minister near Charleston Lake, and I came to know and admire Don. He and I found we had a mutual love of hunting, dogs, and rum, and we spent considerable time together. Don was also there to provide financial advice for some of my business ventures.

On one of our hunting trips, Don accidentally shot his own dog, which he'd named the Boomer, and was completely overcome — first with grief, and then with guilt. I had to carry the German short-haired pointer out of the bushes, and it looked like I might have to carry Don out as well. There was a Leafs home game that night, and the word quickly travelled around Maple Leaf Gardens that Giffin had shot the Boomer. At first, everyone thought he'd shot me!

———

My dear friend Keith Davey hosted a testimonial dinner in my honour at the Westbury Hotel to compensate for the lack of a formal presentation of the Bickell Trophy. Aside from its proximity to Maple Leaf Gardens, it was also my favourite dining spot. I'd come to know the chef, Tony Roldan, so well that I would sometimes assist him in the kitchen; all the while I'd be trying to figure out his culinary tricks.

Telegrams were sent by those friends who could not attend,

such as Prime Minister Pierre Trudeau, Ontario Premier Bill Davis, National Hockey League president Clarence Campbell, and such hockey notables as Punch Imlach, Bobby Hull, Dick Duff, and Harold Ballard. On behalf of Detroit owner Bruce Norris, Carl Brewer presented me with a desk set. Norris was the man who'd convinced me to go into the cattle business, and Red Kelly referred to this in his speech: "Bobby is smart to take up farming because steers are easier to get along with than hockey players." Leaf captain Dave Keon spoke of my diligence in helping the younger players, and added, "Baun is a truly great friend."

Keon left the Toronto Maple Leafs in 1975 after a falling-out with Harold Ballard. He never returned to the Gardens, even after the Leaf organization started to welcome back some of their alumni, and his absence from the closing ceremonies at Maple Leaf Gardens was both sad and conspicuous. My feeling about Keon today is that I only wish he knew how much we all miss him.

I, of course, rose to make a speech of my own. I love doing that, and I acknowledged everyone individually. My childhood coach, George Kitchen, was there, and he was deeply touched by the whole occasion. I asked George to stand up, and then introduced him as the best hockey coach I ever had until Junior A. At that point, Mrs. Kitchen told her husband, "You'd better sit down before your buttons all pop off!"

It was a memorable evening for me, but it also was a sad one. I truly felt this marked a turning point in my life, and in my hockey career in particular.

CHAPTER 15

The Farm, the Bulls, and the Toros

THEY SAY FARM BLOOD RUNS IN THE VEINS, AND PERHAPS NONE more so than mine. So back in 1964, I had begun to look for a farm near Toronto. One of the reasons was that the Baun family had been living in a new home on Ruden Crescent in Don Mills. But Sallie and I shortly grew concerned that we were out of our depth. When our children were getting fifty cents for allowance, while their friends were walking around with $10 bills in their pockets, we knew we were in the fast lane, and we wanted our kids to grow up in a more down-to-earth environment.

Harry Addison wanted me to buy near his place on Leslie Street, due north of the city, but I drove all over the Golden Horseshoe at the western end of Lake Ontario, and finally I settled in the township of Pickering.

In 1967, I bought 100 acres of land near Claremont, Ontario. We took possession on March 17 — St. Patrick's Day, as well as Brian's birthday — and we went to celebrate at George's Spaghetti House. In honour of the day, we wanted to give our farm an Irish name, so I suggested to reporters that people submit names to the newspapers, and that I would donate $1 for each entry to the Hospital for Sick Children or the Princess Margaret Hospital. I had no idea that 3,000 people would send in their suggestions, which meant that the two hospitals split $3,000 between them. The name we chose was Ballybawn, which is Irish for "place of home." It also seemed an appropriate combination of Bob and Sallie Baun.

To design our house, we hired Gardner Cowan, an architect who was well known in Toronto at that time for his exceptional and detailed work. We asked "Gard" for an English Tudor–style home, such as those we'd fallen in love with, and work began on the project while we were still based in Detroit. I tried to get to Claremont once a week to check on the farm as well as the progress of my dream home.

The finished home had twenty-three rooms, and it was built on the rise of a hill. It still stands today, and it's been added to somewhat by a new owner, Alex Chris. With a family of five children, and two adults who enjoyed entertaining, a house this size did not seem unreasonable. I'd hoped to do much of the work myself, remembering my father's words that one of his most satisfying experiences had been building his own home. I didn't have the time to do it all, but I did the next best thing, signing on as a subcontractor. There's a lot of me in that house.

Of course, there was a huge kitchen, where I had lots of room to work. And there was a vast wine cellar that could hold up to 2,000 bottles. Although there were only two storeys, Sallie remembers clearly that, by the time she finished cleaning one end of the house, it was time to start at the beginning again. In time, I added 150 more acres and leased another 1,750. I was truly the farmer I'd dreamed of becoming. We had six hundred head of cattle in the feed lot, five hundred of which were beef cattle. I remember one night when about two hundred got out of their pen. Sallie and I were returning from a night out, and we encountered a friend, Jim Cannon, riding his horse with his dog running along beside. He looked a little the worse for wear, and that's when he told me a third of my steers were running loose around the countryside.

I found the first forty in the driveway of stockbroker Tony Corson. He was stark naked on his front porch, trying to chase them away. I managed to get them moving, but they ended up in Parker's farm, where the entire family's laundry was hanging on the line. The cattle tore under the clothesline, and each one seemed to manage to get a piece of underwear caught on its horns: bras, panties, slips, and pyjamas. It was hysterical — if only we'd had a camera! Eventually, we rounded up almost all the animals. Most turned up within a mile and a half of the farm. I say almost all, because there were half a dozen that it would take us another month to track down.

The children loved it on the farm. Michelle had a horse, Percy, which she'd bought with her own money. Much to our amazement — and mild horror — she made the rounds at one of our Leaf team parties and canvassed all the players. And by the end of the evening, she'd raised enough money. She even managed to pay all of Percy's expenses by getting small jobs and working a bit with her mom at the nursery across the road.

At the back of the property, we had a sugarbush, and we used to make, bottle, and sell the maple syrup. On some occasions, the product was a little watery because we hadn't boiled it long enough.

In 1972 our farm was threatened when the federal government announced plans to build a second Toronto airport in Pickering. According to the plans, the incoming beacon for runway number one would have been on my property, and the airport terminal would have been just a mile away. They put a freeze on all the land within a mile of the perimeter of the airport site, and as a result Ballybawn lost much of its $1,250,000 value. Nearly thirty years later, the airport has never been built, but all the damage done by the government's expropriation scheme is still evident.

By September of 1973, our farming operation was a roaring success, as Canadian beef prices were at their peak. The next year we had six hundred short-keep cattle — cattle that you would buy and bring to market within ninety days — as there was a shortage of those. There were valleys to go with the peaks. On September 9, 1974, my thirty-eighth birthday, we sold our corn futures to the Co-Op for a price that should have netted us $350,000. Instead, the frost hit, and we were only able to rescue enough corn to make $100,000. The remainder had to be used as silage.

In the spring of 1975, we had our usual complement of five hundred calves to feed and fatten. It was the wettest spring in recorded history. I felt I could no longer afford much help, so I did all the work by myself, along with one herdsman and one helper. The three Baun boys also pitched in: they all remember that time as the hardest work they ever did in their lives. They're all hard workers today, so maybe this is where they developed that ethic. Sometimes I'd go three days without sleep just trying to keep up.

By this time the farm had become a real cash eater. It was too big to be classified as a family farm, yet not quite big enough to be a small corporate entity. Some close friends and family had invested in the farm, and the Toronto-Dominion Bank — with whom I had a $750,000 line of credit — was breathing down my neck. It was time to make a tough decision: I would continue to struggle with the farming, but the house would have to go.

The girls were too young to be told, so Sallie and I waited until after they had gone to sleep to break the news to the boys. They would have to help us move the furniture out in the dark of night, in borrowed trucks. Even the oak doors, which I'd bought and arranged to have flown back from Oakland, while I was playing there, were taken down and moved to storage. This, as can be imagined, made a deep impression on all of them.

We moved to much, much smaller accommodations in an empty rented farmhouse down the road. Sallie got full-time work at the nursery across the street, and for a time I did what I seem to do best: sales and signing autographs.

It was three years since my broken neck had ended my hockey career, and I thought the game was well behind me. I was ready to turn my full attention to the cattle I still had on the farm. But Johnny F. Bassett, owner of the Toronto Toros of the World Hockey Association, had other ideas. The team would have a new coach for 1975–76: Bob Baun.

I had watched more Toros games than any others, so I felt I had a good feel for the team. My old friend and teammate Billy Harris had been the coach at the start of the previous season. After a lacklustre start — a time during which Billy's daughter was very seriously ill — the team replaced him with Bob LeDuc. My observation was that the team needed to be a bit more physical.

When Bassett — the son of John W. Bassett, who'd been a member of the Silver Seven until he blew the whistle on Harold Ballard and Stafford Smythe — approached me, he offered me a three-year deal. Instead, I asked for a one-year contract. I didn't want a multi-year commitment, I only wanted to prove to the Toros that I could do the job.

He asked me if there was a salary figure I had in mind, so I did what I'd normally do as a player: I started asking around to find out the going rate. I asked Harold Ballard what the NHL coaches were making, and all he had to say to me was "shove that team up Johnny Bassett's ass." The deal I ended up signing was equal to what Philadelphia's Fred Shero — the highest-paid coach in the NHL — was getting: about $80,000, plus a car and life insurance.

In my first statement to the press, I said I felt the keys to winning were discipline, dedication, loyalty, and enthusiasm. The only way I knew how to play the game was physically, and so I added that "there will be no feather dusters on this team." This was music to the ears of general manager Buck Houle, who'd commented that, "The Toros have been called lovers, sissies, whatever you want, and it hasn't pleased me. We won't have to worry about this now with Bobby. He'll provide team play and discipline, things we've lacked."

I couldn't resist telling a reporter, "Most people thought I had a maple leaf stamped on my backside, but for the last two years I've had bull stamped on my backside. So the transition to Toros won't be too hard."

Before I could begin my new career, I had to wind down the old one: cattle farming was just not meeting expectations — neither mine nor the bank's. I was caught in three traps at once: the cattle market was glutted, the tight grain market was pushing up costs, and the new airport hung over our heads. I organized an auction on my farm for July 4, 1975. A pamphlet we prepared for prospective buyers said, "I'll be coaching the Toronto Toros this fall, and, as a result, I'm pulling out of the cattle business."

I built a special ring for the occasion, and the family, under Sallie's direction, set up a snack bar in the garage. The auction was not a success: in the first eleven sales, prices went from a high of $440, down to $260. I held a brief conference with the auctioneers, and cancelled the rest of the non-event.

I stepped up to the podium, looking and feeling dejected, and said, "I really apologize, but after all that work and effort, I just can't see letting them go for these prices. So go over to the snack bar and have some food on the Baun family." I later told a *Globe and Mail* reporter, Rudy Platiel, "I guess this is just another chapter in the Baun book. There have been quite a few sad chapters lately for that book."

Greg remembers me saying, when I drove him and Jeff back to school, that they would hear all sorts of stories and read things in the newspapers about the Bauns being bankrupt, but they should ignore those reports. I tried to reassure them that everything would be all right.

Although she was only in her early teens, Michelle remembers looking at the crowd of locals, and thinking that they had hopes of getting something for nothing, that they cared little for the outcome as far as I was concerned. She remembers feeling bitter because I'd always been there to help whenever the local farmers had needed it.

With three hundred head of cattle still left to look after, and with no help, I really didn't know what I was going to do. In the end, we travelled across the country, selling the cattle one by one in an attempt to recoup some of the money I owed good friends such as Don Giffin.

"Bobby Baun will find coaching more difficult than most other tutors," George Gross wrote in a piece about the hornet's nest I might be walking into. "For he was the type of player who knew only one way to play — all out. Today's hockey players believe in an entirely new philosophy — gimme. That type of approach is based on offering the smallest and least risky output for the most possible money … When they made players of Baun's type, they threw the mold away."

I did feel that hockey had changed from the game it had been twenty years before. Players expected to be treated more as individuals. Meanwhile, the Europeans had forced us to see that, while we may have had an edge in innate hockey sense, we had not improved our technical, mental, and physical hockey skills. As a result, we had probably lost the head start we'd had on them.

Gross asked me how I planned to motivate veterans like Frank Mahovlich, Paul Henderson, and Vaclav Nedomansky. I replied that I didn't know Nedomansky that well, but Frank and Paul were professionals, and they wouldn't be hard to motivate. When asked about the value of pep talks, I gave a lengthy reply, outlining that I was not Vince Lombardi — my coaching idol — and noting that the successful hockey coaches at the time were Fred Shero and Bob Pulford, both of whom had "game plans which they talked over with their players ahead of time, and not at the last minute."

Gross asked me if I would ever fine a player, and I replied that I would if I had to. He ended by asking if I would be the boss of the team, and I replied, "If I'm not the boss, I'm not the coach."

There was one interesting holdover from Billy Harris's coaching regime, which — although I wasn't fully enthused about it at first — I was going to continue. This was the fact that training camp was scheduled for Sweden. The destination was a town called Ornskoldsvik, which sportswriter Jim Proudfoot referred to as "closer to Lapland than the fleshpots of Stockholm." Harris had felt our focus would be completely on hockey, if only because we'd be unreachable. "Nobody will write to them as who can spell the address, and no one will phone when they can't pronounce the city's name."

Harris assured me that if you sat down to design the perfect training site, this would be it. "A few blocks away there's a sports centre with a full gymnasium and pool. There are running trails through the woods. The hotel is great. And the weather in September is cool, ideal for hard work." He pronounced it "a coach's dream."

Camp would run for twenty-six days, and the Swedish Ice Hockey Federation had scheduled eight games for us against the Swedish National Team. Besides the obvious benefit of getting the players into shape, I saw the trip as an opportunity to learn everything there was to know about my players. I was particularly interested in what was going on between their ears. I don't know how to motivate people unless I understand where their thinking is coming from — their backgrounds, how they were brought up. This is a philosophy I continue to use today when I'm trying to assess people.

I was asked to outline my team philosophy for the Toros

souvenir program. "I'm aiming to build a team which exemplifies the finest qualities of YALE. I want players who have Youth, Attitude, Loyalty and Enthusiasm." I was also hopeful I'd be able to sell my players on the benefits of moderation. In my early days with the Leafs, we were known as the milkshake team. I never had a beer till I was twenty-four, and when I did it was only because Allan Stanley told me I'd never last ten years in the league if I didn't. Of course, I hadn't a clue of how I was going to instil this moderation theory.

The team did not get off to a rousing start, losing its opening game in Quebec City 7–3 to the Nordiques. Quebec-winger Réjean Houle at least gave me the benefit of the doubt: "I know Baun and I've played against him. He'll get that team more defensive. They'll play the way he wants them to play and it won't be so easy for us."

Our home opener at Maple Leaf Gardens was more successful, as we beat the Houston Aeros 6–3. I was also pleasantly surprised at the size of the crowd: 11,996. I was glad that we had started to play some aggressive hockey. I thought we were maybe about halfway there.

I was wrong: we were more like halfway to disaster. After a second game in Quebec City — also a loss — some of my quiet discipline came to the fore. Defenceman Jerry Rollins, who had been knocked out of the game when a slap shot hit him in the forehead, missed the plane the next day. Whether he failed to set his alarm clock, or just didn't hear it, I really didn't care. I made him buy his own ticket and then fined him when he reached Toronto.

Things just went from bad to worse for the Toros. In *The Big M*, a biography of Frank Mahovlich, Gavin Kirk says, "Bobby Baun, who I have the utmost respect for as a person and a player, was a bit of a dictator as a coach. And that was the start of when the old boys club no longer worked. You couldn't rule by the hammer. You had to understand players and talk to players." The only problem was, to me this seemed like mollycoddling the players.

Where Frank was concerned, I found without a doubt that it's hard to coach people you've played alongside for many years. It's hard for the player as well as the coach. One day, Frank wanted to miss a practice so he could go to an art gallery with his wife, Marie. I said no, but the owner, "Johnny F.," overruled me. I felt Johnny F. was undermining my authority as coach, and I could see that he was trying to be one of the guys rather than an authority figure. I thought that if the players felt they could constantly ask favours of him, it wouldn't do the team any good. It went against what I had said earlier: "If I'm not the boss, I'm not the coach."

One night when we were on a road trip to Edmonton, Paul Henderson — who always roomed with Mark Napier — came into my room in tears. It wasn't unusual for players to drop in on me because I had an open-door policy with all of them. At the time, Paul was becoming a born-again Christian, and he was having trouble reconciling hockey with his ever-increasing interest in religion. He felt it was wrong to be earning such a large salary playing hockey, and he was absolutely broken up about it. The only suggestion I could think of to calm him down was to say that he should fly back to Toronto the next day and discuss this with his agent, Alan Eagleson. I knew the Eagle, who was entitled to a percentage of his salary, would have Paul back on the ice in no time.

The WHA was a wild, high-scoring league, where scores of 9–5 or 11–8 were not unheard of. To me this is the kind of hockey that the kids love, because they get to see lots of goals. But for an advocate of defensive play, as I was, it was a sorry imitation of the real thing. Between the calibre of play and the insubordination, the season looked like it was turning into six months of hell. There were other matters that nagged at me, too. For instance, the Toros rented Maple Leaf Gardens from Harold Ballard, who was no friend of the Bassett family, and he'd undermine the upstart team at any opportunity. One of his tricks was to leave the TV lights off until Bassett agreed to pay a much higher rent on the place. I spoke to Bassett and suggested that I quit; it just wasn't working out for the me or the team. He accepted that, but offered to pay me until the end of the season.

Speaking of Ballard, I drove down to visit him numerous times when he was in Millhaven. And on one occasion I mentioned that I'd be interested in a job as general manager — not of the Maple Leafs, but of the arena. I was interested in all aspects of the Gardens' operation — including sports other than hockey, and entertainment events such as concerts. Harold got upset with me — I guess he thought I was after his job, or that of his son Bill. But that wasn't my aim at all. I just like to do different things, keep on improving myself and moving around to new challenges. From that time on, my relations with Ballard were never the same.

Between the loss of the farm and the Toros debacle, these were sad and dreary times for the Baun family. I was also concerned that we might have to uproot my oldest sons, Jeff and Greg, whom we'd been able to send to St. Andrew's College in Aurora, Ontario, a very pricey private school.

Some of my friends' sons were thriving there, so I'd originally taken Jeff over for a look at it and to meet the principal. When I returned home alone, Sallie wanted to know where Jeff was. I quite calmly told her that I'd left him there for a few weeks to try it out. Poor Sallie didn't even have a chance to say a proper "goodbye," thinking he'd only be gone a few hours.

As it turned out, Jeff liked it so well that that we enrolled Greg the next year. They couldn't have been happier with their schooling there. But, along came bankruptcy. Fortunately for them, along came a benefactor, Bill Yuill. He was a St. Andrew's grad himself, and he'd gone on to tremendous success in business in Alberta. He'd also always been an avid sports fan. He had no children of his own, and when he heard about our family's financial problems he offered to pay the balance of their tuition for that year. In the end, he covered their costs every year until they each graduated. He's done the same for many others since. We'll always feel unbelievably grateful for what Bill did. Our third son, Brian, didn't get the chance to go to St. Andrew's, but he was quite happy with his schooling in Brooklin and Pickering.

The Toronto papers reported that both Jeff and Greg had their father's athletic skills, but that they hated to be compared to me. Jeff said it made him nervous when he saw me in the stands during one of his hockey games: he had no NHL ambitions but did want to play for Canada in the 1980 Winter Olympics. That didn't come to pass, but he did go on to play for Tom Watt, who coached at the University of Toronto. Greg, on the other hand, although he played hockey from the age of twelve, was dreaming of a career in the Canadian Football League. His football coach felt his chances were excellent, as he was a mature and competent fullback. He's also found better things to do.

The time had come once again for me to pick myself up, dust myself off, and start all over again. A new housing development was being built near Oshawa, and the developer, Gerry Armstrong, asked if I would come for the weekend and sign some autographs on the site. He was paying $500. Armstrong realized I was in my element dealing with the public, so he asked me if I would like to help sell. What did I have to lose? In six weeks, I sold all the houses. Another development, an enclave of sixty-eight houses called "The Homestead," was starting nearby on Harmony Road in Oshawa. In a period of eight months I managed to sell enough houses to make $120,000, which certainly put me back on my feet again.

Selling houses was great, but I really loved cars, so I decided that that was what I really wanted to do. Of course, I'd had years of experience with Alex Irvine and Harry Addison, to whom I practically became another son. A friend of mine, Michael Sifton, gave me a job at a dealership he owned called McLean Chevrolet Oldsmobile. Bud McLean and I did not get along at first, so he suggested the two of us go away to his ski chalet for a few days and re-assess things. I'd gone through the General Motors management school, so we did up a business plan based on the GM program. Bud agreed with everything we had decided, but then he realized he was doing better selling used cars for cash. Since the boss, Michael Sifton, was away playing polo in Carmel, California. I was somehow expendable.

This was followed by a brief stint in 1978 with Mr. Transmission. I worked in the southeastern United States, between Atlanta and Florida. Then I embarked on my next major career.

My good friend and lawyer, Jim Blaney, had brought an offshoot of an American insurance company, American Family Insurance, into Canada where it would be called Pan-American Family. He wanted me to come on board and sell cancer insurance. I was dubious at first — I knew I was fed up with people selling things door to door, and I was sure most people felt the same way. On the other hand, I thought back to the time when my mother was dying of cancer and no one was dealing with it. The policy Pan American sold would pay out $100 a day for care, and I thought about how helpful that would have been if I'd had such a policy during my mom's illness.

I flew down to the company's head office in Columbus, Georgia, and met the owners, John and Paul Amos. While I sat in the waiting room, an older gentleman caught my eye and, as usual, I struck up a conversation. I discovered afterward that the gentleman was Mark McKee, he was eighty-seven years old, and he was on the company's board. He was also on the boards of thirty other corporations. He'd started out as a "door-knocker" at age sixteen and travelled around, just as my father had done, by riding the rails.

A friendship ensued — which is also not unusual for me — and it lasted until McKee's death in his mid-nineties. I've always been drawn to unusual or eccentric characters, and McKee was certainly one of those. He had eleven children, who stayed with his wife when he got divorced. But he kidnapped one of them, Terry, at age five. First he put him on a farm at Lucknow, and then, at age nine, put him into St. Andrew's College. Terry's brother would be sixty-seven years old before he ever got to sign a company cheque.

Mark McKee was a friend of Howard Hughes, and he was also one of the people who worked to get Mackenzie King elected in the 1920s. Finally, close to the end of his days, he told his wife he was locking himself in his room and she was not to enter for two days. As anticipated, she found him dead.

Inspired by that chance meeting with McKee, I signed on. The job required me to recruit thirty people a month for training seminars, to indoctrinate them into the ways of selling cancer insurance. The first was at Toronto's Royal York Hotel and I was able to get thirty-eight or thirty-nine potential recruits. Unbeknownst to the Amos brothers, they were mainly Baun relatives. A guy named Bill Campbell, from Michigan, gave them a pep talk in which he told them he'd had renewals of up to $48,000 a month.

I never did quite reach those peaks, but I did stay with the company for five years. During that time, I flew 150,000 air miles a year, and drove over 50,000 miles. Most of the travel was between Columbus, Georgia; Toronto; and London, England, still one of my favourite places.

The laws regulating a company like Pan-American changed so that Canadian ownership was required. Charlie Burns, a former Gardens director, took the company over on behalf of Crown Life, and eventually the business withdrew from Canada. For me, this meant it was time to find another livelihood.

During my time with Pan-American, another tragedy touched our lives. Our son Brian, then nineteen, was driving near Calgary on October 10, 1980, and was involved in a single-car accident in which one passenger was killed. Another who'd been sleeping in the back seat survived unscathed. Brian had been out West, working on an oil rig while he took a year off before starting university. The paramedics literally saved his life: there were no vital signs on him at first. They revived him and took him to Calgary General Hospital, where he was kept for weeks recovering from injuries to his arms, legs, and head.

While we were in Calgary, Sallie and I were fortunate to find support and friendship from two sources: Bert Olmstead and his wife, Nora. The hospital staff were wonderful (many of the doctors had trained under the Leaf medical team of Dave Hastings and Tate McPhedron), and the paramedics certainly worked miracles, but there is nothing better than good friends at a time like that.

When Brian was stable enough to fly, we brought him back to Toronto, and he made a complete recovery. He went on to attend the Niagara Parks Horticultural University, and now runs his own very successful landscaping business. Sometimes, there really is light at the end of tunnels.

CHAPTER 16

My Life
After Hockey

I WAS PROBABLY CLOSER TO TIM HORTON THAN TO ANY OTHER member of the Toronto Maple Leafs. In fact, I even lent Tim $10,000 to get his company off the ground. He'd always dreamed of owning some sort of restaurant chain, and there'd been a few false starts. Then along came a policeman from Hamilton by the name of Ron Joyce, and an empire began. As hard as it is to believe, in those days, the world hadn't heard of Tim Horton Donuts. The sad thing is that there's now a whole generation who don't know Timmy for anything but donuts.

Through Tim, I became friends with Ron Joyce, and that friendship intensified when Tim was killed in a high-speed car accident on a bitterly cold night in February 1974. By this time the loan had long since been repaid, and the company was on stable footing.

I remember talking to Tim on the night of the accident. At age forty-four, he was still playing for the Buffalo Sabres, and he was showing no sign of quitting soon. I met up with him at the Gardens, and we were all going to meet up at George's Spaghetti House, but for some reason he never showed up. He was driving a very fast sports car, a Pantera. Very few of them had been manu-factured, and his had been given to him by Punch Imlach as a signing bonus. Ironically, Doug Cole had borrowed the car the week before the crash.

Apparently, Tim got as far as the Tim Hortons head office in Oakville, Ontario. He met with Ron Joyce, had a couple of drinks, and talked about how business was booming. He'd been under a doctor's care for a jaw injury, and was taking Percodan for the pain, which he should never have mixed with alcohol. It's sad to admit, but in those days we weren't nearly as aware of the dangers of driving under the influence of alcohol or medication.

After leaving the office, his car hit a bridge abutment on the Queen Elizabeth Way in St. Catharines, at the unbelievable speed of 140 miles per hour. It flipped over, then righted itself and turned in the opposite direction. Tim was thrown out the driver's side window. I was told there was barely a mark on his body: just a small cut on his forehead, and a scratch on one leg.

I was at the farm when I heard the news; the ringing phone woke me up at 5 A.M. It fell upon my shoulders, and those of Ron Joyce, to help alleviate the burden of planning the funeral that Tim's widow, Lori, faced. All anyone can remember of that terri-ble time is people, people, and more people. Between his Buffalo Sabres teammates, his former Toronto teammates, his wife and four children and all their friends, neighbours, and business asso-ciates, not to mention adoring fans, you can imagine how many people were milling around.

A few years before, my mom had read Lori Horton's tea leaves. Mom dabbled in reading people's palms, tea leaves, and cards. In Lori's case she was chillingly prophetic as she said, "Someday, in the not too distant future, your life as you know it now will suffer a great tragedy and change completely."

After Tim's death, Lori found things more and more difficult to cope with. There wasn't only her own grief to deal with, but that of her four daughters, most of whom were in those awful teenage years. She sank into a serious dependency on drugs and alcohol. The logical and sensible conclusion for Tim's business affairs was for Ron Joyce to buy her shares of Tim Donut Ltd. and continue to operate the business on his own. Joyce bought Lori out for $1 million — he practically had to beg, borrow, and steal to come up with such a large amount, but somehow he did it. He'd tried to convince Lori that she would be better off with payments of between $100,000 and $150,000 a year, spread out over five years. But Lori wanted a million dollars right away and so she got it.

Sadly, for herself, for her daughters, and for Tim's memory, she spent it all rather quickly. The bright side is she eventually got some treatment for her problems and got back on track.

Sober and broke, Lori decided to sue Ron Joyce, saying she had not been in her right mind, citing her drug and alcohol dependency when she accepted the million dollars, and stating that, because the company was really taking off, she felt entitled to more. This was a difficult time for the combatants in the courtroom, but it was also hard on a few others who knew and were fond of both parties.

Of course, I was one of them. I had to testify, and did so on Ron Joyce's behalf. Tim and Lori's daughter, Jeri-Lynn, is married to Ron Joyce, Jr., and she must have been in a horrible bind. I still cringe when I remember Lori's face as she stared across the courtroom at me.

The friendship between Ron Joyce, Sr., and I has lasted and grown over all these years. What impressed Joyce about me when we met at George's Spaghetti House for the first time was my tenacity and my sincerity. He also felt I was an "overall nice human being." Both of us are avid fly fishermen and we have taken a number of fishing trips together.

One memorable trip was to Henik Lake in the Northwest Territories. We flew in and hit a stone on the unfinished runway, which managed to chip the propeller. The blackflies were so thick that we had to wear nets over our faces to protect ourselves. The upside was that we did catch a lot of fish, which we prepared and ate right there.

Ron is proudest of the camps for underprivileged children, which he has started in Tim's memory. His connection with Tim was not solely based in business. They were true best friends, and the mention of his name, particularly in connection with these camps, can easily bring a tear to Joyce's eye. The camps have been operating for over twenty-five years, and in that time Joyce has always been very appreciative of my support and enthusiasm for such a worthwhile cause.

These camps began in Ontario but, as the company's profits allowed, Joyce has been fulfilling his dream of opening them all across Canada. When one was opened in Nova Scotia, Joyce took some favoured supporters there via a chartered Worldways L1011 wide-bodied jet. It was a "super deluxe day," according to Don James. A number of former hockey players, such as Bobby Hull and Pierre Pilote, and their wives, were in attendance.

Don also loves to tell the story of the time that he, Ron, and I did a little Christmas shopping for our wives. Terry Convoy, a former model herself, took us to a restaurant, wined us and dined us, and then had some glamorous models parade around in a series of outfits she thought our wives and daughters would like. She even did the gift wrapping, which is never a favourite sport for men. We left, parcels in hand and seemingly pleased with our purchases. Don got home first, and his wife, June, convinced him to let her open her present. The gift didn't suit her at all. His daughters felt the same way about their gifts. Then the James ladies called the Baun household to forewarn Sallie. Of course, unbeknownst to me, she insisted on opening hers right away, too. Same reaction.

Despite our lack of success, we kept up this method of Christmas shopping for some years. Having fun with the boys was as much the point of the exercise as the actual purchases.

During the summer, the same group would take a cocktail-dinner cruise on Lake Ontario. One year was especially eventful. Ron and I, both very strong men, were on the dock, trying to hoist Don — in his wheelchair — over to the captain, who also appeared to be strong but was caught unaware by a wave that caused the boat to lurch. Poor Don ended up hanging from the lower railing, looking up to the deck where he was supposed to be. Don is never at a loss for words, and he always does his best to put a smile on someone else's face. In this case he proclaimed, "I'm just enjoying the view!" as he gazed directly up some innocent lady's skirt.

When I think of Ron Joyce, I always remember an incident involving another very dear friend, Jim O'Donnell. I first met Jim in 1982 when I was looking for funding for the players alumni. I contracted Alex Chris, who had bought Ballybawn and who was highly connected with Mackenzie Financial. Chris suggested that I talk to Jim, so I called him. Jim agreed to meet me a few days later at the Park Plaza Hotel for breakfast. I told him we needed about $20,000 in seed money. Jim said he believed in the cause and would have a cheque for me that afternoon. He then asked if Sallie and I would be interested in going to Monte Carlo. I said, "Where?" thinking he meant a Monte Carlo night somewhere. He meant the actual Monte Carlo. He treated us to a spectacular trip there, first class all the way.

Later, Jim became interested in Indy car racing, so I suggested to Ron Joyce (Tim Hortons) that he and Jim co-sponsor a car. Joyce agreed to spend $350,000. I got to the press conference before Ron did. I nearly died when I noticed that the only reference to Tim Hortons was a tiny sticker on each door of the car. Ron was quite irate, and I couldn't blame him. I wanted to run and hide.

Jim was the man who first devised the idea of advertising on the boards at hockey rinks. While watching games on TV he would keep track of the number of times the clock was shown on the screen. He arranged advertising for Mackenzie Financial on the clock at Maple Leaf Gardens, and then bought advertising on the boards as well. He knew that seeing the company logo several times during the game would have an impact.

Following suit, I suggested to Ron Joyce that the best place to advertise Tim Hortons was the southeast corner of the rink, the spot most televised.

Jim and Ron became friends. I look upon them as the two greatest marketers in Canada today.

───── ⬤ ─────

In the fall of 1984, Sallie and I decided to take on a Tim Hortons franchise on White's Road in Pickering, a location that had been very familiar to me for most of my life. Neither of us could have dreamed that that donut shop would ultimately destroy our marriage.

There's more to opening a Tim Hortons franchise than putting up the cash. You must attend donut school for eight weeks! While Sallie and I were "students," we stayed at Ron Joyce's apartment in Burlington. I look back upon that time as probably the most fun the two of us ever had. We were away from the children and all our responsibilities, and we could just be silly. The course covered every-thing. We learned to mop the floor properly — and it *must* be mopped properly. I developed quite an attachment to the mop, and I would dance around the apartment with the mop as my partner.

We opened on December 21, and we hit the ground running. Of course, opening up at that time of year was like my hockey days: there wasn't much time for a family Christmas.

It's mind-boggling to look at the facts and figures behind an operation of that kind. (And I'm not sure what it says about me that I still seem to remember them by heart!) A store like ours would go through 6,000 to 8,000 pounds of raw product a week. We'd use an incredible 275 pounds of donut yeast over a twenty-four hour period. We'd sell 200 white and chocolate cakes over a weekend, using 300 pounds of mix. We'd sell 300 pounds of cake donuts in a day, just under half of which — 125 pounds — were chocolate. Add to that, sixty to seventy trays of cinnamon buns and 16 pounds of French crullers. At 3 A.M. all unsold products went in the garbage: there's no day-old food at Tim Hortons.

With the average customer spending $2.20, ours was the first Tim Hortons ever to make $1 million in sales in its first year. It was the top franchise in Canada for four years, and the first store to sell $1.5 million worth of product in a year. All that with only 550 square feet of kitchen space and 1,100 square feet overall.

We were encouraged, so I decided to open a second location at the corner of Westney Road and Bayly Street in Ajax on my own. This did almost as well. You were considered a success if your store did $750,000 a year, but mine always topped $900,000. Next I wanted to open a Tim Hortons franchise with a drive-through concept. Ron didn't like the idea then, but now Tim Hortons drive-throughs are commonplace.

Ron Joyce agrees that the Baun outlets were always the top in his company, and he always found them spectacularly clean. (I'd really taken mop lessons to heart!) There was only one problem: my financial statements were always a disaster, because I've never been much on bookkeeping. I never kept a proper record of what was collected in sales taxes, so the government was always breathing down our necks. Somehow, we managed to stay out of jail. Sallie's bookkeeping was always excellent, so the White's Road location prospered.

My opinion of franchising is that you are buying yourself a job with some good perks. But if it's not a good store, you're buying yourself one godawful job. Unfortunately, I got bored with the business. I would describe it as getting tired mentally. And I guess Sallie was feeling the same way as far as the Baun weakness was concerned. And so we separated, and sold both franchises.

Although it seemed sad to family and friends that our marriage and partnership of so many years had ended, it actually ended up leading to a new beginning. Our problems had always been financial in nature. I freely admit that I have no idea how to budget — and no desire to find out, either. It's not my style. Sallie, on the other hand, is extremely well organized, very good at making and sticking to a budget. And after our experiences in business — especially the devastation of losing the farm — she's not comfortable relying on any man.

We were separated for ten years, but — with all our assets divided — we eventually got back together. Sallie likes to describe the situation as "best friends."

During those ten years, I came to value more than ever my very special friendships. I also had more time to give them. First and foremost, of course, was Don James. The bond between Don and me loosely parallels the friendship exhibited in the movie *Brian's Song*, except fortunately we are both still alive to tell the tale. Our story could also be titled "The Brain and the Brawn." We came together through both school and sports, and when the time came that Don could no longer participate, he loyally attended as many of my Marlie and Leaf games as he could.

Don describes my physical maturing as "the raising of a steer." When we first played shinny together, we were somewhat equal. Don might even have been stronger, given his age. But then I got stronger and stronger, to the point where, as Don puts it, "You could no longer push Bob around. Trying to do so was like trying to move a brick wall." Some claim I am that stubborn as well.

Another, more recent, friendship is with Roy Main. We met at a Grey Cup party hosted by a mutual friend, Del Page, and we discovered some common interests that we've pursued over the past fifteen or twenty years. One of these is fishing. For some years I had taken Roy as my guest to Caughnawana. Roy wanted to reciprocate, so five years ago he took me to a remote fishing camp in the mountains of Wyoming. The scenery there much resembles that in the Robert Redford movie *A River Runs Through It*. The location was Jackson Hole, and the spot where we camped was accessible only on horseback. I'd been assigned a horse called Big John, and he was as stubborn as the proverbial mule.

We slept in tepees for five days without showering or shaving. Our leader, Monty Skinner, a former world-class skier who was in his mid seventies, proved extremely stern. His nephew had climbed Mount Everest, and by the end of the trip we felt as if we'd climbed Everest, too.

The payoff was that the fishing was absolutely incredible, probably the best either of us had ever experienced. When it was time to get back home, the two of us were a pair of grumpy old men. We had to fly from Jackson Hole to Chicago, and then switch planes for Toronto. In the airport at Jackson Hole we argued over which one of us would look after our bags. I looked at Roy and said very tersely, "I don't give a damn about the bags." Given the rift between us, we decided to ask for separate seats. By Chicago I was feeling a little sheepish, so I asked Roy, "Are you ever going to speak to me again?" He thought about it, we both chuckled, and sat together the rest of the way to Toronto.

There were other times when Roy had good reason not to speak to me, but he's always stuck with me. Once we attended a charity auction at Casa Loma, and needless to say the refreshments flowed freely. When the bidding began, I was in fine form, so I bid first on a gold ring, then on an evening at the SkyDome in a private box for eighteen people. Then I got tired, as I usually do after too many drinks, forgot about the bids, and went home, leaving my friends to pick up the tab.

Roy took the ring and sold it, and the eighteen friends all pitched in for the cost of the SkyDome box. Roy remembers that evening because I decided to take my lady friend of the time to the stadium, thinking it would be a great opportunity to introduce her to them all at once.

In the late 1980s, Don James, Roy Main, and Del Page banded together to talk me into holding a celebrity golf tournament. These tournaments are one of the best ways to raise money for charity. Golfers pay to play a round with a sports hero, then afterwards there's a dinner where they can mingle with the other sports celebrities. There's also often a silent auction to bid on donated artefacts or collectibles.

We held the Bob Baun Celebrity Classic at the Emerald Hills Golf Club near Aurora. Over twelve years, with the assistance of Don James and others, we've raised over a quarter of a million dollars for charities, such as Lyndhurst Hospital — a specialty hospital for those with severe physical handicaps — and Bob Rumball's school for the deaf. Harry Rosen always donates jackets for the winners. In more recent years, the tournament has shifted to Scarborough Golf Club and then Cedarbrae Golf & Country Club, in order to lower the overhead and allow a greater share of the proceeds to go to the charities.

After we sold the donut franchises, Sallie and I set about living our lives separately. We both had a lot of settling down, growing up, learning, and adjusting to do. We'd been so young when we got together, and then we had children very quickly. And we did all this while I was part of the hockey world, which is a totally unnatural, albeit exciting, environment. We'd never really had a chance to figure out what we were like as individuals in an adult world, never mind learning what our better half was really like. Now that we've had that chance, some of our best friends — and even our children — tell us that what we have is a love-hate relationship: we can't live together, but we can't live without each other.

Sallie had been my only real girlfriend when I was growing up, so I never really got a chance to sow my wild oats when I should have, when I was single. Now I could. I had a brief liaison with a woman who worked in one of the donut shops, but that was basically a bad relationship for everyone. Then I had a long involvement with my banking advisor, but whenever the question of marriage seemed to be in the air, I was gone.

The Leafs love to tease me about my brief fling with a gorgeous, sexy blonde by the name of Lise Colonyeau. I'd been invited to the wedding of Phillip Giffin, one of the sons of my dear friend Don. The Giffins arranged for another family friend, Russ Bannock, to fly them to Quebec in his private plane. Also on board was their friend, Dr. Barbara Hazlitt, whom I knew through the Giffins.

The bride was from a prominent Montreal family, so this was to be quite an occasion. No one expected that Barb and I would develop a romance on this trip. We'd known each other for years, and, as anyone who knows either of us realizes, we're not at all suited; we were just to keep each other company. It was a great idea until I discovered Lise. Barb was quite unceremoniously ditched. And the Giffins were quite annoyed with me.

The Leafs of my era got wind of the romance when shortly after I travelled to Prince Edward Island for Rick Vaive's golf tournament, and showed up with Lise. Of course they all knew Sallie, and here I was acting like a kid with this glamorous creature. Who knows, they might have been a bit jealous, too. As Billy Harris said, "There he was, running up and down the beach, holding hands with this dreamboat." In due course this relationship fizzled as well.

There was one other short-lived liaison with an interior designer, Betsie Shea. In none of these cases was I prepared to make a real commitment. It would probably always be Sallie.

I did manage to do some travelling in our years apart, including a major trip to Thailand with a friend — for once, it wasn't a woman, it was Ted Irvine. We stayed in a huge, ultra-modern hotel. There were his-and-hers marble spas; a restaurant that seated 3,000, where you put your choice of food in a basket and it's delivered to you, prepared perfectly. I could not believe the manager's office: it had pictures of guess who all over it.

For part of the separation, I lived with my then-widowed sister Marlene and her son Jason. It's the only time I actually lived with another woman!

Through it all, Sallie and I were always together for any family function. We may have arrived and departed separately, but while there, we were together. I bought a house, near Ballybawn, and intended to do grandiose renovations. It started as a 1,600-square-foot house, which I planned to expand to 4,000. The master suite alone — equipped with a Jacuzzi — was to be the size of the original house. I'd been hopeful that Sallie might move in with me, but the day after I bought this house, Sallie bought one for herself, in Pickering.

I'd been trying for years to convince her to take up golf, but she'd expressed no interest. Now that we were apart, she'd taken that up as well. I felt that she was making a statement.

Along the way, we even got divorced. Actually, we still are! One year, we were away visiting friends at their cottage for a weekend and had a really good time. Shortly after we returned, it was Sallie's birthday, so I sent flowers. Later that day, the divorce papers also arrived, from my lawyer — they were never supposed to be delivered that day. Sallie was definitely not impressed with my timing.

When it was clear that Sallie would not move into the house I was working on, I decided to sell. Unfortunately, my timing in the real estate market was just as bad, so I took a considerable loss.

Did the lawn really need cutting three times a week, or was I just lonely? In any case, we got back together again, in Sallie's house, in the fall of 1998. The children all say that they never really felt as if we were ever separated. It's a most unusual situation, but it seems to work — maybe more couples should try it. Sallie has no more financial worries because she invests very carefully and is completely independent. Growing up, her father changed jobs regularly, so this is really the first time in her life that she's felt financially stable. She's also taken an active interest in the stock market and seems to do quite well. She's also having fun with it.

Building on the success of the Leaf wives' bridge club, she has formed a women's investment club (completely above-board, not a pyramid scheme) and they call themselves the "Money Madams."

With five children, twelve grandchildren, countless mutual friends, and basically the same interests — with a particular fondness for golf — we seem to function well as a team. We both also pursue our own separate interests, without in any way hindering or interfering with the other. I still have many irons in the fire; I'm always busy giving speeches or autographing, and in the summer I play in countless golf tournaments across Canada.

All five children are married, and all are very hard workers and have achieved success in their chosen professions.

Jeff, having earned an engineering degree from the University of Toronto, has his own construction business (Baun Construction), which specializes in major renovations that need specialty concrete. He's also in the process of getting another company, Integrated

Kiosks, off the ground, and the future looks promising for that, too. I'd tell you more, but I don't want to jeopardize his success.

Of all our children, Jeff is the most like me in temperament, traits, and habits, and he freely admits that. The biggest problem he's had with me is the same one I had with my father: getting me to come out and say I love him. But he has succeeded. Jeff and his wife, Ann, have two young and very active sons, Andrew and Christian.

Greg was the born football player. He married early, while he was at Queen's University in Kingston, and then he took a job in the Yukon as an arena superintendent. He and his wife realized the marriage was finished, and he drove home, 8,200 miles, without stopping or eating — he was fuelled by nothing but Coca-Cola. He got as far as South River, in Northern Ontario, getting three speeding tickets along the way, and then collapsed in a motel, threatening to commit suicide. He was completely exhausted.

His mom and younger sister Patti jumped in the car and drove up to meet him, while I was glued to the phone, talking with the police about how to handle him. Basically, the answer was to give him food. It was a nightmare, but he is now happily married to a very bright girl, Glenda. They have a son, Lyle, who seems to be following in Grandpa's footsteps with hockey, and two little ballet-dancing daughters, Jessica and Lauren.

Glenda helps with his business, Innovative Building Products, which sells specialty road products — for ice melting and patching. The ice melter is made from magnesium imported from the Dead Sea, and it's completely safe for the environment.

They live in a house overlooking Lake Ontario, near where my parents' last house was, and a few doors from one of my favourite Gardner Cowan homes.

Brian, my third son, was the one who followed my love of art. But while I used to draw hockey manoeuvres on my Grade 5 workbook, Brian had his own room for art in Ballybawn, and he's since become a landscape designer. He is married to Claudia, whom he met while they were both studying landscaping at the Niagara School of Horticulture. She, too, helps him with his work, and they have three children: Erin, Nicholas, and Peter.

Michelle, the $2,500 baby, is a very natural, down-to-earth girl. She married a man she met at my Tim Hortons franchise, Keith Karroll. I was chomping on my cigar, standing in front of the donut shop that was about to open, and looking for a manager. Keith stopped and talked and I hired him on the spot. I did mention one condition of employment: no dating fellow employees. He and Michelle disobeyed that rule, so I fired both of them! They now have two daughters, Jill and Monique. Keith has his own business in home improvements, specializing in four-season rooms. As a teenager, Michelle kept an album of my press clippings when I was coaching the Toros. It starts enthusiastically, then ends abruptly.

Baby Patti is now in her thirties, married to Adrian Brown, and they live in Calgary with their daughter, Colme. Adrian is a primary school teacher, while Patti continues to study for her degree in engineering. She claims that her best memories are of times spent at Charleston Lake at the Giffins' cottage, where I taught all the children to fish and to water-ski. There, probably more than anywhere, I seem more patient with children — and now, with grandchildren — because I am truly relaxed and away from the outside world.

In reflecting back over my 63 years, I realize every aspect, every event, and every person whose life has touched mine has been important to me. My early years out West were as important a part as my life in Toronto. I was blessed with caring, nurturing, and supportive parents, who also gave me two special siblings. I married my childhood sweetheart, and we have weathered our good times and bad, plus added five children who are contributing to this world in their own right, not to mention twelve grand-children. My hockey career was exciting, the Stanley Cups were an irreplaceable time, and the team members have also always been friends. My other careers were a learning experience, sometimes profitable, sometimes not, but I would not trade any of that. But in honest reflection, what has affected my life the most was that goal I scored on April 23, 1964.

Epilogue

That best portion of a good man's life
His little, nameless, unremembered acts
Of kindness and of love.
        — William Wordsworth

My PRIMARY REASON FOR WRITING THIS BOOK WAS TO TRY to give a little direction to parents and children — not that I have all the answers, but I have provided some sort of a track to follow.

Today's younger players are so protected, and don't have the freedom that people of my generation had as youngsters — the freedom to travel on streetcars alone, play hockey in parks, and play in wide open fields without our parents worrying about us. We have to let our young people fly off in their own directions so that they can discover what is right and what is wrong for themselves. A straight line is a good one to follow. Keep it simple.

I have been fortunate to have been able to help out in so many areas, with various charities and children's programs, though I have never been able to help young athletes, boys and girls, as much as I would have liked. But there is still time.

I feel that we should keep children's participation in sports at the school level, where the little people will have equal opportunity. There has to be a better system than the one we have right now.

Canada is certainly falling behind in hockey. Our Olympians are always stretched for money to help them reach their potential.

To current professional hockey players, who have so many choices and different kinds of problems: do not forget where you came from. Whether you're from Europe or North America, remember that you will be alumni in the future.

When we get up in the morning, we should give thanks and appreciate each other with a simple "good morning," and a big smile. Look at the simple flowers in a flower pot, or look out into your garden. That look at the simple things might give you the boost you need for the rest of the day.

Learning to give comes from within; it is the most pleasing way to say "thanks."

Index

Quotable Quotes on Bobby Baun

"Bob Baun challenged anyone, even Hull or Howe. He never went after the small guy and never backed away from the big guys."

— Frank Mahovlich

"I've known Bob since we were kids and I have a great deal of respect for the whole family. I well remember the time he was cut in New York and when he, Sallie, and newborn Brian left the hospital together, happily ever after — well, almost!"

— Billy Harris

"Bob could be my teammate anytime. That goal made him; it defined him."

— Dick Duff

"Bob has always had strong opinions, but he's also very supportive. He is willing to make sacrifices to be successful and for the sake of the team. I'm just glad I wasn't playing against him. He had a great pain threshold, and unlike players today, he played when he was hurt."

— Dave Keon

"Bob, along with Al MacNeil, were the hardest hitting defencemen I ever saw."

— Mike Nykoluk

"Bob gave 150% every time; he was an all-out team man. He always took out his man, even if he hurt himself in the process, and if he was hurt he'd bounce back up. I wish I had him on my team when I coached [in Los Angeles, Pittsburgh, and Toronto], especially when we visited Philadelphia. Whenever we had a game there, my players got the Philly flu. They were afraid of the goons and the ruts at the edge of the ice. Bob would never have done that. He would play no matter what."

— Leonard "Red" Kelly